Abel
8.75

Burke and the Nature of Politics

Burke and the

The Age of the

UNIVERSITY OF KENTUCKY PRESS

Nature of Politics

French Revolution

by CARL B. CONE

To Mary Louise and Tim

Preface

IN ADDITION TO the persons and institutions named in the preface to the first volume, I acknowledge the assistance of the following: Mr. James M. Osborn of New Haven, Connecticut, for permitting me to use the Burke manuscripts in his collection deposited in the Yale University Library; Mr. Alistair Wood, Librarian of the Osborn Collection, for arranging the Burke manuscripts for my use; Miss Rosamond Meredith, Archivist, for making it so convenient to use the Burke, Rockingham, and Fitzwilliam manuscripts in the Sheffield Central Library; Professor Thomas W. Copeland and Dr. John Woods, who freely placed materials at my disposal when I was at Sheffield, and gave of their knowledge and their time; President Joseph E. McCabe of Coe College, Cedar Rapids, Iowa, who made available his unpublished Ph.D. dissertation; Mr. L. H. Marshall of Columbus, Ohio, for sending me a copy of a Burke letter in his possession; Dr. John Brooke, Professor Ross Hoffman, Professor Thomas Mahoney, Dr. Walter Love, Dr. John C. Weston, Jr., and Dr. Peter Stanlis for helpful conversations and other kinds of aid; Irving F. Kanner, M.D., for a diagnosis of Burke's last illness; Miss Dorothy Leathers for typing much of the manuscript; Dean M. M. White and the College of Arts and Sciences of the University of Kentucky for making it possible for me to spend some time in England in 1959-1960; and the University of Kentucky Research Fund Committee for financial assistance for research trips and the purchase of research materials. I am grateful to all named above.

Contents

Illustrations

The Constitution: Domestic and Imperial

CHAPTER I

Introduction

WHEN BURKE DISTINGUISHED between politics as a scramble for places or a struggle for power, he meant quite different things. Office was an end in itself, the pursuit of little persons, whereas power was a noble ambition, to be used for the enlargement of social good. When Burke described the politician as the philosopher in action, he meant that the politician should be guided by prudence or practical reason to seek the good appropriate to man in civil society, the only man in whom Burke was interested. The synonym of social good was justice.

Prudence and experience taught Burke that in politics an individual, such as Lord Chatham, was ineffective by himself. According to Aristotle, man was a political animal, and according to Burke, man was a social being. In society, men belonged to various groups as their needs dictated; in politics, the natural group, whether called faction or party, was the means by which the individual, supported by those he was joined with, sought to give effect to the measures that, according to their judgments, would promote justice. Parliamentary politics, then, was the organized pursuit of justice by contending individuals and parties. In this view, contentions arose from the unavoidable disagreements about actions and policies, not from differences as to the ultimate goal.

In 1765 Burke had become attached to the parliamentary party led by the Marquis of Rockingham. Like others, this party was not homogeneous or monolithic. It was a confederation whose components were more closely affiliated than the constituent elements of other parliamentary parties of the time, but less than the parties of a later age. From the time of its formation, shortly before Burke became attached to it, until the fall of Lord North in March, 1782, the Rockingham party had enjoyed only one year in office, yet in its adversities it had retained a more distinct identity than any other contemporary party. When Lord North's ministry came to its end, the Rockingham party, because of its size, its history, and its relative steadfastness in opposition, seemed to deserve the opportunity to control the new ministry.

Burke's view of party, shaped while his own party was in opposition, was exaggerated by that fact. Because in 1782, as earlier and later, fewer than half of the members of the Commons considered themselves members even of the loose parties of that day, purely party control of the Commons was not possible. Both royal confidence and the support of the unorganized members was necessary to sustain a government, as the fall of Lord North demonstrated. Moreover, strong distrust of parties still prevailed. William Wilberforce, who confused Burke's idea of party with the kinds of "cohesions" produced by the eighteenth-century electoral structure, thought that parties were incompatible with the independence of the Commons. But he was thinking of the independence of individual members, whereas Burke, like Walter Bagehot eighty years later, was thinking of the independence of the House of Commons from either crown or popular influence. He considered party organizations the best security against extramural influences.

Obviously, Burke was thinking of parliamentary parties, not of national or constituency parties. In 1782 the best known ones were those of Lord North, Rockingham, and Shelburne. North's, developed after his accession to power, had enjoyed the king's support as well as that of politicians whose first loyalty was to the king, and that of many of the so-called independent members. The Shelburne party was the old Chatham connection. The Rockingham party was unusual, as it was an opposition party that had survived the natural attrition of years out of office. It had coherence and a program.

Whether members opposed or belonged to the Rockingham party, they recognized its unusual character. Burke had earlier defined a party as a body of men who agreed upon certain principles and desired office in order to give effect to them. He had helped to formulate the principles of the Rockingham party and, assisted by events, the program that would give them concrete form. Burke liked to think of them as the principles of liberty that English history had revealed, the Revolution of 1688 had confirmed, and eighteenth-century Whiggism was defending. If, as everyone now admits, there was no Whig party as a party in Burke's time, there was something that men as diverse as Burke, Rockingham, Fox, the Duke of Grafton, and Horace Walpole accepted as Whiggism—a spirit, a set of prejudices, a collection of attitudes, and a body of aspirations needing reaffirmation and reassertion. To a great extent the political battles of the 1780's, particularly of the years 1782-1784, were fought over the issues and the acts associated with the attempts to give stronger effect to a Whiggism that, to Burke, was still the meaning of English history.

With the French Revolution this struggle took on added significance, because the old Whig principles were challenged more threateningly than ever before. No longer a "generous contention" among English politicians, the struggle of the 1790's was against a dogma, against a doctrine that repudiated the assumptions and traditions that earlier even Burke's domestic political opponents had claimed to accept. If before 1789 Burke had thought that the Whig view of the constitution was at issue, then after 1789 the very foundations of the Christian social order were assaulted. In this crisis the old methods of defense were not sufficient. The tactics of normal parliamentary warfare were useless. In the ideological struggle of the 1790's the incendiary doctrines of the revolutionaries had to be opposed by moral as well as by physical force.

Thus Burke, whose speeches and writings before 1789 had been instruments of parliamentary politics, after 1789 had to be the philosopher. He had always been a philosopher of sorts, better able than most politicians to formulate appropriate generalizations about politics and the constitution as well as the affairs of the

British Empire, so that his occasional pieces retained meaning after the events that brought them forth had become history. These generalizations form a coherent body of thought, but they are scattered through his formal publications, his speeches, and his correspondence. None of these political tracts from 1765 to 1789, not even those on the American problem or the Irish question, constitutes a systematic treatise. His writings on the French Revolution, however, contain his complete political thought. Taken together, they have unity, and one of them, the *Reflections on the Revolution in France,* crystallizes all of value that Burke had said and thought about the nature of man and society. With its publication in 1790 Burke produced a treatise addressed to a specific event, but far transcending it. If he had ever given up to party what was meant for mankind, the universal significance of his *Reflections* redressed the balance.

So it was that in defense of the social order Burke willingly went beyond his customary role as a party politician and a defender of the British constitution to become the champion of the Christian order of western Europe. Had he not risen to this height, the historian would nevertheless have found him noteworthy. But a reconstruction of his pre-Revolution thought, though containing the elements of his political philosophy, would never place him in the first rank as a political thinker.

And so we might fail to perceive that even before 1789 he possessed and applied rather profound principles to the problems he encountered as a parliamentary politician. From Burke's point of view, the contentions over the British constitution arose from the question: in which kind of political and constitutional order was justice more likely to prevail in the Empire and at home. Imperial authority that was too weak to preserve social harmony or was tyrannical, as in India (Burke believed) under Hastings, or corrupt, as in Ireland, or impolitic, as in America, must be reformed and directed toward promoting the well-being of people who lived under the superintendency of the imperial government. Justice for the people of Ireland or India was the same as justice for the people of England, though circumstances might differ from one part of the Empire to another. The French Revolution threatened destruction to the just, Christian order of western

Europe because, Burke insisted, its principles were alien and hostile to the usages and principles of the social order that had developed in Europe through the centuries.

We come then to the old question, what is justice and what did Burke understand by it? Here he drew upon one of the oldest intellectual traditions of western civilization, the natural law, which had passed from Aristotle, the Stoics, and Cicero on to western Europe and thus into the mainstream of Christian moral, legal, and social thought. As understood by Burke from his college studies and his other readings, notably in Richard Hooker, it described a moral order of the universe, created by God and governed by eternal, divine law. Within this universal order existed the worldly social order whose strongest imperative is the moral law, binding men to seek justice in their social relationships, to respect the rights of others, and to perform the duties that their natural endowments of intelligence, free will, and conscience make known to them. Observance, according to the direction of right reason, of the moral law, which is the foundation of the social and political order, has enabled men throughout history to move toward fulfillment of their duty to God, to bring, as their merely human capacities will permit, the social order into closer conformity with the order of the universe. In such a social order, justice prevails, and it is the same among all men, because the mandate of the moral law is in the nature of men. Particular rights and duties, and so particular justice, may vary according to time and circumstances. It is the duty of the political rulers, as Burke said in the *Reflections,* to combine "the principles of original justice with the infinite variety of human concerns" in order to achieve the social order in which justice will prevail.

The affairs of men require the operation of human reason and judgment. That was why Burke insisted that men of superior judgment must govern and, in making "human Laws," must recognize that they are only "declaring" the particular relevance of the principles of "original justice." In all human affairs, Burke said in the *Reflections,* justice is a paramount consideration— "Justice is itself the great standing policy of civil society." And the quest for justice was Burke's career as a Rockingham Whig, as a friend of America and Ireland, as the prosecutor of Warren

Hastings, and as the enemy of the French Revolution. In these characters Burke lived most of his adult life, and especially his last fifteen years.

For two years after the fall of Lord North, England experienced political instability. The second Rockingham administration lasted from March until July, 1782, and when the marquis' death terminated it, the king called upon Lord Shelburne to form a government. In February, 1783, an alliance between North and Fox defeated the preliminaries of the peace treaties, and Shelburne left office. The Fox-North alliance became a coalition government in April. It endured until December, when Pitt the Younger took office. Burke, who was paymaster general in the Rockingham and the coalition governments, never held office again after the fall of the Coalition, and never lived to know another ministry except Pitt's. But in 1794, as he was retiring from the House of Commons, Burke saw with pleasure the consummation of a political realignment that he had advocated for two years as a necessary defense against the threats to domestic order caused by the French Revolution. With the party badly divided by the Revolution, the Portland wing joined Pitt. A Whig rump, led by Fox, with whom Burke had broken in 1791, continued the tradition of opposition.

The four changes of governments between March, 1782, and December, 1783, occurred amid a great debate on the British constitution, specifically on the related questions of the influence of the crown, the independence of the House of Commons, the nature of the electoral system, and the relations among ministers, king, and parliament. Burke believed that the independence of the Commons could only be assured if the influence of the crown was diminished while the parliamentary franchise remained restricted and the distribution of seats in the House of Commons unchanged. Then the men of property—many of them of aristocratic lineage and others with status achieved through hard work and ability—who could resist pressures from the people below or the king above, could control the legislature and the administration. This would provide a stable political order in which liberty and opportunity would be combined with security of property, respect for organized religion, and leadership by the properly qualified, while the gradations of a hierarchical social structure would be preserved. Since 1769 both the influence of the crown and the radical program of parliamentary reform, with its specific assertions about the dependence of the member of parliament upon extramural opinion, had been seen by Burke as threats to the independence of parliament. Burke's well-known defense of the right and duty of a member of the Commons to make decisions about public affairs free of instructions from his constituents (and in consequence, his troubles as member for Bristol from 1774 to 1780) illustrated his concern over the danger of parliament's becoming a congress of delegates incapable of acting upon their independent and informed judgments.

In this view Burke seemed to be the traditionalist insisting upon the preservation of eighteenth-century political and social dispositions. But not entirely. He thought the influence of the crown too strong and the independence of the Commons too uncertain; therefore, while resisting parliamentary reform, he would also curtail further the royal prerogatives that, in the minds of many, still authorized the king to appoint and dismiss ministers and to keep certain offices of state outside the purview of parliament. In order to bring about these changes in the laws and customs of the constitution, Burke fostered the idea of party, the organization of parliamentary politicians that would enable a number of men, by joining together their votes, their talents, and their influence, to control parliament and thus to contest successfully for the curtailment of the royal influence and the independence and power of parliament. The rise of Pitt the Younger was a blow to Burke's hopes, and after Pitt's accession to office was confirmed by the election of 1784, Burke and his friends resumed their careers as an opposition party—the Portland Whigs, or merely "the Party," as they were labeled in the public prints. The Regency crisis of 1788-1789, caused by the king's temporary insanity, was the last opportunity "the Party" had to overturn Pitt, and the king's recovery made pointless the furious parliamentary battle in which Burke played a leading part.

Inevitably, the struggles for power and place in the 1780's affected the great imperial problems of the period, just as they had during the American Revolution. For a year after the fall of

Lord North, the settlement of the American war was a subject of political contention. Then and later the questions of relations with Ireland, the administration of India, and the impeachment of Warren Hastings were deeply involved in domestic politics. In 1782 and 1785 Irish problems were prominent, and throughout the period 1781-1789, the questions of India. The defeat of the Coalition's India bills, drawn by Burke, and the passage of Pitt's India Act in 1784 did not resolve the problem of Warren Hastings. Burke continued to press it. Finally in 1787 the House of Commons passed Articles of Impeachment, and in 1788 the trial began in Westminster Hall, with Burke leading the prosecution before the Lords. Although the specific issues of the Empire can be examined separately, any realistic discussion of them must include the political context within which Burke and his contemporaries had to confront them. Unavoidably then, in the 1780's Burke was fighting on several fronts, but in the same cause, to secure justice and freedom from oppression, as he understood them, for the peoples of the Empire, whether they lived in England, Ireland, or India, or as slaves on the West Indian plantations.

After 1789 the French Revolution was the dominating event and the focus of Burke's life. The former constitutional problem had to take second place to the effort to preserve the institution of monarchy itself, and the nicer definition of its political and constitutional powers had to be postponed. The impeachment of Warren Hastings was under way; it was simply a matter of continuing with the trial before the Lords each spring until the prosecution and the defense had completed their cases. It seems better therefore to consider these sessions as extensions of the Indian debate of the 1780's rather than to intrude them into the history of the revolutionary decade. The Irish question, after some years of quiescence, pushed itself forward again in 1792 and, stimulated by the Revolution in France, remained in agitation during the last five years of Burke's life. Although the issues remained those of the 1780's, they had to be considered in the context of the French Revolution and the politics of the 1790's, which were also deeply affected by the Revolution. In consequence, the Irish problem is an integral part of the history of the 1790's as well as a continuation of the earlier problem.

The unity of the last seven years of Burke's life is provided by the monopolizing influence of the French Revolution. And so the date 1789 clearly divides that period from the decade of the 1780's.

But if convenience is served by dividing Burke's career according to the focus provided by changing times and events, the overriding unity must not be ignored. His aim in politics was the achievement of a just social order, and to this end he directed his efforts and his thoughts. The foundations of his thought and the framework of principles that he erected upon them remained unchanged throughout the variety of events and experiences of his parliamentary career. In each great cause to which he devoted himself, Burke judged events and issues against the constants of morality and justice, for politics was but morality enlarged, and the principles of "original justice" were eternal and uniform.

CHAPTER II

The Second Rockingham Administration

THE FALL OF Lord North's government on March 20, 1782, terminated a distinct twelve-year period in English politics. During the next two years observers saw strange occurrences in the political world—even monstrous and unnatural ones, in the opinions of some persons. The uneasy political and personal relationships of the period were complicated further by the number and gravity of the public questions that Lord North's administration passed on to its successors. Though the American war was virtually over, the naval war with France and Spain continued, even while the beginnings of peace negotiations provoked new international and domestic disputes. Ireland and India clamored for attention, the one demanding the loosening of constitutional ties, the other needing purified administration under closer supervision from the imperial government. The discontented at home cried out for reforms and economy, for greater nobility of spirit among the governors of the British Empire. The humiliated king spoke of sailing off to Hanover. Politicians might scoff that George III was crying wolf again, but they could not shrug off the constitutional issue involved in the recent political upheaval. Along with its adored principles, the Revolution of 1688 had bequeathed to the eighteenth century the problem of adjusting relationships among crown, ministers, and parliament, and Lord North's fall dramatized it.

Burke and the Rockingham party, the leading opposition group during the preceding decade, recognized these problems and thought that they knew what to do about them, even though party opinions were not always unanimously held. The party was ready to concede American independence; for twenty years Burke had pleaded for magnanimous treatment of Ireland; at the moment of Lord North's fall, as the most vigorous member of the select committee, Burke was deeply involved in the study of Indian administration; in 1780 with the support of his party he had brought before parliament a plan for administrative reform at home; and ever since 1770, when he published his *Present Discontents,* he had thought that organized parliamentary parties were a means of reducing crown influence and enhancing the independence of parliament, and that these in turn would increase the dependence of ministers upon the House of Commons.

By the law of the constitution, ministers were the king's servants, but by custom for the past century, the Commons had possessed a decisive, ultimate power that on unusual occasions could overturn the much-admired "balance" of the constitution.[1] If that were admitted, the Marquis of Rockingham was the obvious and deserving successor to Lord North, because he led the largest, best organized, and most clamorous of the opposition parties. Some people, however, thought it unethical, even unconstitutional, to "storm the closet"—that is, to force themselves upon an embarrassed king and to curtail his prerogative to choose ministers. George III left no doubt of his sentiments. He disliked the Rockingham chieftains as persons because they had opposed his governments almost since his accession to the throne, and he abhorred the measures they would insist upon as conditions of taking office.

But the times were unusual. The king's position was weak,

[1] See the important article by W. R. Fryer, "King George III: His Political Character and Conduct, 1760-1784," *Renaissance and Modern Studies,* VI (1962), 68-101. Subtitled "A New Whig Interpretation," this article dissents from some of Namier's and Pares' interpretations and argues that "on several occasions and in various ways," notably in the dissolution of 1784, George III did indeed "infringe the constitutional limits of his station, as they existed in his age," not as they were thought to be by the Victorian Whigs. My first draft of the following chapters on politics in the 1780's was written before Fryer's article appeared; my references to Fryer's article are therefore insertions and additions, rather than original incorporations of his interpretation. If mine is also a "New Whig" view, it was arrived at independently of Fryer's.

because the servants he trusted had been repudiated by a rebellious House of Commons. Even the country gentlemen and the members who had supported Lord North out of a sense of loyalty to the crown, in wrathful despair over the nation's disgrace, had turned against the king's ministers. It was stupid of George to tell Lord North that he had deserted the king who desired to continue to support him. It was mere obstinacy, though he thought it royal duty, to try to salvage as much as he could from the wreckage of North's administration during the unpleasant negotiations for a new ministry. In these days, George displayed "a profound reluctance to accept the plainest implications of his constitutional position."[2]

Like the death of a man who has suffered a long illness, the demise of North's government, though expected, was a shock. Having tried other alternatives, the king reluctantly permitted Thurlow, the Lord Chancellor, to talk with Rockingham even before North's resignation. The conversation was "without any good effect" except to confirm Rockingham's adherence to a well-defined program and his desire for direct negotiations with the king.[3] Besides mutual dislike, an important barrier to agreement was Rockingham's demand for a royal promise of support for his program. Though the idea was not quite new, it was sufficiently novel to offend the king, and the specific terms of the program made it even more distasteful. The king was not yet ready to concede independence to America; Burke's proposed civil list reform struck close to him; and the plans for disfranchising revenue officers and debarring government contractors from the Commons reflected upon the king and his former ministers.

If he needed encouragement to be firm, Rockingham received it from Burke.[4] Apprehensive of possible misunderstandings and fearful of trickery, Burke urged Rockingham to be very explicit, to beware of "general" terms. The marquis' firmness in these early negotiations made North's resignation even more a critical event. Ironically, it gave point to the titles of two plays then at Covent Garden, "The Positive Man" and "Which is the Man?"

2 Fryer, *Renaissance and Modern Studies*, VI, 88.

3 Fortescue, ed., *Corr. of George III*, V, 292-93, 401, the King to Thurlow, March 14, 18, 1782, and Charles Jenkinson to the King, March 18, 1782.

4 Burke MSS, Sheff., B-23, a memo to Rockingham dated March, 1782.

Disagreements among his followers weakened the effect of Rockingham's firmness about his program. Burke, hostile toward royal influence and enamored of an unorthodox idea, argued for an exclusively Rockingham cabinet.[5] This was more than a pretext for monopolizing the spoils of office. It was also Burke's concept of party government. Cabinet unanimity was a requisite for enactment of the party program. This was only another way of describing the basic idea Burke was advocating. He would invade the king's conventional right to choose his ministers, making the choice in fact that of the party. Burke was too radical for his colleagues and allies. Both Lord John Cavendish and William Pitt upheld the prerogative. They would be content with a coalition of opposition groups, though desirous of excluding members of North's administration.[6] Fox disliked the prospect of a mixed ministry mainly because he detested Shelburne. But Burke thought the golden moment had arrived. He bid for the support of the independent members and of the public as soon as North announced the end of his government.[7] Unless the new government, that is, Rockingham's, enjoyed the patriotic votes of the members who had turned out North, the promise of England's regeneration would be unfulfilled. This was the right moment to praise the virtue of the independent members and to flatter them for reflecting the "spirit of the people."

Unlike his wife, Burke did not underestimate the danger of disunity among those who had driven North from office, or the difficulties in satisfying them.[8] The most nagging worry was the king's ostentatious preference for Shelburne, who was not only an opponent of North but also the most generally distrusted politician of the time.[9] Ignoring the implications of his earlier

5 Burke MSS, Sheff., Burke to Rockingham, March 22, 1782.

6 *Morning Chronicle*, March 16, 1782, reporting debate of March 15.

7 *Morning Herald*, March 21, 1782; *Parl. Hist.*, XXII, 1224-26.

8 Burke MSS, Northamptonshire Record Office, Aii29, Jane Burke to [Richard Champion], March 20, 1782 (hereafter Burke MSS, N.R.O.; these manuscripts were referred to as "Burke MSS, Lamport Hall" in the first volume of this study); Br. Mus. Add. MSS 35,525, fol. 2, William Fraser to Robert Murray Keith, March 19, 1782. Three days later, Fraser spoke of the "cruel state of suspense" pending the completion of negotiations. Add. MSS 35,525, fol. 2.

9 *Daily Universal Register* (after Jan. 1, 1788, the *Times*), Sept. 5, 1785, contains an interesting character sketch of "Malagrida," referring to his pursuit of self-interest by means of "duplicity and stratagem"; the article sums up the opinion of contemporaries. There is need of an explanation for Shelburne's reputation.

talks with Rockingham, the king asked Shelburne to form a cabinet and suggested its membership.[10] Shelburne knew that the motley crew recommended by the king could never sail together, and he understood that Rockingham would not accept anything less than the leadership. It was not so much Shelburne's sense of decency as his appreciation of Rockingham's political strength that urged him to advise the king to secure the marquis' support, "cost what it would more or less."[11] The royal pride begrudgingly yielded, assuaged only by the king's insistence upon dealing with Rockingham through Shelburne.

The marquis was in continual consultation with his paladins. They had first to persuade him to overlook the king's preference for Shelburne, putting the case on public grounds. If the marquis refused to form a government, people might attribute his decision to "pique or jealousy."[12] As usual, Burke advocated the extreme course. If the king refused Rockingham's terms, the "whole corps" of the party should disdain office.[13] By March 22, when it appeared that the king had given ground, Burke then insisted on a homogeneous cabinet, "a new system," "*one* ministry," with Rockingham and his men in full control.[14] Two days later the marquis and Shelburne met for their first confrontation.[15] Rockingham presented his program in writing, demanded consent to it "confirmed to him by His Majesty himself," submitted a tentative cabinet list, but offered to continue conversations about men. Shelburne equivocated and, worse, withheld information.[16] The Rockingham leaders were angry. At a large, raucous meeting at

---

[10] Fitzmaurice, *Shelburne*, III, 130-31; *Daily Advertiser*, March 23, 1782.

[11] Fitzmaurice, *Shelburne*, III, 132-33, for the quote.

[12] Russell, *Fox*, I, 234, 239.

[13] Burke MSS, Sheff., B-23, misc. paper.

[14] Burke MSS, Sheff., Burke to Rockingham, March 22, 1782.

[15] Rockingham MSS, Sheff., R1-2003, Rockingham to Shelburne, March 24, 1782; Fortescue, ed., *Corr. of George III*, V, 408, Rockingham to Shelburne, same date, accompanying Shelburne to the King.

[16] Rockingham MSS, Sheff., R1-2004, 2005, Shelburne to Rockingham and Rockingham to Shelburne, March 24, 1782; Liverpool Papers, Br. Mus., Add. MSS 38,218, fol. 45, John Robinson to Jenkinson, March 24, 1782. An example of Shelburne's duplicity is seen in that he never informed Rockingham that the king had given him the appointment of the governorship of Portsmouth. When General Monckton died on May 20, Shelburne appointed the Earl of Pembroke, to the displeasure of Richmond, who had desired the post for his brother. Alison Gilbert Olson, *The Radical Duke* (Oxford, 1961), 68-69.

Thomas Townshend's house that night, they decided to demand an immediate, specific answer from Shelburne and the king.[17]

This display of temper hastened a settlement that Pitt and Shelburne were already reconciled to. The king gave in "unwillingly," pleased only by Thurlow's continuance as Lord Chancellor. More pliant than Burke about appointments, Rockingham accepted Barré, Lloyd Kenyon, Townshend, Dunning, and Lord Camden, and of course Shelburne as Home Secretary. If only the last three were in the cabinet, they, with Thurlow, Grafton, and Conway outnumbered the Rockingham members—the marquis, Fox, Lord John Cavendish, Admiral Keppel, and the Duke of Richmond. Portland as Lord Lieutenant was not in the cabinet.

These arrangements produced some curiously contradictory reactions. Burke could not be entirely satisfied with this approach to a broad-bottomed ministry. Surely, said Lord North, the *Gazette* lied, for could "his Majesty *be pleased* to appoint" Lord Rockingham as First Lord of the Treasury?[18] Horace Walpole was far off the mark to say that the Court had "yielded completely" and that Rockingham had won "without the shadow of a compromise," or to feel able to leave London "without anxiety."[19] Francis Hale was only partly correct in saying that the new ministry had *"Carte-blanche,"* and Philip Yorke ventured the most hazardous opinion of all when he thought "everybody" was pleased.[20] The king stated the most significant fact about the new administration. When he saw Rockingham for the first time on March 27, he was completely frank.[21] He would have preferred a government composed "of the ablest men without selection or party description," but for the sake of amity he "forbore" insisting upon this point. He promised to listen to Rockingham's "recommendation and advice" but reserved his confidence for Shelburne.

In addition to the fundamental cleavage, the ministry showed

17 Br. Mus., Add. MSS 38,218, fol. 50, Robinson to Jenkinson, March 25, 1782.

18 *Walpole's Corr.,* XXIX, 235, Walpole to the Rev. William Mason, April 14, 1782.

19 *Walpole's Corr.,* XXIX, 207-10, Walpole to Mason, March 25, 26, 1782.

20 Br. Mus., Add. MSS 35,525, fol. 21, Hale to Keith and Yorke to Keith, March 26, 1782.

21 Fortescue, ed., *Corr. of George III,* V, 420, and Fitzmaurice, *Shelburne,* III, 136-37.

other seams. Thurlow, who was not to be trusted in any case, was at odds with Richmond over the contractors' bill. Richmond was separating from Rockingham over the issue of parliamentary reform. Unlike the Rockinghams, the Shelburne group were not ready to concede independence to America. Pitt was on the outside, displeased by the offer of a minor office.[22] Should serious differences develop between Rockingham and Shelburne, there would be no doubt of Pitt's preference.

If Rockingham had yielded on men, he was admirably firm about measures. He took office pledged to a coherent program and with the promise of royal acquiescence to it. His victory was in part the consequence of an upsurge of public opinion, though it was as much revulsion against Lord North as enthusiasm for Rockingham. The accession of the Rockingham administration owed more to parliamentary politics than any previous ministerial change in the reign of George III. The conduct of the Rockingham party was to Burke an example of proper parliamentary procedure. "Party is the union of several public men to support ideas of the public good, in wch they are agreed, & they take office or abstain from it or not according as they may best promote their principles. Faction is another thing."[23]

Burke was not among the cabinet ministers. He stood high in the estimation even of his opponents. The king had spoken well of him. Gossip since 1780 had marked him for office. On March 20 Conway mentioned him in the House of Commons as a man "who most likely would be one of those ministers to whom the country looked up for its salvation."[24] Embarrassed, Burke denied such ambitions, "nor had he a right to have any such," considering his rank and fortune. As late as March 25 Burke could write that he formed no part of the cabinet arrangements though he probably would receive some lesser office.[25] Rockingham never thought of a cabinet post for Burke. He made no arrangement for Burke until he had settled the chief appointments. On March 27 the

---

[22] Fitzmaurice, *Shelburne*, III, 136.

[23] Burke MSS, Sheff., undated fragments for a speech. Burke first wrote "many" and then substituted "several."

[24] *Parl. Hist.*, XXII, 1227.

[25] Philip Henry Stanhope, ed., *Miscellanies* (London, 1863), 43-44, Burke to Dennis O'Bryen.

king approved Burke's nomination as paymaster general of the forces.[26]

The reasons for the appointment suggested by one of Burke's early biographers have generally been accepted.[27] Burke preferred the paymastership because in that office he would be best situated to promote his economical reforms; Shelburne's demands for places for his own friends required the sacrifice of Burke's claims to higher office; Burke did not belong to the nobility and had no parliamentary following to lend to the support of the new government. Yet Shelburne's biographer thought Burke "was treated with strange neglect by his friends," as if to say that neither Shelburne nor the king would have objected to giving him a higher post.[28] It is sometimes said that Burke's friends considered him temperamentally unfit for a position of first rank.[29] The paymaster handled large sums of money, particularly in time of war, but he never had to make important policy decisions. Traditionally, the paymaster belonged to the second rank of office-holders; if he had weight in an administration it was not because of the office he held.

There is another story to be told. It reflects honor upon Burke and no discredit upon Rockingham. In an undated manuscript in his papers at Sheffield (B-23), written while ministerial negotiations were still under way, Burke advised Rockingham:

take no thought about any thing for *me*. We talked of compensation for reduction of emoluments [*sic*]; at another time I would have proposed it for Mr. Rigby [the former paymaster] or any other stranger —that office used to be considered as giving, a person who had some pretensions, his Baton de Marechal de France en argent comptant—But now no consideration but for *your* honor—you never stipulated nothing except for my poor lad [Richard, Jr.]—even the office itself may keep cold, & lie for another time, if arrangements should at all require. I can readily consent to lie by, but having second rate pretensions, not to be put below others on that line.

---

[26] Fortescue, ed., *Corr. of George III*, V, 420, Shelburne to the King, March 27, 1782.

[27] Prior, *Burke* (3d ed.), 232.

[28] Fitzmaurice, *Shelburne*, III, 135.

[29] For example, Fox called him an impractical, unmanageable colleague. Rogers, *Table-Talk*, 79-80.

Thus, from the beginning Rockingham intended to give Burke the paymastership.[30] Were it not for the pledge to economical reform, it might appear that Rockingham grasped at the opportunity to relieve Burke of his chronic financial worries. Perhaps he did anyway, not knowing how comprehensive were Burke's plans for Pay Office reform, or thinking that of the former exorbitant perquisites of the office, some might remain after Burke reformed it. If all were eliminated, then the "compensation" Burke mentioned might be arranged. Conventional practice permitted the paymaster to invest the unexpended balances in his custody and to pocket the interest. In wartime, when the balances were large, the profits were correspondingly great. The Commissioners of Public Accounts, reporting on August 10, 1781, recommended abolition of this practice.[31] If Burke and his party embraced this reform, the paymaster would lose his chief source of profit. But during the interval before a new law could take effect, Burke might obtain a considerable sum, as Charles Townshend had done during his short tenure. The *Morning Herald*, referring not to such an interval before a reform but to a short tenure of the traditional office, thought Burke might realize between twenty and thirty thousand pounds.[32] This would be in addition to the £3,000 salary and use of a Whitehall residence.[33]

Actually, Rockingham seems to have thought of the office with its former perquisites. He justified a pension for Barré on the grounds that as treasurer of the navy he would not receive the perquisites he would have enjoyed as paymaster.[34] When it was decided to reform the Pay Office drastically, Rockingham was

[30] On March 20 Lord Hillsborough reported this as rumor to Lord Carlisle, Auckland Papers, Br. Mus., Add. MSS 34,419, fol. 370.

[31] *Commons Journals*, XXXVIII, 577.

[32] April 22, 1782.

[33] "Sixth Report of the Commissioners of Public Accounts," *Commons Journals*, XXXVIII, 704, gives the figure as £3,061/12/7 in 1780. Lucy S. Sutherland and J. Binney, in "Henry Fox as Paymaster General of the Forces," *English Historical Review*, LXX (1955), 237, estimate the sum as just under £3,000. In addition to the basic salary of £3,000, the paymaster enjoyed other perquisites, but his deductions for land tax, pension duty, and civil-list duty just about canceled them. When he inspected the house in Whitehall, Burke joked that the kitchen was much too large for him, however suitable it had been for Rigby, a famous gourmet. *Morning Herald*, April 20, 1782.

[34] Burke MSS, Sheff., Lord John Cavendish to Burke, July, 1782. If this is true, then Shelburne was incorrect in denying that Barré's pension was compensation for not receiving the Pay Office.

prepared to offer Burke a pension. He refused it in order to facilitate the grants to Barré and Dunning.[35] Burke's testimony on this point, made twelve years later, does not go far enough. The *Morning Herald* on June 29, 1782, said that Rockingham intended a pension for Burke but gave up the idea in fear of a public outcry so soon after the grants to Barré and Dunning. A pension to Burke was almost the same as one for himself, added the *Herald*. But toward the end of June, when the cabinet quarrels were so bitter, Rockingham decided to revive the pension. His death killed the project. A few days later the question of Barré's pension came up in the House of Commons. Fox and Frederick Montagu, a member of the Treasury Board under Rockingham, expressed regret that a "most respectable gentleman" had not received the pension he so richly deserved.[36] Possibly when Earl Fitzwilliam, Rockingham's heir, assumed the responsibility of continuing Rockingham's financial aid to Burke, he did so in part because the marquis' untimely death deprived Burke of a pension of £2,000 a year.

Burke did not solicit the paymastership. Rockingham offered it freely, and Burke accepted it without grumbling that he was entitled to more.[37] The salary was increased to £4,000.[38] It is difficult to think of any high office to which Burke's talents recommended him.[39] Throughout the negotiations Burke acted with a stoical sense of duty, willing to serve the party and, if he became paymaster, to serve the nation, even if prospects for greater personal gain had to be sacrificed. Within the party Burke's position did not depend upon the tenure of a public office, nor did his personal relationship to Lord Rockingham. His admission to the Privy Council and his new distinction of Right Honourable had no material meaning. Newspaper reports of his presence at a "cabinet council" on March 28 and at a "council" two days later

[35] Public Record Office, Chatham Papers, 30/8, 118. Burke made this statement in a document submitted to Pitt in 1794 to support his claims for a pension.

[36] *Daily Advertiser*, July 11, 1782; *Parl. Hist.*, XXIII, 135, debate of July 9, 1782.

[37] P.R.O., Chatham Papers, 30/8, 118, Burke's statement to Pitt, 1794.

[38] *Parl. Hist.*, XXIII, 198, a statement by Burke in the Commons.

[39] *Morning Herald*, April 4, 1782, says that Burke desired the Chancellorship of the Exchequer, and deserved it, but had to defer to Lord John Cavendish, who belonged to a great family. It would have been strange if Rockingham had not considered the matter of "connexions"; but there is no evidence that Burke ever showed resentment toward Lord John. In fact, he had great affection for him.

had political rather than constitutional significance.[40] Burke attended because he was a leading party spokesman in the House of Commons, the party's pamphleteer, and a member of the party's board of strategy, and because he was Edmund Burke. That he was also Receiver and Paymaster General of His Majesty's Guards, Garrisons, and Land Forces was quite incidental.

In office for the first time in his career, Burke did what politicians naturally do with patronage at their disposal. Many friends and strangers asked him for his good offices with other members of the administration, as if they understood that for jobs he would prefer members of his family.[41] Boswell, who wanted General Conway to appoint him Judge Advocate of Scotland, was the most bothersome suppliant.[42] Burke's request and Boswell's hopes were lost in the mists of Conway's indecision. Nevertheless, Boswell seemed to blame Burke, "vexed," as he told his journal, "at being neglected" by him. Uneasiness prevailed among the twenty-eight persons holding jobs in the Pay Office until Burke made it clear that there would not be wholesale dismissals. He created a joint deputy paymastership in place of a single deputy and at once appointed his hard-pressed friend Richard Champion and his own son at £500 a year each. Young Richard Burke's election to the Club soon after was not in recognition of his new station nor of his own merits, but rather was a tribute to his father. Burke solicited for his sister, Juliana French, a pension of £200 a year in Ireland, and for a kinsman, John Bourke, a lucrative receivership of the window duties; he obtained for his protégé Walker King the post of private secretary to Rockingham and for the painter Barret a lifetime place in Chelsea College.[43]

Before Burke's appointment to his office, rumors destined him for the secretaryship to the Treasury.[44] This was a case of mistaken

[40] *Morning Chronicle*, March 29, 1782; *Morning Herald*, April 1, 1782.

[41] E.g., Burke MSS, N.R.O., Aii34, Charles Dillon Lee to Burke, April 2, 1782; Burke MSS, Sheff., Henry Goldsmith to Burke, May 24, 1782, Maurice Goldsmith to Burke, May 29, 1782.

[42] Burke MSS, Sheff., Boswell to Burke, March 18, April 18, 1782; Boswell MSS, Yale, Burke to Boswell, Burke to Conway, Conway to Burke, all on April 23, 1782; Pottle, ed., *Private Papers*, XV, 73, April 14, 1782.

[43] Wecter, *Kinsmen*, 71; Magnus, *Burke*, 111; Burke MSS, Sheff., Thomas O'Beirne to Burke and Burke to O'Beirne, Aug. 20, 27, 1782; *Daily Advertiser*, April 1, 1782.

[44] Br. Mus., Add. MSS 35,525, fol. 21, Francis Hale to Keith, March 26, 1782; Add. MSS 34,419, fol. 385, Edward Cooke to William Eden, March 29, 1782.

identity; the position should have been connected with his brother Richard. The manipulation was complicated, and everything about it was embarrassing.[45] Richard, who had tried to avoid controversy by offering to do the secretary's work while dividing the salary with another claimant, David Hartley, must have considered himself extremely well paid when the full salary of £3,000 was settled upon him. In return for it he sifted the papers preliminary to meetings of the Treasury Board, presented the papers in digest form, signed letters for issuing money, "perused" warrants to be signed by the king, and "superintended" parliamentary business for the Treasury Board.[46] The office was not a sinecure, and the political duties were heavy. There is no evidence to suggest that Richard was unsatisfactory in that important office. An effort was also made to take care of Richard for life. Lord John Cavendish, as an act of friendship, was making arrangements to appoint him Joint Receiver of the Land Revenues of Essex at the time of Rockingham's death. Pitt, as the new Chancellor of the Exchequer, was ready to complete the appointment when Thurlow objected to a grant for life. In a huff, Richard withdrew his name, not wishing to embarrass Pitt, he said, and afraid of antagonizing the Lord Chancellor.[47]

Unlike Richard, who was a barrister, poor Will Burke out in India had only one profession, that of office-seeker. "Such is the prejudice against his name and principles, that although he was 10 years in Parliament and under secretary to Gen. Conway, with a fair character for morals and ability, he had not interest sufficient to obtain any station in the Company's Service."[48] So John Bourke had written to Francis five years earlier. The description still fit Will. He had failed to get rich in the service of the raja of

45 Dora Mae Clark, "The Office of Secretary to the Treasury in the Eighteenth Century," *American Historical Review*, XLII, 27 and 43, n. 19; Rockingham MSS, Sheff., R1-2046, Richard Burke to Rockingham, April 14, 1782; *Corr.*, II, 483, Edmund to Will Burke, April 24, 1782. Richard's tenure began on April 6 and lasted until July 15, 1782. He resumed the office on April 5, 1783, under the Fox-North coalition and held it until Dec. 27, 1783. Clark, *American Historical Review*, XLII, 45. The *Daily Advertiser*, April 8, 1782, announced the appointment, calling Richard first secretary to Rockingham.

46 P.R.O., Chatham Papers, 30/8, 231, "Duties of the Secretary to the Treasury."

47 Burke MSS, Sheff., Pitt to Richard Burke, Nov. 7, 1782, Richard Burke to Pitt, Nov. 8, 1782, Richard Burke to Thurlow, Nov. 9, 1782.

48 Francis and Keary, eds., *Francis Letters*, I, 283.

Tanjore. To acquire wealth in order to live well and, more important, to relieve Edmund and free Beaconsfield of its debts were Will's ambitions. When his old friend Lord Macartney became governor of Madras, Will's hopes rose. Macartney's replies to his entreaties were merely polite.[49] Will was not discouraged. As a man of experience in India, he freely offered advice to Macartney, who finally had to tell him to cease interfering with the East India Company's resident at Tanjore and to abandon hopes of an appointment from the Madras government.[50]

Though he did not know it when Macartney rebuffed him, Will had been taken care of. On April 24, 1782, Edmund, already planning to provide for him, asked him to be of good cheer.[51] Burke intended to appoint a deputy paymaster in India, a position already existing in other stations abroad; in India, however, the deputy was to have wider authority than elsewhere, because he was to pay the king's naval forces in the area as well as the land forces. By July 9, after protesting, the Treasury Board and the company approved.[52] By this time the Rockingham administration had ended, but on August 16 Barré, paymaster in Shelburne's government, reappointed Will to the post Edmund had created for him.[53]

This appeared to be pure jobbery. Will Burke had £5 a day as deputy, the opportunity eventually to reside in Calcutta, where he bought a beautiful country house, and a position that as it

[49] Macartney Papers, Br. Mus., Add. MSS 22,457, fols. 16, 102-104, 116-18, Macartney to Will Burke, Jan. 4, 1781, April 10, 1782, May 10, 1782.

[50] Br. Mus., Add. MSS 22,457, fols. 172-75, Macartney to Will Burke, Aug. 1, 1782; Add. MSS 22,458, fols. 116, 117-21, 139, Macartney to John Sullivan, Nov. 27, Dec., 1782, Macartney to Will Burke, Nov. 27, 1782.

[51] *Corr.*, II, 483. Six months might intervene between the time a letter was posted from England and its arrival in India, and an exchange of letters might take a year.

[52] In Burke MSS, N.R.O., Avii22 and Avii25 are copies of the correspondence and documents. In Burke MSS, Sheff., to William Cuppage, May 13, 1792, Will complained that if Edmund could not restore arrangements as he had left them, presumably in 1782, then "It is impossible for me to hold with credit." Whether Will was speaking of the arrangements described in the text above, or of others, is not certain. In 1786 Burke was afraid that the new governor general, Lord Cornwallis, might threaten Will's position. Osborn Collection, Yale University Library, Box 32, #29, Burke to Adam Smith, Dec. 7, 1786.

[53] Br. Mus., Add. MSS 22,429, fols. 225-26, Proceedings of the Select Committee at Fort St. George, Sept. 13, 1783.

turned out lasted for ten years.[54] Actually, the arrangement made sense. Macartney had already complained to Warren Hastings about the absence of "method or arrangement" in the old system of issuing money through army channels.[55] When he learned of the new system for centralizing accounts and payments in the office of the deputy paymaster in India, he thought it would simplify procedures and improve the accuracy of the records.[56] That the new system did not work as contemplated by the Burkes was in part because Macartney, Hastings, and later Cornwallis distrusted Will Burke. For years he disputed with them and never was able to exercise the authority over military finance that his office and instructions from England entitled him to possess. Nor was Will able to gain the profits that his office could have yielded. The governors rebuffed him when he proposed schemes for getting rich that exceeded the bounds of decency though not of his implied power. In 1792, after years of frustration but remarkable persistence, he gave up and sailed for England as poor as when he went to India. He bore until his death the clouded reputation that had always been his greatest obstacle to success.

Burke's care for his kinsmen and friends differed from contemporary practice only in earning for its dispenser more than the customary amount of abuse. Though other appointments were criticized, Will's elicited most of the condemnation aimed at Burke. It drew the attention of persons who were becoming aroused by the growing controversy over India and Warren Hastings. "Asiaticus," who was Hastings' agent John Scott, berated Burke for crying economy while creating a deputy paymastership in India at an expense of £5,000 a year, and worse still, for appointing to the office someone who already enjoyed £8,000 a year as agent for the raja of Tanjore.[57] It vexed Burke to read

54 Hickey, *Memoirs*, III, 214, about the home. In P.R.O., P.M.G. (Paymaster General), 2/33, fol. 229, is a record of a payment to Edmund Burke on account of Will Burke for 146 days' pay, that is, to Dec. 24, 1782, the amount being £730.

55 Br. Mus., Add. MSS 22,455, fols. 32-33, May 22, 1782.

56 Br. Mus., Add. MSS 22,429, fols. 225-26, Proceedings of the Select Committee at Fort St. George, Sept. 13, 1783.

57 *Morning Herald*, Feb. 25, 1783. See also Jan. 6, Feb. 10, March 27, 1783. These estimates were exaggerated three and four times respectively.

this abuse when in fact his brief career as paymaster was one of self-abnegation and an energetic effort to reform an office, "perhaps potentially the most lucrative that a parliamentary career had to offer," the former administration of which was a chaos so "indescribable" that the Commissioners of Public Accounts gave up trying to understand it.[58]

No amount of study would enable the modern student fully to comprehend the details of Pay Office procedure.[59] The surviving records are incomplete, owing partly to the practice, prohibited by Burke's reform statute, of allowing paymasters to remove documents when they left office.[60] The Pay Office, only a century old, was characterized by bureaucratic routines congenial to the interests of its officials. Some details of procedure were trade mysteries known only to the clerks; the paymaster, if new to the office, as was Burke, could not become familiar with them quickly. But the broad principles can be described sufficiently clearly to reveal the problems Burke encountered and the importance of the reforms he sponsored.

As the name of his office suggests, it was Burke's duty to administer the payments to the officers and men of the land forces at home and abroad. Former paymasters had developed "a system of manipulation" for managing the several accounts.[61] In the words of the Commissioners of Public Accounts, describing the office before Burke's reforms, the paymaster was both the officer of account and the banker for the army.[62] The six happiest members of his staff should have been the ones who received fees in addition to their salaries. The parliamentary appropriation for the military services was deposited in the Exchequer. The

---

58 The quotes, in order, are from Sutherland, *English Historical Review*, LXX, 230, and Sir John Fortescue, *A History of the British Army* (London, 1911), III, 521. Perhaps the confusion made it necessary for Burke to retain the staff he inherited.

59 For the Pay Office, see J. E. D. Binney, *British Public Finance and Administration, 1774-1792* (New York, 1958); Sutherland, *English Historical Review*, LXX, 230-57; P.R.O., P.M.G., 2/30, Accounts and Ledgers; P.R.O., Chatham Papers, 30/8, 231, "The Business Done in the Treasury"; the Fifth and Sixth Reports of the Commissioners of Public Accounts, *Commons Journals*, XXXVIII, 572-93, 702-83; *Annual Register*, XXXII, 313-29, 349, summarizing the seventh report of the Commissioners; *London Chronicle*, March 16-19, 1782, containing extracts from the Sixth Report.

60 Fifth Report, *Commons Journals*, XXXVIII, 577.

61 Binney, *Public Finance*, 153.

62 Fifth Report, *Commons Journals*, XXXVIII, 577.

paymaster, using the proper administrative forms, drew upon it virtually at discretion, usually in sums of £1,000,000. Again by an established routine, he made the appropriate payments personally or, in the case of troops stationed abroad, through the appropriate deputy paymasters, of whom there were ten after the creation of the office in India. Some of these accounts were far in arrears, and those for troops overseas unavoidably so.

Even this brief description suggests the possibilities. In the absence of close supervision by the Treasury Board, and because of the delays in auditing that characterized all financial offices at this time, former paymasters, such as Henry Fox and Richard Rigby, had freely requested larger sums than were required to meet immediate demands. Unused balances (which on any December 31 between 1768 and 1780 averaged £585,000) were invested by the paymaster in mortgages or stocks or in other lucrative ways, and the interest was his profit.[63] The gains made by some of Burke's predecessors were fantastic. In 1761 Henry Fox, the father of Charles James, bought government stocks that in two years earned for him £103,000.[64] Although the exact amounts of the profits were not known to contemporaries, they knew the general situation. Politicians eagerly sought the office of paymaster, and successful seekers were objects of envy and subjects for the kinds of rumors that angered Burke. As long as the public only envied the paymasters, opinion condoned their practices. But about 1780, when public and parliamentary opinion was beginning to change, and Burke led the chorus crying for economy in the public services, attention was directed to the Pay Office. In his speech on economical reform in 1780 Burke recommended the obvious remedy, to deposit in the Bank of England the money drawn from the Exchequer. The Commissioners of Public Accounts, appointed by statute in that year as a result of the demands for administrative reforms, turned their attention first to the Pay Office. Their fifth report repeated Burke's recommendation. When adopted as a part of his reforming statute (22 Geo. III, c. 81) in July, 1782, to take effect on the

---

[63] Fifth Report, *Commons Journals,* XXXVIII, 575.

[64] Sutherland, *English Historical Review,* LXX, 244-45, 257. Many other examples could be cited.

following January 1, this provision made the Pay Office merely a keeper of accounts.

In their fourth, fifth, sixth, and seventh reports, issued between April 9, 1781, and June 18, 1782, the commissioners pointed to other evils in the Pay Office. The practice already described delayed the final settlement of a paymaster's accounts. Rigby, who before his death in 1788 managed to compromise his accounts, at one stage in the inquiry pleaded inability to pay in some of his public money because it was out on mortgage.[65] A paymaster was responsible for all the obligations arising during his incumbency until they were settled, so he might even continue to draw from the Exchequer after he left office. Again, the remedy was obvious. The commissioners recommended, and Burke's statute required, that henceforth a new paymaster assume at once his predecessor's accounts and balances (now in the Bank). The statute also enacted a related recommendation of the commissioners providing for frequent examination of the Pay Office accounts by the Treasury.

The commissioners criticized two other features of Pay Office administration, though neither was unique to it. One was the unfathomable complexity of accounting and bookkeeping. Unable to comprehend these mysteries, the commissioners spoke only generally of the need for simplification.[66] Burke's statute made changes which the army disliked. The commissioners devoted their sixth report to the fee system in the Pay Office. All but six of the clerks received salaries only, and none earned more than £100 a year. The lowest annual income among the favored half-dozen in 1780 was £674 a year, of which over half was derived from fees. The entering clerk earned £1,508, of which £1,448 came from fees; the accountant, Charles Bembridge, earned from fees £1,358 of his total income of £1,501; the cashier, John Powell, received £8,389 in 1780, of which only £200 was salary.[67] Powell, who had served under Fox and was one of the executors

65 Binney, *Public Finance*, 152.

66 Fortescue, *British Army*, III, 52; Fifth Report, *Commons Journals*, XXXVIII, 576-77.

67 *London Chronicle*, March 16-19, 1782; *Commons Journals*, XXXVIII, 704, for Powell's income.

of his estate, therefore enjoyed an income in modern equivalents of about $200,000 a year. The commissioners, understandably, were shocked by their discoveries. They urged abolition of fees. Burke's statute, for reasons that were not divulged, did not abolish fees but regulated them and diverted the proceeds to augment other salaries in the office.

During his three months in the Pay Office under Rockingham, Burke probably devoted more time to the study of Pay Office routine and the preparation of its reform than to the transaction of business. His signature was necessary for drawing money and disbursing it, and scattered documents for these purposes bear his name.[68] Otherwise, the veteran employees performed the office work.

Rockingham may have hoped to make Burke rich by appointing him to the office, but Burke himself, the reports of the commissioners, and the fear of alienating a public eager for reforms combined to defeat that intention. The surrender of the paymaster's emoluments, like the reform of the Pay Office, was in Rockingham's program by implication when he began negotiations with George III because Burke had included them in his plan for economical reform in 1780. In 1782 Burke separated the Pay Office reform from the civil list reform. On June 14, in discussing the latter in the House of Commons, he mentioned certain internal reforms already inaugurated in his office in anticipation of eventual statutory reform. Four days later Lord John Cavendish brought in a resolution recommending a fixed salary for the paymaster and another disapproving of large balances of public funds in the paymaster's custody.[69] In fact, Burke was already conducting the business of the Pay Office as the second resolution contemplated.

On June 24 Burke was given leave to introduce the Pay Office reform bill. Hastily drafted under the supervision of a paymaster who could not have mastered the details of the office, the bill

---

68 For example, Burke MSS, Sheff., Hugh Hansard to Burke, Aug. 24, 1782; P.R.O., T64/37, Burke to Lords of Treasury, April 16, 1782, requesting £135,544 for thirty days' subsistence money; H.M.C., *Royal Inst.*, IV, 221, 256, 283, 353, notices of bills drawn on Burke for the forces in North America.

69 *Parl. Hist.*, XXIII, 115-18, 123.

encountered little opposition, because its principles harmonized
with the sentiments of the Commons. The House demonstrated
its attitude when the attorney general tried in a separate motion
to force the former paymaster and treasurer of the navy to settle
their accounts by a stipulated time. Although the motion failed,
the Commons left no doubt of their dislike of the "ancient
practise" of the offices. In such circumstances Burke's bill made
steady progress. Rockingham's death did not affect it, and by
July 10 it had passed both houses.

Burke's act has been called so unworkable that a new statute
was needed in 1783.[70] This statement is unfair. Some of the
criticism, like Thurlow's, was partisan; he had opposed administrative reforms all along.[71] Some army officers and recruiting agents
and a few Pay Office employees disliked having to change time-
encrusted methods or simply did not understand the new procedures introduced by Burke's act. Sir George Yonge, Shelburne's
secretary at war, in a circular to these persons, counseled patience.[72] He anticipated improvements in Pay Office procedure
once the act was understood and in operation. One modern student, whose judgment is based on intimate knowledge of the
British army, thought the disgruntlement of certain army officers
proved the effectiveness of the act.[73] The critics did not dare
condemn its basic principles. These made the Bank of England
the depository, prevented the kind of profiteering former paymasters had engaged in, and ensured prompt settlement of
accounts and balances when a new paymaster entered office.

Nevertheless, experience and the continued investigation of the
Commissioners of Public Accounts suggested amendments.[74] Burke
took the lead in proposing them, though he was not in office. On
February 7, 1783, he asked leave to bring in a bill explaining
and amending his Pay Office act.[75] His speech set the tone for

[70] Binney, *Public Finance*, 157; 23 Geo. III, c. 50.
[71] Br. Mus., Add. MSS 38,218, fol. 134, Jenkinson to ? , Sept. 20, 1782.
[72] Br. Mus., Add. MSS 38,218, fols. 152-53, letter of Dec. 24, 1782.
[73] Fortescue, *British Army*, III, 521.
[74] The Eighth, Ninth and Tenth Reports of the Commissioners, June 19, 1782,
March 31, 1783, and July 2, 1783, revealed the clumsiness of old administrative
procedures, especially in connection with army extraordinaries. *Commons Journals*,
XXXIX, 325-44, 522-674, 1066-1111.
[75] *Daily Advertiser*, Feb. 10, 1783; *Morning Herald*, Feb. 8, 1783.

the debates on the bill. Partisanship was avoided. Burke apologized for the defects of his earlier act and asked for help in correcting them. Barré suggested the abolition of fees.[76] Other speakers promised their help. The amending act left intact the main provisions of the earlier one but altered and expanded the provisions for the handling of payments and accounts.

Although Burke was the prime mover of these acts, they were products of the times. Since 1779 the cry for administrative reform had been heard, along with demands for other kinds. Burke would not accept parliamentary reform because he thought it hostile to the principles of the constitution. Reforms of governmental departments and the reduction of public expenditures were of a different order. They might, and were intended to, reduce the influence of the crown. They would enlarge the authority of parliament. They would alter the constitution. Burke was inconsistent only in the view of persons who think he opposed all constitutional change. He would accept what he considered desirable reforms, even of the constitution, and was eager for them when he thought they promised to enlarge British liberties, increase the independence of the Commons, reduce the influence of the crown, and make government more economical and efficient. Such reforms were in harmony with the traditional principles of the constitution as the Revolution Settlement had defined them. Burke was a monarchist in the sense that he cared for the hereditary monarchy as a part of the constitutional system, but he was also a Whig who was jealous of the independence of parliament and unafraid to restrict the royal prerogative and the influence of the crown. Economical reform, then, was a sound Whiggish reform. The reform of the Pay Office was a statutory reform of an administrative department; its enactment affirmed the authority of parliament over the offices of state. The act achieved its purposes. It struck a blow at the eighteenth-century concept of the privileges of an officeholder, effected economies in the Pay Office, improved the efficiency of its operations, and was

---

[76] Burke MSS, Sheff., Barré to Burke, March, 1783. This became Section 12 of the act. It prohibited the taking of fees by Pay Office clerks after Dec. 25, 1783. The prohibition was not fully enforced until Aug. 4, 1786. *Daily Universal Register*, Aug. 11, 1786,

one of a series of reforms during the next generation that removed from the crown some of the means of exercising influence upon politics and politicians.[77]

The reform of the Pay Office was, however, only one of the achievements of Burke and the Rockingham party during their short administration in 1782.

[77] *Parl. Hist.*, XXIII, 916-17, May 21, 1783 (when Burke said his reform was saving the public £47,000 a year), and XXV, 295, 300, 303, Feb. 17, 1785, debates on reports of the Commissioners of Public Accounts.

CHAPTER III

Domestic Policies

WHEN IT UNDERTOOK its "reformation of English political life," the Rockingham party was twenty years old.[1] By self-appointment and with Burke as its spokesman, it represented venerable Whig principles, those of 1688. In 1782 this tradition meant more to Burke than broad generalizations about parliamentary sovereignty, or literal adherence to the constitutional arrangements prescribed by the Revolution, or platitudes about a balanced constitution. Much had happened since the reign of William and Mary to disturb the so-called balance. Unlike most of his contemporaries, Burke refused to venerate the shibboleth of a balance, for parliamentary sovereignty meant, besides the independence of the House of Commons, ultimately the supremacy of the Commons. Properly, the preferences of the Commons should prevail over those of the king in the formation of a government.[2] To Burke the term "storming the closet" was not opprobrious. His mature Whiggism held that it was parliament's duty to advise the king as to his ministers and was the king's obligation to recognize men who possessed the confidence of parliament and to invite them into office on public rather than private grounds. Unless ministers depended upon parliament rather than upon the king, they could not be held accountable for their measures through ordinary political processes. These principles of political action did not require the reform of the electoral system. Parliament adequately represented the nation—the people incorporated in counties and boroughs, and the economic and professional interests of land, commerce, the law, and the armed services. The agency for giving effect to parliamentary supremacy was party.

If Burke's ideas about party were clearer and more advanced than those of his colleagues, they marked out the line along which the Rockingham party was moving. When Shelburne, speaking the language of most of the politicians of the time, vigorously opposed Burke's attack upon the prerogative, he defined it as a desire to transfer control of the ministry from the king to the leaders of a party.[3] This, he said, would mean a new tyranny, not royal but of a political party, exercised over all who were not members of it. The desire to limit the influence of the crown was widespread in 1782, but not as extreme as Shelburne described it. Shelburne's support of the prerogative, amounting to betrayal of Whiggism, contributed to his later unpopularity among the Rockinghams and their friends.[4] Horace Walpole and the Duke of Grafton, who in their distrust of the prerogative verbally represented the kind of Whiggism that Burke and Rockingham claimed to stand for, thought they saw the issue plainly.[5] Though neither shared Burke's vision of the political party as an agent for determining the opinion of parliament, both desired to reduce the discretion of the king in forming ministries. If the country did not support Rockingham, said Walpole, and if evil men succeeded in undermining his administration, then "the predominance of the crown is incontrovertible"; after Rockingham's death, Grafton was chagrined because the king did not seek the advice of the cabinet but at once offered the headship to Shelburne. Domestic politics in 1782 could be reduced in Walpole's mind to the contest between liberty and the prerogative. This had been the issue of party strife a century before. The Rockingham party was in the true tradition of liberty. Walpole deplored the disunity

1 Namier, *American Revolution*, 484.

2 Burke MSS, Sheff., fragments for a speech, *ca.* 1778. The remainder of this paragraph is a close paraphrase of the fragments.

3 Br. Mus., Add. MSS 34,418, fols. 484-85, Shelburne to the Duke of Marlborough, July 8, 1782.

4 It was, for example, the reason for Grafton's later disillusionment. *Autobiog.*, 322.

5 *Walpole's Corr.*, XXIX, 215-16, Walpole to Mason, April 1, 1782; Grafton, *Autobiog.*, 322, 324.

within the ministry, because he disliked seeing the friends of liberty quarreling over patronage and personalities when their duty was to unite in the cause of freedom.[6]

Walpole magnified the crown's ability to threaten liberty after 1688. But the prerogative power over appointments was a check to the ambitions of parliament. William Pitt understood this, though he took the side of the king and provided a basis for the resurrection of the old Tory partisanship for the crown. Where, he asked, is "the independence—nay, where is even the safety of any one prerogative of the Crown . . . if its prerogative of naming ministers is to be usurped by this House"?[7] In this difference between the Rockinghams and their opponents, a real constitutional issue was involved, and upon its resolution would depend the direction of constitutional development.

The Rockinghams, especially Burke and the marquis, who opposed parliamentary reform, were not inconsistent in desiring curtailment of royal influence and seeking control of the cabinet by the leaders of a parliamentary political party.[8] There was nothing "deceptive" about this. The Rockingham program, it has been asserted, would have removed the crown "from the political arena—as it is today," but would have left authority in a small group of Whig factions rather than in the leaders "of a national party, representing the views of the majority in a wide democratic electorate."[9] This idyllic distinction was mechanical, not substantial. Such a criticism of Burke's and the Rockinghams' ideas seems to assume that party government is impossible and improper unless based upon a universal franchise and national parties, which would be to say that Britain did not possess parliamentary government before 1884, or certainly 1867. The cabinet system clearly locates responsibility. Burke desired to concentrate power and responsibility in party leaders, but no more than Walter Bagehot did he see a necessary connection between party government and democracy, nor any contradiction in terms when responsible government was managed by parliamentary parties.

---

[6] *Walpole's Corr.*, XXIX, 244-45, Walpole to Mason, May 7, 1782.

[7] Quoted in Asa Briggs, *The Age of Improvement* (London, 1959), 85, n. 1.

[8] Fox, who differed from Burke on parliamentary reform, did not use it as an argument for party government nor did he argue the other way round.

[9] Harlow, *The Second British Empire*, I, 235.

It has been asserted that there cannot be "parliamentary government" unless four essentials, all lacking in 1782, are present.[10] These are "a more effective party mechanism than existed" at that time; "a more effective contact between 'ministry' and 'opinion' "; "a civil service outside politics"; and "a pliant monarch" willing to yield the traditional "rights" of the king. National and "effective" party organizations did not exist in England until the 1870's, about the time a nonpolitical civil service was created. "Opinion," in the sense implied, had little opportunity to express itself in national elections until after the extension of the franchise in 1867. Yet England enjoyed its fullest measure of parliamentary government between 1835 and 1867, when only the last of these four "essentials" was present.

Indeed, the classic description of parliamentary government, Bagehot's *The English Constitution* (published in 1867), refers to this period. It has been adopted by textbook writers and fitted to the period following, when Bagehot's cabinet government was giving way to a different system. "*The English Constitution* remains an accurate and vivid account of how Cabinet government worked *before* the extension of the suffrage, *before* the creation of the party machines, and *before* the emergence of an independent Civil Service administering a vast welfare state."[11] The conditions that Harlow and Briggs insist upon as necessary for the existence of cabinet or parliamentary government are those that in fact destroyed the classical system Bagehot described. Cabinet government functioned in its most nearly perfect form when parties were parliamentary parties, the kind Burke desired. His ideal, like Bagehot's, was a party organization resembling a political "club" rather than a "modern machine." Party was necessary to regulate the making and unmaking of ministries, but parties functioned within a House of Commons that had a "real collective life and a general will" and whose members were not beaten by the hammer of party leadership upon the anvil of constituency opinion. Burke saw the need for more effective party machinery within parliament

10 Briggs, *Age of Improvement*, 109.

11 R. H. S. Crossman, "Machine Politics," *Encounter*, XX (April, 1963), 17 (italics by Crossman). Also Lord Altrincham, "A Cure for Westminster," *Encounter*, XX (July, 1963), 82: ". . . Parliament has been losing whatever vestiges of independency it may have had under the Grand Whiggery. . . ."

when few others did, and earlier than his contemporaries he was trying to deprive the crown of the powers that interfered with control of the government by party leaders in parliament. It is not presentism to say that the tendency of Burke's ideas was toward the cabinet government of the midnineteenth century, which did not know, any more than did Burke, an independent civil service, a democratic suffrage, or mass parties.

The cleavage in the Rockingham administration was not merely personal. A profound disagreement over the leading constitutional question of the reign of George III underlay the political struggles that began in the spring of 1782 (if they had not begun earlier) and continued until 1784. To tell the story of the second Rockingham administration only in terms of Shelburne's intrigues with the king, without relating these intrigues to the question of the royal prerogative, denigrates Shelburne too greatly and obscures the aims of Burke and his party. The Revolution of 1688 had been a victory for parliament, but it had not been complete. It had given to the eighteenth century a constitutional system whose rough joints had to be smoothed by the erosions of time and the empirical development of workable customs. Burke's theory of party government was intended to solve the problem of adjusting relations among king, ministers, and parliament in harmony with traditional Whig principles, and to give practical political and constitutional meaning to the independence of parliament, by weakening the prerogative power over ministers.

If Shelburne strove to uphold the prerogative, his methods were hardly frank, and to his contemporaries—especially Walpole—he personified deceit and untrustworthiness. His correspondence with the king and some of his actions justified his colleagues' suspicions and recriminations. The king was also guilty of impropriety when, by collaborating with Shelburne, he was refusing to recognize the "existing shape and logic of the constitutional situation."[12] To the extent that Shelburne informed the king of purely departmental affairs, he was giving effect to his belief that individual ministers might communicate directly with the king instead of through the prime minister about the business of their offices. This was common practice at the time. But Shelburne

---

12 Fryer, *Renaissance and Modern Studies*, VI, 81-82, for the quotation.

went further than this. Some of his communications furnished the king with information that was not strictly office business. As early as April 3, 1782, he told George about the difficulties over the appointment of Lord Howe to a naval command. George was grateful, because he would "know how to suit my language" when he saw Rockingham later in the day.[13]

This was one of many disagreements over patronage, specific appointments, and general policy. If Rockingham controlled patronage "to the exclusion" of Shelburne, then, said the king, the earl would be reduced to subordination within the cabinet.[14] Here again was a constitutional point, involving a basic conception of cabinet composition. At Shelburne's request, the king drafted a statement intended to uphold Shelburne's coequal authority over appointments while ensuring that "no mistake may arise in the conducting of business."[15] George hoped for concurrence between them in the future, but his obvious reluctance to converse with Rockingham at any time left the way open for Shelburne's private approaches. Thus encouraged, Shelburne acted with a boldness that his cabinet colleagues properly resented. For example, he arranged for the appointment of Lord Weymouth to be Groom of the Stole and told Rockingham about it only when the matter was settled.[16] George hoped Shelburne and Thurlow would "concert" to protect him from appearing to do anything more than acquiesce in the reform of the civil establishment.[17]

Before the end of April, the division in the cabinet over these and other matters had become obvious enough to cause speculation about the life of the ministry. If at the beginning it was to the *Morning Herald* (April 2) a "Quintuple Alliance," on April 20 the Bishop of Bangor told William Eden that Fox and Shelburne, leading two distinct parties in the ministry, were talking like prime ministers and seeking higher aid, Shelburne from the

---

[13] Fortescue, ed., *Corr. of George III*, V, 440-41.

[14] Fortescue, ed., *Corr. of George III*, V, 443-44, the King to Thurlow, April 5, 1782.

[15] Fortescue, ed., *Corr. of George III*, V, 444, the King to Shelburne and to Rockingham, April 7, 1782.

[16] Fortescue, ed., *Corr. of George III*, V, 486-87, 493.

[17] Fortescue, ed., *Corr. of George III*, V, 451.

king and Fox from the Prince of Wales.[18] By this time, the "daily jealousies" of Fox and Shelburne were becoming "altercations," and Grafton and Camden, usually thought to be partisans of Shelburne's, were beginning to doubt his Whiggism, were striving to conciliate the two leading antagonists, and were refusing to promise to go on with Shelburne if the ministry fell apart.[19] To other causes of disagreement was added the contention about control of the peace negotiations, and to the personal difficulties in the way of conciliation was added the ill health of Rockingham.

These disputes worried Burke. They, rather than his "wrongheaded" conduct or his "nerves and his farcical grimaces" that Walpole commented on, were endangering the life of the ministry.[20] Burke warned Rockingham of intrigues.[21] By making Thomas Orde his secretary, Shelburne was seeking the support of Henry Dundas, which the Rockinghams had bid for unsuccessfully. Not only would this alliance create a dangerous "cabal" in the House of Commons, but it would enable Shelburne to combine the Scottish with the East Indian interest. Already Shelburne had made friends in the City of London, and he had gained the Duke of Marlborough. Burke also admonished Rockingham. The marquis, perhaps already sicker than Burke realized, had been neglecting the "management of men," he had permitted Shelburne to obtain credit for certain appointments, and he was letting other opportunities slip away.

The distrust was mutual, and the king encouraged Shelburne's. When after May 28 the recall of Hastings seemed likely, Shelburne prepared to promote the cause of Cornwallis. The Rockinghams in a cabinet of June 1 opposed Shelburne's recommendation, and the marquis insisted upon his right to suggest Hastings' successor. Shelburne persisted, and even privately informed the chairman of the Court of Directors of his preference for Cornwallis. The king approved, because he thought the appointment should originate with the Home Secretary. The Rockinghams were attempting to embarrass Shelburne, to "offend" him, but George was confident

18 Br. Mus., Add. MSS 34,418, fol. 427.
19 Grafton, *Autobiog.*, 318-23.
20 *Walpole's Corr.*, XXIX, 241, Walpole to Mason, April 25, 1782.
21 Burke MSS, Sheff., April 27, 1782.

that he was "too well aware of their arts to be ever surprised by them."[22] These maneuvers came to nothing, because the ensuing uproar in the East India Company prevented the recall of Hastings.

There were other causes for disunity in the Rockingham administration. The marquis' insistence upon the enactment of his reform program had left no doubt about the measures that his government would try to pass through parliament; as a result, the ministerial disagreements about measures were revealed clearly. Thurlow's hostility to "everything that is attempted by the new government" was common knowledge even before he openly opposed certain bills in the Lords.[23] On May 14 the *Morning Herald* reported the inability of the cabinet in three meetings to agree on anything.

Seen against this background and considering the shortness of its tenure of office, the achievements of the Rockingham government seem the more remarkable. The sources of the period give the impression of vitality and vigor during the early days of the ministry. By April 15, when hardly two weeks old, the government had begun to act in connection with the peace negotiations, Ireland, economical reform, Crewe's bill and Clerke's bill, and had taken the first threatening actions against Hastings. And toward the end of June, with Rockingham ill and absent, parliament was kept busy carrying through the bills introduced by Burke and his colleagues or actively supported by them.

Of the measures enacted by the Rockingham administration, or begun by it and completed early in Shelburne's, Burke was most intimately associated with the Pay Office and civil list reforms. With his party at last in office, enjoying the support of many of the unengaged members, and encouraged by the reform spirit that was strong during those days, Burke was ready to try for the third time to reform the civil list establishment. Two years earlier it had been novel even to suggest that parliament had any business tampering with the establishment; traditionally, parliament's concern was to provide revenue, and the expenditure of it was left

22 Fortescue, ed., *Corr. of George III*, VI, 49, 51-52.
23 Russell, *Fox*, I, 261, Fox to Richard Fitzpatrick, May, 1782. Walpole told Mason about Thurlow's conduct as early as April 1. *Walpole's Corr.*, XXIX, 215. See also *Morning Herald, passim*, April-May, 1782.

to the king. The defeat of Burke's bill in 1780 was in part owing to the reluctance of many persons to alter the ancient practice or to encroach upon the king's sacred preserves. But by 1782, with the civil list in arrears, the cry for economy louder than ever after two more years of war, and antipathy toward the political influence of the crown still vocal, a different attitude prevailed toward civil list reform. The preamble to Burke's bill, as it was finally enacted, should be accepted literally. It expressed a genuine concern for the importance of paying off the civil list debts and preventing their recurrence.[24]

Burke's motives were mixed. As his conduct in the Pay Office demonstrated, he sincerely desired to benefit the public by effecting economies while improving the efficiency of public administration.[25] The statute emphasizes this point. Burke was also a politician, if not always a skillful one, and he was now happily able to enhance party while serving public interests. The preamble of the statute is also frank about this. One of the purposes of the reform was to improve the security and the independence of parliament—that is, to reduce the influence of the crown. If useless offices were abolished, the royal patronage would be diminished while the public was relieved of certain financial burdens. The Rockingham party was risking little, because the king, in so far as he was able, would resist its efforts to obtain places and pensions for its friends if the establishment remained unreformed. Indeed, a miscellaneous document in the Burke papers at Sheffield admits the importance of the political aims of the reform, the implication being that if the Rockingham party was unable to use the royal influence for its purposes as North had done, then it was better to curtail it as far as possible.[26] But the limitation of the influence of the crown was also a matter of principle, and the process, if it began in 1780, lasted into the next century.

To read the statute is to realize how closely it touched the king and how novel was the principle it introduced. Naturally, the king resented this intrusion into the household. Parliament, now giving effect to the implications of its act creating the Commis-

24 Binney, *Public Finance*, 118-19; 22 Geo. III, c. 82.

25 Binney, *Public Finance*, 120, 270-71.

26 14b. A note on this paper says it was the 1780 plan of reform, carried into effect in 1782 in most respects. See below, n. 46.

sioners of Public Accounts, was asserting that no office in the government or the household should be immune from public inspection and even control. The British government may have begun as an emanation from the household; after 1782 the government was a matter of public concern, and Burke helped to make it so.

Prior to his party's accession, Burke had stated the main principle of the measure in a memorandum to Lord Rockingham.[27] Then for two months he worked on details. Much of the research had been done in 1780, but Burke's proposals were scrutinized again, and new information was sought or was offered gratuitously and sometimes anonymously.[28] Most of the opposition to the reform appeared in the cabinet rather than in parliament, and before June 13, when the bill passed its first reading in the Commons. As early as March 18 the king informed Thurlow of Rockingham's insistence on his acquiescence, at least, in the proposed reform.[29] After the ministry took office, George tried to prevent the reform, first by wondering whether it would affront the royal dignity, and then by preferring administrative or "interior regulations" to a statute.[30] Calling this a trick, Burke persuaded Rockingham to insist upon "the interposition of parliament."[31] Whether he believed Rockingham's assurance that the reform was not directed against him, the king yielded, though he extracted from Rockingham a promise to consult the cabinet before introducing the measure into parliament. The cabinet, as the king had hoped, divided bitterly, and the outnumbered but united Rockinghams prevailed; as Fox said to Fitzpatrick, they were "just as you would expect and wish."[32] And so on April 16 the *Morning Herald* informed its readers that shortly Burke would bring in his measure, "to the great terror of all his Majesty's right honourable cooks, turnspits, and scullions."

27 Burke MSS, Sheff., late March, 1782.
28 For example, Rockingham MSS, Sheff., R 119, a bundle of papers relating to economical reform; Burke MSS, Sheff., letters to Burke, April 1, 16, 23, 26, May 5, 9, 17, June 16, 17, 18, 19, 25, 26, all 1782.
29 Fortescue, ed., *Corr. of George III*, V, 392.
30 Fitzmaurice, *Shelburne*, III, 155-60.
31 Fortescue, ed., *Corr. of George III*, V, 453, the King to Shelburne, April 12, 1782; *Corr.*, II, 466-67, 469-73, Burke to Rockingham, early April, 1782, draft of a conversation between Rockingham and the king, early April, 1782.
32 Russell, *Fox*, I, 252-53, Fox to Fitzpatrick, April 12, 15, 1782.

The formalities of introducing the measure were ludicrous. Fox in the Commons and Shelburne in the Lords presented a "royal" message announcing the king's gracious intention to set an example to the nation by effecting "a Reformation in his Civil Establishment." Shelburne apologized to the king for presenting views with which he could not himself agree; he did it only to prevent a breach in the cabinet.[33] Burke praised the king's wisdom and generosity. Less hypocritically, he pledged the cooperation of the Commons for measures that would increase the dignity of the crown by removing from its presence the insidious influences that formerly surrounded it.[34] The unusual emptiness of this proceeding aroused Walpole to indignation against Shelburne and Burke. The farmers in Walpole's parish would laugh Burke "to scorn for his absurdity."[35]

Though the government was committed to civil list reform, the king and Shelburne still hoped to prune the measure. Shelburne encouraged George to demand information about the "internal Regulations," household arrangements being the king's intimate concerns.[36] Rockingham's firmness defeated this tactic. On May 2, Lord John Cavendish in the Commons and Shelburne, still out of character, in the Lords laid the comprehensive plan before the houses. Four days later the Commons began a detailed examination of it, seemed satisfied that the promise of an annual savings of about £75,000 would result, and gave leave for a bill to be introduced, with Burke as chairman of the committee to prepare it.[37]

After this, the reform advanced steadily. It was read for the first time in the Commons on June 13; two weeks later it passed the Commons; in the Lords it carried the second reading by a vote of 44-0; and on July 11 it received the royal assent. Neither the death of Rockingham in the meantime, nor the opposition of Thurlow, Loughborough, and Stormont caused untoward delay. When the test came, Shelburne, who was at heart a reformer and who no longer had to oppose Rockingham, supported the measure

---

33 Fitzmaurice, *Shelburne*, III, 161-62, Shelburne to the King, April 16, 1782.
34 *Parl. Hist.*, XXII, 1269-71; *Daily Advertiser*, April 17, 1782.
35 *Walpole's Corr.*, XXIX, 241-42, Walpole to Mason, April 25, 1782, and 241, n. 7.
36 Fortescue, ed., *Corr. of George III*, V, 463, 464, 482.
37 *Commons Journals*, XXXVIII, 970-73, 983; *Daily Advertiser*, May 3, 8, 1782.

and expressed the hope that Burke's would be only the first of a series of reforms in government offices. Dissidents dared not oppose the principle or even the details of the bill. Thurlow and Loughborough raised technical objections; Stormont doubted the practicality of a bill framed by a "speculative reformer" who had no administrative experience.[38] The Duke of Richmond defended Burke as a man of "learning, ability, and probity," though the description was not relevant to Stormont's criticism.

The law was drastic. It eliminated one public and nine household offices which have never been revived. It abolished the secretaryship of state for the colonies and the Board of Trade and Plantations on the grounds that the loss of the American colonies rendered these offices superfluous. The creation of another Board in 1786, and the establishment of a new secretaryship of state in 1794, has been placed in evidence against Burke's knowledge of administration.[39] This is hardly conclusive, for both new offices were considerably different in purpose and scope from the ones Burke's bill abolished. Besides transferring to other offices the duties performed by the ones it eliminated, the law also changed the financial practices of the civil list establishment, in order to ensure economy and regularity in the disbursement of money. The restrictions it placed upon pensions and secret-service accounts limited the government's ability to influence opinion.[40] Civil list payments were arranged in classes and were to be made only in the statutory order of precedence. The allowances to the royal family came first and the salaries of treasury officials last. These provisions were intended to prevent civil list debts. In order to pay off the existing debt, the law authorized the issuance of Exchequer bills that would be retired by the savings resulting from the reform.

Drastic though it seemed, the reform was more modest than Burke's proposal in 1780. It did not provide for contractual supply of the royal household and it left undisturbed the Principality of Wales, the Ordnance office, the Duchy of Lancaster, and the mint. Politics may account for some of the differences—

[38] *Parl. Hist.*, XXIII, 140, 142-45.
[39] Binney, *Public Finance*, 119-20; Keir, *Law Quarterly Review*, L (1934), 370.
[40] Arthur Aspinall, *Politics and the Press* (London, 1949), 67, 167.

for example, the charity to the Duchy as a bow toward Shelburne and Ashburton.[41] Burke said he trusted the Duke of Richmond to administer the Ordnance economically, and he did nothing about the mint because the Bank did not desire to take over its functions.[42] There is another reason as a corollary to these. Burke trimmed from the act the parts most bitterly objected to in 1780 in order to ensure passage of the remainder. If opinion came later to desire other reforms, it could have its way.[43] There may have been still another reason that the contemporary documents do not reveal. In 1797, outraged at some "vile lyes" told about him by Fox, Burke said that his reform of 1782 was less extensive than he had wished because Fox had "clipped his wings."[44] This may only mean that Fox was the more astute parliamentary tactician.

Because the reform did not effectively prevent the growth of new arrears in the civil list, both the reform and Burke have been criticized.[45] It was hardly Burke's fault that he could not anticipate the amount of occasional payments—that is, miscellaneous payments not provided by statute—and no civil list contingency fund was established until 1817. Nor could Burke have foreseen the burgeoning of the executive establishment. This was the real cause of future civil list arrears. The solution was not arrived at until 1830, when the household civil list was separated from the civil administration of the government and distinct parliamentary appropriations were made in a true and detailed budget. Burke's reform facilitated these later changes, for it established

41 Keir, *Law Quarterly Review,* L, 372.

42 *Parl. Hist.,* XXIII, 122. Burke was sincere about Richmond and his confidence was justified. Olson, *The Radical Duke,* 74-75. The cartoonists made something of an Uncle Toby out of Richmond because of his passion for fortifications.

43 *Parl. Hist.,* XXIII, 126. On Dec. 19, 1782, Burke obtained leave to bring in bills for the abolition of the Duchy of Lancaster and the Principality of Wales. *Daily Advertiser,* Dec. 21, 1782. But nothing further was done.

44 Windham Papers, Br. Mus., Add. MSS 37,843, fol. 161, Captain Emperor Woodford to Windham, March 16, 1797.

45 Binney, *Public Finance,* 120 and n. 1; Keir, *Law Quarterly Review,* L, 371, n. 12. Binney gives the civil list expenditure as reported on July 6, 1786, as £1,035,876/10/6, whereas the civil list appropriation was £900,000, the excess arising from the "Occasional Payments" of £138,476/4/6. But the report in *Commons Journals,* XLI, 967-75, shows the total, including occasional payments, as £897,400/6/0—that is, £2,599/14/0 under the limit. Binney added the occasional payments twice.

beyond question the authority of parliament to supervise and regulate the civil list. This was one of its most important consequences.

Another was its political impact. William Eden said that Burke's "foolish bill," by curtailing patronage, made it difficult to form or maintain an administration.[46] Though the king, as Burke admitted, evaded one of the intentions of the act by increasing the number of grants of peerages, the reform was one of the means of reducing crown influence and of increasing the independence of parliament. The act was in the tradition of eighteenth-century Whiggism. It was another example of Burke's willingness to inaugurate change when it was in accord with established principles.

Except for the Pay Office and civil list reforms, Burke had little to do directly with the parliamentary measures of the Rockingham administration. The party fulfilled its pledges to disfranchise revenue officers and to exclude government contractors from the House of Commons. Burke supported both measures. They were constitutional laws, altering the franchise and the composition of the House of Commons. They were intended to increase the independence of the Commons and curtail the influence of the crown. They belonged to the Whig order of things, a parliament free from control either by the crown or by the plebs, a parliament dominated by the aristocracy.

These and other measures of the Rockingham government, such as the one expunging from the journals of the House the resolution of 1769 that had expelled Wilkes, were not considered basic constitutional reforms, though in the long run they tended toward a readjustment of the relations between crown and parliament. Burke properly thought of them as being in the tradition of the Glorious Revolution. That revolution had settled the vital question of the seventeenth century, whether the king or parliament would dominate the constitutional system. The Revolution

---

[46] Br. Mus., Add. MSS 34,418, fol. 513, Eden to Loughborough, July 24, 1782. Burke's act eliminated 134 offices in the household and the government. Archibald S. Foord, "The Waning of the 'Influence of the Crown,'" in R. L. Schuyler and Herman Ausubel, *The Making of English History* (New York, 1952), 409. I. R. Christie, *Wilkes, Wyvill and Reform* (London, 1962), 152-53, evaluates the political significance of the act. Burke probably exaggerated the extent to which North had used patronage opportunities.

of 1688 was not a social upheaval. It confirmed the ancient tradition that the king's government should be managed by the upper class, the people who possessed property, especially landed property. In 1711 ownership of land was a qualification for membership in the Commons, required by statute. Participation was a privilege conferred by title and by property, not a right that every man should enjoy.[47] Electoral reform was not an issue in 1688. Before then, the prerogative regulated the system; afterward, by royal default, so to speak—though really in consequence of the Revolution—the system fell under parliamentary control. The Revolution imposed no moral or political obligation upon parliament to use its new power. To Burke and his aristocratic associates, the traditional franchises and electorates were adequate, even admirable. By their operation the true interests of England were found in parliament while the liberties of all Englishmen were or could be protected from the crown and the mass of the people.

In the English tradition, strongly legalistic, men emphasized not liberty but liberties, that is, privileges or exemptions which had no abstract existence. Eighteenth-century Whiggism identified itself with the security of property and the preservation of social gradations because without them liberties could not exist. Liberties were not the same for all Englishmen. They depended upon circumstances, social, legal, economic, and historical, varying with the ranks and fortunes of individuals. Equality, as Burke was to say, did not mean that men had equal rights to equal things. The British constitution, therefore, was properly an aristocratic one in which power was proportionate to property and rank. Under this system England had achieved prosperity and imperial greatness. The degradation she felt in 1782, according to Burke and his party, resulted from the attempt by George III to reassert royal leadership. Hence the reduction of the influence of the crown and the strengthening of parliamentary independence, not the remodeling of parliament itself, were necessary to the revival of England and the enlargement of the liberties of Englishmen.

By 1782 many persons disagreed with this analysis of the state of the nation. Besides the radicals of different shades—Major John Cartwright, Catherine Macaulay, Christopher Wyvill, the York-

---

[47] See David Ogg, *England in the Reigns of James II and William III* (London, 1955), chap. III.

shire Association, or certain Protestant Dissenters—some prominent members of parliament and even a few of the nobility were
demanding one degree or another of parliamentary reform. Some,
like Pitt, thought the weight of the counties should be increased
by disfranchising the smallest boroughs and enlarging the number
of county members. Shelburne, a sincere royalist in the tradition
of Pitt's father, not only would secure the right of the king to
appoint his ministers, and protect him from factions, but would
reform parliament in order that a free and pure representative
system might on the one hand prevent monarchical despotism
and on the other support a true royal leadership of the people
against the tyranny of faction. The Duke of Richmond was less
idealistic, more specific, and democratic in nineteenth-century
terms. He desired annual elections, equal electoral districts, and
suffrage for all males above eighteen years of age.[48]

Burke opposed parliamentary reform as a danger and a decep-
tion. Only people with political skill and knowledge of public
affairs should participate in national political life. The possession
of these was determined, for practical purposes, by a man's station
in life. A member of the propertied classes, enjoying leisure and
the means of obtaining an education, was more likely than the
propertyless man to be able to acquire these qualifications. On
one occasion Burke estimated that there were not more than four
hundred thousand politically literate people. This does not mean
that Burke was contemptuous of the politically illiterate or
oblivious to their needs and wants. On the contrary, it was the
duty of the governing class to care for their interests. There are,
he once said, two voices in the nation, the cool and temperate
voice of the governing class and the clamant voice of the people.
The latter is usually silent, but it cries out when the people feel
"pinching distress," and then wise rulers should hark to it.[49]
Government, Burke said many times, was a contrivance to care
for the needs and the interests of the people (using the word now
in its broadest sense), but it need not and should not be democratic in order to fulfill its responsibilities. The will of the people
and their interest, he asserted, very often differ. Rulers qualified

48 Olson, *The Radical Duke*, 48-49.
49 *Parl. Hist.*, XXII, 1334, April 12, 1782.

by education, status, and experience are better able to determine what is good for the nation than those whose wills and interests only by coincidence happen to agree.

But democratic ideas and a new orientation of politics were being discussed in 1782, and they caused dissension in the Rockingham administration. Before its formation, Richmond "extorted" from the marquis the promise of a committee of the Commons to examine the question of parliamentary reform; he believed that Rockingham was virtually committed to it if they all agreed, an important qualification.[50] He threatened on May 11 to resign from the government unless Rockingham lived up to his bargain.[51] A vote taken on May 7 encouraged him. On that day Pitt asked for a committee to inquire into the state of the representation, explaining with assumed innocence that England was now governed by a ministry anxious "for a moderate reform of the errors which had intruded themselves into the constitution."[52] His motion forced members of the party to commit themselves. Though Burke did not speak, having been persuaded by his friends against stirring bad feelings, Lord John Cavendish, Fox, and Sheridan supported the motion. With Cavendish, Richmond, and Fox in favor of reform, Rockingham was in the minority of his members of the cabinet. The defeat of Pitt's motion, 161-141, indicated that the opinion of the governing class remained hostile to parliamentary reform while being willing to accept administrative reform as sufficient for the needs of the times. But the size of the minority and its composition indicated that many respectable men in the counties shared with urban radicals a growing dislike of the inequities and abuses of the old electoral structure. In this sense, Whiggism was dividing on an issue that, when the crisis of the French Revolution enlarged it, would force a realignment of parliamentary allegiances and promote the growth of parliamentary parties opposed to each other on a large question of public policy. The only other effort of the session was Sawbridge's annual motion for annual parliaments. This time Burke could not be restrained. Attacking Pitt, not

---

50 Doran, ed., *Last Journals*, II, 438, April 4, 1782; Olson, *The Radical Duke*, 60.
51 Rockingham MSS, Sheff., R1-207b, Richmond to Rockingham.
52 *Parl. Hist.*, XXII, 1416, 1429-35.

Sawbridge, "in a scream of passion" he accused the reformers of desiring "to overturn the constitution" and to destroy the perfection of parliament.[53]

Burke did not reserve his opinions for the House of Commons. In September, 1782, he visited Lord Fitzwilliam in Yorkshire.[54] Here the reform movement was strong, agitated by the Yorkshire Association, and here Burke encountered private persons involved in it. Apparently he spoke vehemently, even intemperately, and according to the Reverend William Mason, who was not his friend, Burke antagonized Fitzwilliam's other visitors.[55] If Fitzwilliam enjoyed only a moiety of the influence Lord Rockingham had possessed in Yorkshire, he could blame Burke, and this loss of support he could attribute "to the effect of his friend's eloquence."

On two other occasions before the French Revolution, Burke expressed himself on parliamentary reform. On January 23, 1783, in a debate on a petition from Launceston praying for the intervention of the Commons to force the mayor and council to name additional freemen in order to enlarge the electorate, Burke opposed.[56] By intervening, the Commons would encourage other petitions and open the way to piecemeal reform. Burke preferred to leave "the ancient and venerable fabric of the constitution . . . untouched," for it had "borne the test of ages." This was a specious argument. The petitioners were praying for a restoration of the "venerable fabric," which the local oligarchy had rent by refusing to nominate as freemen persons who met the ancient qualifications. Burke had a great fear of admitting a beginning of parliamentary interference, even though parliament had the authority and would be using it to correct an abuse. This was the position he took on April 18, 1785, when Pitt asked leave to bring in a reform bill.[57] Burke did not speak philosophically or on this occasion oppose the principle of reform. He admitted the moderation of Pitt's plan but feared that acceptance of it would open the door to more radical reform based, like Richmond's notions, upon the pernicious idea of the rights of man.[58]

[53] Russell, *Fox*, I, 257, Sheridan to Fitzpatrick, May 20, 1782.
[54] Osborn Coll., Box 74, #25, Burke to Richard, Jr., Sept. 12, 1782.
[55] *Walpole's Corr.*, XXIX, 281.
[56] *Parl. Hist.*, XXIII, 343, 345.
[57] *Parl. Hist.*, XXV, 469-70.
[58] *Daily Universal Register*, April 20, 1785.

Burke had better reasons than these for opposing parliamentary reform, although they are alien to the spirit of an age which equates liberty and democracy and defines democracy in terms of the franchise. In eighteenth-century England, generally speaking, the governing class thought that the people enjoyed liberty—or the liberties appropriate to their stations. These did not depend upon the privilege (not a right) of voting; indeed, liberty as the absence of governmental coercion might in Burke's view be better preserved by an aristocracy jealous of royal pretensions and independent of coercion by the people. In so far as liberty was the freedom of people to "do what they please," there could not be certainty as to "what it will please them to do." When individuals act in concert, this kind of liberty becomes *"power,"* and when exercised by persons of uncertain "principles, tempers, and dispositions," such power is dangerous.[59] Therefore, political authority should reside in persons the likeliest to be able to avoid abusing it. These were the nation's natural leaders, the people of birth and background, ordained as it were by Providence to guide the nation's destinies, to determine its policies, to promote its interests, and to protect the liberties of everyone. Voting is a mere mechanical device for determining who, among the qualified persons, will exercise leadership and make laws. A democratic franchise that elected qualified men was superfluous, but it was less likely than a restricted electorate to choose freely and wisely among the qualified; such a franchise was therefore dangerous. It was the duty of the well-born, the able, and the educated to protect the liberty of every subject. The House of Commons was preeminently the guardian of English liberties. All Englishmen existed in it, virtually. The king should not have the power "to counteract the wisdom of the Lords and Commons, or, in other words, of the whole nation," nor should "200 peers" be able "to defeat by their negative what had been done by the people of England."[60] Burke was a House of Commons man. That house should be supreme because it represented the whole people of England, even when they did not participate in the election of its members.

One conclusion is inescapable from Burke's discussions of

parliamentary reform. The eighteenth-century political and social order was to Burke the most nearly perfect one that human wisdom and experience could devise. He never suggested that he perceived the beginnings of a profound change of social and economic circumstances that might be incompatible with the eighteenth-century constitution. He was aware of hostile currents of thought and opinion, and he tried to oppose them by argument. But his arguments were destined to have little effect in the long run; they would be submerged, not by the refutations of the natural-rights philosophers but by the exponents of materialism, utilitarianism, pragmatism, and positivism, whose arguments seemed more harmonious than his with the changing economic and social conditions of late eighteenth-century and early nineteenth-century England.

CHAPTER IV

The Fall of the Rockingham Whigs

DURING THE THREE months following its accession to power, the Rockingham administration modified former constitutional arrangements in ways that agreed admirably with Burke's conception of a good political order. By checking further the prerogative power and by resisting parliamentary reform, the administration met two challenges to the independence of parliament, which had alarmed Burke during the preceding decade. The Rockingham administration, then, gave security to property and to the liberties of Englishmen, which were so inextricably tied with it, while assuring continued control of public affairs by men best qualified to exercise it. Happily, too, these triumphs seemed to vindicate Burke's conception of government by party, even though there were serious divisions in the ministry. The fact that the party program was given statutory form, even when the royal confidence was withheld from Rockingham, seemed to indicate that when parliamentary leaders, or a sufficient body of them, were united, they could carry measures through parliament and force the king to accept them. The influence of the crown had been seriously impaired, perhaps permanently, and the radicalism of the American Revolutionary period at least temporarily checked.

But the Rockingham administration was not completely the master of its destiny. It had inherited problems that were distasteful but unavoidable, and in considering them it had to take account of impatient opinions and pressures. One of the most urgent was the chronic problem of Ireland.

It is customary and proper to think of Burke and Ireland together. The well-being of his native land and justice for its people were his concerns for half a century. His knowledge of Ireland and his associations with Irish leaders would seem to qualify him as the expert to whom his party would turn for advice and guidance. Considering the prominent part he had played in bringing about the reforms passed by Lord North's government, men might expect that with the accession of Lord Rockingham, Burke would be able to do even greater things for his country. So it might be something of a shock to realize that Burke had very little to do with the making of decisions on Irish affairs during the Rockingham administration, and still more of a shock to realize that he was not in sympathy with the measures that were adopted. Indeed, not only in 1782 but in 1785 and again in 1795, Burke found himself in disagreement with some of his party friends and deeply disappointed over the decisions that were made. Whatever his reputation, in his own day and since, as an expert on Irish affairs, Burke's party did not depend upon his advice or judgments.

In 1782 they did not even seek them. Burke was little more than an observer of the actions by which the Rockingham administration placed the relationships between Ireland and the United Kingdom on a new footing.[1] It is only part of the explanation to say that he was absorbed with his duties at the Pay Office, with his preparations of the Pay Office and civil list statutes, and with his arduous labors as a member of the select committee on India. The decisions of the Rockingham administration were not the products of deliberate discussions and free judgments, but were agreed upon almost as an unavoidable response to the pressure of events in Ireland. The only alternative seemed to be civil war against the Volunteers, who were prepared under Charlemont's and Grattan's leadership to back up their demands with force. Having at first tried to counsel delay, which Burke also urged,

[1] For a discussion of the achievement of Irish legislative independence, Harlow, *The Second British Empire*, chaps. X, XI. For a discussion emphasizing Burke's role, Thomas H. D. Mahoney, *Edmund Burke and Ireland* (Cambridge, Mass., 1960), chap. IV.

and then giving in to the threat of troubles, the administration had only to settle the arrangements that were forced upon it. These lay officially with Fox and Shelburne; Burke stood outside. He was unhappy over the course events were taking. He did not desire to differ publicly with his party or quarrel with Irish friends whose conduct exasperated him. He therefore merely acquiesced, expressed cautious and generalized opinions, and hoped for the best.

In February, 1782, Burke was in communication with Irish leaders concerning Luke Gardiner's new bill for Catholic relief. In a long letter to Lord Kenmare, leader of the Catholic Association in Ireland, he expressed opinions that Kenmare had solicited.[2] He was blunt and impatient. Though he favored further concessions to Catholics in religious matters, he thought the question of toleration was no longer pivotal. Because it would follow naturally from an extension of political privileges, Burke preferred to concentrate upon the extension of the franchise to Catholics. Unfortunately, Gardiner's bill failed to provide for this. There would be another decade of lost opportunities before the Catholics were enfranchised. Burke also disliked the provision for a system of education for the Catholic clergy; it was inadequate and would enact a "species of tyranny" by denying men the best opportunity to improve their minds. When the bill passed the Irish parliament, shorn of the unwise educational clauses because of his objections, Burke was able to persuade himself that it lifted some vexations from the Catholics and, as he told William Eden, would redound to the credit of Lord Carlisle's viceroyalty.[3] Nevertheless it was a timid measure. In the light of later events Burke was correct in asking for greater boldness and magnanimity from the Protestant rulers of Ireland.

By the time the Rockingham administration took office, the question of Catholic relief had yielded precedence to the problem of adjusting Ireland's constitutional relationship with England.

[2] Burke MSS, Sheff., Kenmare to Burke, Feb. 4, 1782, Burke to Kenmare, Feb. 21, 1782. Burke's letter also in *Works,* IV, 219-39.

[3] Burke MSS, Sheff., Kenmare to Burke, March, 1782; Br. Mus., Add. MSS 34,418, Burke to Eden, April, 1782. Mahoney, *Burke and Ireland,* 116, says that Burke misunderstood the Catholic faith when he placed civil before religious liberty. That may be true theologically but not in reference to politics in Ireland in 1782. Burke, as Mahoney says, was exasperated over the timidity of the Irish Catholics (p. 116).

The essential idea was repeal of the statutory restrictions upon the legislative independence of the Irish parliament. This would amount to Irish home rule. In general, Ireland's position within the British Empire, as Grattan stated in his famous speech of April 19, 1780, would approximate the position of the American colonies contemplated by the instructions to the peace commission sent to America in 1778.[4] In 1780 Burke had thought Grattan mad for introducing the subject in Ireland; in 1782 he thought no better of the idea. But the force of Irish opinion was now irresistible. Grattan's demand was brought before the convention of the Irish Volunteers at Dungannon, where Charlemont presided in February, 1782, and in the Irish parliament in the same month Grattan voiced it again. When the Rockingham administration assumed office, the Irish patriots vehemently pressed their demands.

William Eden raised the subject in the British parliament on April 8 as a means of embarrassing the administration. A displeased House persuaded him to withdraw his motion for repeal of the part of the Declaratory Act of 1719 which asserted the right of the imperial parliament to legislate for Ireland.[5] Burke answered Eden and advised caution without committing himself on repeal. Fox avowed that the administration was considering the Irish problem and asked for time to work out a "solid and permanent" plan. But Eden had forced the government, and Fox brought in the next day a message from the king recommending a "final adjustment" that would satisfy both countries.[6]

Thereafter the business proceeded more rapidly than either Burke or the cabinet desired. Portland, the new Lord Lieutenant, rushed to Ireland with instructions to work out the details of this "solid and permanent" plan, that is, to slow down proceedings. He found Ireland impatient, her leaders unwilling to adjourn the Irish Commons while he took soundings. Grattan, responding to or exciting the general impatience, on April 16 carried an address asserting Ireland's legislative and judicial independence, and the Irish people were already beginning to say that their emancipation

---

4 See Vol. I of this study, pp. 301, 343.
5 *Parl. Hist.*, XXII, 1245-58.
6 *Parl. Hist.*, XXII, 1264.

dated from April 16.[7] Charlemont backed Lord Rockingham into a corner when he expressed confidence in his administration and promised the lasting friendship of Ireland if her rights were restored. Portland, unnerved by the excitement he found in Dublin, now frantically urged speedy action if Ireland was to be kept peaceful.[8]

By this time the Rockingham government had accepted the principle of Irish legislative independence. But they wished for a precise agreement about details. Though this would take time, which they were playing for, it was also a proper caution for men who were establishing a novel imperial relationship.[9] Shelburne, like Pitt later, desired this kind of settlement. And Burke tried to persuade his friends in Ireland that "some clear and *solid settlement*" was preferable to hasty action.[10] Repeal of the Declaratory Act and of Poynings' Law without agreement on precise details of legislative, judicial, and commercial relationships, would create suspicions and uncertainties, and in the end, Ireland would regret her precipitancy.

Though he attended the meeting at Fox's house on May 16 when final arrangements were made for the resolutions to be introduced in parliament the next day, Burke had no decisive part in making them, just as he had had nothing to do with Irish business officially during the preceding month.[11] The first resolution recommended repeal of the Act of 1719; the second desired that the connection between the two kingdoms be placed upon a "solid and permanent footing" by some means that would be "conducive to that important end." The resolutions passed the Lords with only one dissenting vote and the Commons unanimously.[12]

[7] Burke MSS, Sheff., Thomas Burgh to Burke, April 21, 1782.

[8] Rockingham MSS, Sheff., R1-2049, Charlemont to Rockingham, April 18, 1782, R1-2059, Portland to Rockingham, April 25, 1782, R1-2060, Portland to Fitzwilliam, April 27, 1782.

[9] Harlow, *The Second British Empire*, I, 529-41.

[10] Burke MSS, Sheff., Burke to J. H. Hutchinson, April, 1782.

[11] *The R. B. Adam Library*, I, 6, Burke to Portland, May 25, 1782. Burke characteristically overstated the matter when he told Portland that he had heard nothing at all about Ireland. Besides other letters, he received one from Portland himself. The resolutions, offered by Shelburne in the Lords and Fox in the Commons, are printed in *Parl. Hist.*, XXIII, 37-38.

[12] *Daily Advertiser*, May 20, 1782.

Before the end of the Rockingham administration, the parliaments in both countries passed the repeal acts that established Ireland's legislative independence, at least statutorily. But the *"precise* and unambiguous terms" that Burke, Shelburne, and Fox desired, and the definition of the nature of Britain's "superintending power and supremacy . . . in all matters of State and general commerce" that Portland tried to arrange in Ireland, were never agreed upon.[13] It is doubtful whether even these terms would have solved the Irish problem unless followed by changes that would have freed the Irish executive from British control and the Irish Commons from the electoral arrangements that restricted the delusory constitutional independence that it possessed after 1782. The achievements of the Rockingham administration were statutory steps toward the emancipation of Ireland from British authority. Such emancipation was not synonymous with full independence. Few Irishmen desired to imitate the American example. Whether the "Ascendancy," a clique of Irish politicians, controlled the Lord Lieutenant and led the British administration along, or whether, through the Lord Lieutenant, the British cabinet gave orders to the Ascendancy, the Irish parliament was not a free or representative legislature amenable to the will of the Irish people, the great majority of whom were Catholics. If after 1782 legislative independence within the British Empire had been substantial, there would have been no such events as the unfortunate Fitzwilliam mission of 1795 or the later union of the two kingdoms. For the failure to make the constitutional arrangements of 1782 practically significant, the blame must be widely distributed among English and Irish politicians, and Pitt deserves a large share.

Burke never approved of the grant of Irish legislative independence, and in later years he saw it as the cause of continued troubles. In the debate of May 17, 1782, on Fox's motion, he challenged the Irish patriots and Fox too, though he supported the motion as a matter of form.[14] He disliked the talk about Irish "rights" to legislative independence. Ireland had none, anymore

13 Fitzmaurice, *Shelburne*, III, 150, 152, Shelburne to Portland, June 4, 1782, Portland to Shelburne, June 6, 1782.

14 *Parl. Hist.*, XXIII, 33-34.

than had America. He thought England wise to make concessions, but he wanted them to be concessions granted by a magnanimous imperial sovereign. Only the imperial parliament could determine the bounds of its authority. Burke was ready to concede American independence because there was no alternative. But Ireland was still in the Empire and should be subject to Britain's superintending authority. The problem of the years before 1775 was revived—whether British statesmen would be capable of wisely exercising their authority. Burke never abandoned the principle of the Declaratory Act of 1766, nor that of the Act of 1719, though under the force of circumstances he acquiesced reluctantly in giving up the first and repealing the second. He remained an imperialist, but he would temper the exercise of authority with discretion. It was the statesman's problem to render legal subordination tolerable and to govern in such a manner that dependencies would give the "cheerful alliance" that was the strength of the Empire. Justice and Empire were compatible. Indeed, Burke always thought that a generous imperial government was more likely to assure justice for all the people of Ireland than was a junto, a Protestant Ascendancy, which refused to grant political concessions to the Catholics of Ireland out of fear of loss of its own power. Burke dreaded most of all in 1782 the possibility that new legislation, unless accompanied by proper understanding and restraint, might lead to eventual independence of Ireland, the permanent suppression of the Irish people, and the further dismemberment of an empire that had already suffered one grievous hurt.

With these as his genuine beliefs, Burke was not candid when he expressed to friends in 1782 his opinions about Irish legislative independence. He was not really overjoyed, though he told Lord Charlemont he was, and he misled his Irish friend when he expressed himself in words of double meaning.[15] He wrote, "no reluctant tie can be a strong one; . . . a natural, faithful, and cheerful alliance, will be a far securer link of connexion than any principle of subordination borne with grudging and discontent."

15 H.M.C., *Charlemont*, 60-61, June 12, 1782. References to Charlemont's correspondence dated before 1784 are in *12th Report*, app., pt. X, and thereafter in *13th Report*, app., pt. VIII, unless otherwise indicated.

Though an admission that the recent legislation was preferable
to civil war, this was hardly an enthusiastic welcome to the new
order. To Portland, Burke was despondent.[16] The old system
was ended, the imperial link had been snapped, and now the time
for wise and moderate leadership in Ireland had come. Having
failed to reach a solid settlement on details of future relationships,
the men of 1782 created problems for their successors. Ireland
would have to decide what was to be put in the place of the old
imperial connection, and commercial relations would have to be
adjusted. Early in 1783, when the bill renouncing British civil
jurisdiction was passing through the imperial parliament, Burke
referred to the technical problem it dealt with as one of the
thousand difficulties raised by the repeal of the Declaratory Act
of 1719.[17]

Privately, Burke continued to lament the acts of 1782.[18] He
"never liked, as it is well known, that total independence of
Ireland which, without, in my opinion adding any security to its
Liberty, took it out of the common constitutional protection of
the Empire."

Over the American peace negotiations as over the Irish question,
Burke had no official responsibility, and until early in 1783 even
less opportunity to express his opinions. Indeed, since 1780 his
interest had shifted away from America because he considered her
lost to the British Empire. Burke's chief concern with the former
colonies was that their independence be quickly recognized in a
general peace settlement to include a mutually satisfactory basis
for future commercial relations. He did not explain his position
in detail, for during the Rockingham administration disagreements about the conduct of peace negotiations were confined to
the cabinet. Fox and Shelburne, competing for control of the
negotiations, were also at odds over the issue of American independence. On June 30, with Rockingham on his deathbed, Fox
called a cabinet meeting to which he proposed outright recognition of American independence. The cabinet dissented, and Fox
announced his intention to resign, though he did not set a date.

---

16 *The R. B. Adam Library*, I, 6, May 25, 1782.
17 *Morning Herald*, Feb. 20, 1783.
18 Burke MSS, Sheff., Burke to Fitzwilliam, Nov. 20, 1796, Burke to French
Laurence, March 7, 1797, Burke to Thomas Hussey, March [29], 1797.

On the next day, Rockingham died. For Burke and his friends the world turned upside down. Yet, as Charles Jenkinson remarked, "the Convulsions that have happen'd among the Reformers" would have come even had Rockingham lived.[19] That is, the end of the Rockingham administration, though painful in either case, was merely sudden rather than protracted, and the settlement of the American war, so long a concern of the Rockingham party, fell to other persons.

It would be false to distinguish between the personal and the political loss that Burke suffered in Rockingham's death.[20] His life was inextricably bound up with politics, and his friendship with the marquis could not have been formed, much less have endured, except in relation to politics. None of Burke's friendships with aristocrats had the quality of those with men such as Johnson or Garrick or Reynolds. It was common endeavor in the world of parliament and party that lowered the social barriers between Burke and his noble colleagues and supplied the mutual interest that in his other friendships was provided by literature, the theater, and art. These barriers were never leveled. His friendship with Rockingham was sincere but no closer than social circumstances and Burke's acceptance of established rank would permit.

For the magnificent mausoleum, a landmark of the Yorkshire countryside, which Earl Fitzwilliam dedicated to his uncle's memory in 1788, Burke wrote the character.[21] He extolled the marquis' public virtues, his devotion to liberty, his contribution to the art of government through the agency of party, which to Rockingham was "not an instrument of ambition, but . . . a living depository of principle." Burke's description of his private virtues emphasized qualities that made Rockingham's friends respect and admire him. If Rockingham preferred calm friendship to warm affection, his friends and followers did not sigh over his passing and then forget him. The private sources and the records of parliamentary debates for several years contain frequent respectful references to him. The gentlemen of Yorkshire continued to

---

[19] Br. Mus., Add. MSS 38,309, fol. 67, Jenkinson to John Scott, July 10, 1782.
[20] See Countess of Minto, *Life and Letters of Sir Gilbert Elliot* (London, 1874), I, 80, wherein Elliot tells his wife of Burke's grief.
[21] The completion of the ninety-foot monument was a matter of news. The *Times*, Aug. 29, 1788, printed a full description of it.

meet for dinner on his birthday and pay homage to him.[22] And its enemies referred to the "Rockingham party" for years after the marquis' death.

Burke's relationship with Rockingham had been unique within the party in one respect. The marquis had always subsidized Burke, though to what extent no one knows. Burke also owed contractual debts to him. These were canceled by a codicil to the marquis' will.[23] Contemporaries knew generally about these things, and Lord Carlisle therefore expressed surprise over Rockingham's failure to bequeath money to Burke.[24] Possibly Rockingham expected, or even requested, his heir to continue the bounties to Burke; we know that Fitzwilliam did.[25] At any rate, Charles Jenkinson, who noticed Burke's visit to Fitzwilliam in September, 1782, thought that it signified more than friendship, and was glad of it. Though he and Burke disagreed in politics, Jenkinson had always "pity'd his distresses which I fear are great."[26]

Burke's financial plight, intensified by Rockingham's death, prompted him immediately to seek a brash bargain with Horace Walpole in behalf of Richard, Jr.[27] The story is almost incredible except that Walpole had no reason for inventing it. Burke asked him to persuade his brother, Sir Edward, to resign the Clerkship of the Pells so that Lord John Cavendish, before he gave up the Exchequer, could appoint Richard to the sinecure. In return,

[22] I do not know when the dinners ceased, but that of May 24, 1786, was the largest. *Daily Universal Register*, June 1, 1786.

[23] *Corr.*, II, 492, Fitzwilliam to Burke, July 3, 1782.

[24] H.M.C., *Carlisle*, 631, Lord Carlisle to Lord Gower, July 5, 1782.

[25] Magnus, *Burke*, 182, 222, 224, 343, 348. In 1791 Burke refused Fitzwilliam's offer of aid because as a consequence of the French Revolution he felt he might have to criticize the Portland Whigs of whom Fitzwilliam was a leader. Herbert Butterfield, "Charles James Fox and the Whig Opposition in 1792," *Cambridge Historical Journal*, IX, no. 3 (1949), 295. On Aug. 19, 1795, Burke thanked Fitzwilliam for canceling a bond. Fitzwilliam MSS, Sheff., F30i.

[26] Br. Mus., Add. MSS 38,218, fol. 134, Jenkinson to ? , Sept. 20, 1782.

[27] Magnus, *Burke*, 115-16, 318 n. 29; Doran, ed., *Last Journals*, II, 554-56; Russell, *Fox*, I, 451; *Commons Journals*, XXXVIII, 707, 745. Burke eventually succeeded better in another enterprise set in motion at this time. Before the Shelburne cabinet was formed, he obtained for Richard and Walker King joint-survivorships to the office of Receiver-General of the Land Revenues in certain home counties. The warrant was not executed until the coalition government was formed. In 1784 George Rose, secretary to the treasury under Pitt, sought unsuccessfully to purchase their rights to the office. Magnus, *Burke*, 115; P.R.O., 30/8, 115, Richard Burke, Jr., to Pitt, April 22, 1794; MS in Morgan Library, copy of conveyance of Jan. 13, 1797.

Burke promised that Sir Edward would receive the income for life. Walpole refused, and refused again the next day when Richard renewed the plea with an intricate arrangement for Sir Edward. Walpole was indignant over the effrontery, and his account hints of calculation in Burke's failure to abolish the office when he reformed the civil list. It is easy to understand why Burke had his eye on this sinecure. It returned about £7,000 a year to the incumbent, and even more in wartime.

The significance of Rockingham's death for politics generally and for Burke in particular was determined by the actions of the king. For three months he had suffered ignominy, acquiesced in distasteful measures, yearned for the royal freedom, and dreamed of the recovery of his authority. Rockingham's illness had encouraged him to lay plans. He knew that he could count on Shelburne to accept his invitation to become First Lord of the Treasury, and he knew that Shelburne thought it constitutionally proper for the king to make his own decisions about appointments. If this action could be carried off with the approval of public and parliamentary opinion, the king's troubles might be ended and the prerogative restored to its full vigor. His conviction that Rockingham's friends were keeping from him the true state of the marquis' health strengthened the king's desire to be prepared for the critical moment. Whether he was cruel and cynical or merely realistic was not his concern. On the day before Rockingham's death Shelburne told the king of conversations with Pitt and Jenkinson. The earl would want them "in my Government" at almost any price as able men immune to Fox's "Habits, Assiduity and Address."[28] The king approved.[29] If Pitt and Jenkinson would come in and offset Fox, it might not be necessary to dismiss him "at once," but if he felt uncomfortable, Fox would doubtless resign. And if other Rockinghams would remain in a "broad-bottomed" ministry, then a quarrel with them "as a party" might be avoided, whereas control would lie with Shelburne, that is, the king. No wonder then, that the moment he learned of

[28] Fortescue, ed., *Corr. of George III*, VI, 69, Shelburne to the King, June 30, 1782. Had he been asked, Burke would have confirmed this estimate of Pitt. He publicly acknowledged Pitt's talents at Reynolds' dinner of June, 1782. Charlotte Barrett, ed., *Diary and Letters of Madame D'Arblay* (London, 1842-1846), II, 230.

[29] Fortescue, ed., *Corr. of George III*, VI, 70, the King to Shelburne, July 1, 1782, at 7:21 a.m.,—that is, about four hours before Rockingham expired.

Rockingham's death, the king wrote to Shelburne.[30] In strict honesty, if indecently, he wasted no amenities on Rockingham. He merely said as a matter of fact that the office was vacant and that he was offering it to Shelburne.

The king's plans succeeded almost as well as he could have desired. During the few days required to settle details, the Rockinghams lived in torment. First they had to agree upon a successor to Rockingham. Burke, Fox, and Lord John Cavendish preferred Portland to Richmond.[31] This was a blow to the amateur military engineer, who dreamed of building a bridge between Shelburne and the Rockinghams.[32] Richmond stayed in office, though Shelburne continued to identify him with the Rockinghams. The party did not disown him until ten months later.[33] Secondly, the Rockinghams had to decide whether they would join a "broad-bottomed" ministry. The party leaders, including Burke, met with Shelburne on July 4.[34] It must have pleased the earl to see them fight among themselves. Cavendish said that he would not stay in the government; Fox rejected an offer from Shelburne that Keppel thought generous. Burke scorned Ashburton's suggestion for a union of the parties. The Shelburne party, said Burke, consisted of only seven or eight persons. Two days later in a protracted, anguished meeting at Fitzwilliam's house, the decision was made by the two-score members who attended.[35] After bitterly denouncing Richmond for desiring to continue in office, Burke, Fox, and Cavendish announced their intention to resign. For Burke, who had spoken to the group for two hours, this was a retreat from the bold, extreme line of conduct he had been unable to persuade his colleagues to follow. He had pre-

---

30 Fitzmaurice, *Shelburne*, III, 220-21.

31 Russell, *Fox*, I, 342-45; *Walpole's Corr.*, XXIX, 260-61, Walpole to Mason, July 8, 1782.

32 Olson, *The Radical Duke*, 60.

33 Fortescue, ed., *Corr. of George III*, VI, 185, Shelburne to the King, Dec. 14, 1782. Richmond's break with the Rockingham (henceforth the Portland) Whigs did not come until the formation of the Fox-North coalition. The ties had been weakening for a long time. On Jan. 8, 1783, Fitzwilliam asked Burke about certain correspondence that would prove to Richmond the distance his thought had strayed from that of his political mentors, meaning Burke and Rockingham. Burke MSS, Sheff.

34 Fitzmaurice, *Shelburne*, III, 225-26.

35 H.M.C., *Carlisle*, 632-33, Carlisle to Lord Gower, July 8, 1782; *Walpole's Corr.*, XXIX, 260-61, Walpole to Mason, July 8, 1782; Fortescue, ed., *Corr. of George III*, VI, 76-78, Shelburne to the King, July 9, 1782.

ferred to stay in office, to defy the king by refusing to acknowledge Shelburne as prime minister. He had wished to place the struggle upon parliamentary ground. This, he had argued, would strengthen parliament and prevent the revival of the prerogative.[36]

Burke's frustrated desire was perfectly consistent with his notions of party government and his interpretation of Revolutionary Whig principles. He did not accept the opinions held by almost all of his contemporaries about the prerogative right to choose ministers. He was outwhigging his Whig colleagues in advocating a practice that he thought would conform to the spirit of 1688. In effect he was asserting that "balance" in the constitution was a myth, and that in a showdown, the House of Commons had to be superior to the crown.[37] To say that Burke was moved by self-interest is irrelevant, for probably every change in English constitutional practice and principle has served the interest of its advocates.

Burke was too far ahead of his contemporaries. Even Fox and Cavendish would not go with him. In the House of Commons on July 9 Fox conceded the king's right to appoint ministers, and his qualification did not alter the substance of his concession or obscure the clear difference between his views and Burke's.[38] In any case parliament would have overwhelmingly repudiated Burke's constitutional doctrine. It was less radical in logic than it appeared to contemporaries, though it represented a departure from accepted ideas of constitutional convention. Burke's conduct was probably more indecorous than his arguments. The Revolution of 1688 had made it clear that a king who differed with parliament did so at his peril, and if to perpetuate the victory of 1688 it became necessary further to restrict the prerogative, then Burke was prepared to redefine convention—but within the context of the principles of the Revolution. Burke thought he

---

[36] Russell, *Fox*, I, 352-54, Burke to Fox, early July, 1782.

[37] See also Fryer, *Renaissance and Modern Studies*, VI, 99. Fryer does not say that the logic of the constitutional situation was carried this far, but on p. 100, regarding the fall of North, he does say that "in the final reckoning" a House that overturned a ministry would have been able "to prescribe, in effect and more or less precisely, who their successors should be." It is true that the House had not overturned the Rockingham ministry, but Burke would have said that if it had not, the king surely should not.

[38] *Annual Register*, XXV, 184-85.

was advocating a revision that would preserve the eighteenth-century political order. Between this kind of change and that which he opposed during the French Revolution he saw a basic difference, the one a change that conserved, the other a change that destroyed existing political and social dispositions.

After the Rockinghams decided against a fight, Shelburne was enabled to complete his task of forming a government. Parliament learned the results on July 9.[39] In bitter speeches, Fox, Cavendish, and Burke explained the reasons for their resignations. Contradicting Richmond and Conway, they could not believe that Shelburne had "subscribed to those articles of faith" adhered to by the preceding ministry, and they described a Shelburne ministry as a complete change of system and principles. Particular measures excepted, Shelburne admitted the truth of the charge. He reiterated his dislike of parties and upheld the royal prerogative of appointing ministers freely. Burke was especially violent upon hearing this. He "threw a whole basket of invectives on him [Shelburne] collected from the Roman history down to Mother Goose's tales."[40] Shelburne was Cataline, then a Borgia, and finally the wolf in grandmother's nightgown.

Despite the continuance in office of Richmond and Grafton, whose loss to the party was not vital, and of Keppel, the Portland Whigs, with Fox the tactical leader, resumed their normal career as an opposition party. Burke, who underwent "a very sore tryal" during these days, was calling up his whole "stock of Philosophy" in an effort to persuade himself that if Rockingham's dismayed followers could form "some sort of system," their cause would again triumph.[41] They were still a party, opposed to the high view of the prerogative and still in their own minds the heirs of true Revolution principles, but not unanimous in their beliefs about details of the British constitution. Burke had departed the furthest from eighteenth-century concepts of the prerogative. But the party as a whole represented views uncongenial to the king and Shelburne. The members might expect proscription of individuals and a design to destroy the party.[42]

39 *Parl. Hist.*, XXIII, 180-93.
40 *Walpole's Corr.*, XXIX, 264-66, July 10, 1782.
41 Burke MSS, Sheff., Burke to Loughborough, July 17, 1782.
42 *Annual Register*, XXVI, 137-39.

After the prorogation of parliament on July 11, Burke had time at Gregories to reflect upon recent events. His resignation of the Pay Office entailed the loss of an income of £4,000 a year as well as the house in Whitehall, and both Richard Burkes became unemployed.[43] It is unlikely that consolatory letters that he received (from Adam Smith, Boswell, Portland, and William Baker, among others) were necessary to persuade him that he had acted honorably and courageously.[44] At any rate, he did not find himself in an unfamiliar situation, and as in earlier days he turned for pleasure to his farm and to his friends.

Among his new friends were the Burneys. Burke had known Fanny since a chance meeting four years earlier, but not until Reynolds' dinner, given at Burke's request, in June, 1782, were they formally introduced.[45] This was something of a family party with Burke, his wife and son, Fanny and her father, Dr. Burney, Bishop Shipley and his daughter Georgiana, and the bachelor Gibbon, whose seat at the Board of Trade Burke's civil list act would soon eliminate. Georgiana ignored Reynolds' arrangements and took Fanny's intended seat by Burke at dinner. But from across the table Fanny could see him clearly, a tall, graceful, "noble" figure. She was thrilled by his conversation, more varied and copious than Johnson's. If this occasion was characteristic, it is not true that he monopolized conversations almost to the point of rudeness. Perhaps this evening he kept in check his habit of punning, for Fanny did not remark upon it. She mentioned instead his vocabulary, his imaginativeness, and his knowledge, spilling from a full mind.[46] Perhaps she saw Burke at his best; he usually was, in female company.

The friendship formed that evening continued to ripen. When a month later Fanny's novel *Cecilia* was published, Burke devoted

[43] Yet a little later Burke affirmed that the income from his office did not "pay the expenses" he had incurred in holding it. *Corr.*, III, 13, Burke to Joseph Bullock, March 3, 1783.

[44] Burke MSS, Sheff., Smith to Burke, July 1, 6, 1782, Baker to Burke, July 14, 22, 1782, Boswell to Burke, July 19, 1782; *Corr.*, III, 2, Portland to Burke, July 20, 1782.

[45] Madame D'Arblay, *Memoirs of Dr. Burney* . . . (London, 1832), II, 219-20, 227, 228-34, 238, 241; Austin Dobson, ed., *Diary and Letters of Madame D'Arblay* (London, 1904-1905), II, 87-91.

[46] There are many incidental comments about Burke's conversation. They are collected and discussed in Donald C. Bryant, "Edmund Burke's Conversation," *Studies . . . in Honor of Alexander M. Drummond* (Ithaca, N. Y., 1944), 354-68.

three of his now leisurely days to it and told the author of his profit in reading it.[47] The next recorded meeting took place at Miss Monckton's in December. This time Fanny took notice of Jane Burke and was impressed by her "civility and softness of manner" as well as her good spirits.[48] Noticing her husband's look of pleasure when he saw Fanny, Jane accused him of starting a flirtation, and "before my face, too!" Thereafter the Burkes and the Burneys met occasionally, at Mrs. Vesey's and at Reynolds', among other places. On December 18, 1783, Burke called at the Burneys' home to perform his last official act as paymaster in the coalition government, the appointment of Dr. Burney to the post of organist at Chelsea Hospital.[49]

Burke's concern for Dr. Burney was only one example of his desire to promote the artistic and literary careers of deserving men. Another was his attempt during the Rockingham administration to further the career of John Hickey, the Irish sculptor. Hearing that a grateful Irish nation desired to erect a statue of Grattan, Burke recommended Hickey for the commission.[50] The discontinuance of the project because of Grattan's objections in no way reflected on Burke's judgment of Hickey's abilities. When a group decided to erect a monument to Garrick, and Albany Wallis offered to pay for it, Burke secured for Hickey the commission as sculptor.[51]

Burke's circle of friends, political and nonpolitical, changed with the times. He had the capacity to make new friends among younger people to replace older ones who died. William Windham, for example, was one of several young men who were gathering around Burke in the early 1780's.[52] Born in 1750 into an ancient Norfolk family, educated at Eton, Glasgow, and Oxford, Windham was one of those precocious persons like Fox and Pitt who matured in the age of the American Revolution. While in

47 MS in Morgan Library, dated July 29, 1782.
48 Dobson, ed., *Diary and Letters*, II, 137-38.
49 D'Arblay, *Memoirs of Burney*, II, 373-75.
50 H.M.C., *Charlemont*, 61, Burke to Charlemont, June 12, 1782.
51 Greig, ed., *The Farington Diary*, I, 86 and n.; Bryant, *Literary Friends*, 152-53.
52 Mrs. Henry Baring, ed., *The Diary of the Right Hon. William Windham* (London, 1866), *passim;* Robert Wyndham Ketton-Cremer, ed., *The Early Life and Diaries of William Windham* (London, 1930), 226, 263, 284, 295; Julius Parnell Gilson, *Correspondence of Edmund Burke and William Windham* (London, 1910), 4-6; *The Windham Papers* (London, 1913), I, *passim.*

his twenties he became a member of the Club and of the Johnson circle. After taking an M.A. at Oxford in 1782 he served as chief secretary to the Lord Lieutenant in Ireland under the Fox-North coalition. For several reasons, including ill health, he gave up that post in July, 1783. When he earned distinction as one of the few friends of the Coalition newly elected to the House of Commons in April, 1784, he was already a protégé of Burke. He was a gallant man among the ladies and a fine conversationalist. He was at home both with Burke's political associates and with his literary and artistic friends, whether at Brooks's, at the home of Reynolds, or with Malone or Boswell or the Burneys as frequently as with Fox and Portland. Perhaps the best indication of the nature of his friendship with Burke is an incident that occurred in May, 1785. Windham, whether foolhardy or courageous, made a balloon ascent, "the first rational being that has taken flight," said Burke. But before he did it, Windham made his will, leaving his estate to Burke if the original grantee died without issue. Windham remained a devoted follower. More than any politician of the next twenty years he was the faithful exponent of Burke's political thought.

Besides Windham, there were other additions to the Johnson circle. Edmond Malone, who had settled in London in the late 1770's, was admitted to the Club in 1782 and soon became, if he was not already, a warm friend of Burke. Their common interest in literary scholarship and in Shakespeare was an important link between them. It was Malone who, on a visit to Gregories with Reynolds in July, 1789, urged Burke to revise his *Sublime and Beautiful*. The French Revolution did not intrude upon their friendship as it did upon that between Burke and another Irishman, John Courtenay.

Courtenay had entered public life as secretary to Lord Townshend when Townshend was Lord Lieutenant of Ireland. In 1780 he obtained a seat in parliament and thereafter allied with Burke and Fox. He supported vigorously their positions on the leading political questions of the 1780's. A ready, sharp-tongued debater, he was a useful member of the party, always prepared, said the newspapers, with a joke from Joe Miller. He had a taste for literature, published some light pieces, and was accepted by Burke's literary friends as a member of the Club. More than anything he was proud of his wit and displayed it freely in parliament. Some persons thought he had a bad influence upon Burke. On May 16, 1787, for example, Burke tried to be witty like his friend Courtenay, said the *Daily Universal Register* (May 22, 1787), and "as usual, he overshot his mark." Just a few days earlier, Courtenay had scored a hit, damning Wilkes and Lord Hood with faint praise.[53] Wilkes, he said, had raised a spirit for constitutional freedom the like of which England had not seen since the days of Wat Tyler and Jack Cade. Hood deserved congratulations on account of his being "a spectator at the grand victory gained by Admiral Rodney," when he was under Hood's command in the West Indies. The incensed victim demanded an explanation. Burke sweetly supplied an infuriating one: Courtenay had meant to say "Participator." Like Burke's with Fox, the happy collaboration with Courtenay dissolved during the French Revolution.

One of Burke's younger friends, already mentioned, was Sir Gilbert Elliot. Almost the same age as Windham, and like him possessing scholarly interests along with political ambitions, Elliot was a firm political ally of Burke during the 1780's. Various incidents suggest the closeness of his relations with Burke, but a letter of August 14, 1783, reveals a particular intimacy between them.[54] Elliot did not ask whether he might visit Gregories; he simply informed Burke that on his way to London he would stop with his wife, his child, and the nurse. In case Burke had missed them, Elliot wanted him to know that he "stole" from his room in London two copies of the ninth report of the select committee on India and a copy of Isaac Walton. During the crisis of the French Revolution Elliot joined with Burke rather than with Fox.

Even among Burke's female friends, politics had its influence. Throughout the 1780's Burke went occasionally to Mrs. Vesey's salon, a biweekly event. It was there that he kept up his acquaintance with Hannah More, though he also met her at Reynolds' and at Mrs. Montagu's. Hannah found him less agreeable than formerly, owing, she thought, to the pressures of politics.[55] It was

53 *Daily Universal Register,* May 10, 1787.

54 Burke MSS, Sheff.

55 William Roberts, ed., *Memoirs of the Life and Correspondence of Mrs. Hannah More* (New York, 1835), I, 204, 235, 237.

not precisely the strain of business that affected Burke. Hannah sympathized with Warren Hastings when Burke was attacking him. In contrast, nothing could have pleased Burke more than Hannah's unctuous opposition to the leveling influences of the French Revolution. But the "bluestocking" friends meant less to him now. The measure of the change was his more frequent association with Mrs. Frances Crewe. She presided over a political rather than literary salon in her villa at Hampstead and, besides Burke, welcomed his party colleagues Fox and Sheridan. Burke visited at Crewe Hall in Cheshire and Mrs. Crewe visited Gregories.[56] She remained a loyal friend when the French Revolution shattered so many former political associations, and was at Gregories during Burke's last illness.

Of other old friends remaining, two in particular deserve notice. One was Dr. Brocklesby, Burke's friend of longest standing in England. He was often a member of the company who dined at Reynolds' or Courtenay's. When he gave Burke £1,000 outright in lieu of a bequest, he did so out of "veneration" for Burke's public conduct and his "real affection" for Burke's "private virtue."[57] Akin to this one was Burke's friendship with the calm and congenial Reynolds. He and Burke never disagreed about anything, even politics. In March, 1789, Burke dined with him the day after Reynolds had dined with Hastings. Reynolds was almost invariably a member of the company when Burke dined with literary friends or attended the Academy dinner, the Club, or the theater. In May, 1782, and in December, 1786, Burke sat for him. It was typical of their friendship that Reynolds should write a simple note on August 24, 1784, just to say that he wanted Burke to know he had been appointed the king's principal painter.[58]

Far different was Burke's relation with William Jones.[59] Long recognized as an oriental scholar, a member of the Club, a bar-

56 Burke MSS, N.R.O., Burke to Richard, Jr., Sept. 21, 1788.

57 *Corr.*, III, 77-81, Brocklesby to Burke, July 2, 1788, Burke to Brocklesby, July 17, 1788.

58 Burke MSS, Sheff.

59 Garland H. Cannon, "Sir William Jones and Edmund Burke," *Modern Philology*, LIV (Feb., 1957), 165-86; John Shore, First Baron Teignmouth, *Memoirs of the Life, Writings, and Correspondence of Sir William Jones* (Philadelphia, 1805).

rister, and lately a consultant of Burke on Indian affairs, Jones was properly ambitious for a judgeship in India and well qualified by his standing in the legal profession and his unusual scholarly accomplishments. During the Rockingham administration, Burke promised to use his slight influence to obtain a post for the most learned man of the time.[60] It was not enough, though Jones eventually obtained an appointment through Shelburne's intervention.[61] Almost at once Jones carried to completion all of his plans. Now Sir William, he married Anna Maria, a daughter of Burke's friend Bishop Shipley in April, 1783, and immediately sailed with his bride for India. His first letter from Calcutta was in the old spirit of friendship. He requested Burke to intercede with the government in behalf of insolvent debtors in India.[62] "Could the rights or the happiness of mankind be intrusted to better hands?" Jones, however, became an admirer of Hastings.[63] Burke took offense, broke off correspondence with Jones, and thenceforth disliked him as an apostate.

From about 1782 onward, Burke's friendships tended to become more exclusively political. After that year he never attended more than two Club dinners in any year.[64] As literary friends died, Burke made no effort to cultivate new ones. It is perhaps significant that on March 19, 1783, he was elected to Brooks's Club, on the nomination of the Duke of Devonshire.[65] This was the political club to which his party friends belonged, and there was within it a Fox Club, where Burke's real interest lay. He smiled at his brother's facetious warning, "for heaven's sake, be cautious at play!"[66] Burke, of course, neither desired nor could afford to gamble. He was never a prominent member of Brooks's, despite the testimony of hostile caricaturists; indeed, he never kept up

60 Burke MSS, N.R.O., Aviil8, Burke to Jones, April, 1782.

61 Fortescue, ed., *Corr. of George III*, VI, 253-54, the King to Thurlow, March 1, 1783.

62 Burke MSS, Sheff., Feb. 27, 1784.

63 Cannon, *Modern Philology*, LIV, 181, citing Jones to Burke, April 13, 1784.

64 *Annals of the Club, passim.*

65 *Memorials of Brooks's* (London, 1907), ix-xix, 30; Burke MSS, N.R.O., Portland to Burke, March [20], 1783.

66 *Corr.*, III, 17, letter of March, 1783. Burke detested gambling. He once said he had never bought a lottery ticket or won or lost £5 in his entire life. Wecter, *Kinsmen*, 71-72.

his dues after March 21, 1785, and in 1791, after his political break with Fox, he resigned.[67] It is sad to compare Brooks's with the Literary Club, to observe a certain narrowing of Burke's interests and a diminishing desire to maintain or form new nonpolitical friendships.

67 MSS in Morgan Library, one noting a payment of £45/12 on March 21, 1785, and the other, a reminder to Mrs. Burke, Jan. 26, 1802, of an unpaid account of £109/3/6, accumulated since the earlier payment.

CHAPTER V

The Fox-North Coalition

AFTER THE FALL of the Rockingham administration Burke settled his Pay Office accounts and withdrew to Beaconsfield. By August, politics intruded upon farming, and Burke planned a political visit to Lord Fitzwilliam and the Doncaster races. No contradiction in terms was involved. Burke's friendship with Fitzwilliam continued that with Rockingham, both having a firm political basis. As for the Doncaster race meeting, Burke was interested only in the political atmosphere which would envelop it. Eighteenth-century race meetings were political gatherings. The Portland party, like the Rockingham party, was at the same time a political organization and an association of many of the leading turfmen, though its new leader was not the horseman Rockingham had been. But the racing tradition remained a characteristic feature of it.[1] In September Burke made his political visit to the north. Accompanied by Walker King he stopped at Milton, the Peterborough estate of Lord Fitzwilliam, and thence the party went on to Wentworth and to Doncaster. In October Richard, Jr., who had been on circuit in the north, joined them at Wentworth. There Burke met and argued with some of the Yorkshire politicians. In the county where the Association movement had been strong, he offended some persons by his diatribes against parliamentary reform.

Undoubtedly, Burke's conversations concerned preparations for the December meeting of parliament and the relations of the Portland Whigs with other political interests, particularly that of

Lord North. These subjects had occupied some leading politicians from July onward. Their correspondence, even more than Burke's, reveals preoccupation with the possibility that an alliance between North and Fox might come about as a result of the universal dislike for Shelburne. As early as July 14 Loughborough and William Eden were talking about it. Their discussions indicate that knowing politicians saw nothing absurd or monstrous or unnatural in a Fox-North coalition. The Shelburne administration, said Loughborough, deserved no man's confidence; a new government formed of the leaders of the North and Rockingham parties would possess "more character" and more "public confidence" than any other arrangement could attract.[2] The first step, a personal reconciliation of Fox and North, would not be difficult. North was "irreconcileable to no man," and Fox could easily forget his old antagonisms toward North because of his new hatred of Shelburne. More than revenge would be involved. Fox needed North's parliamentary strength in order to realize his ambitions, and North needed office in order to retain the allegiance of his friends.[3] There would be plenty of patronage to go around.

Loughborough was realistic, not cynical. With the end of the American war, a main difference between the Fox and North parties had disappeared from politics, and on most other public questions they could agree. Eden stressed this point, and so did Rigby.[4] According to Eden, Fox had already stated the possibility of agreement with North on all except one or two points, and these were not of pivotal importance. Eden was not spreading rumors; North had just visited him for two days. Given the irresoluteness of North, it might be too early to "form a system," but Eden was trying. Overlooking Portland, he confessed to Loughborough his inability to think of a proper person as titular head of a Fox-North coalition.[5] On two other matters he had little doubt. The Fox and Shelburne parties would remain "utterly irreconcileable," and Fox felt personally congenial toward

---

1 Innumerable snippets of evidence bear on this point. For example, on Aug. 26, 1789, the *Times* reported that the Portland Whigs had set up their "standard" at York races.

2 Br. Mus., Add. MSS 34,418, fols. 496-97, Loughborough to Eden, July 14, 1782.

3 Pares, *George III*, 81 and n. 3.

4 Br. Mus., Add. MSS 34,418, fol. 513, Eden to Loughborough, July 24, 1782.

5 Br. Mus., Add. MSS 34,418, fol. 515.

Lord North.[6] But North remained coy throughout the autumn, as Eden and Loughborough continued to advance their project.

Like the other politicians, Burke was counting heads. Amid the bitter early days of the parliamentary session he assessed attitudes and alignments and by Christmas had completed his analysis.[7] There were three active groups in the House of Commons: the followers of Shelburne numbered about seventy; Lord North's party was twice as large; and the Portland party, whose numbers Burke did not state precisely, was the most numerous of the three, at least on paper.[8] There was always uncertainty in such matters in days when members prided themselves upon their "independence" and when the idea of party still bore some taint. There was a particular reason for uncertainty about the Portland party. The death of Rockingham had removed the personal factor of long-established leadership. Moreover, a party founded on principle, said Burke, could never be quite sure of retaining in a time of trial the support of men who acted only from self-interest. He admitted that a coalition of the two other parties against Shelburne might appear strange. The integrity of the Portland party would be combined with a party lacking principle or a sense of loyalty to its leader, a party desiring only to overthrow Shelburne and return to office under the old system. Burke, more than Eden, for example, emphasized the idea of incompatible systems. Conceding a common desire for places and a common hatred of Shelburne, Burke was not sure whether these feelings provided a strong basis for a coalition. Though second to none in his dislike of Shelburne, Burke was not an active early proponent of coalition, and he continued to think that principle, program, and character were the true bases of party.[9]

6 Br. Mus., Add. MSS 34,419, fols. 18, 24, Eden to Loughborough, Aug. 22, Sept. 3, 1782.

7 E. B. de Fonblanque, . . . *Life . . . of . . . John Burgoyne* (London, 1875), 417-21, Burke to Burgoyne, Dec. 24, 1782.

8 Eden had counted thirty or forty followers of Lord North, but he was thinking only of active men. Br. Mus., Add. MSS 34,419, fol. 18, Eden to Loughborough, Aug. 22, 1782. Earlier Burke had said that the Shelburne party numbered only seven or eight men, but he was speaking derisively. Early in 1783 Gibbon made his famous estimate: Shelburne and the government, 140; North, 120; Fox, 90.

9 *Walpole's Corr.*, XXIX, 280-81, Mason to Walpole, Jan. 18, 1783, speaks of Burke's former and present attacks on Shelburne. Mason's belief that Burke "must have had" a hand in writing certain anti-Shelburne pamphlets is unsubstantiated, but his opinion about Burke's attitude toward Shelburne is correct.

Yet changed conditions might have their effect, and in sharing experiences in opposition, the Fox and North parties would find themselves cooperating, at least, as the Rockingham and Shelburne parties had done before 1782. When he asked John Noble to support two party members in the event of a dissolution of parliament, Burke spoke of a planned attack, "under the guidance of secret influence," upon every member who championed the independence of parliament.[10] The secret influence now operated under the aegis of Shelburne, not North. Ironically, the followers of Lord North would be victims of it. To resist it and to defend the independence of parliament could be a common cause for Fox and North.

Others, less cautious than Burke, continued to work for coalition as the session entered the new year. William Adam, the Scottish lawyer, a supporter of North and a personal friend of Fox, was in touch with important people. On January 3, 1783, he expressed uncertainty about political dispositions, but Jenkinson reassured him on one point.[11] There was no possibility of friendship between Fox and Shelburne.

By the end of January Shelburne's opponents found something specific to attack. The provisional treaties of peace, which Shelburne's administration had negotiated, seemed to some persons to give away to America and to France more than was necessary. Some members of the government were displeased with them. Richmond refused to attend cabinet meetings after he learned of them.[12] Keppel and Lord Carlisle resigned their posts in protest. Grafton gave up the Privy Seal, though for a different reason. He disliked Shelburne's "want of openness" in conducting public business.

The tribulations of the administration and the approach of debates on the treaties brought nearer the time when decisions would have to be made about party relationships. An attempt by Pitt to persuade Fox to promote a reunion of the Chatham-Rockingham Whigs failed, as it should have. Fox has been criticized for destroying this prospect of unity because of his personal

10 Osborn Coll., Box 74, #4, Jan. 1, 1783.
11 Br. Mus., Add. MSS 38,218, fols. 154-56, Adam to Jenkinson, Jan. 3, 1782 [1783]; Add. MSS 38,309, fol. 77, Jenkinson to Adam, Jan. 4, 1783.
12 Olson, *The Radical Duke*, 70, 192-94.

antipathy toward Shelburne.[13] The critics forget that the Chatham
and Rockingham parties traditionally disagreed on many matters
and had never cooperated wholeheartedly. Loughborough and
Eden continued to talk with the frustrated North. Loughborough
found in early February that North would not unite with Fox.
North would criticize the treaty but not divide the House upon
it, and would even consent to some of his friends entering the
government.[14] He probably had little choice on this last point.
Eden was almost ready to concede that a Fox-North coalition was
less likely of achievement than a reinforcement of the Shelburne
government.[15]

Then on February 14 North made up his mind on one matter.
He and Fox formed an alliance against the treaty. The end of
the American war removed the one "cause of the enmity"
between them. Personally they were friends, sharing confidence
in each other's personal integrity. But this agreement only related
to parliamentary conduct with respect to the treaty. It did not
include arrangements for replacing Shelburne if he were forced
out of office. The alliance accomplished its immediate objective.
On February 17 Lord John Cavendish moved an amendment to
the address to the king on the treaty, North spoke ably for the
amendment, and it carried 224-208. On February 22 Cavendish's
resolution censuring the peace terms was supported by North and
Burke and passed 207-190. Two days later Shelburne resigned,
his hard and able work on the peace treaty apparently repudiated.
Never had a minister been "so universally disliked," and no one
lamented his political demise, not even the king, who was bitter
because he thought Shelburne, like North a year before, had
deserted a tenable position.[16] The king seemed incapable of

13 See, e.g., W. E. H. Lecky, *A History of England in the Eighteenth Century* (New
York, 1882), IV, 291, who maintains that Fox needed only to have acted with
"common wisdom" to restore "unity" to the "Whig party"—as if there had ever
been unity, or even a "Whig party."

14 Br. Mus., Add. MSS 34,419, fol. 89, to Eden, n. d., but late Jan. or early Feb.,
1783.

15 Br. Mus., Add. MSS 34,419, fol. 109, Eden to the Duke of Marlborough, Feb. 13,
1783.

16 The quotation, Br. Mus., Add. MSS 35,528, fols. 26-30, Joseph Ewart to Keith,
Feb. 20, 1783. On Feb. 25 Alexander Straton used the same phrase in a letter to
Keith, Add. MSS 35,528, fols. 39-40.

appreciating the strength of parliament or the difficulties a minister faced when the majority, for whatever reason, was hostile.

In these debates over the treaty, Burke for the first time in nearly a year, and almost for the last, expressed himself upon the American question.[17] Though he spoke as a partisan, he expressed some settled views about relations with America that were not incompatible with the position he had taken in the days when the American problem gave him opportunities for winning fame as an orator and as an apostle of magnanimity in the conduct of imperial relations. In 1783 the possibility of American membership in the Empire or the question of granting independence to America were irrelevant. As Burke saw it, and as other opponents of the treaty held, the issue was the unnecessary generosity of England toward an independent America. Burke denounced the surrender of the Northwest Territories and the uncompensated concession of American access to the Atlantic fisheries. If he was hardly realistic about the territorial provisions of the American treaty, Burke was prophetic in his excoriation of the provisions respecting American loyalists. Why even mention them in the treaty if nothing could be done for them? Burke preferred to leave the subject for future negotiations between the two governments.[18] Mainly Burke was interested in preserving the commerce between Britain and the United States.

He was not an avowed free trader. Burke was a protectionist, and like the others of that time, he considered foreign commerce not only as an economic problem but as a form of international rivalry. Although he could say that "a free trade is in truth the only source of wealth," he would not apply the formula indiscriminately but would consider it in relation to diplomatic and strategic factors.[19] With countries between whom and England there existed traditional and substantial friendship or kinship, like America, Ireland, or Portugal, Burke would remove restrictions upon trade as far as consistent with British security. With

17 *Parl. Hist.*, XXIII, 466-69; *Morning Chronicle*, Feb. 27, 1783.

18 Burke sorrowed for the plight of the loyalists, and later he cordially supported Pitt's policy of providing financial aid to them. *Times*, June 7, 1788. See also Burke MSS, Sheff., William Pepperel to Burke, July 10, 1788, thanking him for supporting Pitt.

19 Burke MSS, Sheff., B-81, Misc. papers.

historical enemies, like France, he would be more cautious. Distrust of France was a lifetime passion with Burke. Whether he was opposing the treaty of 1783, the commercial treaty of 1787, French encroachments upon the Netherlands, or the doctrines and aggressions of Revolutionary France, he was manifesting hostility toward England's historic enemy. Thus he told Mrs. Crewe that England's commerce was her life, whereas France could always recover from hard blows because nature had given her the advantage of self-sufficiency.[20] In the House of Commons on December 5, 1787, he spoke warmly in support of Pitt's policy of checking incursions into Holland.[21] It must be a fundamental of British policy, he said, always to be wary of France and to counteract her influence wherever she tried to exert it. His later opposition to the territorial expansion of Revolutionary France was an intensification of his distrust of the foreign policy of monarchical France. This attitude toward France was in the background of his criticisms of the American treaty in 1783.

It was vitally necessary for England to protect her great national interest, commerce; and desire for American friendship and trade must not be permitted to weaken Britain's bulwarks, her protectionist commercial system and her naval supremacy. If American trade could be advanced without endangering Britain's position in Europe, Burke would be agreeable to loosening some of the restrictions upon it. He would have preferred a commercial treaty with America as a part of the general peace settlement, and he criticized the treaty for this omission. Later he voted for the commercial bill prepared by the Shelburne government.[22] Like Shelburne he was willing to treat the Americans for commercial purposes as if they were still in the Empire. He thought William Eden silly for believing that it was possible to prevent the export of machinery or the emigration of artisans, and he would not desire certain other restrictions which Eden wanted in the bill. On one matter he agreed with the protectionist opponents of the bill. He desired to support the merchant marine as an arm of the royal navy. He would not open the West Indian trade to

[20] Rogers, *Table-Talk*, 100.
[21] *Parl. Hist.*, XXVI, 1273-75.
[22] *Parl. Hist.*, XXIII, 612-13; *Morning Chronicle*, March 6, 1783. Shelburne's bill was defeated.

American ships that would replace British shipping unless Britain obtained adequate concessions in return. Here again he was thinking of France as the future danger. Abundance of cheap land would probably keep America an agricultural nation "for a very long time." On the whole, Burke's opposition to the American treaty was directed to details rather than against the principle. It was strongly partisan.

Having said this much, Burke hardly again spoke or thought of America. Once he expressed fear that the American union might not endure. He regarded secession of the Southern states as a distinct possibility, and he was afraid that the "Federalist" party, the party of wisdom and patriotism, would succumb to the forces of democracy.[23] In one sense, he was correct. The Articles of Confederation, to which he was undoubtedly referring, were replaced by the Constitution of 1787. In 1791 in the debates on the Canada Act, Burke spoke of the American constitution as well adapted both to American circumstances and to the American tradition yet with an admixture of British constitutional principles that preserved it from pure democracy.[24] But he did not recommend it for Canada. Clearly, America outside the Empire had ceased to interest him, and after the defeat of Shelburne, a problem that had for fifteen years occupied much of his attention disappeared from English politics, as far as he was concerned.

Following Shelburne's resignation, six weeks passed before a new government was formed. The victorious allies not only had difficulty with the king, who contemplated abdication of, as he saw it, his tottering throne, but also found that it had been easier to defeat Shelburne than to replace him. As early as February 20 the *Morning Herald* emphasized the limited purpose of the coalition against the treaty, and then went on to predict the formation of a government of the former Rockingham party. Portland would head it with Fox at the Exchequer and Burke and Cavendish as secretaries of state. On March 3 the *Herald* made one change. Fox and Cavendish would trade places.

23 *Notes and Queries*, 2d ser., XII, 267; Thomas Somerville, *My Own Life and Times, 1741-1814* (Edinburgh, 1861), 222-23. Burke made the remark in 1784-1785, probably too early to be precise about the name Federalist. Perhaps his auditor, Somerville, added the name later. He wrote his autobiography in 1813-1814.

24 *Parl. Hist.*, XXIX, 365-66; *Times*, May 7, 1791.

These and other remarks suggested that contemporaries expected Burke to figure prominently in any new administration. To expect was not the same as to approve. John Scott lamented to Hastings because the laziness of good men left control of affairs to "adventurers, such as Burke" to whom "politics are a trade."[25] One "Walpole" had a satirical piece in the *Morning Chronicle* of March 1, 1783. He recommended Burke for the management of the House of Commons in the new ministry. Certainly, he argued, Burke was well qualified. "Not supercilious in his deportment, dictatorial in his conversation, or assuming in his consequence; his smoothness will soften, conciliate every temper, and reconcile every jarring interest: his ingenuity will explain the hereditary right of an aristocratick administration to rule us, though *not founded on publick opinion.*" To Burke's qualities of temper and his indiscretions, "Walpole" might have added a tendency toward coarseness and vulgarity in the heat of debate. Thus Burke once attributed to Pitt a strange olfactory sense that enabled him to smell "a ball of horse dung a thousand miles off" but not a dung heap under his window.[26] Burke was an indispensable embarrassment to his party, unqualified for high office and least of all for the management of the House of Commons.

The tortuous negotiations for a new administration spun out amid strange alignments, contradiction, opportunism, and charges of factionalism. The king talked again of a broad-bottomed ministry. He would not submit to control by "any Party"; he preferred an administration composed of "the best of all."[27] He was willing to see North at the Treasury once again. If North declined, then the king would appoint an "independent peer," "named by Myself," a peer who was not connected with "any of the Strong parties that distract this Kingdom."[28] This insistence upon the prerogative right was, of course, one of the points at issue between the king and the Portland party. Lord North's indecision was another cause of difficulties. Through his father, he made known to the king his unwillingness to take the Treasury

[25] G. R. Gleig, *Memoirs of the Life of . . . Hastings . . .* (London, 1841), II, 512, Feb. 21, 1783.

[26] *Parl. Hist.*, XXIII, 958, June 17, 1783.

[27] Fortescue, ed., *Corr. of George III*, VI, 248, the King to Shelburne, Feb. 22, 1783.

[28] Fortescue, ed., *Corr. of George III*, VI, 248, 257, 258, the King to Shelburne, the King to Thurlow, Feb. 22, March 3, 1783.

or "any other office." Eden pleaded with him to join with Fox to form a government.[29] Shelburne's resignation left the leadership of his forces to Pitt, and, warned Eden, Pitt was an avowed enemy. He was also pledged to wild schemes of parliamentary and administrative reforms. Members of the Portland party, in contrast, were reliable and conciliatory. They desired to "atone for past differences," and on public questions were in closer agreement with North than with Pitt. This contemporary analysis stressed the affinity between the North and the Portland parties; agreement between them on measures was more natural than between either and Pitt. Eden was not alone in holding this view. The *Morning Chronicle,* for example, on February 27, 1783, rejected the word "heterogeneous" as an accurate description of a Fox-North coalition, now that the American war had ended. The word more accurately described the Shelburne administration, it said.

Negotiations involving the king proceeded simultaneously with the conversations among the leaders of the parties that had defeated Shelburne. By March 5 the king understood two things. The Portland party would not serve under an "independent Peer," and a ministry composed of North's friends and holdovers from the Shelburne government could not be formed. The king then turned to Pitt, who had remained at the Exchequer as a caretaker, pending the completion of arrangements for a new government. He was patient. His time had not yet come, and he was not going to jeopardize his prospects by acting precipitately. Gradually the negotiations settled more and more upon a Fox-North coalition, with Portland the titular head. By March 18 the king reluctantly but unavoidably agreed to this arrangement. On the next day he consented to receive Portland in order to discuss details. Then the king decided in desperation to try Pitt once more. On March 20 he sent a peremptory note, "Mr. Pitt, I desire You will come here immediately."[30] Three days later they met again, after Pitt responded to an order "to come here in his Morning Dress as soon as convenient for him."[31] But George could not order Pitt to take office. Later in the day he wrote to Portland and to North,

29 Br. Mus., Add. MSS 34,419, fols. 113-14, Feb. 25, 1783.
30 P.R.O., Chatham Papers, 30/8, 103.
31 P.R.O., Chatham Papers, 30/8, 103, the King to Pitt, March 23, 1783.

"I shall not give him [Portland] any further trouble."[32] This was after Portland had demanded the king's confidence.[33] Yet within two days the king tried Pitt again. The conduct of Portland and North made it "impossible" to admit them into his service; that is, they had encroached too far upon the prerogative. Once more Pitt refused the king's pathetic plea to rescue him from this "daring and unprincipled faction."[34]

His ultimate surrender on April 1 the king disguised as a desire to end the "stagnation" of public business. He assured North that there would be no difficulty about arrangements.[35] But at the same time he assured Lord Temple that the Portland ministry "cannot be supposed to have either My favour or confidence."[36] Before many months he expected the Pitts and the Grenvilles to rescue him from his humiliating situation. In the light of events of December, 1783, this letter is worth remembering.

There is good reason for omitting Burke from a discussion of the formation of the coalition government. He had virtually nothing to do with the negotiations or the final arrangements. He had helped to overthrow Shelburne by voting against the peace treaties, but as Pitt correctly said, the votes were against Shelburne.[37] Burke's dislike of Shelburne was personal only in part. It was also founded in awareness of their basic disagreement about constitutional problems and in a desire for revenge against a man who Burke believed had tried to destroy the Rockingham party.[38] To pull down the Shelburne government and "to destroy him was a necessary preliminary to everything that could be desired beneficial for the public." That accomplished, it remained for the king to permit the new government to do what was necessary to bring about England's recovery.

32 Fortescue, ed., *Corr. of George III*, VI, 301.

33 Fortescue, ed., *Corr. of George III*, VI, 299-300; Portland MSS, Portland to the King, March 23, 1783.

34 P.R.O., Chatham Papers, 30/8, 103, the King to Pitt, Pitt to the King, March 25, 1783.

35 Fortescue, ed., *Corr. of George III*, VI, 328-29, memo. by the King; Burke MSS, Sheff., Portland to Burke, April 1, 1783.

36 Fortescue, ed., *Corr. of George III*, VI, 329-30.

37 *Parl. Hist.*, XXIII, 552, Feb. 21, 1783.

38 Magnus, *Burke*, 317, n. 15, quotes Burke's sketch of Shelburne; *Leadbeater Papers*, II, 133, Burke to Richard Shackleton, March 3, 1783.

COALITION DANCE, by James Gillray, April 5, 1783. North, Fox, and Burke; the book in Burke's hand refers to his speech of July 9, 1782, in which he likened Shelburne to the wolf in *Little Red Ridinghood.*

Burke acquiesced in the coalition with Lord North because he knew that the Portland party could not form a government. "Acquiesce" is the strongest word one can use. For the sake of appearances Burke had publicly announced his support for the idea of coalition. On February 24 he argued in the House of Commons for a coalition that would give strong government to the country.[39] It would be foolish to permit memory of an irrelevant past to impede the formation of a government capable of doing good for the country. This kind of half-hearted defense hardly satisfied members who liked to remind Burke and Fox of their recent strong language against Lord North. Burke seemed to be rationalizing the concept of party that he had been expounding since 1770. His colleagues were relieved to learn that he would do this much. Years later Lord John Townshend told Lord Holland that if Burke had openly opposed the coalition, "we must have dropt all idea of the thing," so great was his influence, "I might almost say command, over Lord Rockingham's friends."[40]

Having given his approval, Burke neither sought nor was assigned a part in making the detailed arrangements. He was kept informed of their progress, and on rare occasions he shared in consultations.[41] Early in March he was one of those who talked with North and the king's confidant, Lord Gower. A few days later Burke called on Loughborough, praising Lord North but deploring his attachment to Thurlow.[42] This may have been at Portland's request, for the duke objected to North's partiality for Thurlow and Lord Stormont.[43] As the negotiations proceeded, Burke's attitude toward the idea of coalition changed. Constitutional considerations may have affected it. The defeat of Shelburne and the imposition of parliament's wishes upon the king were victories for parliament and defeats for the prerogative.

39 *Parl. Hist.*, XXIII, 571-72; *Morning Herald*, Feb. 25, 1783.

40 Russell, *Fox*, III, 41.

41 In 1797 Burke, angry at Fox, said he knew nothing about the coalition until it was formed, and then he felt he had to support it. Perhaps he referred to the alliance against the treaty. If he meant the formation of the coalition government, the contemporary evidence contradicts his memory. Windham Papers, Br. Mus., Add. MSS 37,843, fols. 161-62, Capt. Emperor Woodford to Windham, March 16, 1797.

42 Fitzmaurice, *Shelburne*, III, 376; Br. Mus., Add. MSS 34,419, fol. 125, Loughborough to Eden, n. d., but mid-March, 1783.

43 Burke MSS, Sheff., Portland to Burke, March 15, 1783.

If the situation in early 1783 was not precisely like that of a year earlier, a similarity existed. On both occasions Burke's party needed parliamentary allies, and on neither occasion was the king able to resist the strength of the alliance against the government. A second victory over the king, following so closely upon the administrative reforms of 1782, might weaken the prerogative beyond hope of recovery. As Burke's approval of the idea of coalition grew warmer, his confidence increased. On March 22 Boswell found him almost arrogant, delighted because the king was "overwhelmed by a Faction."[44]

By the time he received Portland's letter telling of the king's capitulation and of the likelihood of his own return to the Pay Office, Burke was speaking positive, enthusiastic language.[45] He was happy to belong to such an honorable political coalition. It promised a strong, stable administration "on a firm and broad basis," a government composed of two parties whose similarities were much more striking than their differences. Once again, admittedly, self-interest was present, though justified as being synonymous with the interest of the community.

On the surface Burke was repudiating the concept of party government that he had been advocating for a dozen years. It seems ironic that twice in his career, in 1783 and in 1794, the outstanding apologist for party in his era gave up party for coalition. On the second occasion he worked for it for two years before achieving it. But Burke never said that party excluded the desirability of making new political arrangements when circumstances changed. Nor did he ever think of party as a static thing. Parties were living, growing organisms. Members might drop out, and new members might join. The important consideration was adherence to principles. The Fox-North administration would begin as a coalition whose two members agreed on "grand points," and that would be unity enough. Burke never held that members of a party could always or should agree on all details.

The question then becomes, were there fundamental points of agreement between the Fox and the North wings of the coalition? There was, first, the common dislike of Shelburne, and it would

44 Pottle, ed., *Private Papers*, XV, 175-76, March 22, 1783.
45 *Parl. Hist.*, XXIII, 707, March 31, 1783.

last. Secondly, there was personal friendship among the leaders of the coalition. Malevolence had never existed between North and his former opponents.[46] Politicians, they knew the facts of political life and normally did not carry outside St. Stephen's the antagonisms that appeared within. If North admitted to John Scott that the Rockinghams had "badgered me till they turned me out," he stated the fact without rancor.[47] Thirdly, the end of the American war dissolved a major difference between North and the Rockinghams. That difference had been over policy, not constitutional authority. The Declaratory Act of 1766, a statement of the Rockingham administration on the nature of the imperial constitution, was in fact the basis of North's American policy until 1778.

The question of differences of political systems was more embarrassing. A pamphleteer argued that it was the fundamental incongruity between the Portland and the North party.[48] North, he said, had always stood for a system of secret influence and corruption, which since 1770 Burke and the Rockinghams had attacked. Now, argued this author, it was strange for two such disparate parties to form a coalition. The pamphleteer overlooked some points. The so-called secret influences were the focus of Burke's and his party's diatribes even before North came to the head of the ministry in 1770. After that they identified North as the beneficiary, not the creator, of these influences. They located the ultimate responsibility in the king. And after North's fall, they continued to talk about them, finding them at work in Shelburne's administration. Historians have scoffed at the doctrine of secret influences. Whether they existed is one question; whether the Rockinghams found it politically useful to talk about

46 *Daily Universal Register*, May 16, 1787, debate of May 15, in which Fox defended the coalition of 1783 and explained that the Rockinghams' criticism of North had always been on public grounds. Historians, especially academic ones, sometimes err in accepting at face value the words of politicians. Anyone who has kept an eye on the political fluctuations that go on about him today (I could cite the recent gubernatorial election in my own state) would not be shocked by the Fox-North coalition, despite the criticisms of North made by Fox and his colleagues during the American Revolution. Politics and politicians of the eighteenth century were in certain respects not greatly different from those of 1964.

47 Gleig, *Hastings*, II, 524, Scott to Hastings, July 18, 1783.

48 *The Coalition, or, an Essay on the Present State of Parties* (London, 1783), 14, 15, 34-35.

them is another. In any case the Rockinghams had not made North the architect of the so-called system of secret influence, and when he joined with them in opposing Shelburne, he wiped out the stain of having permitted himself to be the victim of the system. Along with a good deal of rationalization, there was a basic truth in this argument. North had never been completely the master of his administration. Though he had acquiesced in it, he had never approved, as Shelburne did on principle, of a departmentalized administration in which individual cabinet ministers enjoyed direct access to the king.

The twelve-year identification of North with the king obscured some important considerations. In 1783 for the second time within a year a government enjoying the royal confidence had been forced out of office by a hostile majority in the House of Commons. Never before in the eighteenth century had the authority of the Commons over the crown been so effectively asserted. Political events were amending the Revolution Settlement, in so far as it referred to relations among crown, Commons, and ministers. This alteration, in favor of the Commons, was carried further by the administrative reforms enacted during the preceding year. What is often overlooked is that Lord North had given impetus to those reforms. The statute creating the Commission of Public Accounts had been passed in 1780 by North's government. This commission encouraged the series of statutory reforms that hastened the waning of the influence of the crown. Not only had North accepted the new reforms but on many other matters he and Burke and the Rockingham party had agreed, even before 1782. North was an outstanding House of Commons man. Just before his fall, he had told the king bluntly that in England "the Prince on the throne cannot, with prudence, oppose the deliberate resolution of the House of Commons."[49] The views of parliament, he added, "must ultimately prevail." To cite a modern student, the so-called balance of the constitution "had no final validity," and if parliament could overturn ministers, then it could also "prescribe, in effect and more or less precisely, who their successors should be."[50] North did not go quite so far as to

[49] Quoted in Fryer, *Renaissance and Modern Studies*, VI, 86.
[50] Fryer, *Renaissance and Modern Studies*, VI, 100.

say this, but his statement went in that direction. On a leading constitutional problem of the time, North was moving along the Rockingham road, with Burke in the van. And on another—the authority of the prime minister in his cabinet—North was admitting, by 1783, the desirability of strengthening the prime minister's control. On this he was one with the Portland party and directly opposed to Shelburne.

North and the Portland party also agreed on many policy questions. They had cooperated before 1782 in granting commercial and religious concessions to Ireland, yet they remained loyal to the traditional protectionist commercial system. They desired closer parliamentary supervision over the administration of India. If parliamentary reform divided the Portland party, the part of it, including Burke, which opposed reform, agreed with North, whereas the members who like Fox desired reform, did not want to make a party issue of it. Under these arrangements, reform was neither an embarrassment nor a hindrance to the Coalition, and in any case divided the parties to the Coalition less from each other than from Pitt and Shelburne.

Finally, there is a basic fact of political life. All politicians desire office and in seeking it respond to expediency. More than the Portland party, the following of Lord North was a personal union whose members, collected during the years he enjoyed office, would remain loyal to their leader only so long as he had offices to bestow.[51] They were not inured to adversity as were the Portland party; they were summer soldiers, and their needs had to be attended to or they would desert. In joining the Coalition, North did what he had to do, but for the reasons alleged here, the union with the Portland party was not so unreasonable or monstrous as it is customary to depict it. If this were the only political coalition in history, it would be easier to understand the amount of abuse that has been hurled at it. But junction or union of erstwhile enemies is a frequent occurrence in political history, so frequent that it is difficult to see why the Fox-North coalition has customarily been regarded as something unusual or unnatural.

[51] This point is demonstrated by the analysis of the Commons made for Pitt in 1788, after Fox and North had been out of office four and one-half years. The followers of Fox numbered 138, of North, only 17. A. Aspinall, ed., *English Historical Documents* (London, 1959), XI, 253.

In the larger view, the period 1782-1784 was one of a reorganization of English life at the end of a distinct era. The age of the American Revolution was over. Ireland and India were now the major imperial concerns, along with a general eastward orientation of the Empire. A reassessment of commercial policy was impending. Relationships with Europe were being reexamined. And certain domestic problems, such as parliamentary reform, were being agitated. In these circumstances, politicians were realigning themselves, much as they have done in other periods when new problems forced reconsideration of past political affiliations. The coalition of North and the Portland party was one of the three available alternatives in 1783 and the most harmonious one. The differences between the North and Portland parties on parliamentary reform, on the constitution and the prerogative, as well as on personal relationships were much less pronounced than the differences between either of them and the Shelburne party. Indeed, speaking of unnatural alliances, what of the miscellaneous assortment that later came to be the party of William Pitt? Burke asked the question in 1787 when he derided the ministerial party as a miscellany, odds and ends, scraps from a merchant's warehouse to furnish out a peddler's box.[52] When Dundas, Jenkinson, and later Eden, former followers of Lord North, were leaders of Pitt's government, it hardly became the ministerial party to call the North-Portland forces an ill-assorted crew. The "high-prerogative faction," composed of these men, Gower, and Robinson, joined with the remaining Chathamite politicians and the radicals to form a combination of Tories, reformers, and (some would say) republicans.[53]

According to Burke the principles of the Revolution of 1688 defined the political good in England. The Rockingham Whigs, he believed, had throughout their history represented it, and in 1783 Lord North brought his party into the stream of that tradition. As the *Daily Universal Register* said on October 12, 1785, "the honest English Lord North, being united by an happy coalition with the Rockingham principles, and great abilities of

---

[52] *Morning Chronicle*, Feb. 6, 1787. See also Fryer, *Renaissance and Modern Studies*, VI, 88-89, and Pares, *George III*, 122n.

[53] Russell, *Fox*, II, 70.

Mr. Fox, they were again brought into power [in 1783] by the true Whig principle of the revolution." Considering the issues of that time, the statement makes sense, for in the period 1782-1784, the supremacy of the House of Commons and the independence of parliament were in the forefront of politics.

To contemporaries, emphasizing superficialities, the Coalition might appear strange. It was violently abused in pamphlets, cartoons, newspapers, and in parliament. Burke, Fox, and North were represented as an unholy trinity. All of this should have been irrelevant to the king. His duty, "both morally and constitutionally," was to accept the fact that the coalition government possessed "the authority of the House itself."[54] The historian, enjoying the advantage of perspective, should not be misled by surface inconsistencies. If the Coalition was a marriage of convenience, a combination of ill-assorted political banditti, opportunists seeking only revenge and places, it would not have endured. Burke's analysis was correct. There was a basic harmony between the North and Portland parties, and it survived the pressure of later events. Those who deserted Portland on account of the French Revolution were the followers of Fox, not the surviving followers of North. Thus the coalition of 1794 between Portland and Pitt, like the coalition of 1783, was between politicians who agreed on the issues of the day. In 1794 the larger issue was the preservation of social order in Europe as well as England, whereas in 1783 it had been the preservation of the political order confirmed by the Revolution of 1688. In 1794 the domestic issue of the prerogative power was no longer so important as it had been in 1783.

Burke was vulnerable to attack because he supported the Coalition, but he was even more vulnerable because he, his son, and his brother, back in their former offices, were undeniably beneficiaries of the Coalition's triumph. Except for one unpleasant event, his second incumbency of the paymastership deserves little attention. The event attracted much notoriety at the time, brought down upon Burke an extraordinary amount of abuse, and revealed the ease with which his opponents distorted naïve

54 Fryer, *Renaissance and Modern Studies*, VI, 88.

benevolence into connivance at corruption. When Burke was paymaster in 1782, he had retained the two chief officials in their offices, John Powell and Charles Bembridge. Familiar by long experience with the complicated office routine, they had been valuable to him. On June 18, 1782, in the course of a debate on Pay Office reform, Burke, his predecessor Rigby, and Thomas Townshend had testified to the good characters and abilities of both men.[55] Barré, who succeeded Burke, kept them on. But early in 1783 an independent audit of Lord Holland's still unsettled accounts revealed a discrepancy of £48,000 that pointed to a conspiracy between Powell and Bembridge. Since Lord Holland's estate owed this sum in turn to the Exchequer, the state would be the ultimate loser.[56] Barré dismissed both men early in March, 1783. When Burke came into office a month later, he rehired them, though they already lay under charges. He told them that he was acting on the principle that a man is innocent until proven guilty.[57] As "I would not send a Man, of whose good Conduct in office I have personal Experience, in any degree prejudged to his Trial, on grounds which are by no means clear to me, I conceive myself . . . bound in fairness & equity to continue to employ you." But he added that he would "certainly be obliged to remove you" if the charges were proved.

On May 2 the case of Powell and Bembridge was discussed in the Commons for the first time.[58] Pitt remarked that the two men should not have been reemployed. Burke took full responsibility. He explained, somewhat irrelevantly, that his reform of the Pay Office made embezzlement impossible, and then, angry at an interruption, was pulled down into his seat by Sheridan before he committed some irreparable indiscretion. Fox closed the conversation with soothing remarks, justifying Burke's reemployment of the men as an attempt to be fair until the charges were adjudicated.

On May 19 and 21 the affair came once again before the House.[59] The coalition government won the formal vote to

55 *Parl. Hist.*, XXIII, 119.
56 Binney, *Public Finance*, 153-55.
57 Burke MSS, Sheff., Burke to Powell, Burke to Bembridge, April 17, 1783.
58 *Parl. Hist.*, XXIII, 801-804.
59 *Parl. Hist.*, XXIII, 900-908, 911-23.

quash the order for the Treasury minute on the case, by arguing that a prosecution had begun in King's Bench. The debate was embarrassing to the government and especially so to Burke. His justification for rehiring Powell and Bembridge was a sincere statement, but it did not persuade suspicious members. Some of them may have recalled that Powell had engaged in stock speculation in 1769 with Richard and Will Burke.[60] When Conway thought Burke had acted imprudently in rehiring the men, Fox had to agree. Two days later Burke was pressed again. After reiterating his former defense, he admitted his mistake in judgment. Powell had already resigned, and Burke would dismiss Bembridge if the House desired. Only Rigby, who defended the abilities of the men, demurred.

There was more to the affair than Burke's humiliating surrender to the will of the House. People blamed him for Powell's suicide on May 25. In rehiring him, Burke had exposed Powell to the scorn that drove him to kill himself.[61] As for Bembridge, King's Bench fined him £2,600 and sentenced him to six months in prison.[62] Later he appealed to Burke to help him recover a loan he had made to Champion.[63] Burke was indignant. He had only gotten into trouble for his efforts to be kind to people. He wanted nothing more to do with Bembridge, and he feared publicity that would fasten upon his long friendship with Champion. He was considerably relieved when soon thereafter Champion left quietly for America. He never wrote to Champion, though Will Burke did, excusing Edmund on the grounds of press of business.[64] In 1791, when Bembridge imprudently asked for aid in procuring some office allowances he thought he was entitled to, Burke's reply was curt.[65]

The Powell-Bembridge affair produces some conclusions about Burke. There is no evidence for charging him with anything more serious than benevolent indiscretion and excessive trust in

---

[60] Wecter, *Kinsmen*, 96.

[61] Pottle, ed., *Private Papers*, XV, 234, May 29, 1783.

[62] The trial is in *State Trials*, XXII, 1-160.

[63] Burke MSS, N.R.O., Aii103, Aii104, Axiv68, Bembridge to Burke, Burke to Richard, Jr., Oct. 1, 1784, Burke to Champion, Oct. 22, 1784; Burke MSS, Sheff., Burke to Champion, Oct. 3, 1784, Burke to Bembridge, Oct., 1784.

[64] Burke MSS, N.R.O., Aii67a, Will Burke to Champion, Nov. 11, 1788.

[65] Burke MSS, Sheff., Burke to Bembridge, Aug. 29, 1791.

the probity of his friends. Members of parliament, newspaper writers, and caricaturists were not interested in Burke's good intentions, and they exploited his mistake unmercifully for years.[66] The mistake suggests a reason why Burke was not temperamentally suited for administrative work. He permitted his feelings to affect his judgment. On May 21, 1783, during a discussion of the Pay Office affair in the Commons, Governor Johnstone admitted that Burke acted on grounds of humanity when he reappointed Powell and Bembridge.[67] But, said Johnstone, Burke sometimes let his humanity "run away with him," and this tenderness disabled him from acting with the firmness demanded of a statesman. And worse (or is it worse for a man to do this?) Burke gave his trust too readily to other persons.

Obviously, Burke never was comfortable in office. But there was another reason. His mind preferred larger subjects than office routine. What was the business of the Pay Office compared with the well-being of the British Empire in India?

[66] See, e. g., *Parl. Hist.*, XXIV, 357-58, XXV, 374, debates of Jan. 16, 1784, and March 8, 1785.
[67] *Parl. Hist.*, XXIII, 922.

CHAPTER VI

The British Empire in India

APART FROM MAINTAINING its own existence, the leading problem confronting the Coalition was the problem of India. After three years of hard study, by Burke preeminently, English politicians were ready to give it full consideration. Comprehensive measures relating to the administration of India were debated in parliament twice during the life of the Coalition. Both measures were defeated, and with the second, sponsored by the administration, the Coalition was also thrown out. But the Indian problem remained. The government that succeeded the Coalition dealt with part of it. The other part, concerning Warren Hastings, continued to plague the politicians and engross Burke's attention. Probably from 1780 to the outbreak of the French Revolution, India in its various aspects consumed more of the time and attention of parliament, and certainly of Burke, than any other question, domestic, imperial, or foreign. The impeachment of Hastings, in which Burke was the dominating person, was not, in fact, concluded until the sixth year after the French Revolution began.

So complex and controversial was the Indian problem that it is not easily comprehended even when treated in isolation from other events of the period. And such treatment distorts the problem, because the affairs of India belonged to the history of commerce, politics, and the British Empire generally. So many interests were involved, so many persons and fortunes both in England and in India, that the problem aroused intense emotions.

To Burke it was more than an economic and administrative problem. It was a moral question, because it involved justice for the people of India, whom history and Providence, it seemed, had placed under British authority. How could that authority be exercised so that order and justice would prevail in India? The imperial trusteeship that England had assumed imposed obligations on the merchants and the British public, but, more importantly, a responsibility before posterity and before God for the well-being of the people of India.

As an uninterrupted narrative, the story of Burke and India may begin in 1780, with a glance at the earlier period for introduction. As founder and editor of the *Annual Register,* Burke had early demonstrated an interest in India, but hardly a profound and discerning one. His attitude toward the East India Company in the late 1760's was conditioned by the stock speculations of his family and friends. His defense of the company prior to the Regulating Act of 1773 was very personal and partisan. His speeches at that time and a bundle of miscellaneous notes and fragments in the Sheffield manuscripts (9a) reveal the limited scope of his early concern with India. After 1777, because of Will Burke's interests, Burke acquired a personal connection, hardly reaching to the level of affairs of state, with Madras, Arcot, and Tanjore. It was this relationship that moved him to acquire the £1,000 of East India stock that entitled him to carry his fight in Will's behalf into the Court of Proprietors. He held the stock and the membership from October 17, 1780, to February 23, 1782.[1]

About 1780 his interest embraced the affairs of Bengal and the troubles of India generally. Possibly Philip Francis' letters after 1775 were partly responsible, although there is little direct evidence of their effect. More likely, Burke's broadened interest simply demonstrates that Indian affairs were again becoming matters of public concern, especially for members of the East India Company and of parliament. The war, the quarrels in the

[1] Private communication from the Bank of England, Oct. 27, 1959.

Bengal Council, the reappointment of Hastings as governor general, and the question of the renewal of the company's charter would have commanded Burke's attention in any case. By 1780 there was a noticeable difference in his comments on Indian affairs. He talked about the oppression of the Indian people, and he began to wonder whether the charter rights of the company, which earlier he had defended, were sacred after all. At the time of the Gordon Riots in London he scribbled a note comparing the avarice and bigotry in England with that which threatened fifteen millions of souls in India.[2] A little later he began to offer advice to ministers about changes in the government of India and in the conduct of company affairs. On December 27, 1780, John Macpherson told Macartney about Burke's views on India. Burke had proposed to Loughborough a "calm" discussion of Indian affairs. Though his information was faulty and betrayed him into *"unjust"* remarks, about Hastings for example, his intentions were "liberal," and, said Macpherson, if Burke persisted he would do much good "from his *forcing*" the nation to attend to the Indian problem.[3]

If he and his party criticized Hastings at this time, Burke was still relatively dispassionate. Early in 1780, thinking back over the history of the Regulating Act, he reduced his thoughts to writing, and they were incorporated or noted in a plan of reform drafted apparently by Jenkinson.[4] In order to eliminate the kinds of conflicts that had torn the Bengal Council, Burke recommended a veto for the governor general. This was certainly not a pro-Francis or anti-Hastings recommendation. He suggested strengthening the authority of the crown by requiring the directors to submit to it their instructions to, as well as papers from, India. Jenkinson interpreted this advice to mean that "Political Power over the Company's settlement in India would devolve on the Crown." On January 12, 1781, in a meeting with ministers, Burke reiterated these suggestions, and the group agreed that the powers of the governor general and of the crown should be

2 Burke MSS, Sheff., 8b.

3 C. Collin Davies, ed., *The Private Correspondence of Lord Macartney* (Camden Third Series, LXXVII, London, 1950), 68 (italics Macpherson's).

4 Br. Mus., Add. MSS 38,404, fols. 57-99, *ca.* March, 1780.

increased.[5] If these opinions of 1780-1781 contradicted the views he held in 1773, Burke only arrived at them by stages. As late as April 15, 1782, he remained undecided about the precise position of the company.[6] There was a case for government intervention in the affairs of India, and it grew stronger as events and continued study revealed more clearly the nature of the Indian problem. By this time Burke was perhaps the most avid student in parliament.

A deluge of words enveloped the study. The newspapers told tales of misdeeds and scandals in Indian administration. The printers busily turned out the diatribes of paid pamphleteers. The most active publicists were Philip Francis and Major John Scott. Immediately upon their return from India late in 1781 they began zealously to inject fresh vituperation into the developing controversy.

Francis' role in the India struggles of the 1780's and his relations with Burke are matters of some controversy. He took up his duties in India as a member of the Bengal Council in the autumn of 1774. On two occasions in later years he said that he had gone to India with an unprejudiced mind, determined to assist Hastings in the reform of abuses. But when he with the other new councilors, Monson and Clavering, arrived in India and found Hastings "implicated in every abuse, and the leader in most of them," they resolved to oppose him.[7] These statements are falsehoods, refuted by Francis' own letters and other sources. For example, Add. MSS 34,287 in the British Museum is a volume containing notes to Francis, mainly from Clavering and Monson, and some from John Bristow, the resident at Oude. Bristow was a friend of Loughborough (then Wedderburn) and Clive with whom Francis spent much time before departing for India. This volume reeks with intrigue dating from the earliest letter, November 27, 1774. Even before leaving England, Francis had made up

---

[5] Br. Mus., Add. MSS 38,405, fol. 10. In this meeting Burke also offered suggestions for settling the affairs of Tanjore in a manner favorable to the raja and therefore to Will Burke. But it is important to be clear about Will. At this time he had no interests in Bengal or in the larger problems of India except by indirection.

[6] *Morning Chronicle*, April 16, 1782, reporting a Commons' debate.

[7] Francis MSS, India Office Library, MSS Eur., E. 13, p. 700, Francis to Wedderburn (Loughborough), Aug. 7, 1776 (hereafter MSS Eur.); *Parl. Hist.*, XXVI, 922, April 19, 1787; *Daily Universal Register*, April 20, 1787. The quote is from *Parl. Hist.*

his mind about Hastings. To Lord North on February 24, 1774, he spoke of the natives of India as a conquered people, subjected to the sovereignty of Hastings; just before boarding ship he told Henry Strachey of "cabals" that were forming in India against the three new councilors, but "they are not half so determined to resist, as we are to overcome."[8]

The vendetta between Francis and Hastings began at their first council meeting. On October 24, 1774, the new councilors demanded reports on various subjects, perhaps properly, but resolved "to minute his refusal" should Hastings withhold information. At the same meeting, Francis, Clavering, and Monson, constituting the majority of the council, resolved "To take charge of the Treasury."[9] Soon Francis was describing the ruins of "this glorious empire," asking for the removal of Hastings, calling him and the other minority councilor, Richard Barwell, a pair of "abandoned villains," hoping that Ned Burke would support the "honest" councilors, and demanding that the "powers at home" do their duty.[10] Such complaints and threats gained some attention in England. Though careful not to state his own opinions, John Robinson, secretary to the Treasury, found the public concerned about the conduct of Hastings and Barwell, and some people admitting the existence of grounds for censure.[11]

Fate seemed set against Francis. Monson died in 1776 and Clavering in the next year. Thereafter, Hastings controlled the council. A duel with the governor general in August, 1780, was a quietus between them, so Francis said. From the time they shook hands, as Francis lay bleeding on the ground, he was neither Hastings' "friend, nor his foe."[12] Francis was resolved to return to England. Only an event that he no longer expected to occur, his appointment to the governor-generalship, could detain him in India.[13]

Francis sailed for England in December, 1780. He arrived ten

8 MSS Eur., E. 13, pp. 10-11, April 5, 1774, and the 48th page of a letter beginning p. 133.

9 MSS Eur., E. 13, pp. 25-28, Minutes of the agenda for the Council.

10 MSS Eur., E. 13, pp. 37-44, Nov. 30, 1774, to John Bourke; E. 13, pp. 56-59, Dec. 1, 1774, to Welbore Ellis; E. 13, pp. 60-62, Dec. 7, 1774, and p. 106, Jan. 12, 1775, to Christopher D'Oyly; E. 13, pp. 237-44, May 21, 1775, to Lord North.

11 MSS Eur., E. 13, pp. 327-30, Robinson to Francis, Feb. 1, 1776.

12 MSS Eur., E. 14, pp. 505-506, Francis to Major Philip Baggs, Aug. 28, 1780.

13 MSS Eur., E. 18, p. 54, Francis to Col. Gilbert Ironside, Nov. 5, 1780.

months later, full of information for Edmund Burke and with a present for Jane Burke that she said "made her as fine as an *Eastern* Queen."[14] Francis plunged at once into the ferment of Indian politics. On January 17, 1782, he wrote to G. A. Ducarel, "Everything, that could be done by one human creature to support a cause, has been done by me, from the day of my arrival in England. It cannot be very long, before I see the final effect of my endeavours."[15] His object remained the removal of Hastings, and to that "all my efforts tend and shall be directed a few months longer."[16] The few became many months. Five years later, when the impeachment was impending, Francis wrote grimly, "the charges will gibbet their characters [Hastings' and Sir Elijah Impey's] to all eternity."[17]

Francis directed his campaign not only to the politicians but to the public. A pamphleteer so able and a writer so skillful that some people identify him as Junius, he turned naturally to the press. He was pleased to find that Hastings had already appointed his own press agent, Major Scott. A controversy between Francis and Hastings' agent would "spread the question."[18]

Scott had been two months behind Francis in leaving India and arriving in England. The dates suggest Hastings' intention to send a man who knew his affairs intimately and enjoyed his confidence, to attend "to my political interests and . . . [manage] all my public concerns."[19] Hastings asked for Shelburne's support and advised him to turn to Scott for information. Hastings also informed the Court of Directors of Scott's commission, as justification for having given to him "every necessary Information" relative to the Bengal administration. But not even Scott was empowered to "perform any Act in my Name, that shall be construed to imply

14 MSS Eur., F. 6, p. 30, Jane Burke to Francis, Dec. 6, 1781.
15 MSS Eur., E. 19, p. 44.
16 MSS Eur., E. 19, p. 51, Francis to John Bristow, Jan. 15, 1782.
17 MSS Eur., E. 19, p. 70, Francis to George Shee, Dec. 4, 1786. Shee, a nephew of John Bourke, was Francis' secretary in India after 1776.
18 MSS Eur., E. 19, p. 49, Francis to Edward Wheler, Jan. 18, 1782.
19 Clements Library, Shelburne Papers, vol. 98, Hastings to Shelburne, Jan. 26, 1781. Several documents following this letter show how Scott kept in touch with Shelburne on matters pertaining to Hastings, and tried to create ill will toward Burke. For example, a letter of April 28, 1782, accompanying a pamphlet relating to "the public conduct of Mr. Hastings," and a letter of Nov. 21, 1782, warning Shelburne of an intended move of Burke against Hastings.

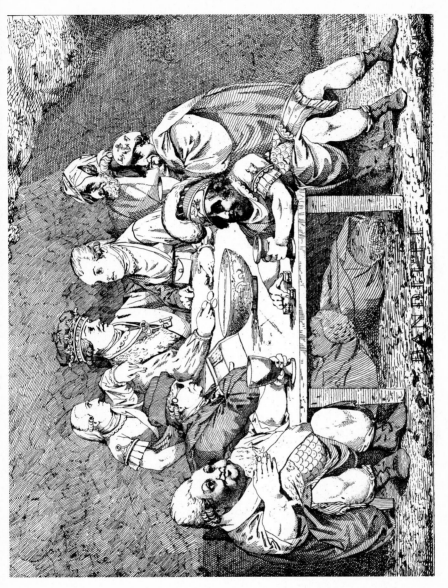

BANDITTI, by *J. Boyne, Dec. 22, 1783.* From left to right, North, Burke, Lord John Cavendish, Portland, Carlisle, Sheridan, Keppel, and Fox; under the table, the bodies of Ashburton (Dunning) and Shelburne.

a Resignation of my Authority."[20] Scott, who had served on the Bengal establishment for fifteen years, during the last two as Hastings' aide-de-camp and one of his private secretaries, described his duties to the select committee on India in the following terms: he was Hastings' agent "for the Purpose of explaining any Part of his public Conduct, which should be an Object of Inquiry, and to enable him to do this, he [Hastings] has furnished him with Copies of the most material Proceedings in *Bengal* for the last Three Years."[21] While Scott was on the high seas, Hastings was hard at work on an account of the transactions at Benares that later would be investigated by the select committee.[22] This was an argumentative piece, an apologia, and not simply a "narrative." It is difficult to believe that it was written late in 1781 rather than in 1787-1788, for it anticipates with remarkable accuracy some of the charges Burke later brought against Hastings. Not only, it seems, did Hastings expect Francis to attack him in England but he expected an inquiry into his administration, and he appointed Scott to defend his interests.

Scott was an incompetent advocate. He hurt Hastings more than he helped him.[23] Francis remarked about the warfare in the press carried on by Hastings' partisans. They had "purchased the press" and had it "in every sense at their command." They were abusing him and Burke enthusiastically.[24] Immediately after the appearance of the select committee's first report, Scott openly accused Burke of seeking to destroy Hastings.[25] Such an accusation could not be confined to Burke; it reflected upon a House of Commons committee. It was an example of tactics that offended many people. The most curious thing about Scott's career for the next decade is that Hastings maintained confidence in him.

20 *Reports from Committees of the House of Commons*, Select Committee, First Report, V, 442, app. 10, Hastings to the Court of Directors, Jan. 6, 1781 (hereafter *H. of C. Comm. Reports*).

21 *H. of C. Comm. Reports*, V, 396-97, Feb. 5, 1782.

22 Hastings, *Narrative of the Transactions at Benares* (Calcutta, 1782); P. E. Roberts, "Warren Hastings and his Accusers," *Journal of Indian History*, III (March, 1924), 108.

23 MSS Eur., E. 19, p. 23, Francis to Wheler, Dec. 25, 1781, describing Scott's performance before the select committee on Dec. 20.

24 MSS Eur., E. 19, pp. 32-34, 40-41, Francis to G. Livious, Jan. 14, 1782, Francis to G. A. Ducarel, Jan. 17, 1782.

25 Sophia Weitzman, *Warren Hastings and Philip Francis* (Manchester, 1929), 146.

Some persons, though they exaggerated, blamed the impeachment upon Scott's persistence and "bullying" of Burke. After Scott obtained a seat in the Commons in 1784, he used it for a forum. Against Hastings' wishes but with the assistance of Thurlow, he also sought a directorship in the East India Company.[26] He thought himself invaluable to Dundas, who after 1784 dominated the Indian Board of Control. Perhaps because he was a nuisance, he managed to extract concessions. The East India Company directors, for example, gave him access to records.[27] In making these pushes, Scott displayed his egotism and stupidity. Speaking of his aspirations for a directorship, he told Hastings, "I fancy I shall accomplish the Point without much difficulty, as I am on the most cordial Terms with the Proprietors."[28] Telling of what he thought were the plans of powerful men such as Pitt, Dundas, and Thurlow to find him a seat in the Commons, he mentioned Thurlow's desire to bring in men of *"knowledge."*[29] Scott professed the utmost scorn for "that reptile Mr. Burke," who was "a contemptible Enemy, even with the assistance of Francis." Though a man of application and certain abilities, Burke permitted his unsound judgment and warped mind to make him appear "ridiculous" in the Commons. More than once, boasted Scott, he "completely silenced" Burke by crushing answers in debate.[30]

If it is hardly to Hastings' credit that he thought Scott's services useful, it is no more to his credit that he was willing to

26 Holden Furber, "Edmund Burke and India," *Bengal: Past and Present*, LXXVI (1957), 18, says that as late as Dec., 1784, Thurlow had an open mind about Hastings. But contrast Scott's letters to Hastings earlier than this date in which he speaks of Thurlow's activities in ways that cannot be reconciled with Professor Furber's interpretation. Gleig, *Hastings*, III, 108-109, Scott to Hastings, Jan. 11, 1784; Br. Mus., Add. MSS 29,166, fols. 115-19, Scott to Hastings, Sept. 14, 1784. Throughout the year 1784 Thurlow was pressing Pitt to obtain a peerage for Hastings. C. C. Davies, "Warren Hastings and the Younger Pitt," *English Historical Review*, LXX (1955), 612; Br. Mus., Add. MSS 29,167, fols. 181-86, Scott to Hastings, Dec. 7, 1784, two letters. See also Add. MSS 29,167, fols. 25-32, Scott to Hastings, Nov. 6, 1784. Scott tells of Thurlow's ignorance about India, but the letter also reveals Thurlow's partisanship for Hastings.

27 India Office Library, Court Book 92, pp. 32, 108, April 24, May 27, 1783.

28 Br. Mus., Add. MSS 29,166, fols. 115-19, Sept. 14, 1784.

29 Gleig, *Hastings*, III, 108-109, Jan. 11, 1784.

30 Gleig, *Hastings*, III, 170, Scott to Hastings, Aug. 15, 1784; Br. Mus., Add. MSS 29,168, fols. 18, 24, Scott to Hastings, Feb. 4, 1785, fol. 72, Scott to Hastings, Feb. 16, 1784 [1785].

pay so much for them. On April 1, 1786, Scott submitted a statement of his expenses between January 1, 1781, and June, 1785, when Hastings arrived in England.[31] They were just short of £21,000, of which £12,523 were personal expenses, and the remainder publishing costs and charges for sending messengers and dispatches to India. Scott thought the statement effectively refuted the gossip about his extravagance. But the talk continued, even in the Commons, where on April 2, 1787, Scott admitted having spent £7,000 in advocating Hastings' cause in print.[32] Before Burke brought formal charges against him, Hastings had spent an enormous amount of money on public relations, and still more before the trial began in Westminster Hall.

The business to which Francis and Scott dedicated themselves was the business in which from 1781 to 1794 Burke was deeply and at times almost exclusively engaged, in close association with Francis until about 1790 and as the object of Scott's vituperation throughout. From his participation in the affairs of India and later in the impeachment of Hastings, he earned an incredible amount of abuse. Next to Fox, he was the favorite subject of the political cartoonists of the 1780's, and many of the savage caricatures of the period portrayed his participation in the India business.[33] The periodicals, newspapers, and pamphlets matched the cartoons in viciousness. The *Morning Herald,* accessible to his opponents, was especially hostile to Burke. On March 27, 1783,

31 Br. Mus., Add. MSS 29,170, fols. 45-46. See also Add. MSS 29,226, a volume of Hastings' accounts from 1774 to Dec. 31, 1785, which shows the amounts drawn by Scott from time to time after Jan. 4, 1781. But the transactions were not one-sided. Hastings also owed Scott money. Add. MSS 29,226, fol. 12, a payment to Scott on Jan. 31, 1782, of £400, which was one year's interest on a bond given at Calcutta. At 10 per cent the bond would have amounted to £4,000. When on the witness stand during the impeachment, Scott was examined about his agency. He described the services he rendered, estimated the expenses at £11,000, and admitted that Hastings paid all of them. *Times,* May 2, 1788. This sum, judging from the context, only referred to Scott's services between May, 1782, and 1785, when Hastings arrived in England.

32 *Parl. Hist.,* XXVI, 859, 883-84. Also *Morning Herald,* April 5, 1787, and *Morning Chronicle,* April 13, 15, 16, 20, 1782.

33 I speak here, not statistically, but from notes and general impressions derived from examination of the collections of caricatures in the British Museum and the Morgan Library in New York. These prints are best used in connection with Mary Dorothy George, *Catalogue of Political and Personal Satires,* V, VI, VII (London, 1935, 1938, 1942 respectively). See also the same author's *English Political Caricatures,* I and II (Oxford, 1959) and Thomas Wright, *Caricature History of the Georges* (London, 1868).

it printed a letter which quoted from a pamphlet called *A Vindication of General Smith*. The extract compared Burke's background with the glorious career of Hastings. Burke was educated at St. Omer, scribbled for the booksellers after he came to England, was an "unprovided-for adventurer" when Rockingham stooped to raise him up, and then, when he got into office in 1782, plundered the Exchequer to the amount of £10,000 a year for himself and his family. A month earlier, "Asiaticus" (Scott) in the *Morning Herald* had emphasized the financial benefits Will Burke derived from Edmund's paymastership. A letter of March 10, 1786, to Hastings from an unknown writer enclosed a piece that he intended to publish, which would expose the "impudent Impostor [*sic*]," the "brazen itinerant Hibernian" who had "obtruded" himself upon England as a "state Quack" possessed of "high flown hypocritical pretensions to Benevolence."[34] The *St. James's Chronicle*, February 19-21, 1789, thought Hastings would triumph over "the Fury of Desperadoes, the Clamour of Enthusiasts, and the Malevolence of Beggars." In the same year, the author of *Begum B-rke to Begum Bow* was happy that the Hastings impeachment had extinguished Burke's fame and glory:

> Wak'd from that dream, where fancy's pencil drew,
> Place, pension, plenty, to my hungry view. . . .
> No more in rage to empty seats I bawl,
> By one side laugh'd at, and despised by all.

Captain Ralph Broome, who wrote as "Simpkin the Second," published some caustic verse during the impeachment.[35] Referring to Burke's absence from the trial on a certain day:

> Some said the disease was increased in his head;
> Some said he was drunk, and lay stretch'd on his bed;
> Some thought he was seized with a fit of the vapors,
> At something that morning in one of the papers—

[34] Br. Mus., Add. MSS 29,169, fol. 508.

[35] Broome had been on the Bengal establishment for some years. Edward Dodwell and James Miles, *Alphabetical List of the Officers of the Indian Army* (London, 1838), 34-35. This notice spells the name Broom. His works included *Letters from Simpkin the Second, to his dear Brother in Wales* (London, 1789) and *Letters from Simpkin the Second to his brother Simon* (London, 1796). The quoted extract is taken from the first of these works, pp. 61-62.

From almost any view, Burke's involvement in the affairs of India dragged him deeply and slowly, for over a dozen years, through a nasty, mean, distressing business that exposed him to abuse, monopolized his time, required arduous labor, and promised no personal reward even if he achieved his purposes. Burke's dedication is not explained by saying that he was led into this great undertaking as the dupe of Philip Francis' desire for revenge. In the early months of 1782, when he had become committed not to the prosecution but to the investigation of the problem of India, he did not and could not foresee where it would lead him. It was on May 1, 1788, that the *Times,* recalling the first sitting of the secret committee exactly seven years before, commented, "little did those who then met, suppose that the result of their deliberations would ever produce so serious investigation" as the impeachment then going on in Westminster Hall. But Burke learned very early that even the first duty he assumed, membership on the select committee to inquire into Indian administration, would be arduous, protracted, and unpleasant. His participation in the investigations of 1781-1783 led him into the path he would follow for nearly the remainder of his life. Burke's work as a member of the select committee, and the nature of its inquiries and of those of the secret committee, are basic to understanding the Indian phase of Burke's life.[36]

The committees were quite independent of the Rockingham administration. Begun before the fall of Lord North, the investigations of the select committee persisted until the end of November, 1783—that is, through the Rockingham, Shelburne, and coalition governments.[37] Philip Francis was right when as early as December 25, 1781, he told Edward Wheler that no administration could stifle the committees.[38]

The select committee ranged widely over the field of Indian administration. Its first report, February 5, 1782, censured the

[36] Furber, *Bengal: Past and Present,* LXXVI, 18, makes the same point.

[37] The eleventh and last report of the select committee was dated Nov. 18, 20, 1783. The secret committee, dominated by Dundas, had a more limited scope, had got under way earlier, and presented its last report, the sixth, on March 6, 1782. This accounts for its and Dundas' leadership on India questions during the Rockingham administration. Both committees, of course, reported to the House of Commons.

[38] MSS Eur., E. 19, p. 26.

East India Company administration in England for its "long continued Inattention" to the "open Disobedience of their Orders," by Hastings and Impey as well as other servants in India.[39] Generally, the committee thought that parliament would have to protect the people of India against officials who could not be reached by ordinary processes, and to that end, such officials ought to be called home and held to account.[40] By the spring of 1782 news of the troubles in Oude and Benares was reaching England, and the select committee decided to conduct an "Immediate Investigation."[41] The second report, June 6, 1782, expressed dissatisfaction with Hastings' conduct up to September 29, 1781, the date of the latest news to reach England; in a supplement issued on April 1, 1783, the committee said its later information, including Hastings' own narrative of the events in Benares and Oude, only confirmed its original judgment.[42] Hastings' treatment of the raja of Benares, Chait Singh, was severe out of proportion to his offenses, if they were offenses, and the "Justice of Parliament" should intervene "as the best Means to recover the national Reputation, Probity, Humanity, and Good Faith." The brief third report, June 12, 1782, returned to the relations between directors and their servants. Knowing of his "irregular" conduct in the past, the committee wondered how the directors could appoint to the Bengal Council such a man as John Macpherson, who had formerly "been guilty of a flagrant Breach of their Trust."[43] In this Burkean language the question was asked of the men who had been chairman and deputy chairman at the time of Macpherson's appointment. Their evasiveness persuaded the committee that the "Disobedience and Corruption of the Servants Abroad . . . may in a great Measure be imputed to Intrigue, Cabal, and Management in Great Britain."[44]

By this time the committee had accepted the necessity of a more comprehensive parliamentary intervention than the Act of 1773

---

[39] *H. of C. Comm. Reports,* V, 402-403; MSS Eur., E. 19, p. 58, Francis to Wheler, Feb. 12, 1782.

[40] *H. of C. Comm. Reports,* V, 415.

[41] *H. of C. Comm. Reports,* V, 447.

[42] *H. of C. Comm. Reports,* V, 483.

[43] *H. of C. Comm. Reports,* V, 631, 636.

[44] *H. of C. Comm. Reports,* V, 636-37.

provided for. Burke not only acquiesced in the first three reports but was a leading member of the committee and probably responsible for some of the language of the reports. He was thus rapidly moving away from the position he had taken on company affairs in 1773. The investigations of the select committee were conditioning Burke to the idea of active official participation in the administration of India.

By July 11, just after the end of the Rockingham administration, the committee issued three more reports, issuing no more until April, 1783. The fourth, June 18, 1782, was very short and unimportant. The fifth, of the same date, reverting to the subject of servants' disobedience, was a detailed attempt to ascertain the truth of certain charges Francis had made in a much publicized letter of October 12, 1780, to the Court of Directors.[45] Two of his allegations involved both Hastings and the directors, the one for violation of company orders, and the others for acquiescing in Hastings' disobedience. It is easy to understand, from the evidence studied by the committee and printed in the report, why Burke was impatient with company administration at home and in India. The sixth report examined the system of administration established by Hastings in Bengal.[46] Some of the details were very technical, and the committee turned to Francis for explanations of them.[47] For very recent events, the committee sought information from Scott, who, it seems, had secured documents unknown even to the Court of Directors. The committee saw in Hastings' innovations, especially those relating to revenue collections, an inordinate increase in the authority of the governor general, in violation of the directors' order of February 5, 1777, which had prohibited administrative changes without their prior consent.[48] Even if these changes were improvements, the committee thought that "the Abuses and Disorders" of the administration of Bengal threatened "utter ruin."[49]

45 *H. of C. Comm. Reports*, V, 655-89, for the report; 690-830, for supporting documents; and esp. 657-58, 664-65.
46 *H. of C. Comm. Reports*, V, 841-78, for the report; 878-1014, for the supporting documents.
47 *Daily Universal Register*, Dec. 12, 1787.
48 *H. of C. Comm. Reports*, V, 847, 859.
49 *H. of C. Comm. Reports*, V, 841.

The six reports had unity and a prophetic quality. After the first one the committee had wondered whether mere "Legislative Regulation" would be as effectual as "Criminal Proceeding" in directing servants to their duties. The committee also wondered whether the enactment of new statutes without "a strict Attention to their Execution" might increase "the Audacity of Delinquents." It was not enough for directors to issue "a feeble Repetition of Orders" when their first instructions were disobeyed. The directors could not be ignorant of the "Suppression" of information and the sending of "garbled Communication" in an "unconnected and irregular Correspondence."[50] In the light of later events, the committee's opinions are very significant. The term "Criminal Proceeding" could include impeachment, and the criticism of the directors anticipated the closer governmental supervision provided both in the Coalition's India Bill of 1783 and in the one that became law, Pitt's Act of 1784.

In performing its labors, the select committee, and Burke in particular, depended heavily upon Francis for information and assistance.[51] To admit his importance is not to say that his influence was decisive. If he directed its attention to certain matters and advised it, the committee also exploited other sources, including the company records and officials, and Major Scott. The committee's reports, and especially the documents they reproduced, created impressions unfavorable to the directors and to Hastings. Though in 1782 Hastings' side of the story had not been told, except by Scott, the directors had testified before the committee and left it dissatisfied. The evidence gathered by the committee, admittedly incomplete, was voluminous. It justified a censure of the directors, a reprimand of Hastings, the promise of a fuller examination when he returned from India, and eventual changes in the East India Company's administration of India.

It is important to notice that the most severe indictment of

---

[50] *H. of C. Comm. Reports*, V, 401, 415.

[51] Examples are found in Impey Papers, Br. Mus., Add. MSS 16,260, fols. 169-71, Impey to Shelburne, Oct. 18, 1782; MSS Eur., E. 19, pp. 31-32, 41, 29, 30, Francis to John Mackenzie, Jan. 14, 1782, Francis to Andrew Ross, Jan. 10, 1782, Francis to Burke, Jan. 11, 1782; MSS Eur., F. 6, p. 2, Burke to Francis, March 12, 1782.

Hastings during the Rockingham administration came not from Burke or the select committee but from the secret committee.[52] It was led by Dundas, whom no one has charged with being a tool of Francis or of the Rockingham administration. This committee extended its view beyond its original commission and ranged far from the military events in the Carnatic that it had been appointed to study. Between June 27, 1781, and March 6, 1782, it presented six reports.[53] Having completed its investigations, it was prepared, earlier than the select committee, to open the Indian question before the House of Commons. This was the real beginning of the new parliamentary consideration of the problem of India. One stage, the remodeling of the administrative system, was completed two years later with the passage of Pitt's Act. The other stage, the proceedings against former administrators, lasted for a decade after that.

With a three-hour speech on April 9, 1782, Dundas inaugurated the new era in the history of India and of parliament. He reviewed the background of the Indian problem, explained the work of the secret committee, and moved the reference of the reports to the committee of the whole house. He confessed that until he had begun his duties as chairman of the secret committee he had paid no more attention to India than a member was likely to give to parliamentary business in which he was not personally concerned or about which he did not feel deeply. To the subject of India only a few men in England had directed wholehearted attention, and hitherto he had not been among them. Neither was the writer for the *Morning Chronicle* nor the editor who, in brackets following the lengthy account of Dundas' speech, admitted that it was not easy to follow because the "subject was so new to us."[54]

Generally, in this and later speeches, Dundas condemned the aggressive actions of company servants in India and the failure of the directors to restrain would-be Alexanders, who preferred "frantic military exploits to the improvement of the trade and

52 Sutherland, *East India Company,* 382-84.
53 The reports are printed in *H. of C. Comm. Reports,* VII, 2-268, 269-589, 591-637, 639-710, 711-1066, VIII, 1-270, 271-1105.
54 April 10, 1782.

commerce" of India.[55] Parliamentary intervention was needed to supply the defect of authority. Pending a permanent provision for Indian administration, Dundas urged strong measures against delinquents. Burke agreed heartily. Parliament should announce its determination to "regulate" the government of India and to punish men who "by their malpractices" had disgraced the British name.[56] He did not define the word "regulation," except to say that he did not mean the complete assumption by government of the administration of India. But Burke was closer to Dundas' position than to Fox's. Fearing that the "interposition of the Crown" would increase the royal influence, Fox preferred to continue the parliamentary investigation while giving the company an opportunity to reform itself and replace disobedient servants with honest men.[57] If Burke saw the danger mentioned by Fox, he did not admit it, or he thought it less important than the effort to enlarge justice for the Indian people.

Whatever the differences about new modeling the administration of India, there was a general desire to proceed against certain individuals. One of them was Sir Thomas Rumbold, a member of the Commons who had served two years as governor of Madras.[58] Upon his return to England in 1780 he found himself blamed for the war in the Carnatic. Dismissed from company service, he came under the scrutiny of the secret committee. Anticipating an attack in parliament, he tried to conciliate Burke, sending him a published defense of his actions and later seeking interviews.[59] Though Rumbold's career had not been the select committee's concern, Burke was interested because Rumbold's authority had touched Tanjore and Arcot and therefore the affairs of Will Burke.

When on April 22 Dundas brought into the House twenty-four resolutions relating to Madras that, if adopted, would require the prosecution of Rumbold, Burke supported them. With "a con-

[55] *Parl. Hist.*, XXII, 1279, April 15, 1782.

[56] *Parl. Hist.*, XXII, 1289, April 15, 1782.

[57] *Parl. Hist.*, XXII, 1286-87, April 15, 1782.

[58] For the fullest account of Rumbold and a defense of his conduct, see E. Rumbold, *A Vindication of the Character and Administration of Sir Thomas Rumbold* (London, 1868).

[59] Burke MSS, Sheff., Rumbold to Burke, March 11, May 5, 1782.

summate Knowledge of his subject," said the *Daily Advertiser* on April 24, he condemned the Madras administration for corruption and mistaken policies. It permitted its servants to lend money to the nawab of Arcot, who, oppressed by his private creditors, in turn oppressed the raja of Tanjore. With Dundas, Burke desired parliamentary intervention to protect the raja and to regulate the finances of the nawab.[60] To Will Burke, Edmund reported that Dundas' speeches were as if Will had made them.[61] Burke brushed aside the defenders of Rumbold.[62] Parliament could choose to be lenient to the oppressors of India, or by punishing them, to protect fifteen million Indian dependents and "save India."

The House of Commons followed Dundas' lead. It gave him leave to bring in a bill of Pains and Penalties, the common-law criminal process being thought inadequate to deal with Rumbold's case. And so the first Indian "delinquent" was called to account.[63]

The next attack was directed at Hastings. It came from both committees. In an effort to wrest the lead from Dundas, the select committee on April 18, 1782, drawing upon its first report, brought ten resolutions before the Commons.[64] Sulivan, as chairman of the East India Company, was criticized for failing to send promptly to India the Judicature Act of 1781; Hastings, for creating, without authority, a new superior court of civil jurisdiction; and Elijah Impey, for accepting the headship of it when he was already a judge of the Supreme Court in Bengal. The committee of the whole passed the resolutions against Hastings

---

[60] Parl. Hist., XXII, 1309, 1320, April 22, 29, 1782; *Daily Advertiser,* April 24, 1782.

[61] *Corr.,* II, 485, April 24, 1782.

[62] *Parl. Hist.,* XXII, 1317, April 29, 1782.

[63] Rumbold escaped conviction. Changes of ministries delayed proceedings; Rumbold's defense, begun late in Shelburne's administration, was skillfully conducted by one of the ablest lawyers of the time, George Hardinge, and after June 2, 1783, the bill was not debated again. Though not formally dropped until December 19, 1783, when Pitt had assumed office, in effect the action was taken on the initiative of the coalition ministry, on a motion by John Lee, the coalition attorney general. Burke had been convinced by Rumbold's defense, and later showed respect for him. Burke's position changed also as his hostility against Hastings mounted, so that in any conflict of testimony, he tended toward Rumbold's side. Finally the settlement of the nawab of Arcot's debts by Dundas in 1784-1785 completed the reversal of Burke's position. The Rumbold affair was part of the background of the Arcot debts which prompted Burke's famous speech in 1785.

[64] Sutherland, *East India Company,* 384; *Annual Register,* XXVII, 56.

and Impey, and General Smith promised to ask the House to request Impey's recall from India.[65] In the meantime, Dundas brought in a new set of resolutions and recaptured the lead in the chase, with Hastings his quarry. His resolutions, more comprehensive than Smith's, culminated in a demand that the directors recall the servants "chiefly concerned" in discrediting British honor in India.[66] The committee of the whole house urged the Commons to request the directors to recall Hastings for having acted "in a Manner repugnant to the Honour and Policy of this Nation."[67]

The scene of the struggle over Hastings then shifted to India House, which under the Act of 1773 possessed the power of recall. Hastings' friends rallied energetically to his support. On June 19 the Court of Proprietors resolved that compliance with the Commons' request without a thorough investigation of the charges would diminish the prestige of the company, and reminded the directors that they alone could not remove Hastings.[68] In reference to this event, Major Scott gleefully informed Hastings of the demise of Burke's "popularity." "Our illiberal opponent Burke is sunk, never, I hope, to rise again."[69]

The death of Lord Rockingham did not affect these proceedings, for at no time had they been in the hands of the Rockingham administration. Shelburne, for political reasons, found it expedient to promote the proceedings.[70] He bluntly told Scott of

[65] *Parl. Hist.*, XXII, 1313-14, April 24, 1782. The House voted on May 3 to ask the crown to recall Impey. Weitzman, *Hastings and Francis*, 149. Before he could have known of the order for recall, Impey complained to Shelburne about the select committee's report. Br. Mus., Add. MSS 16,260, fol. 171, Oct. 12, 1782. He was certain that Francis, who in 1780 opposed the creation of the court, had primed the committee, and he was fearful of a "popular assembly" influenced by "a man of Mr. Burke's ability, perseverance & industry." Besides Shelburne, Impey enjoyed the support of George Dempster and Governor Johnstone, who accused the committee of partisanship and ulterior motives. *Parl. Hist.*, XXIII, 197, July 11, 1782. Because of his delay in returning to England, the select committee took up the matter on November 12, 1783, during the Coalition. *Daily Advertiser*, Nov. 14, 1783, reporting debate of Nov. 12. General Smith asked for papers on the Impey recall, Burke seconded, and the motion carried without opposition. But by this time, Impey was preparing to return to England, and in June, 1784, he arrived to face criticism and abuse and eventually to appear before the House of Commons.
[66] *Parl. Hist.*, XXII, 1291-1302 for the texts of the resolutions.
[67] *Commons Journals*, XXXVIII, 1032, May 28, 1782.
[68] India Office Library, General Court Minutes, VI, 210-11.
[69] Gleig, *Hastings*, II, 486, 495, June 26, Aug. 29, 1782.
[70] Sutherland, *East India Company*, 386-90.

his intentions to press the directors, and on October 14 they voted 13-10 for Hastings' recall.[71] Then the Court of Proprietors by an overwhelming vote of 428-75 asked the directors to rescind their action.[72] On November 22 the directors complied.[73]

So ended the first engagement in the long war against Hastings. The governor general was safe only for the time being. His opponents did not intend to give up the attack. Of Francis' hostility there had never been any doubt. If previously Burke had not been persuaded, now he was.[74] The enmity of Dundas and the coolness of Shelburne also worried Hastings' partisans. The Rockingham party had not yet dedicated itself to the campaign against Hastings, but it had followed the lead of Burke, Dundas, and the committees, and after July, 1782, in opposition again, it was likely to be more determined. Many members of parliament who were not partisans had been stirred by the revelations of the two committees. The company administration had been severely criticized. The inadequacy of the Regulating Act of 1773 had been revealed. Regardless of Hastings, something had to be done about the administration of the British Empire in the East.

Of course, individuals had played their parts in exciting opinions. But one must not underestimate the influence of events in giving focus to opinions and substance to personal actions. The Indian question had been crying out for attention, and as the American war ended, consideration of it would not have been postponed. The parliamentary investigations had begun, for example, before Francis and Scott returned from India. If the committees' reports were garbled, that was in large part because the masses of materials were confused, contradictory, and to men just beginning their studies of India, not entirely comprehensible. One did not have to be an avowed enemy of Hastings to find in

[71] The *Morning Herald*, Feb. 17, 1783, spoke of Shelburne's influence upon the directors.

[72] India Office Library, General Court Minutes, VI, 225, Oct. 31, 1782; *Daily Advertiser*, Oct. 26, Nov. 1, 1782. The proprietors' meeting of Oct. 24, which decided to ballot on the question, lasted nine and one-half hours.

[73] *Daily Advertiser*, Nov. 25, 1782.

[74] Years later the king told Sylvester Douglas that Sir George Shee was the person who had influenced Burke against Hastings. Bickley, ed., *Diaries of Douglas*, I, 392, Aug. 19, 1804. So far as I know, this is a unique reference to Shee.

the documents reasons for doubts, suspicions, and criticisms of Indian administration, of Hastings, and of the directors. Until someone presented Hastings' side of the story more adequately than Scott did, it is not surprising that the committees and members of parliament were shocked. No advocate, no profound knowledge of India, was needed to identify the tergiversations in the testimony presented before the committees. The examples of willful violations of orders by company officials, and news of the fantastic events in Oude, Benares, and the Carnatic, which came while the investigations were going on, seemed to justify the conclusions reached by the committees.

In July, 1784, Burke described the development of his thought about India. By that time he not only was hostile toward Hastings but was indulging in the intemperate language afterward characteristic of his writings and speeches about India. He averred that he had never felt a personal animus toward Hastings and that except for partisan disapproval of Hastings' friendship with the North administration, he had even felt, when the select committee first came into being, "a strong prepossession in his favour," having previously heard so much praise of him. Impey's friends, in fact, had accused him of partiality to Hastings. Burke said "the discoveries" he had made "in the Company records," and the additional knowledge of Indian affairs gained from his work on the committee had persuaded him that Hastings was "the scourge of India."[75] This statement, made to the House of Commons, was corroborated by George Dempster.[76] A few months later Burke told Thurlow precisely the same thing.[77] A modern student adds, "Anyone who has worked in the baffling masses of papers in the India Office records on this period can easily see how a man of Burke's strong and unstable emotions could feel that here really was evil—corruption which outshone any type with which he was familiar at home."[78] Besides such emotions, Burke possessed a rich imagination and warm humanitarian concern for all who suffered or seemed to suffer under oppression. Once

[75] *Parl. Hist.*, XXIV, 1214, 1271.
[76] *Parl. Hist.*, XXIV, 1271.
[77] Furber, *Bengal: Past and Present*, LXXVI, 18, citing Burke to Thurlow, Feb. 28, 1785.
[78] Furber, *Bengal: Past and Present*, LXXVI, 18.

aroused, his nature would not let him stop. The difference between him and all others who were concerned in the business of India and Hastings was measured by his deeper passion and his greater ability to desire intensely the well-being of humanity. Nor was Burke altogether misguided. Hastings' character and his conduct were not unimpeachable.

It was in 1782-1783 that Burke became convinced. Neither the end of the Rockingham government nor Shelburne's humiliation by the Court of Proprietors discouraged Burke or dissuaded parliament from pursuing the attack on Hastings or the study of the Indian problem. The mails from India, for example, brought to him the same passionate pleas that Macartney was sending to other persons in England. "Lose not a moment, apply the remedy without delay, send able men, honest men, and practicable men to govern India."[79] Burke agreed. In April, 1783, Major Scott said that Burke's main interest was to send new men to India rather than inaugurate constitutional changes.[80] This charge was misleading. Burke saw no sense in establishing a new system of government and then giving it over to men who were already under severe criticism for mismanaging the old one.

And so he continued to attack Hastings. On February 17, 1783, Hastings' name popped up in the debate on the American treaty.[81] Burke admitted his abilities but thought his ambitions had very nearly ruined the British Empire in the East. Eventually he might be proved a "great delinquent." This implied threat became specific on April 25, when Burke "pledged himself to God, to his country, to that House, and to the unfortunate and plundered inhabitants of India, that he would bring to justice, as far as in him lay, the greatest delinquent that India ever saw."[82] When Burke called Hastings to account, he would provide the House with a list of Hastings' crimes. If there is any doubt about the time when Burke resolved to bring in his list, there can be none about the date when he publicly committed himself to do it. By the

[79] Br. Mus., Add. MSS 22,458, fols. 54-59, 80, Macartney to Burke, Oct. 18, Nov. 5, 1782. The Macartney MSS in the Br. Mus. contain copies of his letters on this theme to friends in England.

[80] Sutherland, *East India Company*, 393, n. 6.

[81] *Parl. Hist.*, XXIII, 467-68.

[82] *Parl. Hist.*, XXIII, 800-801; *Morning Herald*, April 29, 1783.

spring of 1783 he had dedicated himself to the cause of justice for the people of India. His speeches on the subject thereafter revealed an intensity, a commitment, an emotional involvement that had not been present earlier.

Burke's passion against Hastings was not the extent of his concern with the Indian problem. Changes of men had to be accompanied by a general reform of the government of India and of the company.[83] The renewal of the select committee on December 21, 1782, implied that the changes would come. Burke plunged into his work with the clear intention of dominating the committee. He told Francis that he did not know whether he could carry it with him (where?), but with Francis' help he would try.[84] Though in some manner the central authority in India had to be strengthened and the supervision of the state over company affairs improved, Burke anticipated disagreement over the detailed provisions for giving effect to these fundamental principles.

In the Shelburne administration Henry Dundas assumed responsibility for drafting legislation that would establish a new system of government for India. He drew freely upon others' labors, including Burke's and the committees'.[85] Not until April 14, 1783, after the fall of Shelburne, did Dundas ask for leave to introduce his India bill. Judging from the past, there was no reason for believing that his views on India would be uncongenial to Burke and the Coalition. The government, however, did not intend to permit an outsider to take the lead in Indian legislation. The bill was "tacitly withdrawn," said the *Annual Register;* the government said that it was introducing its own bill.[86]

Dundas' proposals were not lost forever. His bill was the basis for some parts of Pitt's India Act of 1784, and its intention was

[83] *Parl. Hist.,* XXIII, 647, 796-98, debates of March 12, April 25, 1783.

[84] MSS Eur., F. 6, pp. 3, 4, 5, Burke to Francis, Dec. 29, 1782, Feb. 8, May 28, 1783. On March 31 Boswell breakfasted with Burke. Francis dropped in. If he had come to talk about India, he avoided the subject in Boswell's presence. They talked about Chatham. Pottle, ed., *Private Papers,* XV, 188-89.

[85] Sutherland, *East India Company,* 391-92; transcript by Thomas W. Copeland of Burke to Dundas, March 1, 1783, in Melville MSS in National Library of Scotland. In this letter Burke urged protection for the raja of Tanjore and other native princes. He said that experience proved that revenue payments were more regular when the administration of a country was in native hands.

[86] *Annual Register,* XXVII, 54-56.

identical. With some of Dundas' desires Burke agreed, especially the investigation of the claims of Tanjore and the Arcot debts and the confirmation by statute of the possessions of the raja of Tanjore.[87] The provisions for strengthening the authority of the Bengal government over the other presidencies resembled in general the proposals Burke had confided to Jenkinson in 1780. Dundas' desire to recall Hastings made them more acceptable. Of Dundas' suggested qualifications for a governor general, birth, ancestry, independent fortune, and talents, Burke thought only the last was necessary. An able man, even of "middling rank," would do. This is a curious point in view of Burke's alleged deference to the claims of the aristocracy to govern England. In general, Burke and Dundas were not far apart concerning the administration in India. But Burke, as his own bill was soon to show, preferred to locate superintending authority at home in parliament rather than in the crown.

When Dundas was rebuffed, the coalition government took charge of the Indian problem. Though the grand inquest of the affairs of India was not a strictly partisan matter, and the seventh report of the select committee on April 23, 1783, would have appeared regardless of changes of administration, it nonetheless happened that the second series of reports, beginning with the seventh and ending on November 18, 1783, with the eleventh, appeared during the Coalition's tenure. In this last period of its activity, the committee was influenced more strongly than ever by Burke. He wrote two of its reports, the ninth and the eleventh. They are among the great papers in the history of British administration in India.

The seventh report returned to the subject of company administration at home and relations with servants in India.[88] The irregularities, for which Sulivan was largely blamed, amounted to "Neglect of Duty."[89] The preparation of this report coincided with the campaign for a company election in which there would be a Sulivan list of candidates for directorates. Without trying to deter Burke, Lord North informed him that he intended to

[87] The main points of the bill are outlined in *Parl. Hist.*, XXIII, 757-62; see also Sutherland, *East India Company*, 392-93.
[88] *H. of C. Comm. Reports*, VI, 3-17.
[89] *H. of C. Comm. Reports*, VI, 12.

support the Sulivan interest.[90] In the Commons, some members objected to printing the report on the eve of a company election.[91] Burke's denials persuaded no one that the report was not intended to influence the election. John Scott called it Burke's "diabolical attempt" to injure Sulivan's chances.[92] If that was his purpose, Burke failed to achieve it.

The eighth report, June 13, 1783, returned to Hastings.[93] On February 14, 1783, the directors had censured him for his treatment of Fyzoolah Khan, a Rohilla chieftain. Three years earlier Hastings had requested the nawab of Oude to make demands of Fyzoolah Khan that exceeded his treaty obligations to the nawab. Hastings had not yet taken threatened punitive action against Fyzoolah Khan when the directors passed their censure.[94] Hastings, they said, had committed "an Act of Injustice," and still more, had complicated relations with the nawab of Oude so that the choice now lay between wronging the Rohilla chieftain or violating a new treaty with the nawab. The committee found Hastings in a vulnerable position. Whether there were extenuating circumstances or whether state necessity could justify Hastings' action would not be known until his story could be told. But on the evidence it possessed, the committee had reason for holding Hastings culpable and for thinking he deserved more than a slap on the wrist from the directors. Why not some kind of proceedings to expose the truth, especially in view of Hastings' involvement in other questionable incidents?

The famous ninth report of June 25, 1783, discussed some of these questions. It revealed even more decisively that Burke had made up his mind about Hastings and India—that is, if he was indeed the author of the report. On this point the testimony of Francis is authoritative.[95] He said without qualification that

---

90 Burke MSS, Sheff., March 25, 1783. North had just written a letter in support of Sulivan to be circulated among his friends. Gleig, *Hastings*, II, 517-18, John Scott to Hastings, March 23, 1783.

91 *Parl. Hist.*, XXIII, 717-23.

92 Gleig, *Hastings*, II, 517, Scott to Hastings, March 23, 1783.

93 *H. of C. Comm. Reports*, VI, 21-41.

94 *H. of C. Comm. Reports*, VI, 32-33.

95 Francis and Keary, eds., *Francis Letters*, II, 358, 388, Francis to "a friend," March 15, 1785, Francis to Sir Robert Chambers, April 27, 1791. In MSS Eur., E. 19, p. 88, there is a separate sheet following this letter, which, from internal evidence, was probably written in 1813.

not only was Burke the author but that only he was capable of writing such a magnificent paper. It was a masterpiece of which "I wrote a very small part" and "as to the composition, corrected the whole." Though Burke derived "every" idea in it ultimately from Francis, this information was "dilated on & expanded by a superior power," and therefore the report was "the sole undoubted property of the commanding master-mind of *Edmund Burke*." In another statement Francis identified the minor passages he had written at Burke's "own desire."[96] Francis went further. He attested to Burke's authorship not only of the ninth report but of the eleventh as well, and said that Burke wrote "most" of the other reports of the select committee.[97]

This testimony suggests two remarks. First, it is difficult to imagine the prodigiousness of the labors Burke had performed on the Indian problem even before the end of 1783. In addition to attending the meetings of the committee, preparing for them ahead of time, and studying the information and the documents they uncovered, he digested the materials and wrote the reports, two in full and undetermined portions of the others. During half of the year 1783, for example, he wrote two reports that comprise three hundred pages of his octavo works and, as we shall see, spent the summer and autumn preparing the famous India bills. Secondly, whether Francis primed him with information, Burke made it his own and henceforth would use it for purposes which he had now decided upon.

The ninth report displays Burke's opinions about Hastings and India.[98] It opens with a summary. The state of company affairs was "disordered"; the natives lived amid "Depression and Misery"; and "This Mismanagement has . . . arisen from dark Cabals, and secret suggestions to Persons in Power." This situation arose immediately out of the defects of the Act of 1773 and out of the

[96] MSS Eur., F. 8, pp. 37, 38, 39, a paper of 1808 discussing Bisset's *Life of Burke*, and p. 47, a sketch of Burke.

[97] Corroborative of this statement is Burke's remark of March 22, 1786, in a debate in the House of Commons, when he thanked T. B. Rous for "his powerful assistance in drawing up the first report of the select committee." *Parl. Hist.*, XXV, 1275.

[98] *H. of C. Comm. Reports*, VI, 45-91, for the report, and pp. 91-484, for supporting documents. This report is also in *Works*, VIII, 3-215. The difference in pagination arises from the differences in format. The reports are in folio volumes. The texts differ only in capitalizations, punctuation, and spellings.

maladministration and corruptions of company officials at home and abroad. Ultimately, the fault lay in the failure of the imperial government to exercise its responsibility for the good order of the Empire.

The Regulating Act was unfortunate because it was based, not on the information proved by the committee of 1772-1773, but on speculation and "general Ideas." As he had when speaking of ineffective American policies, and as he would when condemning the French Revolution, Burke attributed mistakes of policy and maladministration to the refusal of politicians to take facts, circumstances, and history into account when making decisions. In his earliest treatise Burke had expressed contempt for political metaphysicians who, by preferring speculative rules of uniform conduct, contributed to the ills of that revolutionary age. The prudential statesman, guided by practical reason, considered circumstances and the probable consequences of their adoption before choosing the means that seemed most likely to accomplish the end desired. "Seemed most likely," because at best there was an "unavoidable uncertainty" in all calculations of human conduct.[99]

The goal of British imperial administration was hardly a matter of choice. It was ordained by eternal and universal law. It was justice, whose principles were the same everywhere, the good order and well-being of the people of the Empire, and in this instance the people of India. Therefore the means to be employed for achieving justice should be determined by the needs of India, not by the speculative reasoning of English politicians ignorant of her history, traditions, and circumstances. Just as Britain had failed in its government of the American colonies to give first place to the eternal principles of justice and humanity, so hitherto the company and its servants, exempt from imperial restraints, had placed profits for themselves ahead of "the Prosperity of the Natives." Only if the people of India were happy, prosperous, and peaceful could British imperial administration justify itself.

The Act of 1773 did not furnish the proper means to justice. The qualifications for membership in the Court of Proprietors neither discouraged factions nor promoted "Integrity of Conduct."

---

[99] Francis P. Canavan, *The Political Reason of Edmund Burke* (Durham, N. C., 1960), for a clear discussion of Burke's idea of prudence.

The provisions respecting the Court of Directors, contrary to the intention of the act, diminished their authority and encouraged the disobedience of company servants, who were left free to oppress the people of India. The unhappy history of the Supreme Court of Bengal was an excellent illustration of failure to follow the rules of prudence. The court was in effect an alien institution in India. Hindustan was treated as if it was a "province of Great Britain" instead of a civilization with its own history and culture. Yet in some instances when it should not have, the court functioned upon principles "too remote from the constitution of English tribunals." The provisions regarding the Bengal Council were especially defective. Burke attributed some of the difficulties of the years after 1774 to the act itself. Rival ambitions or conflicting personalities did not account for all of the troubles between Hastings and Francis. The Act of 1773 did not give sufficient authority to ministers. Britain was not properly exercising her imperial responsibility. This was Burke's hindsight, and it caused him to abandon his earlier opinions about the sanctity of the company charter. Now, in absolute contradiction of his former beliefs, but in harmony with his new knowledge of Indian affairs, he was a clamant advocate of close governmental supervision of company affairs. While prepared to enlarge the authority of ministers, he did not desire to enhance the influence of the crown. He hoped to strengthen parliamentary control. Here his constitutional views were pertinent. If ministers were to become more dependent upon the Commons, then ministerial supervision of company affairs would mean closer parliamentary control.

All of this Burke illustrated by a scorching condemnation of the commercial policy that hitherto the company had pursued. Much of his discussion was technical, but the lesson was clear. The company's profits came from the Indian people; the "Plunder" of India, especially of Bengal, produced dividends for company stockholders. What was worse, in recent years the company trade had become a "Vehicle for Tribute," and the company itself had been reduced to the role of "Agents and Factors" to the private traders who conducted commercial operations between India and England.

These pernicious commercial endeavors profoundly influenced

the character of the political administration of India. The committees' investigations clearly revealed the failure of the company to enforce obedience to its instructions. Hastings was only the best known person who had violated company orders as well as the principles of decency and humanity. Thus, reformation of Indian administration was all of a piece. Parliament must intervene to reorganize the company's commercial system, its constitution, and the administrative arrangements in India, all "in the strictest Obedience" to the imperial government. This conclusion and the whole of the ninth report must be kept in mind if one is to understand the purpose and the provisions of the controversial India bills that Burke wrote and the coalition government tried to enact.

The remainder of the ninth report was a bill of particulars against Hastings and other company servants in India. Because some of these allegations appeared in the later impeachment charges, it is only necessary to mention them as a reminder that the impeachment of Hastings was at least in part a consequence of Burke's experience as a member of the select committee. It is worth asking whether there would have been an impeachment without the two committees. Burke's main argument in his attack upon Hastings in the ninth report was the governor general's disobedience of company orders. He described some of his censurable deeds: the strange "resignation" of Hastings in 1775-1777, which turned out not to be a resignation at all; the dismissals of Bristow, Fowke, and Mahomed Reza Khan and Hastings' refusal to obey the directors' orders to restore them to their posts; the violations of company regulations with respect to commercial contracts. Such "uniform and systematical" disobedience was also defiance of parliament because it violated the Act of 1773.

The ninth report was many things. It was quite different from earlier reports and much more characteristically Burkean, in that it was a history of the East India Company and of British administration in India—perhaps the first that many politicians had read. It explained the reasons for and suggested the plan of reform that Burke would soon embody in parliamentary bills. A list of allegations against Hastings, it anticipated some of the impeachment charges. It was an implied attempt to analyze the character of Hastings and an intimation that willfulness, arbitrariness, deviousness, unwillingness to take responsibility for his actions when they were criticized, and a lust for power "characterized" him and therefore his administration.

The tenth and eleventh reports, July 10 and November 18, 1783, directly attacked Hastings.[100] The tenth report furnished one of the leading impeachment charges, the treatment of the begums of Oude, dramatizing primarily the resumption of their jagirs (government revenues from a tract of land assigned with power to collect and administer). This act, said the report, was "totally unnecessary to the restoration of the peace of the country," and whatever the obscurities surrounding it, it was essentially "the act of the Governor General." In this report an interesting point emerged, one that is vital to an understanding of subsequent proceedings against Hastings. The select committee, apparently anticipating the argument of "state necessity" or "reason of state," refused to accept it as a valid justification of Hastings' administration.[101] Undoubtedly, Burke urged this point in committee sessions. To him, the argument could be used to justify any action. To employ it in defense of immoral or illegal actions was to undermine the foundations of civil society.

The eleventh and last report of the select committee returned to the question of Hastings' disobedience of company orders and the Act of 1773. This time Hastings was accused of accepting presents on three occasions and then attempting to conceal or to misrepresent his actions. Thus, that he had accepted two lacs of rupees from Chait Singh, a fact not known to the committee when it wrote its second report on the transactions in Benares, was a "complication of fraud and cruelty" admitting of "few parallels." Another transaction, involving Hastings' request for compensation for the three lacs of rupees that he said he had advanced to the company service out of his private funds, was "covered with the thickest obscurity." Hastings' three accounts of the episode were full of contradictions; if one was accurate, the

---

100 *H. of C. Comm. Reports*, VI, 487-576 and 579-84. The eleventh report, with a few extracts from the long appendix, is in *Works*, VIII, 219-304.

101 *H. of C. Comm. Reports*, VI, 502.

other two "must necessarily be false." The third transaction related to Hastings' appointment of Munny Begum as the guardian of the nawab of Bengal. It appeared to the committee that money was passed in this transaction. On this low note the important series of committee reports ended.

It is difficult to exaggerate the significance of the work of the select and secret committees. Their effect upon Burke's career has already been emphasized; their influence in directing public attention to the Indian problem also must be stressed. But it remained for the coalition government to take the bold step of staking its existence upon the passage of Indian legislation. When the Coalition at last produced a strong majority in the House of Commons, the first "determined attempt" was made to deal with the Indian problem.[102] That attempt could not have been made without the preliminary work of the committees and their success in drawing attention to their labors by their well-written and heavily documented reports.[103]

When the Coalition's India bills were before the House of Commons in November and December, 1783, both Fox and Burke paid tribute to the committees.[104] Fox claimed that the bills were based upon their prodigious work, and that that having been done, it was now left to parliament to draw conclusions from their investigations and take the actions necessary to reform Indian administration. Burke agreed. The bills were the product of three years of "laborious Parliamentary research," that is, the research of the two committees that reported to the House of Commons. Whatever one thinks of the committees' interpretations and methods, there can be no doubt of their diligence. Boswell, for instance, upon visiting the committee room with Burke, was pleased to see it such a businesslike place.[105]

Burke had a pivotal part in transferring the Indian problem to the floor of the House of Commons. It is difficult to imagine any government's evading the question after the work of the committees, yet there is agreement that Burke drove the Coalition

---

102 As to the Coalition's parliamentary strength, see A. Aspinall, ed., *Later Corr. of Geo. III* (London, 1962), I, xxii-xxiii.
103 C. H. Philips, *The East India Company, 1784-1834* (Manchester, 1940), 23.
104 *Parl. Hist.*, XXIII, 1189; *Works*, II, 433.
105 Pottle, ed., *Private Papers*, XV, 185, March 27, 1783.

and thus parliament onward.[106] His "passionate and intemperate activity," so characteristic when he felt the need for action, was a vital influence in forcing the Coalition to take a calculated risk.[107] If the government succeeded, much credit would come to it; if the various opposition groups, including powerful East Indian influences, defeated the bills, the king might be able to force the government out. Eden and Loughborough agreed in fearing the opposition and the king. Said Eden, the bills would either make or break the administration; said Loughborough, that "curse of India" would be the ruin of the administration and the country.[108] Fox was under no illusions. Though we are strong in parliament, he told Lord Northington, the Lord Lieutenant, an India bill will be dangerous.[109] Many members of parliament had a personal interest in Indian affairs or connections with the company. On no other issue could various opposition groups coalesce more readily. Nevertheless, Fox had survived a quarrel over the Prince of Wales's establishment that, taking place during the recess, would have provided the king and Lord Temple with their opportunity if they had been inclined to press for anything at that time, and so he anticipated the future with greater confidence. Since the weakness of the Coalition was the royal dislike and since Coalition strength lay in parliament, its survival until the session began would mean the passing of a dangerous period. This consideration persuaded Fox, influenced strongly by Burke, to face the challenge of India even at the risk of the administration's life.

Contemporary opinion made Burke the author of the bills. He was, after all, the party's India expert. At India House the measure for reorganizing company administration was called "Burke's Bill."[110] The actual writing seems to have been done by others after Burke returned from a month's tour with his family

106 Sutherland, *East India Company*, 397.

107 Russell, *Fox*, II, 78, quoting a remark of Lord Holland.

108 Br. Mus., Add. MSS 34,419, fols. 296, 305, Eden to Morton Eden, Nov. 21, 1783, Loughborough to Eden, Nov., 1783. Loughborough thought the detailed provisions of the bills provided materials for attacks.

109 Northington Letter Book, Br. Mus., Add. MSS 38,716, fols. 69-73, July 17, 1783.

110 C. H. Philips, "The East India Company 'Interest' and the English Government, 1783-4," *Trans. Royal Hist. Society*, 4th ser., XX (1937), 85; Weitzman, *Hastings and Francis*, 156; Sutherland, *East India Company*, 397; Thomas Moore, *Memoirs of . . . Sheridan* (Philadelphia, 1825), 287.

in Devonshire, Wales, and at Bath.[111] A letter from Arthur Pigott, written in October, asked Burke for materials on India, and a note on the manuscript, in Burke's hand, says that Pigott completed the bill from his drafts.[112]

Perhaps the internal evidence is more important than the external. There were two bills, and both reflected the reports of the select committee and Burke's opinions. The one respecting administration in India has received less attention than the bill relating to company arrangements in England. It deserves notice as a revelation of Burke's views about the internal problems of India.[113] It made authorities in England supreme over company servants in India. It clarified the superintending power of the Bengal presidency over all other company posts. But unlike Dundas' bill, it restricted the authority of the governor general in Bengal. He could not act independently of his council and without express permission from England could not enter into treaties of alliance with native princes or cede or exchange or acquire territories in India. In harmony with the opinions of Francis and of Dundas, the bill undertook to adjust native land-holdings in favor of the ancient holders and to protect them in their possessions. Finally, like Dundas' bill, Burke's enjoined a settlement of the tangled affairs of Tanjore and Arcot.

Except for the limitations upon the governor general, this bill resembled Dundas' in its tendency toward centralization of authority in Bengal and then in the authorities at home. It contained one defect that later experience showed would have been fatal. With the memory of Hastings' conduct uppermost in his mind, Burke not unnaturally desired to limit the independence of the governor general. The history of India after 1784 justified the powers that under Pitt's acts of 1784 and 1786, opposed by

111 Sutherland, *East India Company*, 395; Burke MSS, N.R.O., Axv128, Richard Burke, Sr., to Champion, Sept. 13, 1783. Burke spent "a long time" during the evening of Oct. 7 telling Johnson of the journey, with which he seemed to be much pleased. G. B. Hill, ed., *Letters of Samuel Johnson, LL.D.* (New York, 1892), II, 340, Johnson to Mrs. Thrale, Oct. 9, 1783.

112 *Corr.*, III, 22. See the excellent discussion in Sir George Cornewall Lewis, *Essays on the Administrations of Great Britain from 1783 to 1830* (London, 1864), 99-101. The conclusion is that "the conception and elaboration" of the bill were Burke's and that Pigott was the legislative draftsman who reduced Burke's work into "correct technical form."

113 *Parl. Hist.*, XXIV, 62-85, for the texts of both bills.

Burke, the governor general received. Events demonstrated the impossibility of governing India closely from England in that age of slow communication.[114] But these events occurred under a forward policy. Burke advocated an essentially defensive policy with respect to the native princes, and such a policy did not demand a powerful governor general. Burke desired the purification of administration in India and the protection of the interests of the natives. He opposed British territorial expansion. If he failed to consider the administrative aspect, his opponents did not point out this weakness of the bill, choosing instead to criticize its political implications.

The furor centered around the "Bill for vesting the Affairs of the East India Company in the hands of certain Commissioners." Naturally, parliament and the company became stirred up because it affected people at home so intimately. It was a drastic bill, even if characterized by "simplicity, efficiency, and responsibility."[115] In that respect, if not in its details, it should have satisfied Pitt's demand for a "vigorous" bill, suited to the "exigency" of the Indian situation. The bill eliminated the old functions of the Courts of Directors and Proprietors, and transferred to a board of seven commissioners or directors control over company affairs, properties, and servants at home and abroad. This meant patronage as well. The original seven commissioners, named in the bill, were to serve four-year terms. Lord Fitzwilliam agreed to be chairman of the board, to establish a *"temporary dictatorship"* to set company affairs in order.[116] *A commissioner was removable by the king upon address by either house of parliament;* the king could fill vacancies and make subsequent appointments. The bill named nine assistant directors, all company proprietors, to manage commercial affairs under the "orders and directions" of the commissioners. They were removable either by the king acting on address of either house of parliament or by any five of the commissioners. Every six months the

---

114 Philips, *East India Company*, 300.

115 *Annual Register*, XXVII, 61.

116 Portland MSS, Fitzwilliam to Portland, Nov. 16, 1783 (italics Fitzwilliam's). Earl Fitzwilliam proposed an interesting alternative, namely, that the government buy out the company stockholders. In 1858 when the company was abolished, stockholders received Indian bonds in exchange for their stock. Dividends were paid out of Indian revenues.

commissioners were to give an accounting to the proprietors, and at the beginning of every session to the Treasury Board for submission to parliament. Here again was centralization of control, but in a board of commissioners strictly responsible for their trusteeship to parliament.

On November 18, 1783, Fox obtained leave from the House of Commons to introduce the bills. At once the storm broke, in and out of parliament. It is difficult to say how much the directors knew about the bills before this time. It is commonly accepted that Burke and Fox erred in failing to consult with the company while drafting them. Of course, Burke's general views on India were well known through the committee reports. The chairman of the Court of Directors, Sir Henry Fletcher, a member of parliament, had been consulted by administration leaders for some weeks. As he was named as one of the commissioners in the bill reorganizing company administration, he must have given prior consent.[117] If Fletcher knew the contents of the bills, it is safe to assume that he informed the eight other friendly directors. But there is nothing about the bills in the minutes of the directors or proprietors until November 19, when Fletcher officially informed the directors of the proceedings in parliament.[118] The directors, of whom fifteen were hostile to the bills, resolved to advertise a meeting of the Court of Proprietors to be held two days later and to order the company solicitor to prepare a petition to the Commons praying for relief from the threats they were exposed to.[119]

Henceforth opposition grew. The proprietors met frequently, with a large attendance, and the directors daily.[120] The proprietors, loyal to Hastings and fearful for his future, urged the majority of the directorate into a firm stand against the government.[121] The company petition, which Fletcher had to present

[117] *Morning Herald*, Nov. 3, 1783, reported the conferences.

[118] India Office Library, Court Book 92, pp. 563, 569.

[119] Philips, *East India Company*, 24, for the division in the directorate.

[120] India Office Library, General Court Minutes, VI, 289-93, 295-97, 299, 302, also meetings of Nov. 21, 25, Dec. 6, 9, 16, 19, 1783; *Daily Advertiser*, Nov. 20, 24, 28, 1783.

[121] On Jan. 11, 1784, Scott reported a rumor to Hastings. If the Coalition bill had passed, the government would have proceeded against him with charges of peculation based on the 11th Report of the Select Committee. Gleig, *Hastings*, III, 106.

to the Commons, found the bills destructive of the constitution (apparently that of England) and subversive because they authorized the confiscation of company property. The petition prayed for an opportunity for the company to be heard against the bills. The company also circulated widely a statement demonstrating its financial soundness.[122] This was an answer to Fox's argument justifying the attack upon the company on the grounds of its financial difficulties.

The hostile directors and the proprietors gained much support, especially in the business community. Hitherto the coalition ministry had had twenty of the thirty-one votes of the "Bengal Squad." Twenty-one of the twenty-seven members who were classified as belonging to the company, the City, and the commercial interest had supported the Coalition. Now, six of each group deserted the ministry.[123] On November 27, the Lord Mayor, the aldermen, and the commons of London petitioned against the unconstitutionality of the bill and prayed for its rejection; on December 2, a Common-Hall at the Guildhall voted to oppose the bill.[124] Vitriolic newspaper writers and savage political caricaturists attacked the leaders of the Coalition. Fox later admitted that James Sayers' famous caricature of Carlo Khan (Fox) leading the elephant (North), heralded by Burke the trumpeter, had had a powerful influence.[125] Pitt also testified to the effectiveness of this caricature; when he took office he gave Sayers a job at the Exchequer.

Besides the opposition of company and City, there was the force of public opinion to which Sayers had appealed. As so often happens when a complex matter becomes the subject of popular debate, the real issues were lost amid emotion and unreason. In the extramural discussions, the bill was not considered on its merits, but was judged evil because it was sponsored by the so-called monstrous Coalition, which, it was charged, would be able to perpetuate itself in office by annexing the patronage of the company. Public opinion was incompetent to judge the difficult problem of India, but it was easily aroused to detest the Coalition

122 *Daily Advertiser*, Dec. 8, 1783; Philips, *Trans. Royal Hist. Society*, XX, 88.
123 Philips, *East India Company*, 24.
124 *Daily Advertiser*, Dec. 1, 3, 1783.
125 Philips, *Trans. Royal Hist. Society*, XX, 89.

of North and Fox. The intensive propaganda campaign against
both the Coalition and the bills linked them together, and whatever was done to influence opinion inflamed it against both. This
propaganda, so strongly felt by contemporaries, has affected historians' judgments ever since.

No more than among the public did the bills receive a fair
hearing in parliament. The king's friends, led by Jenkinson, the
members influenced by Pitt, and the Hastings corps under Governor Johnstone deliberately obscured the issues and appealed to
prejudices.[126] As Sheridan said, bitterly, never was a bill "so
little examined, so generally misunderstood, and so confidently
misrepresented."[127] The parliamentary opposition harped on the
coalition theme, to the exasperation of Fox and Burke. "The
coalition," said Fox, "is . . . a fruitful topic," traduced by uninformed persons outside parliament and within by men of "rank
and parts" who should not stoop to such tactics.[128] In their
attempts to arouse prejudice and passions, the opposition know-
ingly spoke a good deal of nonsense. "It is doubtful" if Pitt and
Thurlow, or Grenville, for example, really believed everything
they said.[129] Both Grenville and Pitt, echoing others, called the
bill an attack upon the constitution of England, an attempt to
create a system of despotism.[130] It was an invasion of chartered
rights; it would simultaneously increase and destroy the influence
of the crown; it would give to a party, the Coalition, control of
such tremendous patronage power as to enable it to perpetuate
itself in office. This last point made sense, at first hearing. The
relatively new phenomenon of the East Indian patronage had
excited the cupidity and imaginations of politicians in recent
years and was the basic cause of the great vendettas and confusions
that had characterized company politics since the 1760's.[131] The

---

126 This classification of the opposition to the bill was made by the *Morning
Herald*, Dec. 2, 1783.

127 R. B. Sheridan, *A comparative statement of the two bills for . . . India . . .
by Fox and Pitt* (London, 1788), 6.

128 Quoted by P. E. Roberts in *Cambridge History of the British Empire* (New
York, 1929), IV, 198.

129 Philips, *Trans. Royal Hist. Society*, XX, 88, for the reference to Pitt and
Thurlow.

130 *Parl. Hist.*, XXIII, 1225, 1279.

131 Pares, *George III*, 26.

identities of the seven commissioners seemed to give point to the arguments about patronage. Loughborough admitted this, and he knew Lord North worried about it.[132] Thurlow suggested the possibilities when he described the commissioners as "four gentlemen to be named by Mr. Fox, and three persons whom nobody calls gentlemen, by Lord North."[133]

Fox and Burke led the defense of the bills in the House of Commons. Fox made too much of the company's financial distresses; his answers to the political and constitutional arguments were sounder. Burke on December 1 made the greatest of all the speeches on the subject. It was a three-hour effort that Wraxall, not his admirer, thought the finest speech he had ever heard in the House of Commons.[134] It was also Burke's first major speech in Commons on the subject of India. Hitherto his work had been confined to party circles and to committee investigations and reports. Henceforth, the floor of the House and later Westminster Hall were the scenes of his India labors.

The speech may not impress modern readers so strongly as it did contemporaries. It contains some fine passages, was carefully prepared, well organized, and clearly thought out; it sounded authoritative and met head-on the opposition's objections. Yet something is lost in the reading—the excitement of the moment, the profundity of the issue at stake, possibly the effect of Burke's delivery, and certainly his growing passion after the calm introduction. The middle portion of the speech would seem irrelevant except that by a conscious effort Burke imposed relevance upon it, demonstrating that the long recital of Hastings' misdeeds and company misrule was an argument, if not for the bill under discussion, at least for the reform of Indian administration and the reorganization of an "incorrigible" company. If "in its present state, the government of the East India Company is

132 Br. Mus., Add. MSS 34,419, fol. 305, Loughborough to Eden, Nov., 1783.
133 Quoted in Keith Feiling, *The Second Tory Party, 1714-1832* (London, 1938), 156. The seven commissioners were Lord Fitzwilliam, Frederick Montagu, Sir Henry Fletcher, Robert Gregory, Lord Lewisham, George Augustus North (son of Lord North), and Sir Gilbert Elliot.
134 Printed in *Works*, II, 433-536. John L. Mahoney, *The Burke Newsletter*, nos. 3 and 4 (1963), 210-19 analyzes the speech from the standpoints of composition and rhetoric.

absolutely incorrigible," then an extreme remedy was justifiable. All political power and commercial privilege is in "the strictest sense *a trust*: and it is of the very essence of every trust to be rendered *accountable,*—and even totally to *cease,* when it substantially varies from the purposes for which alone it could have a lawful existence." The purpose for which political power exists is not the "private benefit of the holders"; the company charter, even if originally intended to confer benefits upon stockholders, could no longer be justified on such narrow grounds of self-interest. Events of recent years had made the company a great political power, and more than before, its first concern, and surely that of the imperial government, should be "the interest and well-being of the people of India."

Burke admitted that the bill attacked the company charter, but not "the chartered rights *of men*." He conceded the existence "of an original right in the subject" that "can never be subverted" except at the risk of destroying society itself. But these "natural rights," anterior to charters, independent of them, were not the same as chartered rights. Charters might describe and protect them, but they could not create rights, which were in the order of nature by act of Divine Providence as a means to the attainment of justice. Burke was not speaking of pre-civil rights, but of those rights that people possess within the historical social order, rights that are compatible with social existence and necessary to social well-being because they impose duties as well as confer exemptions.

This brief reference to a natural order indicates Burke's awareness of a natural law that was the basis of human justice, but he did not develop the argument. He turned instead to a discussion of legal rights, implying, without trying to demonstrate, that to be valid they must correspond to natural rights. His main interest was to show that these natural rights were made secure by human law, and in the case of England by certain basic charters, "great public instruments," like Magna Charta. The charter of the East India Company, however, was not one of these charters; indeed, it conferred privileges that were incompatible with natural rights and was *"the very reverse"* of the great historical charters that secured English liberties. It was a charter of a subsidiary character, granted by parliament. For the exercise of the privileges conferred by it, the company was accountable to parliament. When the company abused its trust, and when "the abuse is proved, the contract is broken, and we reenter into all our rights, that is, into the exercise of all our duties." It was now the duty of parliament to assert its authority in order to provide for the people of India "a real chartered security for *the rights of men,* cruelly violated" under the subsidiary charter of the East India Company.

Burke made no effort to disguise or excuse his reversal since 1773, when he had so vehemently defended the chartered rights of the company. He simply knew more about the problem of India in 1783. Since the passage of the Regulating Act, the events that he described in this speech, and had explained in the ninth report of the select committee, justified the extreme remedy which his bill would apply to the Indian malaise. The Dundas bill would have left to manage Indian affairs the same directors and proprietors who had neglected their duties in the past. Burke's bill, taking account of circumstances, would be a complete reform because it would be a total change of system and men.

Burke's bill would increase the authority of the government, but of a particular branch of it. If, to reform India, it was necessary to increase the influence of the crown, Burke would sanction that, for his interest was good government, "let it come from what quarter it will." But that necessity did not exist. True to his Rockingham creed, true to the principles of 1688, and true to himself, Burke preferred to increase the influence of parliament. Herein he was consistent with the course of recent events and with the spirit of reform that he had done so much to promote since 1780. Yet the crown was not ignored, for the bill gave to the king the power to fill vacancies and name future commissioners.

An interesting part of Burke's speech answered the charge that the bill promoted the interest of party. Both Pitt and Jenkinson had protested the grant of power to a "junto," independent of the crown. Burke's answer was consistent with his earlier views, and it reveals an amazing prescience. At first he was sarcastic in calling the "objection against party" a "party objection," made by opponents who feared that if they succeeded to office they would not enjoy the "clandestine influence" that earlier ministers had possessed in company affairs. And what, he asked, should a minister do if he has powers of appointment—name to office his enemies, who will use their authority to undermine his work? Passing by the probity of the commissioners themselves, Burke came directly to the heart of the matter. Supposing one party gained by the patronage the bill created. What, precisely, he demanded, is wrong with party government? "The kingdom is divided into parties, and it ever has been so divided, and it ever will be so divided." Reform cannot wait for a time when "no party can derive an advantage from it," for that time will never come. And if any party is to derive such advantage, it should be the party that "alone in this kingdom has its reputation, nay, its very being, pledged to the protection and preservation of that part of the empire."

Burke was speaking of a matter essential to the conduct of representative government, namely, responsibility. To him, party was an instrument not only for carrying on government but for locating responsibility. If a party (or a coalition) controls a majority in parliament and then forms a government, along with the advantages of power it assumes responsibility for its actions. In this speech, as in his pamphlet of 1770, Burke was expounding the lesson politicians were slow to learn about accountability and trusteeship as the bases of political power—that power conferred trusteeship for the well-being of the governed and carried with it responsibility to parliament and the electorate for the exercise of that trusteeship.

It has been asserted that the provisions for appointing the commissioners contained an administrative defect.[135] Their appointment for fixed terms raised the possibility of friction between them and some new government. But certain provisions in the act, and the realities of political life, could have prevented or mitigated this friction. The commissioners were removable by

---

135 Sutherland, *East India Company*, 399. It is interesting to speculate about the extent to which the Board of Commissioners anticipated a modern board set up to control a nationalized enterprise. After writing this sentence, I discovered a remark to the same effect in J. Steven Watson, *The Reign of George III, 1760-1815* (Oxford, 1960), 263.

the king, who could dismiss them upon address of either house of parliament in order to satisfy a government he liked. In the exercise of certain functions, the commissioners needed the permission of the Lords of the Treasury, the Admiralty Board, and the Ordnance Office and in all cases were required to communicate documents to the ministry and obey their orders.[136] Indeed, the intimacy between commissioners and ministry would almost have required, as a practical matter, the resignation of the commissioners should a new and hostile ministry assume office. In case of friction a government could use its majority in either house to remove disagreeable commissioners. Certainly Pitt's Act, setting up the so-called nonpartisan board of control, did not guarantee that there would be no friction, nor prevent the exercise of government influence in patronage matters, nor discourage the board of control from building up its own interest. Under Dundas' leadership, the board of control steadily acquired far greater authority over the company than the author of the Act of 1784 had intended. And finally, in 1858, when the company was abolished and a secretary of state for India replaced the board of control, that secretary came to exercise the superintending authority that Burke's commissioners would have possessed. In 1858 was established the clear, undivided party responsibility that Burke was seeking, but it operated more smoothly through a cabinet member than it would have through Burke's commissioners. Nevertheless, what was established in 1858 was party responsibility. By that time, of course, the patronage problem had ceased to exist because of the creation of the Indian Civil Service. But it is not fair to charge Burke with failure to solve the patronage problem. A nonpartisan civil service did not exist in the eighteenth century. The exercise of patronage power was a fact of political life accepted by Burke and all of his contemporaries. He did not suggest the abolition of patronage; it was one of the rewards of politics. But the achievement of party government would enable people to locate responsibility for the conduct of political affairs by ministers and their appointees alike.

One cannot determine the effectiveness of Burke's speech. Perhaps it had no influence at all. Often members had admired

---

[136] Sheridan, *Comparative statement*, 28-30.

his speeches but voted against him. The vote of 217-103 for the motion that Burke's speech supported is not attributable to his effort. Throughout the course of the bill in the House of Commons the Coalition enjoyed a steady majority of about two to one, and the bill passed the third reading 208-102. Up to this time the king had not expressly committed himself. But far from intimating dislike of the bill, he had, said Eden, "held out a contrary idea."[137]

On December 10 Fox carried it to the House of Lords. People not in inner circles anticipated a smooth passage. The *Morning Chronicle* had considered Indian affairs "now settled," after the bill passed the committee stage in Commons; the *Morning Herald* thought that the bill would pass the Lords with a majority of about thirty, though Richmond, Shelburne, and Camden might offer stout opposition.[138] On December 11, the *General Advertiser* had Lord Temple conceding passage of the bill.

Lord Temple must have been amused to read this. The usual story is correct—that upon the royal authorization Temple spread the word of the king's vow of eternal hostility toward any peer who voted for the bill. But this is only part of the story. Political realities underlay this action, and other people besides Temple were involved in it. As early as December 1 Temple, Thurlow, and whoever else Temple included in the word "we" had agreed upon the best method of defeating the bill and expelling the coalition ministry.[139] They rejected the use of the royal veto or an assertion of the prerogative to throw out the government while the bill was in the Commons. They advised the king to wait for a moment when the bill "shall have received more discountenance than hitherto" and predicted that when the bill went to the Lords, the moment would come, if the king made known "his wishes"; an indubitable expression of them would "raise difficulties so high as to throw it [out], and [leave] His Majesty at perfect liberty to choose whether he will change them or not." Obviously

137 Quoted in Aspinall, ed., *Later Corr. of Geo. III*, I, xxiv. Eden wrote this letter on Dec. 16.

138 Dec. 5, 1783, for both papers.

139 Buckingham, Second Duke of, *Memoirs of the Courts and Cabinets of George the Third* (London, 1853), I, 288-89. On these pages is printed the memorandum of Dec. 1, 1783, which is summarized in the following sentences.

the primary objective was the overthrow of the coalition government; the discrediting or defeat of the India bill was a means to an end.

Thereafter the secret campaign against the bill and the government got underway. On December 3 Richard Atkinson told John Robinson that all was in readiness "for the blow" if the king would strike it.[140] This was only two days after Burke's great speech, and a week before the Commons passed the bill. "A few resolute men," Robinson, Jenkinson, Pitt, and Dundas, working with the Committee of Nine Proprietors, headed by Atkinson, Sulivan, and Johnstone, had been encouraging the opposition in the company and assessing the parliamentary situation. By December 8 Robinson had completed his canvass of the House of Lords. He reported that a firm disavowal of the act by the king would defeat it. Not only that, said Robinson a few days later, but with patience and tact and the royal confidence, Pitt could win a majority in the House of Commons. By this time the king had assurance that Pitt would undertake to form a government and had, after a long conference with Temple, given Temple the famous authorization to reveal the royal opinions.[141]

These maneuvers soon became known. The *Morning Herald* of Monday, December 15, mentioned the rumored opposition of "a great personage." The *Morning Chronicle* of the same date said the rumor had been reported two days earlier, and gave details of the weekend gossip. Under Lord Temple's aegis, a "daring and unconstitutional attempt" would be made to flout the will of the Commons. Already cabinet lists of a new administration were being circulated. By this time responsible politicians were giving credence to the rumor. In the House of Lords on December 15 Portland mentioned it, Richmond described it, and Temple haughtily acknowledged a conference in which, as an hereditary counselor and a peer of the realm, he had given the king advice unfriendly to the bill.[142] Supporters of the ministry differed about the portent of all this. Burgoyne told of Fox's

---

140 Philips, *Trans. Royal Hist. Society*, XX, 90. Besides this article, pp. 90-94, see also Philips, *East India Company*, 25, and Sutherland, *East India Company*, 404-407.
141 Aspinall, ed., *Later Corr. of Geo. III*, I, xxv.
142 Adolphus, *History of England*, IV, 62.

continued confidence in his position.[143] The king's opposition would influence only the trimmers, and their desertion would not defeat the bill. If it passed, the king would not veto it. In any case, the ministry's strength in the Commons would dissuade the king from attempting to form a new government. On December 16 William Eden predicted the imminent entrance of a new government.[144] The king's name was being dropped among the Lords Spiritual, the Lords of the Bedchamber, the Scottish peers, and a few others susceptible to royal influence. This maneuver had been delayed deliberately in order to make the blow a surprise and therefore heavier. Eden expected a majority of eight against the government when the motion for commitment of the bill was voted upon, and he was certain that the Coalition would not be able to survive the defeat, despite their great majority in the Commons. Loughborough was less gloomy.[145] He reported some resentment among the bishops; if they remained firm, the government was not lost. In fact, at a dinner at Portland's house, the party leaders studied the list of peers and concluded that if only the "false cards" defected, the government would win.

Eden was the better prophet. On December 17, while the House of Commons was debating the constitutionality of the rumored action of the king and resolving by a majority of two to one that to report the royal opinion on a measure pending in either house was a high crime and misdemeanor, the House of Lords was defeating the motion for commitment of the bill by a vote of 95-76.

The king lost no time in bringing the ministry down. On December 18 he ordered Fox and North to give up their seals of office. He discouraged a personal interview because that would be "disagreeable."[146] On the next day the other ministers, including Burke, received letters from Lord Temple informing them that they could no longer be of service to the king.

With the end of the coalition government came the end of an eighteen-month struggle for the independence of parliament. If

143 Br. Mus., Add. MSS 38,716, fols. 142-44, to Northington, marked "Secret," Dec. 15, 1783.

144 Br. Mus., Add. MSS 34,419, fol. 310, to Morton Eden.

145 Br. Mus., Add. MSS 34,419, fol. 313, to Eden, probably Dec. 17, 1783.

146 Buckingham, *Courts and Cabinets,* I, 290.

the king could maintain the new government in office in defiance of the wishes of the majority of the Commons, then the influence of the crown and the prerogative power had recovered vitality. The end of the Coalition was also the failure of Burke and his friends to solve the problem of India. If he intended to continue the fight, as he had committed himself to do, he would have to carry it on in his customary role as a member of the opposition. The difficulty of doing that successfully was appalling.

CHAPTER VII

The Crisis of the Constitution

By taking office with the royal blessing, Pitt preserved the king's victory over the Coalition. At the same time, Pitt served his own ends. Had not the king's great sense of relief over the Coalition's defeat made him less suspicious than usual, he might have wondered whether his prerogative was yet in safe hands. Though Pitt's insistence upon the prerogative right to appoint ministers was known, he entered into the First Lordship of the Treasury as an exponent of parliamentary and administrative reforms and as a former participant in the attacks upon the influence of the crown. If the king could have read Temple's letter of July 21, 1783, to Pitt he might have wondered whether the "schoolboy" minister would be as tractable or even as trustworthy as he anticipated.[1] Temple cautioned Pitt against accepting office under arrangements that would restore the initiative to the king and leadership to Thurlow and Gower in a ministry acting upon the king's ideas. But the king's detestation of North and Fox and the absence of a realistic alternative obviated the necessity of Pitt's complete surrender to the royal will.[2]

It remained for the future to reveal the nature of the relationship between Pitt and the king. Meanwhile, the king was the encouraging mentor, colleague, and father to his struggling minister during the painful early weeks in office.[3] Never had he been so kind to a minister, giving paternal advice, pointing out hopeful signs, and in every way acting the part of the elder statesman. "We must be men," he told Pitt on January 25. On February 15 the king thought that the Lords and the people were on the side of government. When the efforts of some independent members failed to promote a coalition, the king on March 2 expressed pleasure, for a workable union among Pitt, Portland, and Fox had never been feasible. Finally, when parliament was dissolved, the king demonstrated by financial and other aid that he was determined to secure a majority for Pitt. If Fox could seek "bad votes" in Westminster, then, said the king on April 13, we must adopt "similar measures . . . rather than let him be returned."

For Burke, the dismissal of the Coalition, the accession of Pitt, and, most important, the unusual circumstances under which this transfer of power occurred were more than episodes in a political skirmish between ins and outs. They represented another phase of the constitutional struggle over the prerogative, the authority of the Commons, and the relationship between ministers and parliament. In this struggle, Burke's side had recently scored two victories over the crown. Now the triumph of the king showed that the Coalition had been unable to consolidate the position first gained by the Rockingham ministry. If with the king's aid Pitt remained in office, the resurgence of the crown and the conduct of the House of Lords might nullify the gains won by the administrative reformers and the political opponents of the king in 1782 and 1783.

This was the opinion Burke is supposed to have expressed to Jean Baptiste Cloots, who visited Gregories just after the fall of the Coalition.[4] Seven years later Cloots recalled Burke's dissatisfaction with the British constitution and his willingness to reform it radically by curtailing the power of the Lords and by limiting further the royal prerogative. That is why Cloots in 1790,

---

1 P.R.O., Chatham Papers, 30/8, 117.

2 Aspinall, ed., *Later Corr. of Geo. III*, I, gives me the general impression that after they obtained their parliamentary majority, Pitt and his ministers paid no more attention to the king than propriety demanded, keeping him well enough informed to humor him and make him think that he was as important as he had been in the 1770's. Of course, the comparative political stability after 1784 permitted the king to be less active than he had been in the 1760's.

3 See the king's letters from Dec., 1783, to April, 1784, in P.R.O., Chatham Papers, 30/8, 103.

4 Burke MSS, Sheff., Cloots to Burke, May 12, 1790.

remembering Burke as a radical, was surprised to find him unfriendly to the French Revolution.

The constitutional battle of 1784 had to be fought in the political arena. It was easy for the opponents of the Coalition to categorize the Portland-North forces as an unholy alliance of two bands of self-seeking politicians. The caricaturists pictured them as political banditti, plotting strategy in the cave of darkness or assaulting the gates of the Treasury. Always prominent in the caricatures were the lean, scholarly figure of Burke, dressed in Jesuitical garb or Quixote-like armor or both, the dark, heavy countenance of Fox, and the innocent, porcine features of North. But abuse, artistic and verbal, is one of the hazards of politics, and it did not discourage the opponents of Pitt's government. Fox led the political attack, which his talents as a debater fitted him to do. Burke was much less active, and though he contributed to the argument, he did not figure prominently in the parliamentary debates, in the backstage conferences, or in the open political maneuvering. Indeed, he was unusually quiet during the period between Pitt's accession and the dissolution of parliament at the end of March, 1784.

At first it seemed that even with the royal confidence Pitt could not sustain his minority position in the Commons. On January 1 Loughborough could not find a "trace of any desertion" among the opposition.[5] He spoke too soon. On January 12 a division in the Commons found the Coalition majority reduced to thirty-nine, and on January 23 to eight. Meanwhile, Pitt was blandly denying opposition assertions that his continuance in office was unconstitutional. It was unusual perhaps, but as long as the appointment and dismissal of ministers belonged to the king, Pitt contended that he was acting constitutionally, and serving the nation at a critical time. The opposition argued in vain that it was the business of the Commons to judge whether a minister was useful to the country. On February 27 the king dismissed this assertion by rejecting the address, written by Burke, asking for Pitt's dismissal. And when on March 8 the opposition carried a similar address by only one vote, it was clear that Pitt had won the battle in the House of Commons.

5 Br. Mus., Add. MSS 34,419, fol. 322, Loughborough to Eden.

The steady growth of ministerial strength brought to an end the half-hearted negotiations for a coalition between Portland and Pitt. The victory of Pitt refuted the contention of the independent gentlemen who advocated coalition, that the crisis required the union of all parties. Burke had never been impressed by their argument, and he opposed the coalition on other grounds. A union with Pitt could not be one between equals. It would destroy the remaining identity of the old Rockingham party and would mean also capitulation to a minister of whose conduct and measures Burke and his party could not approve without surrendering their principles. The king had accepted Pitt with an understanding that he would leave parliamentary reform an open question for the members of his administration. Burke would not go this far. On January 16, when a Yorkshire freeholders' petition for reform was brought into the Commons and tabled, Burke made his first extended speech about the political situation produced by the change of ministries. In company with Lord North he expressed his fears of the effect of reform upon the constitution. On this issue North was a congenial ally. He used Burkean language in admonishing against fundamental constitutional reforms to remove "warts" or "little excrescences" from the body politic. He did not desire to transform a representative body such as the House of Commons into a congress of ambassadors.[6]

Besides his objectionable views about reform, Pitt held high prerogative ideas about the dependence of ministers upon the king. A minister who, according to Burke, entered office "by means the most disgraceful and unconstitutional," and remained in it against the will of the Commons, the highest authority in the nation, degraded that body and subverted the Revolution Settlement.[7] A coalition with such a minister would not be a reunion of two ancient branches of the Whig Revolution party, as some liked to say, but would be the destruction of Revolutionary Whiggism. It would take control of the government from the propertied, responsible minority who by wealth, training,

[6] See North's speech of June 16, 1784, *Parl. Hist.*, XXIV, 989-90, for a repetition of these sentiments.
[7] *Parl. Hist.*, XXIV, 355, Jan. 16, 1784.

education, and the tradition of 1688 were the trustees of political power in England. Burke must have been as pleased as the king, if for different reasons, when early in March talk of coalition ceased. There is no evidence that he attended the last-ditch attempt at coalition—which really was its funeral—a grand ball at Carleton House, where the Prince of Wales entertained the Portland nobility, the cluster of independent members, and some of Pitt's followers.[8]

With rare acumen and after careful study of the political situation by his experts, Pitt obtained a dissolution of parliament on March 25. Burke was the most furious of all the opposition members. Sitting for a safe constituency, he opposed the dissolution not from self-interest but on grounds, he said, of national interest. There was no need to appeal to the electorate on a matter of which the House was the competent and proper judge. Pitt was acting dangerously in seeking an alliance between the prerogative and the populace. Even though the electorate was small, there was at the moment a surge of outdoor opinion. The dissolution had been ostensibly a response to popular petitions.[9] Under such circumstances Pitt was appealing over the heads of the Commons and encouraging a division between parliament and the people.[10] This view, to Burke, was not inconsistent with his position during the petition movement of 1769. Then, a dissolution had been called for in order that the electorate might chastise a majority subservient to royal influence; in 1784 the election might produce a majority subservient to the people, even those who had no vote.

In either instance the independence of the House of Commons was threatened. Like Jenkinson, Burke thought that at this time the contest was between the majority of the Commons on one side

---

8 *Daily Advertiser*, March 12, 1784.

9 For public opinion, see Mrs. Eric George, "Fox's Martyrs: The General Election of 1784," *Trans. Royal Hist. Society*, 4th ser., XXI (1939), 133-68.

10 Burke MSS, Sheff., fragment for a speech, 1784. Fox felt the same, even though he stood for the popular constituency of Westminster. Professor John Millar, who considered himself a Whig in the 1688 tradition, writing in 1796, called the dissolution an attempt to revive the prerogative and a blow at Commons' control of ministers. But his conclusion differed from Burke's. If the appeal in 1784 was to the electorate of rotten boroughs, then parliamentary reform offered the best protection from the prerogative power. William C. Lehmann, *John Millar of Glasgow, 1735-1801* (Cambridge, 1960), 392.

and on the other a mélange consisting of the king, a majority of the Lords, the City, and the merchants, and militant groups of the populace.[11] It was bad enough for some members of his own party to forsake their aristocratic commitments by obligating themselves, like Fox, to the masses in a tumultuous popular constituency.[12] But it was even worse when, with the blessing of the king, a government placed itself at the disposal of the populace. Indeed this was, as a modern scholar says, the reintroduction of the abandoned "plebiscitary element into the resources of the Crown" as well as a violation of the Septennial Convention, which restrained the exercise of the prerogative power of dissolution until a parliament had nearly run its statutory life of seven years.[13]

An election under such circumstances would result in a kind of popular tyranny. The inevitable corollary would be the destruction of the mediating "aristocratic independency" of the Commons. The prerogative plebiscite was only one threat. The other was created by Fox and Sheridan, who were also trying to gain the support of the populace. At issue were the venerable Rockingham principles that placed the rank, property, and talents of an aristocratic party between democracy and tyranny. Burke was uneasily aware that the ascendancy of Fox might change the character of the Rockingham party, and if its "aristocratic independency" was weakened, then there would be no barrier to alliance between the crown and the people.[14]

For Burke personally, the election offered neither the risks nor the expenses that some of his friends encountered in larger constituencies. Malton would do Lord Fitzwilliam's bidding. There was at Bristol a flurry of interest in him. Despite the rebuff he had met there in 1780, a party of his friends had remained active.

11 Br. Mus., Add. MSS 38,309, fol. 89, Jenkinson to John Stables, Feb. 7, 1784.
12 Olson, *The Radical Duke*, 70, 192-94.
13 Fryer, *Renaissance and Modern Studies*, VI, 89-93. But Aspinall, ed., *Later Corr. of Geo. III*, I, xxv, justifies the dissolution on the grounds that the Commons elected in 1780 were "chosen" by Lord North. If this argument has any validity, it supports Burke's view of the necessity for harmony between ministers and the Commons.
14 Osborn Coll., Box 74, #24b, proof sheets of the 1791 *Annual Register*. This account of the political history of the preceding decade suggests that the breach between Burke and Fox in 1791 had a history going back to 1780, when Fox embraced parliamentary reform and the Westminster constituency.

In December, 1783, they had succeeded in electing Richard Burke as recorder, a post he held until his death, serving, according to his biased brother, with distinction.[15] Pitt's calculators were impressed by Richard's victory, and they wondered whether this evidence of the Burkes' continued strength in Bristol might encourage Edmund to contest the parliamentary seat for Bristol.

If so, they thought that they could beat him if they spent enough money.[16] If Burke ever seriously considered standing for Bristol, his correspondence is silent. He had little more to do with that city.[17] But he was remembered there. Inscribed on the pedestal of his statue erected in 1894 is a sentence from his speech in Bristol in 1780—"I wish to be a member of Parliament to have my share of doing good and resisting evil."[18]

Burke found Malton perfectly congenial. When he presented himself in early April, 1784, his constituents willingly did their duty to Lord Fitzwilliam. There were no "outcries against aristocracy." There was strong antiprerogative feeling in the north, if an incident at Doncaster races later in the summer meant anything. When the orchestra played "God save the King," half the company refused to stand.[19]

From Malton Burke went on to Glasgow for his installation as rector of the university.[20] He had been elected on November 15, 1783, in succession to Dundas. He traveled by way of Edinburgh, where he spent a few days in sightseeing and visiting eminent Scotsmen. Adam Smith was his constant companion, and he saw much of the young philosopher Dugald Stewart. On the trip from the capital to Glasgow, Burke and Smith passed the night at the seat of the Earl of Lauderdale in Midlothian. The installation

15 Wecter, *Kinsmen*, 73.

16 W. T. Laprade, ed., *Parl. Papers of John Robinson, 1774-1784*, Camden Third Series, vol. XXXIII (1922), 106, 110.

17 Underdown, "Burke and Bristol," 440-41.

18 *Works*, II, 421. The story about the statue is told in Henry J. Spears, ed., *Life of Edmund Burke—Published on the Occasion of the Unveiling of the Statue presented by Sir William Henry Wills, Bart., to the Citizens of Bristol* (Bristol, 1894).

19 Burke MSS, Sheff., Fitzwilliam to Burke, Sept. 15, 1784.

20 A full account is given in John Rae, *Life of Adam Smith* (London, 1895), 387-91. See also *Corr.*, III, 23-25, William Leechman to Burke, Dec. 6, 1783; Burke MSS, N.R.O., Aii91, Dundas to Burke, April 7, 1784; Boswell MSS, Yale, Boswell to Burke, April 10, 1784; Pottle, ed., *Private Papers*, XVI, 50-51, April 10, 1784.

was held on April 10. It was preceded by a breakfast to which
the ubiquitous Boswell managed to get himself invited, and in
the company were Smith, Stewart, and Professors Andrew Dalzell
and John Millar. Boswell was thrilled with the ceremony. He
thought that Burke looked handsome in the Lord Rector's gown
and that he spoke appropriately in accepting the honor. On the
day after, Burke, Smith, and Lord Maitland visited Loch Lomond.
Then they toured the famous Carron ironworks before returning
to Edinburgh, where Burke spent several more days with his old
and new Scottish friends.

The Lord Rectorship was not merely honorary. It even had
political significance. Lord Fitzwilliam, for example, interpreted
Burke's election as a defiance of the political influences that
controlled Scotland at this time.[21] If this is true, these influences
did not try to embarrass Burke in his office. One of his first items
of university business was the appointment of a new professor of
practical astronomy. Burke presented the faculty petition recommending Patrick Wilson to the Home Secretary, his old friend
Tommy Townshend, now Lord Sydney, and the king made the
appointment.[22] Burke's political connections served the university well on another occasion. A troublemaker on the faculty,
Professor John Anderson, had made various allegations against
his colleagues and desired a royal visitation as a means of settling
the differences. Burke favored it at first but was dissuaded by
his Glasgow friends. Out of all proportion to its significance the
affair worried the faculty. It dragged into Burke's second term as
rector, to which he was elected in November, 1784; it was at last
settled when the ministry, acting on the advice of Dundas and
Sydney, dismissed Anderson's charges and refused the visitation.[23]
Burke's political differences with the government did not impair
his position as the advocate in London of the university's cause.

21 Burke MSS, Sheff., Fitzwilliam to Burke, April 25, 1784.
22 Burke MSS, Sheff., William Leechman to Burke, June 16, 1784, Lord Sydney
to Burke, July 19, 1784; Osborn Coll., Box 20, #11x, Burke to Lord Sydney, July 3,
1784.
23 Burke MSS, Sheff., John Millar to Burke, Aug., 1784, Jan. 19, April 17, Nov. 13,
1785, William Leechman to Burke, Feb. 16, May 1, May 14, 1785; Burke MSS,
N.R.O., John Millar to [?], n. d. but early fall, 1784, William Richardson to Burke,
Aii99a, Aug. 14, 1784, William Leechman to Burke, Aii109, Nov. 15, 1784, John
Millar to Burke, Aii110, Nov. 15, 1784. Also, Lehmann, *John Millar*, 46, 71.

His two-year association with Glasgow University brought Burke into closer contact with Scots than ever before. He received two additional honors almost at once, the freedom of the city of Glasgow and election to the Royal Society of Edinburgh, the latter on Smith's nomination and over several political black-balls.[24]

From his Scottish visit Burke returned to a new political world. The election had been a triumph for Pitt and the king, and a disaster to the Portland Whigs. Some estimates had as many as 160 supporters of the Fox-North coalition suffering martyrdom. At best, the minority was less than a quarter of the full House. The first real test in the new House demonstrated Pitt's strength on a partisan question. Three times the opposition was defeated on motions relating to the contested election for Westminster, where Fox, though second on the poll, had not been seated pending a scrutiny of the returns. One vote, on May 18, went against the opposition 233-136; two others found the government victorious 195-117 and 178-90. This last division on June 8 ordered the High Bailiff to proceed with the scrutiny. Fox, having been elected for another constituency, was fighting not for a seat in Commons but for the retention of the preferable seat for Westminster, and the issue was purely political.

The new parliament evinced contempt for the opposition and disrespect for Burke. He tried to avoid political speeches in order to concentrate upon constitutional issues, but he found it difficult to gain a hearing. On May 25, for example, angered by teasing remarks from the Treasury bench, he called the ministry "a parcel of boys," then asked pardon so vehemently as to nullify the effect of his apology.[25] Burke was being made aware that he belonged to the old order, not only on account of his age but, it seemed, because his Whiggish ideas were anachronistic. The new radical-ism repudiated him and mocked him. On June 16, for example, "the young members" baited him again. Their interruptions caused him to fly into "a violent passion," after which he gave up,

[24] Burke MSS, N.R.O., Aii96, Patrick Colquhoun to Burke, July 24, 1784, Aii97, Andrew Dalzell to Burke, July 20, 1784; Rae, *Smith*, 393; *Trans. of the Royal Society of Edinburgh*, I (1788), 95.
[25] *Parl. Hist.*, XXIV, 939-40.

muttering about the disorderly conduct of the House.[26] The time had passed, it seemed, when he could by "wit, argument, and satire, so finely blended and so strongly carried on" keep the House "in a burst of laughter the whole time."[27] A member of a badly beaten minority and suddenly an old man without hope of office again, ridiculed by "boys" who openly expressed their impatience with his newly recovered readiness to speak, Burke seemed to have lost the great constitutional campaign which in 1782 had been so near success.

On June 14, when Burke presented a remonstrance and gave a two-hour speech, he admitted that his effort was in the nature of a coroner's inquest into the death of the late parliament. He did not intend his remonstrance as a party program, although with Lord Fitzwilliam he agreed on the need for one in the present state of disorder and dismay.[28] When William Baker asked why he had not concerted his action with the party, Burke did not reply directly. His answering letter reveals his despair and shows that his speech was really a lament.[29] For twenty years, he told Baker, the Rockingham party had labored to secure the independence of parliament, and now Pitt had restored royal control almost overnight. It would take another twenty years to make up the lost ground, if it could be done in that time, for unfortunately the people—that is, the voters—had acquiesced in Pitt's conduct. The remonstrance, then, was not a party document. It was a plea for what Burke believed to be the most desirable constitutional system for England. For that reason the remonstrance and the accompanying speech deserve more attention than Burke scholars or historians generally have given to them.[30]

Burke's effort revealed the philosophical politician rather than the political philosopher.[31] It was a practical disquisition upon the British constitutional system, but with a clear implication of

26 *Parl. Hist.*, XXIV, 1001; H.M.C., *Rutland*, III, 109, Thomas Orde to the Duke of Rutland, June 17, 1784.

27 *Parl. Hist.*, XXIII, 267, Dec. 6, 1782.

28 Burke MSS, Sheff., Fitzwilliam to Burke [June 13], 1784.

29 Burke MSS, Sheff., Baker to Burke, June 20, 1784; Copeland transcript from Hertford County Record Office, Burke to Baker, June 22, 1784.

30 The remonstrance is in *Works*, II, 543-76.

31 *Parl. Hist.*, XXIV, 943ff.

Burke's idea of the good social order in England. It was a
Whiggish declaration of the independence and the supremacy of
the House of Commons, a vigorous attack upon the manner in
which the prerogative power had recently been abused, and in
its animadversions upon the malevolent work of "secret advisers,"
a throwback to the *Thoughts on the Cause of the Present Discontents* and a revival of the Rockingham bogey of secret influences. It denied the assumptions of the parliamentary reformers, expressed confidence in the traditional representative character of the House of Commons, and asserted the constitutional
propriety of ministerial subordination to the House. It attacked
the contemporary *mystique* of a "balanced" constitution, so congenial to the aesthetic preferences of a society that revered classical
and geometrical order. Burke's speech advanced the unorthodox
claim that imbalance, or a readjusted balance in favor of the
Commons, was the best security for English liberties.[32]

Burke, therefore, was continuing the political themes he had
been developing since the late 1760's, and most emphatically
addressing himself to the issue of the independence of parliament
and the authority of the Commons. If the sense of the people
"must always govern the legislature of this country"—if, that is,
the Commons should take cognizance of it, though not bow to it—
was the franchise wide enough and the distribution of representation equitable enough adequately to collect the sense of
the nation? Burke argued that it was, provided the electorate
remained free to express itself. Recent events revealed a deliberate
effort to mislead the people into antagonism against the House of
Commons. Members were not delegates but representatives,
whose duty it was to form independent judgments upon public
affairs and even to resist the claims of the people when the people
needed protection against unscrupulous interests. Here Burke

---

32 Fryer, *Renaissance and Modern Studies*, VI, 78-79, 99-101, vigorously attacks
the idea that the so-called "balance" was real. Fryer does not cite Burke as one
who scoffed at the idea that there was a balance, but he quotes Hume to this effect,
as well as Fox and North. It is worth remarking that the balance had changed at
other times. The balance of the eighteenth-century constitution was certainly not
the balance that Charles I argued for in his "Answer" to the Nineteen Propositions
of the Long Parliament in 1642. John Rushworth, *Historical Collections* (London,
1691), IV, 725-35.

found the danger. Once again the influence of "secret advisers" was forming a "prerogative party in the nation."

Such machinations undermined the constitution. Although the crown possessed certain prerogative powers, such as the power to dissolve parliament, the exercise of them ought not be abused or be used in favor of any set of ministers against the wishes of the Commons. In fact, Burke was asking for the political neutrality of the crown. Continued abuse would justify further limitations upon the prerogative—"Necessary reformations may hereafter require, as they have frequently done in former times, limitations and abridgements, and in some cases an entire extinction, of some branch of prerogative." Perhaps we should remind ourselves that the speaker was Burke, the so-called defender of the *status quo*. It was specious, he said, to talk about a "just balance" among the three parts of the legislature, King, Commons, and Lords. That doctrine was a "fiction." The fact was that the Revolution of 1688 had established beyond doubt the supremacy of the Commons. The prerogative was subject to statutory definition; parliament could clip it, if it chose. Parliament expected the king to accept its advice "concerning his Majesty's servants" instead of flouting it. And those servants "should yield to Parliament" rather than attempt, by abusing the prerogative power of dissolution, to "new-model" parliament "until it is fitted to their purposes."

This was bold doctrine. In effect Burke was threatening retribution against the king. But this was neither new nor inconsistent. For years he had been attacking the prerogative power and the influence of the crown. In 1784 he was trying to explain that whatever the political implications, he was expounding his mature constitutional doctrine. The Revolution of 1688 had made parliament sovereign, for practical purposes, but had left in the crown the authority to appoint and dismiss ministers. During the eighteenth century experience showed that this separation of the executive from the legislature was clumsy and that it provoked embarrassments and uncertainties. By vesting control of the ministry in the Commons, Burke hoped to locate there the practical administrative authority that he thought the Revolution Settlement implied. Burke was a House of Commons man who earlier than any other politician of his time made the doctrine of responsible government his credo.[33] He did this knowing that in the past the threat to liberty had come from the crown. The Revolution had sought to preserve English liberties by achieving the supremacy of parliament.

In the 1780's Burke saw another threat to liberty. Radicalism urged the location of ultimate authority in the people and desired the reform of parliament in order to make it conform to popular opinion. The eighteenth-century aristocratic order was being attacked from below, and it was in double jeopardy if radicalism allied itself to the crown. In the longer view, Burke was fighting a losing cause. Within a few years the French Revolution would encourage the forces of radical democracy. Within a century the changing economic and social conditions in England would enlarge the political power of the people. Burke's aristocratic system, operating through an independent Commons controlled by parliamentary parties, would give way, as Bagehot feared it would and as after 1867 it did, to a democratic system operating through national, constituency parties. These parties would become the agencies for alliance between the people and, not the king, but the prime minister.[34] But the result would be the one that Burke feared from an alliance between radicalism and the king. The independence of the House of Commons would be diminished if not lost. The political and constitutional history of England since 1784 is an extended commentary on the judgments Burke offered in that year.

That the House neither debated nor divided over Burke's motion for his remonstrance indicated the absence of opposition support for it or government interest in it. This indifference reflected weariness with a subject that had been debated off and on since the preceding December. The election, whether manipulated or a genuine expression of electoral opinion on the constitutional issue, in fact closed the debate. As Viscount Palmerston

33 See Donald G. Barnes, *George III and William Pitt, 1783-1806* (Stanford, Cal., 1939), 106, 267.
34 See Lord Altrincham in *Encounter*, XX, 82-84. Recently, he says, power has passed from the "oligarchy" that had captured it from the king in the seventeenth century to the prime minister. "Universal Suffrage has strengthened the executive *without* making it democratic."

said, the election resulted in the triumph of the prerogative over the House of Commons.[35] The king's dismissal of the coalition government, Pitt's retention of office during three months in the minority, and finally the dissolution of parliament at a shrewdly calculated time had all been approved by the voters. Burke and his party had been thoroughly discredited, their cause disavowed, and their conduct censured. Their political prospects were once again forlorn.

[35] Watson, *George III,* 272, n. 1.

CHAPTER VIII

The Politics of Empire

THE ELECTION OF 1784 settled for the time being the constitutional issue that had dominated parliamentary politics for the past two years. The problem of empire, the questions of India and Ireland, remained. Pitt seemed to have the parliamentary strength as well as the inclination to confront the problems. In January, while still in the minority, he had lost an Indian bill by only eight votes in the Commons. His tactful negotiations with the interested persons had soothed some who had opposed Burke's bill.[1] After Pitt's candidates won in the April elections to the Court of Directors, circumstances were even more propitious. Then the government's triumph in the parliamentary elections assured the passage of his bill.

Pitt's bill, introduced on July 6, was based upon Dundas' bill of the preceding year though modified somewhat as a result of discussions with the company; nonetheless, it was largely Dundas' work.[2] It withheld from the governor general the control of the Bengal Council that Dundas' bill would have granted, but it gave to Bengal authority over the Madras and Bombay presidencies. Instead of a third secretary of state, preferred by Dundas, the bill provided for a Board of Control composed of two cabinet officers and four privy councilors, and to this board was given a superintending authority over the political, though not over the commercial, affairs of the company. The letter of the bill left the patronage power with the directors. Skillful drafting gave it the appearance of avoiding the controversial features of Burke's proposals. "It was a clever, dishonest bill, which successfully concealed from the East India interests the Ministry's intention of effectively subordinating the Court of Directors as a political power."[3] It was so "deliberately vague" that through the years the board had little difficulty in increasing its administrative authority. The bill was theoretically defective but politically shrewd in separating control of commerce from politics. But in the end it worked, as much because it was amended in 1786 to enable the governor general to dominate the Bengal Council and because Dundas, who at once gained the leadership of the board, made it work, as because of its inherent merits. Pitt's India Act achieved what Burke's had aimed at achieving—that is, the establishment of government control over the affairs of the company, though the crown rather than parliament exercised immediate supervision. Pitt's Act differed from Burke's "more in form than in substance," permitting the company to exist but curtailing its autonomy. As Atkinson finally admitted to John Robinson, Pitt's Act applied to the company a "coercive regulation very similar in its principle" to that which Burke's bill intended.[4]

Burke's failure to oppose the bill strenuously in the Commons is not immediately clear. Membership in the minority seldom had discouraged him from speaking upon subjects about which he felt strongly. The disaster of the recent election, reemphasized by the vote of 271-60 on the motion for going into committee on Pitt's bill, may have produced one of his temporary states of depression. In fact, having already melodramatically threatened

1 Philips, *East India Company*, 25-31; Ind. Off. Library, General Court Minutes, VI, 308-13, 334, 335-36. After the bill was laid before parliament, the minutes are silent, reflecting the company's silence. Also *Daily Advertiser*, July 16, 21, 1784, speaking of concessions made by Pitt as a result of company representations made privately, and Burke MSS, Sheff., Francis to Burke, July 20, 1784, to the same effect.

2 Philips, *East India Company*, 33-34; Sutherland, *East India Company*, 408-409, 414. Elijah Impey told Hastings that the bill was entirely Dundas' work. Thurlow never saw it until its second reading in the Commons. Br. Mus., Add. MSS 29,166, fols. 5-6, Sept. 1, 1784.

3 Philips, *East India Company*, 34.

4 Philips, *Trans. Royal Hist. Society*, XX, 95, 100.

to quit the House forever, he absented himself during many of the debates, leaving to Fox and to a disgruntled Francis the burden of opposing.[5] When finally he spoke, on July 28, on the third reading, his objections were quibbles, and came too late to have effect.[6] He complained in a general way that the bill would not correct the evils revealed by the committee reports. It failed to eliminate opportunities for misconduct of company servants in India, and it left the administration at home divided and therefore weak. Like the directors, Burke did not see the possibilities that the bill opened to a vigorous Board of Control, or he underestimated, like the directors, the ability and ruthlessness of Dundas. In any case his opposition was half-hearted and peevish; he complained that his speech was not supported by his own party, as if the third reading was the time for vigorous opposition.[7]

Clearly, Burke was discouraged and indifferent. The prospect of another indefinite career as a minority member was the more displeasing because he was growing self-conscious about his age. If he was not an old man at the age of fifty-five, there was great disparity between his and the ages of the leaders who sat opposite. Pitt and William Grenville were twenty-five years old and Dundas forty-two. On July 30 Burke complained of "indecent" treatment from "juvenile statesmen" who received with levity and "laughter" his piteous accounts of the sufferings of the Indian people.[8] Grenville taunted him for expecting deferential treatment out of respect for his age. This must have been especially irritating, coming from the son of the man whom Burke had formerly delighted in baiting. It was indeed a new generation that had come into power with Pitt. Considering the strength of the ministry, its success with its India Act, the youth, vigor, and ability of its leaders, and the king's confidence in it, Burke may have wondered what besides wishful thinking persuaded William Eden to predict a short life for Pitt's government.[9]

[5] Burke MSS, Sheff., Francis to Burke, July 20, 27, 1784, in which Francis' displeasure at Burke is evident though not explicit; H.M.C., *Rutland*, II, 123, Thomas Orde to Rutland, July 9, 1784.

[6] *Parl. Hist.*, XXIV, 1209-10.

[7] Osborn Coll., Box 74, #23, Burke to Sir Gilbert Elliot, Aug. 3, 1784.

[8] *Parl. Hist.*, XXIV, 1266, 1270, 1271-72.

[9] Burke MSS, Sheff., Eden to Burke, May 13, 1784.

There was no merit in lethargy when the nation still had great business before it. The India Act did not touch the business of Warren Hastings; that was Burke's major objection to it. Shaking off his depression, Burke renewed his attack upon Hastings. The House was still interested in him; often during the debates on the India Act there had been irrelevant controversy about the governor general. Major Scott defended Hastings every time he got to his feet. Like Thurlow, he thought that Burke, Francis, and their friends were looking for opportunities to "misrepresent" Hastings' actions. Burke leaped into the controversy. Answering Scott, he welcomed the opportunity to prove the allegations made against Hastings in the recent reports, and he moved for a committee of the House to inquire into their truth.[10] Later he asked for papers on Oude. Scott, with bravado, seconded the motion. It carried, and the Hastings affair entered a new stage.

Hastings' stock had recently risen. First there had come good news of the end of the Maratha war. Then the fall of the Coalition seemed to give assurance of a safe future for Hastings.[11] From a conversation with Pitt, Scott had persuaded himself of the minister's friendliness. In this congenial atmosphere he seems to have thought that his only remaining duties were to refute all attacks upon Hastings, to clear him of all suspicions, and to prepare the way for his triumphant return. Having already resigned, Hastings was thought to be merely awaiting the arrival of his successor before returning to receive the honors Scott was accumulating for him. These would include the peerage that Thurlow was soliciting.

There was much misunderstanding, and Scott was the worst deceived of all. Pitt's refusal to recommend the peerage, following upon his India Act, strongly suggested his reservations about Hastings. Hoping to be reappointed as governor general with enlarged powers, Hastings told his wife as soon as he read the Act that fifty Burkes, Foxes, and Francises could not have conspired to produce a bill more injurious to him, the company, and

10 *Parl. Hist.*, XXIV, 1210-12, July 28, 1784.
11 Davies, *English Historical Review*, LXX, 609-21. This and the next paragraph draw upon this article.

the national honor.[12] In a long letter to Thurlow he tore Pitt's Act apart.[13] He foresaw accurately that the Board of Control would dominate the directors. It would be better to abolish the Court of Directors outright, as Burke's bill would have done. If Hastings seemed to agree with Burke on the need for centralizing authority in England, he went far beyond Burke in desiring to make the governor general virtually a dictator in India, though ultimately responsible to authorities at home. In a letter that he never sent, Hastings rebuked Scott severely for supporting Pitt's Act.[14] It denounced him and ruined his career. It killed his desire to continue as governor general. He ended with a curious remark. He wished that he could recall a letter he had sent to Pitt. He seemed to regret having been so frank with a man who he now thought was neither honorable nor virtuous.

That letter, dated December 11, 1784, dealt mainly with the office of governor general.[15] He should be "absolute and complete within himself"; his power could not be "too despotic," considering circumstances in India. Granting the need for a strong governor general in India, which Hastings' defenders have asserted, Hastings' description of such a man was a description of himself. It does not make him a lovelier person, and it confirms Burke's conviction that Hastings was arbitrary, egocentric, and jealous, as governor general.

Burke did not know Hastings personally before his return from India in 1785. His judgments hitherto had been formed from the information, some of it prejudiced, given to him by people who knew Hastings, and from the materials assembled by the committees. Their reports, Hastings' manuscripts, and other sources give a strong impression that Burke's judgment was not far off the mark when it ascribed to Hastings an authoritarian character, a readiness to justify his conduct by the argument of state necessity,

12 Sydney C. Grier, ed., *The Letters of Warren Hastings to his Wife* (London, 1905), 413.
13 Br. Mus., Add. MSS 29,169, fols. 148-65, Dec. 5, 1785. If this letter was misdated from 1784, no further comment is needed. If the date is correct, then it must have been written in anticipation of the amendment of Pitt's Act in 1786. The letter contains a statement of Hastings' preference of a totally new bill to an amendment of the act of 1784.
14 Br. Mus., Add. MSS 29,167, fols. 265-66, Dec. 27, 1784.
15 Printed in Davies, *English Historical Review*, LXX, 616-18.

and a tendency to blame others when things did not go to his liking. The Regulating Act of 1773 disappointed him because it failed to give to the governor general the authority to override the council and to conduct the diplomatic and military affairs of India.[16] He blamed other councilors for the quarrels in the council, adopting the unattractive, whining tone that revealed his frustration. He wrote on December 4, 1774, to Lord North that "this unhappy difference did not spring from me," and would not have occurred if the majority had "brought with them the same conciliatory spirit which I had adopted."[17] He was confident that North was displeased to see "the measures which you had so wisely planned" thwarted by the persons sent to India to administer them.

As time passed, Hastings' bitterness increased, with consequences apparent in the complex events that figured in the impeachment. To give an example from evidence available to the select committee, the commander at Bidjeygur in 1781 acted with Hastings' explicit consent when he distributed the booty among his troops.[18] When Hastings later learned of its great value, he was angry. "A very uncandid advantage" had been taken of a letter he had written in haste. This was a minor event, but it reveals his tendency to quick resentment, which later commentators noticed and which undoubtedly alienated Macartney. When he opposed Hastings on certain matters of policy, "Hastings misconstrued Macartney's honest criticism for opposition. He had met with opposition so often, and in so many directions, that he had now become totally incapable of enduring it."[19] Macartney seems to have noticed something else in Hastings. Says a modern authority, "there are many indications that [Hastings'] character had deteriorated. Embittered by years of factious opposition he could no longer brook the slightest deviation from his plans."[20] Thus, his retribution against John Bristow as resident in Oude was "a counsel of desperation." "Hastings' hatred

16 E. Monckton Jones, *Warren Hastings in Bengal, 1772-1774* (Oxford, 1918), 154.
17 Gleig, *Hastings*, I, 473-75.
18 Gleig, *Hastings*, II, 428, prints letters connected with the episode.
19 A. P. Dasgupta, *The Central Authority in British India, 1774-1784* (Calcutta, 1931), 157.
20 Davies, ed., *Private Corr. of Macartney*, xvi.

of Bristow blinded his political vision. He had suffered so much from opposition that he could no longer brook any deviation from his plans."[21]

It is pertinent to ask how many years of opposition Hastings faced in Bengal. Monson died in 1776, after which Hastings controlled the council. General Clavering died in 1777, and Francis left India in 1780. Hastings was in the minority for only two years; thereafter, the opposition might object but could not check him. He was in complete control in Bengal when he performed his most arbitrary and ruthless acts in Oude and Benares. Hastings' difficulties with the Madras and Bombay presidencies arose in part from the constitutional uncertainties of company administration in India. But his complaints about these problems suggest that his reactions to "opposition" were natural tendencies of his character. Considering only the fact of his conduct, there was reason for Burke and others in England to be uneasy over Hastings' administration.

His letter to Pitt in December, 1784, reflects his character. He was unduly suspicious, quick to take as a personal insult a measure enacted by Pitt's government without any intention of aspersing him. Hastings' reaction was typical. First he impulsively wrote a letter of criticism, which he regretted as soon as he sent it. Then he left India almost at once, sailing for England on February 6, 1785. If he could not be governor general upon his own terms, he would not be governor general at all.

It would be interesting to know why Hastings regretted sending the letter to Pitt if he intended to return to England. If he feared that he had alienated a man whom Scott thought their friend, he was mistaken. Pitt was neither pro- nor anti-Hastings at this time.[22] His doubts about the administration of India reflected, not dislike for a man he did not know personally, but

21 C. C. Davies, *Warren Hastings and Oudh* (Oxford, 1939), 246. Contemporaries said the same thing. Thus, Sir George Staunton, Secretary to Macartney, told him of Macpherson's statement that Hastings was irritable, owing to the long opposition he had faced in his council. Staunton to Macartney, Feb. 24, 1782, printed in George Thomas Staunton, *Memoirs of . . . Sir George Leonard Staunton, Bart.* (privately printed, 1823), 266.

22 Generally, for Pitt's impartiality, see Davies, *English Historical Review*, LXX, 609-21, and espec. 614-15.

the persuasiveness of the material accumulated by the select and secret committees.

By the autumn of 1784 it was apparent that Burke was preparing to renew the attack upon Hastings. He was encouraged by Macartney's letters. As earlier, Macartney described the wretched state of affairs in India and the need for good, honest company servants. His letters reflected his unpleasant relations with Hastings. To various correspondents he predicted the loss of Britain's Asiatic empire unless parliament enacted reforms and punished delinquents. He complained of the actions of the Bengal government which not only would drive him from his post but "which, I think, have an evident Tendency to plunge the Company anew into the stresses of War."[23] If Macartney did not convince all these persons, he at least reminded them of the Hastings problem. Francis continued his campaign too, not only in parliament but in private meetings with Burke and others, who demonstrated "their attachment to the Cause" by listening to his accounts of the latest scandalous news from India.[24]

There was a semblance of a party against Hastings, identified with the Portland Whigs and the parliamentary opposition, led by Burke, Fox, and Francis. On August 7, 1784, just a few days after Burke had reopened the subject, Fox told Francis of his desire to recall Hastings and to impeach him.[25] Because of Pitt's honest neutrality and Dundas' past performances, it could not be said that the government constituted a pro-Hastings party. Scott still hoped for Hastings' peerage, though Pitt said nothing could be done while the "ridiculous and absurd" charges against him remained on the journals of the House.[26] Scott correctly understood Thurlow's partiality for Hastings.[27] Thurlow admitted his ignorance of Indian affairs and professed to Burke his desire to

---

[23] *Corr.*, III, 26-28, Jan. 31, 1784; Br. Mus., Add. MSS 22,460, fol. 197, to Burke, fols. 181-82, to Loughborough, fol. 191, to Dundas, fol. 187, to Ellis, fol. 187, to Eden, fol. 188, to Johnstone, fols. 193-94, to Fox, fol. 195, to North, fol. 189, to Sandwich, all dated July 28, 1784.

[24] Burke MSS, Sheff., Francis to Burke, April 29, 1784.

[25] MSS Eur., D. 20, Francis diary, Aug. 7, 1784.

[26] This is Scott's phrase, allegedly quoting Pitt. Br. Mus., Add. MSS 29,166, fols. 41-43, Scott to Hastings, Sept. 4, 1784.

[27] Br. Mus., Add. MSS 29,166, fols. 41-43; Add. MSS 29,167, fols. 25-32, 181-86, Scott to Hastings, Nov. 6, Dec. 7, 1784.

learn more about the man who was being talked about so much.[28]
But he had already committed himself for the peerage, he had
challenged Pitt to detail Hastings' delinquencies, and he implied
sympathy when he told Burke that the governor general had no
"friends" in the ministry, among the directors, in the Board of
Control, or among the opposition. Indeed, said Thurlow, they
were "declared enemies."

If this was the true state of affairs when parliament was
prorogued in August, 1784—if Hastings had only a few isolated
friends supporting him and a party against him, and if the recent
India Act was understood to be, in effect though not intentionally,
a censure of his administration—then Burke might be optimistic
about his chances of forwarding the "Cause" in the next session.

Burke spent the recess at Gregories. A visit from Shackleton,
in London for the annual Quaker meeting, was the pleasantest
event during the interlude. Shackleton's daughter Mary accompanied him. Awestruck during her visit and ecstatic with the
memory of it after her return to Ballitore, she rhapsodized about
it in a poem.[29] It was not so much the beauty of the "mansion"
at Gregories that impressed her as the hospitality, "connubial
love," "parental fondness," wit, good conversation, and all that
was "sublime and beautiful." The poem pleased Burke, not as
an artistic endeavor (as his letter of thanks to Mary makes clear
to a modern reader if it did not to her), but for the effort to do
what "great artists" should—that is, improve their observations
"up to the standard of perfection" in their own minds.[30] Had
Mary visited Gregories six weeks later, after a gang of London
thieves purloined the family silver, she would have been able to
write about philosophy there. We cannot replace our loss, Jane
Burke told a friend, so our guests will have to bring their own
utensils and accept us as poor but honest people.[31]

The joy of seeing Shackleton was offset by dismay over the

28 Burke MSS, Sheff., Thurlow to Burke, Dec. 17, 1784; MSS Eur., D. 20,
Francis diary, Dec. 14, 1784.

29 Burke MSS, Sheff., Shackleton to Burke, Sept. 22, 1784. This is the poem
mentioned in vol. I, chap. V of this work.

30 Osborn Coll., Box 39, #15, B43, Burke to Mary Shackleton, Dec. 13, 1784.

31 Burke MSS, Sheff., Jane Burke to Charles O'Hara, Jr., Nov. 3, 1784. This was
the son of Burke's deceased Irish friend. Also *Annual Register*, XXVII, Chronicle,
202. The robbery occurred Sept. 28, 1784.

approaching demise of Johnson. After a late summer tour, which included a stop at Chatsworth, where Richard Burke, Jr., was visiting the Duke of Devonshire, Johnson returned to London in November, to make his will and prepare for death. His friends, including Windham and Burke, were solicitous in their attentions. A few days before Johnson's death on December 13, 1784, Burke paid his last visit. Boswell had the account of it from their old mutual friend, Bennet Langton. Calling in Bolt Court, he "found Mr. Burke and four or five more friends sitting with Johnson. Mr. Burke said to him, 'I am afraid, Sir, such a number of us may be oppressive to you.'—'No, Sir, (said Johnson,) it is not so; and I must be in a wretched state, indeed, when your company would not be a delight to me.' Mr. Burke, in a tremulous voice, expressive of being very tenderly affected, replied, 'My dear Sir, you have always been too good to me.' Immediately afterwards he went away. This was the last circumstance in the acquaintance of these two eminent men."[32]

Burke was at Gregories when Johnson died. Reynolds summoned him to town to serve as first pallbearer.[33] The funeral was on December 20; the services were held in the Abbey at noon, and afterward the members of the Club gloomily dined amid a descending dusk.[34] Burke was a member of the committee that erected a monument to Johnson in St. Paul's Cathedral, the fitting place for one whose life was in London, not Westminster.

In October, 1784, Burke attended a gathering of party leaders in London. It was a pleasant but lethargic meeting.[35] No one had a plan of conduct for the coming session; everyone was willing to leave the future to chance. If Burke had a program, he did not reveal it when after the Christmas holidays he moved to London in preparation for the opening of parliament. The *Daily Universal Register* pretended to know his thoughts. He would bring forward some calculations on the window tax "to clog the wheels of the State waggon."[36]

[32] Boswell's *Johnson* (Modern Library ed.), 1185.

[33] Burke MSS, Sheff., Reynolds to Burke, Dec. 18, 1784.

[34] In his letter of Dec. 18, Reynolds said that the Club would dine at Lord Palmerston's. Windham's diary speaks of a dinner at Reynolds'. Bryant, *Literary Friends*, 162.

[35] Br. Mus., Add. MSS 37,843, fol. 5, Burke to Windham, Oct. 14, 1784.

[36] Jan. 8, 1785.

To oppose for the sake of opposition and to make the administration aware that parliamentary opposition still survived was about all that Burke and his friends would be able to do unless fortuitous events occurred. The beginning of the session offered nothing propitious. Burke commented on the unusual brevity of the speech from the throne. The opposition lamented the omission of references to the extraordinary proceedings in Ireland and to the Westminster election scrutiny; North wanted to know whether the speech hinted at parliamentary reform.[37] Burke followed this lead by predicting the death of the constitution if reform was passed. He also moved a reference to the affairs of India in the Commons' address on the speech. Pitt defended the speech while praising Burke's qualifications to judge the difference between a long and a short one. The House accepted the address without a division. Scott reported to Hastings that the opposition numbered only fifty on opening day and would never rise above one hundred.[38] He did not anticipate Pitt's bad calculations.

The first serious business to come before the House was the Westminster scrutiny. Since June 8, 1784, when it had been resolved upon, tedious and almost endless examinations of voters in the Westminster parishes had been going on amid a tangle of technicalities. By early February, 1785, interrogations had touched only one-fourth of the voters. At that rate the proceedings would continue for another two years, and Westminster would be without one of its members for that period. At first the Commons seemed to enjoy wrangling about details of the scrutiny, and on February 9 had the added pleasure of hearing a fine maiden speech from Windham. But discontent soon manifested itself, when an administration motion defending the scrutiny passed 174-135. Subsequent divisions revealed that the scrutiny was tiring other members besides the Portland Whigs. On February 21 the administration was able to defeat a motion to end the scrutiny by only nine votes in a House of nearly two hundred.[39] Though on March 9 the House rejected 242-137 a

---

[37] Portland doubted that it did. Burke MSS, Sheff., Portland to Burke, Jan. 25, 1785.

[38] Br. Mus., Add. MSS 29,168, fol. 19, Feb. 4, 1785.

[39] *Daily Universal Register*, Feb. 23, 1785.

motion to expunge from its journals the resolution calling for the scrutiny, Pitt was ready to drop it. He got out of the business as gracefully as he could by promising a statute, passed later in the session, to regulate elections and scrutinies. Fox had the pleasure of taking his seat for Westminster and later of recovering damages of £2,000 from the High Bailiff.

It is not clear why Burke said so little during this contest. It is doubtful that he remained tactfully silent because Pitt's position was so obviously embarrassing. Perhaps it was because he had never approved of Fox's engagement in Westminster and did not desire to appear to approve, even for party reasons. But he must have been pleased to witness Pitt's humiliation. He was certainly overjoyed a month later when Pitt's motion for parliamentary reform was defeated 248-174. In this struggle the vote cut across government and opposition divisions. Pitt's defeats on the Westminster scrutiny and parliamentary reform did not signify the recovery of the opposition or the decline of administrative strength.

There was probably a better reason for Burke's reticence early in the session. During the first two months he was preoccupied with the notorious business of the debts of the nawab of Arcot. This provided an opportunity to attack Pitt's government from another direction and, in one of his most celebrated speeches, to drag across the floor of the House of Commons the reputations of company servants in India, including Hastings. Undeniably Burke's interest in the nawab of Arcot originated in Will Burke's employment by the raja of Tanjore, who had been at odds with the nawab for years. In 1781 in the Court of Proprietors Burke had fought against Paul Benfield, one of the creditors of the nawab, and ever since that time he had brooded over the sordid financial history of the Carnatic. The nawab, a wastrel, had granted assignments on his land revenues to his various creditors, many of them company servants. When he became governor of Madras, Macartney forced the nawab to grant to the Madras government the management of the Carnatic revenues in order to guarantee that the company would receive the payments owing to it for the troops which protected the Carnatic. The alarmed creditors and their dupe, the nawab, appealed to Hastings. Having reverted to his traditional policy toward native princes now that peace prevailed in the Carnatic, and anxious for the support of the Arcot interest in England, Hastings retracted his earlier approval of Macartney's arrangement and ordered the Madras government to restore control to the nawab. This was one of the causes of Macartney's quarrel with Hastings, and one of the reasons he wrote so bitterly to Burke and other persons in England about the need for purifying Indian administration. When Macartney appealed to England, the nawab's debts entered company and parliamentary politics. Several directors and, in July, 1784, thirteen members of parliament, were among the nawab's creditors.[40]

Though his appeal failed, Macartney's action aroused parliamentary interest. Burke and Fox inserted in their India bill a clause ordering an investigation and settlement; Pitt dared not omit a similar provision in his Act, despite the opposition of the directors. After the passage of his bill, the problem was handed to the new Board of Control. After a cursory investigation in the autumn of 1784, Dundas arranged the settlement. It established three classifications of the nawab's debts and a plan for repayment that gave to the claims of private creditors precedence over the company's.[41] To Burke, rightly, this was a sordid deal intended to repay the Arcot interest for their support of Pitt in the general election of 1784.[42] He at once tried to learn the details. From

[40] Philips, *East India Company*, 36. See also H. Dodwell, "Warren Hastings and the Assignment of the Carnatic," *English Historical Review*, XL (1925), 375-96. Dodwell blamed the confusions of the Regulating Act of 1773 for the difficulties between Bengal and Madras, but he also admits, p. 396, the degeneration of Hastings' character by this time, his readiness to use force to accomplish his objects if anyone opposed him, and his unsavory alliance with Benfield.

[41] The division of the debts followed a suggestion made to Pitt in April, 1784, by John Call, an agent of the Arcot creditors. Philips, *East India Company*, 38-39.

[42] Philips, *East India Company*, 38-39. Holden Furber, *Henry Dundas* (Oxford, 1931), 52, absolves Dundas of collusion with the Arcot interest for corrupt purposes, but does not discuss the political pay-off that Philips describes. Yet Furber, p. 52, n. 4, cites a letter of Oct. 3, 1802, in which Dundas calls certain debts of 1802 "better founded in justice" than those of 1784, and then, p. 52, says investigation showed the new debts to be 95 per cent fraudulent. Philips, *East India Company*, 40, n. 6, affirms the fraudulent nature of the later debts. In "The East India Company Directors in 1784," *Journal of Modern History*, V (1933), 479-95, and esp. pp. 481-82, Furber admits that the settlement of 1784 was a *quid pro quo* for election support in 1784 and on p. 482, n. 16, revises the judgment given in the earlier biography of Dundas cited above. Furber says that the settlement in favor of the private creditors doubtless "was the price paid by Pitt and Dundas" for the aid of Atkinson and the Arcot interest in the 1784 election.

Thurlow he received a vague denial of accurate knowledge but an affirmation of willingness to discuss the settlement.[43]

If morally indignant, Burke and Fox also saw the political opportunities the settlement offered to them. Early in the new session they brought it before parliament, when Fox asked for papers.[44] He accused the administration of denying information to the House and of violating its own India Act by making a settlement without holding a "special inquiry." The motion was intended to give Burke the opportunity that, judging from the quality and thoroughness of his speech, he was awaiting. His "Speech on the Nabob of Arcot's Debts" proves that he had been busy since October, 1784.[45]

The speech was a political attack upon the administration and a plea for right and justice in the government of India. The settlement was wrong in itself, unjust to the raja of Tanjore, to the people of Madras, and to the company. Burke also questioned the propriety of the manner in which the settlement had been made. The Board of Control had usurped from the directors the authority to arrange the settlement, and in further violation of the India Act had done it without the thorough investigation stipulated by the Act. These proceedings alarmed Burke; they suggested a tendency to "make ourselves too little for the sphere of our duty" in India. The result would be "the shameful dilapidation" of the remainder of our "great empire."

The central portion of this speech attempted to unravel a network of intrigue, corruption, and obfuscation. The real culprits were the nawab's private creditors, Paul Benfield and company. Dundas, Pitt, and other ministers were their willing agents. The victims were the people of the Carnatic, whose taxes, by Dundas' settlement, were pledged to the payment of the nawab's greedy creditors. Burke explained why it was that after condemning the creditors in the reports of his Committee of Secrecy, Dundas arranged a settlement of which they were the beneficiaries. Besides sitting for the notorious borough of Cricklade, Benfield, this "public-spirited usurer," sent to the former parliament seven members who supported Pitt. Burke did not know to "how many

43 Burke MSS, Sheff., Thurlow to Burke, Dec. 6, 1784.
44 *Parl. Hist.*, XXV, 162-65, Feb. 28, 1785.
45 Printed in *Works*, III, 1-210.

others" besides Benfield and Atkinson the ministry was obligated, but he implied that "general opinion" knew of them. Dundas was the most callous participant in this sordid affair. As chairman of the secret committee he had eagerly published its reports to serve his political interest. Having attained power, he became timid, and thought frankness about Indian politics "highly dangerous." There was no doubt, said Burke, that "concealment" became "prudence" because Dundas did not want the world to know how "he chooses to dispose of the public revenues to the creatures of his politics."

This speech was a clever but ineffective attack upon the probity of the administration. It contained some gorgeous exaggeration, for example of the devastations Hyder Ali's troops had worked upon the Carnatic.[46] It displayed Burke's characteristic vulgarity of expression. Dundas, once so forthright and now so timid, was by his settlement "exposed like the sow of imperial augury, lying in the mud with all the prodigies of her fertility about her, as evidence of her delicate amours." The speech was a valiant effort to explain the inexplicably confused financial affairs of the nawab of Arcot. It failed to persuade Burke's hearers; the motion for papers was defeated 164-69. For whatever satisfaction it might give Burke's admirers, the future vindicated his efforts. Dundas did not answer Burke's political charges, and later he admitted that the government was under "necessity" when it made the decision that was a bonanza for the nawab's creditors.[47] A thorough investigation of the earlier debts would have shown what a later inquiry revealed about debts accumulated after 1784, that most of the creditors' claims were fraudulent. Burke was correct in accusing the ministry with attempting to conceal a dishonest transaction. Perhaps his own avowal to Thurlow of freedom from "private interest and private malice" was self-righteous.[48] But if a politician pleads for honesty in the administration of public affairs, and if he attacks subterfuge and concealment of corruption, he serves the public even though he is inspired by party motives.

If in condemning the Arcot settlement Burke tried to serve both

46 Davies, ed., *Private Corr. of Macartney*, ix.
47 Philips, *East India Company*, 40. Also Furber, *J. of Modern History*, V, 481-82.
48 *Corr.*, III, 36, Burke to Thurlow, March, 1785.

party and public, his conduct with respect to Ireland in 1785 has been considered partisanship in its least savory form. No one has offered a persuasive apology for him, and the latest student of the problem of Burke and Ireland deplores his opposition to Pitt's commercial plan for Ireland.[49] Perhaps there is more to say upon the subject, not by way of exonerating Burke from charges of partisanship, for that cannot be done, but by way of understanding more fully his position on the Irish proposals. That can only be done against the background of Burke's views of commercial policy.

As Burke had said at the time, the grant of legislative independence to Ireland in 1782 was not by itself the solution of the Irish problem. It might have opened the way to a settlement if imperial statesmanship had been adequate to the demands of the times. The legislation had left unresolved the political problem within Ireland and that of commercial relations between Ireland and the United Kingdom. During the years 1783-1784, Ireland was agitated by discussions of parliamentary reform. This was a more inflammatory subject there than in England because of the religious implications. The agitation failed and by 1785 receded, to the relief of Burke as well as the Pitt administration. Burke did not oppose reform for religious reasons; he would, as he had made clear in 1782, give the vote to Catholics who otherwise qualified under existing franchise requirements.

Simultaneously there began another agitation, stimulated by the economic hardship of the years since independence. Ireland's manufacturers desired tariff protection against imports from England. Failing to obtain it in the spring of 1784, they and the politicians pressed for amendment of the regulations that bore against Ireland in her trade with England. Lord North's earlier legislation had made only a beginning at removing such inequities. Remembering Burke's role in obtaining that commercial legislation, his conduct in 1785 appears inconsistent. But neither Burke nor North had ever desired to impair the navigation system, as Pitt's original proposals in 1785 would have done. When in office in 1783, Fox and North had rejected their Lord Lieutenant's

49 Mahoney, *Burke and Ireland,* 150-51.

suggestions for a further relaxation of commercial restraints. On November 1, 1783, Fox flatly told Lord Northington that the earlier concessions to Ireland closed the account forever.[50] Burke and his friends were earnest protectionists as well as "genial buccaneers." When they eagerly seized for partisan purposes the opportunity Pitt gave them in 1785 to inflame "English jealousy on one side of the water and Irish pride on the other," they were also consistent with their basic beliefs about British commercial policy.[51]

In Ireland in the summer of 1784 statesmanship prevailed over recriminations and substituted good sense for provocation and retaliation. On May 13 the Irish Commons had passed a resolution favoring a comprehensive and liberal plan for commercial relations between Ireland and the United Kingdom. John Foster, the Irish Chancellor of the Exchequer, aided by the Irish Secretary Thomas Orde, transformed this resolution into a plan for a commercial settlement. Pitt heartily approved. Unfortunately for Foster's plan, Pitt desired a much more comprehensive settlement of Irish affairs. In return for granting commercial equality, he hoped to extract from Ireland a contribution toward imperial defense and, taking advantage of the resurgence of good will, to push through a temperate parliamentary reform. This would be made palatable to the Irish Ascendancy by *"excluding the Catholics from any share in the representation* or the government of the Country."[52] The Catholic question apart, his proposals seemed generous. But his enlargement of Foster's limited plan provided the opposition in England with emotional arguments that were also advanced vehemently and bitterly in Ireland. Pitt ignored the warnings of his Lord Lieutenant, the Duke of Rutland, of Foster, and of Orde. He rejected Rutland's assertion, which anticipated Fox, that to demand a contribution to imperial defense would make Ireland think she was "at the Devotion of

---

[50] Harlow, *The Second British Empire*, I, 561. This volume contains the best account of Pitt's trade proposals, pp. 558-616.

[51] Harlow, *The Second British Empire*, I, 562, for the quotations only, not for the conclusion.

[52] Harlow, *The Second British Empire*, I, 564-65. The quotation is from Pitt to Rutland, Oct. 7, 1784, and the italics are Pitt's. In the light of later events, it is interesting to notice Pitt's attitude toward the Catholics.

the British Government.''[53] Pitt's belief in the rightness of the enlarged plan, a point not disputed by the Irish government, misled him. His conduct illustrated an argument Burke frequently employed. The politician who begins with a proposition that is right in itself permits its virtue to hide the circumstances and practical difficulties. One of these was the pride of the Irish in their newly won legislative independence.[54]

Confident that Irish objections could be overcome, and insistent that the contribution to imperial defense was necessary to the success of the commercial proposals in England, Pitt pushed ahead with his plan. He mentioned it in the King's Speech on January 25, 1785. Burke took notice of the allusion. While approving the desire to settle commercial relations with Ireland, he deplored the neglect of the more urgent affairs of India. In February the plan, embodied in eleven resolutions, passed the Irish parliament. The opposition was strong, and more ominous because of Grattan's hostility. Consequently, acting upon its own initiative, the Irish administration accepted his demand for a qualification setting forth conditions regulating the financial contribution. Though this amendment did not emasculate the plan, Pitt was furious over it, and the parliamentary opposition overjoyed. Since Pitt, now appearing as an inept tactician, was already in trouble over the Westminster scrutiny, the Fox-North forces thought they had a good chance of bringing him down. They resolved to oppose the commercial propositions vigorously, both in and out of parliament. The king had earlier predicted that Lord North would "undoubtedly easily" arouse the merchants, the manufacturers, and the people against the plan.[55] Yet between January 29 and March 8, testimony of the commercial and manufacturing interests before the Committee on Trade and Plantations revealed little apprehension of adverse effects of a mutual reduction of duties on trade between the two countries.[56] The later opposition of the same interests was evoked, as Harlow says, by "cleverly organized political propaganda."

[53] Quoted in Harlow, *The Second British Empire*, I, 573.
[54] Harlow, *The Second British Empire*, I, 572.
[55] Harlow, *The Second British Empire*, I, 581-82, n. 33.
[56] Harlow, *The Second British Empire*, I, 593-98.

Burke began the parliamentary discussion in England on February 21 with some peripheral objections in anticipation of the question that Pitt had announced for the next day.[57] He demanded postponement of full debate until the House acquired sufficient information for judging the proposals. He sought an explanation of the reason for introducing the plan first in the Irish parliament, taking this to be an affront to the imperial parliament. This hortatory device evoked varied responses, including abuse from one newspaper that remarked facetiously upon the strangeness of the spectacle—an Irishman the only member of Commons who stood up for the honor of England.[58] Like succeeding debates, the abuse grew warmer. Burke became a parricide, like Sheridan and Courtenay opposing generous offers of commercial advantage to the land of his birth. How different now, said his opponents, were his sentiments and conduct compared with his earlier avowals of love for his native land.[59]

The opposition to the commercial proposals during March and April grew steadily more powerful and better organized. The commercial and manufacturing interests reversed themselves and formed against the plan a country-wide organization headed by Josiah Wedgwood. They bombarded parliament with petitions and protests, kept up a steady newspaper campaign, encouraged the writing of pamphlets, and appeared at the bar of the Commons to testify against the government's plan. They repeated arguments that Burke had scoffed at in 1778 and 1779 concerning the unfair competition of cheap Irish goods. The protectionists who believed in the old navigation system, and had rejected Shelburne's scheme for admitting the United States into the imperial commercial system, rallied against the admission of Ireland because they feared the difficulties of enforcing the navigation acts throughout that island. Fox and his colleagues skillfully exploited these fears and the ancient protectionist prejudices, which it must be said they shared. By early May, 1785, the opposition in and out of parliament was so powerful that Pitt feared for the life of his government.

[57] *Daily Universal Register,* Feb. 22, 1785.
[58] *Daily Universal Register,* Feb. 23, 1785.
[59] *Daily Universal Register,* March 5, April 4, 1785.

In the debates in the English Commons, and in the organization work outside, Burke played an inconspicuous part.[60] The reasons are not at once apparent. Perhaps he felt embarrassment because of the seeming inconsistency of his conduct, and because of his Irish background. Perhaps he preferred to concentrate his efforts upon an anonymous reply to the official pamphlet of George Rose, Secretary of the Treasury. There has been some doubt whether Burke or Thomas O'Beirne wrote the *Reply to the Treasury Pamphlet*. Though Burke's correspondence does not remove it, other evidence makes Burke the author. One of the pamphleteers who answered the *Reply,* probably Sir Richard Musgrave, attributed it to Burke.[61] There is a remarkable similarity between the arguments in the *Reply* and Burke's known opinions about the protectionist system and about certain features of the Irish proposals. One piece of external evidence and a great deal of internal evidence, leaving aside stylistic resemblances, make a strong case for Burke's authorship of the pamphlet.

The *Reply* repeated arguments that Lord Sheffield had published in February, 1785.[62] The opposition had performed a public service in exposing the true meaning of the proposals. North's reforms had not impeached the navigation system. They opened trade between the plantations and Ireland as an end in itself, not as a preliminary to opening British markets to Irish producers or to Irish shippers who would bring foreign colonial products into England labeled as the produce of the British West Indies. The grant of Irish political independence had never contemplated concessions that would ruin British trade and industry or destroy the navigation system. It is difficult to reconcile Burke's disavowals of partisanship in 1785 and his emphasis upon

60 The newspaper accounts of the debates have Eden, Fox, Sheridan, and North the leading opposition speakers. Except for the comments in the pamphlet shortly to be discussed, there is little information about Burke's opinions either in his correspondence or in the accounts of parliamentary debates. The discussion in Mahoney, *Burke and Ireland,* chap. V, tells little about Burke's opinions, presenting instead the opposition arguments and then identifying Burke's position with them.

61 *An Answer to the Reply to the Supposed Treasury Pamphlet* (London, 1785), 3-7.

62 *Observations on the Manufactures and Trade of Ireland.* As he had when opposing the American trade proposals, Sheffield concentrated upon a defense of the navigation system.

Irish competition with statements he made in 1778-1779. Though he had not then seen incompatibility between the trade conces-sions and the protectionist system, in 1785 he expressed fear of Irish competition and found the economic interests of Ireland and England in conflict.

The remainder of the *Reply* was honest and consistent with Burke's earlier position. He opposed Pitt's plan mainly because he was a protectionist, not a free trader. In 1785 he agreed per-fectly with his earlier exceptions to Shelburne's proposals regard-ing American trade and reaffirmed his faith in the traditional imperial commercial system. He believed also that the scheme for an Irish contribution to imperial defense was delusory under the conditions that the Irish parliament had inserted into the plan, and thus it did not have "equity, equality, or reciprocity for its basis."[63] In that case, as Burke said in the Commons on May 19, he would have to give his preference to England when its interests clashed with Ireland's.[64] The most effective parts of the *Reply* were those that appealed to traditional protectionist sentiments. These, with rare exceptions, still dominated the thought of En-glish politicians. It was Pitt's fatal mistake to underestimate the strength and universality of the devotion to the old navigation system, and it was the strength of this devotion that supported the parliamentary opposition.[65]

Under a mounting pressure that became almost universal op-position in England, Pitt made concessions. These were embodied in altered resolutions laid before the English Commons on May 12, 1785. The amendments obligated the Irish parliament to re-enact Britain's navigation laws, prohibited direct trade between Ireland and the regions included in the monopoly of the East India Company, maintained Britain's authority to regulate Irish exports to the West Indies and North America, and modified the provision for the financial contribution. In effect, these changes meant "the virtual surrender of Ireland's right to legislate for

---

[63] *Reply*, 90. Burke forced Pitt to admit on May 19 that his hopes of a revenue from Ireland had to depend on the chance that expanding Irish prosperity would raise hereditary revenues beyond the sum that had to be attained before Ireland would contribute to the support of the navy. *Daily Universal Register*, May 20, 1785.

[64] *Parl. Hist.*, XXV, 649.

[65] Harlow, *The Second British Empire*, I, 590-91.

herself in commercial matters."[66] Pitt was now in an impossible position, vulnerable to the charge that the provision for an Irish contribution to the navy amounted to British taxation of Ireland. Burke explained this on May 19 and raised the specter of the American Revolution.[67] The opposition formulated a new accusation that was bound to excite Ireland. The injunctions concerning commercial regulations infringed upon Ireland's newly won legislative independence.[68] Fox said Ireland would be reduced again to the position of a colony.[69]

At this time Burke separated himself from the parliamentary opposition. Apart from the revenue provisions, the commercial changes seemed to satisfy him. Though Ireland enjoyed legislative independence, she could possess "no other independence . . . without reversing the order and decree of nature: . . . she must for ever remain under the protection of England, her guardian angel."[70] If, in establishing such protection, the imperial parliament imposed commercial restraints that would preserve the navigation system and yet provide a sound basis for Irish well-being, then Burke would be satisfied. It is interesting to notice that his remarks on May 19 were confined to the provisions for the financial contribution. Otherwise, unlike his party, he approved of the altered plan.

This he made clear in a letter of May 13 to Sir John Tydd.[71] At first glance this letter embarrasses the biographer of Burke. It contradicts the conclusions of all who have written about Burke's role in this episode.[72] Because the letter seems to reverse Burke's previous position on the trade proposals, the pertinent passage deserves quotation.

I hope you on your side know and approve the substance, at least, of the amendments; for if you should not acquiesce in them, I do really

66 Harlow, *The Second British Empire*, I, 592.

67 *Parl. Hist.*, XXV, 647; *Daily Universal Register*, May 20, 1785; Mahoney, *Burke and Ireland*, 148.

68 *Annual Register*, XXVIII, 19-20.

69 J. Holland Rose, *William Pitt and National Revival* (London, 1911), 261.

70 *Parl. Hist.*, XXV, 650, May 19, 1789.

71 Grattan, ed., *Memoirs*, III, 251-52. It is interesting to observe that in this letter Burke uses "we" to refer to the House of Commons and "they" when speaking of the "Opposition." He completely dissociates himself from Fox and North.

72 Even Mahoney, *Burke and Ireland*, does not mention this letter or refer to it in his notes.

fear that your situation is most critical indeed. This is the only moment, in my idea, for Ireland to fix her happiness, commercial and political, upon a solid and firm base. If pertinacity, or an ill-understood punctilio should be suffered to step in, to prevent the operation of the good sense of your country, and prevent our now coming to a final settlement upon some system that may connect the two countries permanently, and for ever lay asleep every motive of jealousy and dispute, every man, either of wisdom or feeling, will soon have reason to regret the day when the question was first stirred among us, and that anything was done to let all *loose from the bands of the old situation,* before due consideration was had upon what should be those of the new. But it is idle, my pressing upon you my private and crude sentiments, ill-digested and inadequate as they must be on a subject of this extensive and very comprehensive nature; but I own I do feel the utmost anxiety upon what may prove the termination of it. What we do upon Thursday next, you may rely upon receiving information of from me.

Burke's apparent reversal is not unexplainable. His initial hostility to the Irish commercial proposals was directed against the financial clauses and the breach of the protectionist system contained in the proposals sent over from the Irish parliament. Unlike his colleagues, he had said virtually nothing about the infringement upon Ireland's legislative independence. Indeed, he had always been cool to it and on May 19 had repeated his opinion that it should not be limitless. Pitt's alterations, announced on May 12, did not remove Burke's dislike of the revenue scheme, but allayed his fears about the safety of the navigation system. Consequently, he was able to hope that the amended resolutions would pass the Irish parliament, though he remained doubtful that the Irish hereditary revenues would ever approach the minimum sum of £656,000 that must be attained before a revenue would be forthcoming. But his doubt was expressed more as a question than an assertion. Pitt remarked upon the good spirit in which he had sought information.[73] Thereafter the burden of opposing the plan fell upon Fox, North, Sheridan, and Eden. They, not Burke, supplied the arguments that were employed to defeat Pitt's amended commercial plan when it was returned to the Irish parliament in July.

[73] *Daily Universal Register,* May 20, 1785.

Throughout, there was the dilemma of reconciling Ireland's political autonomy with membership in a mercantilist empire. When Pitt altered the proposals in order to assure Irish adherence to the navigation system, the British opposition at once raised the cry of infringement upon Ireland's political autonomy. It was a neat trick and an effective one for Fox to cry, "I will not barter English commerce for Irish slavery."[74] When Thomas Orde on August 12 asked for leave to introduce a bill in the Irish Commons based on the resolutions that had been returned from England, his majority was too small for comfort, being 127-108. The Irish opposition, especially Grattan and Flood, used arguments previously employed by the opposition in England. The administration gave up, and the project upon which so much effort had been expended was dropped, forever.

Historians and biographers have agreed in condemning the British opposition for their factious narrowness in destroying Pitt's commercial plan. But partisanship is not by definition dishonesty. In their defense of the old navigation system, Burke, Fox, Eden, Sheffield, and their cohorts were probably sincere and clearly consistent with views long held and often expressed. It is not so much their technical arguments that are to be reprobated, for there was a certain logic to them. The terms held out to Ireland were not absolutely consistent with her legislative independence and did limit the discretion of her parliament in respect of the financial contribution and commercial regulations. Pitt asked Ireland to make some prudent concessions in order that she might remain within the closed commercial system of the Empire. These were the kinds of reasonable adaptations to circumstances that Burke normally thought a statesman should make, and which, after May 12, he thought had been made. Nevertheless, by insisting upon the maintenance of the protectionist system on terms laid down by Britain, Burke helped make it impossible for the Irish parliament to consent. Nineteenth-century experience would demonstrate that legislative independence and commercial autonomy went together in the British Empire.

Burke himself said nothing about the episode in retrospect. He made no effort to join with his party colleagues in celebrating

74 *Parl. Hist.*, XXV, 778.

their success. At Manchester in early September, the mercantile
and manufacturing interests honored the "Rockingham" party
for their devotion to the interests of the country.[75] In an enthusiastic procession, the people paid to the Earl of Derby the supreme
tribute of pulling his carriage by hand, and later, at a banquet in
honor of Derby and Fox, the assembled merchants drank toasts
and sang in tribute to them. Burke, who was in Scotland, was
not mentioned.

While concerned with India and Ireland, Burke's attention
was called to a different kind of imperial problem. It was one
which would become more prominent as the humanitarian movement directed its efforts to the alleviation of misery among people
at home and in the Empire. Burke was not in the 1780's a leader
of any organized humanitarian group, but he had a reputation for
doing good works, and he supported efforts to promote them.
His humanitarianism was an aspect of his passion for justice;
people had a right to decent treatment.

When Burke manifested his humanitarianism in 1785, he
played a minor part in making the decision which resulted in the
expansion of the British Empire into the Southwest Pacific. The
loss of the American colonies had intensified the penal problem
in England by ending the transportation of convicts to the main-
land colonies. The West Indies could not receive the large
numbers whom the inadequate English prisons and the hulks in
the Thames were unable to accommodate but whom the harsh
criminal law nevertheless condemned to transportation. The ideal
solution, which Burke advocated, was a radical reform of the
wholy body of criminal law. In the *Annual Register* for 1767
(pp. 316-20) he had reviewed favorably Beccaria's *Essay on Crime
and Punishment,* praising the book for "the eloquence and tenderness" with which it pleaded "the cause of humanity." In parliament in 1789 he urged "a revision of the whole criminal law,
which, in its present form, . . . [was] abominable."[76] Specifically,
he desired reform of the law relating to imprisonment for debt, to
prison administration, and to the transportation of convicts to the

---

[75] *Daily Universal Register,* Sept. 13, 1785.
[76] Quoted in Leon Radzinowicz, *A History of English Criminal Law and its
Administration from 1750* (New York, 1948), 340; *Times,* May 29, 1789.

colonies.[77] He thought the law failed to distinguish between trivial and grave offenses, especially when it sanctioned the death penalty or transportation for offenses that were not felonies.

If Burke was ahead of his times in asking for revision of the criminal law, he found an opportunity at least to ameliorate the system of transportation. In 1784, when ministers were pondering the difficulties created by the loss of the American colonies, John Call, a government official, suggested the establishment of a penal colony in New South Wales or New Zealand.[78] As time passed without a decision, the convict problem became more acute. Burke apparently heard of ministerial discussions about a penal colony in West Africa. On March 16, 1785, he anticipated a government announcement by opening the subject in the House of Commons.[79] In an impassioned speech he exposed the cruelties of the penal-transportation system. Its evils violated "every principle of justice and humanity." Burke also denounced the government for its apathy and its secrecy. Where were they going to send these convicts? He hoped not to Gambia, for that would be a ministerial sentence of death.

Burke's speech carried beyond the walls of St. Stephen's to Newgate itself. One prisoner wrote him a letter confirming his description of the horrors of transportation and saying that his case was like that of countless other wretches.[80] If this letter moved Burke, so also did one from Eugene Keeling, who pleaded with Burke to intercede for his two sons who were awaiting transportation.[81]

On April 11 Lord Beauchamp raised the subject again in the Commons, trying to force a positive statement from Pitt.[82] He got instead a typical official answer; it would be better to postpone discussion, said the minister, pending the submission of a report. Burke, referring again to rumors, protested against establishment of a penal colony at Gambia. He refused to be cowed by Pitt's sarcastic suggestion, characteristic of the "expert," that Burke was

---

77 Radzinowicz, *Criminal Law*, 35-36, 339-41.
78 Br. Mus., Add. MSS 29,106, fols. 27-28, Call to Warren Hastings, Sept. 2, 1784.
79 *Parl. Hist.*, XXV, 391; Rose, *Pitt and National Revival*, 434.
80 Burke MSS, Sheff., C. Peat to Burke, March 18, 1785.
81 Burke MSS, Sheff., April 2, 1785.
82 *Parl. Hist.*, XXV, 430-32.

presuming without knowledge of the facts. Burke argued that it was not only the destination that was at issue but the entire system of transportation. Because of the danger of pestilence, "the public safety" was involved, and that, "no less than a humane regard to the individuals in question, called for the interposition of parliament."

Burke's suspicions of Pitt's lack of candor were correct. On July 28 appeared a report recommending a penal colony on the Gold Coast.[83] Burke protested violently and "probably" with effect, says Pitt's biographer.[84] At any rate, the government abandoned the project, perhaps because it did not desire more opposition when it was already in trouble over the Irish trade proposals. Burke was sufficiently practical to realize that he was asking for too much when he recommended the abolition of transportation. In the debate of April 11 he had suggested Botany Bay as an alternative to West Africa, if there had to be transportation. The government had already unenthusiastically considered Botany Bay; after giving up, or being forced to give up, the Gold Coast project, it reconsidered. Pitt's biographer again is generous to Burke; "possibly" his and Lord Beauchamp's protests caused the change of plans. In January, 1788, the first convicts were landed on Australian soil. "Possibly" Burke was one of those who promoted the beginnings of settlement in Australia.

The session of 1785 had been much concerned with problems of empire, but even before the adjournment Burke's attendance slackened. With little taste for the last debates on the Irish trade proposals, he withdrew to Gregories, but not to isolation. Burke's estate was something of a Mecca, and at this time especially for visitors from France, where Burke's reputation seemed to be higher than it was at home. In 1784 Burke had had three visitors from that country, the Abbé Raynal, Cloots, and in November an old Paris schoolmate of Sir Gilbert Elliot. This was the Count de Mirabeau.[85] He and Burke held long and vigorous conversa-

---

83 Rose, *Pitt and National Revival*, 435.

84 Besides Rose, 435, see Wraxall, *Memoirs*, IV, 110.

85 Bryant, *Literary Friends*, 305-306; Louis Barthou, *Mirabeau* (London, 1913), 111; Greig, ed., *The Farington Diary*, I, 5; Burke MSS, Sheff., Elliot to Burke, Nov. 22, 1784. This letter established the date of the visit as Nov. 23 rather than early 1785, as formerly believed.

tions, though each was uncomfortable in the language of the other. Burke had to use English words to fill out his French, but even this awkwardness did not destroy his eloquence. Mirabeau went away much impressed, calling Burke his friend. He was charmed rather than alienated by the warmth of Burke's frank conversation. As for Burke, in 1791 in anticipation of a visit from the Abbé Maury, he offered to have his house "purified and expiated" because Mirabeau had once visited in it.[86]

Such visits continued in 1785. That of Madame de Genlis in July was immediately disagreeable.[87] Besides her own obnoxious personality she brought to Gregories a company of servants as demanding as their mistress. Among her eccentricities was an inability to sleep except in absolute darkness; Burke had to arrange for a carpenter to nail blankets over the windows of her room. Even the equable Reynolds, who journeyed the twenty-five miles to meet her, was critical. For all of her haughtiness, she admired Burke. She was the person who sent to Gregories another Frenchman destined to have some influence upon Burke's career. Writing on October 12, 1785, she begged to introduce Jean DePont, the intendant of Metz.[88] He was accompanied by his nineteen-year-old son, Charles Jean François. Not only did Burke have them for three days but he arranged for entertainment elsewhere. He obtained tickets for the Lord Mayor's Guildhall dinner and prevailed on Richard, Sr., to accompany them.[89] They returned to Paris in time to give to Richard, Jr., a letter of appreciation to his father.[90] This was not the end of the acquaintance with Charles DePont. He was the young man who asked Burke for his opinions on the French Revolution and to whom, in consequence, Burke addressed the *Reflections on the Revolution in France*.

Between the visits of Madame de Genlis and the DePonts, in August and September, 1785, Burke made another trip to Scot-

---

[86] *Corr.*, III, 199, Burke to Captain Woodford, Feb. 11, 1791.

[87] Bryant, *Literary Friends*, 306-307.

[88] Burke MSS, N.R.O., Axxiiil. See also H. V. F. Somerset, "A Burke Discovery," *English*, VIII (1951), 171-78, and Hans A. Schmitt and John C. Weston, Jr., "Ten Letters to Edmund Burke . . . ," *J. of Modern History*, XXIV (Dec., 1952), 406-408.

[89] Wecter, *Kinsmen*, 74; Burke MSS, N.R.O., Aii56a, F. Buller to Burke, Nov. 10, 1785.

[90] Burke MSS, N.R.O., Aiie, Charles DePont to Burke, Jan. 15, 1786.

land in company with Richard, Jr., and his young friend William Windham.[91] On the way they visited Lord Fitzwilliam at Milton and Sir Gilbert Elliot at Minto. In Edinburgh Burke resumed his pleasant associations with Smith and Dalzell. He met the historian Robertson, the Scottish friend of the Prince of Wales, Henry Erskine, and John Sinclair, the young member of parliament who was destined for fame as an agricultural expert. He also met the poet John Logan, whose "Ode to the Cuckoo" he thought was the most beautiful of all lyric poems. On September 1 Burke was installed at Glasgow for his second term as rector, though because of the lateness of the ceremony he had only three more months in the office. The highlight of this second Scottish journey was a two-week trip with Windham through the Highlands, during which he visited the Duke of Argyll at Inverary. Burke returned to England by way of Wentworth Woodhouse, in better health than he had known for many months.

Richard, Jr., had left his father in Edinburgh on the return journey in order to take ship for Holland en route to Paris.[92] The ship encountered a terrific storm. The newspapers reported it lost and Richard drowned. According to Fitzwilliam, Burke's distress was indescribable during two days of uncertainty. You know, said Fitzwilliam, how Burke dotes on his son. By the time the story reached Ireland, it had Burke dying of grief over Richard's loss. Shackleton was ready to believe its truth. But only the storm was real, and as Burke was pleased to tell Shackleton, none of the consequences "manufactured" by the "great artists in the newspapers" had occurred. So it was with even greater pleasure that Burke read his son's accounts of his movements in Parisian society, at court, and in the company of such as the Duke D'Orleans and Madame de Genlis.[93]

By this time Warren Hastings had been in England six months.

---

[91] Osborn Coll., Box 88, #40, Burke to Walker King, July [1785]; Rae, *Adam Smith*, 396; Pottle, ed., *Private Papers*, XVI, 281, Sir William Forbes to Boswell, Sept. 16, 1785.

[92] Burke MSS, Sheff., Fitzwilliam to Richard Burke, Sr., undated but early Oct., 1785; Burke MSS, N.R.O., Aii55, Shackleton to Burke, Oct. 18, 1785; *Corr.*, III, 36-37, Burke to Shackleton, Oct. 26, 1785.

[93] Burke MSS, Sheff., Richard, Jr., to Burke, Nov. 9, Dec. 25, 1785.

CHAPTER IX

The Impeachment of Hastings: The Commons

In a document written in Warren Hastings' hand appears a laconic statement dated June 16, 1785, saying that on this day he arrived in London and that in the Commons Burke announced his intention to bring accusations against him during the next session.[1]

The disposition of parliamentary forces was not unfavorable to Burke's purpose. Though Pitt had suffered defeats during the session, they did not indicate that he was unable to carry on the nation's business. He retained the king's confidence and enjoyed the general support of many members who had deserted him on one or another particular question. These independent members could be useful to Burke. If they felt no obligation to support Pitt on every occasion, even on matters close to his heart, then upon one on which he was neutral, like the Hastings question, their independence was unrestricted. Indeed, even Pitt's dedicated followers would be at liberty on such a question. Burke's chances of persuading parliament to support proceedings against Hastings depended more than was usual upon the merits of the case he could make.

John Scott misrepresented the situation when he told Hastings that parliament was tired of the Indian business and that Burke and his friends, held universally in contempt, were so sick of it they wished they could drop it.[2] Indian affairs had appeared in the Commons during the session, but not so often as to bore members. On certain occasions the proceedings had been interesting. On February 24, 1785, Burke and Scott quarreled. Burke attacked Scott as Hastings' agent; Scott called Burke the representative of Will Burke, the agent of the raja of Tanjore. Burke boasted of his championship of the raja. Four days later, when he spoke about the affairs of Arcot, he supported strongly the raja's interest. Perhaps a report of this reached India. On December 30 Will Burke complained to Richard, Jr., of journalistic errors that identified him as the person who inspired Edmund in the business of India.[3] He admitted, however, that he had not been harmed by Edmund's espousal of the raja's interests.

Suggestions of favoritism angered Burke because he liked to believe that he was approaching the Hastings affair objectively. A man's personal feeling should not be a consideration in public affairs. On "any Indian question," he averred to Francis, he would give his vote "for justice in the first place," and only after that to Francis and Fox.[4] Justice should be the aim of imperial statesmanship, whether in the Orient or in the West, both as a positive good and in the retributive sense. It was his desire, he told Sir George Staunton, to bring to justice the culprits who were destroying India and a large part of mankind.[5] But some persons wondered whether Burke would be able to achieve his desires, being, as a pamphleteer said, no longer a "formidable opponent."[6]

Hastings' return from India stimulated interest. His appearance at court, soon after his arrival and after Burke's announcement in the Commons, attracted attention.[7] Observers noted the king's courteous conduct and wondered whether it meant a peerage for

1 Br. Mus., Add. MSS 29,219, fol. 2, "Chronology of Hastings' Impeachment." Actually it was on June 20 that Burke promised a motion regarding the conduct "of a gentleman just returned from India." E. A. Bond, ed., *Speeches of the Managers and the Counsel in the Trial of Warren Hastings* (London, 1859-61), I, xxxv.

2 Br. Mus., Add. MSS 29,168, fols. 182-88, 210, Scott to Hastings, March 9, 16, 1785.

3 P.R.O., Chatham Papers, 30/8 118.

4 MSS Eur., F. 6, p. 9, Burke to Francis, Nov. 23, 1785.

5 Osborn Coll., Box 88, #27, June [7], 1785.

6 H.M.C., *Rutland*, III, 199, Chatham to Rutland, April 13, 1785; [Nathaniel B. Halhed], *Detector, A Letter to . . . Burke* (London, 1783), 7-8, 9, 76-77.

7 *Daily Advertiser*, June 23, 1785.

Hastings. There were reasons for doubt; against Thurlow's open espousal of his interest, Pitt's coolness and Dundas' neutrality were setoffs. But the peerage was not all that occupied Hastings. When on January 4, 1786, just before the new session began, Hastings and a "great number of East India Chieftains" dined with Thurlow, they surely talked about Macartney's recent arrival in England and wondered what had been going on in the enemy camp since the August prorogation.[8] Before November, nothing. Upon returning from his Scottish trip, Burke told Francis that the time had come to resume the battle of the Bay of Bengal.[9] Then his guests and his near prostration over the false report of his son's drowning had intervened. On November 23 Burke said he had done nothing on India.[10]

Thereafter Burke gave precedence to the prosecution of Hastings. In a letter to Francis in early December he outlined a procedure. The object to be sought was "justice," meaning not the conviction of Hastings, which "we all know to be impracticable," but proceedings that would result in his condemnation. The campaign, therefore, should not be modeled after a case in a law court. It should be planned in the manner best calculated to "acquit and justify" Hastings' prosecutors in the eyes of contemporaries and of posterity. There would be no difficulty in establishing "fact by evidence." The problem would be to prove "*criminality*," for "Guilt *resides* in the *intention*." That would be difficult before parliament, "a bribed tribunal" where politics and parties were so "jumbled and confounded" that perfect agreement was impossible. Burke recommended a shotgun campaign, not limiting the charges to three or four, but seeking to establish "a *general evil intention,* manifested through a long series and a great variety of acts." He was not concerned that on one or another charge "Lord Titius or Mr. Caius" would be unable to go with him. The "substance" of the case lay in "the multitude and the perseverance in offenses" which might be established against Hastings.[11]

8 *Daily Universal Register,* Jan. 6, 1786.
9 MSS Eur., F. 6, p. 7, Sept. 30, 1785.
10 MSS Eur., F. 6, p. 9, Burke to Francis.
11 *Corr.,* III, 38-45, Burke to Francis, Dec. 10, 1785. Italics Burke's.

These sentiments explain much about the proceedings of the next months. Burke had to take account of the difference between his situation and that of Fox, who as the head of a party desired to "march with the whole body in an orderly array upon the expedition before us." Fox preferred to confine the charges to a few well-documented offenses that the party could support unanimously, and to present them as if in a court of law. Not having Fox's responsibilities, Burke did not consider the attack upon Hastings as a party maneuver. He was interested in the "cause, and not the support." To establish the one would create the other. Characteristically, Burke thought of an appeal to men's passions, their humanitarianism, their sense of justice, and their dislike of oppression. His arguments, like his case, would not be disciplined by logic, strict relevance, or legal rules of evidence. Like his writings and speeches, his arguments in the hearings in the Commons would be attempts to persuade by exposition. The web of rhetoric would catch up all whose emotions could be appealed to. If this was not the way to conduct a judicial proceeding, no matter. Burke was never confident of victory. If the case reached the Lords in the form of an impeachment, it would be heard, he said, by a body whose members had prejudged it.

This difference between Fox and Burke explains the doubts of some Portland Whigs as the new session approached. Like Fox, some members hesitated about getting involved in anything less than a strong legal case. This uncertainty within the party was resolved just before the session began on January 24, 1786. The sources, even Burke's correspondence, are vague about details. London gossip said that at a "great meeting" of the party at Portland's house, Burke's colleagues tried to dissuade him from continuing the campaign against Hastings, but instead, he persuaded them against their better judgments.[12] This tale, which exaggerates Burke's influence in the party, is not easily reconciled

12 Gleig, *Hastings*, III, 276, for the quotation and the version that the meeting occurred a day or two before the session began. Gleig offers no documentation. Rose, *Pitt and National Revival*, 228, repeats the story. In Br. Mus., Add. MSS 29,225, fol. 138 are some extracts from unidentified publications. Here the meeting is dated after the opening of parliament, and it is implied that Scott's provocation of Burke on opening day forced the party to decide the matter, thus making a party campaign of it.

with what we know of the work that had been going on for months in anticipation of the meeting of parliament. It may, however, reflect the hesitancy of some members of the party.

The debate on opening day indicates that the party had reached agreement. It is not accurate to say that Hastings, who prompted him, and Scott, who challenged Burke to name the day when he would bring in charges, must assume "the responsibility for renewing the strife."[13] When Burke later said that he was "called upon and driven to the business," he referred not to Scott's provocation but to the mounting indignation of five years' study of Indian affairs.[14] Only in a formal sense was Scott's challenge the "dignified & decent" beginning of this "great work," as Hastings facetiously remarked.[15] Indeed, it was Fox who took the lead on opening day. He attacked the minister for omitting reference to India from the King's Speech, and he praised Macartney, an object of the Bengal Squad's hatred.[16]

Burke told Scott and the House of his intention to choose his time to bring in accusations. Not until February 17 did he make his next move, "with extraordinary ability," reports Boswell, but "by oratorical sallies" that lessened "the solemn effect."[17] Burke was vague because he was not ready to delineate the charges. He desired to establish the image of an earnest searcher for truth, to create an atmosphere of tension, and to tease uncommitted members into eager anticipation. For the benefit of members who had entered the Commons in 1784, he requested the reading of two of Dundas' resolutions of May 28, 1782, which had censured Hastings and demanded his recall. Then he narrated, briefly for him, the history of Hastings' governor-generalship and the efforts of the select and secret committees to penetrate into it. Finally he revealed his plan of procedure. By a process of elimination he concluded that an impeachment, in Blackstone's words "the most

13 As does Rose, *Pitt and National Revival*, 228.

14 Wraxall, *Memoirs*, IV, 257-58, for the quotation.

15 Br. Mus., Add. MSS 29,219, fol. 2, Jan. 24, 1786, "Chronology."

16 *Parl. Hist.*, XXV, 1009-11. See also *Daily Universal Register*, Jan. 19, 1786, for Macartney.

17 Pottle, ed., *Private Papers*, XVI, 160, Feb. 17, 1786. Burke's speech lasted three hours. *Daily Advertiser*, Feb. 20, 1786. The debate, continued on Feb. 20, is in *Parl. Hist.*, XXV, 1060-95.

solemn grand inquest of the kingdom," best fitted the dignity of the House and the importance of the Hastings affair.[18]

Burke altered the usual procedure in impeachments. Instead of moving first for an impeachment and then for a committee to frame the charges, he called for papers dated after 1781. The information presented to the House would shape the charges and only then would he ask for an impeachment. Pitt objected mildly to "fishing for evidence" and hinted that Burke was afraid his information would not support charges. This was not quite fair. Hastings' tenure had lasted for two years after the select committee completed its work, and the committee could not have known of events in India during the six months preceding its termination. Aware of the analogy between an impeachment and grand jury proceedings, Burke and Fox stressed the differences, in an effort to emphasize their desires for fair play. A grand jury hears evidence ex parte.[19] Under the procedure suggested by Burke, Hastings and his friends would offer defense in the House before it decided to impeach. This, said Fox, was a "deviation . . . in favour of the supposed delinquent, who thus enjoyed a chance of acquittal" by the House of Commons.

This point has not been sufficiently stressed. It is well known that the House of Lords in 1795 acquitted Hastings, and because of this Burke has been censured for bringing charges in the first place. It should be remembered that before the Lords received the charges, the Commons had to pass them. It did so only after exhaustive deliberations on the evidence presented to it. It is one thing for a grand jury or the House to decide that the evidence before it is sufficient to justify a trial, and quite another for a trial jury or the House of Lords to decide whether the evidence warrants a conviction.[20] In persuading the Commons to vote the impeachment, Burke won the greatest parliamentary

18 As commoners could not be impeached for capital crimes, the sentence in Hastings' case could not be death. *Daily Universal Register,* Feb. 20, 1786. But Burke was not seeking that. The *Register* reminded readers that a pardon could not bar an impeachment.

19 As explained by the Speaker on April 23, 1786. *Morning Chronicle,* April 24, 1786.

20 One who did distinguish between the preliminaries in the Commons and the trial before the Lords was A. Mervyn Davies, *Strange Destiny* (New York, 1935), 373-74.

victory of his career. Its magnitude is not diminished by the eventual decision of the Lords.

The debate of February 17 and 20, 1786, promised that the task of persuading the Commons would be formidable. The strength of the East Indian interests, the appeal of Hastings' argument of reason of state, the Commons' understandable distaste for dragging further through the morass of Indian affairs, and the inertia of members (notably Dundas) who were willing to let well enough alone with Hastings back in England were barriers that seemed very high.[21] When Burke and Fox reminded him of his antagonism toward Hastings in 1782, Dundas said that he had sought nothing more than Hastings' recall. Pitt, who upheld Dundas on this point, professed an open mind. Hastings' "innocence or guilt must be proved by incontestable evidence," he said. If Burke could "bring fully home" the charges he was going to make, then Pitt "would wish to bring down upon him [Hastings] the most exemplary punishment."[22]

Pitt's demand for evidence, unlike Scott's demand for charges, had to be taken seriously. Burke believed that he could meet the challenge and was heartened by Pitt's statement that he was entitled to all the relevant material he desired in order "to elucidate the subject." Without a division, the House agreed to Burke's motion for certain Indian correspondence. But he sometimes met rebuffs. On March 3, by a vote of 87-44, the House denied his motion for papers on the Maratha treaty when Pitt and Dundas pleaded the necessity for safeguarding state secrets.[23] Pitt opposed discreetly, but Dundas exposed himself to Burke's scorn by preferring to let Hastings alone rather than "hazard the welfare of the country." Three days later Burke's next request for papers met the same fate for the same reason.[24]

These refusals neither disconcerted Burke nor made him displeased with his progress during February and March, 1786. As he told Sir Gilbert Elliot, the administration, for its own reputation, could not hold back everything. Burke had obtained most

21 Dundas' self-defense is supported by Furber, *Dundas*, 37-41.
22 Pitt's impartiality is affirmed by C. C. Davies, *English Historical Review*, LXX, 609-15.
23 *Daily Universal Register*, March 4, 1786; *Parl. Hist.*, XXV, 1183-97.
24 *Parl. Hist.*, XXV, 1197-1202.

of the papers he asked for, and was in a position to go on "power-fully."[25] But he still felt himself in some "peril." Would he be able to persuade enough members that Hastings had committed crimes rather than political errors?[26]

Hastings' friends hoped to protect him by forcing Burke into precipitate action. Scott, in the Commons, urged decision as an act of mercy to Hastings.[27] The Speaker exonerated Burke from blame for delays; in fact, the company was producing papers as rapidly as possible. He ruled superfluous Scott's motion urging the directors to speedier responses. Meanwhile, Hastings was cultivating support, for example by entertaining influential persons. On the night of February 22 at his house in St. James's Place, he gave a supper and a ball for some of the nobility.[28]

At this time Macartney's refusal of the governor-generalship created the problem of finding a suitable appointment. Cornwallis finally accepted the offer, conditional upon amendments of the India Act that would strengthen the governor general's authority. The opposition fought the amending act. In the committee stage, Burke delivered against it one of his "most animated and eloquent" speeches.[29] To empower the governor general to overrule his council was a libel on the British constitution because it was an admission that only a tyranny could produce good government. Burke also objected to the provision for trying Indian delinquents as circumvention of the ancient right of jury trial.

Burke's opposition may have been partisan, but his emphasis upon constitutional liberties was consistent with his Indian policy. He opposed arbitrary government on principle; to legalize it for India was to repudiate the lessons of English history. There is no call for condemning Burke because later governors general used their great authority without abusing it. India was fortunate that Britain sent men of character to rule her. And some would argue that abuses of power did occur. Burke hated tyranny in any form. The people of India as much as the English people deserved

[25] Minto, *Elliot*, I, 102-103, Feb. 20, 1786.
[26] Br. Mus., Add. MSS 29,169, fols. 432-34, Jonathan Scott to George Nesbitt Thompson, Feb. 25, 1786.
[27] *Daily Advertiser*, Feb. 27, 1786.
[28] *Daily Universal Register*, Feb. 23, 1786.
[29] *Daily Universal Register*, March 23, 1786; *Parl. Hist.*, XXV, 1273-80.

security against arbitrary power. Burke knew that his arguments had little appeal. But they demonstrated that his attack upon Hastings as upon this amending act was directed against excessive concentration of power, which, if misused, meant abuse of the trust under which Britain held her imperial authority.

The pressure upon Burke to produce the charges finally became too great to resist. Though he was not ready, he brought in nine charges on April 4. Before the end of the month he produced twelve more, and on May 5 the twenty-second.[30] His apology for their length was a rebuke to the Commons. He had intended to be more precise, but the House had frustrated his desire to be deliberate.[31] He had to "take in and state every thing" for fear of omitting anything important. It was actually to Burke's interest to scatter his charges, arousing suspicions and making it easier for members to find justification for an impeachment.[32] The charges were compiled from a vast quantity of material at great expense of thought and labor. Though the work of a group, Burke gave them final form and presented them to the House. They are printed in his *Works*.[33]

Only Hastings' militant friends complained of their verbosity. When Fox explained that eventually specific charges could be presented to the Lords as articles of impeachment, most members were satisfied. Ominously for Hastings and interestingly to the uncommitted, Pitt thought the charges contained "great criminal matter and such as it was highly incumbent upon the House to investigate."[34] Burke's "mildness and simplicity" baffled and disarmed men who usually opposed him. The *Daily Universal Register* found him philosophical, patient, and reasonable, instead of characteristically "warm, unguarded, and irritable."[35] Then, there was something impressive in the circumstances. It took courage to assume the role of accuser against a powerful man; even success in his venture would not bring rewards to Burke. If there was resentment and prejudice behind his conduct, there

30 *Commons Journals*, XLI, 483-536, 568-95, 612-23, 627-29, 648-55, for the charges. *Daily Advertiser*, May 10, 1786.
31 *Parl. Hist.*, XXV, 1395, April 26, 1786.
32 Davies, *Strange Destiny*, 375-76.
33 VIII, 307-486, IX, 3-325.
34 *Parl. Hist.*, XXV, 1395-96, April 26, 1786.
35 April 12, 1786.

was also principle and belief in "moral standard."[36] Burke was not inspired solely by "malevolence," as nearly everyone believes Francis was.[37] If caricaturists and pamphleteers attacked Burke, other persons were impressed that one of the great men of European politics was closing his "long and splendid career with a great public prosecution" that would wash the stains from the British character.[38]

Burke and Francis enjoyed the respectful attention they were receiving. As Francis said, "Two months ago, no Man living would have believed it possible it could ever get so far."[39] The labor had been exhausting; he and Burke had been slaves to their work. And the end was remote. He and Burke, "two Individuals, against the whole Kingdom & against every Power & Influence in it" would persevere. "The Event is in the Hand of God." But they were confident, for "It is His own Cause."

The charges covered the whole ground and, for understanding, required a knowledge of Indian affairs possessed by few members of parliament. Those that eventually became articles of impeachment will be examined later. Here it need only be said that they and the others referred to the Rohilla war, events in Benares and Oude, relations with Indian princes other than the ones involved in those affairs, the Maratha wars, and various aspects of the administration of Bengal in which financial improprieties were alleged.

On April 26 Scott offered a petition from Hastings praying for an opportunity to defend himself at the bar of the Commons. The Speaker set Hastings' appearance for May 1. In consequence Hastings produced a complaint that his defenders have echoed. "I had but 5 incomplete days to reply to a volume that could not be read in less than one."[40] In fact, he had been gathering materials for a defense for many years, even before there was any

[36] Wraxall, *Memoirs*, IV, 251, 301.

[37] This is the word used in Br. Mus., Add. MSS 29,225, fol. 139, and by many writers since.

[38] *Daily Universal Register*, April 10, 1786.

[39] Francis and Keary, eds., *Francis Letters*, II, 363, April 15, 1786. Francis said the same thing to John Bristow. MSS Eur., E. 19, pp. 68-69, April 15, 1786. He was thanking Bristow for sending some papers on Indian affairs.

[40] Br. Mus., Add. MSS 29,219, fol. 2, "Chronology." Keith Feiling, *Warren Hastings* (London, 1954), 339, says, "For five days he and his friends were hard driven, composing the defence."

prospect of an impeachment. He had composed his apology for the events in Benares in 1781 while still in that province. During his voyage from India he had spent much time in organizing materials that could quickly be adapted to any purpose. In 1786, by April 12, the House had received sixteen of the charges. Moreover, it was not Burke who set the day of May 1. He and Fox had desired to hear more witnesses before Hastings appeared. Other persons dissented. Jenkinson said that "then," meaning at once, was the fittest time to hear Hastings; Pitt accused Fox and Burke of trying "to prevent, if possible, Mr. Hastings from being heard at the bar *forthwith*"; and George Hardinge thought it imperative that Hastings be heard "as soon as he could be ready."[41] When the Speaker announced the date, Scott, without protest, said that Hastings would be ready.[42]

The shortness of time may have worked to Hastings' discomfort, but not in the way that his defenders have suggested. Hastings and his friends needed time, not to gather materials, but to give better form to the long, discursive, psychologically miscalculated document they produced.[43] Perhaps time was not a factor at all; Hastings and Scott were verbose persons. Beneath the superficial dignity of the defense was self-pity and the hurt tone that so often marked Hastings' complaints against persons he thought had frustrated him. As Francis remarked, Hastings was appealing beyond the House to public opinion.[44] As he and three readers who spelled him droned on, Hastings seemed unaware that he was losing his audience. He was not embarrassed when at 11 p.m. Pitt interrupted to propose continuation of the reading on the next day. When the reading ended, Burke exuded graciousness.[45] He urged every member to give to the defense his "grave and deliberate judgment." Hastings, oblivious to his failure, thought he had triumphed over his accusers. In a pathetic letter he revealed his capacity for self-delusion as well as his motives in

[41] *Parl. Hist.*, XXV, 1405-406, 1413, April 26, 1786. Italics mine.
[42] *Daily Advertiser*, April 28, 1786; Br. Mus., Add. MSS 29,219, fol. 2, April 26, 1786.
[43] The defense is in *Commons Journals*, XLI, 668-733. Because Burke added a charge on May 5, Hastings was permitted to reply to it on May 10. The statement is in *Parl. Hist.*, XXV, 1415.
[44] *Observations on the Defence made by Warren Hastings, Esq.* (London, 1787), 1.
[45] *Parl. Hist.*, XXV, 1416.

desiring to be heard.[46] Thinking that Burke was beginning to impress people, Hastings had directed Scott to ask for the hearing. All of his friends except Thurlow advised against an appearance before the House. But note, Hastings boasted, how much wiser he was than they. He was heard attentively! His defense "instantly turned all Minds to my own Way." He would hold the captured ground. His credit with the public was at its highest. He was beginning to anticipate an early termination of the business in the Commons; if it ever got to the Lords, Hastings expected to triumph over a man who had "thrown away ye Cloak of Shame" and would be "most foully discomfited."

Burke had better reason to be pleased over Hastings' performance. He and his friends had displayed themselves as magnanimous seekers of truth. Hastings had only delayed matters for two sittings. After the defense, no one suggested quashing the proceedings, as Hastings and his friends had hoped.[47] If he were indeed so sensitive a person, he would have felt the irony of the situation when, as soon as he had finished reading and the House ordered the printing of the document, it permitted Burke to call the first witness on the charge relating to the Rohilla war.

This charge described various actions that Burke hoped to prove were high crimes and misdemeanors. Having violated the company injunction in 1773 by entering with the nawab of Oude into a verbal agreement directed against the Rohilla people, Hastings provided company troops, which the nawab used in 1774 to defeat the Rohillas and then, it was alleged, to treat them cruelly. Hastings, the charge asserted, made no effort to restrain the nawab from devastating the country. Thereafter, Hastings attempted to conceal these transactions from the company. When they learned of them, the directors condemned Hastings. During the month of May, 1786, the prosecution elucidated this charge with documents and witnesses. By June 1 Burke was ready to move that it contained grounds for accusing Hastings of high crimes and misdemeanors.[48]

46 Br. Mus., Add. MSS 29,170, fols. 60-63, Hastings to George Nesbitt Thompson, May 20, 1786.

47 *Annual Register*, XXVIII, 133-34.

48 *Daily Advertiser*, May 5, 16, 20, 1786; Burke MSS, Sheff., Burke to Sir William Bolts, May 5, 1786, Philip Crespigny to Burke, May 18, 1786; *Parl. Hist.*, XXVI, 37.

In leading on this charge, Burke assumed a role congenial to his talents. Hastings' alleged ruthless conduct and the awful events of the Rohilla war inspired Burke to pathos and fine sentiments about justice and humanity.[49] He opened soberly, as the gravity of the occasion demanded. He was acting deliberately after studying Indian affairs intensively for five years and after considering carefully every step he had taken since 1781. He admitted anger but not passion—a "uniform, steady, public anger" justified by concern for "national" and "imperial" interest. It was an anger inspired by a sense of trust for the well-being of the people of a great empire, an anger that drove the imperial statesman to make justice prevail over power and to establish "a set of maxims and principles to be the rule and guide of future governors of India."

It was an important debate that Burke opened on June 1. It continued until 3 a.m. on June 2, was resumed that evening, and lasted all night. The vote on the charge took place at 7:30 in the morning of June 3. Many members spoke. North told of his reactions to news of the war when he had been head of the government; Fox made a long and able speech. But during the debate it became clear that policy, not justice, was the issue for Hastings' defenders. They asked members to choose between state necessity and justice. When they could not refute an accusation by facts, they answered by appealing to reason of state. In its tenth report, July 10, 1783, the select committee had anticipated such a defense when it observed "that if this principle was to be admitted, no power nor no subject in *India* could be secure from the violence and injustice of our Governors in India."[50] Now, in 1786, George Hardinge deplored a "tendency . . . to adopt those pernicious principles . . . that in the administration of public affairs, no sort of weight ought to be given to the calls of conscience or of honour, and that morality and good policy were totally incompatible with each other."[51]

The argument from necessity was effective. It countered the only part of the charge that was proven, Hastings' disobedience

---

[49] *Parl. Hist.*, XXVI, 37-42, for an abbreviated version of his speech.
[50] *H. of C. Comm. Reports*, VI, 502.
[51] *Parl. Hist.*, XXVI, 48-49.

of the letter of company orders. The atrocities, the "extermination" of the Rohillas, the devastations, and the extent of Hastings' responsibilities, were not proven then nor have they been since.[52] The charge was rejected, 119-67.

This defeat strengthened Burke's determination. Seeing no advantage in delay, and overcoming Fox's reluctance, he forced action on the Benares charge.[53] Four years before, the second report of the select committee had raised difficult questions about Hastings' treatment of the raja of Benares, Chait Singh. If since then men's memories had dimmed, Hastings' recent defense had brightened them. Judgment on this charge depended upon an understanding of the raja's position in Benares. By a treaty in 1775, the company became the recipient of the tribute that the raja owed as a zamindar. A later agreement between him and the Bengal Council used the word *zamindar* without defining it; Hastings desired but failed to obtain a stipulation to the effect that "no other Demand be made upon" Chait Singh than payment of his tribute.[54] Later it became convenient for Hastings to consider Chait Singh a ruler who, besides the tribute, was liable to additional demands by his sovereign in emergencies.[55] In 1778, in wartime, Hastings demanded money from the raja. Their agreement did not "preclude that Right, which every government inherently possesses, to compel all its Dependencies to contribute by extraordinary Supplies to the Relief of extraordinary Emergencies."[56]

The various parts of the Benares charge grew directly and indirectly from the uncertainty about the status of Chait Singh. "A false interpretation of the exact position of Raja Chait Singh" was the presupposition of those who thought the demand upon him was unwarranted.[57] There was room for doubt because the

---

[52] P. E. Roberts, *History of British India* (2d ed., Oxford, 1938), 174-78; Davies, *Hastings and Oudh*, 41-61; and the pioneer study, Sir John Strachey, *Hastings and the Rohilla War* (Oxford, 1892).

[53] MSS Eur., F. 6, p. 15, Burke to Francis, 1786, probably early June.

[54] *H. of C. Comm. Reports*, V, 456.

[55] Davies, *Hastings and Oudh*, 124-26. See also Davies, ed., "The Benares Diary of Warren Hastings," *Camden Miscellany*, XVIII (Camden Third Series, LXXIX, London, 1948), vii-viii.

[56] Quoted in *H. of C. Comm. Reports*, V, 466.

[57] Davies, *Hastings and Oudh*, 117-18.

final agreement (sunnud or *sanad*) of 1776 did not specifically cancel the raja's earlier exemption from extraordinary demands, and Hastings was aware of this. In his *Narrative* of the Benares insurrection he cited not the final draft but an earlier one, and thus "It looks very much as if Hastings deliberately suppressed the second *sanad* in this publication."[58]

In any case Hastings demanded money from Chait Singh in 1778 and in the following two years. In 1781, desperate for funds for the war and angered by the raja's procrastinations, Hastings went to Benares in order to make him pay for his "past delinquencies." The charge laid before the Commons described Hastings' intention "to execute the wicked and perfidious design by him before meditated and continued."[59] During this visit occurred the spectacular events that almost cost Hastings his life, resulted in the flight of Chait Singh from Benares, and produced the other grounds for accusing Hastings, in his "tyrannical arrogance," of acting "contrary to the fundamental principles of justice."[60] After telling a lurid story of Hastings' misdeeds, the charge asserted that he was "guilty of an high crime and misdemeanor in the destruction" of Benares.

Many members of the Commons must have been puzzled by the intricacies of this episode. If Hastings correctly described the position of Chait Singh, why did he, shortly before going to Benares, write to Scott about reducing the raja "to the condition of a zemindar"?[61] Pitt, seeing the issue, asked Hastings for a definition of the word.[62] In consequence, Pitt accepted the right to demand extraordinary pecuniary aid from a zamindar. In his response to Pitt, Hastings included some remarks about the nature of sovereignty. Knowing no superior, a sovereign power may act unjustly, but act he can, for the only check against him "is in his own Breast." This was Hastings' ultimate defense for all of his actions as governor general.

[58] Davies, *Hastings and Oudh*, 126, n. 2.

[59] Burke, *Works*, IX, 355.

[60] Burke, *Works*, IX, 357, 360.

[61] Gleig, *Hastings*, II, 383, April 28, 1781.

[62] Br. Mus., Add. MSS 29,202, fols. 32-37, is the rough copy of the paper Hastings prepared for Pitt, dated June 11 or 12, 1786. Hastings' Diary, Add. MSS 29,219, fol. 4, gives the date of composition as June 8, and adds that he also sent to Pitt a separate paper prepared by David Anderson.

Other controversies arose out of the inquiry into Hastings' visit to Benares. There was disagreement then that has never been resolved about the condition of Benares—whether it was in a state of rebellion, whether Hastings treated Chait Singh cruelly, and whether he decreed punishment out of proportion to his transgressions.[63] One of the most interesting sidelights, as mentioned earlier, was Hastings' *A Narrative of the Insurrection which happened in . . . Benares . . . with an Appendix of Authoritative Papers and Affadavits*.[64] Suspicions about Hastings' motives in writing the *Narrative* are heightened by his remarks about the affidavits. Impey, it seems, suggested them. It had not occurred to Hastings that verification beyond his own testimony would be necessary to quiet opinion in England. In his defense on May 1, 1786, Hastings described the affidavits as proofs for the satisfaction "of others." The prescience stimulated by an uneasy conscience and revealed in the *Narrative* existed for months before news from Benares reached England.

In the debate on the Benares charge, Pitt's speech was decisive. His judgment turned on an almost ludicrous point. He conceded Hastings' authority to demand aid from Chait Singh and to enforce its payment, but he believed that the fine levied upon him for noncompliance was "beyond all proportion exorbitant, unjust, and tyrannical," unguided "by any principle of reason and justice." Pitt supported the motion that in this charge there was "ground for impeaching" Hastings. A vote for the motion was not a commitment to a final vote for impeachment. That would not be called for until the remaining charges had been aired. If at the end an impeachment was voted, Pitt thought that the Benares charge should form one of the articles.[65] Pitt's biographer says flatly that passage of this motion "led to the impeach-

---

63 For conflicting views, see Davies, *Hastings and Oudh*, 123-68, Roberts, *J. of Indian History*, III, 91-134, esp. 93-111. Davies' summary judgment is that Hastings was justified in making demands upon Chait Singh, that he made mistakes of judgment, and that he cannot be "entirely" exonerated from blame. But none of these constituted high crimes. Roberts raises many questions about Hastings' conduct, says that "searching enquiry" was necessary, and appreciates that Hastings' accusers had adequate motivation for bringing charges, but he feels that in the end impeachment was not the proper action.

64 Printed by Order of the Governor General.

65 *Parl. Hist.*, XXVI, 111, June 13, 1786.

ment of Warren Hastings."[66] There has been much debate about Pitt's motives and judgment.[67] The latest opinion, ironically, affirms the king's, given immediately afterward. In a kind letter he said that he would have been disappointed had Pitt failed to vote his convictions.[68] In 1955, C. C. Davies wondered if the speculation about Pitt's motives had not missed the point. After studying the evidence, Pitt "honestly" voted that on this charge there was ground for impeachment.[69]

Burke felt intense relief. If the motion had failed, the proceedings probably would have stopped, though it is preposterous to think, with Hastings, that Burke would have received punishment for his "Baseness & Falsehoods."[70] His parliamentary career would have suffered, however, and he might have been derided into oblivion. The passage of the motion was a personal triumph, a vindication of years of effort, and perhaps Burke's greatest specific parliamentary victory.

On July 11, after five days of testimony on the charge relating to the begums of Oude, the House postponed further consideration until the next session. The vote on the Benares charge ensured continuance, whereas the disposal of only two out of twenty-two charges meant that the end would not come as quickly as members had hoped. Some of Hastings' friends were losing their earlier confidence, and other persons wondered whether Burke might have caught something in his wide net. Writing to Cornwallis late in the year, Dundas confessed respect for Burke's imposing mass of evidence, some of it damning, and surprise at the weakness of Hastings' defense.[71] Their success was a tonic to the Portland Whigs. On August 12, the Prince of Wales's birthday, seventy-four gentlemen who dined together drank toasts to Portland, Fox, and other "distinguished patrons of liberty."[72] Burke was not overconfident. The party had got off with their

66 Rose, *Pitt and National Revival*, 233.
67 Various theories are discussed in Weitzman, *Hastings and Francis*, 186-87.
68 P.R.O., Chatham Papers, 30/8, 103, the King to Pitt, June 14, 1786.
69 Davies, *English Historical Review*, LXX, 615.
70 Br. Mus., Add. MSS 29,170, fols. 131-33, Hastings to George Nesbitt Thompson, July 18, 1786.
71 Furber, *Dundas*, 41-42.
72 *Daily Universal Register*, Aug. 15, 1786.

reputations and had, to some extent, aroused the nation's conscience. But it had been difficult to keep up interest and attendance; Burke worried about the next session.[73] The *Daily Universal Register* thought about it too (October 9, 1786). Perhaps a sifting committee should go through the evidence, for the business was becoming so protracted that already it had "sickened the public ear." Although a statement such as this might have displeased Burke, he would have been delighted to know of Hastings' discontent. He complained of Burke's success in jumbling the charges so that a clear-cut decision could not be formed. How could "a Mob of giddy & uninformed Men" decide a matter so confused and so complex? Burke might gain a majority from among members who would find guilt in one or another accusation.[74] One person was intensely happy. Speaking of Hastings and Impey, Francis thought that whatever the outcome, "the charges will gibbet their characters to all eternity."[75]

Between parliamentary sessions Burke went to Ireland.[76] It was his first visit in twenty years, and it would be his last. It lasted only three weeks and was meant to be a "frolic." Richard, Jr., accompanied his father. They landed in Ireland on October 7, spent a few days in Dublin with such prominent persons as Charlemont, the Duke of Rutland, who was still lord lieutenant, and George Ponsonby, and then had a day at Ballitore. Though it was forty-five years since Burke had lived there as a schoolboy, some of the villagers he had known were still alive. He was especially delighted to reminisce with old William Gill, who had been a servant at Ballitore school during his schooldays. Burke did not attempt to see his sister in Galway. The trip had been planned as a short one. By November he was back in England pleased by his reception in Ireland and eager to talk about it.

---

[73] Burke MSS, Sheff., Burke to O'Beirne, Sept. 29, 1786.

[74] Br. Mus., Add. MSS 29,170, fols. 188-99, Hastings to David Anderson, Sept. 13, 1786.

[75] Francis and Keary, eds., *Francis Letters*, II, 368, Francis to George Shee, Dec. 4, 1786.

[76] H.M.C., *Dropmore Papers*, I, 270, Earl of Mornington to W. W. Grenville, Oct. 8, 1786; Burke MSS, Sheff., Lord Earlsfort to Burke, Jan. 17, 1787; Pottle, ed., *Private Papers*, XVII, 9, Nov. 16, 1786; H.M.C., *Rutland*, III, 360, Reynolds to Rutland, Dec. 2, 1786; Osborn Coll., Box 88, #43, Burke to Juliana French, Oct. 12, 1786.

He was also flattered by election to a unique honorary member-ship in the Royal Irish Academy.[77]

This trip reminds us that Burke's interests in Ireland were not only political but personal and historical as well.[78] As a writer of history who distinguished between it and antiquarianism, whose thought patterns were strongly historical, whose political ideas were reinforced by historical content, he had long desired that students of Irish history use reliable source materials. Scholarly study was necessary for all who desired to understand the problems of Ireland. The source materials, especially for the modern period, were available. When in 1769 Burke sent to Dr. Thomas Leland two volumes of Irish manuscripts from the collection of his friend Sir John Sebright, he initiated a series of events that culminated in the gift of Sir John's entire collection to Trinity College, where scholars might use it. Though Burke never claimed more than the original discovery of the manuscripts in Sir John's home, he was something more than—as he described his part—the sexton who rang the bell for the sermon.

The preacher, to continue Burke's figure, was Colonel Charles Vallancey. Besides his pivotal role in bringing Sebright's decision to fruition, Vallancey was engaged in historical and antiquarian studies in Ireland. Without overlooking the unsubstantial parts of Vallancey's labors, Dr. Walter Love's studies have challenged some of the derogatory judgments formerly passed upon him. By profession a military engineer, Vallancey was a self-taught, energetic, controversial champion of the "Oriental" system for explaining the origins and splendor of ancient Irish history. The other system, the "Scandian," held that Ireland remained barbaric until civilizing Northern influences penetrated the country.

Burke, who desired to avoid this controversy, nevertheless found himself involved. The year after his visit to Ireland, he received the Reverend Thomas Campbell at Gregories.[79] Mutual friend-

---

[77] Burke MSS, Sheff., Burke to [?], n. d. but early 1787; H.M.C., *Charlemont*, 194.

[78] Two indispensable accounts are by Walter D. Love, "Edmund Burke, Charles Vallancey, and the Sebright Manuscripts," *Hermathena*, no. XCV (1961), 21-35, and "Edmund Burke and an Irish Historiographical Controversy," *History and Theory*, II (1962), 180-98.

[79] John Nichols, *Illustrations of the Literary History of the Eighteenth Century* (London, 1848), VII, 773, Campbell to John Pinkerton, Feb. 6, 1788.

ships and a common interest in Irish history eased their acquaintance. Having been disappointed in Leland's *History,* published
in 1773, Burke encouraged Campbell to continue with his and
loaned him four volumes of manuscripts.[80] Upon returning to
Ireland, Campbell, disregarding Burke's advice against controversy with Vallancey, engaged in a newspaper dispute involving
the interpretation of a letter from Burke to Vallancey. In 1789
Campbell published his *Strictures on the Ecclesiastical and Literary History of Ireland,* a collection of controversial pieces. He
dedicated it to Burke, without permission, so far as known. In
the next year Vallancey published a volume that dragged Burke
again into the dispute.

Disgusted, Burke apparently severed relations with both men.
When in 1792 Richard, Jr., was in Ireland, Burke told him to get
from Campbell the four volumes of manuscripts loaned in 1787.[81]
"Let him not triffle with you. I have triffled in giving them to
him." The absence of these volumes from the sale catalog of
Burke's library suggests Richard's failure to perform his commission. Burke was impatient with the disputants, though he never
thought the subject of the dispute unworthy of attention. Anti-
quarians could be useful persons provided they based their judgments upon thorough research in the sources. Burke's views
about the study of Irish history illustrate his judgments about
history as a discipline. It was important because it was useful, the
degree of present utility being a measure of the values of historical study. Moreover, the historian was worthy of the name
only when he strove for accuracy and based his judgments upon
reliable sources.

As in Ireland during his visit, so in England when parliament
opened in January, 1787, Burke's reputation stood very high.
Sir Gilbert Elliot thought that he was enjoying the favor of
fortune.[82] "Called mad, and *worse,*" he had accomplished a
political miracle. By the force of "truth, and by his single vigour"
he had persuaded his party, the prime minister, and a majority

[80] Nichols, *Illustrations,* VII, 773, 801, Campbell to Pinkerton, Feb. 6, 1788,
Campbell to Richard Gough, Feb. 9, 1788.
[81] Burke MSS, Sheff., March 20, 1792.
[82] Minto, *Elliot,* I, 122, Elliot to Lady Elliot, Feb. 3, 1787.

of the Commons to support the Benares charge. At the moment that Elliot was writing his letter in the House, Burke, enjoying an ease he had not known before in the Commons, was "lolling on the Treasury Bench" chatting with ministers.

This pleasant description meant nothing about politics in general. The votes on the Hastings charges did not describe the relative strength of government and opposition or the views of independent members on other questions. The Portland Whigs were only about one-seventh of the House, having gained only five votes between sessions. They had little that was tangible to offer recruits. As the *Daily Universal Register* explained (January 6, 1787), with "volunteering" in politics a thing of the past, the party had no chance against "the Minister's Regulars," who were on full pay. The truth of this statement was demonstrated early in the session in the struggle over the commercial treaty with France.

In addition to its political implications, this struggle revealed basic conflicts over commercial and foreign policy in an age of changing ideas and changing conditions. Late in 1785, after months of uncertainty and pressure, William Eden, one of the organizers of the Coalition, deserted it.[83] Eden's self-interest coincided with his desire to use his talents for diplomacy, and he accepted an appointment to negotiate a commercial treaty with France. Aided by the advice of English manufacturers, whose good will Pitt was seeking after the rebuff on the Irish trade proposals, and by a French government eager to appear congenial while advancing its interests in the Netherlands, Eden concluded a treaty that on the whole was favorable to English commercial prospects.

It was debated in the House of Commons in February, 1787. As a purely commercial proposition it promised early economic advantages to England. The opposition had to focus upon the long-run diplomatic and political implications of the treaty. The debates aroused tempers. On February 5 Burke attacked Pitt for abusing Fox.[84] Inevitably, the subject of the Fox-North coalition was dragged in. If Pitt disliked coalitions, asked Burke,

83 Br. Mus., Add. MSS 34,419, fol. 459, the Duke of Marlborough to Eden, Jan. 12, 1785, fol. 124, Pitt to Eden, Oct. 16, 1785.
84 *Parl. Hist.*, XXVI, 358-59; *Daily Universal Register*, Feb. 6, 1787.

looking at Eden, what about Pitt's with the person who negotiated the treaty? Burke passed off the laughter of the backbenchers on the government side as a "species of insult" to which he was accustomed. Pitt retorted angrily. Unable to match Burke in "abuse and personality," he deplored the efforts of that "disappointed" man to reduce others to his level of wretchedness. The Speaker had to call Pitt to order.

The debate was not entirely a matter of personalities and irrelevancies, nor was the treaty altogether obscured by the "metaphors" of Burke, the wit of Sheridan, or Courtenay's humor.[85] Indeed, Burke spoke well, though the praise he received for efforts that were inferior to those of his days of "meridian splendor" revealed that he was pitied as a man whose reputation was evaporating and whose abilities seemed to be declining.[86] Burke concentrated upon the political dangers of the treaty. He thought that England risked much for the sake of a small and delusive commercial gain.[87] This was not an arrangement between two countinghouses but a treaty between nations who had friends, enemies, and interests in the world, the first to be cultivated, the second to be distrusted, and the third to be preserved. Burke feared the loss of Portugal's ancient friendship. He feared and suspected France. He doubted the prudence of seeking commercial gain that would strengthen the economy and the commercial competition of France. A true protectionist, Burke conceived of international commerce as a form of economic warfare. He was not impressed by the apparent advantages to English manufacturers. Naturally they would think of their immediate gain and ignore the larger issues of policy. England was about to join herself "with that power against which nature designed us as a balance" in the European arrangement. France was England's traditional and inevitable rival. Burke deplored the vogue, encouraged by this treaty, for idolizing France and things French.[88] French involvement in the disturbed politics of the Low Countries, of which Burke and his colleagues talked a great deal, proved that England must be wary of trusting the historic enemy who

---

[85] *Daily Universal Register,* Feb. 15, 1787.
[86] *Morning Chronicle,* Feb. 24, 1787.
[87] *Annual Register,* XXIX, 91-92; *Parl. Hist.,* XXVI, 358-59.
[88] *Daily Universal Register,* Feb. 23, 1787.

was preparing for war against her.[89] This was a political treaty, not a commercial treaty, and England must never sacrifice her national interest for the promise of temporary commercial gain.

The opposition failed to prevent the ratification of the treaty. Their gloomy prophecies appeared exaggerated in 1788 when, as a result of decisive intervention by Prussia and internal rearrangements in the Netherlands, the French advance was checked. England then strengthened her position by treaties with the United Provinces and Prussia. The debate on the French commercial treaty reveals two important things about Burke. First, he was hardly a disciple of Adam Smith on commercial policy. Secondly, his basic dislike for France antedated the French Revolution. He had always felt this dislike and frequently expressed it, and that is one reason why he was easily aroused when the Revolution came. If he feared monarchical France and considered her a steady enemy even in times of official peace, a revolutionary France was still more to be distrusted and dreaded.

Although if Burke was on the losing side in the debate over the French treaty, his strength relative to the impeachment of Warren Hastings remained undiminished. It was encouraging to receive expressions of good will, promises of support, and proofs of the interest that people in Europe as in Britain were taking in the Hastings affair.[90] It was also stimulating to see his friends, far from becoming weary, growing more enthusiastic for the attack. When Fox and Windham had visited Gregories during the preceding Christmas season, Burke had thought that they felt "about India nearly as I could wish, & as we do ourselves."[91] Elliot was ready to assume responsibility for a charge, and Sheridan, according to Portland, was warming to the subject of the begums of Oude. General Smith, who was assisting him, predicted that Sheridan would be magnificent.

One thing should have worried Burke more than it appeared to. There were already many indications that Hastings' defenders would rely upon the argument of state necessity, as Hastings himself had done for years. In that event an impeachment, let

89 *Morning Chronicle*, Feb. 22, 1787.

90 E. g., Burke MSS, Sheff., Lord Buchan to Burke, Dec. 25, 1786, Unknown to Burke, Jan. 12, 1787.

91 MSS Eur., F. 6, p. 16, Burke to Francis, Jan. 2, 1787.

alone an eventual conviction, would be difficult to obtain from politicians who customarily found the justification of a policy in its success, utility, advantage, or mere convenience. Specifically, Hastings had saved the British Empire in India, and of what effect was a lofty moral argument against that indisputable fact? An admiring editor of Hastings' papers repeated this argument many times:[92] Hastings in Benares "obeyed a political necessity, to which, circumstanced as he then was, it became his positive duty to render all other considerations subservient"; "He was bound to save the empire, let the effort cost what it might"; to save the Empire, he had to sacrifice "personal feelings, as well as the property, and in some instances the rights, of individuals." A contemporary writer devoted an entire pamphlet to this kind of reasoning.[93] Necessity and the preservation of society is a law of nature and the ultimate, overriding justification for the actions of statesmen. Major Scott approved Hastings' seizure of the treasures of the begums of Oude because "Without money the Empire in India must have been lost."[94] A governor general "cannot do in India as a minister does in Great Britain." "Our empire in India must be preserved by the exertions of the moment, proportioned to the danger of the moment." "I have ever understood that circumstances may arise, which would render it meritorious even to plunder a mosque, or a zenana." Pitt admitted the force but not the universal validity of the argument from necessity.[95] There were some crimes so great that necessity could not justify them, and then the problem was to decide between the degree of the necessity and the enormity of the crimes. George Dempster said that governors were sent to India "to act at discretion as the necessity of the case required; . . . and for what they did upon the principle of state necessity, they ought not to be held amenable"; Samuel Smith added that if a governor, in acting to preserve the state, committed "some errors," he ought not to be chastised if he succeeded in saving the state.[96] Lord

---

92 Gleig, *Hastings*, II, 432, 433, 434.
93 *An Appeal to the People of England and Scotland in behalf of Warren Hastings* (London, 1787).
94 *Parl. Hist.*, XXVI, 316-30.
95 *Parl. Hist.*, XXVI, 333, 1135-36, 1140.
96 *Parl. Hist.*, XXVI, 339, 341.

Hood enlarged the argument by asserting that a public man must do things for which a private man might be condemned.

Burke despaired to see morality discarded. It was deplorable to hear men assert that standards differed in England and in India and between a man in public life and one in private life. Burke had a right to wonder what the effects of unabashed pragmatism would be upon English public life. Neither Pitt nor Hastings desired to go as far as Hastings' defenders in employing the argument from state necessity. Pitt did not intend to judge Hastings' guilt or innocence by this doctrine, though he would take it into account for the purpose of deciding upon Hastings' punishment should he be found guilty.[97] Hastings, who had used this defense when in India and still admitted its validity, did not desire that his services to England should be used in 1787 as a setoff in defense against Burke's charges.[98] Burke thought it his duty to expose the nature of British administration in India in the hope that men might learn to act under the compulsion of morality as well as positive law.

The long fourth charge (the third to be presented to the House) laid upon Hastings the responsibility for the events that made up the tangled and controversial story of the begums of Oude. They were the mother and the grandmother of the nawab of Oude, from whose father they had inherited lands and treasure. Because Hastings had failed to extract money from Chait Singh, because the nawab had been unable to pay the huge arrears of his subsidy to the company, and because the begums had "openly espoused the cause of Chait Singh," Hastings in September, 1781, agreed to a treaty with the nawab.[99] It embodied a proposal inspired by Nathaniel Middleton, the British resident, to resume the begums' lands and confiscate their treasures. Later it became necessary for Middleton and Hastings to goad the nawab into carrying out the arrangement. By February, 1782, the seizures had been made, and two eunuchs, the begums' ministers, were imprisoned for their refractoriness in meeting the nawabs' demands. They stayed in prison throughout the year. These events

[97] *Parl. Hist.*, XXVI, 699-700.

[98] According to Pitt, *Parl. Hist.*, XXVI, 699-700; Br. Mus., Add. MSS 29,202, fol. 32.

[99] The quotation is from Davies, *Hastings and Oudh*, 138.

occurred against a background of legal and political controversy
—whether it was wise for the company in 1775 to guarantee the
begums' lands and treasure, whether under Moslem law the
begums had any right to them in the first place, and whether,
indeed, Hastings was correct in asserting that the begums' alleged
assistance to Chait Singh in 1781 dissolved the company guarantee
and justified the seizure of their properties. On the first point,
it was the council majority, led by Francis over Hastings' protests,
that had given the guarantee. On the second point, it was true
that the begums had no legal right to inherit the property. As
to the treachery of the begums, there is disagreement. Even if
they had encouraged rebellion, the question of policy remains.
Hastings seems to have anticipated trouble about this. At Impey's
suggestion and with his aid, he gathered affidavits to prove the
begums' complicity. The leading modern authority believes that
the begums were involved in the rebellion.[100] But this conclusion
is based on sources more readily available to the modern scholar
than to contemporaries; Hastings founded his defense upon the
affidavits. They were hardly persuasive. Many of them were
virtually worthless as evidence, and they tend to create suspicions
of Hastings' veracity. They cause one to wonder whether Hastings
was busily gathering opinions that he might use should it become
expedient to charge the begums with rebellion. Hastings said
that he gathered the affidavits on Impey's suggestion because he
had not previously thought that verification of the begums'
complicity, beyond his own testimony, would be necessary to
quiet opinion in England.[101] In the autumn of 1781 Hastings
must have anticipated adverse opinion when the transactions became known in England.

Besides the controversial matter, there was material in the story
of the begums ideally suited for the purposes of Burke, Sheridan,
and their colleagues. It was easy to embroider the facts, to appeal
to emotion and humanitarian instincts in talking about the
hardships endured by the eunuchs and the humiliations imposed
upon the begums. These opportunities Sheridan exploited fully.
He opened the charge before the House of Commons on February

100 Davies, *Hastings and Oudh*, 172-73.
101 *Narrative*, 54.

7, 1787, with a five and one-half hour speech. He succeeded in influencing men's minds as well as their hearts. Sheridan's efforts frightened Hastings' friends. Though it was only midnight, they succeeded in winning an adjournment. Pitt approved, because he thought members ought to reflect upon Sheridan's persuasive speech before voting. When the pause ended, Pitt voted for the charge, deliberately and on the basis of evidence.[102] Whether other members were this judicious, 175 voted for the charge against only 68. To Hastings this was proof that the impeachment would go to the Lords.[103] Burke told the Commons that they had, in fact, made their decision for impeachment even before considering the remaining charges.[104] Pitt, however, reminded the House that it would have to vote separately whether to impeach.[105]

It was almost a foregone conclusion that they would. The *Daily Universal Register* (February 24, 1787) conceded the victory to Burke. "The match over *St. Stephen's course,* betwixt the two famous horses *Justice* and *Hastings,* is now decidedly in favour of the former; *crossing* and *jostling* was tried in vain by the jockey of the latter: but Burke, who is rider of the first horse, has clearly the *whip*-hand.— N.B. This match is not for the *King's* plate!" In retrospect, Hastings saw Pitt as the villain whose influence decided the question of an impeachment.[106] If this was true, there seemed little purpose in the "elegant entertainment" given by Hastings on March 6 at the Crown and Anchor, where among the company were members from both houses of parliament, or in the grand dinner and rout at his home on March 21.[107]

Hastings did not give to Pitt or Dundas the credit they deserved for judiciousness. Even Dundas, by this time, admitted that against his will he would have to support the impeachment. When he and Pitt studied the evidence "minutely," he told Archibald Campbell, they had to concur—"there is no help for it."[108] Dundas told Cornwallis the same thing, adding that neither he nor Pitt

---

[102] *Parl. Hist.,* XXVI, 307, 332.

[103] Br. Mus., Add. MSS 29,170, fols. 387-92, Hastings to John Shore, Feb. 19, 1787.

[104] *Parl. Hist.,* XXVI, 675-78.

[105] *Morning Chronicle,* Feb. 20, 1787.

[106] Br. Mus., Add. MSS 29,219, fol. 5, March 2, 1787; Add. MSS 29,170, fols. 405-406, Hastings to George Nesbitt Thompson, March 29, 1787.

[107] *Daily Universal Register,* March 8, 23, 1787.

[108] Quoted in Furber, *Dundas,* 42.

was happy over being forced to this conclusion by the evidence.[109] Acquiescence, however, did not commit him or Pitt to an active part. Burke complained because their lukewarmness would weaken the prosecution.[110]

The evidence of which Dundas spoke was not only that that was adduced to support the charges previously discussed but also that brought forward during March and early April. One by one the charges were debated. By varying but strong majorities the House decided that in his treatment of certain native princes, in his disposition of contracts, in his acceptance of presents, in his financial administration, and in his relations with the company directors, Hastings had furnished grounds for impeachment.

By the end of March Burke and Francis were preparing to ask for the general decision for impeachment. If that should pass, the articles would have to be framed and provisions for management of the proceedings agreed upon. Thus, on March 24, Francis pleaded with Sir Thomas Clavering in memory of his brother the general, to give his vote for the resolution of the committee of the whole house to the effect that the charges, listed one by one, contained grounds for impeachment.[111] "Forgive me if I speak passionately," said Francis, but every vote will count, even if Pitt and Dundas support the resolution.

Meanwhile, Burke gathered information from the company records, pressed the directors for correspondence that remained in private hands, and discussed frequently with Dundas the procedures to be followed in carrying the business eventually to the Lords. Fortunately, the chairman of the directors at this time was John Michie. In the old days he had supported Rockingham, and now he served well in laying Burke's requests before the Court of Directors and seeing that Hastings' friends, and Hastings himself, were notified to turn over to the court the company correspondence remaining in their possession.[112] Burke

109 Ross, *Cornwallis*, I, 281, March 21, 1787.

110 Furber, *Dundas*, 42, 43, 312, Dundas to Burke, March 26, 1787, Burke to Dundas, April 1, 1787.

111 MSS Eur., E. 19, pp. 72-73.

112 Burke MSS, Sheff., Burke to John Michie, March 14, 1787, Michie to Burke, March 16, 30, 1787, Thomas Morton to Burke, March 21, 31, 1787; Ind. Off. Library, Court Book 95A, pp. 1073, 1086, 1095, 1111, 1126-27, 1128-29.

tried to involve Dundas as much as he could.[113] This, a non-partisan, was a "National Cause," and in the "interest of justice" Burke hoped Dundas and Pitt would give their full support. Self-interest should move them to cooperate, for the life of the ministry was at stake. If Hastings escaped indictment, his interest would become so strong in England that no government would be able to withstand the efforts of that "corrupt combination" to seek revenge. Burke knew what he was doing when he mentioned the threat to the ministry. Dundas and Pitt were displeased by the earlier opposition of the Indian interest, and when that interest reacted unfavorably to the vote on the Benares charge, it "probably ruined whatever chance Hastings had of ministerial support."[114] This is not to accuse either minister of partisanship but merely to indicate that when the time came to decide on the impeachment itself, they would not go out of their ways to favor Hastings. Burke and Francis had exaggerated their difficulties. On April 3, without a division, the House found grounds for impeachment in nine of the twenty-two charges considered by the committee. Burke moved for the appointment of a secret committee to frame the articles of impeachment. Respecting the ministry's desire to remain aloof, he confined the nominations to his friends, including Fox, Sheridan, Francis, Windham, and Elliot. They were voted on separately and accepted, all but one. By a division, 96-44, Francis was rejected.

The drafting of articles of impeachment was a complicated task. Burke, as chairman, worked with the committee's lawyers, including his brother Richard, presided over meetings at which witnesses were examined, and spent long hours studying records at India House, where a room was prepared for the committee's use.[115] There was, moreover, still another charge to be debated, the fifteenth, relating to revenue administration in Bengal. Francis led in a complicated and technical debate. To Burke, Francis' performance was brilliant, and next morning before

113 *Corr.*, III, 48-49, March 25, 1787.
114 Philips, *East India Company*, 53.
115 Ind. Off. Library, Court Book 95A, pp. 1145-48, 1165-66, Court Book 96, pp. 12-13, 22-24, 31-36, 50, 53-54, 124-25, 148-49; MSS Eur., E. 47, p. 2; Clements Library, Melville Papers, Burke to Dundas, April 5, 1787; *The R. B. Adam Library*, I, 11, Burke to Dundas, April 7, 1787.

breakfast he wrote a note of congratulation to Mrs. Francis.[116] Not everyone was so highly impressed. Pitt saw no moral wrong in Hastings' revenue arrangements; the crime would consist, if it were proven, of Hastings' acceptance of presents. And this was what Francis was asserting. Much of his speech described "a scene of profligate, abandoned peculation, which perfectly accounts for every part of Mr. Hastings' conduct in this transaction."[117] Francis' judgments reflected fundamental disagreement with Hastings' revenue policy and the role of the zamindars in its administration.[118] Subsequent revenue administration in India showed that Hastings had not solved the problem, but also indicates that its relative newness when he encountered it in 1772, and its fearful complexities, would have made the first British efforts merely tentative. Pitt was correct in seeking criminal actions not in the policy itself but in the alleged peculative administration of it. Whether members of the House understood the problem clearly enough to make this distinction, they were sufficiently impressed by Francis' efforts to vote 71-55 that in this charge there was ground for impeaching Warren Hastings.

The closeness of the vote reflected the uncertainty of the House. If, as the *Daily Universal Register* (April 9) chided, Major Scott had been unable to prove that Hastings was "immaculate," the House was less certain than Burke that the revenue charge was one of the most obvious and atrocious examples of Hastings' criminality.[119] Perhaps another reason for the smallness of the vote and of the majority was the failure of ministers to take much interest in the charge. The concluding events of this stage of the proceedings came soon, because the House was growing impatient. Gilbert Elliot desired to introduce the case of Sir Elijah Impey. Burke told the House that he had advised Elliot against bringing it forward at this time. Pitt's concurrence and the

---

[116] *Corr.*, III, 56-58, April 20, 1787.

[117] *Parl. Hist.*, XXVI, 970.

[118] The best modern study, B. B. Misra, *The Central Administration of the East India Company, 1773-1834* (Manchester, 1959), in chaps. III and IV, where it discusses these matters, confines itself to the policy and efficiency of Hastings' revenue arrangements. See esp. pp. 181-84, for the basic differences between Francis and Hastings and a judgment upon Hastings' experiments, and pp. 171-82, for a discussion of the zamindars.

[119] *Corr.*, III, 54-55, Burke to Dundas, April 20, 1787.

obvious disfavor of the House persuaded Elliot to give up without a struggle.[120] Then Burke reported for the committee on articles of impeachment, and the seven articles he produced were ordered to be printed.[121]

The great decision, on the second reading of the articles, took place on May 9. It was the focus of the prosecution that had begun in 1781 and the consistent conclusion to the action the House had taken in May, 1782, when it passed Dundas' condemnatory resolutions against Hastings. The five intervening years merely linked these decisions of the House. Burke did not speak. Despite the general reputation he bore, recently noticed by the *Daily Universal Register* (April 9), for being unable to hold his tongue, he sometimes had moments of discretion, and this was one of them. His colleagues were equally tactful. They emulated Lord North's example of leaving the floor to their opponents and to the uncommitted. Hastings' supporters, Lord Hood, Wilkes, Alderman Townshend, and Nathaniel Smith, synthesized their previous scattered arguments in one more great plea for the doctrine of state necessity. Dundas tried to be lofty. He cited Blackstone in comparing the vote of impeachment by the Commons with an indictment by a grand jury. The Commons must be certain of the truth of their indictment and must not try to shift their responsibility onto the House of Lords. For himself, he was not fully persuaded that the two requisites of a crime were present in Hastings' actions, the overt act and the "vicious intention."

Pitt rebuked his colleague. Admitting a rough analogy between a grand jury and the Commons, he protested against pushing it as far as Dundas had. Otherwise, the House would limit itself too closely in considering the larger problem with which impeachments had to be concerned. He thought Dundas had undervalued the "consequence or magnitude" of the Hastings affair. He rejected arguments from state necessity and the attempts to balance Hastings' mistakes against the services he had rendered to England. The fatuousness of this kind of argument, said Pitt, almost excused the indiscretions and violent language of Burke

120 *Parl. Hist.,* XXVI, 1019, April 24, 1787.
121 *Parl. Hist.,* XXVI, 1031.

and the other prosecutors. Pitt "could not expect that gentlemen, when reciting what they thought actions of treachery, actions of violence and oppression, and demanding an investigation into those actions, should speak a language different from that which would naturally arise from the contemplation of such actions."[122]

As he had throughout, Pitt displayed understanding of the arguments and desires of both prosecution and defense, and an unusual ability to distinguish between relevance and irrelevance, hyperbole and sober statement. The only question before the Commons was whether to send the articles of impeachment to the Lords. There was no need for reviewing the evidence again. In it were justification for the impeachment and "very reasonable grounds" for thinking the Commons would make good the charges. Pitt concluded this persuasive speech with a judgment that must have given Burke immense satisfaction. "Upon the whole, the House could no otherwise consult their honour, the duty which they owed their country, and the ends of public justice, than by sending up the impeachment to the House of Lords."[123] This statement expressed Burke's objectives—not persecution for its own sake, not revenge in a spirit of vindictiveness against a man named Warren Hastings, but justice and honor, justice for the people of India, justice in the name of humanity, and honor for the reputation of England and the British Empire. The vote for the articles was 175-89.

On May 10, without a division, the House accepted Burke's motion "That the said W. Hastings, esq. be impeached of High Crimes and Misdemeanors." Frederick Montagu moved that "Mr. Burke do go to the Lords," and at their bar, in the name of the House of Commons and the Commons of Great Britain, impeach Warren Hastings, and inform the Lords that articles of impeachment would be presently exhibited. Heading a procession of the Commons, Burke marched to the Lords' chamber and "solemnly impeached" Warren Hastings. He then handed the accusation to the Lord Chancellor, who read it and laid it on the table amid silence. On May 11, adhering to forms, Burke reported to the House that he had obeyed its commands. On May 14, "Mr. Burke

122 *Parl. Hist.*, XXVI, 1138.
123 *Parl. Hist.*, XXVI, 1143.

carried the Articles of Impeachment up to the Lords."[124] On the same day, the Commons agreed to Burke's resolution that the sixteenth charge on misdemeanors in Oude contained matter for impeachment, and three days later Burke took the Lords another article of impeachment.[125] By May 28, Burke had presented twenty articles of impeachment to the Lords. A week earlier, despite protests, Burke's motion was adopted that the sergeant at arms take Hastings into custody. With great solemnity he was handed over to the custody of the Gentleman Usher of the Black Rod. The Lords admitted him to bail after some difficulty in deciding upon an amount of money proportionate to "the magnitude of the charges." Hastings was given permission to employ counsel and ordered to prepare his answers to the charges.

And so, on July 1, a month after the close of the session, Burke, at leisure momentarily at Gregories, wrote to Thomas Burgh.[126] He and his friends had successfully completed the first stage of a long journey. In deciding for the impeachment the House of Commons had vindicated him and his party. Although the election of 1784 discredited the coalition government, in Burke's view the House had repudiated that event. In consenting to prosecute the "delinquent" that it was elected to protect, it had adopted the views of Burke and the Coalition regarding India. Burke was even optimistic now. His case was strong, he believed, and only the bishops would be unreliable in judging according to the evidence. If the trial was a great public event in Westminster Hall, the Lords, including the bishops, would not dare to rebuke the Commons by acquitting Hastings.

124 *Parl. Hist.*, XXVI, 1150.
125 *Daily Advertiser,* May 19, 1787.
126 Copeland transcript from Osborn Coll.

CHAPTER X

The Impeachment of Hastings: The Lords

BURKE HAS BEEN much criticized for prosecuting Warren Hastings. The criticism has obscured his remarkable victory in persuading the House of Commons to undertake the impeachment. The Commons, of course, had proved nothing against Hastings. Their charges were allegations. It has been argued that the "anachronism" of an impeachment was not called for; an inquiry, and if the evidence warranted, an expression of "temperate disapproval" of Hastings' actions, and then an acknowledgment of his services, would have been the appropriate course.[1] But the crimes alleged against him, if proved, were too serious to be disposed of by a "temperate disapproval." An impeachment was not an "anachronism" to men of the eighteenth century. The debates in the spring of 1790, when parliament was trying to decide whether a dissolution terminated an impeachment, make this very clear. To avow disapproval and to reward Hastings with a high honor would be strangely inconsistent. Even Hastings' friends could not have been satisfied with such an action. The "disapproval" would remain on the records, and doubts would forever linger in men's minds. Having come so far by the end of the 1787 session, it was necessary to clear Hastings' name or to condemn him.

The magnitude of Burke's victory during the first six months of 1787 appears greater when considered against the state of politics at that time. If there was political bias in the attack upon

Hastings, it was not enough to explain the Commons' acceptance of the charges. The forces opposed to Pitt's government were a minority, doomed, as Burke had to admit, to remain in that position so long as Pitt possessed the royal confidence. No ministry could stand without the king's favor, and royal backing alone could attract the support of about one-third of the members of the Commons.[2] Even though the Commons had voted the impeachment, the opposition had no reason for thinking it had gained ground.[3] Besides the untrustworthy testimony of the newspapers on this point, there was the history of the session itself, which Lord Hawkesbury summed up for Cornwallis by saying that the opposition existed, but lacked the power to do any "mischief."[4]

But they could make a noise. On October 10, 1787, in memory of past glories, in hope of triumphs to come, and specifically to celebrate the anniversary of Fox's election for Westminster, they met at the Shakespeare Tavern to eat a buck donated by Earl Fitzwilliam. With Fox as toastmaster, they drank to the people of England, to freedom all over the world, to the friends of freedom in the House of Lords, in London, Middlesex, and Yorkshire as well as to those who had lost their seats in 1784, to the Duke of Portland and the Whig interest, to the House of Cavendish, to Aldermen Sawbridge and Newnham, to the Prince of Wales, and to Burke and Sheridan, laboring in the cause of justice and humanity.[5] Burke, back from a summer in Beaconsfield, gave a short talk, acknowledging the honor of being linked in this noble cause with Sheridan and the assembled company.

By this and other scraps it printed, the *Daily Universal Register* refuted its scornful statement made a month later that the Hastings business was no longer heard of or thought of unless it

1 P. E. Roberts, "The Impeachment of Warren Hastings," *Cambridge History of the British Empire* (Cambridge, 1959), IV, 309.

2 Pottle, ed., *Private Papers*, XVII, 95, April 14, 1788; Aspinall, ed., *English Hist. Doc.*, XI, 253. The document cited herein gives to the "Party of the Crown" 185 members who would support any minister "not peculiarly unpopular."

3 *Daily Universal Register*, May 30, 1787. After it became the *Times*, it continued to support Pitt. It supported the impeachment and it disliked Scott, but it was not militant toward Hastings.

4 Br. Mus., Add. MSS 38,310, fol. 1, July 23, 1787.

5 *Daily Universal Register*, Oct. 12, 13, 1787.

was at Gregories or at Crewe Hall, where Sheridan had passed the summer. In fact the accusers and the defense had spent a busy summer in preparation for the impeachment. Both parties had permission to study the records at India House and to make copies of needed papers.[6] With his counsel, Hastings worked at Drapers' Hall, preparing the voluminous reply to the charges, which he would deliver to the Lords on the second day of the session.[7] Burke, too, had worked hard. A fortnight before the opening of the session, Jane Burke thought he would be "tolerably" prepared.[8] Besides the presentation of his case, he had to arrange for the conduct of the trial.[9] He was anxious to conduct the trial in the glare of publicity. "Shut us up in a little chamber," he told Burgoyne, "and our cause is damned from the beginning." To Dundas, Burke was perfectly frank about this. Besides the practical convenience of Westminster Hall, which was much larger than the Lords' chamber, its spaciousness would enable the managers to make the impeachment as public and as solemn as possible. Not wishing to appear defeatist, Burke predicted to Dundas that publicity would guarantee victory, and then the "condemnation" of Hastings would clear the way for "some ostensible measure of Justice." His desires for Westminster Hall were gratified, but Dundas reiterated the ministry's intention to have no part in the management of the trial.[10]

The first days of the new session of parliament were filled with formalities in which men sought omens. The attendance was meager when the Lords heard Hastings' long reply to the Commons' charges. The *Daily Universal Register* thought that this looked bad for Hastings.[11] But when the Commons received a copy and Burke proposed a committee to prepare a replication, the House, over Burke's vigorous protests, refused to accept his nomination of Francis as a member. Burke complained to Dundas, trying once again to persuade ministers that if Hastings was

[6] Ind. Off. Library, Court Book 96, pp. 138, 571; 96A, pp. 655, 672.

[7] *Daily Universal Register*, Oct. 26, Nov. 9, 1787.

[8] Burke MSS, N.R.O., Aii264, Jane Burke to Richard, Sr., Nov. 19, 1787.

[9] *Bengal: Past and Present*, XXIX, 201-202, Burke to Dundas, Oct. 11, 1787; De Fonblanque, *Burgoyne*, 446-47, Nov. 7, 1787; Copeland transcript from National Library of Scotland, Burke to Dundas, Nov. 1, 1787.

[10] Burke MSS, N.R.O., Axiii, Burke to Richard, Sr., Nov. 21, 1787.

[11] Dec. 3, 1787.

acquitted, he would threaten the life of Pitt's government.[12] On December 11, on Burke's motion, the committee, having presented the replication, was transformed into the Committee of Managers. Again an effort to obtain Francis' appointment failed, by a vote of 122-62. As a consolation, on December 18 the committee wrote what amounted to a letter of unanimous confidence, informing Francis of their intention to continue to seek his assistance.[13]

As usual, Burke's lamentations over the exclusion of Francis were exaggerated. The sources do not reveal an untoward dependence upon Francis from this time forward, nor even as much consultation with him as Dundas suggested might be proper. In fact, Burke and the other managers were sufficiently masters of their material that they did not need Francis' help so vitally as in the beginning, when they were new to the Hastings business. The occasional letters between Burke and Francis during the impeachment were perhaps less numerous than might be expected because much of their consultation was personal. Some of the letters suggest that Burke was not writing to Francis in search of aid but simply because he found comfort in talking about the things he was doing.[14] The minutes of the Committee of Managers do not record Francis' presence at the twenty-six meetings that occurred between December 6, 1787, and the opening of the trial on February 13, 1788, or at the less frequent meetings that were held usually on trial days and occasionally in between.[15] Still, some allowance has to be made for tradition, and Francis' contacts with the managers were noticed by contemporaries. They could have multiplied the numbers of these meetings or exaggerated their importance as, undoubtedly, Simpkin the Second did when he wrote:

12 *Corr.*, III, 60-66, Dec. 7, 1787.

13 MSS Eur., F. 6. The committee, with Burke as chairman, consisted entirely of Burke's friends and partisans. Dundas had said this was perfectly proper. The members were Fox, Sheridan, Thomas Pelham, Windham, Sir Gilbert Elliot, Charles Grey, William Adam, John Anstruther, Michael Angelo Taylor, Lord James Maitland, Dudley Long, Burgoyne, George North, Andrew St. John, Col. Richard Fitzpatrick, Courtenay, James Erskine, and Welbore Ellis.

14 E. g., MSS Eur., F. 6, p. 19, Burke to Francis, Jan. 3, 1788.

15 Br. Mus., Add. MSS 24,260, 24,266 are MS volumes of the committee minutes. Beginning in 1789 the minutes merely record the meetings. Earlier they revealed the business that was transacted, including the reading of reports, interviews with witnesses, and discussions about materials to be requested from India House.

Then Francis comes sneaking, with grief in his heart,
At not being indulg'd with a MANAGER's *part*—
Tho' he now and then steals to the Managers' BOX,
To suggest a shrewd Question to BURKE and CHARLES FOX.[16]

The correspondence and the official records concerning the impeachment suggest that after December, 1787, Francis' role diminished, whereas Burke's leadership became more important. Indeed, Simpkin referred to him as "that powerful Chief." He presided over the meetings of the managers, grappled with the problems created by witnesses like Nathaniel Middleton, whose convenient lapses of memory were as irritating as the deficiencies of his records and as much an object of gossip, drew up the orders to the Court of Directors for records that the managers wished to consult, studied these records so thoroughly that some of them he virtually indexed, and finally, when the trial began, directed the strategy and tactics of what Simpkin called "that powerful Troop," the managers.[17] On both sides a sense of desperateness and urgency marked the final preparations. Hastings was meeting regularly his counsel, Edward Law, Thomas Plumer, and Robert Dallas, all of whom were destined for distinguished careers in the law. Major Scott indefatigably gathered materials that were needed to support the defense.[18] As the opening approached, Burke confessed to Sheridan that "I feel a little sickish. . . . I have read much—too much, perhaps—and, in truth, am but poorly prepared. Many things, too, have broken in upon me."[19] This was meaningless self-deprecation. As early as January 6, 1788, at Gregories, with the aid of the King brothers, he was working on his opening speech, which he intended would last for three or four sittings.[20] As usual when under strain Burke invoked the name of God, who would, he prayed, "send *us* a good deliverance."[21]

16 *Letters from Simpkin to his dear brother,* 2.
17 MSS Eur., F. 6, p. 19, Burke to Francis, Jan. 3, 1788; Ind. Off. Library, Court Book 96A, pp. 789, 816-17, 877-78, 883, 884, 912-14, 938-39, 977-78, 1069-70, 1230, 1239-40, containing requests for papers from the managers and signed by Burke; *Letters from Simpkin to his dear brother,* 1.
18 E. g., Br. Mus., Add. MSS 29,171, fol. 63, Law to Hastings, Dec. 20, 1787.
19 Moore, *Sheridan,* 312, n. d., but early 1788.
20 Burke MSS, Sheff., John and Walker King to Richard, Sr.
21 MSS Eur., F. 6, p. 19, Burke to Francis, Jan. 3, 1788.

Yet the prosecutors of Hastings found this the time to bring up the case of Sir Elijah Impey. There was more than coincidence between it and Hastings' trial. Sir Bland Burges called it an attempt to excite the public, inflame emotions, and confuse the issues.[22] When on April 24, 1787, Sir Gilbert Elliot so easily was dissuaded from bringing on the Impey affair, Burke acquiesced for a patently specious reason. If friends who could assist Elliot against Impey were then fully absorbed in the Hastings business, that situation certainly prevailed in December when they permitted Elliot to proceed.[23]

Burke and his friends miscalculated in thinking that the attack upon Impey would support the proceedings against Hastings. Elliot brought six charges against Impey. In three of them, Hastings was involved. Only one was thoroughly investigated. It involved the raja Nandakumar (or Nuncomar in Burke's usage), whom the Supreme Court of Bengal, with Impey as Chief Justice, had sentenced to death in 1775 for forgery. The execution removed the man who had accused Hastings of receiving a bribe and whom Hastings had accused of conspiring against him. On the surface it appeared that Impey had been Hastings' tool. Their subsequent intimacy strengthened such suspicions. If the charge against Impey stood up, Hastings would appear a conspirator in a miscarriage of justice.

Before the House of Commons on February 4 and 7, 1788, Impey presented a persuasive defense.[24] Then followed several sessions, including the interrogation of witnesses, in the committee of the whole house, and it was not until three months later, with the trial of Hastings already underway, that the House decided the question. Burke, though not the leader of the attack, took an active part, his long speech of May 27 being as much a diatribe against the East India Company for failing to prosecute Impey as it was an elucidation of the charges against him. After an all-night sitting, the House voted 73-55 against impeaching on

22 Br. Mus., Add. MSS, 29,171, fols. 80-88, Jan. 5, 1788.
23 Burke supplied materials to Elliot. Osborn Coll., Box 74, #23, Burke to Elliot, Dec., 1787.
24 *The Speech of Sir Elijah Impey, . . . at the Bar of the House of Commons* (London, 1788). Much of the defense was technical. It is easy to imagine members getting lost in detail while listening to Impey.

the charge involving Nandakumar. The other charges were never pursued.

To admit the attackers' ulterior motives is not to say that they had no other reasons for proceeding against Impey. Until recently it was thought that Sir James Stephen had exonerated Impey.[25] But two articles, one presenting new evidence concerning the political background in Calcutta and the other examining technical legal aspects of the matter, force a reconsideration of Stephen's judgments.[26] Although Miss Sutherland finds "no direct evidence" of Hastings' collusion with Impey, she thinks that political considerations in India in 1775 "played a big part in the decision to proceed forthwith" in a criminal accusation against Nandakumar. If Hastings was literally truthful when he denied interfering in the business, he nevertheless spoke "with an economy of truth," because he was involved in the political warfare in Bengal apart from which the case had no meaning. As for Impey's conduct of the trial, Derrett has some harsh things to say. To the extent that Impey erred on a legal point, there was a miscarriage of justice; Nandakumar was guilty of the charge, but not on the grounds Impey chose. His blithe disregard of doubts about the applicability of English law show him "insensitive to the requirements of strict justice." For these reasons, says Derrett, the attempt to impeach Impey makes "much more sense" than was formerly believed.

The attack upon Impey was not irrelevant. Burke always thought of the impeachment of Hastings as an effort to secure justice for the people of India. The same sentiment underlay the assault upon Impey, whatever else was involved. There is now reason for believing that justice may have been denied to Nandakumar, who was a victim of Bengal politics. Although Burke's correspondence does not reveal his reaction to the failure of the charge against Impey, he never disguised his feelings. During the Hastings trial he adverted to the case of Nandakumar and

[25] *The Story of Nuncomar and the Impeachment of Sir Elijah Impey* (London, 1885).

[26] Lucy S. Sutherland, "New Evidence on the Nandakuma Trial," *English Historical Review*, LXXII (1957), 438-65; J. Duncan M. Derrett, "Nandakumar's Forgery," *English Historical Review*, LXXV (1960), 223-38.

accused Hastings of murdering the raja, through Impey's agency. The violent reaction to this indiscretion in 1789 and the censure laid upon Burke by the House of Commons suggest that the failure of the impeachment against Impey was the first loss that Burke suffered in the campaign against Hastings.

If Burke intended to prepare men's minds for Hastings' trial by impeaching Impey, he desired to instill in them by the fittings of Westminster Hall the sense of dignity and awe appropriate to the grandeur of the proceedings. He should have been pleased by the arrangements. At one end of the Hall in front of the passageway to the House of Lords was the Lord Chancellor's box, where Thurlow sat under a rich canopy. On his right was the royal box, which the king never occupied. To the Chancellor's left was the princes' box. Before the Chancellor were the judges on woolsacks, in front of them the earls, and facing them the prisoner's box, where Hastings sat through the weary days and interminable speeches of a procedure that would last until 1795. On Hastings' right and left were the boxes of the managers, counsel for both sides, and functionaries. On the sides sat the other peers and the bishops. Surrounding the principals were the seats and the galleries for members of the House of Commons, peeresses, and on days of special interest the fashionable world of London. Since only 1,100 spectators could be accommodated in the public galleries, on gala days tickets of admission went at scalpers' prices. The sight must have been impressive, with the Hall draped in crimson cloth, the peers and judges in their robes, the managers in court dress, and the public garbed in the brilliant colors of eighteenth-century dress. To be mercenary about all of this, as some critics soon became, it cost £3,758 to prepare Westminster Hall for the trial.

The East India Company was represented in a utilitarian way by the cartloads of books and documents hauled from the City to be available when managers or counsel might call for them.

Empty, Westminster Hall fitted out for the trial was grim; on February 13, 1788, filled to capacity with the interested and the curious who were there to see and to be seen, the Hall presented a colorful, noisy spectacle. Among those who chatted while wait-

ing for the proceedings to begin were William Windham and
Fanny Burney.[27] They disagreed amiably about the trial. Windham thought Burke had won a great victory in pressing the charges
through the Commons against "every check and clog of power and
influence." Fanny, who admitted she knew nothing about India
and little of Hastings except that she had met him and liked him,
had firmly prejudged the event. She considered Burke a "cruel
prosecutor . . . of an injured and innocent man!" Windham
disliked Hastings. There was in him a streak of "ambiguity";
Burke thought so too and called this lack of candor by a Persian
word that suggested a penchant for intrigue and evasiveness.
Windham was impatient with Fanny's misplaced sympathy.

Three of the first lawyers of the time represented Hastings.
Two of them, Plumer and Dallas, were more than hired counsel.
As East India Company stockholders they had successfully defended Hastings in the Court of Proprietors in 1782.[28] Against
such legal talent the managers had to conduct their own case,
being limited to using their counsel only for advice.[29] The
advantage to Hastings of this technical rule was apparent throughout the trial, as Windham anticipated it would be. Windham
was dissatisfied with the formal proceedings during the first day.[30]
He thought that Lord Thurlow revealed partisanship for Hastings
in his opening address when he labeled as allegations what
Windham thought were facts. And why, asked Windham, should
Major Scott sit next to the Speaker in the Commons' galleries,—
that is, when he was not skipping about from one person to
another like a "grasshopper"?

The eager spectators were disappointed by the proceedings of
the first two days. After the thrill of the initial ceremony when
Thurlow addressed the prisoner and Hastings made his response,
the clerks spent the remainder of the afternoon and all of the
next reading the charges and the answers. Thus ended the first
of what would turn out to be 148 sittings, extended over seven
years.

[27] Barrett, ed., *Diary and Letters of Madame D'Arblay*, IV, 46-73.
[28] *Proceedings at the India House, relative to Warren Hastings, Esq.* (London,
1782), 59-76.
[29] *Times*, Jan. 25, 1788.
[30] Barrett, ed., *Diary and Letters of Madame D'Arblay*, IV, 56-60.

The trial the spectators had been waiting for began on February 15. The galleries had been filled for three hours when Burke opened for the prosecution. Speaking two to three hours on each of four days, he concluded his speech on February 19, setting the pattern for long-winded repetitive eloquence and offering the promise of a protracted trial.[31] Some of Fanny Burney's friends called the speech a "farce," "ranting," or "mere words." Boswell thought Burke had spoken astonishingly well; Hannah More thought him "abusive" and "vehement," reaching at times the "highest pitch of eloquence and passion."[32] As Burke thundered against vice that "withers" the understanding of the public man and "makes his mind paralytic," Hannah found herself looking at Fox and Sheridan. They seemed "quite free from any symptoms of palsy." Hastings made an abstract of Burke's speech. He recorded errors of fact and statements that he sarcastically said Burke knew to be false.[33] Everyone, said Mrs. Thrale, was talking about the speech.[34]

Burke attempted "to open a general view." Against the historical background, he accused Hastings of "crimes" of deliberation proceeding from "a heart dyed deep in blackness—a heart corrupted, vitiated and gangrened to the very core." The administration of such a man could only be "one whole system of oppression, of robbery of individuals, of destruction of the public, and of suppression of the whole system of English government." This trial would decide "whether millions of mankind shall be miserable or happy," governed unjustly or justly, and whether Britain would exercise wisely, before God, the trust her position imposed upon her. Not state necessity but morality and justice furnished the precepts by which men carried out their trust as governors. "The laws of morality are the same everywhere"; they are of the universal moral order established by God, with which, so far as human reason could enable men to do it, the social order must be brought into conformity. Deriving his

31 The speech is printed in *Works*, IX, 329-493, X, 3-145. Also Bond, ed., *Speeches*, I, 1-182.
32 Pottle, ed., *Private Papers*, XVII, 68, Feb. 18, 1788; Roberts, ed., *Memoirs of Hannah More*, I, 287.
33 Br. Mus., Add. MSS 29,219, fols. 33-44.
34 Balderston, ed., *Thraliana*, II, 709, Feb. 19, 1788.

inspiration not from motives of vengeance against a man whom he frankly admitted he detested, but from the teachings of the natural-law tradition, Burke impeached Hastings in the name of the British House of Commons and the people of Great Britain and of India, "in the name and by virtue of those eternal laws of justice which he has violated," and thus in the name of "human nature itself."

From this lofty position the managers were at once displaced. When Fox began by blithely explaining the managers' plan to dispose of the charges one by one, Hastings' counsel objected vehemently. They preferred that the prosecution complete its case before the defense began. The Lords adjourned to discuss the problem and take the advice of the judges. This was to become standard procedure as other disputes occurred. Thurlow and Loughborough took opposite sides, as they would throughout the trial. Thurlow won the first skirmish. The Lords voted 88-33 to follow the procedure desired by the defense, on the grounds that the charges overlapped and could not be separated clearly enough to permit a verdict on one before considering the next. By this decision, it became possible for each peer to consider the evidence as a whole before voting on any charge—to permit his judgment of the body of the evidence to affect his decision on a particular charge. The verdict of the Lords on this point was a victory for Hastings, possibly a decisive one, thought the *Times*.[35] It was also a reminder that the trial was a judicial proceeding, not a philosophical disputation.

The managers were humiliated and Fox was chastened, but on February 22, with the help of Charles Grey, he introduced the Benares charge eloquently and confidently.[36] The matter he adduced had been threshed out earlier by the select committee and during the debates in the Commons. What was new for Fox was his point of reference, explained in language that Burke had already used. "There are general laws of morality and justice, which pervade every constitution in the world, and which are impressed upon the mind of every individual man." The charges against Hastings were based upon facts, but the "reasonings on

---

[35] March 6, 1788.
[36] Bond, ed., *Speeches*, I, 183-306.

those facts" had to be informed by "the general principles of law that pervade the world." Some of the peers doubtless wondered whether they were schooled for such reasoning. The more discerning probably saw that Fox and Grey were talking not about "high crimes and misdemeanors" but about mistakes of policy and judgment. If Hastings' decisions had been inhumane, were they offenses for which a court could convict?

Following these speeches the managers presented evidence to support their accusations.[37] Then at the end of February, after the eleventh sitting, the Lords adjourned the trial until the judges returned from the assizes. On Lord Derby's plea, the date for resumption was fixed so that the trial would not have to compete with the Newmarket races.[38] Satirists made much of this opportunity. The pause gave time for other sarcasms. Lord Mornington complained to the Marquis of Buckingham that the trial had already cost £5,000; the managers' counsel, including Richard Burke, Sr., were costing the government ten guineas a day. And so, said Mornington, "Make your own calculations of the probable expense of this business, and of the patronage which it has placed in the immaculate hands of the great orator."[39]

On April 11, the day after the trial was resumed, the prosecution concluded its case on the Benares charge. John Anstruther's summation, though it repeated information already in the possession of the Lords, reads impressively.[40] Anstruther was a barrister; his trained mind was reflected in his handling of the evidence. He drew plausible deductions from it and, as was appropriate to a summing up, led his hearers to doubt the candor and suspect the motives of Hastings while he exposed contradictions in the evidence that came from Hastings' writings.

It was a mistake for Burke to follow Anstruther.[41] Though he spoke surprisingly briefly, he made himself ridiculous, furnishing a caricaturist with an idea when he deplored the "ridiculous"

37 The detailed proceedings are recorded in *Minutes of the Evidence Taken at the Trial of Warren Hastings Esquire* (London, 1788-1794). Also useful is *The History of the Trial of Warren Hastings . . .* (London, 1796).

38 Br. Mus., Add. MSS 29,219, fol. 9.

39 Buckingham, *Courts and Cabinets,* I, 357, March 4, 1788.

40 Bond, ed., *Speeches,* I, 307-61.

41 Bond, ed., *Speeches,* I, 362-67.

torment imposed upon Chait Singh's minister. The poor fellow was deprived of his hookah. This was as if a man were deprived of his snuff box, said Burke indignantly. People might ask whether this was a "high crime." With this ludicrous bit the prosecution ended its case on the first charge.

By this time the managers' strategy was clear. They were not only attempting to build up a factual case but were also trying to establish a basis of principle. Ever since 1787 Hastings' friends, when they could not deny the truth of an allegation, had tried to justify his misdeeds on grounds of reason of state, just as Hastings had done. The managers needed an argument that, unlike positive law or company instructions or the concept of moral relativity, would be impervious to the doctrine of state necessity. The speeches of Burke and Fox had already shown, and speeches yet to come from William Adam and other managers would also show, that the prosecution had decided to base its case ultimately upon the principle of natural law and natural justice. Its members' classical educations and, in certain instances, training in the Roman law, led them easily to this as the best argument against reason of state.

This clash of principle was in the minds of the managers who presented the second charge. The first two, William Adam and Thomas Pelham, on April 15 and 16, did an able job. Adam tried to impeach the validity of materials adduced in the House of Commons in defense of Hastings and then to establish the criminality of Hastings' actions.[42] He thought that Hastings "manufactured" his *Narrative* in anticipation of an investigation. He attacked the affidavits collected in Benares in 1781-1782. They were ex parte, based for the most part on hearsay. Finally, he appealed to justice. He denied Hastings' view of the geographical nature of morality, opposing to it "the immutable nature of right and wrong." Hastings, he charged, was guilty of "a deviation from that system of morals which must pervade the universe, which must embrace every creature, which, like the principle of gravitation, pervades the universe throughout," and makes right and wrong the same in India as in England. In this

42 Bond, ed., *Speeches*, I, 368-435.

A CONVENTION OF THE NOT-ABLES, *by Henry Kingsbury, April 28, 1787.* Storming the gates of the Treasury, from left to right, North, Burke, the Prince of Wales, William Adam, George Hanger, and Fox.

forceful speech, Adam placed upon Hastings the responsibility for the mistreatment of the begums, even though the acts were performed by his agents.

On the next day Pelham continued the attack. He also made Hastings responsible for the misdeeds committed in Oude. Skillfully he revealed inconsistencies and contradictions in Hastings' *Defence*. Then he excoriated the plea of state necessity. Under it any act of tyranny could be justified, Pelham asserted.

The examination of witnesses during the succeeding sessions was intended to illustrate Adams' and Pelham's assertions. Elijah Impey, who had been in Benares at the time of the rebellion, was the chief witness. His testimony was not nearly so persuasive as his appearance before the House of Commons in his own defense. It could hardly have helped Hastings' cause.[43] When asked whether Hastings had composed the *Narrative* in anticipation of an inquiry, he admitted lamely that although prosecution had not been expected, some kind of inquiry had been anticipated, because the events in Benares were so extraordinary. When asked the time at which he decided there would be an inquiry, he was not sure whether before or after he solicited the affidavits, but "certainly, something very near the time."

Q. What induced you to go to Lucknow upon this Business?

A. . . . I did it for the Purpose of authenticating to the English Nation the Facts in the Benares Narrative [of Hastings]. I thought . . . that Affidavits taken by me would have a greater Weight than Affidavits taken by any Common Person: I thought it my Duty, both to give all the Assistance I could to the Governor-General, . . . and . . . to authenticate to the English Nation what the Situation of those Affairs was.

Further questioning established the fact that Impey, as a judge, had no official duties in Oude. Asked whether these measures were in preparation for future proceedings, Impey contradicted himself:

A. It was to authenticate past Events, without any View of Justification: it had nothing in my Mind to do with future Measures.

43 *Minutes of Evidence*, II, 622-51, May 6, 1788.

The affidavits, Impey thought, better than a plain narrative, would establish Hastings' probity. The managers did not ask to whom the affidavits would be more convincing.

When the taking of testimony was concluded, Sheridan came forward to sum up the evidence on the second charge.[44] His speech on the begums of Oude, a four-day effort, was in substance the one he had given a year before in the House of Commons. It is customary to admit that it was a great dramatic effort, complete with the histrionics of his sinking, ill, into Burke's arms.[45] It rehearsed material covered more judiciously and reasoned more closely by Adam and Pelham, and it contained much exaggeration. Certainly it pleased spectators who had paid as much as fifty guineas to witness the show. It had some effective parts—for example, that which discredited Impey's testimony. The review of the history involved in the charge was reasonably sober; it was on the fourth day that Sheridan reached the emotional climax, the mistreatment of the begums and their eunuchs. Yet a connecting thread ran through the long speech. Sheridan never forgot his chief purpose, to define Hastings' responsibility for the events in Benares and Oude. He rejected the plea of state necessity; it was, in any case, a "skulking, quibbling, pilfering, prevaricating" kind of state necessity. On the whole an attempt to read the speech objectively today leaves one with the impression that it contained a good deal more substance and much less Gothic horror than is commonly thought. Possibly something is lost in the reading; hearers were strongly affected even when they were not favorably impressed. Women fainted as Sheridan described the events in Oude. But one must remember that in appropriate surroundings genteel women were supposed to faint. Without a blush the same delicate creatures enjoyed vulgar prints, raw gossip, and crude jokes.

Sheridan's performance left Captain Ralph Broome impressed only by its length and ludicrousness:

> Dear Brother, at last I've the pleasure to say,
> That the Orator clos'd his Oration this day.
> Tho EDMUND *his Chief,* who supposes the strength

---

44 Bond, ed., *Speeches,* I, 481-729.
45 Feiling, *Hastings,* 357.

And effect of a SPEECH correspond with its length,
In a whisper observ'd—"Now you find yourself stronger,
You might as well speak for a *week or two* longer."[46]

But Sheridan had finished, and the Lords adjourned the trial until the first Tuesday of the next session. Judging from the regularity of their sittings except during the assizes, the Lords had suffered from the delusion of an early ending. But by the end of the session they must have had second thoughts. In thirty-five sittings the managers had completed their presentation of only the first two charges; eighteen more remained before the defense would begin. If boredom was setting in among the public, disaffection was beginning to plague the managers. Burke persuaded them to be patient. They agreed, but in private remained discontented. Sheridan told the Duchess of Devonshire that he was tired and wished Hastings would run away, with Burke after him.[47] The managers had also to endure the jibes of the public prints. The *Times* offered in "Sporting Intelligence" an account of the run for the Oude Plate. Sheridan's "Pathetic" won over Burke's gray horse, "Weeper," Anstruther's filly, "Puzzle-cause," and Fox's aged horse, "Blow-bellows."[48]

By this time another kind of criticism had appeared.[49] As early as April 10 the Lords of the Treasury expressed concern over the mounting expenses of the trial. The Commons at least three times asked for an accounting. Burke was angry that people should haggle over a few thousand pounds when the national honor was involved. The Commons were not impressed; on May 20, by a vote of 60-17, they called for a statement more detailed than the generalized account Burke had previously rendered. On June 6 some members brought up the subject again. Burke talked of the dignity of the House; Fox called for the continued confidence of the Commons; Pitt and Dundas, somewhat archly, thought that the managers were entitled to the confidence of the House, and the matter was dropped for the time being.

Criticism was to be expected, and there was other work to do.

---

[46] *Letters from Simpkin to his dear brother*, 29.
[47] Walter Sichel, *Sheridan* (New York, 1909), II, 170.
[48] July 4, 1788.
[49] *Corr.*, III, 73-75, Burke to Speaker of the House of Commons, May 1, 1788: Br. Mus., Add. MSS 24,266, fols. 289-90, 291-98, 360-63; *Annual Register*, XXX, 169-72.

Burke spent the summer preparing for the resumption of the trial at the next session.[50] By mid-October Sir Gilbert Elliot was at Gregories, discussing with him the imminence of the session, set for November 20. But the king's illness and a great struggle over the Regency intervened. The trial had to be postponed until April, 1789. Hastings, in the meantime, was complaining of the delay and petitioning the Lords for a speedy resumption of the trial. His mounting expenses threatened financial ruin; for the first year of the trial he had incurred costs of nearly £ 30,000.[51] Burke was not impressed with these plaints, though he was as anxious as Hastings to get on with the proceedings. Delays wearied everyone. On April 11, 1789, William Scott, one of the managers' counsel, resigned because of the press of his financial affairs.[52] Other defections threatened. Burke's brave words on April 21, when at last he opened the charge on presents and bribery, were intended to allay the growing uneasiness about the duration of the trial. "How long is this business to continue? Our answer is, it is to continue till its ends are obtained."[53]

That this would be in the distant future was likely when Burke, after speaking for two days, announced that he was only half finished with the opening of the sixth charge. Simpkin probably expressed the prevailing mood:

> With this declaration their Lordships were struck,
> And thought themselves born to exceeding *hard luck.*
> That THEY should *be Peers* in such turbulent times,
> Of enormous *long speeches,* IMPEACHMENTS, and CRIMES.[54]

Burke's specific accusations were intended to create a presumption of guilt against Hastings in his administration of Bengal, and at the same time to destroy his character. The acts Burke detailed, such as the receipt of three and one-half lacs of rupees (about £ 35,000) from Munny Begum (the "prostitute" whom Hastings appointed as guardian over her stepson, the young nawab of Bengal) or the "bribe" of three lacs received from the

---

50 MSS Eur., F. 6, p. 22, Burke to Francis, Sept. 14, 1788.
51 Br. Mus., Add. MSS 29,224, fols. 94, 96.
52 Burke MSS, Sheff., Scott to Burke.
53 *Works,* X, 151.
54 *Letters from Simpkin to his dear brother,* 66.

Raja Nobkissen, were "vices, which gender and spawn in dirt and are nursed in dunghills, [and] come and pollute with their slime that throne which ought to be a seat of dignity and purity."[55] By participating in corruption and countenancing it in his agents, Hastings polluted the whole of the India service. Some of this corruption he attempted to "conceal," and some he tried to disguise with euphemisms. Part of the money received from Munny Begum was an allowance for "entertainment" when Hastings visited the court, and some of his plunder he said he accepted for the company's use. Burke rejected these rationalizations. Hastings had violated company orders. His devious conduct in these matters, his lack of candor with the directors, and his procrastination in carrying out directions from England were all presumptive of guilt.

This speech revealed a basic defect of the managers' presentation of their case. Presumptive and proved guilt were not the same. The actions Burke had described as presumptive guilt had yet to be proven as crimes. If the crimes must be vast in order to justify the impeachment, the task of proving the charges would be the more difficult. The depth of Burke's passion and the intensity of his efforts to impress the judges with the awfulness of Hastings' conduct betrayed him into hyperbole. By attempting too much, he placed the Lords on guard, and his indiscretions became exaggerations harmful to his cause.

Thus, on April 21, when describing the execution of Nandakumar, Burke not only brought in something that was not contained in the charge but did it in an offensive manner. Hastings, he said, "murdered this man by the hands of Sir Elijah Impey." This was an extreme statement. The House of Commons had already refused to impeach Impey. Now, Burke was repudiating that decision and inviting from Hastings the petition of protest that Major Scott presented to the Commons on April 27. The disorderly debate that followed occupied four sittings of the Commons and forced a postponement of the proceedings in Westminster Hall. Burke tried to bluff, by inviting the Commons to discharge him from his responsibility in the impeachment if they lacked confidence in him. The Commons refused to be led away

[55] Bond, ed., *Speeches*, II, 10.

from the issue. On May 4 they voted 135-66 that Burke ought not to have spoken the words about Hastings, in effect refusing to the managers a discretionary authority to introduce matter foreign to the impeachment charges.

At this point, supported by the Commons' censure of Burke, the defense inaugurated a policy of delay. Hastings' counsel repeatedly objected to the presentation of evidence by the managers on various technical grounds. The objections often referred to the managers' efforts to bring in evidence on matters not alleged in the charges. Burke and Fox advanced laymen's arguments. Their concern was with justice, and they were impatient of legalities. Thurlow offered some general explanations about the rules of evidence. The judges who sat in the Lords and controlled the decisions on these matters continued to think and decide as men trained in the law. Whether the managers liked it or not, the House of Lords in an impeachment would proceed according to the rules of evidence followed in the common-law courts. The managers, of course, were neither ignorant nor naïve. They were trying to create the impression of monstrous, presumptive guilt, and the more evidence they could slip into the record, whether relevant or not, the better for their case.

Throughout the remainder of the session the trial consisted of the presentation of evidence, documentary and oral, on the bribery charge. On July 8, 1789, a week before the fall of the Bastille in Paris, the Lords adjourned the trial until the next session. Fifty-four sittings had been held, the equivalent of three months if business had been done on every weekday.

During the summer and autumn of 1789 the news from France was so exciting and, to Burke, disturbing, and the gossip was so concerned with a forthcoming general election that men had little time to think about the impeachment of Warren Hastings. But occasionally they remembered it and commented about it, now with boredom and now with bitterness. Burke was frustrated. He accused the queen of protecting Hastings. He charged the lord chief justice, Baron Kenyon, with partiality because of his opinions on legal technicalities.[56] Burke's relations with Fox and Sheridan were becoming strained; it was embarrassingly

---

[56] H.M.C., *Charlemont*, 100-102, July 10, 1789.

difficult for him to persuade them to maintain their interest in the impeachment.[57] They were falling into the game played by Hastings' counsel and were permitting themselves to grow weary because of the delays in the trial. Burke wished that his friends could see how vital was success in the impeachment to their common character. Sometimes Burke feared the trial would evaporate in indecision. When in these moods he "totally" despaired, he wished there was some "honourable retreat" from the business.

The prosecutor, often portrayed as gloatingly vindictive, was in greater agony than Hastings, for whom pity is often expressed. While Burke was at Gregories preparing materials for the resumption of the trial, the defendant was enjoying London. He had moved from a furnished house in Wimpole Street to Park Lane and had decorated his new home "with all the magnificence of Eastern taste."[58] Such extravagance by a man who pleaded poverty outraged Burke as much as did Hastings' presence at social affairs.[59]

Adding to Burke's unhappiness was his knowledge of plans to end the impeachment prior to a judgment. Sir John Sinclair was thinking of a motion to that effect, but doubted whether he could win over the ministry, those *"hollow friends"* whose sincerity he did not trust.[60] Many of Hastings' friends felt animosity toward ministers who, they thought, were using the impeachment to serve political interests.[61] The administration intended to remain neutral concerning the conduct of the impeachment and its continuance, even though they felt that the managers had made mistakes and were proceeding too slowly.[62] Only upon specific points, like that concerning Nandakumar, would they take a position. Pitt was satisfied to let the impeachment continue because it kept occupied two forces opposed to his government, the Hastings interest and Burke's party.

During the session of 1790 the proceedings consumed thirteen

[57] MSS Eur., F. 6, pp. 24, 25, 26, Burke to Francis, Nov. 15, Dec. 11, 17, 1789.
[58] *Times,* Dec. 19, 1789.
[59] *Parl. Hist.,* XXVIII, 787, May 11, 1790.
[60] Br. Mus., Add. MSS 29,172, fols. 4-7, Sinclair to Hastings, Jan. 2, 1790.
[61] Br. Mus., Add. MSS 29,171, fols. 57-60, Col. Thomas Pearse to Hastings, Jan. 24, 1790.
[62] Burke MSS, Sheff., 9b, W. W. Grenville to Walker King, April 14, 1790.

more sittings, all confined to the charge relating to presents. Much time was again taken up by haggling over rules of evidence. On April 29 Burke complained for two hours of the hardships the Lords' rulings imposed upon the managers.[63] Finally, even he saw the need for compromise. On May 11 he presented two resolutions to the Commons. The second was a point of honor, declaring the intention of the House to complete the impeachment. The first authorized the managers, for the sake of practicality, "to insist only upon such and so many of the said charges as shall appear to them the most conducive to the obtaining speedy and effectual justice against the said Warren Hastings."[64] Pitt approved and so did the House, or a fraction of it, 48-31. In consequence, the trial of Warren Hastings was confined to the three charges upon which evidence had already been presented and to parts of three others relating to presents, bribery, and contracts. The managers never took up fourteen of the original twenty charges, and of the six they presented in whole or in part, four related to financial mismanagement or corruption.

Then the ingenious Major Scott popped up. He reminded members that the life of the present parliament would doubtless end with the session of 1790. He followed with a letter printed in Woodfall's *Diary* on May 20 in which he accused the managers of protracting the trial so that it could not be concluded before the dissolution. The House on May 28 reprimanded Scott for having libeled it. This reprimand did not chasten him any more than did the ridicule hurled at him during the summer. The *Times* made him responsible for Hastings' troubles; Scott's speeches and writings "operated as so many strong counts in the indictment against his employer"; the *Times* understood that at last Hastings had ordered his agent to remain silent.[65]

Scott had raised a question that was in many minds. Though it could not be discussed officially until the new parliament assembled, it was anticipated long before the session began. As early as August the *Times* was insisting that a dissolution did not terminate an impeachment.[66] Using language like Burke's, the

63 *Times*, April 30, 1790.
64 *Parl. Hist.*, XXVIII, 790.
65 Aug. 26, 28, 1790.
66 Aug. 24, 26, 1790.

Times found the honor of England, the interest of the Empire, and justice for the people of India involved in the continuance of the impeachment.

With this constitutional question as a talking point, and with the growing tension between Burke and some of the managers, notably Fox and Sheridan, over the French Revolution, persons who a year before had hoped to end the impeachment now had a pretext and reason for confidence. The *Times* reported rumors about their strategy but expressed confidence in Pitt's determination to defeat it.[67] Burke knew that the attempt would take the form of a legal argument. He was resolved to settle the question early in the new session. Pitt agreed to let the Commons decide it.[68] Burke, Fox, Pitt, and Dundas were on the same side and for the same reasons. If a dissolution could abate an impeachment, the privileges of the House were in jeopardy. Only the Commons could decide the nature and extent of their privileges. When the order of the day calling for a consideration of the state of the impeachment was read in the newly elected parliament on December 17, Burke moved a factual but pregnant resolution, that an impeachment "is now depending."[69] Burke had not been better in debate nor heard more enthusiastically for many years.

The approval of the motion did not settle the constitutional issue. On February 17, Burke, Fox, Pitt, and about one hundred members of the Commons appeared before the bar of the Lords with a request for a date for the resumption of the trial.[70] If the size and gravity of this delegation were supposed to persuade the Lords to renew the trial without examining the "great constitutional question," the mission failed of its purpose. Despite earlier rumors to the contrary, the Lords considered the problem for three months.[71] In a debate of May 16, Thurlow and Loughborough took their usual positions, for and against Hastings. The debate did not end until 3:30 a.m. on May 17, when the

[67] Nov. 18, 27, 1790.

[68] *Corr.*, III, 178-79, Burke to Francis, Dec. 4, 1791. The *Times* on Dec. 11 reported Burke's presence at No. 10, Downing Street, on the preceding day.

[69] *Parl. Hist.*, XXVIII, 1035. The subsequent three-day debate is on pages 1035-170.

[70] *History of the Trial of Hastings*, part IV, 41.

[71] On Jan. 29, 1791, the *Times* had been "credibly informed" that the Lords would not even discuss the subject.

Lords resolved to resume the impeachment on May 23. This was a rare defeat for Thurlow during the impeachment, but he was defending a weak position.

In the meantime other ways of halting the impeachment were being explored. Pitt had suggested a compromise. Having vindicated its privileges by deciding to continue the impeachment, the Commons could with honor consider separately the question of the duration of the trial. This was virtually an invitation to revive the efforts to end the impeachment. Hastings, of course, distrusted Pitt.[72] He disclaimed any intention of directing a campaign to terminate the trial. He preferred to force Pitt to expose himself for the "personal & inveterate Enemy" that he had always been and to deny him an opportunity to ruin Hastings "under the mask of Candour & even of kindness." The eminent lawyer George Hardinge argued learnedly against the continuation of the impeachment, in a pamphlet addressed to Burke.[73] Captain Ralph Broome joined in the attack upon the impeachment.[74] It would drag on for years, and even if it continued to the end, no benefit would come either "from Mr. Hastings' acquittal or condemnation."

To Burke the argument from expediency was irrelevant.[75] The object of the impeachment remained as valid as it had been in the beginning. Burke had labored eleven years on the business of India—it was "the greatest object for which I live"; and God willing, he would see it through to the end. Whatever the outcome, acquittal or conviction, "Mr. Hastings shall not escape judgment." Burke did not mean that the impeachment was a personal vendetta to be carried on to satisfy his pride; it was a crusade to be continued until its purpose, justice for the people of India, was obtained.

On this point, at least, Burke seemed to be victorious. The trial was resumed on May 23. A week later the managers con-

---

[72] Br. Mus., Add. MSS, 29,172, fols. 275-76, Hastings to Col. Norman Macleod, April 14, 1791.

[73] *A Series of Letters to the Right Honourable Edmund Burke* (3d ed., London, 1791).

[74] *An Elucidation of the Articles of Impeachment* . . . (London, 1790); *An Examination of the Expediency of Continuing the Present Impeachment* (London, 1791), 89-90.

[75] Burke MSS, Sheff., Burke to [?], undated, but *ca.* 1791.

cluded their case, with Sir James St. Clair Erskine summing up
the evidence on the fourth charge, and with Burke delivering a
"very short speech."

Hastings then tried another tack. He petitioned the Lords to
conclude the trial during the present session, pleading the hardship and expense which he had endured. Grenville opposed. It
was impossible to determine in advance how long the defense
would take, and he was not willing to deny the managers the
opportunity for rebuttal to which they were entitled. The Lords
agreed, and the trial continued. They had proved their determination to be fair to both sides, and they were now ready to give to
the defense the opportunity to prove the sincerity of their complaints about the length of the trial.

By their conduct, as soon became clear, the defense betrayed
themselves. They were just as verbose as the managers had been.
They quickly revealed the speciousness of Hastings' plea to the
Lords to end the trial during the session. And Hastings himself
had resorted to a gesture of magnanimity that he must have
known the Lords would not and could not accept.

Hastings began for the defense on June 2, 1791. The speech,
which he read, contained a variety of matter. After complaining
of the hardships and inconveniences he had suffered, he offered
to accept the Lords' "immediate judgment" without presenting
a defense. He would be confident of acquittal because the
prosecution had not supported their charges with evidence and
he knew that the Lords would not be influenced by the managers'
oratory. But then, instead of stopping to obtain the Lords'
answer to his plea, he began to defend himself. The prosperity
of India refuted the accusation that he had ruined the country;
the affidavits of Indians attesting to his character and their affection for him denied the assertion that he had oppressed the
people; financial data would refute accusations of mismanagement;
and, to sweep together the remainder, when his actions had been
culpable—for example, in disobeying orders of the Court of
Directors, or in the affairs of Benares and Oude—his vindication
would be found "by the necessity of the case, and by the event."
Every government in time of danger had to resort to extraordinary measures. "And of that necessity Government only could

judge." Hastings concluded with a bit of emotional pleading and a repetition of his offer to accept immediate judgment.

The Lords returned to their own chamber, where they decided upon their answer to Hastings. The trial would continue.

When it resumed on February 14, 1792, Hastings' counsel at last took charge. Plumer and Law consumed the eight sittings between that date and April 26 with speeches, mainly upon the Benares charge and the doctrine of state necessity. Not until the ninth sitting of the session, and the eighty-first of the trial, did the defense proceed to adduce evidence and examine witnesses. It is hardly accurate to say that the managers were the only loquacious participants in the trial.

Burke was as irritated now as formerly people had been with him.[76] Law and Plumer, he complained, were wasting more time than ever the managers had; clearly, they intended to drag on the proceedings until everyone was worn out. And that time seemed to be approaching rapidly. The sittings, though still long, were shorter than formerly, beginning about 2 p.m. instead of at noon, but continuing until 5:30 or 6 p.m. They were sparsely attended. As early as 1790, for example, only seven managers, thirty-one peers, and about a dozen of the Commons attended.[77] By 1792 only two or three or four managers and thirty or forty peers appeared regularly. On June 6, 1792, Burke was the only manager present at the time when the court was supposed to open.

In a long letter to Dundas on March 22, 1792, Burke reflected upon the impeachment.[78] He accused Hastings and Scott of trying to take over the management of the trial. First they imposed delays and then they complained of the cost to the public.[79] He protested Scott's insinuations about padding of the expenses and mismanagement of the trial. Hastings desired to prevent the trial from coming to judgment, and his tactics revealed "a policy of conscious guilt." Because Burke was isolated politically from former colleagues on account of the French Revolution, Hastings was hoping to separate him from the other managers by suggesting

[76] *Corr.*, III, 426, Burke to Richard, Jr., March, 1792.

[77] *Times*, Feb. 19, 1790.

[78] Burke MSS, Sheff.

[79] A statement submitted by the managers' solicitors on March 8, 1792, said that to that date the trial had cost the nation £36,960. *History of the Trial of Hastings*, part V, 15n.

that the impeachment was "the private business of one Mr. Burke." Hastings, said Burke, was "a mean and pernicious" man. His intrigues must be checked by a clear statement from the government that the impeachment was the business of the whole House of Commons and would be carried to judgment regardless of expense. It was perfectly true that Burke had a large stake in the outcome—"What but some irresistible sense of duty could induce me to continue so unthankful, unfruitful, & unpleasant an occupation" in which he had spent twelve years? But more important, the impeachment involved the public honor of England. If Dundas and Pitt did not think so, then "throw me off, & let me shift for myself."

Burke was indulging in self-pity, and he misread the conduct of Dundas and Pitt. They had done nothing to justify his suspicions that they were ready to give up the trial. They had always made clear their intention to avoid interference in the conduct of the trial, yet they had also opposed the efforts to end it. It had been in Burke's hands throughout, and there it would remain. Burke would have been resentful if they had tried to interfere with the management.

The trial droned on through the session of 1792 with Hastings and his counsel contradicting each other. While the members of the defense counsel were making long speeches, presenting documents, and examining witnesses, Hastings was preparing another petition to the king. On May 30 Sir John D'Oyly presented Hastings' prayer for the continuation of the present session until the trial ended.[80] But when the last sitting of the session terminated on June 12, the defense had only finished its evidence on the Benares charge.

The impeachment was only one cause of Burke's chronic state of mental depression. Everywhere he turned, he met disappointment. The affairs of Europe and of Ireland made him unhappy. His political isolation tormented him. His private concerns were in disorder. And now it appeared that the impeachment was not a purging influence upon East India administration. When in the autumn of 1792 Sir John Shore, a friend and former associate of Hastings, was appointed to succeed Cornwallis, Burke was enraged.

---

[80] Copy in Br. Mus., Add. MSS 29,223, fols. 27-33.

He protested vehemently and futilely to Dundas and Francis Baring, chairman of the Court of Directors.[81] To Lord Fitzwilliam, Burke confessed his despair.[82] Some of his former friends among the managers had deserted him; the ministry persecuted him; the trial of Hastings, which he had hoped would check "rapine & tyranny" in India, would not accomplish its purpose. This event "has about beaten me to the ground."

It was curious. Hastings was also feeling sorry for himself.[83] All the power and influence was on the side of the prosecution; Hastings had no friends in high places; the managers were dragging out the trial in order to prolong his agony. Supposing, he asked himself, that the accused had been a friend of Burke or Fox. What a furor they would have raised, "how would Heaven & earth have been invoked to pour down Vengeance on ye heads of his oppressors, clubs instituted to collect subscriptions to parly. petitions . . . [to] avert the impending ruin of the constitution!" Mrs. Hastings felt the same way. She once told Boswell that she had shot a tiger in India and would like to do the same to a tiger in England.[84]

Yet the end was approaching, and well it might, before all of the participants disappeared. Before the opening of the sittings in 1793, Lord Loughborough replaced Lord Thurlow as lord chancellor, and he would preside over the impeachment. Since 1788 there had been 121 changes in the peerage. At the opening, 186 peers had been present; on February 15, 1793, 26 peers formed the procession into Westminster Hall to resume the trial. But they were destined to achieve a sense of accomplishment. On May 28, 1793, the one hundred and seventeenth day of the trial and the twenty-second of the session, the defense closed its case, having in this session disposed of the charges on the begums of Oude and on bribery, corruption, and presents.

When the Lords appointed a day only a week distant for the managers to reply, they protested vigorously. The time was too short. Their protest touched off in the Commons a review of the

81 Burke MSS, Sheff., Burke to Dundas, Oct. 8, 1792; Burke MSS, N.R.O., Dundas to Burke, Oct. 19, 1792; Br. Mus., Add. MSS 29,172, fols. 458-60, Burke to Baring, Oct. 14, 1792, Baring to Burke, Oct. 17, 1792.
82 Burke MSS, Sheff., Oct. 5, 1792.
83 MS in Hastings' hand, Br. Mus., Add. MSS, 29,225, fol. 18.
84 Pottle, ed., *Private Papers*, XVIII, 269, March 22, 1794.

conduct of the trial. Burke, as usual, felt that the arbitrary order of the Lords offended the managers' and the Commons' dignity. But he revealed to Dundas a better reason.[85] Haste at this point would surely result in the acquittal of Hastings. Dundas agreed, blaming the Lords for the protraction of the trial. Each year since 1788 they had adjourned the trial in midsession during the assizes, as though they were incapable of proceeding without the judges. The Lords were beseeched from both sides, the Commons asking for delay and Hastings, in a new petition, for dispatch. Lord Grenville summed up the situation. Everybody was blaming everybody else for the long duration of the trial. Upon investigation, he was sure, it would be found that all concerned shared in the responsibility. Recalled to their senses and reminded by Grenville that having gone this far they must go on to the end, doing what was right and proper, the Lords agreed to resume the trial at the next session.

Although the proceedings in 1794 were to begin with the prosecution's reply, other interruptions occurred. The defense asked for the privilege of presenting Lord Cornwallis, just back from India, as a witness. The managers consented, asking in return for an examination of William Larkin, the accountant general, who was also fresh from India. Then, because of Cornwallis' "indisposition," the Lords twice postponed proceedings. Men must have wondered whether the end of the trial was as close as they had thought. Finally the trial resumed on February 25, though Cornwallis had not fully recovered. Hastings offered to waive his examination of the noble lord. The day was spent in quibblings between the managers and the defense counsel, as though both parties were as fresh as they had been in 1788, and the day closed with the Lords adjourning to consider a question of evidence. Two days later the Lords ruled against the managers on the admissibility of certain evidence, and Burke, as he had been doing from the beginning, lamented the failure of the Lords to explain the principle upon which they based their decision. Once again, as so often before, he was called to order for indiscretion. And then the defense objected to another attempt to offer certain evidence. When the Lords rose to retire on this

[85] *The R. B. Adam Library,* I, 19, Burke to Dundas, June 7, 1793.

question, Hastings begged their indulgence to hear another of his pleas for a speedy decision. Burke remarked that Hastings had said all of this five years earlier. On March 1, the managers lost another argument over the admissibility of evidence. On the same day, the Lords adjourned the trial for five weeks because they deemed it "absolutely impossible to go on without the judges," who had to proceed on circuit. Altogether this was an unpromising beginning for the session that men thought would see the end of the impeachment. It was almost comical, it was not quite ludicrous, it was all legally proper, and the Lords continued to show admirable patience.

By the time the judges returned, Cornwallis had recovered his health and was ready to appear. This event stimulated the largest attendance in years. The spectators may have been disappointed. There was little in Cornwallis' testimony to cause excitement or give comfort to either the defense or the prosecution. Both asked questions whose answers they anticipated, and each canceled out the impression created by the questions of the other side. Another witness than Cornwallis might have been handled more roughly; in the past Burke had reprimanded witnesses who responded as he did. Burke read aloud a passage from an official letter, only to be told by Cornwallis that "I cannot take upon me to recollect the words of a letter that I have written five years ago."[86]

All this time the Commons had been growing increasingly impatient. Confident that the fault was not the managers', Burke moved for an inspection of the Lords' journals. The long report on the causes of delays that was brought into the Commons on April 17, and discussed two weeks later, was largely Burke's.[87] The report, in effect a history of the trial, was a persuasive exoneration of the managers.[88] It upheld fairly Grenville's remark concerning the general responsibility for the delays. Inclusive of March 1, 1794, the proceedings had consumed 118 days. They had been spent as follows:

[86] *History of the Trial of Hastings*, part V, 95.

[87] Bond, *Speeches*, IV, xxxiv.

[88] It is printed in *History of the Trial of Hastings*, Supplement, i-xliv, and in *Works*, XI, 3-153.

Published 1788 by WM Holland No Oxford St   The POLITICAL-BANDITTI, assailing the SAVIOUR of INDIA.

THE POLITICAL BANDITTI ASSAILING THE SAVIOUR OF INDIA, by *James Gillray, May 11, 1788.* Burke, North, and Fox attacking Hastings.

3   reading articles of impeachment, defendant's answer, debate on
     rules of procedure
19   managers' speeches, opening and summing up
51   managers' evidence, documentary and oral
22   speeches of defense counsel, opening and summing up
23   defense evidence, documentary and oral
___
118

Certainly the defense had had its days in court. Between sittings
there had been long delays caused by reasons for which the
managers could not by any reckoning be held accountable. Then,
the material of the trial was so vast in bulk that much time was
necessary for its presentation. Finally, "and principally," the
defense had raised sixty-two objections. These had given rise to
numerous debates during the trial. On twelve occasions the
Lords had referred questions to the judges.

This explanation, requiring only two pages of the report,
would have answered the intentions of the House. But Burke
desired to express himself about something that had made him
unhappy throughout the trial. The report was a protest for the
record against the judges' domination. Basically, Burke objected
to the application of rules of evidence and procedures used in
the common-law courts. The judges, he said, should have been
treated only as technical assistants, whose advice the Lords were
free to reject. The trial was being conducted by the High Court
of Parliament acting as a court of first instance and bound only
by its own law and usages. Burke's argument was honestly
consistent with his lifetime solicitude for the dignity and freedom
of parliament and his contempt for the narrowing effects of
formal legal training and the technicalities of judicial administration. His preference for liberal rules of procedure was the natural
preference of a layman who quickly sees legal niceties contributing to "a failure of justice" but refuses to appreciate the
reasons that underlie the rules of evidence. Burke was also
correct in contending that the learned defense counsel had used
effectively for their purpose the rules of evidence under which
justice was administered in the ordinary courts and which were
followed during the impeachment.

While these events were taking place in the House of Commons, the trial was resumed in Westminster Hall. The end was in sight. On May 6 the managers announced that they had "totally closed their evidence." They still had to make some speeches. Charles Grey replied to the defense's evidence on the Benares charge in a two-day speech; Sheridan reviewed for the third time the case of the begums and, to the surprise of his listeners, did it in one afternoon; Fox answered the defense on the three charges relating to corruption; and Michael Angelo Taylor spoke on the fourth charge relating to contracts.

And last came Burke. Just as in 1788 he had opened the impeachment with a general speech, so now he closed it by speaking to all of the charges during nine sittings between May 28 and June 16.[89] Had it been their first time through the business, the Lords would have been interested; it was in fact their eighth time over the ground, and only about two dozen could bear to traverse it again. The literary and forensic quality of the speech could not compensate for the staleness of its contents.[90] The vulgarity of the epithets repelled the audience. "We never said [Hastings] was a tiger and a lion; no, we said he was a weasel and a rat."[91] For the last time Burke tried to destroy the argument based upon reason of state. Hastings might have performed great services but "Merit cannot extinguish crime."[92] The law of nature governed all men for eternity. Hastings should be judged according to the canons of that as well as of English law, for the object of the impeachment was more than the punishment of an individual. The object was the attainment of justice for the people of India and the preservation of the honor of England.

There is one thing, and one thing only, which defies all mutation,— that which existed before the world, and will survive the fabric of the world itself; I mean justice,—that justice which, emanating from the Divinity, has a place in the breast of every one of us, given

[89] *Works*, XI, 157-445, XII, 3-398. Also Bond, ed., *Speeches*, IV, 331-774.

[90] One listener thought parts of it dull, whereas other parts, especially the last one, were "beautifully composed and admirably delivered." Greig, ed., *The Farington Diary*, I, 54.

[91] *Works*, XI, 221.

[92] *Works*, XII, 368.

us for our guide with regard to ourselves and with regard to others, and which will stand, after this globe is burned to ashes, our advocate or our accuser before the great Judge, when He comes to call us for the tenor of a well-spent life.

Burke's last words to the Lords, and his admonition, were, "May you stand a sacred temple, for the perpetual residence of an inviolable justice!"

And so ended the one hundred and forty-eighth day of a trial whose beginning and ending took place in different worlds.[93]

It remained for the House of Commons to do one more thing. Decency and consistency demanded it. On June 20 Pitt moved the thanks of the House to the managers. He hoped for unanimity but did not expect it. He vigorously defended the managers against accusations of delaying the trial, repeating arguments Burke had furnished in his report. If one counted days and hours only, one would see that the trial had not been inordinately long, considering its importance, even though seven years had elapsed. Pitt's speech indicated his belief that Hastings deserved impeachment. After Dundas seconded the motion, a heated debate ensued. The opponents of the motion singled out Burke as the manager whose conduct they most intensely deprecated. As the debate narrowed upon him, Windham, Fox, Sheridan, and Francis, forgetting the French Revolution, rushed to his defense. After this sharp, personal clash ended with the defeat of the previous question, Pitt's motion carried 50-21.

Burke had sat quietly hearing himself abused and praised. Now he spoke. It was to be his last appearance in the House that he had entered twenty-nine years before. He expressed the managers' gratitude for the thanks of the House, the highest reward any man could receive. Burke's career was the proof of the sincerity of this moment. His brief defense of the conduct of the impeachment blurred the dignity he had shown throughout the evening. Nevertheless, so touching was the occasion, for it was no secret that Burke intended to retire from the House, that the *St. James's Chronicle* could remark on Burke's speaking "in his usual dignified and impressive manner."[94]

93 *St. James's Chronicle*, June 17-19, 1794.
94 June 19-21, 1794.

On the next day Burke applied for the Chiltern Hundreds. His parliamentary career had ended. It is necessary, in trying to form some judgment of Burke's motives in impeaching Hastings, to remember that he always considered the impeachment one of his greatest public services. Because of it he stayed on in the House of Commons for at least three years longer than he had wanted to.[95]

Lord Fitzwilliam, of course, knew of his intention, but Burke owed him official notification.[96] "My Engagement with the publick is fulfilled, & the House has declared itself satisfied with my Endeavours to do my Duty." Burke was leaving public life; he was too old to continue in a "Situation of struggle & contention"; he desired to depart before "the little powers of mind & body that I possess have quite forsaken me." Before he departed, he wished to thank Lord Fitzwilliam for enabling him to continue in the position where he could combat the two great evils of the times—"Indianism & Jacobinism."

It is difficult to believe that Burke impeached Hastings because of personal malevolence and for party reasons. Hastings, to him, represented evil; he had abused power; he had violated the laws of eternal justice. To bring him to account was a leading purpose of the last decade of Burke's public life.

The events in the House of Lords during the spring of 1795 constituted a separate episode, even though they were an integral part of the impeachment and were the concluding stage of it.[97] The process of arriving at and announcing the Lords' decision deserves more attention than historians have given it. The Lords, in systematic fashion, reviewed Hastings' career for the ninth time. No one can accuse them of making a hasty decision. They acted with dignity and propriety; they deliberated in good temper but with solemnity, as though always conscious that their actions involved the honor of England and of parliament. Upon Thurlow's suggestion they left it to the conscience of each peer to decide whether he had attended enough sessions to enable him

---

95 As early as Jan. 31, 1791, the *Times* had Burke ready to retire from parliament as soon as the trial ended. Osborn Coll., Box 74, #24A, Burke to Dudley North, Dec. 28, 1796.

96 Burke MSS, Sheff., June 21, 1794.

97 *Debates in the House of Lords, on the Evidence delivered in the Trial of Warren Hastings, Esquire* (London, 1797).

to vote intelligently upon Hastings' guilt or innocence. For the
sake of clarity and order, again following Thurlow's recommendation, the peers subdivided the original charges upon which
evidence had been heard. Thus, fourteen articles of impeachment
were at once dispensed with, and the remaining six were separated
into sixteen criminal allegations with a vote to be taken on each.
It would be difficult to find in English history an instance when
the integrity of the House of Lords shone more nobly.

After making these sensible decisions about procedure, the
Lords reviewed the evidence. Though their preferences had long
since been revealed, this was the first time that Thurlow and
Loughborough had had the opportunity to act as advocates, the
former lord chancellor for Hastings and the present lord chancellor
for the managers. The review of the evidence was almost a running
debate between them, with other peers interjecting remarks and
opinions from time to time. Thurlow held the initiative throughout. He introduced the subject matter, reduced the mountain of
evidence to the essential and relevant points, and perhaps made
fully intelligible for the first time the mass of material presented to
the Lords since 1788. Without being obnoxiously partisan he directed the presentation in Hastings' favor, and his summaries sometimes amounted to pleadings for Hastings. The reader of the volume
of debates cannot but be impressed by Thurlow's performance.
It would be no exaggeration to say that he, more than Hastings'
counsel, played the pivotal role in the defense, and he did it at a
time when it counted most. More than once during the debates in
March and April, individual peers remarked upon the persuasiveness of Thurlow's summaries of the evidence. It is fitting that
the frontispiece of the volume of debates is Thurlow's portrait.

Thurlow made much of the argument from state necessity. The
Lords "must reflect on the situation in which Mr. Hastings was
placed"; he had used his power with the intention of promoting
the public good and in the fulfillment of his duty to preserve the
British Empire in India.[98] Loughborough refused to believe that
ends justified means.[99] Hastings should be judged according to

---

[98] *Debates in the Lords,* 5.
[99] *Debates in the Lords,* 7, 19.

objective moral standards; his intentions or his objects were irrelevant to the nature of his conduct. The principle of sovereignty upon which Hastings acted was alien to the British constitution. This basic conflict ran throughout the debates. The verdict upon Hastings was strongly influenced by the choice between the argument from necessity and the moral argument.

This choice in turn was influenced by the peers' conception of the House of Lords as a high court. The charges against Hastings were too inattentive to the distinction that a judicial body has to make between positive and moral law. As Thurlow said at the outset, "the zeal of the agents who drew the articles, had certainly outrun their discretion."[100] It may be true that a violation of moral law is a crime against the natural order, but unless the act is also a violation of common or statute law, the state has no cognizance of it. Thus, said Thurlow, in discussing the allegations concerning presents, it was not a crime at common law for a superior to receive a gift from an inferior.[101] There must also be some corrupt consideration as a motive for giving or taking the present, and the corruption must be proved. The charge against Hastings merely assumed that the fact of the gift constituted a crime. There could be no conviction on such a charge, any more than on the charge relating to contracts. The managers may have demonstrated that certain individuals made fortunes from the contracts awarded by Hastings, but they had not proved collusion between Hastings and the beneficiaries. The story of the contracts might raise doubts about the ethical conduct of certain gentlemen in India. But the House of Lords was a court of law. Regardless of the managers' suspicions, they had not presented the evidence that would convict a man of high crimes and misdemeanors.

A third consideration arises out of these debates. There was a sentimental predisposition in favor of Hastings. The impeachment had endured for seven years; Hastings had spent a great deal of money in his own defense; there were some who felt that he had already suffered enough. Although pity should have been irrelevant, it existed, and in the absence of indisputably damaging

---

100 *Debates in the Lords,* 4.
101 *Debates in the Lords,* 192-93.

evidence, or in the presence of any doubts of guilt, or when two learned lawyers might disagree about the evidence, then, as Lord Walsingham said, the safest thing was to take "the mildest side" and lean in favor of the defendant.[102] There was another kind of predisposition in favor of the defendant. William Markham, the Archbishop of York, thought that the attack upon Hastings concerned trifles.[103] What were one and one-half lacs of rupees (£15,000), anyway? The Lords acted as though they were trying a "horse-stealer" instead of a "gentleman." Moreover, the Lords should consider the services Hastings had rendered. The absurdity of this argument, enlarged when advanced by a clergyman, was obvious. Loughborough promptly disposed of the Archbishop: he did not have to remind the peers that Markham's son had served Hastings in India. Still, it would be interesting to know how many of the peers felt as did Markham.

By April 13 the Lords had gone through the evidence, voting *singulatim* that the Commons had not made good the charges. Then a procedural question arose. Up to this point the debate had been in committee of the whole house, and the committee had to report back to the Lords. Loughborough desired that the report lie on the table, because the Lords would not give the final verdict until they assembled again in Westminster Hall to vote publicly and individually on each question. But Thurlow was anxious to commit the Lords as far as he could and argued for a vote on each resolution of guilt or innocence as a matter of record. Thurlow won, though the Earl of Lauderdale thought it desirable to remind the peers that such votes were not binding prior to the balloting in Westminster Hall.

The scene in Westminster Hall on April 23, though lacking the novelty of the opening day in 1788, was as much the center of London's attention. The crowd was perhaps the largest of any session of the trial. The drama of solemnity, the anticipatory hush before the awful decision was rendered, made this the most tense day of the trial. The questions to be voted upon and their wording had been decided in the House of Lords a week before. Now each peer was upon his conscience, to decide whether he

---

102 *Debates in the Lords,* 281.
103 *Debates in the Lords,* 229-30.

should vote at all and then to vote as his best judgment directed. He would place his hand upon his right breast and respond to each question, "guilty" or "not guilty," "upon my honour." There would be one question on the Benares charge, one on the charge relating to the begums of Oude, six on presents, seven on contracts, and the sixteenth would embrace the residue.

Twenty-nine peers were present in their robes—they were the ones who would vote. The first question, on the Benares charge, was called. One by one the peers pronounced their judgments. The first fourteen said "not guilty"; Lord Carnarvon said "guilty"; and then the sixteenth vote was "not guilty." This was a majority. The vote on the charge was 23-6 in favor of acquittal. On the second charge, the begums of Oude, the vote was identical. On none of the remaining questions were there more than five votes of guilty, and on two of the questions there was a unanimous verdict of acquittal.

The lord chancellor then informed Hastings, who stood at the bar, that "you are acquitted of the articles of impeachment, . . . and you are discharged, paying your fees." There was some slight applause from the galleries, but it quickly subsided as though the spectators had become abashed at violating the sanctity of the occasion.

Mr. Hastings bowed and withdrew, and the peers adjourned to their chamber. Edmund Burke had not been present.

The *St. James's Chronicle* ended its account of the scene in Westminster Hall by hoping that the judgment would "put an end to all disputes on the Subject."[104] The disputes have never ceased.

Burke showed his displeasure with the acquittal by opposing the East India Company's desire to compensate Hastings for his legal expenses and to grant him a pension of £4,000 a year retroactive to June 24, 1785.[105] Nearly a year passed before the arrangements were completed. When he heard that they had been, Burke dashed off letters to Dundas, Loughborough, Lord

---

104 April 23-25, 1795.
105 The story of this episode is conveniently summarized in *History of the Trial of Hastings,* Supplement, 274-330. Hastings' legal expenses were about £71,000. Also MS in Yale Library, Burke to Dundas, May 13, 1795; Burke MSS, Sheff., Dundas to Burke, May 14, 1795.

Fitzwilliam, and Windham.[106] To Dundas he expressed disappointment that the Board of Control had not checked the "gang of thieves," the directors and proprietors. He threatened to petition the House of Commons to explain to them how the reward to Hastings impugned their honor and betrayed the managers of the impeachment. The letter to Loughborough was less a protest against the compensation than an apologia for Burke's promotion of the impeachment. By implication Burke accused Loughborough of thinking he had some personal interest in the impeachment; in any case, since 1780 he had been generally accused of "personal animosity" against Hastings. This he indignantly denied. He had never seen Hastings until 1785, he had had no previous relations with him, had owed him no favors nor had Hastings owed any to Burke. There had never been any party or political difference between them. Burke's interest during fourteen years of incredible labor had been to obtain justice for an oppressed people. He had failed, and now the result of his labors was a pension for Hastings to be extracted from the people he had oppressed—for the revenues of the company came out of the labor of the Indian people.

It seemed to Burke that all had been in vain, and the awards to Hastings merely emphasized the defeat. The acquittal condemned "whole tribes and nations" to oppression, because the purification of Indian administration would never be achieved. By some "incomprehensible dispensation" God had placed the Indian Empire in the hands of the British people. They were abusing their trust and using their power and wealth to gratify "the lowest" of their "passions."[107]

A vast, controversial, partisan literature has been written about the impeachment and its background. Apparently, none of the authors of this literature has asked himself a very simple question, namely, how would he have voted had he been a peer who sat throughout the trial in Westminster Hall? In the first place,

106 The letters to the first three are in Burke MSS, Sheff. Those to Fitzwilliam and Dundas are dated March 6, 1796, the one to Loughborough is undated and exists in two drafts, one in Burke's hand. It is probably of the same date. The letter to Windham, also March 6, 1796, is in *Windham Papers*, II, 5.

107 *The Epistolary Correspondence of the Right Hon. Edmund Burke with Dr. French Laurence* (London, 1827), 54-55, Burke to Laurence, July 28, 1796.

such a peer, in order to be perfectly judicious, would have to forget the years before 1788 when the question of India and Hastings was argued in the House of Commons, the Court of Proprietors, in the newspapers and in pamphlets. He would not have asked what were Burke's motives and the motives of the other managers. He would have accepted the decision of the House of Commons, after eight years of investigation and debate, that there was impeachable matter in the mass of documents and testimonies they had reviewed. He would have understood that the articles of impeachment carried by Burke to the House of Lords were accusations that were to be proved or disproved. He would have seen it as his duty to hear evidence, to sift it, and then to decide, on the basis of the evidence, whether Hastings was guilty or innocent of the crimes alleged in the charges.

Such a peer would have to remember other things. In listening to the speeches of the managers in opening and closing, he would remind himself that these speeches were, so to speak, the efforts of lawyers to influence a jury. So too with the speeches of the defense counsel. It would not be the duty of the peer, as of later historians, to conduct his own investigation of the historical sources and to base his judgment of Hastings upon independent research; only the evidence presented at the trial was pertinent. Finally, in attempting to find a verdict in this evidence, he would have to try to avoid being influenced by the premises upon which the prosecution and the defense based their arguments, in the one instance the principles of moral law, and in the other, reason of state.

If he achieved such perfect objectivity, then the peer would ask himself only one question—what does the evidence presented at the trial direct me to do? If one reads the eleven volumes of the minutes of evidence and decides on that evidence alone, one must vote as the majority did, for the acquittal of Warren Hastings.

Having done that, and being at leisure, the peer could then reflect upon the matters that he had excluded from his mind while trying to arrive at an unprejudiced judgment. He should have learned enough during the trial to believe that Mr. Burke had had sufficient reason in the history and records of the Hastings

administration for seeking impeachment. Burke's attack upon
Hastings was perfectly explainable in terms of his character.
Personal or party motives were, at most, of secondary importance.
Since two years elapsed after the passage of Pitt's India Act before
Burke began proceedings in the House of Commons, there was
sufficient time for him and his friends to understand that an
impeachment launched as an attack upon Pitt's government was
foolish. By leaving the entire business to the managers, Pitt and
Dundas skillfully avoided getting involved in it. The neutrality
of the government meant that it had no stake in the outcome.
Even a brief and successful prosecution of Hastings would not
have altered party fortunes. The most the Portland party could
hope for was to win some favor if they convicted Hastings, but
that would not be sufficient to change the political balance. If
Pitt had opposed the impeachment, that would have been the
end of it. Pitt supported the impeachment, with the results that
have been explained.

If he knew Burke well, the peer would understand his passion
for the moral law, his conviction that politics was morality
enlarged. He would know, and the trial would make clearer,
that some of Hastings' actions that were not crimes under
statute and common law were nevertheless breaches of morality.
To Burke, such actions were crimes against humanity and the
law of nature, and the author of such actions deserved punishment. But it was not for the House of Lords as a high court of
English law to convict a man of these types of crime. A sympathetic peer would commiserate with Burke in the impossibility
of the task he had set for himself. While all men, informed by
their consciences, admit the existence of right, they find it difficult
not to soften the absoluteness of the concept by appeals to utility
and expediency. And in the secular world, the divine law is not
always so apparent as is the rule and necessity of the state, because
divine sanctions are not so immediate or imminent as the force
of secular power or the urgencies of physical self-defense. It does
not denigrate Burke or his philosophy, nor does it weaken his
sincerity, to say that he had no choice but to base his prosecution
of Hastings upon the doctrine of natural law. The impeachment
illustrated his way of relating the doctrine to the needs of the

social order. It was the only argument he could use against Hastings' defense. The doctrine of reason of state had no superior as a purely secular argument. Burke had to appeal to a higher authority, and it could only be the spiritual, supernatural authority of divine law.

Burke lost. It is often alleged in the histories that in the long run he did not fail, that the impeachment had a salutary influence upon future Indian administrations and that Burke therefore infused in the imperial administration the doctrine of trusteeship; the purity and integrity of Indian administration and generally of British colonial administration are testimonies to Burke's triumph. It would be pleasant to be able to believe this. The House of Commons Committee on Aborigines, 1835-1837, declared, "He who has made Great Britain what she is will enquire at our hands how we have employed our influence."[108] In 1923 the Colonial Secretary wrote that His Majesty's Government "regard themselves as exercising a trust on behalf of the native populations . . . the objectives of which may be defined as the protection and advancement of the native races. . . . it is the mission of Great Britain to work continuously for the training and education of the African towards a higher intellectual, moral and economic level."[109] These are certainly Burkean sentiments. But to find their origin in the impeachment of Hastings is to identify resemblances with cause and effect. It still remains to adduce evidence that Burke's impeachment of Hastings had these beneficent effects.

Burke's impeachment of Hastings was one of his great causes. It does credit to his memory; it was a considerable part of his life; it was a major historical event. If his efforts ended in failure, he was not ashamed, nor had he any reason to be.

[108] Quoted in *Cambridge History of Brit. Empire,* III, 7.
[109] *Cambridge History of Brit. Empire,* III, 7.

CHAPTER XI

The Regency Crisis

WHEN THE DEBATE on Warren Hastings in 1787 was transformed from an extended inquiry by the House of Commons into a trial before the House of Lords, it lost for all practical purposes whatever political significance it might have possessed. Except for occasional disputes over delays or costs or the effect of a dissolution upon an impeachment, the House of Commons had no part in it. Because the government had adopted a neutral position, the trial presented no issues between the Portland party and the administration.

This mutual tolerance did not extend beyond the impeachment. On other issues warfare continued, accompanied by the abuses and vituperation to which the growing newspaper press and the developing art of caricature made notorious contributions. Both sides had their journalistic supporters and constantly strove to recruit new ones.[1] The *Times* was pro-Pitt even before January, 1789, when during the Regency crisis it went on his subsidy list for £300 a year. The opposition had failed to gain a half-share of the paper, although it had offered £4,000 and had promised printing business. Sheridan had bought the support of the *General Advertiser* four years earlier for £300 a year, and he wrote for the *Morning Herald*. In the desperate days of the Regency crisis, Carlton House, the Prince of Wales's establishment and "party" headquarters, ended the *Morning Post's* hostility by buying the paper. Louis Weltje, maître d'hôtel for the Prince, became joint lessee. The *Morning Chronicle* favored Pitt for £400 a year until, coming under new ownership in 1789, it went over to the opposition. Burke knew about these maneuvers but seems to have had nothing to do with them. He appreciated the influence of the press, but his own experiences caused him to doubt its integrity. In self-defense he had adopted an attitude of indifference toward the press; otherwise he could not have endured the abuse he had suffered from it.

Seldom was the abuse so personally insulting or so viciously distorted as that which in 1784 drove him to sue Henry Woodfall of the *Public Advertiser*. For Woodfall's insinuation of undue partiality for homosexuals, arising from Burke's opposition to the use of the pillory for men convicted of sodomy, Burke won damages of £100. Usually the abuse had a political reference or, at worst, talked of private affairs that were public knowledge. On June 5, 1787, Burke was at Beaconsfield, said the *Daily Universal Register,* "busy in preparing a few lean kine and ragged sheep for the Smithfield market." Everyone knew that Burke was an enterprising farmer; the *Register* was reminding readers of his chronic pecuniary distress. On September 25, 1787, the *Register* found Burke still immured at Beaconsfield, not studying how to provide good government for England, political "fate" having decreed that he could not, but deep in the "Fathers." His favorites were St. Augustine and Machiavelli. In the evenings Burke composed elegies in honor of Lord Rockingham and speeches in favor of *"distracted* virtue." The reader was asked to imagine *"honest* Edmund the *reformer,* in a black leather chair, with the representation of *Ignatius Loyola* on the right hand, and the *bribe to the Samnites* on the left."

During the spring and summer of 1788 the *Times* carried on its campaign of ridicule. Like the caricaturists it dressed the Foxites in the buff and blue of the American Revolution. On May 3 it reported a Foxite council of war at which Burke lamented the theft of money intended for the pay of the buff and blue mercenaries, that is, " 'to clothe the naked, and feed the hungry,' to stop the cries of patriotic distress, and satisfy the

---

1 Aspinall, *Politics and the Press,* 74-75, 270-78.

wants of wit and satire." Later in the meeting the impeachment was mentioned, and Burke went into convulsions weeping for the begums. Finally, the council resolved to apply to their ducal patrons, Portland, Devonshire, and the young Bedford, to relieve the financial emergency. At another meeting, said the *Times* on May 7, the party was planning a campaign on the budget. Burke brought in a "Hasty Sketch" of a plan that he prefaced with a speech on the history of British public finance from Egbert of Wessex in 819 to the present, with apologies for omitting Cromwell and the Interregnum. The company approved Burke's sketch, though Courtenay wished to insert some jokes from Joe Miller. Fox ended the meeting by agreeing with Burke that the remedy for England's ills was a change of ministry. A Foxite ministry, the *Times* later remarked, would be led by a trinity.[2] The leader would be three persons in one, existing on ducal bounty. The three had complementary abilities: Fox had the greatest lung-power, Sheridan the keenest wit, and Burke, the handsomest, was their equal in verbosity. He was a "master of words to swell a paragraph of four lines into a volume of argument."

These themes, Burke's hypocrisy, inconsistency, and frustration, and the intimations of his Catholicism remained favorites of the political caricaturists as well as the newspapers. Year after year Sayers, James Gillray, and others continued to caricature the world of politics and fashion. Their drawings, sold in the print shops, chronicle the period. One, subtler than most, deserves reflection. It was published early in 1789 as the frontispiece to the verse satire *Gynomachia,* a violent attack on Burke. The picture, sold separately, represents two ladies, each wearing Burke's head. One is his moral conscience, which is accusing the other, his political conscience, of permitting Burke to follow "selfish, iniquitous ends" (p. 12). The *Monthly Review,* when noticing the book, was sorry to see Burke's "political conduct attacked with so much severity."[3]

The Portland party answered this abuse in kind. The best known retaliation was the *Rolliad,* a series of satires in verse and

2 July 1, 1788.
3 LXXX (1789), 463.

prose that appeared from 1785 to 1789 and demonstrated the considerable talents available to the party.[4] The *Rolliad* took its name from John Rolle, a vulgar leader of the squadron of young members in the House, the "smoking and spitting" detachment who so often and so maddeningly interrupted Burke's speeches and at times forced him into desperate silence.

> Great ROLLO's heir, whose cough, whose laugh, whose groan,
> The' Antaeus EDMUND has so oft o'erthrown;
> Whose cry of "question" silenc'd CHARLES's sense;
> That cry, more powerful than PITT's eloquence;[5]

In a debate of March 19, 1787, for example, Burke protested because he could not be heard for the coughing on the ministerial side.[6] George Dempster replied blandly that coughing was a very ancient privilege of the House.

The contributors to the *Rolliad* were members of a Foxite group called the "Esto Perpetua Club," and particularly Thomas O'Beirne, Richard Fitzpatrick, Joseph Richardson, George Ellis, Sheridan, and his brother-in-law Richard Tickell. One other young contributor was at this time becoming a protégé of Burke. This was French Laurence, an Oxford M.A. and in 1787, at the age of thirty, a doctor of civil law. He was already assisting on the *Annual Register* or was on the eve of doing so in succession to Walker King.[7] In the election of 1784 he had given journalistic support to Fox; by 1785 he was helping Burke in the preparations for the Hastings business. At his age and that stage of his life, the idea of the *Rolliad* appealed to him. His considerable talents and his admiration for Burke made him "the most prolific of the contributors."[8]

[4] *The Rolliad, in two parts; Probationary Odes for the Laureateship; and Political Miscellanies* (London, 1795). This edition contains only part of the satires; Sichel, *Sheridan*, II, 86-96.

[5] *The Rolliad*, xii.

[6] *Daily Universal Register*, March 20, 1787.

[7] Copeland, *Our Eminent Friend Edmund Burke*, 107-14. It now seems clear that Burke not only gave up the editorship of the *Annual Register* but also the writing of the Historical Section in February or March, 1766, and that from then until 1793 Thomas English was the editor. William B. Todd, "A Bibliographical Account of *The Annual Register*, 1758-1825," *The Library*, 5th ser., XVI (June, 1961), 104-20.

[8] Sichel, *Sheridan*, II, 90.

The victims of the *Rolliad* were the members of the administration and their supporters. It was Laurence who reminded readers of Pitt's youth. "Alas! that flesh, so late by pedants scarr'd/Sore from the rod, should suffer seats so hard."[9] The *Rolliad* mocked the Duke of Richmond, a notoriously parsimonious person who spent government money lavishly on fortifications:

> Hail, thou, for either talent justly known,
> To spend the nation's cash—or keep thy own;
> Expert alike to save, or be profuse,
> As money goes for thine, or England's use.[10]

The "JOURNAL of the Right Hon. HENRY DUNDAS" was an effective bit of satire.[11] It stressed his authority over "those damned fellows the Directors," whose lavish dinners he enjoyed. After one of the dinners he took home "twelve dozen of their claret." Of a director who grumbled at this, Dundas wrote, "A very troublesome fellow that—remove him." When Dundas did not have authority to employ troop transports at company expense, he "ordered PITT to bring in a Declaratory bill!" Then Dundas "Wrote to Ross [Cornwallis' secretary], enclosing the copy of a letter to be sent to me from Lord C-----ll-s requiring more King's troops." The *Rolliad* left no doubt who was governing India. Of William Eden who left the Coalition for Pitt in 1785, the *Rolliad* said:[12]

> Then give him a place, O dearest Billy Pitt O!
> If he can't have a whole one, O give a little bit O!

If the government writers chastised the Prince of Wales, the opposition did not spare his father.

> Hail, inexhausted boundless spring
>   Of sacred Truth and holy Majesty!
> Grand is thy form—'bout five feet ten,
> Thou well-built, worthiest, best of men;
> Thy chest is stout, thy back is broad—

9 *Rolliad*, 45.
10 *Rolliad*, 144.
11 *Rolliad*, 135-48.
12 The two following quotations are from Sichel, *Sheridan*, II, 90-92.

> Thy Pages view thee and are awed!
> Lo! how thy white eyes roll!
> Thy whiter eyebrows stare!
>   Honest soul!
> Thou'rt witty as thou'rt fair.

But the "honest soul" was the central political figure of the age. His illness in the autumn of 1788 raised the political stakes to the highest point. The king's illness was both physical and mental. No one could say when he would recover, and some added, if at all. The constitutional system could not function without a king, yet the man still lived. A regency was in order; the efforts to provide for it provoked a political and constitutional crisis.[13]

In retrospect it was possible to trace suggestions of the king's illness back to May, 1788. Beginning in the autumn, his infirmities became more pronounced, though as late as November 3 he was able to write to Pitt, and on November 5 Pitt replied, flattering himself that "a Continuance of Quiet will in a short Time remove the Remains of your Majesty's Complaint."[14] London was full of rumors which by that time included talk of insanity. The *Morning Chronicle* berated the parliamentary opposition for exaggerating the king's malady when everybody knew that he was recovering.[15] The opposition took no chances of being caught unprepared. They badly needed Fox who was in Italy, and they sent an express urging him to hasten home.[16] Already there was talk of a regency to be proclaimed as soon as parliament assembled on the scheduled day, November 20.

Attention centered upon the Prince of Wales because of his intimacy with Fox, Sheridan, and the opposition. For the first time in the reign the reversionary interest, so much a factor

13 Among the useful sources on the regency crisis are Buckingham, *Courts and Cabinets*, I, 427-57, and II, 1-131; H.M.C., *Dropmore Papers*, I, 360-425; Harlow, *The Second British Empire*, I, 616-27; Lecky, *History of Ireland in the Eighteenth Century* (London, 1909), II, 467-84.

14 P.R.O., Chatham Papers, 30/8, 103, the King to Pitt, 101, Pitt to the King. This was the last exchange until Feb. 23, 1789, when the king, "with infinite satisfaction," was able to "renew" the correspondence though not to carry on business. P.R.O. 30/8, 103, the King to Pitt.

15 Nov. 8, 1788.

16 *Times*, Nov. 13, 1788.

before 1760, suddenly became of overriding importance. With the prince as regent, the rise of the opposition and the decline of Pitt, probably his downfall, seemed inevitable. But there might be an alternative. Anticipating precisely the position that Pitt would take, the *Morning Chronicle* of November 8 denied that because he was the heir apparent the prince had a right to the regency. Parliament would have to decide. The *Times* did not agree with a "distinguished lawyer" who thought that the prince could assume the reins of government without waiting for parliamentary action, but it expected parliament when it assembled to proclaim immediately the prince as regent with full authority to exercise the prerogative powers.[17] The *Times* only hoped that, like Prince Hal, the regent would abandon his former companions of the bottle, the gambling table, and the racetrack.[18] The *Times* was referring to a scheme of Loughborough's, who was the "distinguished lawyer."[19] Promoted by the Comptroller of the Prince's Household, Captain John Payne, the plan envisaged virtually a seizure of power by the prince. But it was too bold for him and for Sheridan, and in any case, it was not proper to act before Fox returned. Burke was not in town for the early consultations.

As the date for the meeting of parliament approached, the *Times* defined the problem as a decision about the proper moment to proclaim the regency.[20] There could be no doubt "respecting the legality of the Prince of Wales' succession, and his right to be sole regent." Perhaps the prince's exemplary filial conduct during the early days of the king's illness influenced some people. The "Youth who discovers, in this, as on every other occasion, a most tender heart, and a strong sympathy to all in distress, must make a gentle and just ruler."[21] Evidently the *Morning Chronicle* had doubts about its denials of the prince's rights.

If, as most politicians believed, the royal prerogative encom-

---

17 Nov. 13, 14, 1788.

18 Nov. 15, 1788.

19 Charles Chenevix Trench, "The Royal Malady: Some Aspects of the Regency Crisis, 1788-9," *History Today*, XII (June, 1962), 388.

20 Nov. 17, 19, 1788.

21 *Morning Chronicle,* Nov. 17, 1788. This kind of nonsense appeared in all of the newspapers during the days before parliament met.

passed the appointment and dismissal of ministers, then there was cause for alarm in government circles. As a practical matter, the crown had to consider the disposition of political forces in exercising this power. In 1782 the Commons destroyed a government that enjoyed the royal confidence; in December, 1783, the king dismissed a ministry that had just carried an important measure through the Commons, and then he sustained a minority government until an election gave it a firm parliamentary basis. But the appearance of mastery after the election of 1784 was deceptive. Only a minority of the Commons were committed followers of Pitt or of Fox and North. The tradition of independence was still strong. Upwards of two hundred members adhered to the crown. Therefore Pitt's strength depended much upon the confidence of the king and of the independent members. But the king's incapacity and the accession of the prince to the regency might encourage enough shifts of allegiance to alter seriously the parliamentary balance of power, even though royal confidence in Pitt had not diminished. "Ratting" was a normal thing when the reversionary factor operated.

Even before the king's illness became serious, Pitt had endured moments of anxiety. The most recent had been in the preceding spring, when he had exposed himself to danger in pushing through a bill to remove doubts concerning the power of the Board of Control to order the East India Company to pay troops deemed necessary for the defense of India.[22] The bill was part of the contest between the board and the company directors that had been going on ever since the India Act of 1784. In 1788 Pitt faced the combined opposition of the East India interest and the Foxites. For a few days in March his government was unsteady. "There were doubts," said Dundas' daughter, of the ability of the administration to carry the bill; the opposition, General James Grant told Cornwallis, thought they might "overset" the ministry.[23] Never had Pitt faced "such a push"; he had to call in "auxiliary troops" from Scotland and from "the outposts"; and he saved the bill only by accepting amendments to it. At one stage his majority was only about fifty in a well-attended house.

[22] Philips, *East India Company*, 57-61.
[23] Furber, *Dundas*, 70-71; Ross, *Cornwallis*, I, 374.

There were doubts whether, if he suffered defeat, the royal confidence would be able to sustain him.

During the prorogation the opposition scored a triumph that further improved their spirits. When Lord Hood accepted a seat at the Admiralty Board, he had to stand for reelection in Westminster. Suddenly, opposition appeared, and a bitter contest ensued as the Foxites pushed the candidacy of Lord John Townshend. Burke, who had been ill, offered to help during the election, but Portland urged him to conserve his strength, which was more important to the party than winning the Westminster election.[24] Portland's advice contained a half-truth; the rest of it was that Burke's talents would not be useful in such a constituency as Westminster. It was ducal money, especially Bedford's, which won the election of Townshend, whined the *Times*.[25] The *Times* consoled itself by describing the "Party" as "foolish old Peers, gay, giddy, dissipated young Lords, and a club of avowed sharpers, drunkards, and gamblers." The Westminster victory encouraged the party to look forward hopefully to the future and, a good two years in advance, to begin preparations for the next general election. Burke visited Fitzwilliam and the Duke of Devonshire to discuss prospects during October. The Duke of Norfolk, as "canvasser general," spent an encouraging season traveling up and down England in the party's behalf.[26]

In short the opposition already was gaining confidence when the king's illness presented them with a heaven-sent opportunity. Their parliamentary strength, far from being contemptible, was sufficient to make Pitt's concern a genuine worry over the prospect of the prince's becoming regent. An analysis of the House of Commons by Pitt's secretary added to his discomfort.[27] The

---

24 Burke MSS, Sheff., Portland to Burke, July 24, 1788. Burke asked Dr. Burney for his support. Unable to give it, because of his daughter's position at court, Burney was embarrassed. Burke assured him that he was under no obligation just because he was beholden to Burke for his post at Chelsea Hospital. "God forbid that worthy men, situated as you are, should be made sacrifices to the minuter parts of politics." Burke never deluded himself about the roughness of politics, but he disliked its crudities. MS at Yale Library, Burke to Burney, Aug. 1, 1788; Burke MSS, Sheff., Burney to Burke, Aug. 8, 1788; D'Arblay, *Memoirs of Burney*, III, 122.

25 Aug. 27, 1788, and various references throughout this month.

26 *Times*, Oct. 7, 1788.

27 Feiling, *Second Tory Party*, 167; Barnes, *George III and Pitt*, 198-99; Aspinall, ed., *Eng. Hist. Documents*, XI, 253.

largest group consisted of 185 members, the "Party of the Crown," including "all of those who would probably support his Majty's Governt under any Minister not peculiarly unpopular." The question would be, was Fox so peculiarly unpopular that none of these men would support him if the prince regent brought him in? Then there were 108 independents, of whom about 40 considered themselves a kind of third force, ready to rescue the king from both Pitt and Fox. Pitt's followers numbered 52, of whom only 20 would be returned in an election held when Pitt was not minister. The rest of Pitt's strength came from the 10 Scots led by Dundas, the 15 East Indians, and the two groups of 9 men that followed the Marquis of Lansdowne and the Earl of Lonsdale. Lonsdale could hardly be counted on; indeed, urged by the Prince of Wales, he deserted Pitt during the regency crisis. Against this mixed majority there were 138 Foxites and 17 members who continued to support Lord North even after he absolved them from their allegiance early in 1788.[28] According to the *Times* (May 31, 1788), the opposition was a motley group. It was nevertheless more formidable than a party could be when composed of "a crazy Painter, a broken apothecary, a hunting Parson, a Gunner's Mate, five Publicans, four Tavern-keepers, an Auctioneer, two Scotch lawyers, half a dozen poor authors, three Dukes, four Earls, and about twenty-five Commoners."

This background explains why the regency question was so critical. It also explains the political tactics and the arguments of both sides. If Pitt fought desperately to shackle the proposed regency and the opposition strove to maintain the regent's freedom to exercise the prerogative powers, the reasons are plain. The regency crisis was hardly a moral cause, and Pitt was not Sir Galahad. He was simply a politician, trying to hold on to his power. The opposition were the "outs," trying to wrest it from him. Both sides rationalized their positions to make them appear principled.

On November 20, while Fox was still four days from London though traveling night and day to get there, parliament assembled because there was no authority competent to extend the earlier

[28] *Times,* Jan. 9, Feb. 6, 1788.

prorogation.[29] Amid uncertainty, each house adjourned for two weeks. On December 3 the Privy Council, of which Burke was a member, met to examine the king's physicians. In preparation for the meeting, Burke sought information from the unreliable Captain Payne.[30] Though he would have liked to talk with Dr. Richard Warren, the prince's physician who was in attendance on the king, Burke decided to be discreet. He nevertheless seemed to be well prepared for the meeting. He asked more questions than any other councilor.[31] Fox, ill ever since his return, did not attend the council. The king's physicians testified that although he would eventually recover, they could not say when that would be, and for the present he was incapable of performing public business. On December 8 the Commons, like the Lords, appointed a committee to question the physicians. Pitt excluded Burke from it, though the opposition had nominated him.[32] The committee heard only what the Privy Council could have told it. Partisanship revealed itself in these sessions. Rightly suspicious of Dr. Warren's political bias, the government placed its credence in the testimony of Dr. Francis Willis, an acknowledged authority on mental illness whom the queen had called in on the case. On the whole, Willis was optimistic about the chances of recovery, though uncertain about the time when it would come.

During this interval, political intrigue and speculation became intense. The newspapers contained many letters offering advice about the proper actions in such an unusual situation. The Marquis of Buckingham and his correspondents talked of dissension among the opposition.[33] The prince had spoken impatiently of Portland and Burke; Sheridan's intimacy with the prince was provoking jealousy among others in the party, especially the "old Rockinghams." The *Times* thought that the problem of a regency would be quickly settled once parliament

29 Pitt had already explained this to Burke. Burke MSS, Sheff., Pitt to Burke, Nov. 15, 1788. Possibly Burke hoped to delay matters until Fox arrived.

30 Copeland transcript from Royal Archives at Windsor, Burke to Captain Payne, n. d., but early Dec., 1788.

31 H.M.C., *Carlisle*, 659, George Selwyn to Carlisle, Dec. 4, 1788.

32 Barnes, *George III and Pitt*, 187.

33 H.M.C., *Dropmore Papers*, I, 374, Buckingham to W. W. Grenville, Nov. 23, 1788; Buckingham, *Courts and Cabinets*, I, 451, II, 15, Grenville to Buckingham, Nov. 11, 1788, Lord Bulkeley to Buckingham, Nov. 25, 1788.

got down to business.[34] On November 26 the prince called Fox
to Windsor; on the next day the cabinet met there with the
prince, and Fox urged Malmesbury to return to England because
his presence would be necessary if things took "the turn which I
expect"; after that the king was moved from Windsor to Kew,
which was closer to London.[35] Thurlow was beginning to act
suspiciously.[36] On Fox's return from Windsor Thurlow sent for
him at 11 p.m., and they talked into the next morning. The Lord
Chancellor was said to have grown suddenly popular among the
opposition. The gossip about secret meetings among the opposition and in the government was so widespread and so confident
that the sessions might as well have been held in taverns and on
the streets. The cabinet lists that were circulated indicated a
complete turnover.[37] The opposition would form the new ministry, and Burke would again be paymaster. Nineteen new peerages
would assure a majority for the new government in the Lords.
And if Burke's party took office, they would have patronage to
bestow unless restrictions were placed upon the regent's appointing powers. Eager persons were announcing their availability.
O'Beirne, unhappy in the country living that Portland had
secured for him, thought he deserved if not a bishopric then at
least a place that would enable him to provide for his family.[38]

Early in the crisis, Burke was relatively inconspicuous. The
press directed its attention to the party leaders who would obtain
ministerial posts. Burke was in good spirits, and conducting
himself discreetly. He restrained his resentment at being omitted
from the committee of December 8, leaving himself in a position
to offer statesmanlike advice. He urged the wisdom of a careful
examination of the physicians; he advised the Commons to be
watchful of their rights; he warned against quarreling with the
Lords; and like Pitt, he hoped that the regency would be settled
speedily.[39]

But approaching were the days of bitterness when men would

34 Nov. 20, 27, 29, 1788.

35 *St. James's Chronicle,* Nov. 27-29, 1788; Earl of Malmesbury, ed., *Diaries and
Correspondence of James Harris, first Earl of Malmesbury* (London, 1844), II, 434.

36 *Times,* Nov. 28, Dec. 1, 1788.

37 *St. James's Chronicle,* Dec. 2-4, 4-6, 1788; *Times,* Dec. 10, 1788.

38 Burke MSS, Sheff., O'Beirne to Burke, Dec. 8, 1788.

39 *Times,* Dec. 9, 1788.

argue the question of rights—the prince's right to the regency and parliament's right to make provision for it. On December 10, after the report on the physicians' testimony, Pitt moved for a committee to search for precedents. Fox saw no need for delay. In the absence of the king there was no parliament. It merely remained for the two houses to determine when the prince should assume the station that his hereditary right as heir to the throne entitled him to.[40] Pitt professed to be shocked. Actually he was delighted at Fox's blunder. Did Fox mean to say that parliament, or the two houses, had no rights? That "was little less than treason to the constitution of the country." Unless by the decision of the two houses, Pitt declared, "the Prince of Wales had no more right (speaking of strict right) to assume the government, than any other individual subject of the country."[41] At this point Burke entered the debate. Characteristically, he placed upon Pitt's remark an extreme interpretation and gave it a personal meaning by denouncing the prime minister as a competitor for the prince's rights.[42]

On the next day in the Lords the debate continued. Loughborough spoke in the words of Fox, Thurlow in those of Pitt.[43] As in the Commons, each speaker pushed the argument closer to the point of irreconcilability. When the Lords finished their debate, that point had been reached. It is difficult to see how this situation could have been avoided. Both sides desired control of the government. Each favored the constitutional position that most closely harmonized with its political interests. The disagreements about constitutional law increased the confusion.[44] When on December 12 Pitt announced the government's intention to circumscribe the regency, he took the position that political necessity dictated. By making it the first order of business he took

40 *Parl. Hist.*, XXVII, 706-707, 711-12.
41 *Parl. Hist.*, XXVII, 709.
42 *Parl. Hist.*, XXVII, 714.
43 *Parl. Hist.*, XXVII, 669-72.
44 These disagreements continue. Trench, in *History Today*, XII, 391, thinks that Fox "had the better case"; Holdsworth, *History of English Law*, X, 440-42, thought Fox's position was probably constitutionally improper. If, since the Revolution of 1688, there had been no doubt of parliament's power over the kingship, it remained true that the king was a part of parliament. Pitt's procedures throughout amounted to an assumption of power by the two houses outside the constitution, unless one accepts fiction for fact.

from the opposition their chance to seize the initiative. They never found another.

With political self-interest so obvious, both sides embarrassed themselves. Pitt's casuistry in insisting that by limiting the regency he was preserving intact for the king's recovery the royal prerogative to appoint ministers could not disguise his real purposes. His earlier interpretation of the king's constitutional powers over ministers taunted him. His championship of the rights of the Commons, though strong in its popular appeal, repudiated his earlier conduct and avowals. The opposition also tried to conceal embarrassment behind brashness. In asserting the regent's right to exercise the prerogative powers, they seemed to be forgetting their Whig ancestry, their former championship of the Commons, and their traditional hostility to the power of the crown. Remembering their anger in 1783 over the fall of the coalition ministry, they could hardly argue consistently in 1788 that if the regent dismissed Pitt, he was only acceding by anticipation to the wishes of the Commons. But why worry about consistency when it was not unlikely that the Portland-Fox party, with the regent's support, would also acquire the support of the Commons? Amid the confusions about the rights of parliament and the right of the prince and the prerogative rights, it was easy to make it appear that Pitt was expounding and Burke and Fox were abandoning the genuine Whiggery of the Revolution of 1688.[45]

As so often happened, Burke was in disagreement with his party over tactics. He was in accord on the theoretical question of the prince's right, but he favored bold, even radical actions. But by the time the debate over rights occurred, on December 10-11, the opportunity had gone by. Burke had proposed to Fox that the prince in person before the Lords officially inform the two houses of the king's condition and then ask their advice and assistance. But his friends, including the prince, thought that this scheme, almost as much as Payne's, resembled usurpation. The result was that the opposition confined itself to talk, merely opposing, while the government used its majority to advance its plans to limit the regent's freedom to promote the interests of

---

45 *St. James's Chronicle,* Dec. 11-13, 1788.

his friends. As for Burke, according to his account, thereafter he "was little consulted."[46] Had the opposition adopted Burke's proposal they would have been no worse off or no more unpopular than they were in verbalizing about rights. They would have forced Pitt to introduce the question of right and to take up immediately the conditions of a regency, a stage which was not reached until after mid-December.

By that time the committee on precedents had reported, and Pitt had proposed a future day for a committee on the state of the nation. Fox objected. He recommended that the two houses acknowledge the prince as regent with full powers to exercise the prerogative for the duration of the king's illness. Burke's original suggestion had at last impressed Fox, but too late. When Sheridan showed displeasure with Fox's remarks, thus intimating the prince's views, Pitt easily got his way. The committee on the state of the nation was appointed for December 16. The opposition was divided, the prince was displeased, and Pitt was in command.[47]

Pitt brought three resolutions to the debate that began on December 16. These outlined the government's plan for a method of enacting legislation that would enable the two houses to establish and define a regency. The second resolution, expressing Pitt's intention to pursue the issue, asserted the right of the two houses to settle the question of a regency. The debate extended through three sittings. On December 22 Burke expressed himself.

His speech was important, not because it influenced his audience, but because in it he discoursed upon the constitution and began the intellectual journey that would end in 1794 when he and some of his friends, in the interest of preserving the monarchy, joined Pitt and in effect became Tories.[48] In this speech Burke was not sure, and cared little, whether the views he was about to express were labeled Whig or Tory. They were the true constitutional doctrine of the wise men who had settled the principles

46 *Corr.*, III, 81-84, Burke to Fox, Nov., 1788, and 90-91, Burke to Windham, Jan. 24, 1789. The later letter shows that Burke remembered correctly the advice he had given in the earlier letter to Fox. The difference between Burke's proposal and the plan of Payne and Loughborough is important. Burke's would not have begun to operate until after the two houses assembled.

47 *Times*, Dec. 18, 1788.

48 *Parl. Hist.*, XXVII, 819-26.

of the constitution in 1688. The Revolution had reaffirmed the principle of the hereditary monarchy even while it changed the order of the succession as an act of self-preservation against a delinquent monarch. The act was not a precedent for any time and occasion. The necessity of 1688 did not exist in 1788. Pitt's proposal jeopardized the monarchical principle for purely political reasons. The limits of the prerogative might be changed. Burke had always been among the readiest to change them, but only by the consent of a full parliament—that is, of the king in agreement with the Lords and the Commons. He was readier than most politicians to contend "for the constitutional propriety of the king's submitting, in every part of his executive government, to the advice of parliament."[49] This could mean in choosing ministers as well as in performing other acts of state, but it should not be done "from faction and caprice," as Pitt was doing. Under no interpretation of advice or limiting the prerogative did the two houses have the constitutional power to do what Pitt desired.

The English constitution provided for a hereditary monarchy. The prince's right to the regency was a constitutional right. To deny him the regency, or to set new limits upon him by a simple act of the two houses, was to overturn the constitution at a time when no overwhelming necessity existed to justify such a revolution. This speech of 1788, connecting the former days of opposition to the later period of the French Revolution, found its principle of unity in the nature of the British constitution. It consisted of a hereditary monarchy united with the Lords and the Commons. Burke had always been a friend to the hereditary principle, even while he had attacked the prerogative powers. During the French Revolution he would ignore the problem of the prerogative in the interest of defending the institution of monarchy, because in the 1790's that was the issue. Within these limits, Burke's arguments were not contradictory, nor did it make any difference whether they were called Whig or Tory. As Burke said in 1792, extending the thought expressed in 1788, if "they are Tory principles, I shall always wish to be thought a Tory."[50]

Burke's indiscretions in this speech suggested awareness of the

49 *Corr.*, III, 97, Burke to Windham, Jan. 24, 1789.
50 Maggs Catalogue 365, lot 118, Spring, 1918, Burke to Laurence, April 13, 1792.

practical difficulties raised by his arguments. In speaking of the power of the crown to create peers, he suggested the revival of the title of Marquis of Rockingham. His friends had to drown him out with their outcries until he realized his mistake. The remark was revealing. Formerly, Burke had insisted upon the supremacy of the Commons, yet the prerogative power to create peers, if used to strengthen the Portland party in the Lords, might also strengthen that house against the Commons. Burke had formerly attacked the prerogative power over ministers, yet his colleagues were counting on that power to bring them into office. To be perfectly in agreement with his arguments of 1784, Burke, after asserting the prince's right to an unrestricted regency, would have had to add that the making of ministries was the Commons' business and that the prince regent should respect the Commons' authority. In that case, the advantage to the Portland party might be delusory. But the facts of political life had to be recognized. The influence of the crown existed, and if it was used to aid Fox, that was only what Pitt had contended for in 1784. Burke could have spun out such rationalizations if necessary; all the politicians were rationalizing their difficulties. The point was that they were trying to make self-interest appear to be devotion to principle.

As a sober historical discourse, Burke's two-hour speech had merit. When he insisted upon the monarchical nature of the English constitution, his point was emphasized by the difficulties that parliament was trying to resolve. In 1788 as in 1688 the system could not work without a king. In 1788 the only necessities were political—for Pitt to keep office by restricting the regent's powers, and for the opposition to try to obtain it by preventing restrictions.

Despite his assertions that he was nonpartisan, Burke's speech impressed his audience by its partisanship.[51] No one believed him when he denied a desire for place. His indiscretions also marred his effort. Even before he reached the part in which he referred to peerages, his hearers thought him "Wilder than ever"—"He is Folly personified, but shaking his cap and bells under the laurel of genius."[52] Possibly his opponents exaggerated his "violence,"

51 *Daily Advertiser,* Dec. 24, 1788.
52 Buckingham, *Courts and Cabinets,* II, 71, 73, Sir William Young to Buckingham, Dec. 22, 23, 1788.

but the frequency of references to it cannot be ignored. Burke
was passionate, felt deeply, and acted immoderately. A hostile
view would have it that the prospect of another turn in the
Pay Office, with a pension of £2,000 a year on the Irish establishment and a job for brother Richard naturally excited him, first
with anticipation and then with the rage of dwindling hopes.[53]
A charitable view would attribute Burke's indiscretions to his
anger at Pitt's attempt to hold on to office and to his sense of
outrage at what he thought was an insult to the prince and a blow
at hereditary monarchy.

When it came to a division on the motion that Burke had
opposed, both sides mustered their full strength. It was a fair
test, and Pitt won 268-204. The opposition must have been
disappointed if it was true that 240 of them had recently attended
a rally at Portland's house.[54]

The opposition press made much of associating Burke's wildness
with his part in judging the king's illness. He had tried to study
insanity by visiting institutions in London and by reading.[55]
These efforts were cruelly misrepresented. Simpkin was especially
vicious:

> You remember, perhaps, that I formerly said,
> 'Twas suspected that EDMUND was *touch'd in the Head;*
> Some thought my assertion was matter of sport,
> But now all the PAPERS confirm the report;
> They describe him one day full of spirits and gladness,
> The next like a *Spectre,* dejected with sadness,
> In the BOOKSELLERS' SHOPS, seeking *Books* upon MADNESS;
> At ST. LUKE'S and in BEDLAM inspecting the Cells,
> To see in what comfort INSANITY *dwells . . .*
> To the TOWER some whisper'd a motion to send him,
> But others more tender, lamenting his case,
> Thought BEDLAM by far a more suitable place.[56]

The *Times* had Burke visiting Mrs. Harrison's lunatic asylum.[57]
Particularly he wanted to know the proportion of patients over

---

[53] Minto, *Elliot,* I, 260-63, Elliot to Lady Elliot, Jan. 10, 1789.
[54] *Times,* Dec. 16, 1788.
[55] His library contained several volumes on the subject.
[56] *Letters from Simpkin to his dear brother,* 51-53.
[57] Jan. 19, 1789.

fifty years of age who recovered. Curious, thought the *Times,* that Burke needed to gather information on a subject with which he was already "intimately acquainted." Then the *Times* issued a correction (January 24). Burke had been *sent* to seek advice from Mrs. Harrison concerning his own unstable condition. Imagine, said George Selwyn, "Burke walking at large, and he [the king] in a strait waistcoat!"[58]

Another examination of the physicians was held early in January and Burke participated, apparently acting obstreporously during the lengthy session. On one occasion, the *Times* reported, Dr. Willis looked steadily at "Paddy Burke," who "ceased ranting instantaneously."[59] Perhaps Dr. Willis might enter the House of Commons and work the same magic there. But he was not a member, so Burke was free to declaim against the report. It did not settle doubts about the king's recovery.[60]

The opposition could do no more than object and delay. They could not counter Pitt's scheme of action. On December 22 the House approved his plan for a commission under the great seal to open parliament so that a bill defining the regency could be enacted. This was a procedure tantamount to "a counterfeit representation of the royal signature," complained a group of opposition peers. On December 30 Pitt gave more detail to the prince. Among the specific restrictions to be imposed upon the regent, the most important from the political viewpoint concerned patronage powers. Pitt's letter warned that even the limited powers might be "re-considered" should the king's illness be protracted. To Pitt was written the famous reply of January 2, signed by the prince after a party conclave approved it.[61] Responsibility for the authorship has been given to both Burke and Sheridan.[62] Sichel, relying upon the Duchess of Devonshire's

58 H.M.C., *Carlisle,* 660, Selwyn to Carlisle, Dec. 5, 1788.

59 Jan. 17, 1789.

60 *Daily Advertiser,* Jan. 15, 1789.

61 Burke MSS, Sheff., William Adam to Burke, Dec. 29, 1788.

62 Prior, *Burke* (3d ed.), 304-307, printing the letter in full, says Burke wrote it; Adolphus, *History of England,* IV, 343, agrees, on the authority of Elliot and of Moore's biography of Sheridan. A. Aspinall, ed., *The Correspondence of George Prince of Wales 1770-1812,* I, 1770-1789 (London, 1963), 439, n. 1, relies on Elliot and makes Burke the author of the basic draft, which was amended before being given the final form, which was sent to Pitt. Aspinall prints fragments of preliminary sketches by Burke, 430-35, and the final letter. 436-39.

diary, makes Sheridan the author.[63] According to the Duchess, both Burke and Loughborough wrote drafts, but because Burke's was too passionate and Loughborough's too cold, Sheridan wrote one based upon these, and Fox approved it. In the Burke Manuscripts at Sheffield (B-15) there are two finished copies of the letter, neither in Burke's hand, and an incomplete rough draft, and in the Prince of Wales' manuscripts there are fragments by Burke. This inconclusive evidence does not refute the Duchess' testimony, nor is Sir Gilbert Elliot's account wholly incompatible with hers, for he has Sheridan improving upon Burke's original. The difference is one of degree and definition, but the best judgment is that Sheridan's alterations were emendations rather than changes so radical as to constitute a new letter.

The letter that was sent over the prince's signature clearly represents Burke's views about the necessity for maintaining the prince's dignity even while he capitulated. The prince "apprehends" that the plan "must have been formed with sufficient deliberation to preclude the probability of any argument of his producing an alteration of sentiment in the projection of it." The prince had to make known his dislike of a scheme for "dividing the royal family from each other" and for withholding from him the "powers and prerogatives of the crown [which] are vested there as a trust for the benefit of the people." The "plea of public utility ought to be strong, manifest, and urgent," in order to justify "an experiment" to ascertain with how little executive authority the government of the country could be carried on. These were the sentiments and the words of Burke respecting long-held views of the nature of the prerogative. Neither sacred nor untouchable, it deserved respectful treatment.

The protest was futile, of course. By January 23 parliament had defined the limitations to be imposed upon the regent. The opposition were not only beaten but disorganized.[64] Fox was seriously ill and Sheridan out of favor. Burke could not take the place of Fox as leader in the Commons. The dinners and other meetings at Carlton House were noisy, recriminatory, indecisive

---

[63] *Sheridan*, II, 190-91, 422.

[64] *Times*, Jan. 3, 12, 20, 21, 24, 26, 1789; *St. James's Chronicle*, Jan. 10-13, 1789; *Daily Advertiser*, Jan. 20, 30, 1789.

affairs. Burke thought it likely in these circumstances that the prince, when regent, would ask Pitt to stay in office, and Pitt was acting as though he expected to remain.[65] Burke could think of little but a return to the conduct of the party during the American Revolution, that is, secession. He was foolish enough to think that if its members sulked in their tents, the party would win popular support.

There were other signs of Burke's hopelessness. The *Times* on January 27 remarked upon his comparative silence in the Commons; when he did speak, said the *Times* two days later, "little attention was paid" to him. This statement referred to his bitter speech of January 27, in which he opposed the plan to lay before the prince the resolutions limiting the regency. During the next two days, Burke and other party leaders met at Carlton House to consider the prince's reply to the resolutions.[66] The letter was still another admission of defeat. The prince's sense of duty, it said, left him no choice but acceptance of the regency with its distasteful restrictions. He hoped that the regency would be only a temporary arrangement, pending the king's speedy recovery, and would do no permanent damage to the dignity of the crown.

At this stage, the Portland party had only one hope. The regency bill, introduced on February 3, was intended, as Lord Hawkesbury (Jenkinson) put it, to prevent the prince regent from doing anything the king could not undo when he resumed the throne. But it did not specifically restrict the conventional prerogative power to dismiss and appoint ministers. Such a provision would have been unthinkable, even though it might have given Pitt temporary security. Politics, not law, would determine the exercise of this power, and Hawkesbury expected the prince to dismiss Pitt when the bill passed.[67] In the new administration, according to James Macpherson, Burke would be appointed to the Board of Control, and then "the fat will be in the fire."[68] Perhaps the prince would refuse to make the appointment because it would create ill will. Burke seemed to expect the

65 *Corr.*, III, 89-101, Burke to Windham, Jan. 24, 1789.
66 *Times*, Jan. 29, 31, 1789.
67 Br. Mus., Add. MSS 38,310, fol. 31, Hawkesbury to Cornwallis, Jan. 6, 1789.
68 H.M.C., *Abergavenny*, 70, James Macpherson to John Robinson, Jan. 29, 1789.

post, or something else, along with a change of administration. He virtually promised William Burroughs to do something for him as soon as the prince assumed the regency.[69] This was only one of many instances of speculations and maneuvers concerning the distribution of offices in the anticipated new administration.

If the passage of the regency bill was all that stood between the Portland party and office, it seems difficult to understand why they chose to oppose rather than to hasten its enactment. The prospect of a Foxite ministry had not seriously weakened Pitt's position; the opposition had not previously defeated Pitt; there was no likelihood that they would be able to do so now in order to get a regency bill to their liking. Naturally, the opposition would have preferred a regent who could support them with freedom to exercise the influence of the crown. Yet everyone understood that a limited regency would remain influential, sufficiently so to bring the Portland party into power. The opposition was too greedy. They would have served their interest better if they had hastened proceedings from the beginning. Their conduct manifested a belief that the king's illness would continue, that they could afford to sacrifice haste for a better bargain, if they could make one, and that, taking a hint from Pitt, they were establishing the rationale for an amendment of the regency bill when they took office.

If Burke expected his party to take office, then it appears that he meant his passionate objections to the regency bill. It degraded the prince, "excommunicated the House of Brunswick," and located a revived divine right in Pitt. Even when attacking the household and the prerogative, Burke had insisted upon maintaining the dignity of the hereditary monarchy. His unwillingness to employ euphemisms and his willingness to draw frank conclusions from the uncompleted thoughts or the coy hints of other speakers does not alter the fact that he was indiscreet and improper, even "low and vulgar," said the *St. James's Chronicle* (February 7-10, 1789). If his enemies called him deranged, the prince did not consider him so. In urging his presence at a meeting at Loughborough's, the prince spoke of the need for his

69 H.M.C., *Charlemont*, 87, Burroughs to Charlemont, Jan. 31, 1789.

advice, "at all times, & particularly" at this crisis when the regency bill was in the committee stage in the Commons.[70]

Possibly the crisis the prince mentioned was the one that Pitt had been hoping for all along. The prince had known of the king's steady recovery since the beginning of February, though it was not until February 19, when the regency bill was in the committee stage in the Lords, that Thurlow gave public notice of it. The king's improvement threw calculations askew and brought the proceedings on the regency bill to an end. The Lords adjourned upon Thurlow's announcement, and when they reconvened on February 24, it was to hear a report of continued improvement and to pass a motion for another adjournment.

Burke and his friends were baffled and discomfited. It was a useless and begrudging qualification to say that the king was only better, not fully recovered.[71] Burke was the most disappointed member of "the Party," according to the *St. James's Chronicle*.[72] His disgruntlement and "indecent" conduct made him "Odious in the Eyes of all Mankind." His own party disapproved of his conduct. His reputation had sunk to its lowest point, for now people were speaking of him not in anger but in pity. By March 10, when the king announced his own recovery and issued a commission for the opening of parliament, it appeared that Burke's political career was at an end. All he had to look forward to was some way of bringing Hastings' impeachment to a close and then retiring to oblivion in the bucolic peace of Beaconsfield.

By this time the Irish friends of Burke's party had also been discomfited. Strengthened by the temporary adherence of some who anticipated being on the winning side, and by the unpopularity of the Marquis of Buckingham's administration, they had assumed control when the Irish parliament met on February 5. Basing their actions on the constitutional realities that since 1782 only the Irish parliament could legislate for Ireland, and that the crown was the only link between the two countries, not "a new

---

70 *Times,* Jan. 30, Feb. 11, 1789; *St. James's Chronicle,* Feb. 7-10, 1789; Burke MSS, Sheff., the Prince to Burke, n. d., but marked received Feb. 8, 1789.
71 Osborn Coll., Box 74, #25, Burke to Thomas Burgh, Feb. 24, 1789.
72 Feb. 21-24, 1789; *Times, passim,* late Feb., 1789.

executive authority, invented by a British Administration for its own purposes," they had passed an address to the prince requesting him to assume the regency with full jurisdiction and prerogatives.[73] Burke approved of this procedure, though he did not think the victory presaged opposition control in Ireland.[74] When the Lord Lieutenant refused to transmit the address, Grattan proposed the appointment of a delegation to present it to the prince in London. Charlemont was a member. The mission was a pitiful thing. Even before it left Ireland, the king's recovery was public knowledge. Officially, all that could be done was to record in the journals of the Irish Commons that the prince had received the address and had extended proper civilities to the delegates. The possibility of two incompatible regencies evaporated.

While the delegates were in London, Burke and his friends had to show them honor. Dispirited, they could only do it privately. On March 1 Earl Spencer was host to the delegates, the prince, the Duke of York, Portland and Devonshire, Fox, Sheridan, and Burke; on the next day the same group dined at Carlton House; on March 3 they gathered in Grosvenor Square at Lord Fitzwilliam's; two days later the Duke of York gave a dinner, and later in the evening the company supped at Devonshire House in Piccadilly.[75] The members of this unhappy group must have grown tired of one another's company. At last on March 12 the Irish delegation received the prince's final answer to their address. Burke was at Carlton House for this occasion and the delegation's leave-taking.[76] The Irish Commons received back their delegates, accepted the prince's answer, and salved their pride by passing Charlemont's resolution that the Irish parliament had a right to designate Ireland's regent.[77]

The rest was aftermath. The *Times* (March 3, 1789) reported that the firm of F——, B——, S—— and Company had gone bankrupt

73 The quotation is from Harlow, *The Second British Empire*, I, 617.

74 Osborn Coll., Box 74, #25, Burke to Thomas Burgh, Feb. 24, 1789; Prior, *Burke* (3d ed.), 310, Burke to Charlemont, April 4, 1789. The little that is known of an understanding between Fox and Grattan suggests that if Fox came into power, Grattan and his friends would control Ireland. Harlow, *The Second British Empire*, I, 621-22.

75 *Times*, March 2, 3, 1789; *Daily Advertiser*, March 2, 3, 4, 6, 1789.

76 *Daily Advertiser*, March 13, 1789.

77 Burke MSS, N.R.O., Aii68, Charlemont to Burke, March 24, 1789.

and was selling out its stock of goods, including eighty new blue and buff patriotic frocks. Men continued to talk about the regency and to seek or evade retributions. The prince and the Duke of York were angry over their mother's protective attitude toward the convalescing king; Burke and his friends even met to consider whether political action was warranted. Burke favored strong measures, but, said Lady Elliot, cooler heads in the party rejected his bad advice.[78] If Burke's name, said the *Times,* was stricken from the list of privy councilors in retaliation for his conduct during the crisis, his "Sublime Highness" would retire to a Capuchin convent.[79]

The nation welcomed the king's recovery, thereby manifesting the prince's unpopularity. The procession to St. Paul's for the thanksgiving services on April 23 and the illuminations and celebrations were genuine expressions of public joy. Pitt was the beneficiary. The opposition were weakened and discredited, no member among them more than Burke.[80] He deserved pity, "poor man, whose faculties are in some measure deranged."[81]

The opposition almost deserved their fate. They had created and exacerbated their own difficulties. They erred in the beginning when they raised the question of right. If they expected the prince to dismiss Pitt and bring them into office, they should not have given Pitt the opportunity to delay proceedings. The opposition made themselves appear inconsistently the advocates of the prerogative to be used by the prince for their selfish purposes. They enabled Pitt to stand forth simultaneously as the protector of the rights of parliament and the defender of the royal prerogative in the interest of George III.

Burke's position was not altogether illogical. When he asserted the prince's claim to the regency as heir apparent, Burke was defending the hereditary principle.[82] He was not discussing the nature and extent of the prerogative power. If there was no

78 Minto, *Elliot,* I, 290, Elliot to Lady Elliot, March 28, 1789; Lady Elliot to Elliot, April 3, 1789.
79 April 22, 1789.
80 Br. Mus., Add. MSS 28,310, fol. 36, Hawkesbury to Cornwallis, April 22, 1789; Wraxall, *Memoirs,* V, 316.
81 *Times,* May 8, 1789.
82 *Corr.,* III, 399, Burke to William Weddell, Jan. 31, 1789.

intention to name anyone but the prince, it was useless to talk about parliament's power to choose as regent anyone it pleased; if parliament could exercise such a right for political reasons, then indeed the hereditary monarchy was in danger. Parliament's proper course, in Burke's view, was forthwith to name the prince as regent and ask him to assume the administration. In taking this position, Burke was not denying his earlier career. In his attacks upon the prerogative in 1782-1784 he never questioned the hereditary principle; in 1788-1789, in asserting the sacredness of the principle, he was not obligating himself to hold the prerogative sacrosanct. England still has a hereditary monarchy even though the sovereign exercises the prerogative powers only upon the advice of ministers.

When in the French Revolution Burke championed hereditary monarchy and the constitution of king, Lords, and Commons, he was acting consistently. His ardent defense of monarchy after 1789 was quite separate from the question of the prerogative. What was important in the 1790's was to preserve the institution itself. The prerogative and the relationships among crown and parliament and ministers could wait for settlement in calmer times. And for his defense of the hereditary principle during the French Revolution, George III was deeply grateful.[83]

[83] Butterfield, *Cambridge Historical Journal*, IX, 294.

PART TWO

The French Revolution

CHAPTER XII

The Making of a Philosopher

IN THE PREFACE to the first of these two volumes on Burke and the nature of politics, it is said that had he died before the French Revolution, we would not think of him as a political philosopher. His career until 1789 was that of a party politician, though an unusual one. His opponents admitted his learning; they caricatured him as a scholarly figure; they acknowledged his mastery of prose style. His abilities supported the accepted idea of him as a philosophical politician who could raise debates to the level of generalization and bring facts within the compass of principle and historical perspective.

In the issues that he discussed before the French Revolution, Burke had identified some of these principles. The domestic conflicts had raised questions about the nature of the political, constitutional, and social order of England. By his contributions to the debates on these questions, Burke had committed himself to the ideal of a hierarchical social order knowing degree and rank but admitting of social mobility—a political order in which the minority exercised power as a trust for the protection of the liberty and property of all people, a constitutional order in which liberties appropriate to men's stations in life were protected by institutional arrangements comprising a limited monarchy, an independent judiciary, and a sovereign parliament. Such a constitutional system was a golden mean between royal absolutism of the kind that the men of 1688 had feared and a democracy of the kind that parliamentary reform might bring. Burke abhorred both extremes because they had tyrannical potentialities. Touching all parts of the political, constitutional, and social orders was the principle of establishment. Religion was the basis of civil society, and an established religion was the fitting and necessary expression of social unity, civic harmony, and moral consensus. The three orders, founded upon religion, were aspects of the total moral order of human society.

Such a society had as its object the good,—that is, justice. Because God had created and ruled the universe, there was an eternal principle, a universal law, a perfect moral order, metaphysical in nature, within which existed the historical, mundane, and, by definition the imperfect, social order. Man, a finite creature, was incapable of perfection, but not of improvement. Right reason and his religious conscience enabled man to possess the idea of perfection and to distinguish between good and evil, justice and injustice. It was man's duty to strive for the one and oppose the other. The politician, the public man, the member of parliament, the king's minister held an imposing trust. And if he governed an empire like the British, which included people of diverse histories, traditions, customs, and social dispositions, the trust was the more imposing and the more difficult to fulfill.

It is evident from his writings and speeches that Burke thought the eighteenth-century order that he knew either approximated this ideal or was susceptible of improvements that would enable men to approach more closely to it. The principles of that order were sound. They had been formed through history and experience, and they had been tested by crises. If injustice still existed, as in Ireland or India or in England, it was not so much because the structures and the assumptions were defective as because men had failed to fulfill their trusts, to keep steadily in view the end of social aspiration, which was justice. Burke's career had been dedicated to teaching men their duties as the trustees of power, and to bringing about modifications in the political and constitutional structures that would enable public men to perform their duties.

Although these thoughts are found in Burke's pre-Revolutionary expressions, the historian or the student of political philosophy would not be deeply concerned about them if Burke had not lived to witness the French Revolution and express himself about it. Indeed, it is from his writings on the French Revolution that the student looks backward to Burke's other works and finds in them meanings that otherwise would escape him or would seem to have only secondary importance. The *Reflections on the Revolution in France* (1790) and later writings gave Burke his stature as a political philosopher. His early essays, the *Sublime and Beautiful* and the *Vindication of Natural Society,* were important in themselves, but not as important as they became when their author became known as the author of the *Reflections.* The *Sublime* revealed the nature of Burke's mind. The *Vindication,* quite consistently with the *Sublime,* exposed his hostility to the rationalism, the materialism and secularism, and the perfectionism—the unhistorical, social engineering of the philosophers, whom he called political metaphysicians. In his occasional political tracts from the 1760's to 1789 he expressed the doctrines of the natural law, of the moral order of the universe, and of the religiously oriented and historically developed social order. In such an order morality was based not upon opinions, which constantly change, but upon the whole nature of man, which is always and everywhere the same. The nature of man being fundamentally religious, as Burke would emphasize in the *Reflections,* it followed that morality had its basis in religion. But none of these earlier writings, nor all of them, would support the reputation as a political thinker that Burke earned by his writings on the French Revolution.

That is why the appearance of the *Reflections* is the moment for discussion of Burke's political philosophy. This is not to say that Burke's political thought had not been formed before 1790 but that he had given only partial expression to it before that time.

The crisis of the Revolution, in fact, forced Burke to become a political philosopher, that is, to expound within a single book the ideas that he had earlier acquired and formulated but had never set forth in comprehensive fashion. To Burke, the Revolution was the consequence of ideas, of the false principles that he had been resisting for the preceding thirty years.[1] The man who published the *Vindication* in 1756 was well prepared to discern

1 The debate over the causes of the Revolution is an old one. Whether Burke attributed too much to the influence of ideas is another question.

very early the nature and the dangers of a Revolution that, as he said as early as October, 1789, had Voltaire and Rousseau for its legislators. If ideas stimulated the Revolution, and if it propagated false ones, then it was necessary to oppose them by expounding sound ones. The times and the crisis called out the philosopher in Burke.

Burke's revolutionary writings had a broader meaning than his previous tracts, except for the *Sublime* and the *Vindication*. If before 1789 Burke had assumed a natural law and a moral order in the universe, his references had been in relation to particular problems—America, Ireland, or India. But the French Revolution was an event of greater significance. It had a universality unique among all of the problems that Burke had encountered. The Christian community of Western civilization felt most immediately the impact of the principles of the French Revolution. But as the history of the nineteenth century demonstrated, Burke was correct in thinking the Revolution a pivotal event in modern history.

Not only the quality and the content of Burke's revolutionary writings, then, raised him to the level of a political philosopher, but also the importance of the crisis absorbing him. Burke's writings on the Revolution make his thought a subject of interest to the twentieth century because our age experiences still the influence of the French Revolution.

CHAPTER XIII

The Challenge to Civilization

ON JULY 10, 1789, two days after the conclusion of the second installment of the Hastings impeachment and four days before the storming of the Bastille in Paris, Burke wrote to Lord Charlemont a kind of valedictory: "There is a time of life in which, if a man cannot arrive at a certain degree of authority derived from a confidence from the prince or the people which may aid him in his operations and make him compass usefull objects without a perpetual struggle, it becomes him to remit much of his activity."[1] With the end of the Regency crisis, which revealed the lack of popular confidence that Burke mentioned, vanished the momentary prospect of better political fortune. The impeachment remained Burke's only public commitment. However it ended, having fulfilled his self-imposed duty to mankind, he would withdraw into the rural retirement that political discouragements, declining health, advancing age, and undiminished abuse made attractive to him.

Abuse, his companion from the beginning of his parliamentary career, was now mixed with a form of derisive pity for an old, defeated man. It is not easy to believe that Burke could shrug off newspaper attacks because they came from sources that he considered corrupt and uninfluential.[2] The cumulative effect of abuse in the press and in the House of Commons must have been considerable over a period of years. When Wilberforce told the Commons that he had heard Burke speak "in *his better days*";

when Pitt added that Burke's "temper was gone with his character"; when a "Country Gentleman" accused him of prostituting his talents in the service of a despicable faction; when a handbill was posted at Whitehall reporting, like a medical bulletin, that Burke was "calmer this morning but tendency towards unquietness"; when it was said that his fame had fallen, "never more to rise"; when he was called a bore, soured and senile—he must have felt the vituperation more keenly because it played on a new theme, the approaching end of his parliamentary career.[3]

Throughout the year 1789 nothing occurred to give Burke a lift of spirits. Until autumn the Hastings impeachment, the summer's farming at Gregories, and party business engaged his attention. So that he would be constantly reminded of the impeachment, quipped the *Times,* he gave Indian names to his farm servants.[4] With Burke among them, party members were thinking much of politics and the inevitable election that all believed Pitt would call in 1790. The activities of individual members and of groups within the party revealed this interest. The Whig Club, founded in 1784, was little more than the Portland Whigs in another guise, a faction motivated by self-interest, said Henry Beaufoy.[5] The club still smarted from the satires provoked by its decision at the meeting of November 4, 1788, the anniversary of the birthday of William III, to erect a commemorative pillar at Runnymede.[6] Burke was a member of the committee, which never completed its assignment. The club, which met each month to serve as a kind of Portland caucus, and to plan recruiting maneuvers, continued to be active. It inspired the founding in 1789 of a Whig Club in Dublin to help keep the Irish opposition together after the debacle of the Regency crisis.[7] The need for extraordinary efforts to improve internal harmony and gain seats in the Commons of both England and Ireland

1 H.M.C., *Charlemont,* 101.

2 Mrs. G. A. Bell, ed., *The Hamwood Papers* (London, 1930), I, 257-59, Burke to Lady E. C. Butler and Lady Sarah Ponsonby, July 30, 1790.

3 *Morning Chronicle,* Feb. 6, 1787; *Times,* Feb. 19, Aug. 3, 1789, Jan. 18, 1790; George, *Catalogue of Satires,* VI, 608.

4 July 31, 1789.

5 *Morning Chronicle,* Nov. 8, 1788.

6 *St. James's Chronicle,* Nov. 20-22, 1788.

7 Burke MSS, Sheff., Charlemont to Burke, July 4, 1789.

had been demonstrated by recent events. On January 3, 1789, for example, in what was as nearly a party vote as this period witnessed, Grenville beat Sir Gilbert Elliot in a contest for the speakership, 215-144.

The Portland party continued to associate itself with the Prince of Wales during the summer and autumn. On June 5 Burke and Fox were with him at Carlton House, probably to discuss the continued split within the royal family.[8] Late in August, 1789, the prince attended the York races, as much for political purposes as for the racing. The Portland party, the "Newmarket Jockies," made every race meeting a Whig rally where the party standard was set up. Lord Fitzwilliam was the host in Yorkshire. There were dinners, theater parties, political meetings, and rounds of visits, and most of the party leaders were present, though not Burke. The prince and his friends had a happy time; there were plenty of women and gambling tables, according to the *Times,* and the proper arrangements were made to ensure that the prince's horses won.[9]

There were other political influences to be courted. Burke, as a practical politician, was especially solicitous about the Protestant Dissenters, a "sharp and eager description of men" who were "powerful enough in many things, but most of all in elections."[10] If the Whigs could not win their support, they ought to take advantage of every opportunity to "neutralize the acid" of the Dissenters. Burke was anxious to oblige Joseph Priestley, whose desires to dedicate some scientific publications to the Prince of Wales had not been communicated to him by Fox. Burke urged Fox to push forward the business; Priestley was an eminent scientist and, more to the point, a leader among the Dissenters. The request, a "strong overt act" of reconciliation after the coolness of 1784, ought to be honored. Apparently, Burke did not trust Fox to attend to the favor and wrote to the prince himself. The prince responded graciously, begging Burke to explain to Priestley that the neglect was merely an oversight.[11]

Burke's concern about the Dissenters arose from his regard for

8 *Times,* June 6, 1789; *Daily Advertiser,* June 6, 1789.
9 Aug. 31, 1789. See also the *Times* for Aug. 21, 26-29, and 31, 1789.
10 Russell, *Fox,* II, 359-60, Burke to Fox, Sept. 9, 1789.
11 Burke MSS, Sheff., Capt. Payne to Burke, Sept. 28, 1789.

their numbers and influence, that is, from political expediency, not from deep sympathy or friendship. In 1787 he had neither spoken nor voted on Henry Beaufoy's motion to repeal the Test and Corporation Acts, partly because he was still piqued at Dissenting criticism of him in 1784.[12] In 1789, when Beaufoy repeated his effort, a Bristol Committee solicited Burke's support.[13] If he attended the House, Burke promised to vote for the bill, in conformity with his "known principles," but he was ill and so deeply involved in trying to serve the "cause of humanity" in India that he could give no promises. He took this position even though he knew certain Dissenters and was aware of their political influence. That influence, he added in a note of May 9, explaining his failure to attend the Commons, had been made clear when the Dissenters did not support Fox in 1784. These memories prompted Burke in September, 1789, to urge Fox to court the Dissenters.

This incident reveals the politician in Burke. Electoral victory was worth almost any effort. Burke could have had no illusions about the basic disagreement between his principles and the Dissenters', or the danger of placing the party under obligation for their electoral influence. Even more significant was his indifference or obliviousness to Dissenting sympathy for the French Revolution. That the Dissenters had not yet expressed it vehemently does not excuse Burke from being aware that the affinity had to exist. The only explanation is that up to this time the Revolution had made upon Burke no stronger an impression than the doubts he expressed in letters of August and September.

Other sources reinforce this impression. Burke had never concealed his distaste—indeed, dislike—for France. During thirty years as a journalist and a member of parliament he had often shown distrust and antipathy toward the historic rival and enemy of the British Empire. Judging from his reticence during the preceding year and in the six months following the convocation of the Estates-General, it appears that Burke gave little thought to the

---

12 Burke MSS, Sheff., Burke to Richard Bright, May 8, 1789; Joseph E. McCabe, "The Attitude of Edmund Burke (1729-1797) toward Christianity and the Churches" (Unpublished thesis, University of Edinburgh, 1951), 191. President McCabe kindly permitted me to read his personal copy of the thesis.
13 Burke MSS, Sheff., Richard Bright to Burke, May 5, 1789.

meaning of an event that was the first of its kind in 175 years, or to the actions of the Third Estate when the assemblage took place. Allowing even for his discouragement and mental depression, it is remarkable that the man who later was to see so much more in the French Revolution than his contemporaries, whose life was to be so completely transformed by it, and whose reputation, in the end, was to depend so heavily upon his reaction to the Revolution, should have been so indifferent to its early stages. The contrast between his attitude and the excitement of Fox and Sheridan is striking. Perhaps Sir Gilbert Elliot's light-hearted comment in the fall of 1788 expressed Burke's mood during the following year.[14] The distresses of the French were almost amusing, said Elliot, and if they remained confined to the court and kept France from disturbing the peace of her neighbors, then there might be no cause for alarm.

The one person in contact with him during the preceding year who was greatly stirred by events in France and may have communicated with Burke about them was the American, Tom Paine. But even about this there is no epistolary evidence. Paine had introduced himself to Burke—or rather, had been introduced by letters from Henry Laurens and from a secretary of Cardinal de Brienne—when he arrived in England early in September, 1787.[15] Besides promoting his iron bridge, Paine was working for peace between England and France. The problem of foreign relations as Burke saw it at that time involved a basic British interest that would be best served by being always wary of France and by counteracting her influence wherever she tried to extend it. At the moment she was trying to do this in the Low Countries. Burke approved Pitt's policy of checking French ambitions by seeking friendship with Prussia and supporting the Stadholder.[16] If by opposing direct negotiations with France, Burke disagreed with Paine's ideas, no coolness developed.

A year later, after returning from France, Paine visited Gregories and undoubtedly discussed his trip. Burke took "the great American Paine" to dine with him at Portland's nearby estate.[17]

14 Burke MSS, Sheff., Elliot to Burke, Sept. 28, 1788.
15 Alfred Owen Aldridge, *Man of Reason* (Philadelphia, 1959), 120-21.
16 *Parl. Hist.*, XXVI, 1273-74.
17 MS in Harvard Library, Burke to John Wilkes, Aug. 18, 1788.

In October, when Paine was in Yorkshire on business, Burke met him there and introduced him to Lord Fitzwilliam.[18] Paine was not boasting when he spoke of his "intimacy" with the leaders of the parliamentary opposition. He preferred Burke and his friends to the administration, because he disliked Pitt and his foreign policy.

The Regency crisis interested Paine. He predicted an early change of governments, to be followed by better Anglo-American relations and improved prospects for general peace.[19] It is curious to find that the man who later wrote the republican tract *The Rights of Man* echoed Burke's contention for the prince's right to the regency and attacked Pitt's assertions about the authority of parliament.[20]

In correspondence with Jefferson who was in Paris, Paine received information about the Revolution. He may have passed it on to Burke. But the old story is not true that he immediately included, in a letter of his own, Jefferson's famous letter of July 11, 1789.[21] Paine did not write to Burke until January 17, 1790, and it was that letter that contained the excerpt from Jefferson's.[22] So far as the extant correspondence reveals, Paine had nothing to do with Burke's original doubts over the French Revolution. But the letter of January 17, in conjunction with other events, had a strong influence upon Burke at a crucial time.[23]

It was during the last months of 1789 that Burke's views on the Revolution took firm shape. More than any previous revolutionary event, the fall of the Bastille aroused his interest, and that is as much as can be said about it. Not until August 9 did he express any opinion about the Revolution, and then he was neither hostile nor passionate.[24] He was uncertain whether "to blame or to applaud." When he called it a "French struggle for liberty," he seemed to be admitting that the old regime needed

18 Copeland, *Our Eminent Friend Edmund Burke*, 156-57.

19 Aldridge, *Man of Reason*, 123.

20 Aldridge, *Man of Reason*, 124.

21 This episode is described in Copeland, *Our Eminent Friend Edmund Burke*, chap. V, and with an important correction, by Aldridge, *Man of Reason*, 127-30.

22 Burke MSS, N.R.O., Aiv73a, a copy. Also a copy in Osborn Coll., Box 74, #24A.

23 Robert A. Smith, "Edmund Burke's Crusade against the French Revolution" (Unpublished dissertation, Yale University, 1955), 106-10, ascribes even greater influence to this letter.

24 H.M.C., *Charlemont*, 106, Burke to Lord Charlemont.

reforming. But he was not sure whether in France there was sufficient "wisdom," combined with "authority," to restrain the "spirit" that prompted the attack upon the Bastille. If that outburst of "the old Parisian ferocity" was "character rather than accident," if it meant the absence of the "natural moderation" that kept freedom orderly, then Burke was ready to doubt whether France would form a "solid constitution." "What will be the event, it is hard, I think, still to say." Burke was not an enemy of the Revolution from its outset; he could easily become one if subsequent events enabled him to decide between "character" and "accident." Burke had never shown much confidence in the political wisdom of Frenchmen of any description. His later sympathy for the victims of the Revolution and his preference for them over the Revolutionaries was more a reaction against the Revolution than a long-standing admiration for the people who governed pre-Revolutionary France.

Six weeks later his judgment was considerably more formed. The events of late July and August, the formation of the National Guard and the Commune of Paris, the "Great Fear," the famous session of August 4, and the issuance of the Declaration of the Rights of Man revealed more of the "character" of the Revolution. Unlike Windham, who had just returned from Paris predicting the peaceful adoption of a new constitution, Burke was unwilling to believe that the Revolution was nearly ended.[25] He was not jesting when he expressed relief over Windham's *"safe"* return from "the Land of Liberty." The security of everyone was uncertain in a country where, as he said sarcastically, people had thrown off "the Yoke of Laws and Morals." Doubtless a paper constitution could be written, but whether the government it provided for could command obedience, especially in matters of taxation, would be another matter. The National Assembly appeared to be omnipotent only because it was engaged in a work of destruction and because no armed royalist party existed to oppose it. As Lefebvre has said, it was obeyed "on condition that it agreed with public opinion."[26] No constituent assembly, said Burke,

[25] Burke MSS, Sheff., Windham to Burke, Sept. 25, 1789; Br. Mus., Add. MSS 37,843, fols. 15-16, Burke to Windham, Sept. 27, 1789.
[26] Georges Lefebvre, *The French Revolution from its Origins to 1793* (London, 1962), 134.

could create institutions to replace the ones it had destroyed; time, history, and experience, not legislative decrees, formed governments. This letter assumes significance as a prediction of conflicts to come and a suggestion of the theme of the *Reflections on the Revolution in France.*

Still more clearly in October and November Burke perceived the ominous "character" that he feared. Popular discontent, provoked by intimations of a royalist reaction and an aristocratic conspiracy, was inflamed by economic crisis. When a "mentality of insurrection" again expressed itself in an appeal to arms, the "character" of the Revolution was "transformed" into a "civil war."[27]

By this time, in response to the request of his young friend Charles Jean François DePont, Burke was ready to hazard some reflections upon the Revolution.[28] DePont, only twenty-three years old, had learned to admire Burke during his visit to Gregories with his father in 1785. Enthusiastic about the prospects for greater liberty in France, he hoped that Burke would be able to "assure him that the French are worthy of being free, that they know how to distinguish liberty from license," and that "the Revolution now begun will succeed." Burke's long reply, like his letters to Charlemont and Windham, was restrained. The absence of passion suggests that into November, 1789, Burke neither hated nor feared the Revolution. He expressed himself cautiously; the deficiency of his knowledge about the "political map" of France forbade "a positive opinion." At this stage, therefore, he hoped DePont would not read disapproval into his doubt and hesitation.

DePont had asked for his thoughts on liberty. Of course the French were "deserving" of it. Men only forfeited their "right" to it when they abused it by ceasing to act as rational creatures. Burke defined liberty as *"social* freedom" under "wise laws" and

27 Lefebvre, *French Revolution,* 116. It is interesting to notice the stress that Lefebvre, like Burke, placed upon the "character" of the Revolution.

28 Burke MSS, N.R.O., DePont to Burke, Nov. 4, 1789; *Corr.,* III, 102-21, Burke to DePont, after Nov. 4, 1789. The editors of *Corr.* assigned Burke's letter to the wrong person. For the learned discussion that settles the identity of DePont, establishes him as the person to whom Burke addressed the *Reflections,* and distinguishes him from Pierre-Gaëton Dupont, who translated the *Reflections,* see Somerset, *English,* VIII, 171-78. See also Schmitt and Weston, *Journal of Modern History,* XXIV, 406-407; Copeland, *Our Eminent Friend Edmund Burke,* chap. VI.

"well-constructed institutions," in a society where the *"will"* of any man or group cannot be "set above reason and justice." If France developed a constitutional order that combined security of life and property with freedom of expression and opportunity for the individual, so that a representative legislature and an independent judiciary could responsibly and without coercion fulfill their trusts to the people, then she would "most merit the applause of all discerning men." This was neither a unique nor an imaginative description; it came straight from Burke's reading of English history. Burke thought that the "name or form" of the kind of government he described was a matter of indifference. If—and he was uncertain of this—in France a "democracy, or rather collection of democracies" became "the future frame of society," he as a citizen of a "qualified monarchy" would not withhold approval, provided the substance of liberty was preserved.

So much for ideals. But Burke was uneasy. France "may be yet to go through more transmigrations." He wished the National Assembly would pay less attention to "theories" of the rights of man and more to "man in the concrete." He did not approve of separating the "merits of any political question" from the men who were to give effect to it. Morality, honor, and "common liberal sentiment" deserved greater respect. Except as a last extremity, men should not create new evils in trying to remove existing ones. There might be some "positively vicious and abusive government" that could be changed only by violent means, yet it seldom was true that reform required resort to extreme measures. Men need not aim at perfection; indeed, by their nature, "human contrivances" fall short of perfection. An "imperfect good" is a good containing defects. Given time, the political virtues of prudence and moderation would help men to remove defects in the constitutional order.

This letter, as nearly a concise statement of his principles of political conduct as anything Burke ever wrote, falls naturally into two parts. The first, describing the ideal representative, constitutional order, drew its inspiration from English experience. Those difficult words "liberal" and "conservative" are irrelevant. Burke was describing the good society, and defining justice. In the second part of the letter he applied to a given historical situation the rules of prudence, expressing concern with the concrete and the practicable, admitting the complexity of society and the limitations of men, and recommending willingness to work with the materials at hand to attain a feasible common good. Burke did not like the signs he saw in France. The French were resorting to means that would make difficult the attainment of the object they sought for. In pursuit of a chimera, "theoretical perfection," they were disregarding prudence and moderation. Their revolution did not seem to be achieving a reformation. In subverting a government they did not seem to be recovering freedom. Burke felt sorrow and regret because instead of turning their opportunities for reformation to good purpose, the French were preferring "the full perfection of the abstract idea."

The most remarkable thing about this letter is its indecisiveness. For over thirty years Burke had felt and occasionally expressed hostility to the doctrines of the *philosophes*. But his contact with them had been only in their literary formulation. Only in the abstract or as theoretical propositions had he been able to fear the consequences of materialistic rationalism, of secularism, of the emphasis upon natural rights, of the perfectionist theories of human self-sufficiency, and of the contempt implied in them for history, prescription, tradition, and revealed religion. By November, 1789, there was sufficient evidence at hand, for example in the Declaration of the Rights of Man, to justify the view that the French Revolution was inspired and informed by principles of the nature of man and society that Burke had always considered false. If that was true, then it is surprising that Burke's early reaction to the Revolution was so mild, and that it would be a while longer before he became violent against a Revolution that boasted Voltaire and Rousseau as its legislators. If the principles underlying the Revolution were so dangerous as Burke later asserted, he should not have had to await events to confirm the fact. He should have been eager to attack the Revolution the moment its ideological foundations were revealed. That Burke discerned them earlier than most persons does not modify the contention that if his philosophy was formed even before the Revolution, he should have been alert to danger earlier than he was.

The conclusion is inescapable that Burke's former hostility to the "political metaphysicians" had been to a great extent rhetorical. Neither in the American Revolution nor in the problems of Ireland and India had he seen them at work, though he talked about them. He had viewed the American problem, for example, as one of imperial, constitutional relationships and practical administrative grievances, not as a great ideological assault upon an established social order. He had, therefore, never physically encountered the philosophy he detested until the French Revolution. His dislike of that philosophy had never been tested in the world of practical politics or international relations. His reticence and hesitation up to the end of 1789 were the products of uncertainty, and the uncertainty endured until the shock of events transformed it. Events clarified his thinking, removed his indecisiveness, and enabled him to make up his mind about the evils and dangers of the Revolution. Even parliamentary reform became a different kind of problem than it had been in the early 1780's.

Burke came to understand in the winter of 1789-1790 the difference between theories of man and society as intellectual exercises and as the springs of actions, the events being more inexorably the consequences of ideas than his experience had ever before revealed to him. That is why, in the end, he had to write the *Reflections.* For the first time in his career he found it necessary to expound fully a philosophy that formerly he had expressed at random, in scattered passages and allusions in his comments on the problems he had encountered along the way. In that sense, Burke as a thinker matured under the traumatic impact of the Revolution when events demonstrated what formerly he had believed but never experienced. Of necessity he at last became a philosopher, opposing to one theory of man and society another whose ultimate reference was no more susceptible of empirical verification than the one he attacked.

The events that transformed Burke into the anti-Revolution philosopher were already occurring at the time he wrote to DePont. They removed remaining doubts about the character of the Revolution and taught him to regard it as an assault upon England and upon the moral basis of the Christian order of Europe. By the early part of 1790 it had become a monstrous, immoral thing, in fundamental conflict with the social order Burke knew. Henceforth he could think of the Revolution only with fear, disgust, and implacable hostility.

The first of these events occurred in Paris on November 2, 1789, when the National Assembly took over the estates of the church, that is, put them "at the nation's disposal." At first, Burke reacted against the financial plans based upon the church and crown lands, though he did not predict outright disaster, and to Philip Francis he was willing to concede that they might work.[29] But during the next few months additional measures of the National Assembly made it clear to Burke that the first action had been more than an expedient intended to relieve a financial crisis; it was the first part of a systematic confiscation of property and a basic reorganization of the ecclesiastical life of France. The suppression of the religious orders in February promised that the secular clergy would be dealt with soon thereafter.

In England there were people who not only sympathized with the French Revolutionaries but were urging England to imitate them, or so Burke understood the reform enthusiasts. One man seemed to Burke to speak for all of them. He was Dr. Richard Price, the eminent dissenting minister who, on November 4, preached to the Revolution Society the celebrated sermon *A Discourse on the Love of Our Country.* Price saw and hailed the French Revolution as "the beginning of the reformation of the governments of Europe."[30] This was the theme of his sermon, an exhortation to complete the work of reform implied but left unfinished by the Revolution of 1688. He asked for disestablishment of the Anglican Church, religious freedom, and parliamentary reform; urged his dissenting colleagues to strive for these goals; and warned the rulers of Europe, and England, to "Restore to mankind their rights; and consent to the correction of abuses, before they and you are destroyed together." After the sermon, the Revolution Society sent to the National Assembly a congratulatory address moved by Dr. Price. The society, wishing

[29] Burke MSS, N.R.O., Axiv74a, Burke to Fitzwilliam, Nov. 12, 1789; *Corr.,* III, 121-22, Burke to Francis, Dec. 11, 1789.

[30] Quoted from a letter of Price to Jefferson, July 12, 1789, cited in Carl B. Cone, *Torchbearer of Freedom* (Lexington, Ky., 1952), 179.

the Revolution well, were happy to see France encouraging other nations to assert the rights of mankind and to reform their governments.

Burke's reaction to Price's sermon was not immediate. He was at Gregories when it was delivered and had not read it in its pamphlet form when later he came to town and dined with Walker King and some others, including certain Dissenters.[31] He was still seeking their electoral support. One of them told him that the Dissenters could never be reconciled to the Whigs as long as Fox led them. Burke responded heatedly, and after a long, unpleasant conversation, in which he defended Fox and the party, he went home and read Price's sermon. He found it shocking, both for its attack upon Fox and for its "seditious principles." A subsequent conversation with Sheridan strengthened Burke's animus against the Dissenters, though he had yet no idea of the extent to which their principles were infecting his own party.

But he was already angry at them and fearful when, in a letter of December 29, DePont referred to the "authority" of the Revolution Society's approval of the Revolution, explained away violence in France as a necessary preliminary to reformation, asked Burke for charitable judgments, and again urged him to "write me a few words on the subject."[32] Without trying to be secretive, Burke at once began a letter, which he hoped to publish in the spring.[33] His object was limited, and is suggested by the title which was advertised in the *London Chronicle* of February 16, 1790, and the *Times* of February 20.[34] Already in the press and "soon" to be published by Dodsley, it would be called "Reflections on certain proceedings of the Revolution Society of the Fourth of November, 1789, concerning the affairs of France, in a letter from the Right Honourable Edmund Burke, to a Gentleman in Paris."

A comparison between this title and that of the work published (not in the spring, but on November 1, 1790) indicates, as Burke

[31] *Corr.*, III, 394-97, Burke to William Weddell, Jan. 31, 1792.
[32] Burke MSS, N.R.O., Aiia. Burke had not sent the Nov. letter.
[33] See Burke's preface to the *Reflections*.
[34] The notice in the *London Chronicle* is quoted in Bertram Newman, *Edmund Burke* (London, 1927), 207n.

said in his preface, that the subject gained upon him as he wrote and its "importance required rather a more detailed considera- tion. . . ." The title eventually became "Reflections on the Revolution in France *and* on the Proceedings in Certain Societies in London relative to that Event: in a Letter *intended to have been sent* [italics added] to a gentleman in Paris." The transposi- tion of priorities is explained by the "expansion" of Burke's sentiments and their turn to "another direction," as he said in his preface, while the word "intended" refers to his decision to retain the epistolary form even though he enlarged the scope of his work.

But these changes do not mean that Dr. Price became a straw man. He and those he spoke for were becoming a dangerous influence in the country. It was not possible to consider the new campaign for repeal of the Test and Corporation acts as a simple renewal of earlier demands for freedom.[35] Among the Dissenters there was now "a faction" proceeding "systematically, to the destruction of this Constitution in some of its essential parts," and there was a settled intention to "draw us into a connexion" with France.

It was at this time that Paine's letter arrived. His description of events in France supported the judgment that the Revolution was not a sequence of spontaneous occurrences. Paine spoke of the National Assembly's "plan" for a complete change in govern- ment. He saw no likelihood of a counterrevolution. The French Revolution was not an isolated phenomenon but a "forerunner" of other revolutions. On reading this, Burke had to conclude that false philosophers were systematically endeavoring to give effect to their dangerous doctrines. A plot in France, a plot in England, and threat of plots elsewhere in Europe—there could no longer be any doubt of the character or the inspiration of the Revolution.

And Burke no longer left doubts of his opinions. It was about

35 Burke MSS, Sheff., Burke to Richard Bright, Feb. 18, 1790. This was a reply to Bright's request for Burke's support in the campaign. Bright to Burke, Feb. 4, 13, 1790. In the Sheff. MSS is a copy of a printed letter from Samuel Fletcher to Thomas Plumbe, Feb. 27, 1790, explaining why he was withdrawing from the Dis- senters' campaign. Repeal was only a first move, he said; an attack upon the Church of England would follow.

this time that he began making himself socially disagreeable, disrupting private gatherings by his passionate attacks upon the Revolution. Whether at a meeting of the committee on Johnson's monument or at the Club, Burke made himself "unpleasant."[36] More serious were the squabbles with his party associates. The *Times* had Burke and Sheridan quarreling at the home of a peer.[37] But it was the debate in the House of Commons on February 9 that signaled the real breach in the party. This was the first public expression of Burke's opinions about the French Revolution.

The subject was the army estimates.[38] Instead of a slight increase, Fox thought the times and the need for economy justified a reduction. France was not a threat to England, and as he had said four days earlier, the recent exemplary conduct of the French soldiers reinforced his confidence. Pitt was also sympathetic to France and hoped that when domestic tranquility returned, she would be a "less obnoxious" neighbor. But like Grenville, he thought the government would be neglecting its duty if it altered the nation's defense establishment every time the wind changed. Up to this point the discussion had been conducted in good temper; Burke changed that and the emphasis of the entire debate.[39] His early remarks, in rebuttal of the government arguments, supported Fox's demand for a reduction while agreeing with all previous speakers that France was not a present military danger. Indeed, he went further than they, doubting that "she might speedily rise again" after the destruction the revolutionaries had accomplished. Though the military power of France was temporarily gone and, with it, danger from an external attack upon England, the "influence and example" of France, made stronger by her proximity, alarmed Burke. In her "present distemper" the threat of a spreading French contagion was imminent. There was "a danger of [England's] being led through an admiration of successful fraud and violence, to an imitation of an irrational, unprincipled, proscribing, confiscating, plundering, ferocious, bloody, and tyrannical democracy. On the

36 Pottle, ed., *Private Papers*, XVIII, 24, 27, Jan. 23, Feb. 2, 1790.
37 Feb. 11, 1790.
38 *Parl. Hist.*, XXVIII, 337-74.
39 His speech, printed in *Parl. Hist.*, XXVIII, 351-63, is also in *Works*, III, 213-30. It was published almost immediately after delivery.

side of religion, the danger of this example is no longer from intolerance, but from atheism."

It was Burke alone who spoke of the danger from ideas and from those in England easily influenced by them. The danger was to the English constitution of king, Lords, Commons, and church, and therefore to the social order of a Christian community. In calling attention to the French distemper, Burke did not mean to associate Fox with those "wicked persons" in England who had already demonstrated their infatuation for France. But he gave fair warning. He "would abandon his best friends, and join with his worst enemies" to resist the contagion of France. He was not an enemy to change or reformation. His entire career refuted the thought. But he would distinguish between reform and changes that, like those in France, "unnecessarily tore to pieces the contexture of the state." Instead of freedom, the French were establishing a democratic species of tyranny under the name of the rights of man and with the aid of those citizen-soldiers whom Fox praised and Paine's letter extolled.

Burke concluded his speech with a reference to his weariness and his desire for a peaceful termination of his political career. This was not to be. In fact, before the evening ended, he experienced the first bitter consequences of the debate over the French Revolution. Fox followed him with a genuinely affecting speech. He praised Burke, acknowledging his debt to the man who had been his political mentor. He denied any great affection for the French Revolution but avowed sympathy for a people struggling for freedom. He hoped that the results of the Revolution would be a blessing for both France and England. Burke responded appreciatively. He knew that Fox disliked "dangerous and unconstitutional procedures"; he only desired to warn England against persons whose enthusiasms were not tempered by the knowledge and judgment of a man such as Fox.

It seemed that the danger of a quarrel had passed when Sheridan picked up the apple of discord and tossed it onto the floor of the House of Commons. He attacked Burke's speech point by point, justified the French Revolution, and gloried in it. His speech was provocative and personal. Burke responded in the same way. He declared an end to both his political association and his friendship with Sheridan. If this breach foreshadowed a larger political divorce, Pitt encouraged it when he picked up a suggestion Burke had made. He defended Burke and acknowledged the similarity of their fundamental beliefs about the British constitution and the French Revolution. This was the first, faint hint of the political realignment that occurred four years later.

The immediate problem was the state of the opposition. Members of the party were appalled at the rift between Burke and Sheridan. But with Portland taking Burke's side and with Derby, Porchester, and Queensbury favoring Sheridan, it was difficult to mend the rift. Sheridan himself made the first concession by calling on Burke.[40] They shook hands and then went to Portland's, where, with Fox, they discussed the quarrel. Burke was the obdurate one, and the conference failed. On February 11, Richard, Jr., represented his father at another meeting at Burlington House and that night still a third was held. Burke remained implacable. Possibly, as Dr. Samuel Parr told Mrs. Sheridan, the rupture had other causes, but they were much less important than the basic disagreement over the French Revolution. About that, Burke had committed himself. Henceforth, his writings, his speeches, and his actions had one great purpose—to persuade England and Europe to join him in opposing the Revolution. Certain favorable reactions to the stand he had taken on February 9 suggested that some people might listen to him.[41]

Within three weeks Burke found another opportunity to discuss the subject that now dominated his thoughts. On March 2, Fox moved the repeal of the Test and Corporation acts.[42] The division on the motion was another indication that the Revolution was reshaping political alignments in England. Fox, conceding the former unpleasant state of his relations with the Dissenters, was happy now to assume, at their request, the management of a business so intimately their concern. He did this because, with the Dissenters, he believed in civil and religious liberty and thought this enlightened age the time to establish it. It was anachronous any longer to consider the church in danger from

40 Sichel, *Sheridan*, II, 202-12; Moore, *Sheridan*, 283-84; *Times*, Feb. 11, 12, 1789, for the rest of this paragraph.
41 Burke MSS, Sheff., Thomas King to Mrs. Burke, March 5, 1790.
42 *Parl. Hist.*, XXVIII, 387-452.

either dissent or popery and it was therefore anachronous to impose religious tests for participation in civil affairs. Although he spoke generously for toleration, Fox made the mistake of dragging in the French Revolution and Dr. Price. He was happy to see a "neighboring nation," returning to "first principles," restore the rights of men. He was pleased to find an "enlightened philosopher" in England rising above "local attachments" to demand freedom for the entire human race. He was sorry that his good friend Burke differed from him on this question. As for himself, Fox would forever stand for liberty, whoever opposed him.

After this it was impossible to debate the motion on its merits. Burke took up Fox's challenge. In 1787 and 1789 he had abstained from voting on this question because he was unable to decide whether an extension of toleration would endanger the principle of establishment.[43] Now he opposed repeal, because changed circumstances made it dangerous. He desired to be fair, and he acknowledged the integrity of Fox. But he feared that Fox was too much influenced by an abstract principle. To Burke, toleration was not a right but a privilege extended by the state. Those who asserted a right of toleration were misled, like the Dissenters, by the vision of natural rights, those original rights that were incompatible with the existence of society. There was neither security nor liberty in the kind of presocial existence that the natural-rights philosophers dreamed of. It was society that, by its laws and institutions, gave security and freedom from oppression. In giving effect to its "great and most beneficial purposes" society had the help of "the church." In England this meant the established church, an instrument, as Burke had said in 1773, as important for contributing to social peace as for conferring spiritual benefits. In times like the present he considered it unwise to do anything under the guise of toleration that would weaken this vital part of the constitutional and social structure of England. Presented briefly in his speech, these were ideas that Burke was incorporating in the *Reflections*, which he was writing at this time.

The remainder of Burke's speech discussed the enemies of the

---

[43] Toward the end of the speech, he said he would have voted for repeal.

church. He cited the works of Priestley, Robert Robinson, and Price in evidence of an intention among some of the Dissenters to destroy the established church.[44] If the House wished to postpone a decision in order to conduct a thorough inquiry, and if it revealed that Burke mistook these Dissenters, then he would "hold himself bound to vote for the repeal." Either he was confident that his offer would not be accepted or he was sure of the accuracy of his judgments. At this time he was enlarging them in written form. The vote against repeal, 294-105, assured him that the *Reflections* would find a large, sympathetic audience.

During this session, on issues that would later become more important, Burke assumed positions that were strongly influenced by his attitudes toward the Revolution. When Flood raised the question of parliamentary reform, he argued for it on the grounds that the inadequacy of representation was a cause of war. Burke rejected the notion that peoples, unlike governments, were naturally pacific.[45] Later, he would be able to use the French Revolution as an illustration of this contention. Burke was chagrined to find his opposition to the Revolution cited as evidence for his abandonment of venerable Whig tenets. He rejected this notion, showing by his support of the proposal to increase the Speaker's allowance that his concern for the Commons' independence and his jealousy of the influence of the crown were as strong as ever.[46] His sympathy for the plight of the royal family in France and his concern for the security of the hereditary monarchy in England were not inconsistent with his steady distrust of the prerogative and his desire to limit the influence of the crown. Already Burke was learning that in opposing the Revolution he was exposing himself to the danger of having his beliefs about the British constitution misrepresented.

By the time the session ended on June 10 a person who had attended to Burke's speeches would be able to anticipate fairly accurately the principles, the substance, and possibly the passion

---

44 Two weeks earlier Burke told Richard Bright that he no longer doubted the existence of "a considerable party . . . proceeding systematically" to the destruction of the Constitution and the Church. *The R. B. Adam Library*, I, 12-13, Feb. 18, 1790.

45 *Parl. Hist.*, XXVIII, 477-78.

46 *Parl. Hist.*, XXVIII, 511.

of the pamphlet he was known to be writing. Even such an attentive listener would not be prepared, however, for the length, the depth of thought, the vivid imagery, and the imaginative interpretations it would reveal. While he was writing it, only a few persons knew how much it was engrossing him. Never before, perhaps, unless when writing the *Thoughts on the Present Discontents,* had he worked so carefully and deliberately. Early in the writing he laid out in brief the order of his ideas and suggested them in words and phrases to serve as keys when later he wrote in full amplitude. The preliminary sketch of the central portion of the *Reflections,* in the hand of Richard, Jr., remains among Burke's papers.[47] When compared with the final form of the pamphlet, it reveals that Burke built the *Reflections* around a central theme. In developing it he adhered closely to his early outline. He emphasized ideas that would evoke an emotional response; faithful to the teaching of the *Sublime and Beautiful,* he was concerned with the feelings of his readers. This concern probably accounts for the hyperbole of the *Reflections* and for the relative unconcern with factual accuracy.

Various letters written between February and October, 1790, also revealed the expansion of his ambitions and the progress of his writing. Some of his sources of information were biased, and as he admitted, his knowledge of events in France was imperfect.[48] But he was not engaged in a work of historical research. It was not the accuracy of all details that he was concerned about. He was combatting a set of pernicious principles, and his task was to set against a false philosophy the true philosophy of the nature of man and society. His success in doing this would determine the value and influence of his work. Before the end of February he had written much of the pamphlet and some of the proof sheets had been sent off. This was, however, about the time he was finding it obligatory to expand the scope of his work. The promise of early publication was annulled.

[47] J. T. Boulton, "*The Reflections:* Burke's Preliminary Draft and Methods of Composition," *Durham University Journal,* n.s., XIV (June, 1953), 114-19. This article suggests that what was true of the central part of the *Reflections* would be true of other parts if preliminary sketches of them were studied. Also Smith, "Burke's Crusade," 159.

[48] Burke MSS, N.R.O., Aiv74, Burke to [?], after Feb. 9, 1790.

He had proceeded far enough to ask Francis' judgment on the portion he had written. Francis' criticisms were frank, reflecting his own opinions and those of mutual friends who were hesitant to be candid.[49] Considering the importance of a work intended for "all Europe," Francis disliked the loose writing and the undiscriminating choice of topics. Did Burke really want to distract himself from the larger issues by engaging in a pamphlet war with Price and the Dissenters? Were sarcasm and insinuation in good taste? Had he sacrificed good sense to emotions when he indulged in "pure foppery" over Marie Antoinette? Francis chose these examples as warnings against inviting controversy and ridicule over insignificant matters. He was not attempting to persuade Burke to abandon his work. He was urging him to be more judicious, to be "grave, direct, and serious," to avoid the ludicrous role of Don Quixote, and to discipline himself severely in performing perhaps "the most distinguished . . . and most deliberate acts" of his life. This was honest advice, and particularly impressive coming from a person who was sympathetic to the Revolution.

Francis must have been both amused and angered at the stupid letter he received next day from Richard, Jr., enclosing a much longer one from his father.[50] Richard felt that Francis had mistaken the "warmth" of his father's manner for the "heat of his mind." He had not written hastily or without deliberation. Everything he said, though "adopted on the spur of the occasion," was nevertheless the result of long meditation and "philosophical experience." Men of lesser minds, like Francis and himself, simply could not comprehend the depth and the direction of Burke's thought. They should realize that "his folly is wiser than the wisdom of the common herd of men." And so Richard asked Francis to desist from "any further written communication of this kind" when there was not time to indulge in leisurely adjustment of opinions. No wonder that Burke's friends detested his son. Francis, having been asked for an honest judgment, was told by young Burke to say nothing if he could not flatter.

Burke's letter was less peevish, though hardly pleasing to

49 *Corr.*, III, 128-32, Feb. 19, 1790.
50 *Corr.*, III, 132-34, and 134-41, both dated Feb. 20, 1790.

Francis. It began humbly enough. Burke appreciated a friend who would "dare" to give him advice and hoped that he could correct whatever there was about his manner that intimidated other friends. Francis should know from experience that his advice was appreciated even if not always accepted. Burke admitted the looseness of composition, but that was appropriate to the epistolary form, which he had decided to continue. He agreed also about the need for stylistic improvement. In the more fundamental matters, the "political opinions and moral sentiments," he had to dissent from Francis' advice. He was aware that he was inviting attack and even ridicule. He knew of the defects of the queen's virtue; must he therefore approve the Revolutionists' treatment of her? He genuinely lamented the decline of chivalry, because it pointed to the decline of manners. He was willing to risk, though he was not intending, controversy with the revolutionaries at home and abroad. He felt compelled to expose the dangers from the "wicked principles" and the "black hearts" of such "calumniators, hypocrites, sowers of sedition, and approvers of murder and all its triumphs." Burke was warm to his task. His friends who disagreed with him might as well remain silent. He was preaching a great crusade.

About this time Burke received a sample of the kind of criticism, though not yet vicious, that Francis had warned against. Captain Thomas Mercer, a new Irish friend, was disturbed to read in the newspapers of Burke's opinions on the Revolution and, somewhat presumptuously, undertook to correct them. Burke replied lengthily to a letter whose contents and author hardly deserved so much attention.[51] The letter is more important for its revelation of Burke's state of mind than for its repetition of earlier remarks about the Revolution. His readiness to reply showed that whatever the intentions he expressed to Francis, he would permit himself to get involved in controversy with persons who disagreed with him. He was condescending and irritated; he spoke to "My dear Captain Mercer"; and he made sarcastic comments about phrases extracted from Mercer's letter. He even challenged Mercer to break off their friendship if their disagree-

---

51 Mercer's letter is in Prior, *Burke* (3d ed.), 344-45, Feb. 19, 1790; Burke's reply in *Corr.*, III, 141-60, Feb. 26, 1790.

ments became too unpleasant. The gist of the letter is contained in the famous statement "The tyranny of a multitude is but a multiplied tyranny," and in the refusal to expect a "mild" settlement of a revolution whose beginning was so "rapacious and bloody."

Despite interruptions occasioned by the demands of attendance in the Commons and the third installment of the impeachment, Burke worked hard to complete the book so eagerly awaited by the public. By mid-April he was submitting portions to his friends. Sir Gilbert Elliot liked it and thought it would do good.[52] Windham read the first part approvingly, though he had some doubts of the fairness of some of Burke's judgments or the accuracy of certain facts.[53]

While busy with his writing, Burke remained attentive to the troubles within his party. The general election in June did not greatly disturb him, though it necessitated a trip to Malton to meet with his agreeable constituents and receive their obedient votes.[54] The election results were less disturbing to the party than the continued disagreements over the French Revolution. Burke and Portland strongly disapproved of the July 14 dinner at the Crown and Anchor, where Sheridan, of the party leaders, met with other enthusiasts, while Burke remained at Beaconsfield, "retouching" the book that would widen the rift in the party.[55] More than other party leaders, Burke had stressed agreement upon principles as a bond of party unity. He did not see how the party could continue to ignore the implications of the existing disagreements or the threats to the constitutional order. More bluntly, this meant that the party could not much longer avoid choosing between Burke and Sheridan, that is, making up their minds about the party stand upon the Revolution.[56] Sheridan's efforts to lead the party into cooperation with the Revolution Society and the parliamentary reformers must be resisted, and quickly, or Fox would succumb to the Piper's revolutionary tunes. Burke, said his son, was full of fears about the future of the

52 Minto, *Elliot*, I, 357, April 24, 1790.
53 Br. Mus., Add. MSS 27,843, fol. 19, Burke to Windham, Oct. 27, 1790.
54 Osborn Coll., Box 74, #23, Jane Burke to Sir Gilbert Elliot, June 11, 1790.
55 *Times*, July 27, 29, 1790.
56 Burke MSS, N.R.O., Aiv71a, Richard, Jr., to Fitzwilliam, July 29, 1790.

party. But better to divide it than to permit the destruction of the constitution.

Through the summer Burke continued to work on his pamphlet, taking notice as time permitted of new events and publications.[57] By early September he had finished it and then took a vacation, visiting Bath and touring the Malvern Hills. Late in October he passed out advance copies among his friends. This printing probably contained errors of fact, which he would correct in later editions. He had written from memory of some documents that he was unable to check at Gregories.[58] A few factual errors would not vitiate the substance or the tenor of the book. He would not admit to making "misrepresentations" or to consciously exaggerating. He was ready to concede an imperfect knowledge of French affairs and for that reason, as well as because he was writing to warn an English audience, he had avoided a detailed account of events in France.[59] But he would stand behind his judgments. He was apologetic to Philip Francis.[60] After their unpleasantness of February, Burke had not submitted any more of his manuscript for Francis' criticisms; there was a basic disagreement between them about the Revolution, and there was no point in irritating the difference.

Even before the book appeared in England, Burke made arrangements for a French translation. The *Times* announced this fact on October 27. His friend, Pierre-Gaëton Dupont, who had the proofs, was already working upon it. In a letter to Burke, he took exception to the description of Henry IV of France.[61] Burke would not soften the language; his portrait of Henry was, he said, "strictly true," and the *Memoirs* of Sully corroborated it.[62] The matter was important, because those who denigrated royal power desired to create an image of Henry that would serve

57 E. g., the letter from Anacharsis Cloots, published as a pamphlet on May 12. Smith, "Burke's Crusade," 173.
58 Br. Mus., Add. MSS 37,843, fol. 19, Burke to Windham, Oct. 27, 1790.
59 Copeland transcript of letter in P.R.O., Burke to Calonne, Oct. 25, 1790. Calonne's *Etat de la France* was seen by Burke on Oct. 23. Not until the third edition of the *Reflections* was Burke able to take notice of it. Smith, "Burke's Crusade," 163.
60 MS in Harvard Library, Burke to Francis, Oct. 27, 1790.
61 Schmitt and Weston, *Journal of Modern History*, XXIV, 406-409, Oct. 27, 1790.
62 *Corr.*, III, 155-62, Burke to Dupont, Oct. 28, 1790.

their purposes. Louis XVI would have done well to emulate the "vigor" and "foresight" of his ancestor. Refusing to retract, Burke made a concession. If Dupont desired, he might print Burke's letter as an appendix. Its message was intended as much for the public as for Dupont.[63]

Burke's reaction to Dupont's criticism was the same as his responses to Francis' and Windham's in February and September, or to Dr. Brocklesby's fear that he had been a little too rough on good Dr. Price.[64] His book contained not hasty or ill-considered opinions but measured judgments of the Revolution and its impact upon England. He had used carefully chosen language, and if it was strong or even emotional, he had intended it should be. "My reasons are solid," he told an unknown correspondent, for wanting the book published at once.[65]

For all of his confidence, Burke may have had a doubt. At least, he asked, "God send me a good deliverance."[66]

He would soon know. "This day is published . . . Mr. Burke's long expected Treatise" said an advertisement in the *Times* of November 1, 1790.

---

[63] Instead of doing this, Dupont added a footnote in the first French edition, taking notice of the discussion. Schmitt and Weston, *Journal of Modern History*, XXIV, 409, n. 16. Burke's desire to make the letter known is established also by the fact that in 1791 he revised it and published it as a pamphlet, and in between had permitted its publication in the newspapers. Copeland, *Our Eminent Friend Edmund Burke*, 235.

[64] Burke MSS, Sheff., Brocklesby to Burke, Nov. 1, 1790.

[65] Charles M'Cormick, *Memoirs of Burke* (London, 1797), 339n., Oct., 1790.

[66] Br. Mus., Add. MSS 37,843, fol. 19, Burke to Windham, Oct. 27, 1790.

CHAPTER XIV

Reflections on the Revolution in France

FROM ALMOST ANY point of view Burke's prayer for the *Reflections* was answered. Whether by "good deliverance" he meant quantity of sales, number of editions, warmness of praise, bitterness of condemnation, the number of published replies, or its influence upon English and European opinion, the *Reflections* has had it, not only in Burke's time but ever since. It has been included, of course, in the numerous editions of his *Works,* and excerpts have been printed in occasional anthologies. During the Burke revival of the last generation, new anthologies of Burke's writings and new editions of the *Reflections* have appeared. In New York in 1959 was published a paperback "authentic" text, edited by William B. Todd and derived from the "Seventh Edition" of 1790, the "last attended and revised by the author."[1] The reissues indicate a continuing demand for the *Reflections.* More people are reading it in our day than at any time before. The book is used in college courses in history, political philosophy, and English, and it is a basic reference for all who are interested in Burke's political ideas.

The *Reflections* is recognized as one of the great works of Western thought and its author as one of the great political thinkers of the modern era. Like all of Burke's set pieces after he entered public life, it was written as a tract for the times, but the nature of this supreme crisis both in his thought and in Western civilization gave it an enduring value. Burke even here was not a detached thinker; he still was arguing a case. But as always he was placing particular problems against a background of principle concerning the nature of man, society, and government. Over the period of forty years in which he discussed the problems that England faced, he expounded a coherent body of thought, though he never developed it in a single, systematic philosophical treatise. His writings "had a general taste or tincture of philosophy," he told Francis, and that was what he valued most in them.[2] To understand Burke, one must be aware of the historical situation which informed each of his writings, study all of them, then finally develop intellectual order from the scattered discussions according to the principle one discerns to be implicit in them.[3]

The writings of the Revolutionary period are of course essential for this effort. Without them, the student would not understand Burke; with them alone, he could. Of all Burke's writings, the *Reflections* is most nearly the complete exposition of his political and social philosophy. His basic, inner beliefs were here completely exposed—a fact that we may attribute to the coincidence of the crisis of his age with the close of his career. He was sixty-one and nearing the end of his life when he wrote the *Reflections*. He had not acquired a new set of political principles and social assumptions in the course of less than a year. He found the French Revolution wholly inimical to settled principles that he had revealed along the way when he wrote about the problems of America, Ireland, and India. He did not really add to them in his subsequent writings. But he now presented them with a unique intensity and sense of urgency not only because he no longer had the politician's need to mask his position, but because he saw Europe in terrible and violent revolt against the very tradition he felt was sanctioned by God and man. Here it is necessary to distinguish between the English Revolution of 1688,

1 P. vi. Footnote references are to this edition.
2 MSS Eur., F. 8, p. 46, a sketch of Burke by Francis, written in 1812.
3 A useful summary is Charles Parkin, *The Moral Basis of Burke's Political Thought* (Cambridge, 1956). Canavan, *Political Reason*, and Peter J. Stanlis, *Edmund Burke and the Natural Law* (Ann Arbor, 1958), are analytical as well as expository. I do not include a bibliography of writings on Burke's thought. Canavan and Stanlis contain selective bibliographies, Stanlis' the more extended.

which Burke admired, and the French Revolution. The former he did not consider a complete social revolt. Unlike Dr. Price, for example, Burke did not believe that the principle underlying the Revolution of 1688 made revolution a principle of government. Any such analogy drawn between the Glorious Revolution and the French Revolution was false. Therefore, Burke felt that he had neither abandoned old principles nor adopted new ones when he stood forth as the opponent of the French Revolution. A measure of the difference between him and the men of the Enlightenment was that he, never misled by superficial ratiocination, saw more deeply than they into the nature of human nature and understood more clearly the falseness of the assumptions about man and society on which the Revolutionary intellectual structure was erected.

If the *Reflections* lacked the systematic quality of traditional philosophical inquiry, Burke did bring to its composition the seasoned orator's feel for audience response, a natural ability to deal logically with large issues, and the high order of literary talent he had early displayed. The result was a work developed with a sure touch and a grand passion that produced an overwhelming rhetorical effect.

Burke opens with a theme of direct concern to his British readers—the threat to the institutions of England that he felt was posed by the sermons of such men as Dr. Price and the fulminations of the Revolution Society. In the next difficult section, Burke is both persuasive and eloquent in holding that the Revolution of 1688, to which he had always been partisan, did not establish revolution as a natural political instrument. Burke argued that the Glorious Revolution restored a just social balance rather than overturned a social order. Far different was it from the cataclysm of 1789, which with "self-evident" illusions about the nature of man and a fine-spun logic about "natural rights" was assaulting the whole tradition upon which Western civilization was based. In the remainder of the book, Burke turns his devastating and prophetic ire upon the situation in France. With the insight of one experienced in parliamentary leadership, Burke attacks the composition, the principles, and the conduct of the General Assembly and measures adopted by it.

He lingers over its unrealistic financial schemes and their threat to the institutions of property and religion. The last third of the book analyzes the constitutional measures that, as they accumulated, became finally the Constitution of 1791—the provisions for the legislature, local government, the executive, the judiciary, the military, and, once more, public finance. Using the bizarre nature of these measures as a text, Burke held them up as a warning to Englishmen not to regard lightly their well-wrought treasure, the British constitution.

In Burke's hands, the looseness of construction of the *Reflections* became its strength. Slowly, with a somber fervor that carried his readers with him, he paused for brilliant insights into what he felt to be lofty but insecure superstructure of the Revolution. There was scope for enlargement and elaboration of the grandeur of the British tradition, for illumination and gorgeous metaphor, for passages of reflection that revealed in clear and moving phrases his noble conception of the organic nature of the community and the duty of men to preserve it. Burke's method was the method of an artist to whom long and profound experience had furnished insight that gave concrete shape and vitality to the essentially intuitive principles always at the root of his life and thought.

Aided by other works of Burke, the modern reader of the *Reflections* may identify the natural law as the foundation of Burke's thought.[4] Burke did not attempt to expound the doctrine. He assumed knowledge of Cicero, the Stoics, Aristotle, and Hooker, even if his readers did not know St. Thomas or some of the textbook treatises.[5] Burke's statements merely showed the relevance of the natural-law teachings to particular problems without proving their validity. If aware, he was unconcerned over the "inconsistency" between his metaphysics and his epistemology.[6] He accepted the existence of a "metaphysical order intelligible

[4] The fullest exposition is in Stanlis, *Burke and the Natural Law.* See also Louis I. Bredvold, *The Brave New World of the Enlightenment* (Ann Arbor, 1961), and esp. chaps. I and VI.

[5] Canavan, *Political Reason*, app. A, discusses the texts Burke probably studied at Trinity College. For examples of the ease with which some of Burke's contemporaries used the language of natural law, Fox, for instance, or North or William Adam, see Bond, ed., *Speeches*, I, 190, 191, 433, and the *Times*, May 9, 1788.

[6] Canavan, *Political Reason*, 45, 210-11.

to the human mind," an order in which immutable law, of divine origin and anterior to positive law, describes the nature of moral duty and provides the measure of justice in the social order. This premise grounds Burke's philosophy in principle. In relating practice to principle, however, he employs an empirical method, argument from circumstance.[7] This attentiveness to circumstance has tempted some interpreters to consider Burke a utilitarian— even an apologist for expediency. Man, who is God's creation, is endowed with reason—not the abstract reason of speculative philosophy concerned with the ultimate truth of a metaphysical proposition, but the right reason of the natural law, which is concerned with the good or evil of human actions measured against the norms of the natural moral order. Right reason, abetted by revealed religion and the church, urges man to seek good and to conform to duty in his social and political conduct. Duty would not be forgotten or separated from rights, as Locke had separated rights and law; justice would consist of enjoyment of rights but also would require performance of moral obligation in the social order to which men belonged. The world would therefore be preserved from the moral anarchy into which natural-rights doctrines and Rousseauan sensibility would lead it. Perhaps nothing was more repugnant to Burke than notions of social and moral relativism; they were fundamentally and necessarily at war with all desires for social and moral order.[8]

In the *Reflections* Burke reaffirmed the existence of a natural moral order and gave it specific reference.[9] Power is legitimate only when it is expressed "according to that eternal immutable law, in which will and reason are the same." Public officials, entrusted with the power of the community, should use it as "an holy function." To ignore, as the National Assembly did, the doctrine of prescription, which "is a part of the law of nature," is to threaten the security of property and therefore to be in "contempt of this great fundamental part of natural law." The confiscation of property by the National Assembly separates

---

[7] Richard Weaver, *The Ethics of Rhetoric* (Chicago, 1953), 57-58, 68-73.

[8] Stanlis, "Burke and the Sensibility of Rousseau," *Thought*, XXXVI (Summer. 1961), 246-76, is an excellent treatment of this subject. Also Bredvold, *Brave New World of the Enlightenment*, chaps. III and IV.

[9] *Reflections*, 114, 117-18, 186-87, 192.

"policy from justice. Justice is itself the great standing policy of civil society. . . ."

A student of the natural law might wonder whether Burke was aware of the finer discriminations in the doctrine. He learned it from both classical and Christian sources and synthesized them in a way that indicates disregard of certain distinctions and contradictions, or suggests misleadingly that the tradition of natural law remained an undifferentiated body of thought through-out the centuries.[10] Thus Burke passed over the medieval empha-sis upon the interpretative aid of a universal church and seemed unconcerned about the autonomy and the secularism of the classical view. Modern scholarship does with Burke's conception what he himself never attempted, that is, engage in the exacting pursuit of definitions, distinctions, and classifications. To Burke the tradition in its eclectic, undifferentiated form was a valid foundation for a right view of the nature of man and society. He would leave the metaphysical and logical disputations to the schools while, as befitted the politician, the philosopher in action, he related general principles to the practical problems of politics.

Following Aristotle and the Stoics, Burke found the natural order of human relationships not in some precivil state of nature, but in civil society itself. Even if there had been a state of nature, its existence was irrelevant to the problems of man in society, and in any state since Adam, man was a fallen creature. The rights and duties derived from natural law relate to men living in a social order whose moral precepts, in Western civiliza-tion, have been interpreted by revealed religion and the teachings of Christianity. These statements indicate the extent to which Burke's social philosophy was synthetic.

It is at once apparent why Burke was in fundamental disagree-ment with the individualism of the Enlightenment and of the social-contract theory. He had to hold the natural-rights philoso-phers in contempt as legislators and to berate the National Assembly for following their legislative models. At the beginning

10 See, e. g., Will Herberg's review of Stanlis, *Burke and the Natural Law* in *Modern Age,* I (Summer, 1959), 328, and James F. Davidson, "Natural Law and International Law in Edmund Burke," *The Review of Politics,* XXI (July, 1959), 483-94.

of his literary career, in his *Vindication of Natural Society,* Burke had taken his position, and in the *Reflections* he reaffirmed it. With the apostles of "the rights of men" and with "the clumsy subtilty of their political metaphysics," Burke had no communion.[11] He was interested in "the direct original rights of man in civil society."[12] These were the *"real* rights of men," and persons who adhered to "pretended rights" would destroy the social order in which alone men's rights have meaning. These real rights are the advantages men derive from civil society, living by the rule of law that is "beneficence," and thus obtaining justice. A man has a right to his property, inheritances, and the fruits of his industry, "a right to a fair portion of all which society, with all its combinations of skill and force, can do in his favour." Men have equal rights in these matters, but "not to equal things"—not to an equal share of power, authority, and direction . . . in the management of the state," but to equal opportunity in proportion to their abilities and their social contributions. Thus political activities and the so-called civil liberties are not inalienable rights but are the internal arrangements of a civil society. They are regulated by "convention," which is its law, although declaratory positive law, which should be in harmony with natural law, may modify and shape convention. The natural rights of the revolutionaries, which did not even suppose the existence of a civil society, had no place in Burke's thought. "Men cannot enjoy the rights of an uncivil and of a civil state together."

Other differences between Burke and the philosophers are apparent. From his point of view their concern with rights distorted the nature of society, giving to it an atomistic quality that seemed to force each man, jealous of his individual rights, into perpetual conflict with the social order from which he could not escape. Burke, with his emphasis upon the social aspects of human existence, was concerned with the preservation of civil harmony. The obligations of justice took precedence over individual rights; in a good order, men's civil rights were aspects of justice and were the more secure because complete justice re-

11 *Reflections,* 69.
12 *Reflections,* 70.

quired attention to men's duties to their fellows. To a degree, ✦
Burke's concepts of justice were, like natural rights, pronounce-
ments or assertions validated by a priori references. But only
to a degree. His list of "real rights" has a strong traditionary
character, is clearly derived from historical experience, and found
its ultimate verification in the English common law and the
political consensus that Englishmen had arrived at by the beginning of the eighteenth century. In short, to Burke the eighteenth-
century social order, even with its acknowledged defects, was a
good order, because empirical processes had produced social
dispositions that he was able to believe were approximations to
the divine moral order.

If the "extreme rights" of revolutionary "theorists" were
"morally and politically false," so were the principles of the
French Revolution. Its consequences were necessarily evil because it was based upon a philosophy of man and society that
was fundamentally incompatible with a moral, social order. The
Declaration of the Rights of Man exposed the principles and
tendencies of the National Assembly and prepared him to expect,
though he waited for events to verify, the destructiveness of
their works. Such men, to whom art and nature were antithetical,
could not understand society, and were not fitted to be social
architects.[13]

Civil society, a work of nature and of art, by Burke's definition ✦
embraced the entire complex of human relationships.[14]

Society is indeed a contract. Subordinate contracts for objects of
mere occasional interest may be dissolved at pleasure—but the state
ought not to be considered as nothing better than a partnership
agreement in a trade of pepper and coffee, calico or tobacco, or some
other such low concern, to be taken up for a little temporary
interest, and to be dissolved by the fancy of the parties. It is to be
looked on with other reverence; because it is not a partnership in
things subservient only to the gross animal existence of a temporary
and perishable nature. It is a partnership in all science; a partnership
in all art; a partnership in every virtue, and in all perfection. As the

13 Bredvold, *Brave New World of the Enlightenment*, 135-38.
14 *Reflections*, 117-18. For a discussion of the misunderstandings of this long
passage, see Stanlis, *Burke and the Natural Law*, 73-74 and 275, n. 95. Outside the
context of the natural law, the passage, Stanlis argues, is necessarily misinterpreted.

ends of such a partnership cannot be obtained in many generations, it becomes a partnership not only between those who are living, but between those who are living, those who are dead, and those who are to be born. Each contract of each particular state is but a clause in the great primaeval contract of eternal society, linking the lower with the higher natures, connecting the visible and invisible world, according to a fixed compact sanctioned by the inviolable oath which holds all physical and all moral natures, each in their appointed place. This law is not subject to the will of those, who by an obligation above them, and infinitely superior, are bound to submit their will to that law. The municipal corporations of that universal kingdom are not morally at liberty at their pleasure, and on their speculations of a contingent improvement, wholly to separate and tear asunder the bands of their subordinate community, and to dissolve it into an unsocial, uncivil, unconnected chaos of elementary principles. It is the first and supreme necessity only, a necessity that is not chosen but chooses, a necessity paramount to deliberation, that admits no discussion, and demands no evidence, which alone can justify a resort to anarchy. This necessity is no exception to the rule; because this necessity itself is a part too of that moral and physical disposition of things to which man must be obedient by consent or force; but if that which is only submission to necessity should be made the object of choice, the law is broken, nature is disobeyed, and the rebellious are outlawed, cast forth, and exiled, from this world of reason, and order, and peace, and virtue, and fruitful penitence, into the antagonist world of madness, discord, vice, confusion, and unavailing sorrow.

There is no place in this concept of society either for the social-contract theory of Locke or for philosophic anarchism.[15] Society is both natural and artificial. There is no contradiction here because, said Burke, art is man's nature. Society is shaped and molded by men; the social conventions defined by historical experience are just as natural as the human relationships existing in a mythical state of nature. Ideally, this society was to resemble as closely as finite man could make it the perfection of the natural, moral order of the universe, which, through the dispensation of divine providence, sinful men knew was "the source and original archetype of all perfection."[16] Improvement and

---

[15] Bredvold, *Brave New World of the Enlightenment*, 140-43.
[16] *Reflections*, 104.

moral progress, though not continual, were not impossible through the long range of history. By the "disposition of a stupendous wisdom, moulding together the great mysterious incorporation of the human race, the whole, at one time, is never old, or middle-aged, or young, but . . . moves on through the varied tenour of perpetual decay, fall, renovation, and progression."[17] No single generation made great leaps from one state to another; progress was gradual. The men of the eighteenth century were wiser than their ancestors only as they had inherited the accumulating wisdom of the generations and not because their moral norms were different. "We know that *we* [Englishmen] have made no discoveries; and we think that no discoveries are to be made in morality; nor many in the great principles of government, nor many in the ideas of liberty. . . ."[18] The "private stock of reason" in any generation is small; men would do well to "avail themselves of the general bank and capital of nations, and of ages."[19]

All of this Burke conceived within a framework of religion. "He who gave our nature to be perfected by our virtue, willed also the necessary means of its perfection—He willed therefore the state—" as the institutional means whereby harmony between the social order and the natural, moral order was to be approached.[20] This passage combines Christian and Platonic influences. By "perfected," Burke meant improved, for man, finite and a sinful creature, could not achieve perfection. The state, as the instrument of social harmony, had the duty of promoting justice among sinful men. The state had a religious foundation. God created man as "a religious animal."[21]

Religion, "the basis of civil society, and the source of all good and of all comfort," gives moral direction to inherited wisdom.[22] In England or in France, admitting denominational differences, a national church was a part of the traditional social order, so deeply involved in the life of society and so closely connected with the government that any description of the state had to

17 *Reflections*, 38-39.
18 *Reflections*, 104.
19 *Reflections*, 105.
20 *Reflections*, 119.
21 *Reflections*, 110.
22 *Reflections*, 109.

include the church. They "are ideas inseparable." Suddenly to remove the church from its historic place in the life of people would be violently to disrupt the social order. Burke rejected William Warburton's theory of an alliance between church and state as separate, sovereign entities.[23] Their historical and ideal relationship was too intimate for that; Burke preferred to follow Hooker and the Elizabethan concept. To Burke the idea of a church establishment was vital; it was this which made him so sympathetic to the Catholic Church in France. The attack of the National Assembly was not against Catholicism only but also against the principle of establishment and therefore against one of the pillars of the social order.[24]

Though man possessed reason, and continuity or "unchangeable constancy" enabled him through history to remain in touch with the experience of the ages, he had not been abandoned when God willed the means of perfecting his nature. Running through the *Reflections*, as through Burke's other writings, is an implication, made explicit only occasionally, of the watchful presence of God, "the Supreme Director of this great drama."[25] With the theological problem involved here, Burke did not concern himself. He preferred to admit the presence of divine providence, to concede that its identity and operation, like so much in human experience, were mysterious, and, as with the natural law, to accept its existence as an act of faith without attempting explanations.

Burke was not fatalistic. His doctrine of providence did not vitiate free will.[26] Possibly the Revolution was itself an instance of divine intervention, yet Burke opposed it with all of his energy. His career refuted any of his statements that seem to suggest mute acquiescence in any given situation. The individual may find himself in a certain place in the social order, first of all through birth, and he will also find duties attached to that place. But he is neither consigned permanently to that place, if virtue, ability, intelligence, and even accident may enable him to attain another

23 McCabe, "Attitude of Burke toward Christianity," 148-49.
24 *Reflections*, 108-12, 120, 178-84.
25 *Reflections*, 97.
26 Canavan, *Political Reason*, 177-88; John C. Weston, Jr., "Edmund Burke's View of History," *The Review of Politics*, XXIII (April, 1961), 227-28.

one, nor, unless he accepts the compulsions of social convention, morality, and public service, forced to perform the duties attached to that station. Determinism was not a part of Burke's doctrine of providence, nor was pessimism. But mystery was, as well as a kind of humble acquiescence when human knowledge and wisdom could not explain historical events. Burke never claimed that man was capable of understanding the workings of providence.

Burke's faith formed his doctrine of providence and the natural law, and his beliefs about the religious constitution of man and society. With few exceptions, scholars have not questioned the sincerity of his religious faith. In his speeches and writings, and especially in his correspondence of the 1790's, he frequently invoked the name of God. This is not conclusive evidence. More important is the "religious consciousness" that was present in his writings throughout his life.[27] This presence strikes forcefully the person who reads much of Burke. As with other aspects of his thought, Burke did not attempt to explain or justify his religious faith. The existence of God was a self-evident fact to anyone who would look about him; Burke viewed the world within a religious framework.

Christianity, he wrote in 1760, was "not a speculative science but a practical obligation."[28] By his own admission he gave up the study of theology because it led to confusion, and simply embraced and held fast to the Church of England.[29] This statement suggests more than Burke meant. He did not fear confusion; he simply did not think it necessary to resolve in consistent terms that which he was ready to embrace by faith. His study of theology was not an attempt to resolve agonizing, youthful uncertainty. The story of his early life does not reveal a religious crisis that was ended by conscious commitment to the Church of England. There was never a later period of doubt about this commitment. Burke's early religious study was a part of his pursuit of knowledge. The cynic might even suggest that in view of the statute book and Burke's political ambitions, he was fortunate in escaping mental turmoil. He did not have to make a choice between

27 McCabe, "Attitude of Burke toward Christianity," 52.
28 McCabe, "Attitude of Burke toward Christianity," 174, citing *Annual Register*, III, 206.
29 McCabe, "Attitude of Burke toward Christianity," 53-61.

religious conviction and political self-interest. He lived at ease within the Church of England; when at Beaconsfield, he is said to have attended Sunday services faithfully; his reverence for his church was partly doctrinal and strongly social and liturgical.[30] He loved the Church of England because it was two hundred years old, was woven into the texture of English life, and was by law and convention indissolubly (it seemed) a part of the English constitution. Burke was a disciple of Hooker.

Shortly after the appearance of the *Reflections,* in a letter to an unidentified person he wrote that the Church of England "harmonizes with our civil constitution, with the frame and fashion of our Society, and with the general temper of the people. I think it is better calculated . . . for keeping peace amongst the different sects, and of affording to them a reasonable protection, than any other System. Being something in a middle, it is better disposed to moderate."[31] At the same time Burke would grant tolerance to other sects; they existed and could only be extirpated, if even then, at the risk of civil disorder. Twenty years earlier, Burke had said the same thing to the House of Commons.[32] In matters of religion he would, "unless the truth were evident indeed, hold fast to peace, which has in her company charity, the highest of the virtues." In these statements, Burke relegates doctrinal matters to an inferior place; he revered the Church of England as an instrument of social peace.[33] Burke rarely, and then briefly, discussed Anglican or any other doctrine. Nevertheless, it is difficult to accept Lord Acton's judgment that Burke was not sincere in his religious belief.[34] Burke's writings carry conviction; they are filled with a sense of immanence and acceptance of moral

[30] Thomas Somerville thought Burke excessively partial to Episcopal church government and forms of worship. But Somerville was Presbyterian. Somerville, *Life,* 222. The church attendance is mentioned by S. C. Carpenter, *Eighteenth Century Church and People* (London, 1959), 165, but without documentation. On April 10, 1792, Elliot told his wife of strolling through the Buckinghamshire countryside on a Sunday morning while Burke was at church. Minto, *Elliot,* II, 10.

[31] Copeland transcript of MS belonging to Miss E. S. Scroggs, Jan. 26, 1791.

[32] *Works,* VII, 14.

[33] Father Canavan admits that Burke made statements in which he seemed to subordinate religious truth to political convenience, but he does not think that they represent Burke's deepest convictions. *Political Reason,* 48.

[34] H. G. Schenck, *The Aftermath of the Napoleonic Wars* (London, 1947), 6 and n. 4, for Acton's judgment.

duty based upon religious faith. The "evidence seems unimpeachable that Burke's personal religion was sincerely held and
that his moral convictions were loyally adhered to throughout his
life."[35] By none of his works is this verdict more strongly supported than by the *Reflections.* But if anyone should prove Acton
correct, then the *Reflections* would be a great imposture and
Burke's talk about the natural law and divine providence mere
verbiage.

Burke's doctrine of providence assigns to God a transcendent
and ultimately inscrutable influence upon the affairs of men.[36]
History, therefore, does not conform to scientific laws of development that are wholly intelligible to man. Good and evil are not
the moral relatives of a historical process containing its own
rationale. That which exists is not right by virtue of being; it
may be evil for purposes known only to God. In the *Reflections,*
Burke insisted upon the evil of the Revolution; he did not show
the despair over combatting this evil that later, in moments of
anguish and ill health, he gave way to. His refusal to secularize
the doctrine of providence encouraged his despair, because he
wondered whether the Revolution was a divine judgment. Had
he seen the Revolution as a secular phenomenon explainable by
intelligible laws of historical process, its evil would have been
devoid of moral significance. But Burke's despair was not pessimism because God had not redefined good and evil. The Revolution was, as Burke saw it in 1790, the beginning of a long time
of troubles. His doctrine of providence, because it was based on
faith, spared him fear that the "ordered continuance of that
divine evolutionary process" had ceased forever.[37]

The record of history and Burke's view of the nature of history
also rejected that conclusion. Though he talked about decay and
regeneration as historical phenomena and predicted that some
popular general in France would establish a military dictatorship
in place of the democratic anarchy that would succeed to the
democratic tyranny already being established, he did not hold a
cyclical theory as an inexorable law of development. Nor did he

---

35 McCabe, "Attitude of Burke toward Christianity," 105.
36 Canavan, *Political Reason,* 180-81.
37 As Magnus, *Burke,* 62, thought he feared.

accept a biological analogy of infancy, adulthood, and decline. In fact, Burke had no self-sufficient explanation of historical causation. He knew as a matter of historical record that nations and governments grew, flourished, and fell, but this record did not mean that changes were unavoidable necessities. Mere historical accident could account for them; changes might be intelligible if sufficient information were available; if in the end the explanation escaped men, it was known to God.

History was to Burke the cumulative experience of mankind. He did not, however, study a universal history; his concern was with the histories of particular groups of men, that is, nations, England or France, or societies, the Christian society of Western Europe.[38] This is not to say that Burke was denying the feasibility of the study of universal history. For example, his statement that religion is the basis of civil society is a proposition of universal relevance. But his own historical interests were directed to restricted fields because the particular problems he encountered were those of a nation, an empire, or Western Europe. The English constitution or the European world of the eighteenth century were the achievements of over a thousand years of history. Burke was unusual among his contemporaries in his respect for the Middle Ages. It was a creative, if a rude, age. It produced, for example, Magna Carta, parliament, and the common law, the spirit of chivalry whose passing he deplored in the *Reflections,* and St. Thomas, and it turned the ancient natural-law tradition into a Christian doctrine. In fact the basic principles of morality were fully developed, and of those of government and liberty a great part was known, "long before we were born."[39] Yet Burke did not doubt that in many respects progress had occurred. In more recent times, man had made material, scientific, artistic, and literary improvements. The eighteenth century was the beneficiary of the wisdom and work of its ancestors under the transcendent beneficence of divine providence.

Burke's view of progress was developmental and evolutionary. It was also empirical, uncommitted to any theory or laws of social progress. Improvements or "correctives" are the "results of various

38 Weston, *Review of Politics,* XXIII, 203-29.
39 *Reflections,* 104.

necessities and expediences." Prudence or practical reason suggests a remedy; "errors and deviations . . . are found and computed, and the ship proceeds in her course."[40] In this kind of growth, some of the past is found in the present, and the present, if men are wise, will always be kept in touch with the past. The French Revolution was a denial of a truth verified by all of human experience. The members of the National Assembly, complained Burke, did not think historically but only contemporaneously, as though each generation were self-sufficient.

The British constitution was to Burke the outstanding example of this kind of historical evolution.[41] In the *Reflections* he frequently contrasted British with French conduct, always to the credit of the former. Burke seemed to have forgotten that in the seventeenth century England was considered a politically unstable country. Nevertheless, she had experienced a constitutional evolution from Magna Carta to the Declaration of Right, and Englishmen held their liberties "as an *entailed inheritance*" from their forefathers. This was the happy effect of following nature, which is "wisdom without reflection, and above it." This appealing phrase tells much about Burke's mode of thought and sharply distinguishes him from the rationalists he opposed. Some matters, Burke was saying, defy intellectual analysis; nothing, they insisted, should be immune from the test of reason, least of all political and ecclesiastical institutions.

The idea of inheritance included the "principle of conservation" and the "principle of transmission." "People will not look forward to posterity, who never look backward to their ancestors."[42] British constitutional history was not the only example Burke might have cited to illustrate his view of progress, but it was the clearest, it coincided with his own political interests, and it was apt because the Revolution Society and the National Assembly were concerned with constitutional problems. The

40 *Reflections*, 212-13.

41 I warn against interpreting the word in a Darwinian sense. Late nineteenth-century historians used Darwinian terminology. Even today historians speak of the "growth" or "development" or "evolution" of the constitution. The word "making" more accurately describes Burke's meaning because it admits of men's creative activity. Growth then becomes the accumulation of creative acts.

42 *Reflections*, 37-38, for the three preceding quotations.

British constitution was also the perfect example because, through centuries of historical experience, it had been adapted to fit the temper and the nature of English society. The Revolution of 1688, as he explained in the early part of the *Reflections,* was the grand, permanent settlement made within the inherited framework. Further adjustments, as Burke's political career demonstrated, could be made in harmony with the principles of that settlement.

In this, Burke thought more like a common-law historian than like a philosopher.[43] His view of history was almost what has been called "Montesquieuian."[44] The wisdom distilled from it could not be reduced to doctrinaire first principles. In this respect Burke's thought belonged to an English tradition which antedated him and has continued to our own day; it did not anticipate Continental philosophical historiography.[45] The men of 1688 naturalized their Revolution on historical grounds. Their eighteenth-century admirers did likewise. Burke's historical approach stressed the legal foundations of English society; concepts of property rights and liberties were inherited, as well as the governmental institutions that gave force to the aspirations of society. This way of thinking was peculiarly congenial to the common lawyers like Coke, Matthew Hale, and Blackstone. Burke had studied the common law. He once began a history of it. He venerated the common law (if not always certain lawyers or the methods of teaching it). The history of the law neatly illustrated his empirical and historical cast of mind. Matthew Hale, the seventeenth-century legal historian, used language Burke might have used; the common law is "immemorial custom in perpetual adaptation," though like Burke's origins of society, its origins are lost in the mists of time.[46]

There is no understanding of Burke's thought or of the *Reflections* without an examination of his view of history. Of all

43 J. G. A. Pocock, "Burke and the Antient Constitution—A Problem in the History of Ideas," *The Historical Journal,* III (1960), 125-43.

44 John C. Weston, Jr., *The Burke Newsletter,* III, 91.

45 For a discussion of British empirical historiography, see W. H. Walsh, "History and Theory," *Encounter,* XVIII (June, 1962), 50-54.

46 Pocock, *The Historical Journal,* III, 136-37. Pocock carefully avoids placing Burke in debt to Hale, though he suggests that Burke had read him.

the intellectual disciplines, history was the most congenial, his favorite and lifelong study. It provided his mode of thinking about the problems that he confronted as a politician. The historical approach brought him into contact with the concrete, enabling him to avoid abstractions, speculative reasoning, and doctrinaire dogmatism. It could be reconciled with his basic assumptions about the nature of man and society. It was compatible with the natural-law tradition. When it failed to furnish complete explanations of human experiences, the doctrine of providence was available to supply deficiencies. History did not furnish laws of human development; religion defined moral principles. History furnished examples and illustrations, models to follow and warnings to heed. Knowledge obtained from history enabled men to connect the past with the future through the present. Men were not meant to live like "the flies of a summer," the generations linked only by the reproductive process.[47] History was the collective memory that kept unbroken "the whole chain and continuity of the commonwealth."

It is the historical emphasis in his thought that refutes persons who find in the anti-revolutionary crusader the opponent of change and the apologist of reaction. Burke's career before 1789 was only part of the answer to this charge; the *Reflections* itself was an answer. Burke was anxious to explain his "philosophy" of change. It was not a philosophy expounded through logical progression of ideas. It was historical, because to Burke the occasion, quality, and extent of change were to be determined in relationship to inherited "presiding principle," to "times and occasions, and provocations," to circumstances and necessity.[48] Certain occasions might require drastic, dangerous change. A chain of circumstances might lead to "a grave and overruling necessity"—but a necessity "in the strictest moral sense"—for resisting constituted authority.[49] No formula in advance of the circumstances can locate the line between obedience and resistance. If present abuses and calculated consequences make it clear that "the prospect of the future" will be "as bad as the

[47] *Reflections*, 115.
[48] *Reflections*, 34-35, 74, 210.
[49] *Reflections*, 19, 30, 34-35.

experience of the past," then a revolution will be justified, but only as "the very last resource of the thinking and the good."

The *Reflections* is permeated with Burke's idea of change. It is a vindication of gradualism, itself a concept of change. Burke nowhere suggests that change is anything but an active rule of political conduct. He would follow principle and historical experience in admitting change, but change should not be the last-ditch conversion of retreating resistance. The wise legislator does not wait for change to force itself upon him. In initiating it, he should proceed with "prolific energy," but energy without haste.[50] Change is a rule of life—"a state without the means of some change is without the means of its conservation"—but change, to be beneficial, must follow the precepts of "conservation and correction."[51] Burke's ideal statesman combines a "disposition to preserve" with "an ability to improve."[52] That was the kind of change England experienced at the Restoration and Revolution when, after a momentary loss of the "bond of union" with the past, the connection was restored in a "regenerated" constitution, which kept "inviolable" the old principle but "altered the direction."[53] This was understatement. As we shall see, there was more to the Revolution of 1688 than Burke was admitting in the *Reflections*.

If his explanation of change was an apology for the Revolution of 1688, it was no argument against the cause of the French Revolution. "Necessity" is not amenable to mathematical computation or objective definition. Necessity is something men feel. The English may have felt it in 1688, the French did in 1789, and who was Burke to say that the feelings of the French were spurious and those of the English well founded? Burke never made a good case against the original need for the French Revolution.

His case against the conduct of the Revolutionaries was weightier. He stated it in part in terms of the principles of practical statesmanship. When initiating change, the statesman who acknowledges the force of prejudice and the validity of prescription

---

[50] *Reflections*, 210.
[51] *Reflections*, 23.
[52] *Reflections*, 193-94.
[53] *Reflections*, 23-24.

honors the principle of conservation. Prejudices are "untaught feelings" that contain "latent wisdom," and the older they are, "the more we cherish them."[54] The mind of man is not a blank tablet upon which environment writes impressions. Man is born with a "mass of predispositions" that may be altered or disposed according to place and time.[55] The quality, content, and force of these "predispositions" will differ among individuals and genera-tions, though there will be a core that represents the consensus of society's experience. There might be blind prejudices, just as there are wise ones: blind prejudice is obstinacy; wise prejudice is a "trembling sollicitude" that resists rash innovations.[56] The statesman, informed by history and circumstances, learns to dis-tinguish between them, and Burke provides formulas.[57] The "grand prejudice" is Christianity.[58] In short, prejudices are the experiences of individual minds that, through long periods of time, have coincided. Custom, habit, and affection are not perfectly synonymous words, but they are all parts of prejudice, and another part is reason. Prejudice is a safeguard against precipitate, rash, and doctrinaire reform.

Prescription is a different thing, a principle of natural justice operating within civil society.[59] It is easy to parody the idea into a justification for immorality, cruelty, plunder, and crime, pro-vided the wrongs occurred at some distant time in history. Prescription might also be used as an argument against the validity of recent change. Yet to Burke it was "a part of the law of nature."[60] The expressed contempt shown for it by the National Assembly was a major cause of his hatred of the Revolution.

Here again Burke used a concept familiar to common law as a maxim of society and government. If prescription—that is, long usage and possession—gave title to the authority of government and to the possession of property, it did not justify abuse of power or the violation of trust, and by itself was not a competent defense against reform and improvement. Burke had made this

---

54 *Reflections*, 105.
55 Basil Willey, *The Eighteenth Century Background* (New York, 1941), 249.
56 *Reflections*, 116-17.
57 Canavan, *Political Reason*, 74-81.
58 *Works*, VI, 367.
59 Canavan, *Political Reason*, 120-30; Stanlis, *Burke and the Natural Law, passim.*
60 *Reflections*, 186.

clear when he promoted economical reform. But he asked men
to consider what society would be without prescription.[61] Property
would become insecure, and with it, liberty. All authority,
constitutional and social, would dissolve. Each generation, each
individual, in the absence of prescription, would feel free to cast
off all restraints. The ensuing social anarchy would resemble a
mythical state of nature wherein will and physical force would
dictate the rules of social relationships and alter them at convenience. Burke's doctrine of prescription reveals a profound
understanding of the delicate and complex nature of society. Men
are born into a society whose order is already established, and
much of that order depends upon an instinctive, unthinking
adherence to prescriptive claims. Burke was afraid that the
National Assembly, by its contempt for prescriptive rights, was
setting an example that, if it spread, would destroy the social
order of Europe.

Burke's doctrines of providence and prescription and his views
on change gave to the public man an influence in shaping
institutions and forming the social order. Freedom of choice was
the power of making decisions; Burke held that the individual
made personal decisions, the public man made decisions affecting
the lives of many people and even the destinies of nations and
empires. The wisdom of these decisions depended much upon
the virtue of prudence. Again Burke used a familiar word in a
special sense.[62] Sometimes he used it to mean caution or decorum,
though never timidity, but there was also a prudence of "an higher
order," and this was the "first of all virtues."[63] It was "a part of
wisdom" that became a duty when the object was the well-being
of multitudes; it was the virtue that enabled men "to unite into
a consistent whole the various anomalies and contending principles that are found in the minds and affairs of men"; it was
the virtue that reconciled means with ends, recognized and
avoided "errors and deviations" in social and political relationships, and, considering the "ignorance and fallibility of mankind,"

---

61 *Reflections*, 186-87.
62 Canavan, *Political Reason*, is an enlarged and varied discussion of Burke's
concept and its application. Also Stanlis, *Burke and the Natural Law, passim.*
63 *Reflections*, 7-8, 74.

taught men to respect the wisdom of their ancestors when endeavoring to reconcile the present with the past.[64]

Prudence was subordinate to principle and moral philosophy because it affected not the ends but the means to ends.[65] It assumed the ends established by religion and natural law. It was concerned with concrete actions in relation to the circumstances, needs, and abilities of men. Although this kind of prudence embraced that rare quality common sense, in its "higher order" it also included reason, intelligence, and knowledge. A better term than common sense, because it implies these other attributes, would be political reason or practical reason, and this further implies a contrast with speculative reason. "It is thus the function of prudence to supply the deficiencies of principle in meeting the demands of practice," and this is achieved by adapting means to ends according to circumstances and in recognition of the consequences of the actions that are chosen.[66] The virtue of prudence was as conspicuously absent in the conduct of the National Assembly as it was present in the men who made the Revolution of 1688.

The British constitution of the eighteenth century had evolved as prudence acted upon principle through centuries of English national experience. Burke never said that the British constitution ought to be exported, for then a rule of political reason would be violated. It was the manner of achieving it rather than the copying of its structure that he recommended to France. The British constitution provided for the needs of men, which was what governments were supposed to do, and in that sense its principles were worthy of attention. Under it there was a "manly, moral, regulated liberty" that was "combined with government; with public force; with the discipline and obedience of armies; with the collection of an effective and well-distributed revenue; with morality and religion; with the solidity of property; with peace and order; with civil and social manners."[67] English liberty was given institutional form in four establishments, church, mon-

64 *Reflections,* 208-209, 213, 307.
65 Canavan, *Political Reason,* 24, 208.
66 Canavan, *Political Reason,* 25, 27.
67 *Reflections,* 6-7.

archy, aristocracy, and democracy, and Burke desired that each exist in the degree it then existed, "and in no greater."[68] This was the kind of unfortunate, exaggerated statement that enabled Burke's opponents to say he desired to maintain the *status quo.*

But did he? When he said "no greater," he meant in relation to the social circumstances of his day. If these changed? Everything Burke said about prudence and change left the door open to modification and adaptation according to circumstances. These "give in reality to every political principle its distinguishing colour, and discriminating effect. The circumstances are what render every civil and political scheme beneficial or noxious to mankind."[69] Burke's main point about the "right" of men to participate in government was that it was not a natural right at all.[70] The end of society was justice; the means of achieving it were to be determined by prudence, recognizing circumstances and social convention. The form that the government should assume, and the participation of men in government, that is, voting and holding office as civil functions, were "to be settled by convention"; and conventions were not fixed irrevocably. Under radically changed circumstances such as Burke did not envisage—an industrial, urban nation and universal education—it is unlikely that Burke could or would have continued to oppose parliamentary reform. He opposed it under the circumstances of the eighteenth century, to which his arguments were adapted, for he believed that representation in parliament then was "perfectly adequate" to the purposes of government.[71] "I reprobate no form of government merely upon abstract principles. There may be situations in which the purely democratic form will be necessary. . . . [and even] clearly desireable."[72] Except for a few theoreticians, the men of the nineteenth century who voted for parliamentary reform did so for practical reasons, the kind Burke talked about. And if they did not always do it happily, they nevertheless recognized the necessity of doing it. Twice in three years, for

68 *Reflections,* 110.
69 *Reflections,* 6.
70 *Reflections,* 70-71; Stanlis, *Burke and the Natural Law,* 53.
71 *Reflections,* 67.
72 *Reflections,* 152.

example, the Duke of Wellington yielded to the pressures of an overwhelming necessity.

In making such concessions to circumstances, Burke did not think that he was abandoning his principles of the nature of man and society. Such admissions as these did not imply that he would become reconciled to the philosophy of the French Revolution, to rationalism, secularism, and materialism. It was these he opposed in the first place; the deeds of the revolutionaries he detested, but they were the consequences of false principles. He might have learned to acquiesce in parliamentary reform in the way that Macaulay did, as an adjustment to social changes. He would never accept reform as an imperative of the rights of men. Thus Burke did not wish "to confine power, authority, and distinction to blood, and names, and titles. No, Sir. There is no qualification for government, but virtue and wisdom, actual or presumptive. Wherever they are actually found, they have, in whatever state, condition, profession or trade, the passport of Heaven to human place and honour. . . . Every thing ought to be open; but not indifferently to every man." But, asked Burke, quoting Ecclesiasticus, "how can he get wisdom that holdeth the plough, . . . and whose talk is of bullocks?"[73]

This was the body of thought that informed Burke's judgment of events in France and provoked his doubts and fears about the ability of the National Assembly to settle the constitution of France. He admitted that he made errors of factual detail. Even if he had not, his judgments about the character and tendency of the Revolution would not have been different. Modern historians, like his contemporaries, both French and English, have found the *Reflections* replete with errors. To Godechot it has no value as a tract on the Revolution; Cobban calls it "ill-informed. . . . prejudiced, violently unfair, grossly unhistorical."[74] Its importance is in the history of thought. It is not a work of history, but it is one of the great books in the history of ideas. It was the first book to develop a body of counterrevolutionary doctrine, and so it "set the terms" not only of the debate over

[73] *Reflections*, 58, 59.
[74] Jacques Godechot, *La Contre-Révolution* (Paris, 1961), 66; Alfred Cobban, *The Debate on the French Revolution, 1789-1800* (London, 1950), 5.

the French Revolution but of subsequent debates concerned with the problems of political and social change and the nature of man in society.

The Revolution to Burke was based upon a specious philosophy, a false view of history, a dangerous, relativistic morality, and a misunderstanding of the nature of man and society. The atrocities he abhorred in the Revolution were not accidents. They were in character, the inexorable consequences of a morality of sensibility, which passed itself off as benevolence but was destructive of the moral rules of a social order seeking harmony with the natural moral order.[75] Englishmen had not yet become the "converts" of Rousseau or Voltaire or Helvetius; "Atheists are not our preachers; madmen are not our lawgivers."[76]

In France it was otherwise. The character and composition of the National Assembly and the beginnings of the popular revolution meant that power had become located in persons who could not use it wisely. The revolutionary actions threatened the ancient social order; the attacks upon property, the church, and the other bases of society contained dread meanings for Burke. The destruction of the old constitution made prudential reform impossible. French fiscal policy would invite economic disaster. And the people in England who approved of all of this and wished to emulate the French must be restrained from having their way, for they too were intoxicated by a false philosophy, misguided by it and by their antihistorical thought.

Upon all of these subjects Burke wrote fully, presenting the philosophy this chapter has summarized. Whether he was in error on some matters is a problem of historical judgment. Philip Francis did not think that the French possessed an ancient constitution that could be reformed.[77] Burke thought otherwise and built the *Reflections* upon that belief. France had prospered under the old regime and this prosperity did not reveal "the character of a government, that has been, on the whole, so oppressive, or so corrupt, or so negligent, as to be utterly unfit

[75] Stanlis, *Thought*, XXXVI, 265. Burke was not thinking of the mob violence inspired by fear of retaliation by counterrevolutionaries but of a violence growing from the character of the Revolution and the principles on which it was based.

[76] *Reflections*, 104.

[77] *Corr.*, III, 162-70.

for all reformation."[78] This kind of reasoning is not a matter of error in scattered factual detail but of generalized historical judgment. Was Burke also wrong about that? Admitting the force of his empirical injunctions, did he misinterpret the circumstances, which, in politics, should count for everything? Was the eighteenth-century British constitution so perfect an instrument of social order as he believed, and was the old regime in France worth reforming? The fact is that the eighteenth-century constitution was amended in the nineteenth century. As for the constitution of the old regime in France, resistance and counterrevolution strengthened that belief of the National Assembly that it was past reforming. The constitution of 1791, whose provisions Burke scorned, never received a fair test, and the counterrevolution that finally caused its death was stimulated by Burke himself.

But the essence of the Revolution he saw clearly. "Better than any of his contemporaries, he perceived the most essential and enduring aspects of the revolution in France."[79] It was a revolution of ideas; the social order of the eighteenth century was threatened by it, the age of chivalry and all that. It was "a revolution in sentiments, manners, and moral opinions," and it could be dated from October 6, 1789.[80] The preciseness of this date suggests the reason why Burke was several months in making up his mind. The march on Versailles and the humiliation of the royal family meant more to Burke in revealing the true character of the Revolution than the fall of the Bastille. Burke was soon to urge war, hoping for a victory that would preserve the world he knew. Swords would leap from their scabbards, not to defend the queen, but to assault the Revolution. But even if peace had been preserved, the days of that world were few. Mr. Watt's steam engines were already at work. Another kind of revolution was beginning, gradualist in point of time but profound in its social consequences. To all of this, Burke was oblivious.

[78] *Reflections,* 160-61.
[79] Lefebvre, *French Revolution,* 189.
[80] *Reflections,* 96-97.

CHAPTER XV

The New and the Old Whigs

BY DESIGN AND as effect, the *Reflections* influenced three over-lapping realms of opinion. First, Burke had directed his book to parliamentary opinion, especially that of his own party. He was anxious for publication by November 1 because parliament was to convene on November 25. Members of parliament must make up their minds about the Revolution. In deciding on that issue members of his own party would be choosing between moving in the direction Sheridan was leading or following the "old & safe course" of loyalty to the British constitution.[1] Not since the early eighteenth century had there been in English public life a cleavage over the principles of social order. Not only the followers of Pitt and of Portland but independents as well were going to have to choose, and their decisions would profoundly influence the course of party and political history. Burke intended that the *Reflections* influence the choice.

Secondly, the *Reflections* would help the public to judge the Revolution.[2] The Dissenters and others who were energetically trying to persuade public opinion must be exposed and their doctrines refuted. The bulk of opinion would be silent, while "petty cabals," making great "bustle and noise," would mislead people at home and abroad into thinking that they spoke for England.[3] "Half a dozen grasshoppers under a fern make the field ring with their importunate chink, whilst thousands of great cattle, reposed beneath the shadow of the British oak, chew the cud and are silent." These "loud and troublesome insects of the hour" must not be allowed to give the impression that they were "the only inhabitants of the field."

Finally, Burke addressed the *Reflections* to European opinion.[4] He dreaded the "contagious nature" of the principles and manners of the revolutionaries. The governments of Europe could not be safe so long as "this strange, nameless, wild enthusiastic thing" existed in their midst. The Revolution was the great issue of the times, involving in a conflict of ideas the interests of party, country, and Europe. If Burke's party and then the country succumbed to revolutionary doctrine, England would not be able to serve the cause of Europe. Burke was humble about his part in this struggle against the Revolution. A "private man," without authority in the state or influence with its rulers, he was becoming steadily more estranged from even his party colleagues. Nevertheless, he intended to devote himself for the rest of his life to the antirevolutionary crusade that the *Reflections* announced.

The beginning was auspicious. The *Reflections* was immensely popular and widely read. Within the first six days, 7,000 copies were sold; by November 29, the day Dupont's French translation was published in Paris and an edition appeared in Dublin, 12,000 copies had been sold in England; by February, 1791, 10,000 copies had been disposed of in Paris, and 6,000 of pirated editions in Lyon and Strasbourg; shortly after, Friedrich Gentz decided to translate it into German; in 1791 it was translated into Italian; though banned by the Inquisition in Spain simply because it discussed the subject of revolution, it circulated there and was translated; by 1797 James Dodsley, Burke's publisher, had sold 18,000 copies.[5] Working furiously to keep up with demand,

1 Fitzwilliam MSS, Sheff., F115a, Burke to Fitzwilliam, June 5, 1791, speaking of his purpose in writing the *Reflections*.

2 Fitzwilliam MSS, Sheff., F115a, Burke to Fitzwilliam, June 5, 1791.

3 *Reflections*, 103.

4 *Corr.*, III, 185, 192, Burke to John Hampden-Trevor, Jan., 1791, Burke to the Marquise d'Osmond, Jan. 8, 1791.

5 Osborn Coll., Box 39, #16, Richard Burke, Sr., to Shackleton, Nov. 8, 1790; Minto, *Elliot*, I, 366, Burke to Elliot, Nov. 29, 1790; Burke MSS, Sheff., Arthur Browne to Burke, Nov. 30, 1790, Anthony Leonetti to Burke, July 30, 1791; Godechot, *La Contre-Révolution*, 73; Schmitt and Weston, *Journal of Modern History*, XXIV, 413-14 and n. 41. Gentz completed his translation early in 1793. Burke MSS, Sheff., Gentz to Burke, Feb. 8, 1793.

Dodsley issued five unrevised impressions by mid-November, 1790, five revisions before the end of the year, and four more in 1791.[6] Thomas Percy, a nephew of Burke's friend Bishop Percy, with Burke's approval issued a digest as a six-penny pamphlet.[7] The pecuniary return is not accurately suggested by these figures. Though no advance agreement about royalties existed, there is record of a receipt from Dodsley dated May 26, 1791, for £1,000; eventually Burke may have earned about £2,000 from the *Reflections*.[8] Remembering the absence of international copyright and the changes in the value of money, the *Reflections* paid Burke very well—perhaps the equivalent of forty to fifty thousand dollars today. The value of the *Reflections* to Burke's reputation is incalculable.

Burke's manuscript correspondence contains many letters of praise from friends and strangers.[9] Other contemporary sources add to the admiring chorus. Burke was especially pleased to receive the king's plaudits and asked the Duke of Clarence to lay "this faint expression of my gratitude at his Majesty's feet."[10] In writing to Mary Berry, Walpole was even more enthusiastic about the *Reflections* than he had been in a letter to Burke.[11] The book exceeded all expectations; it had dealt the Revolution Club a fatal blow; Walpole heard Gibbon admire it "to the skies" and say that he liked even the discussions of religion. Sir Gilbert Elliot thought the book contained the "fundamental elements" of all political knowledge.[12] Lord Camelford told George Hardinge what Burke would have been pleased to hear, that the argument of the *Reflections* was unanswerable, and that it would do "infinite service" in showing Englishmen the dangers of "meta-

6 *Reflections*, v. See also William B. Todd, "The Bibliographical History of Burke's *Reflections on the Revolution in France*," *Library*, 5th ser., VI (1951), 100-108. Highly technical, this article shows that neither author nor publisher anticipated the extent of the demand.

7 Burke MSS, Sheff., Percy to Burke, Feb. 28, March 12, 1791.

8 Matilda Betham-Edwards, ed., *Autobiography of Arthur Young . . .* (London, 1898), 428; Bickley, ed., *Diaries of Sylvester Douglas*, I, 266; H.M.C., *Morrison*, Part II, 484b.

9 Burke MSS, Sheff., Nov. and Dec., 1790, various letters.

10 Burke MSS, Sheff., Feb. 8, 1791.

11 *Walpole Corr.*, XI, 131, 146, 168-70, 209, letters of Nov. 8, 18, Dec. 20, 1790, Feb. 26, 1791.

12 Burke MSS, Sheff., Elliot to Burke, Nov. 6, 1790.

physical speculations."[13] Mrs. Piozzi predicted for the *Reflections* a longer life than its critics would desire.[14] When on December 11 Dublin University conferred upon Burke an honorary LL.D., it recognized "the powerful advocate of the Constitution" and "the friend of public order and virtue" as well as a man of "transcendent talents and philanthropy."[15] There was talk of an honorary degree from Oxford, and the *Times* thought Cambridge ought to honor Burke.[16] Neither university acted, but the resident fellows at Oxford sent an address of approbation.[17] The Anglican clergy were on the whole enthusiastic. After all, said the *Times*, "It is not every person who will say so much in their favour."[18] From parliament when it opened Burke doubtless would receive praise, predicted the *Times*.[19]

These comments were sincerely meant. The noisy opposition to the *Reflections* must not be permitted to drown out an important remark. Not so much because of the book's philosophic premises but because of its defense of the established social order and constitutional system, it harmonized with the ideas and the prejudices of most of the people who governed England. It came at a time when they were ready to receive it. The book eloquently expressed the silent assumptions of Whitehall and St. James's, of Oxford and the cathedrals, of the great country homes, of the quarter sessions, and even of many of the town halls, that is, of a very large part of eighteenth-century England.

But the *Reflections* was a controversial book, and the reactions were not uniformly favorable. The Abbé Jean Maury caught Burke in factual errors and disputed his prediction of a long period of troubles for France.[20] William Coats, a Glasgow merchant, disliked Burke's opposition to parliamentary reform and

13 Nichols, *Illustrations*, VI, 122, Nov. 19, 1790. Camelford was Thomas Pitt, a cousin of the prime minister.

14 Balderston, ed., *Thraliana*, II, 792, Dec. 13, 1790.

15 *Notes and Queries*, 4th ser., II, 32; *Times*, Dec. 23, 1790; Osborn Coll., Box 74, #24A, Burke to Hutchinson, Dec. 18, 1790.

16 Dec. 8, 10, 11, 1790; Minto, *Elliot*, II, 153-54, Elliot to Lady Elliot, July 3, 1793.

17 *Corr.*, III, 180, Burke to Windham, Dec. 21, 1790. Smith, "Burke's Crusade," 206, suggests that Oxford hesitated because of uncertainty about Burke's standing at court.

18 Nov. 30, 1790.

19 Nov. 25, 1790.

20 Burke MSS, N.R.O., Aix55, Maury to Capt. Woodford, Nov. 11, 1790.

pointed to inconsistencies in his views.[21] The Glasgow *Mercury* of November 11 lamented the death "at an advanced age, of the Whiggism of the R't. Hon. Edmund Burke."[22] Lord Macartney reported the shock of disappointment felt by a presbyterian neighbor, a former admirer of Burke's positions on the American Revolution, on economical reform, and on the impeachment of Hastings.[23] Richard Shackleton was not able to hide his embarrassment.[24] When he said he admired the book, he meant only as a literary effort; he knew too little about politics and philosophy to be able to judge it. But on one point he could not dissemble. He thoroughly disagreed with Burke on the principle of religious establishment. An important French reaction was that of François-Louis-Thibault de Menonville, a member of the National Assembly who sat center-right.[25] Along with political wisdom, particularly concerning the British constitution, the *Reflections* contained much that De Menonville could not accept. He wondered whether Burke was not too ready to export the British system. Burke had expressed some unfair judgments for which factual errors were not responsible. The National Assembly was not a "gang of assassins," nor did it lack moderate members.[26] Mostly, De Menonville feared that Burke's diatribes would strengthen the extremists.

Another French critic was DePont.[27] He regretted having so badly misjudged Burke. He thought Burke quite wrong about

21 Burke MSS, Sheff., Coats to Burke, Feb. 26, 1791.

22 Quoted in Henry W. Meikle, *Scotland and the French Revolution* (Glasgow, 1912), 52.

23 Staunton, *Memoirs*, 330-31, Macartney to Staunton, Dec., 1790.

24 Osborn Coll., Box 39, #16, B/50, Shackleton to Richard, Sr., Dec. 21, 1790.

25 The letter, dated Nov. 17, 1790, survives in the Royal Archives at Windsor Castle. Written in English, it has been translated into French and annotated by Godechot, "Une première critique des Réflexions sur la Révolution française de Burke," *Annales historiques de la révolution française* (July-Sept., 1955), 217-27. De Menonville had a long military career. He died in 1816. See also Copeland, *Our Eminent Friend Edmund Burke*, 211-16, who, however, wrote before the MS letter was found.

26 Burke modified his statement in later editions. Copeland, *Our Eminent Friend Edmund Burke*, 211.

27 Burke MSS, N.R.O., Aix21a, DePont to Burke, Dec. 6, 1790, published in Feb., 1791, as "Answer to the Reflections of the Right Hon. Edmund Burke by M. Depont." See the *Times*, Feb. 9, 1791. The first three pages of the pamphlet explain the earlier correspondence between Burke and DePont, pp. 3-16 contain the letter of Dec. 6, and pp. 17-36 consist of notes.

the old regime and the causes of the Revolution. Burke's support of the forces of reaction endangered peace by encouraging counter-revolution. So far as we know, Burke did not reply. The correspondence ended. One French historian, noting the criticism from France, has wondered whether the sale of the *Reflections* there owed more to curiosity than to acceptance of Burke's views.[28] But even if the philosophic heirs of Burke appeared in France only after 1815, the tide of emigration carried to the Rhineland and England many persons whose bitterness was even more intense than Burke's.

The *Reflections* did not terminate Burke's friendship with Philip Francis, though there was an initial exchange of criticism and defense.[29] Francis expressed frankly his dissent from Burke's judgments of the Revolution and the old regime. Since "I am not likely to alter my opinions," Burke replied, let us avoid this subject and attend to the impeachment, "on which I have the happiness of more agreement with you." Inevitably, their future relationship was more formal.

More than these private ones, certain public reactions suggested a hardening division in English opinion after the *Reflections* appeared. Ironically, its publication revived demand for Price's *Discourse*.[30] The Revolution Society began to divide; Lord Stanhope and Lord William Russell, who disliked the egalitarian tendency of the meeting of November 4, 1790, over which Price presided, quit the society, though Stanhope remained a friend of the Revolution.[31] Other secessions followed. The ardent Dissenters were more determined than ever to present their views. They packed the City Debates in Cornhill on November 8 and 9 and the Westminster Forum on November 10 and 17, when the disputants considered whether Burke's sentiments on Dr. Price and the Revolution Society reflected the spirit of liberty for which he was formerly known.[32]

28 Godechot, *La Contre-Révolution*, 71-72.

29 *Corr.*, III, 162-70, 172-77, Francis to Burke, Nov. 3-4, 1790, Burke to Francis, Nov. 19, 1790.

30 *Times*, Nov. 11, 17, 22, 1790.

31 *Walpole's Corr.*, XI, 131 and n., Walpole to Mary Berry, Nov. 8, 1790; *Times*, Nov. 5, 1790.

32 *Times*, Nov. 8, 17, 1790.

The *Reflections* appeared at an unpropitious time for harmony in Burke's party. Relationships within it had been uneasy for personal reasons since the Regency crisis, a year before Burke and Sheridan quarreled over the French Revolution.[33] Since then, the division had become wider, and continued friction over matters of policy and principle would be disruptive. During his career as a party man Burke had always (some would say hypocritically) identified party and principle, equating his party's position with the national interest.[34] Now there were some, like Sheridan, who would commit the party to a course that Burke considered inimical to England's well-being. It was becoming difficult to assemble the party harmoniously. Sheridan's absence from the annual summer meeting at Portland's seat, Welbeck, soon after the party leaders disapproved of his prominent part in the July 14 anniversary dinner of the friends of the French Revolution, seemed to suggest the split between the Pall Mall and Portland groups.[35] Burke objected on principle, Fox from expediency and, said the *Times,* because he was jealous of Sheridan's popularity at Carlton House, whereas Portland, Fitzwilliam, and Devonshire were apprehensive of Sheridan's growing reputation among the Irish Whigs. Fitzwilliam agreed with Burke that it was desirable to check the tendency for some in the party to fall into "the trammels of Dr. Price."[36] Though appearances were kept up at social gatherings, members regarded one another suspiciously. A week after the original quarrel with Sheridan, it had been rumored that Burke would join with Pitt.[37]

Despite the uneasiness, the party held together during the election in June, 1790. Opinions about the Revolution did not strongly affect the voting. The customary local influences determined the outcomes in contested constituencies. How much old forms prevailed is indicated by the fact that nearly one-fourth of the new house "were peers, or sons or brothers of peers."[38] Dissenters who were angry at Burke did not vent their dislike

[33] *Times,* Feb. 16, 1790.
[34] *Daily Universal Register,* Jan. 13, 1787, contains a flattering "character" of Burke, stressing this point.
[35] *Times,* Feb. 15, July 21, Aug. 22, 1790. Also July 3, 1788, for a similar meeting.
[36] Burke MSS, Sheff., Fitzwilliam to Richard Burke, Jr., Aug. 8, 1790.
[37] *Times,* Feb. 18, 1790.
[38] Feiling, *Second Tory Party,* 183.

against his friends. Some of the party had supported the Dissenters' campaign for repeal of the Test Acts, whereas Pitt had opposed it and parliamentary reform as well. If there was any concerted action by the Dissenters, it was against him, and it was of slight importance.[39] Pitt met parliament in November probably stronger than he had been in June.

There was no clear, unwavering line of division in parliament between government and opposition forces. When "Marcus Brutus" in the *Times* lamented the absence of stanch independents making individual decisions about the national interest and charged all but a half-dozen members with having resolved beforehand to support either Pitt or the opposition, he was speaking fancifully.[40] In a general way there was a government side and an opposition side, but the members were not organized in two distinct parties, disciplined by conceptions of party interest or informed by party principle and program. Pitt's majority could vary greatly in size, especially on questions of foreign affairs, or on issues that touched many members' personal interests, such as the slave trade.

The situation was on the eve of change, and by early 1791 no one saw this more clearly than Burke. Yet he knew that the change could force a realignment of members in parliament. It had been twenty years since he had described "party" as a body of men united on principles of public policy. Since that time and until the French Revolution, Burke had been able to consider his party thus united on most issues. It had survived disagreements over repeal of the Test Acts or over parliamentary reform. But the French Revolution was a different matter. The signs of disruption were unmistakable; the issue involved the "cause of social order."[41]

Probably no individual was more responsible than Burke for bringing the issue into focus. His *Reflections* and his later writings explained and emphasized the necessity of choosing upon it. His parliamentary conduct set an example. His efforts among party leaders, especially the aristocratic ones, helped persuade them to make the choice and accept the consequences. Burke's

---

39 Feiling, *Second Tory Party*, 183.
40 Jan. 5, 1790.
41 Pares, *George III*, 8.

old definition of party still applied, but in the light of the new issues, its application would break up the old opposition party. It became increasingly clear after the publication of the *Reflections* that the Portland Whigs were not a body of men united on principles of public policy. Their struggles to resolve their dilemma had effects that "were never wholly lost," particularly as they affected the history of parties.[42]

By the fall of 1790 one could indulge in the malicious compilation of outlandish lists purporting to show the dissolving effects of the Revolution. The "Whigs of 1790" included, among others, Sheridan, Fox, Burgoyne, Stanhope, Major Hanger, the Reverend Doctors Price and Andrew Kippis, and Napper Tandy, a leader among Irish friends of the Revolution.[43] Burke would have agreed with this classification insofar as it reflected opinions of the Revolution. He told Elliot that Fox and Sheridan disliked the *Reflections* but that the main body of aristocratic Whigs stood by the old definition of Whiggism.[44] Burke worried about the differences between traditional Whig tenets and the new Whig articles. The *Times* was not spreading an idle rumor when it predicted that on account of the Revolution, Burke, Fox, and Sheridan would never "draw together again in the *team* of Opposition"; its division of the opposition into the Portland and the Prince of Wales' parties pretty well confirmed Burke's statement to Elliot.[45]

As a foretaste of what was to come, certain newspapers prior to and during the parliamentary session of 1790-1791 abused Burke mercilessly. If this scurrility did not alienate Burke from all the party, it intensified the differences between him and the Sheridan-Fox section. Whether he was an old man living in new times he could not understand, he did on February 17, 1791, take the oath that he was over sixty years of age and thereby gained exemption from serving on committees to deal with election disputes.[46] It was vicious to call this action proof of senility or to suggest that senility explained his increasing irascibleness.

---

42 Pares, *George III*, 195.
43 *Times*, Oct. 26, 1790.
44 Minto, *Elliot*, I, 365-68, Burke to Elliot, Nov. 29, 1790.
45 *Times*, Nov. 26, 30, 1790.
46 *Commons Journals*, XLVI, 187; *Times*, Feb. 23, 1791.

Burke was especially vulnerable to charges relating to his financial condition. Even the *Times,* which had admired his *Reflections,* participated in the orgy. Burke, "the old *entailed pensioner"* of Lord Fitzwilliam, was about to become a pensioner of the king.[47] His more frequent attendance at the levees and drawing rooms at St. James's might be used as evidence against him. In any case, people noticed that the king was gracious to him, on one occasion late in 1790 thanking him in the name of all gentlemen for supporting the "cause of the Gentlemen."[48] Mrs. Burke, who told this story, exaggerated her husband's reputation. She said that he was held in great "respect and veneration" on both sides of the House. There were individuals on both sides who felt this way toward Burke; there were many who did not; and former friends and opponents were only in the process of reversing positions.

Burke encouraged these reversals by continued attacks upon the Revolution both in the press and on the floor of the House. One of each occurred almost simultaneously in May, 1791. He had written a pamphlet as a letter, dated January 19, in reply to De Menonville. Burke left it to the recipient to publish it or not.[49] Its length and its contents suggest that Burke desired publication, despite having spoken of the "inutility" of saying anything more on the Revolution. After learning that De Menonville was publishing the letter, Burke sent copies to Grenville and the king, though he had promised he would not circulate the letter prior to publication.[50] It would be interesting to know whether he anticipated Grenville's appointment as foreign secretary two months later. Early in May the letter was published in Paris and on May 21 in London as *A Letter to a Member of the National Assembly, in answer to some Objections to his book on French Affairs.*[51]

[47] *Times,* Sept. 25, Dec. 2, 1790, Feb. 10, 1791.

[48] Copeland transcript of MS in Mitchell Library, Jane Burke to Will Burke, March 21, 1791.

[49] *Corr.,* III, 193-94, 202-203, Burke to Mme. D'Osmond, Jan. 25, 1791, Burke to Chevalier de la Bintinnaye, March, 1791.

[50] Burke MSS, Sheff., De Menonville to Burke, March 11 and postscript of April 27, 1791, Grenville to Burke, March 23, 1791, James Bland Burges to Burke, May 6, 1791.

[51] *Works,* IV, 3-55; the *Times,* May 20, 1791, announced its publication for "tomorrow," but on May 24 said, "This day is published."

Burke had two purposes in writing the *Letter*.[52] First, as the title suggested, he was defending the *Reflections*. He reiterated the arguments it had advanced and embellished them with references to events that had transpired since its publication. More importantly, he desired to show "the utter impossibility" of a counterrevolution in France, unless assistance came from abroad. The *Letter* therefore moved a step beyond the *Reflections*, or made specific certain of its implications. It advocated war against the Revolution. There was no one in France capable of serving the cause of monarchy as General Monk had served it in England in 1659-1660. The "act of power" that would restore control in France to the "sound part of the community" must come "from without," from neighbors acting "on motives of safety to themselves."[53] "The hell-hounds of war, on all sides, will be uncoupled and unmuzzled," and considering the characters of the men in control in France, it will be vicious, uncivilized war. Burke was reconciled to this, for no country in Europe was secure while France was ruled "by a college of armed fanatics, for the propagation of the principles of assassination, robbery, rebellion, fraud, faction, oppression, and impiety."[54]

Although these sentiments, which he also expressed privately, filled Burke's mind during the spring of 1791, he did not spill them out in the House of Commons until May 6, just before the publication of the *Letter*. Prior to that time his conduct in the House was almost decorous, and his relations with Fox were peaceful. Together he and Fox defended the proposition that a dissolution did not terminate an impeachment, and both supported a bill extending the privileges of Catholics. Only by remote implication did Burke bring in the French Revolution, when he spoke of the desirability of gradual reform, of which the bill was an example.[55] On the Russian question, they opposed a policy that they called an affront to Russia. Burke argued the Russian side from the principle of preserving the balance of power. Like Fox, he did not think the Russian conquest of a Turkish fortress

---

52 See, e. g., *Corr.*, III, 203-204, Burke to De la Bintinnaye, March, 1791.
53 *Works*, IV, 16-17, 36-37.
54 *Works*, IV, 17.
55 *Parl. Hist.*, XXVIII, 1370-72.

endangered the balance, as Turkey was not a part of Europe and the Russian conquest was inconsequential.[56]

Until April 15 surface harmony existed between Burke and Fox and within the party. It was Fox who then disturbed it and Burke who destroyed it, though the rupture had to come sooner or later. It appears almost as though Fox deliberately provoked the quarrel. His later contention, that but for the abrupt ending of the debate of April 15, a quarrel at that time would have cleared the air and a reconciliation would have been possible, suggests this interpretation.[57] But if Fox believed that, he was probably wrong. Between him and Burke the difference over the Revolution was too profound for compromise.

On April 15 Fox spoke again on the Russian question and the balance of power. Russia did not threaten it, and France, the greatest danger in the past, was now a peaceful nation, happy in its new constitution. Burke, visibly aroused, rose to reply, but the call of "question" from all sides ended the debate.[58] Nevertheless, he made plain his intention to answer Fox during the forthcoming debate on the Government of Quebec bill. On April 21 Fox called on Burke in Duke Street in an attempt to dissuade him from reopening the controversy.[59] Burke refused and even outlined the speech he would make. The conversation was calm; Fox and Burke continued it as they walked to the House. When they arrived, they learned that Sheridan had moved a postponement of the debate. Burke commented briefly. He praised Fox, lamented the occasion for differing from him, and vowed that he had tried to avoid altercation. He had forborne mentioning the Revolution in the House for over a year. But Fox had begun the controversy, and Burke would speak, for he held his principles and patriotism dearer than friendships.

56 *Parl. Hist.*, XXIX, 75-79.
57 *Parl. Hist.*, XXIX, 219n.
58 *Parl. Hist.*, XXIX, 249.
59 It is not clear whether before Fox arrived Burke had met with Pitt and Grenville, as he had been requested to do at 11:30 that morning. Burke MSS, Sheff., Grenville to Burke, April 20, 1791. In any case, Burke supported the bill on grounds the same as theirs. Horace Walpole said that the Prince of Wales was supposed to have written to Burke for the purpose of preventing controversy. *Walpole Corr.*, XI, 263, Walpole to Mary Berry, May 12, 1791. If the prince wrote, the letter has not been discovered.

The stage was set for the drama enacted on May 6.[60] When the committee opened on a motion to discuss the bill in details, Burke was the first speaker. The subject being a government for Canada, Burke thought it proper to talk about the French Revolution, which had furnished one example of constitution-making. When the Revolution became the focus of his speech, his friend Baker called him to order. Fox, whose speech of April 15 had not been a model of relevance, agreed with Baker; the tears that Fox shed later in the debate were hardly congruous with the ironical, deliberately provocative remarks he made in supporting the point of order. When Burke tried to resume, his young colleague Michael Angelo Taylor raised a point of order. Burke started to justify his remarks, and another colleague in the impeachment, St. Andrew St. John, cried order again. When Burke resumed, cries of "order" and "go on" arose. He continued briefly until another party member, John Anstruther, spoke to order. After four more interruptions, Lord Sheffield moved that it was out of order to discuss the French constitution. If these maneuvers were not preconcerted, Burke's tormenters had quickly fallen in with a spontaneous tactic.

Then Pitt intervened and began the debate on Sheffield's motion. Fox spoke at length. He blamed Burke for initiating the disorders and then once more praised the Revolution. This was turning the knife in the wound. At last Burke had a chance to be heard. Though hurt and angered by the treatment his former friends had given him, he began with deliberation and restraint. He desired to discuss, not personalities, but principles of government and the facts of the Revolution. What he said was not new, but he said it bitterly. He excoriated the principles underlying the Revolution and found that the actions of the National Assembly followed inexorably from them. Fox, at last aware of what was happening, whispered audibly that there was no loss of friendship in his controversy with Burke. But he and his friends, having prodded Burke this far, could hardly be innocent of the consequences. Burke said their friendship had to

---

[60] The dramatic and disorderly debate took place on May 6, 11, 12, and 16; the altercation between Burke and Fox, on the first two days. *Parl. Hist.*, XXIX, 364-430.

end. Fox was weeping when he got up to speak. Without recanting his opinions about the Revolution, he pleaded for Burke's continued friendship. If not that, then he hoped for an eventual reconciliation, when tempers had calmed and the occasion for the quarrel had passed. Burke's reply was unyielding. Pitt at last brought the debate to an end but not before he had taken Burke's side on the rules of order, on the Revolution, and personally. He thought that Burke deserved England's gratitude.

On May 11, when the debate resumed, Burke took the quarrel beyond the point of reconciliation, having brooded over it for nearly a week. He talked about his virtual banishment from the party, reaffirmed the doctrines he had espoused in the *Reflections,* and stormed at the Revolution. Fox replied and Burke answered, declaring his willingness to stand alone. A footnote in *Parliamentary History* says, "Thus ended the friendship between Mr. Burke and Mr. Fox—a friendship which had lasted for more than the fourth part of a century."[61]

The tragic nature of this episode touched contemporaries. In commenting upon it they forgot personal dislikes for the moment. The clash had been dramatic but not histrionic. Both men, said Walpole, "were in earnest and *sincere.*"[62] They had to be admired, said the *Times,* for the moment unbiased, Fox for his manly effort to maintain friendship and Burke for his "Roman firmness" in placing duty ahead of desire and sentiment.[63] It was sad to find Burke and Fox sending regrets to Lord Kenyon because they did not want to meet at his dinner party.[64] The *Times* hoped that the friendship would someday be reestablished but doubted that it would.

A merely personal quarrel could have been reconciled. Both men desired reconciliation. But a certain embarrassment impeded early attempts, and the longer reconciliation was postponed, the more difficult it became.[65] A renewal of friendship might suggest that Burke's antipathy to the Revolution was moderating. Fox was known to be a warmer, more flexible person, and people

61 XXIX, 426.
62 *Walpole Corr.,* XI, 263, to Mary Berry, May 12, 1791.
63 May 10, 1791.
64 *Times,* May 11, 1791.
65 *Corr.,* III, 303, Burke to Richard, Jr., Sept. 1, 1791.

would be less likely to see in any alteration of his personal conduct an indication of a change of principles. He had, as Burke told Francis, a "facility of his temper, which yields to proximity."[66] Burke was probably equally impulsive and even more sentimental and would be likelier to experience a sudden evaporation of hard resolution. Some anecdotes suggest this.[67] But reconciliation never took place, though both men remained regretful of the rupture and each continued to reserve a special place in his affection for the other.

The rupture was permanent because, as the *Annual Register* said, it was over an issue of the greatest political significance.[68] The public was fascinated. The City debates at Cornhill considered whether Burke was the patriotic guardian of the constitution or the advocate of arbitrary power; at Coachmakers' Hall in London a large audience was asked whether Burke or Fox or Pitt had the greatest knowledge of the constitution and had it most at heart.[69] The caricaturists found the quarrel particularly stimulating. In the "Volcano of Opposition" Fox is consoled by Sheridan while Burke declaims, and calls are sent out for Dr. John Monro, the expert on insanity; Burke, the apostate, in "Political Playthings," is receiving an earl's coronet from Pitt; Burke, "The Uniform Whig," is depicted again as an apostate.[70]

The aristocratic leaders of the party were in a dilemma. They needed Fox for his practical, political abilities, but they agreed with the message of Burke's *Reflections,* though they had been tactfully silent about it. They were afraid to disavow Fox openly for fear of destroying the party, but how could they repudiate Burke and remain true to themselves?[71] Burke prepared a paper to assist Portland in conversation with Fox, but Elliot declined the commission to communicate it to the duke.[72] He thought

---

66 Francis and Keary, eds., *Francis Letters,* II, 376.

67 H.M.C., *Charlemont,* 279, Dr. Alexander Haliday to Charlemont, Aug. 7, 1796; Rogers, *Table-Talk,* 79; Peter Burke, . . . *Life of . . . Edmund Burke* (London, 1854), 257-58; Castalia Countess Granville, ed., *Lord Granville Leveson Gower, Private Correspondence* (London, 1916), I, 166.

68 XXXIV, iv-v.

69 *Times,* May 12, June 2, 1791.

70 Cartoons in British Museum print room, nos. 7863, 7865, 7913, and George, *Catalogue of Political Satires,* VI.

71 Burke MSS, Sheff., Richard Burke, Jr., to O'Beirne, May 6, 1791.

72 Osborn Coll., Box 74, #23, MS dated May, 1791.

Burke misjudged Fox, and he did not desire to encourage a rupture between Fox and Portland. Always the watchful Pitt was ready, as in the debates of May 6 and 11, to exploit differences within the party. It is easy to imagine the nervousness of the grandees who sat in the gallery of the Commons while Burke and Fox quarreled—Portland, Devonshire, Carlisle, Rawdon, and Porchester.[73] The aloof Fitzwilliam, who respected Burke, and, as far as his nature would permit, loved Fox, worried in private.

Aware of the impact of the quarrel upon the party and conscious of the attention of the noble lords sitting above, Burke made a point during the debate of talking about the idea and the nature of party. Once again he defined "party" as a group of men bound by principles. When in opposition they had the duty to oppose ministerial actions that might threaten the constitution. The members should be "disciplined troops," sharing with their leader a common purpose and striving to give effect to it. The implication was clear. Fox's principles and conduct would undermine discipline, destroy party unity, and leave Portland a leader in name only. A party led by Fox would embrace the principles of the Revolution, and there would be no room in it for persons who did not accept them. What, for example, were the party's noble leaders to make of the item in the *Morning Chronicle* of May 12 that read Burke out of the party, placed Fox at its head, and identified with it the "pure doctrine" of Fox? On the next day the *Times* carried the thought further. It did not blame Burke for leaving the party that had inherited the principles of Fox; it trusted that Burke would continue to defend the constitution against its detractors, and the Portland section of the party from its radical wing.

Whether Burke misunderstood Fox and exaggerated the dangers to the British constitution, many contemporaries were beginning to believe that events in France justified the alarms. Friends of the Revolution were indisputably active in England. Replies to the *Reflections* were appearing in large numbers and numerous editions. The best known was Paine's *Rights of Man,* the first part of which was published in March, 1791. It became at once

73 *Times,* May 7, 1791. Stanhope was present, but he hardly belongs with this group.

immensely popular.[74] There was also a group of reformers in the party. Neither the party leaders nor Pitt's government nor the friends of the British constitution could be quite certain whether they were as dangerous as Burke thought.

To add to the uneasiness, Burke's *Letter to a Member of the National Assembly* appeared just after the breach with Fox. The difference in the party over the Revolution could no longer be dismissed as an argument about theory or an event that was distant. Burke was making the Revolution a question of foreign and military policy. If some members would not be as ready as Fox to dismiss the *Letter* as "mere madness, and especially in those parts where he is for a general war, for the purpose of destroying the present government of France," then the division in the party would have to extend to foreign relations.[75]

At this time, as though awed by his own boldness, Burke displayed ambivalence. On May 10, a day between the two debates on the Quebec bill, Elliot moved for a committee of the whole house to consider repeal of the Test Acts as they applied to Scotland. Burke knew of the campaign for repeal; he knew that Windham favored it and that Fox, Sheridan, and Anstruther had participated in the planning of the strategy. But he remained quiet "for prudential reasons"; he disliked the plan, but he did not want to become involved in another intraparty quarrel.[76] When he could agree with his friends, he was willing to speak. On May 12, the day after his quarrel with Fox, he supported Charles Grey's motion for a committee to inquire into imprisonment for debt.[77] He did so for humanitarian reasons and because the proposed legal reform would protect creditors and debtors alike.

The tragedy of Burke's situation was appalling. Isolated in the House of Commons, outside he avoided the company of his remaining friends in order to relieve them from the embarrassment of his presence. As a preliminary to withdrawing from the

74 Burke MSS, Sheff., "Verax" to Burke, May 16, 1791, R. Beauchamp to Burke, June 8, 1791; *Times*, June 16, 1791, for example.

75 Russell, *Fox*, II, 298, Fox to Lord Holland, May 26, 1791.

76 Somerville, *Life*, 226-51, esp. 250-51. Dundas and Pitt opposed the motion, and it lost 149-62.

77 *Parl. Hist.*, XXIX, 512-14.

THE IMPEACHMENT, OR, THE FATHER OF THE GANG TURN'D KING'S EVIDENCE,
by James Gillray, May, 1791. Burke denouncing Sheridan and Fox as "abettors of Revolutions."

party, he asked Lord Fitzwilliam to cease giving him financial compensation for services to it.[78] The *Morning Chronicle* had already separated him from it, and his resignation from Brooks's Club seemed to confirm the statement. When "the world is threatened with great changes," and he and the party disagreed about their nature and meanings, Burke might as well desist from trying to impose his views upon his friends. He had thought they approved of his *Reflections* because it supported their principles and interests. But Fox had disabused him of these fancies. Fox had deliberately provoked him, and when Burke had refused to accept his test of membership in the party—sympathy for the Revolution—Burke had had to leave. When the party "to a man" in the House of Commons applauded Fox, and Burke found himself there without a friend, the time had come to leave. Lord Fitzwilliam might as well begin to think about the disposal of Malton. If the Hastings business could be concluded during the next session, Burke then could vacate his seat. All he asked was Fitzwilliam's friendship.

While Fitzwilliam mulled over this sad letter, at Milton and later at Wentworth with his guest, Fox, there was plenty to occupy the minds of party members who remained near London. Already the friends of the Revolution were preparing to celebrate July 14, and they invited the Whig Club to join them at the Crown and Anchor on that day.[79] The invitation was not intended as a blow at Burke; nevertheless, if the club accepted, he would feel it. His friend John Coxe Hippisley presided over the embarrassed meeting, which finally found a formula for refusing the invitation. This action may not have indicated agreement with Burke's views, but it showed that some members of the party did not want to mix with the friends of the Revolution because of uneasiness about their politics. Burke did not mean to indict the whole party, or even a large portion of it, though his strong feelings sometimes led him into exaggeration. People who merely wished the Revolution well ought to be distinguished from those who would import its principles. There were perhaps "half a score" of Whigs in parliament who strongly sympathized and

[78] Fitzwilliam MSS, Sheff., F115a, Burke to Fitzwilliam, June 5, 1791.
[79] *Times,* June 14, 1791.

two or three more who leaned dangerously toward the Revolution. Burke wanted to prevent this articulate and aggressive minority from assuming leadership; he wished to force the lethargic members to declare their true affection for the British constitution.[80] Party leaders might be influenced by "go-betweens" misrepresenting as public sentiment the opinions of small numbers outside parliament.[81] Burke admitted that he was piqued by the humiliating treatment he had received, but he retained "great affection" for the party as such, knew that at bottom its sentiments were sound, and hoped that when the danger was understood, the party would play its proper role in preserving order in England.[82]

Events, as well as his own proddings, might help the party, especially its "equestrian order," the middle group, to overcome their indecisiveness.[83] In June the news of the flight, capture, and humiliation of the French king was the topic of conversation. When he fled from Paris he left behind a document that bitterly denounced the revolutionaries and all their works and asked Frenchmen to rally around him. The news of the king's escape provoked outbursts of "universal" joy in England, that of his capture "real, unaffected, and general" sorrow.[84] To Burke the event "furnished new motives, and clear grounds of justification" for intervention by the European powers. To Englishmen not yet ready to go so far, it nevertheless seemed that every dispatch from France confirmed Burke's judgments of the Revolution.

But were its friends in England so dangerous? What was one to make of the Birmingham riots of July 14-17?[85] The mob, crying "Church and King," had broken up the dinner of the friends of the Revolution, mainly Dissenters, and then had burned and pillaged. They destroyed two Dissenting chapels, including Priestley's, his home, his library and laboratory, and

80 *Corr.*, III, 225-26, Burke to Richard, Jr., Aug. 5, 1791.

81 *Works*, IV, 189-90, "Appeal from the New to the Old Whigs."

82 *Corr.*, III, 218-19, 226, Burke to François-Claude-Amour, Marquis de Bouille, July 13, 1791, Burke to Richard, Jr., Aug. 5, 1791. The marquis was involved in the plot for the escape of Louis XVI. When it failed, he went into exile.

83 *Works*, IV, 190-91.

84 *Corr.*, III, 219, Burke to De Bouille, July 13, 1791.

85 The *Times*, beginning July 18, carried long accounts of the event, mixing rumor, fact, and fancy so that a reader would hardly know what to believe. Generally, the *Times* seemed to think there was provocation for the riots, though it specifically said it could not condone bloodshed or wanton destruction of property.

other houses as well. The riots lasted from Thursday through Sunday. Had the mob been set off by an inflammatory antichurch and antiking handbill circulated by the "Presbyterean [*sic*] Party"? Had the first toast drunk at the dinner been "Destruction to the present government—and the king's head upon a charger!" Priestley, the author of a reply to Burke's *Reflections,* had gone at once to London, where he issued a long letter about the riots.[86] He denied the statements about the toast, he knew nothing of an inflammatory handbill, he had not been at the dinner. He reaffirmed his sympathy for the French Revolution. He acknowledged his desire for "an improvement" of the British constitution, but denied that this would be the subversion of it.

A great controversy grew up around the Birmingham riots and Priestley.[87] Without wishing to relax vigilance over the English friends of the Revolution, Burke condemned the riots.[88] Mob actions were wrong in themselves and, besides, were ineffective. Such tactics would discredit the cause of the constitution. Those who desired social order should not try to preserve it by illegal actions that challenged the rule of law. Legal remedies were available. Grand juries could preserve order and search out factious associations. And at the top, the "weighty men of all parties" should take a strong stand for the constitution and against the Revolution.

But how could they do that when the Whig party was in disagreement about the constitution and principles of revolution, both British and French? It was time that the British constitution

86 *Times,* July 21, 1791.

87 Historians have treated Priestley sympathetically, but he was capable of dissembling. In a letter to the *Morning Chronicle,* March 7, 1793, he flatly denied ever belonging to a political society or signing any of their papers. He made this statement in answer to a charge of Burke's. But on June 27, 1791, he invited James Watt to join the Warwickshire Constitutional Society and enclosed a printed copy of the principles of the society. Watt declined the invitation because he disapproved of the society's principles. A week after his reply, the Birmingham riots occurred. E. Robinson, "New Light on the Priestley Riots," *The Historical Journal,* III (1960), 73-75. Even before the riots, Thomas Somerville thought Priestley was not straightforward in his sympathies. When he met him in Johnston's bookshop in London, Somerville thought his "enthusiastic admiration" for the revolutionary leaders "rendered his pretensions to religious principle suspicious and equivocal." At this time, Somerville was himself a friend of the Revolution, though he seems to have had doubts about the religious policy of the National Assembly. Somerville, *Life,* 232, 264.

88 *Corr.,* III, 222-23, Burke to Richard, Sr., July 24, 1791.

was explained. It had been said that Fox spoke the "pure doctrine" of the Whig party; Burke contested this. In the *Reflections*
he had tried to interpret the meaning of the Revolution of 1688,
but even in his own party it seemed he had not been attended to.
He decided to try once more to explain that the doctrines of the
"new" Whigs, such as Fox, were not the "old" Whig doctrines
that until the French Revolution the party had abided by. He
spent the summer finishing a pamphlet that he must have begun
about April, when Fox opened the great debate. The *Times* on
June 27 expected its publication within a week, identifying it
probably with the book on the constitution that it had had Burke
writing as early as February 21.[89] The work was published on
August 3. Burke settled on the title only two weeks before that.
He called it "An Appeal from the New to the Old Whigs, in
consequence of some late discussions in Parliament relative to the
Reflections on the French Revolution."

Though parliament would not meet for six months, the time
was favorable in other respects for the pamphlet's purposes.[90]
Written in the third person and published anonymously, its
authorship was obvious to the readers Burke intended it for. It
repeated some points discussed in the *Reflections* and enlarged
upon others, to all of which the events of the past year gave
added force. Burke's purpose in the *Appeal,* as in that book, was
to emphasize the evils and dangers of the Revolution. There was
also some new matter to discuss, especially the episode of the
Quebec bill debates and the allegations of inconsistency between
his conduct in the old days and now. Burke's theme was Whiggism
in both its historical and its contemporary applications.

In defending himself, Burke vindicated the "old" Whigs. He
denied the charge of inconsistency, recalling views on various
public questions since he had entered parliament that showed
a steady adherence to basic principles of the constitution and of
political action. These were true Whig principles; it was his
detractors who had betrayed the Revolution of 1688. Though in
the *Reflections* he had devoted many pages to the Revolution of

89 On June 16 the *Times* described it as a history of the constitution from the
beginnings to the Revolution of 1688.

90 Burke MSS, Sheff., Burke to Richard, Sr., July 24, 1791. The "Appeal" is in
Works, IV, 61-215.

1688, in the *Appeal* he went over the ground thoroughly. The Whig "Fathers" who managed the impeachment of Dr. Henry Sacheverell in 1710 based their prosecution upon the principles of 1688 and explained them at length during the trial. Burke quoted long extracts from their speeches in order to show the difference between them and the "new" Whigs.

The "new" Whigs embraced the principles of the late Dr. Price (who had died on April 19, 1791) and other enlightened philosophers of political metaphysics. Theirs was a simple constitutional interpretation. The people are sovereign; their will legitimizes their acts and makes positive law supreme.[91] It follows from this, as Dr. Price expressed it, that people may depose kings, overthrow governments, and form new ones "at their pleasure." Government in this kind of majoritarian democracy is only a matter of counting heads to ascertain the omnipotent majority. Burke considered this absurd; "rational freedom" and the rules of morality would give way to pure expediency, judged merely contemporaneously.

The "old" Whigs held different doctrine. There was an original contract, not as a contemporary agreement but "implied and expressed," in the ancient constitution providing for king, Lords, and Commons in proper relationship. James II had violated it, the Revolution recovered it, and the act found its necessity in the circumstances of danger to the traditional order. In 1688-1689, not only was the ancient constitution recovered but it was preserved.

Considered only with reference to the historical fact of the Revolution of 1688, Burke's interpretation was wrong. Except formally, the "ancient constitution" was not restored by the Revolution Settlement. Although the Bill of Rights imposed only one new limitation upon the royal prerogative, the other limitations, though previously asserted, had been ineffective, and their reassertion in 1689, made effective by the surrounding circumstances, seriously altered the balance of the constitution. The eighteenth-century constitution that Burke revered was not the

---

91 *Works,* IV, 120-21, 170-71. Later, Fox expressed this very succinctly. In the light of 1688 he "could not admit the right to do all this but by acknowledging the sovereignty of the people as paramount to all other laws." *Parl. Hist.,* XXX, 310, **Feb. 1, 1793.**

ancient constitution, or that under which the seventeenth century had lived; the sovereignty of parliament after 1688 was a reality, no longer merely an aspiration.

The remaining question was how to give effect to the sovereignty of parliament after it had been achieved. The electoral process operated ambivalently in its eighteenth-century form. To Price and his friends it implied the sovereignty of the people. In desiring to broaden the franchise they would, in fact, have altered the old theory by making government representative of people rather than of interests. To that extent they were departing from the assumptions that underlay the Revolution Settlement while following its implications to their conclusion. What was involved here was a disagreement about the theory of representation, whether it was virtual or actual, of interests or individuals. Burke upheld the traditional view of virtual representation that he had expressed during the controversy with America and to his Bristol constituents. Price and his friends spoke for the radical idea, which would become the mainstream of the changing course of representation. The conflicting beliefs about the nature of representation were bound to produce incompatible interpretations of the meaning of the Revolution of 1688.

When they talked about "misconduct" as a justification for changes in government, the radicals were not in basic disagreement with Burke. He used the word "necessity"; they could accept it. The only questions were, what constitutes "necessity," and who decides when it has arisen? Burke's talk about an "overwhelming necessity" that is not chosen, but chooses, is a play upon words. The necessity that chooses is the self-evident fact, but self-evidence is relative to the observer. The reformers would not accept Burke nor persons who thought as he did as the ones who were to decide when to proclaim a self-evident necessity. Burke left himself vulnerable to the charge that he thought England had seen the last of necessity in 1688. More than in the *Reflections*, Burke seemed in the *Appeal* to rule out further constitutional and social change. He seemed to be uneasily aware of this when he berated the National Assembly for making the new French constitution virtually unamendable. But when he spoke of the English constitution being "inviolably" fixed in king, Lords, and

Commons, he was not thinking in Hobbesian terms.[92] The original compact, to use a figure of speech, could be altered with the consent of all the parties. Since Burke's time England has done this. The constitution of 1963 still recognizes king, Lords, and Commons, and there is still in England an established church, but this constitution is as different from the one Burke knew as was his from that of James I.

Philosophically and sociologically Burke's argument is the stronger one. What he really meant is to be understood by reference to his view of the nature of man and society. In the *Appeal* he repeated, though in briefer form, the discussion developed fully in the *Reflections*. He assumed once again the existence of a natural moral order and the working of divine providence; he described the complexity of society; he admitted change under the control of a principle of conservation that kept in view circumstances, the *"necessity"* of the case." Prudence remained the first of virtues that, under providence, tutored the statesman. Art was formally defined as "man's nature," and society, a natural thing, was also a work of art. Throughout the *Appeal,* as in the *Reflections,* Burke did not argue as a philosopher from his premises about the natural moral order. He assumed its existence and went on to argue from circumstance and precedent like the historian or the lawyer. He would affirm "nothing universal" on any moral or political subject. "The theory contained in this book is not to furnish principles for making a new Constitution, but for illustrating the principles of a Constitution already made. It is a theory drawn from the *fact* of our government."[93]

Once again he spoke as the advocate of a prudential, circumstantial gradualism that honored the principle of historical continuity, itself a fact of life for which doctrinaire universals could not be substituted. The *Appeal* presented to the Whigs "their constitutional ancestors" and "the doctors of the modern school."[94] Burke had chosen between them; the Whigs would have to choose. Compromise was impossible.

[92] *Works,* IV, 121.
[93] *Works,* IV, 207.
[94] *Works,* IV, 214.

Burke, who had been at Margate since mid-July for his and his wife's health, read eagerly the letters he received about the *Appeal*. On the whole he was well pleased, though it was not accepted as enthusiastically as the *Reflections* nor was the sale as large.[95] Still, within two weeks a third edition was in preparation. Some people told Burke they liked it better than the *Reflections,* an opinion he did not share.[96] He had sent out prepublication copies to important persons, including the king and the Prince of Wales. From some of them he heard promptly. Lord Camden, who had always considered himself an old Whig, admitted that he had never thought upon the subject so carefully as Burke; after reading the *Appeal* he would be better able to instruct others on the true doctrine.[97] The Bishop of Salisbury sent the king's approbation; shortly after, Burke was at Windsor, where the king saw him and talked with him for a quarter of an hour.[98] Undoubtedly they discussed the pamphlet, but whatever the subject, the fact of the conversation was noticed and condemned by some members of the party. Sir William Scott, the great civil lawyer, had heard only praise for the *Appeal*.[99] More to the point of Burke's interest, Scott thought it would have a powerful influence upon opinion. Around Whitehall, where Burke had hoped there would be a sympathetic audience, everyone praised the work, said Thomas King.[100] Beilby Porteus, Bishop of London, thought the *Appeal* completed "that noble Political Structure" whose foundations had been laid in the *Reflections*.[101]

But these were peripheral opinions. Burke was more concerned about reactions within the party. There is little about this in his correspondence. In talking with Lord Stormont, Burke gathered that "the party is incurable," refusing to admit any "disease" in it

95 *Corr.,* III, 234, Burke to Richard, Jr., Aug. 10, 1791.
96 *Corr.,* III, 274, Burke to Richard, Jr., Aug. 16, 1791.
97 *Corr.,* III, 228-29, Lord Camden to Burke, Aug. 5, 1791.
98 *Corr.,* III, 232, 293, Burke to Richard, Jr., Aug. 9, 25, 1791; Burke MSS, Sheff., Bishop of Salisbury to Burke, Aug. 7, 1791; *Times,* Aug. 24, 25, 26, 1791.
99 *Corr.,* III, 230-31, Scott to Burke, Aug. 6, 1791.
100 Burke MSS, Sheff., Aug. 4, 1791. King was too enthusiastic. Dundas, e. g., was noncommittal, merely acknowledging receipt of the copy Burke sent him. Burke MSS, Sheff., Aug. 12, 1791. Lord Hawkesbury praised it. Burke MSS, Sheff., Aug. 12, 1791.
101 Burke MSS, Sheff., Porteus to Burke, Aug. 9, 1791.

except the personal, imprudent quarrel between him and Fox.[102] Stormont thought Burke had misrepresented Fox and the opinion of the party. Fox did not wish the destruction of the constitution; the party rejected the doctrines of Paine; there was no basic disagreement on principles between Burke and the party. Burke had inflated a misunderstanding into an embarrassing appearance of a serious breach in the party. Burke was ready to admit that the party had not succumbed to French doctrine, but by a "mistaken prudence" it had remained silent, had not denounced the Revolution, had not separated itself from those in the country who wished well for the Revolution, and therefore had given tacit support to the enemies of the British constitution. No good purpose was being served by trying to preserve within the party a mute unanimity that could be misinterpreted to mean "common adherence to sentiments odious to the best of them."

The difference in the Portland party was mainly a difference of understanding of the meaning of the French Revolution. Charlemont, for example, disavowed the "french philosophy," disliked some of the actions of the National Assembly, and did not want England to emulate the French example.[103] But he had to rejoice when he saw the French people emancipated from the tyranny of the old regime. Obviously, Burke had made no impression upon him nor had he convinced him that the tyranny of a multitude was the worst of all tyrannies. Even Lord Fitzwilliam seemed to agree with Stormont. Since Burke's letter of June 5 Fitzwilliam had been silent. This was wise. When at last he wrote (the letter is missing, but Burke referred to it in his reply) he was conciliatory. Apparently, he rejected Burke's offer to surrender his stipend and his seat for Malton, and otherwise he tried to soften Burke's asperity. Burke was grateful and relieved.[104] However, he remained adamant about "that man" (Fox) and sent a copy of the *Appeal* to justify his position.[105] Fitzwilliam seemed immune to persuasion. On the one hand he praised the *Reflections* in a way indicating his desire to make his

102 *Corr.*, III, 235-37, Burke to Richard, Jr., Aug. 10, 1791.
103 *Corr.*, III, 251, Charlemont to Burke, Aug. 13, 1791.
104 Fitzwilliam MSS, Sheff., F115a, Burke to Fitzwilliam, Aug. 4, 1791.
105 Burke MSS, Sheff., Laurence to Burke, Aug. 8, 1791.

opinions known; on the other, he was cordial to Fox. When Fox visited Wentworth in August, Fitzwilliam had an opportunity to witness a demonstration of popular enthusiasm for him at York races.[106] Burke thought this cordiality a "slap" at him.[107] One thing was clear to Fitzwilliam. If the difference between Fox and Burke did split the party, a significant portion of it would go with Fox, and Fitzwilliam's choice would disrupt one of his friendships.

Burke could not appreciate why people were not alarmed about the Revolution. His cries of danger, his call to arms, had not evoked the response he had hoped for. Private commendations of his writings were not enough. Men of substance must commit themselves publicly, even if speaking out meant "hurting Fox."[108] The minority who opposed Burke in England were active, vocal, aggressive, proselyting spirits. More pamphleteers attacked than defended Burke. In the pamphlet war, the friends of the Revolution seemed to outnumber its opponents. Even if people were getting sick of the abuse heaped on Burke, there was no indication of a reaction in his favor.[109] On the continent the counterrevolution was dissolving in bickering and indecision. The Declaration of Pillnitz, August 27, was a timid thing; its "then, and in that case," deferring action until the other monarchs of Europe joined forces with the king of Prussia and the emperor, was an invitation to procrastination. To a group of French nobility who asked when they would be back in France, a despondent Burke replied, "Never."[110] In England, as Burke saw it, the lethargy in his party only encouraged the friends of the Revolution and did nothing to stimulate the government into action. The questions of party, England, and Europe had to be joined. But it was doubtful that that could be accomplished by the efforts of one man, the only man in France or England who at that time was "aware of the extent of the danger, with which we are threatened."[111]

---

106 *Times*, Aug. 17, 1791; Burke MSS, Sheff., William Weddell to Burke, Aug. 27, 1791.
107 *Corr.*, III, 303, Burke to Richard, Jr., Sept. 1, 1791.
108 *Corr.*, III, 274, Burke to Richard, Jr., Aug. 16, 1791.
109 *Times*, Sept. 7, 1791.
110 Butler, *Reminiscences*, I, 149.
111 Butler, *Reminiscences*, I, 150.

CHAPTER XVI

The Whig Dilemma

THE INTRAPARTY CONFLICT that Burke helped provoke was more than a family quarrel. If the public was interested because it had strong views about the personalities involved, it also understood the larger political meanings. The party reaction to Burke's attacks upon the Revolution belonged in the context of two other great debates that the French Revolution stimulated. One concerned reform in England, particularly parliamentary reform —the means of achieving the kind of freedom that some persons thought the Revolution was bringing to France. There seemed to be a bond of sympathy and purpose, a mutual influence, which reformers hoped would enlarge liberty in both countries. To one such as Burke, who opposed parliamentary reform and the Revolution as well, the connection between the two movements was doubly dangerous. To the reformers of England Burke was a prime object of bitter criticism.

The other debate, in which in 1791 Burke became deeply engaged, concerned the means of combatting revolutionary ideas. Burke proposed a radical solution, to stifle the ideas at their source by extinguishing the Revolution itself. He recognized that this was something more easily said than done; yet without depreciating the difficulties, he always insisted that counter-revolution was practicable. England must be prepared to assume her share of the responsibility. She was a part of the monarchical Christian order of Europe. The revolutionary attacks upon religion and monarchy were bound to affect England, the more so in Burke's mind because the English reformers were inspired by revolutionary ideas. If counterrevolution on the continent had to take the form of armed intervention, England should assist it, and at the same time carry out the domestic phase by suppressing the reform movement. England could not effectively do her duty if a section of the Whig party and a part of the public encouraged the English reformers and the French revolutionaries. The political logic of this situation seemed to Burke to require firm action by the government and support of it by all persons interested in preserving the existing social order. The issue was sharp enough to Burke in 1791 and to other people later to suggest a realignment of political interests in England on the basis of opinions about reform, counterrevolution, and war—that is, ultimately on the question of preserving the traditional order.

The debate that Burke's early revolutionary writings stimulated revealed widespread discontent with the British constitution that he adored. Early in the Revolution, some Englishmen believed that it would be an example to all the world. Major John Cartwright thought that the French were asserting not only their rights but "the general liberties of mankind."[1] Dr. Price expected the French Revolution to encourage reform in the governments of Europe, meaning, in England, repeal of the Test Acts and parliamentary reform. This became the theme of many of the numerous replies to the *Reflections*.[2] Besides presenting the case for reform, Burke's opponents, in numerous pamphlets, attacked him personally for the apparent inconsistency of his conduct, wondered about the purity of his motives, and assailed his ignorance of conditions in France. They vigorously defended the National Assembly, excused the excesses of the revolutionaries, and justified the Revolution on the grounds of necessity and philosophy. There was no French constitution worth amending, they argued. In order to achieve freedom the French had to destroy the old regime and build anew.

---

1 Letter of Aug. 18, 1789, quoted in Cobban, *Debate on the French Revolution,* 41.
2 Stanlis, *Burke and the Natural Law,* 275, n. 94, numbers forty-eight replies to the *Reflections* and Burke's other writings on the Revolution. I read a score of them for two articles, "Pamphlet Replies to Burke's *Reflections*" and "English Reform Ideas during the French Revolution," *Southwestern Social Science Quarterly,* XXVI (1945), 22-34, XXVII (1947), 368-84. These articles and Stanlis' bibliography identify the replies, so I forbear listing them here.

The pamphleteers revealed various philosophical predilections. They ranged from the millenarianism of Price through the natural-rights, contract theories to the newer tendencies toward utilitarianism. In some of the pamphlets, like Priestley's and Paine's, there was a mixture. Jeremy Bentham rejected natural rights and carried to its conclusion the doctrine of utility based upon identification of the interests of individuals. When incomplete, political identification of the interests of governors and governed could be promoted by universal suffrage.[3] William Godwin, assuming the pristine goodness of man, went to the extreme of philosophic anarchism. In most instances, the replies postulated the sovereignty of the people and found in their will the supreme source of authority. From this, the demand for parliamentary reform immediately emerged, for under the unreformed constitution the will of the people was not freely or fully expressed.

If reformers agreed about the need, they differed in details, as John Thelwall, the popular lecturer sadly admitted.[4] Neither Godwin nor Paine spoke for the parliamentary reformers and really did not belong among them. Godwin appealed to a coterie of literary people; Paine's republicanism had a practical persuasiveness, especially to the lower classes, which did not truly represent the reformers' real desires. Fox doubted if many people "agreed with the general tendency" of the *Rights of Man*. It was a "performance totally different from all ideas of reform."[5] The Reverend Christopher Wyvill, the veteran Yorkshire reformer, repudiated Paine specifically because he aimed not at amendment but at the destruction of the English constitution.[6] The majority of reformers believed they could accomplish their purposes within the framework of king, Lords, and Commons. Few among them were ready to apply Paine's constitutional or social teaching. But his directness had a stimulating emotional appeal. When Tom

[3] Burke too recognized a natural identity of interests, but chiefly in economic affairs. ". . . the benign and wise Disposer of all things, who obliges men, whether they will or not, in pursuing their own selfish interests, to connect the general good with their own individual success." "Thoughts and Details on Scarcity" (1795), *Works,* V, 141.

[4] *The Rights of Nature* (London, 1796), 40.

[5] *Parl. Hist.,* XXIX, 1315, April 30, 1792.

[6] *A Defense of Dr. Price, and the Reformers of England* (York, 2d ed., 1792), preface.

Hod, in reading the *Rights of Man,* discovered that he did not enjoy liberty, equality, or happiness, he cried, "I'm for a constitution—and organization—and equalization—and fraternization."[7] Whatever these words meant, they implied too much to some people. Where, for example, James Mackintosh and some others asked for parliamentary reform in order to avert revolution, Paine desired an English revolution. His radical spirit had its appeal, but his political thought was becoming dated. The nineteenth-century reform movement in England was stimulated by Benthamite utilitarianism and adopted by Whig common sense, and in the second respect it could be more readily accounted for in Burke's terms than by a philosophy of natural rights.[8]

The significance of the pamphlet literature written in reply to the *Reflections* arises from its connection with existing political discontent, which the French Revolution stimulated and Burke exacerbated. The replies for the most part were throwbacks to the radicalism of the 1780's, which had in large part been middle class and Dissenting. The later intensity of popular agitation owed something, however, to economic discontent as well as to political ideas. Between 1785 and the Revolution, the parliamentary reformers had been quiet. Price's sermon found them stirring again. The efforts in 1790 to secure repeal of the Test Acts and to obtain a parliamentary reform failed, partly because they were inadequately organized and also because the Revolution was dampening parliamentary interest or providing an excuse for opposing reform. These failures suggested the need for better organization among the reformers. But in place of a united, national, reform organization, they formed local societies advocating different programs.[9] The Revolution Society, the original object of Burke's scorn, played little part in the reform move-

---

[7] Hannah More, "Village Politics" (1793), *Works* (London, 1836), II, 222.

[8] For an interesting discussion, N. C. Phillips, "Burke and Paine," *Landfall,* VIII (March, 1954), 36-46.

[9] On the history of reform and the societies, see Simon Maccoby, *English Radicalism, 1786-1832* (London, 1955), John Binns, *Recollections of the Life of John Binns* (Philadelphia, 1854), Philip Anthony Brown, *The French Revolution in English History* (London, 1918), W. P. Hall, *British Radicalism* (New York, 1911), Henry Jephson, *The Platform* (New York, 1892), W. T. Laprade, *England and the French Revolution, 1789-1797* (Baltimore, 1910), G. S. Veitch, *The Genesis of Parliamentary Reform* (London, 1913), and Graham Wallas, *The Life of Francis Place* (New York, 1919).

ment.[10] It never had a specific program; its membership began to scatter after the appearance of the *Reflections*. The French chargé d'affaires in London reported on February 4, 1791, that "Burke's pamphlet has united the entire English nation against us," and this exaggerated statement, though referring to France, suggests disapprobation of all who sympathized with her. At the dinner of July 14, 1791, at the Crown and Anchor, nine hundred persons were reported present.[11] This was not a Revolution Society celebration, though many of the diners belonged to the society. After this the Society declined. Its meeting of November 4, 1792, was its last.

The names of its members appeared on the lists of other societies which had more precise reform objectives. One was the Society for Constitutional Information, revived by Horne Tooke in 1790 after a lapse of five years. It drew largely from the middle class and included a generous proportion of Dissenters and professional men. It had a counterpart in the Manchester Constitutional Society, which in October, 1790, expressed its credo as the sovereignty of the people, freedom of opinion, and "a speedy and effectual reform" of parliament.[12] In March, 1792, this society voted its thanks to Paine, but without approving republicanism, it demanded a "complete reform in the present inadequate state of the Representation."[13] The Sheffield Constitutional Society, founded four months earlier, according to its own statement was composed "chiefly of the manufacturers of Sheffield" and boasted approximately two thousand members.[14] The language of these constitutional societies was often more incendiary than their programs. Something like Pitt's proposal of 1785 would have satisfied most of their members, who hoped a moderate reform would forestall such extreme demands as universal suffrage.

One of the most interesting phases of the reform movement of the 1790's was the emergence of a militant working-class organization. Its humble genius was Thomas Hardy, a London shoemaker.

---

10 E. Pariset, "La Societie de la Révolution de Londres," *La Révolution Française* (Oct., 1895), 297-326. The *Times*, Jan. 1, 1791, facetiously reported the demise of the society. The report, although premature, was prophetic.

11 Maccoby, *English Radicalism*, 51, n. 1.

12 Capel Lofft, *Remarks on the Letter of . . . Burke* (Dublin, 1791), app., 65.

13 Maccoby, *English Radicalism*, 53.

14 Maccoby, *English Radicalism*, 52.

The London Corresponding Society, which he founded in January, 1792, became by the end of the year the nerve center of a network of communicating societies formed of twenty-four local divisions.[15] Between its members and Paine was strong sympathy, but the society's program was only a revival of the more radical reform ideas of the 1780's—universal suffrage and annual elections to parliament. Talk of this kind of reform had not formerly inspired terror, even in Burke; in 1792 it did, because, presented sometimes in intemperate language, it was judged against a different background.

Throughout the history of the reform movement some members of parliament had been its active proponents. Their stations in life made them personally respectable and won for them hearings that were denied other reformers. In April, 1792, some members of parliament, among them even former colleagues of Burke, organized a society called "The Friends of the People."[16] On April 30 Charles Grey announced that in the next session the group would bring in a bill for a moderate reform that would be the best security against subversion of the constitution. Though no motion was before the House, a discussion ensued. Burke denounced the idea of a reform.[17] No grievance had been described for which it would be a remedy. There was no guarantee that such a reform would be the last, for there were in England people who were in correspondence with the revolutionaries, plotting the subversion of the constitution. Did moderate men think they could unite with some of "the worst men in the kingdom" and still be able to guide a safe course? This was not the time for "visionary reforms." Dundas, as vigorously as Burke or Windham, denounced associations like those at Sheffield and Manchester, which aimed at "nothing less than the overthrow of the constitution."[18] Responsible members of parliament should

15 Maccoby, *English Radicalism*, 69 and n. 2.

16 *Parl. Hist.*, XXIX, 1303-309, for the list of members who signed the address at the Freemason's Tavern. Besides members of both houses of parliament, Dissenters, men of commerce, and literary people joined. Some, like George Rous, Thomas Christie, and James Mackintosh, had written replies to the *Reflections*. Among the members of parliament were Philip Francis, William Baker, John Courtenay, Dudley North, Sheridan, and Grey. Fox did not join.

17 *Parl. Hist.*, XXIX, 1317-24.

18 *Parl. Hist.*, XXIX, 1337.

A Uniform Whig.

"I preserve consistency, by varying my means, to secure the unity of my end." Burke's Reflections P. 85d

A UNIFORM WHIG, *by James Gillray, Nov. 16, 1791.* Satirizing Burke's self-proclaimed consistency; Burke represented as an apostate, having gone over to the Court (bust of George III), with the intimation of financial reward.

be aware of the danger to their own reputations when they espoused the same cause as the disciples of Paine. Dundas' speech reflected the growing uneasiness among ministers, who were receiving disturbing reports about the reformers. Lord Gower had witnessed a fete in Paris attended by two deputies from the Manchester Constitutional Society; Lord Auckland knew Dutch ministers who wondered whether the societies in London, Norwich, and Sheffield represented a popular enthusiasm for France that might make it difficult for the British government to take a firm stand against revolutionary propaganda.[19]

This debate of April 30, 1792, was one of the few occasions on which Burke had spoken publicly of the reformers since the appearance of the *Appeal*. He had, however, remained convinced of their incendiary influence and their connections with an international conspiracy. A week after the Birmingham riots he had thought the judges "should directly censure the circulation of treasonable books, and factious federations, and any communication with wicked and desperate people in other countries."[20] The unpopularity of the reform societies among the governing classes did not make them less dangerous. Indifference toward them reflected over-confidence in England's security. "A storm" could destroy it, or it could be undermined by the continued intercourse between the "Anglo-Gallican clubs" and the French Revolutionaries.[21] In translating the "delirium of a low, drunken alehouse club" into an alliance with the people of England, the National Assembly proclaimed the proselyting spirit of the Revolution and converted the treasons of Englishmen into "plain aggression" by France.[22]

By the spring of 1792, to Burke and to an increasing number of Englishmen, events were confirming the warnings of the *Reflections* and the *Appeal*. But Burke did not dwell in an ivory tower, merely telling other people what they ought to do. Always the philosopher in action—the politician—he was ready to work for

[19] H.M.C., *Dropmore Papers*, II, 266, 268-69, Gower to Grenville, April 27, 1792, Auckland to Grenville, May 15, 1792.

[20] *Corr.*, III, 223, Burke to Richard, Sr., July 24, 1791.

[21] *Corr.*, III, 224-25, 268, 454-55, Burke to Richard, Jr., Aug. 5, 16, 1791, March 23, 1792; "Thoughts on French Affairs," *Works*, IV, 346, 369-70 (Dec., 1791).

[22] "Thoughts," *Works*, IV, 370-71.

the counterrevolution as well as to write and talk about it. Often in the past he had been unable to accomplish his purposes because he was in opposition. By the early months of 1792 his position was even weaker because his party was divided and he was in disfavor with a portion of it, almost dissociated from it.[23] Fitzwilliam declared himself in complete accord with Burke but would confine himself to private efforts to oppose the Revolution. He desired to continue his stipends to Burke but was met with refusal. The payment had been a kind of compensation for services to the party, but the party had repudiated Burke. It was no longer the aristocratically independent party that Burke had known, immune from either popular or court influences. Even Windham had been touched by the French madness. Portland was distant. Although the king and the Duke of York seemed kindly disposed, at Carlton House Burke was "in disgrace." The friendship of a man such as Fox with his "wonderful abilities and amiable disposition" was not easily replaced. However, Burke now knew who were his friends. He might retain them because, having "left all politics, I think, for ever," there need be no new controversies.

Party as an agency through which to achieve public ends therefore was no longer available to him. He would work outside party, virtually alone, and by other means promote the public interest as he saw it. That meant to encourage the counterrevolution on the continent and to try to persuade Pitt's government to join others in supporting it. Burke acted as a private person. In treating with the counterrevolutionaries in Europe he involved himself in negotiations that might have compromised Pitt's government. Ministers were extraordinarily tolerant of his officiousness. Fortunately for his reputation, the indiscreet negotiations were without consequence, while later events enabled him to emerge from his campaign for an anti-Jacobin crusade with the reputation of a seer rather than a busybody.

23 Burke MSS, Sheff., Fitzwilliam to Burke, Sept. 18, 1791, Burke to Fitzwilliam, Nov. 21, 1791, Fitzwilliam to Burke, Nov. 26, 1791, Burke to Richard, Jr., Jan. 1, 1792; H.M.C., *Charlemont*, 184, Burke to Charlemont, Dec. 29, 1791; Maggs Catalogue 365, lot 118, Spring, 1918, Burke to Laurence, April 13, 1792; *Corr.*, III, 383-409, 415-16, 445, Burke to William Weddell, Jan. 31, 1792, Burke to Richard, Jr., Feb. 19, March 20, 1792.

Shortly after the publication of the *Reflections* Burke became convinced that the Revolution was not going to collapse from its inner confusions or its financial difficulties. Though morally false, its principles were vigorous. Unless "over-turned" by the "vigorous interference of foreign powers," the "Revolution of doctrine and theoretic dogma" would continue to be a danger to all the states of Europe, the example, the inspiration, and the active leader of subversive factions in other nations.[24] No government that valued order and its own security could remain neutral or rely upon orthodox border defenses, which were useless against ideas. The Revolution must be destroyed in order to eliminate the source of the infection that threatened Europe. The annexation of Avignon in September, 1791, which aroused indignation among European sovereigns but did not appear to threaten their vital interests, was to Burke a demonstration of a new technique in international relations—"exciting sedition . . . and then, under an idea of kindness and protection, bringing forward an antiquated title . . . and annexing Avignon . . . to the French Republic."[25]

If the European monarchs had not yet felt it directly, there was one group whose members had experienced the impact of the Revolution. These were the émigrés. To the first noble and princely group that began their wanderings in the summer of 1789, congregating at last in the environs of Coblentz, there was added another group, noble, clerical, and bourgeois, which left France after the failure of the king's flight. Bickering amid poverty and false optimism, under the leadership of Calonne and the king's brothers, the Comte d'Artois and the Comte de Provence, they sought the aid of the emperor and the king of Prussia and hoped that England would join in the effort to destroy the Revolution by helping them advance into France at the head of a triumphant army.[26] Grenville's advisers, partly because they

24 "Thoughts," *Works*, IV, 319, 322-24, 354, 369-70, 375-76; Burke MSS, Sheff., B-10, Feb., 1791.

25 "Thoughts," *Works*, IV, 334. Burke refused to recognize France as a monarchy under the Constitution of 1791. He was nearly a year in advance of events in calling France a republic.

26 Malmesbury, ed., *Diaries*, II, 437-38, 443, Malmesbury to Portland, Oct. 3, 1790, Oct. 20, 1791.

distrusted the intentions and political wisdom of the émigrés, preferred vigilant neutrality.[27]

Burke therefore was virtually alone in his desire for English intervention. His writings and correspondence and his meetings with certain émigrés in London revealed his sympathy for their plight and his desire for counterrevolution. The émigrés over-rated his influence with the administration. Calonne, who had lived in England off and on for two years, should have understood Burke's position in English politics. Nevertheless, he personally solicited Burke's aid and advice in the émigré campaign, after failing to obtain a commitment of aid from Pitt. When Burke was resting at Margate in July, 1791, Calonne asked for an inter-view to discuss a matter of great importance; Burke explained his private position and suggested coldly that Calonne should take his secret to Grenville.[28] Perhaps Burke disliked the hint of intrigue or feared involvement in something beyond his authority. He could hardly have opposed Calonne's ultimate purpose, having just urged upon Dundas the need for a decision "in the foreign system so far as it regards France."[29]

Whether Calonne misunderstood the political situation, he certainly understood Burke. He gained the interview and won him over to an arrangement that flattered his exaggerated notions of his son's abilities and Richard's inflated opinion of himself. Though pessimistic of the outcome, Burke consented to Richard's going unofficially to Coblentz.[30] "God direct him," said Burke.

But to what purposes? Scattered statements in Burke's cor-respondence during August and September suggest Richard's goals.[31] Generally, he and his father hoped to persuade the British government to stand forth in support of the émigré cause. Richard might advise upon the means of opening intercourse between the princes and the court in England. Since March Burke

27 H.M.C., *Dropmore Papers*, II, 118, 167-68, 186, 192, Lord Mornington to Grenville, July 3, 1791, Auckland to Grenville, Aug. 18, Sept. 7, 1791, Grenville to Dundas, Sept. 14, 1791.

28 Burke MSS, Sheff., Calonne to Burke, Burke to Calonne, July, 1791.

29 MS in Morgan Library, Burke to Dundas, marked received, July 4, 1791.

30 *Corr.*, III, 220-22, Burke to Richard, Sr., July 24, 1791.

31 *Corr.*, III, 205, 220-21, n., 258-59, 265-66, 272-73, 295-98, 305-307, 348-49, 350-51, Burke to De la Bintinnaye, March, Oct. 2, 1791, Richard, Jr., to Burke, Aug. 16, 26, Sept. 2, 1791, Burke to Richard, Jr., Aug. 16, Sept. 26, 1791.

had desired the appointment of an émigré agent to London. The improvement and enlargement of the channels of communication in order to influence policy seemed to be the main purpose of the mission. The émigrés also desired, through his son, Burke's advice about the form and spirit of a restored monarchy in France and before that, about the tone and contents of any declaration the émigrés might issue preparatory to a march toward Paris. Richard thought the mission might advance his personal ambitions.[32] It was to Richard's interest to establish useful connections, since his father's career was coming to its end; his problem was intensified by the split in the party. If some of his new connections should ultimately govern France, Richard would benefit. But the venture was a risk. It might open the door to other opportunities; it might alienate Pitt and Grenville.

It is correct to describe the mission as a failure. Considering all the circumstances, including Richard's personality, failure was the only possible outcome.[33] Neither Burke's rhetoric nor Richard's diplomacy could influence the stubborn, arrogant émigrés or the policies of the governments of Europe. In a more limited sense the mission did have consequences. A first fruit was the appointment, upon Richard's recommendation, of the Chevalier de la Bintinnaye as agent in London for the princes, to communicate with Burke and, if the opportunity arose, directly with the government. When the Chevalier came to England in September, Burke introduced him to ministers.[34] He proved to be an embarrassing, impecunious guest, without status and quick to take offense. Burke had to reprimand him. There would be many more such vexations in dealing with émigrés. Through his son, Burke obtained firsthand information about dispositions in Europe, learning, for example, to place no trust in the emperor.[35] The meeting at Pillnitz between the emperor and the king of Prussia, which occurred while Richard was in Coblentz, produced

32 Burke MSS, N.R.O., Axiii18, Richard, Jr., to Will Burke, May 16, 1792.

33 Calonne later spoke "very slightingly of young Burke." Malmesbury, ed., *Diaries*, II, 448, entry of May 26, 1792.

34 H.M.C., *Dropmore Papers*, II, 193, Dundas to Grenville, Sept. 15, 1791; *Corr.*, III, 354-55, Burke to De la Bintinnaye, Oct. 13, 1791; Burke MSS, N.R.O., Aiil, Burke to Calonne, n. d., but late 1791.

35 *Corr.*, III, 347, 356, Burke to Richard, Jr., Sept. 26, 1791, Burke to De la Bintinnaye, Nov. 2, 1791.

only the declaration, which was so hedged about with conditions as to be meaningless. Likewise, Burke became aware that his own government would not be prodded into action. There was no dissembling about policy. Dundas wrote very plainly to Richard, Jr., and Grenville and Pitt told Burke when they dined and talked an entire evening, that the government intended to continue in its course of neutrality.[36]

In his discouragement, Burke was ready to cease his efforts for British intervention. Had he known of the ministers' private opinions of the Burkes, he would have been still more discouraged. To his face respectful, behind his back they were contemptuous, especially about his son. With a suggestion to send it to the king for his amusement, Dundas passed to Grenville a letter from Richard. Grenville told the king it was not worth the effort to decipher the bad handwriting. It amused Dundas to hear that England's refusal to commit herself to the princes' project had made the emperor cool, or that if the Revolution continued, Burke would not give twenty years' purchase for an annuity on the existence of the country.[37] Yet Grenville consented to see the Chevalier de la Bintinnaye, with whom Dundas had refused to discuss foreign politics.[38] Encouraged by this, Burke tried again to persuade Grenville that England held the key to Europe's future.[39] Dundas tried to pry from him Fitzwilliam's and Portland's opinions about Fox's triumphant visit to Yorkshire.[40] This was just after Burke found Pitt and Grenville firmly attached to a policy of neutrality, as if they were, to use Auckland's phrase, "spectators in a theatre."[41]

Richard's mission, from which he returned at the end of September, gave Burke an opportunity to express himself upon a subject that is important to an understanding of his views on the Revolution. Calonne had desired his advice about a settlement

36 *Corr.*, III, 336, 342-43, Dundas to Richard, Jr., Sept. 20, 1791; Burke to Richard, Jr., Sept. 26, 1791.

37 H.M.C., *Dropmore Papers*, II, 190-93, Dundas to Grenville, Sept. 13, 1791, Grenville to the King, Sept. 14, 1791, Dundas to Grenville, Sept. 15, 1791.

38 H.M.C., *Dropmore Papers*, II, 193, Dundas to Grenville, Sept. 15, 1791; Burke MSS, Sheff., Grenville to Burke, Sept. 17, 1791.

39 *The R. B. Adam Library*, I, 14-16, Burke to Grenville, Sept. 21, 1791.

40 Burke MSS, Sheff., Dundas to Burke, Sept. 26, 1791.

41 A. W. Ward and G. P. Gooch, eds., *The Cambridge History of British Foreign Policy* (New York, 1922), I, 208.

of French affairs after the counterrevolution. This he offered to the Chevalier de la Bintinnaye and to his son.[42] He desired a restoration of the forms of the old regime but in a system that would be in spirit and in function a constitutional monarchy like the British system. He would abolish *lettres de cachet* and other means of arbitrary imprisonment and would provide guarantees for the liberty and the security of the people. Having once replaced "a sort of despotism" by "a sort of anarchy," France "should not change back from anarchy to despotism." A revived Estates-General, freely elected and voting by order, should, with the king, control taxation. Public money should be protected from "abuse and malversation." The restored church should purge itself of abuses. Though he might prefer the old one to the revolutionary regime, he would hope to avoid a choice between the two. He could not in "clear conscience" support a counter-revolution that aimed only at "the re-establishment of a monarchical despotism."

Burke's list of desired reforms was in fact an indictment of the old regime. Though he thought the former constitution amenable to reform, he admitted more frankly than in either the *Reflections* or the *Appeal* the need for it. By the end of 1791 he was more militantly than ever the foe of the Revolution and less positively the champion of the old regime. He was still the gradualist, but willing now to accelerate the process of change in response to overwhelming necessity. If he had been as moderate in the *Reflections* as in the letter to his son, he would have disarmed some of his opponents. But he created the misunderstandings, for the impact of the *Reflections* was quite different from this letter. Indeed, the reforms he now projected were so fundamental, and would so radically have changed the character of the ancient French constitution, that they can hardly be called reforms. Even if enacted peacefully, they would have been more a revolution than England's in 1688-1689. They were also unrealistic and suggest that Burke either forgot his own injunctions about circumstances or misjudged the characters and minds of the French king, the king's brothers, and the émigrés. It is doubtful whether

42 *Corr.*, III, 348-51, Burke to Richard, Jr., Sept. 26, 1791, Burke to De la Bintinnaye, Oct. 2, 1791.

they would have accepted the kind of constitution that he described. Their threatening commentary to the Declaration of Pillnitz suggested vengeance, should they recover authority in France, rather than the reforms that Burke recommended. If he had doubts about the émigrés, Burke had none about the character of the Revolution. He chose to work for the cause of counter-revolution because there could be no compromise with the principles of the Revolution.[43]

The Coblentz mission was not Burke's only attempt at personal diplomacy. When thanking Catherine of Russia for approving his writings on the Revolution, he went on to solicit her aid to help preserve the world "from Barbarism and Ruin." But he decided to request ministers' approval before sending the letter. Grenville, Pitt, and George III admired it—and advised against sending it. Burke acquiesced, somewhat sarcastically.[44] Earlier he had sketched a letter to Marie Antoinette, urging her to keep up her courage, to "have nothing to do with traitors," to strengthen Louis XVI against the new constitution, and to be patient while Europe hastened to the rescue. Through the Duke of Dorset, formerly ambassador to France, Burke hoped to persuade the Austrian ambassador, Count Mercy-Argenteau, who was in correspondence with the queen, to send the letter. Burke's draft was condensed and put into cipher, but Burke doubted that Mercy ever sent it. Alternatively, he hoped that the British government would urge Louis to be firm.[45]

Finally, Burke established communications with high ecclesiastical authorities. His well-known indignation over the treatment of the church and the clergy in France was appreciated in papal circles. A letter to that effect came from the Archbishop of Nisibi, the papal nuncio at Liége.[46] It told Burke of the French annexation of Avignon. Burke replied at once.[47] This letter was

43 Burke MSS, N.R.O., Aii1, Burke to Calonne, n. d., but late 1791.

44 Burke MSS, N.R.O., Aiv45, Burke to the Empress, Nov. 1, 1791, Aiv40, John King to Burke, Nov. 11, 12, 1791, Grenville to John King, Nov. 12, 1791, Aiv43, Burke to John King, n. d., but after Nov. 12, 1791.

45 *Corr.*, III, 283-88, Duke of Dorset to Burke, Aug. 20, 1791; also Burke's rough sketch, a copy of the condensed letter, and a note by Burke.

46 Burke MSS, N.R.O., Nov. 21, 1791.

47 Burke MSS, N.R.O., Dec. 14, 1791, printed in *The Dublin Review* (now the *Wiseman Review*), CCII (Jan., 1938), 139-42, in the article "Edmund Burke, England, and the Papacy," 138-48, by H. V. F. Somerset.

the fullest statement he had yet made about the Christian unity of Europe. Against the "Empire of Anarchy and irreligion," all descriptions of Christians must unite. They must discard prejudices, intolerance, and the "beaten routine of old systems" if they would combat successfully revolutionary tactics "unprecedented in the annals of Europe." The annexation of Avignon was an act of aggression against all European governments. The pope, a prince of high rank, could help in mobilizing opinion in the war of ideas. Implicit in his letter was the question of regular diplomatic intercourse between England and the papacy.

By the autumn of 1791 Burke envisaged a great crusade against the Revolution in which the military and spiritual forces of all of Christian Europe would ally, but as long as England refused to participate, the enterprise would remain visionary. It appeared that England was ready even to recognize the new order in France. The practical question of recognition arose when in September Louis accepted the new constitution and on October 1 the newly elected legislature assembled. Citing Vattel, Burke stated the alternatives.[48] As the French government was illegal by the standards of moral law and of history and had been accepted by only a part of a divided France, England could refuse to recognize it, or she could ignore all legal questions and extend de facto recognition. England's decision, Burke advised, should be a policy matter, based upon consideration of her own self-interest. In spite of his earlier decision to avoid further discussion of French affairs, in December, 1791, he drew up for the benefit of ministers a lengthy argument against recognition of the new French government.[49]

He argued from a single premise. France was experiencing not a political revolution but a revolution of doctrine. Based upon principles alien to European experience, it was incompatible with the existing European order. The French Revolution was by nature a propagandizing, proselyting revolution, irreconcilable with European peace and order. No European government could be secure while the Revolution endured, for it was in league with incendiary groups in every nation. Burke discussed the situation

48 "Thoughts," *Works,* IV, 317.
49 *Corr.,* III, 413-15, Burke to Richard, Jr., Feb. 19, 1792; "Thoughts," *Works,* IV, 315-77.

in each country, finding Germany and Switzerland particularly vulnerable to revolutionary propaganda, and England dangerously exposed to it. Recognition of the French government would encourage it to spread its propaganda even more boldly. With a last word of warning, Burke would be done with the subject of France, "I believe, forever." "I wind up all in a full conviction within my own breast, and the substance of which I must repeat over and over again, that the state of France is the first consideration in the politics of Europe, and of each state, externally as well as internally considered."

Burke submitted his paper to ministers who still had it at the end of February, 1792.[50] "No comment from any quarter. It is plain they wish to be rid of my interference in any thing." That was because the government had resolved firmly upon neutrality. Among those who corresponded with Grenville on foreign affairs, only his brother, the Marquis of Buckingham, and Lord Auckland seemed to have reservations about the wisdom of neutrality. Buckingham wondered whether the French spirit might eventually affect England.[51] Auckland, more belatedly but before the continental war began, feared that if the French did not soon settle their affairs, Europe was endangered.[52] Though England had not yet been seriously infected by French ideas, leveling doctrine tinged some of the language heard in parliament. There was, Auckland feared, "a reasonable probability" that he would see Europe descend to barbarism. Burke was no longer quite alone in his judgments of the Revolution, but upon the official policy of the government his opinions had made no discernible impact, and when he expressed them, he seemed to meddle in ministerial business. Burke rejected this notion. Though a private person, he was talking about a matter of concern to every British subject, indeed to all of mankind. This was the justification for his private diplomacy.

The King's Speech at the opening of parliament on January 31, 1792, was in a sense a reply to Burke.[53] It did not mention France.

50 *Corr.*, III, 413-15, Burke to Richard, Jr., Feb. 19, 1792.
51 H.M.C., *Dropmore Papers*, II, 209, Buckingham to Grenville, Oct. 9, 1791.
52 H.M.C., *Dropmore Papers*, II, 262-63, Auckland to Grenville, March 24, 1792.
53 *Parl. Hist.*, XXIX, 744-46. This speech pretty well reflected the emphasis of Grenville's diplomatic correspondence during the preceding year.

It noticed with satisfaction the settlement of affairs in the Low Countries and eastern Europe—or the promises of settlement—and for the rest of it, "the general state of affairs in Europe, appear to promise to my subjects the continuance of a general tranquillity." England might safely reduce her military and naval establishments. Members of both houses seemed to agree. The brief debates on the addresses in response to the speech revealed some interest in the problems of eastern Europe, Turkey, and India, but none whatsoever in France. That country was not even mentioned by any of the speakers. On February 17 Pitt, in a debate on public finance, said that "unquestionably there never was a time in the history of this country, when, from the situation of Europe, we might more reasonably expect fifteen years of peace, than we may at the present moment."[54]

As far as Pitt and parliament and most people (except Burke) were concerned, the idea of war, the French Revolution, English sympathies for the Revolution, and the growth of the reform spirit in England were closed subjects. Burke's warnings went unregarded; the evidences of dangers abroad and at home signified nothing but his susceptibility to self-delusion. Perhaps he was thinking of his own failures and wrote with a touch of envy when, shortly after this time, he described Reynolds as a person for whom "every thing turned out fortunately."[55]

Reynolds had died on February 23. He had visited Beaconsfield in the autumn of 1791 and fallen ill soon afterward. Burke attended regularly at his bedside, one of the persons permitted to visit him. He wrote the obituary notice for the newspapers and took charge of the funeral. As a beneficiary of Reynolds' will, Burke received a legacy of £2,000 and found a debt of the same amount canceled. As an executor, he shared with Malone and Metcalfe the task of disposing of Reynolds' collection of paintings by old masters.[56] He also was guardian to Reynolds' niece, Mary Palmer. She resided at Gregories for a few months, before marrying Burke's friend and neighbor Lord Inchiquin. Later, when Malone was preparing Reynolds' works for publication, he asked

---

54 *Parl. Hist.*, XXIX, 826.

55 *Corr.*, III, 424, Burke to Richard, Jr., March, 1792.

56 Greig, ed., *The Farington Diary*, I, 93. The sale took place at Christie's on March 12, 13, 14, 1795,

Burke's assistance. Burke pleaded illness, his inability to speak with authority of Reynolds as an artist, and the difficulty of saying anything about a life so calm and benign.[57] In the end Burke offered some comments on Reynolds' powers of generalization and of his evenness of temper and disposition. This was three years after Reynolds' death, and again he seemed to envy a man who could live so tranquilly.[58] This envy, of course, was not realistic, for it was not Burke's nature to live placidly. His life had been a succession of controversies and involvements in great affairs of state. He sought them out because he believed it the duty of his station in life to try to give effect to his conceptions of the public good.

That is the explanation of his career as an anti-Jacobin crusader. The rebuffs he received about the time of Reynolds' death discouraged him but neither silenced nor intimidated him. During the spring of 1792 events gave him new opportunities to express himself. They did not, however, so fully vindicate him as to embarrass ministers or cause them to reconsider their rejections of his counsels. A month after April 20, when France declared war on Austria, George III issued a Declaration of Neutrality. Burke could consider it an answer to his neglected "Thoughts on French Affairs." It was also proof that his writings on the French Revolution had exerted no discernible influence upon those who formed British foreign policy. While deploring the war, England intended to remain neutral, as a spectator of a war and a revolution, trusting France to respect her desire for peace. The government refused to negotiate with the two missions sent from France, and it rebuffed approaches from the continental enemies of France. The war did not seem to involve vital British interests. The administration contemplated a speedy allied victory. Perhaps the time would come, after Paris fell, when England could mediate, though on what terms it was too early to say.[59] As for Burke, he was merely a readable Jeremiah, like the prophets of old, eloquent but bothersome.

The outbreak of the war affected Englishmen's views on certain

57 MS in Morgan Library, Burke to Malone, May 22, 1795.
58 Leslie and Taylor, *Reynolds*, II, 637-40; Bryant, *Literary Friends*, 80.
59 H.M.C., *Dropmore Papers*, II, 281, 291, Grenville to Auckland, June 19, 1792, Grenville to Gower, July 13, 1792.

domestic questions more strongly than their opinions on foreign policy. Matters that had worried Burke since the winter of 1789-1790 became in the spring of 1792 major concerns of the government and of many Englishmen. One was the increasing activity of the various reform societies. Another was the publication in February of the second and more incendiary part of Paine's *Rights of Man*. Its attack upon the British constitution invited the government's prosecution, made it easier for opponents to identify reform with revolution, and confirmed Burke's judgment that reform at this unpropitious time was an assault upon the constitution. He had an opportunity to say this, in the debate of April 30 on Grey's notice of intention to move for parliamentary reform in the next session. The theme of the debate, over Fox's protest that the argument was irrelevant to the merits of the issue, was the connection between reform and subversion. Pitt called reform a "preliminary to the overthrow of the whole system of our present government."[60] Burke identified reformers with the French Revolutionaries—"the worst traitors and regicides that had ever been heard of."[61] Though by "regicides" he meant murderers of the *institution* of monarchy, his use of the word was prophetic. Burke's position was no longer isolated. A year before, when he had talked like this, members either "flew at him" or "flew from him"; now they were eager to support him.[62] A mood favorable to repressing agitation for reform was developing in minds that were growing fearful for the safety of the established order.

It was still possible to isolate some questions from the background of the French Revolution. The slave trade was an example. Though on one side of this issue mercenary interests were uppermost, on the other humanitarianism predominated and overrode differences arising from conflicting views of the Revolution and parliamentary reform. The campaign for the abolition of the slave trade is not ordinarily considered one of Burke's great causes, but it deserves more than the usual casual notice given to it in connection with Burke's career. While a discussion

60 *Parl. Hist.*, XXIX, 1311-12.
61 *Parl. Hist.*, XXIX, 1317-24.
62 *Corr.*, III, 499, Richard, Jr., to Will Burke, Aug. 17, 1792. I have changed the tenses of the verbs in the quotations.

of it amid the events of the spring of 1792 would appear to be a digression, the debate of April was a discernible stage in the history of the movement and in the story of Burke's participation in it. This was his last opportunity as a member of parliament to participate in the effort to abolish the slave trade.

In 1780 Burke had taken up the subjects of slavery and the slave trade where he and Will Burke had left them in 1757 with the publication of the *European Settlements*. He drafted a brief sketch for a regulatory code that must have required considerable thought and research.[63] In 1780 there was no organized agitation

against the slave trade, and no apparent reason to explain the revival of Burke's interest in the subject. He was, so to speak, between causes, having conceded American independence and not yet become immersed in the Indian problem. During the winter of 1779-1780 he had embraced economical reform, but he did not envisage a long crusade. If he needed something to keep him busy, he could always find it in Ireland, but he did not care to agitate the constitutional problem nor did he desire to carry commercial reforms much further. In 1780 Burke was relatively free to embrace a new cause and may have thought for a moment he had found it in the slave trade. During the next year, however, political conditions changed, opposition hopes of overthrowing Lord North began to rise, and at the same time Burke became deeply involved in the Indian question. And so he filed away the sketch and devoted himself to other causes.[64]

The campaign against the slave trade opened a few years later under the direction, not of party leaders, either government or opposition, but of dedicated souls, some Quakers, others Evangelicals, and a few members of parliament. Burke knew some of them well, notably Hannah More and Wilberforce. Some of his good friends, Reynolds, Boswell, Windham, and Langton, were among the persons who helped to strengthen Wilberforce's resolu-

---

[63] Some of Burke's ideas were culled from Spanish colonial experiences. W. L. Mathieson, *British Slavery and Its Abolition* (London, 1926), 17n.

[64] Robert Isaac Wilberforce and Samuel Wilberforce, *The Life of William Wilberforce* (London, 1839), I, 152-53, think Burke gave up the project because political conditions were unfavorable. Reginald Coupland, *Wilberforce* (Oxford, 1923), 92, says Burke feared that he might split his party. Coupland cites no evidence; perhaps he rephrased the Wilberforces' statement.

tion to lead a nonpartisan crusade in parliament.[65] If he was Pitt's close friend, Burke and Fox were his earnest supporters in this enterprise. It deserved support from men on both sides of the House and received it, just as it was opposed by men on both sides of the House. To Burke it was "the cause of humanity," and "the principles of religion and morality" supported it. But he refused to be doctrinaire. He thought outright abolition not yet practicable, and he feared unfortunate secondary effects if statutory abolition was prematurely imposed. This opinion illustrates Burke's willingness to prefer the prudent course to a theoretically desirable remedy that might threaten social peace. He would keep in view the greatest good as an ultimate goal. Nevertheless, in 1788 he supported the resolution for outright abolition and opposed a tactical maneuver for postponing legislative action. He thought the House should inquire into the subject itself instead of handing its investigatory responsibilities to a committee of the Privy Council.[66]

When the slave trade was before the House in that year, in 1789, and in 1791, the opponents of abolition were in the majority. The pygmies, as the saying went, outnumbered the giants—Pitt, Burke, Fox, and of course Wilberforce. In April, 1792, when the question was again introduced, Dundas offered alternative resolutions. Amended by the House, they looked toward gradual abolition. While this proposal was under consideration, Burke dug out of his papers the "Sketch of a Negro Code" he had drafted in 1780; now he sent it to Dundas along with an explanatory letter.[67] He would not separate slavery from the slave trade. A "gradual abolition of slavery" "ought to go hand in hand" with whatever regulations were imposed upon the trade. For the time being, he thought regulation and reform both of the trade and of slavery preferable to abolition, because the problem was so vastly complex. Regulation could be "a beginning of a course of measures" that later parliaments could adopt as experience and circumstances directed. In preparation for an ultimate abolition,

---

65 Coupland, *Wilberforce*, 93-94.
66 *Times*, May 10, 1788.
67 *Works*, VI, 257-89. The letter prefaces the sketch. Burke said he could not find the abstract of it he had made in 1788.

he would introduce "civilization and gradual manumission." His "Sketch" suggested rules to cover the trade in West Africa, the ships engaged in the trade, the treatment of slaves in passage, and the management of slaves in the West Indies. His rules provided for education, instruction in "religion and morality," and the encouragement of family life among slaves. These and other regulations should be sternly enforced. The plan was paternalistic and in that respect congenial to the humanitarians, who continued to invoke Burke's authority in support of their cause.[68] Later statutes of the imperial parliament and enactments of colonial assemblies contained provisions resembling Burke's recommendations for more humane treatment of slaves. In 1822 Wilberforce said Burke's plan was workable, though it did not go far enough.[69] On July 9, 1823, Lord Bathurst, as Colonial Secretary, transmitted instructions for the more humane treatment of slaves. His dispatch reads like an expansion of Burke's "Sketch."[70]

The debate over the slave trade was an exception proving the rule that for Burke every reform question found its ultimate reference in the French Revolution. This was demonstrated again on May 11 during a debate on Fox's motion for the repeal of certain penal statutes limiting freedom of expression of religious opinions. A petition from a group of Unitarians prompted the motion. There was no question, said Fox, of the abstract justice of toleration, nor were there grounds for thinking, even in 1792, that the enlargement of toleration and civil rights was unsafe policy. His speech expounded ably the theory of toleration, though it recognized the power of the state under certain circumstances to restrict freedom of opinion. Fox's concession enabled Burke to concentrate upon the policy and prudence of the proposal, upon the circumstances that the statesman must always take into account but that Fox had avoided.[71]

Dismissing natural rights as irrelevant to the problems of men in civil society, he stated the issue as the preservation of the

68 E. g., Wilberforce in 1804 and 1807. Hansard's *Parl. Debates,* 1st. ser., II, 558, IX, 135, 139.

69 Wilberforce and Wilberforce, *Life of Wilberforce,* V, 157.

70 Mathieson, *British Slavery,* 131-33, and generally chap. II.

71 *Works,* VII, 41-58. The version in *Parl. Hist.,* XXIX, 1381-95, derived from newspaper accounts, is much less philosophical than the one printed in *Works.*

Christian commonwealth of England. He presented the pure doctrine of Richard Hooker. Church and state were one society, not the alliance of separate, sovereign entities. In theory, this teaching excludes religious pluralism and if carried to logical ends is antithetical not only to religious freedom but even to toleration. In practice, England had learned to grant exceptions and admit a practical toleration. Acceptable to Burke on prudential grounds, such grants did not vitiate the state's power to superintend the religious opinions and practices of the people. With the privileges already enjoyed by the various denominations in England he was not concerned. These privileges had a prescriptive title, and they were possessed by Christian communities.

But who were the Unitarians? They were unknown to the records of parliament. By definition they were not Christians, though Burke did not labor this point. He described the Unitarians as he knew them from their petition and from his knowledge of contemporary events. Except negatively, he was unable to define their religious tenets. The truth was that they were a political faction pledged "to dismember the christian commonwealth"; the opinions they desired to circulate were political, not religious opinions. The Unitarians would destroy the established church and the British constitution. They were proponents of French, republican principles; they were disciples of Paine. "Mr. Burke then went into a description of almost every event that had taken place in France since the Revolution" and contended that persons in England who sympathized with the Revolution desired "to subvert and overturn every establishment, political and religious, of every kind," and wished "to extend that destruction to all nations."

The arguments of Fox and North, who supported the motion, may be more congenial to the modern view, but Burke's argument, supported by Pitt, prevailed by a vote of 142-63.

Burke's speech was significant. His Elizabethan identification of church and state would not support a theory of toleration. Because he was two centuries removed from the age of Hooker, he could accept a practical toleration consisting of concessions by established constitutional authority, acting from prudential consideration of social circumstances and the public good. He rejected the idea of religious freedom as an absolute right. It was impossible in the abstract to define precisely "the ultimate rights" of the state in guarding its safety. Societies, like individuals, give priority to self-preservation when the circumstances require. Whether this would be right or wrong would depend, like all practical moral questions, upon surrounding circumstances and possible consequences. The statesman, whose object is "the happiness of the whole," must avoid sacrificing "any part of the ideal good of the whole," but he must calculate happiness in relation to feelings and sentiments, not theoretical rights. Where the doctrine of reason of state made the safety of the state the end in itself, Burke's object was social well-being, to which the safety of the state was a means.

To introduce absolute, inalienable rights into the question made it insoluble, perhaps even theoretically. Burke was willing to concede that the "good man" might find it necessary to reject certain ways of saving the commonwealth. The statesman does the best he can, acting upon circumstances as he finds them, trying to avoid oppressive legislation while seeking the greatest good. In 1792 the statesman had to balance danger against alleged injustice. Burke thought the danger to the commonwealth overwhelming, and he was not persuaded that the Unitarians were suffering, as, for example, were the Catholics in Ireland. He did not believe that the refusal of unrestricted freedom of opinion to a militant, infidel minority was a violation of principles of natural justice.

The vote on Fox's motion showed that the pamphlets, addresses, resolutions, speeches, and conversations concerning reform and revolution were beginning to worry members of parliament and the government. As Henry Mackenzie said, there was a very seditious spirit at large, and Burke had done much to stimulate it.[72] The popular ferment was spreading, but reactions were occurring both among private people and among ministers as the reform societies became bolder and more vocal. Easily driven into panic, the governing class was alarmed as much by the novel stirrings of the urban working class as by the language of the

72 H.M.C., *Home*, 137-38, March 26, 1792.

reform societies.[73] Even Wyvill, the old reformer, was uneasy over this new fermentation and its "Painist" tendencies. From various sources, including its own agents, the Home Office received disturbing reports. Fitzwilliam and the Duke of Norfolk told of agitations in Yorkshire, especially in Sheffield. Personally and through members of his family, Dundas gathered information about agitations in Scotland.[74] It has been customary to deplore and even to ridicule the sense of fear among the governing class of England during the French Revolution, and even to ask whether it was genuine. The agitation of 1792, unlike the usual kind of eighteenth-century disturbances, had a basis in principle. It was conducted against the background of a war declared by an actively propagandist government.

On May 21 the government took its first repressive action, by issuing a royal proclamation against seditious writings.[75] After promising to repress them "as far as in us lies," the proclamation warned the people to be on guard against attempts at "the subversion of all regular government within this kingdom." The debates in parliament, from which Burke was absent, revealed two conflicting views, one justifying suppression and the other denying the dangers. Charles Grey made another point. The proclamation was a mean political trick, conjured up by the master politician, Pitt, in an effort to divide the opposition and proselyte some of its members.

Grey's accusation was neither an exercise of imagination nor a wild shot that happened to strike the target. The idea of a union with Pitt, or at least of support of his suppressive measures, was in the air. For a year past Burke had been trying to prove that the tenets of the New and Old Whigs were irreconcilable. As he told Lord Fitzwilliam, he never doubted his distaste for the views of the "modern Whigs."[76] Burke would say the same thing of Portland. He recognized the practical, political reasons why the group hesitated to break with Fox, but he also knew of the

[73] Butterfield, *Cambridge Historical Journal,* IX, 298-307.
[74] Furber, *Dundas,* 79.
[75] Text in *Parl. Hist.,* XXIX, 1476-77; debated in the Commons on May 25 and in the Lords on May 31, *Parl. Hist.,* XXIX, 1476-1534.
[76] Fitzwilliam MSS, Sheff., F115a, Burke to Fitzwilliam, Sept. 28, 1791.

increasing uneasiness in the party. The strain in his own relationship with Portland and Fitzwilliam was caused by these same
political stresses. Burke was confident that principles, by whatever
label, would in the end prove stronger ties than political expediency. If the party broke up and the Foxites kept the Whig name,
Burke would not object. If his union with Portland and Fitzwilliam was on the basis of Tory principles, then "I shall always
wish to be thought a Tory."[77] Not that Burke would admit to
having changed his principles. Men who thought alike on the
nature of civil order and the maintenance of the British constitution would have to unite to preserve them, regardless of past
politics and party names.

The debates of April 30 and May 25 revealed clearly that
opinions on the new issues cut across former parliamentary
divisions. Events were vindicating Burke. "The ranting declama-
tions of aristocratic pride and exuberant genius" had become
prophetic wisdom and prescient understanding that "the very
existence of civil society was in danger."[78] Men were beginning
to admit that, unlike Burke, they had been "seduced" by the
love of liberty and had failed to see the force and character of
the Revolution.[79] As opinions of the Revolution changed, political
alignments adjusted themselves accordingly. Thus, during the
evening preceding the debate on parliamentary reform, some
Old Whigs met at Portland's house and decided to oppose the
New Whigs and the Friends of the People when Grey introduced
the subject the next day.[80] The Old Whigs meant only to
emphasize their intention to retain Portland as their titular head.
Nevertheless, on the issue of the debate they were supporting Pitt
and, so to speak, the principle of social order. The time was
approaching that in March Burke had told Fitzwilliam had not
come "yet, at least," the time when his full reconciliation with
Fitzwilliam and Portland would occur.[81]

77 *Corr.*, III, 445, Burke to Richard, Jr., March 20, 1792; H.M.C., *Morrison,* part
II, 485a, Burke to Dr. ———, April 16, 1792. Maggs Catalogue 365, lot 118,
identifies this as a letter to Dr. French Laurence dated April 13, 1792.
78 Somerville, *Life,* 264, 266.
79 Burke MSS, Sheff., Mackintosh to Burke, Dec. 22, 1796; Minto, *Elliot,* III, 378n.
80 Butterfield, *Cambridge Historical Journal,* IX, 307.
81 *Corr.*, III, 445, Burke to Richard, Jr., March 20, 1792.

And so, in the spring of 1792 a tug-of-war began within the Whig party, and Burke's importance revived. Instinct told Portland and Fitzwilliam that they agreed with Pitt on what was best for the country; friendship, habit, memory, and wishful thinking persuaded them that Fox did not really believe in the French Revolution and would soon right himself. Fox himself tried to convince Fitzwilliam that their differences of opinion were inconsequential, that their mutual agreements were basic and their principles fundamentally hostile to Pitt's.[82] Fox had been shrewd in refusing to join the Friends of the People, though his speeches showed his sympathy for reform, and he was outspoken against the second part of the *Rights of Man*. As calm an observer as Sir Gilbert Elliot distinguished between Fox on the one hand and Francis and Sheridan on the other.[83]

These differences provoked fears for the future of the party and embarrassed personal relations within it.[84] Perhaps observers read false significance into Burke's movements, but those of a politician as controversial as he earned attention. His presence at the first levee of the season at Carlton House, his fairly regular visits to Portland's, his absence from a political dinner at Fitzwilliam's, and his "general absence" from the House of Commons for the first two months of the session provoked speculation.[85] On April 5 Elliot set out for Gregories, with some trepidation because of the stiffness in his relations with Burke. "The French question" engrossed Burke, and he spoke freely about it. This confidence flattered Elliot, because with other leaders of the party, notably Portland, Burke avoided the subject for fear of unpleasantness. While Elliot was at Gregories, Portland dropped in. The conversation was congenial but self-conscious.

Encouraged by the debate on parliamentary reform and by Burke's ostentatious crossing of the floor of the Commons while Fox was speaking on May 11, Pitt was ready to take advantage of the uncertainty in opposition ranks. He invited Portland and his

---

82 Butterfield, *Cambridge Historical Journal*, IX, 297, March 16, 1792.

83 Minto, *Elliot*, II, 2-3, 15, 17, Elliot to Lady Elliot, March 24, April 20, May 1, 1792.

84 Minto, *Elliot*, II, 6-11, 17, 18, 20-21, Elliot to Lady Elliot, April 5, 9, May 1, 7, 1792.

85 *Times*, Feb. 9, 21, 28, March 16, 1792.

followers, as men desirous of preserving peace and order, to attend the Privy Council and to assist in framing the proclamation against seditious writings.[86] For political reasons the Portland group rejected the invitation to the Privy Council but offered some acceptable suggestions about alterations in the wording of the proclamation.[87] Portland's friends preferred to act "in concert" with the administration rather than "in conjunction." Fox had been wary of Pitt's invitation, thinking it an attempt to divide the party, and for the moment Portland heeded him. There was another way of looking at the duke's conduct. Its indecisiveness was characteristic, said Grenville's brother, but it might also suggest that Portland was looking for some tangible reward for his patriotism.[88]

Portland's indecisiveness was not only inner weakness but the result of too much conflicting advice.[89] He knew that some of his friends desired office, especially Loughborough, who was waiting for the imminent dismissal of Thurlow. At the same time Portland was suspicious of Pitt. Fox meanwhile was suggesting an alternative. Let the party remain in opposition but allow individual members freedom of action on particular measures, for example, religious toleration, the slave trade, or even parliamentary reform. This proposal indicates the notions of party unity shaped by the adversities of a long period of opposition and makes more understandable the reluctance of Portland and Fitzwilliam to endorse actions that would break up the party. There was in the Portland party a concept of unity and discipline unusual in the eighteenth century, and it derived in large part from over twenty years of tutelage by Burke. But Burke was now thinking of a larger problem, the role of his party in a time of national emergency, when its leader was unable to make up his mind. Said Burke, "We had killed Patroclus, and were now fighting for his dead body."[90]

One of these skirmishes occurred on the night of June 9 at

[86] P.R.O., *Chatham Papers*, 30/8, 102, Pitt to Portland, May 9, 1792; Butterfield, *Cambridge Historical Journal*, IX, 310; Minto, *Elliot*, II, 23-25, May 14, 1792.

[87] P.R.O., *Chatham Papers*, 30/8, 168, Portland to Pitt, May 9, 13, 24, 1792.

[88] H.M.C., *Dropmore Papers*, II, 271, Buckingham to Grenville, May 17, 1792.

[89] Barnes, *George III and Pitt*, 243.

[90] Quoted in Barnes, *George III and Pitt*, 243.

Portland's house. Burke, Fitzwilliam, Loughborough, and Malmesbury thoroughly and frankly discussed the problem of a "junction" with Pitt, and its implications.[91] They agreed that the
times "called out for a junction," but they saw "disagreeable"
difficulties, especially because of Fox. Burke desired guarantees
for Fox's behavior in the future; Fitzwilliam was uneasy about
his record of association with the parliamentary reformers and his
sympathy for the Revolution; Fox distrusted Pitt; Portland would
not think of any arrangement with the ministry that did not
include Fox; Pitt could not accept Fox. The meeting served only
to emphasize the pivotal importance of Fox.

The *Times* leered at the party's embarrassments.[92] It had some
virtues—the head of Fox, the heart of Portland, the meekness of
Fitzwilliam, and the writings of Burke. But in each instance the
virtues were offset by defects—the "Obstinancy" of Fox, Portland's
"too easy Surrender of his own opinion to the will of others,"
Fitzwilliam's "too gentle Subservience to Political Party purposes,"
and the violence of Burke.

Other conversations within the party and with Pitt were
indecisive.[93] After the dismissal of Thurlow, Loughborough had
a personal reason for desiring a "junction." Of the remaining
leaders, only Burke was prepared to abandon Fox in the interest
of coalition if Fox refused to give guarantees; except Loughborough, none saw more clearly than he that Pitt and Fox could
not be accommodated in the same government. As he told
Malmesbury, the party could not do with Fox or without him.
Pitt told Portland and Loughborough that it was not his own
objections to Fox but those of his cabinet colleagues that forced
him to give up the effort. On the other side, old party ties still
held, especially the bond with Fox, and so the negotiations for a
coalition were broken off.

91 Barnes, *George III and Pitt*, 244; Butterfield, *Cambridge Historical Journal*, IX,
311-12; Malmesbury, ed., *Diaries*, II, 453-54.
92 June 22, 1792.
93 *Corr.*, III, 520, Burke to Will Burke, Sept., 1792; Malmesbury, ed., *Diaries*,
II, 455-67; Barnes, *George III and Pitt*, 245-46; Minto, *Elliot*, II, 44-52, 53, William
Elliot to Elliot, June 29, July 11, 1792; *Times*, June 26, 1792; Fitzwilliam MSS, Sheff.,
F31a, Portland to Fitzwilliam, June 27, 1792; Portland MSS, Nottingham University,
Portland to Loughborough, July 21, 1792; Butterfield, *Cambridge Historical Journal*,
IX, 312.

At least three persons, Burke, Loughborough, and Pitt, wanted to hold the door ajar. Burke thought Loughborough's occupancy of the lord chancellorship could help to link the government and the Old Whigs. Even when the office was placed in commission, they did not consider that the idea of coalition was dead. Pitt's conduct encouraged them. He courted Portland's support. Not only did he and Grenville favor the duke's successful candidacy for election as chancellor of Oxford but Pitt obtained from the king "full authority" to offer him the Garter made available by the death of Lord North.[94] The king was willing to show any "marks of distinction to the respectable part of the party, provided it was not accompanied with too much power." Clearly, a coalition would not be easy to arrange. Fox would be unacceptable to the king as well as to members of the cabinet, and the disposition of offices would be a delicate and combustible problem. The naïve willingness of the Duke of Leeds during July and August to accept headship of a government with Pitt and Fox as secretaries of state, emphasized the difficulties.[95] Showing political common sense and considerable insight, the king flatly rejected the idea. Until Portland and his friends took firm decisions, discussions of ministerial arrangements were premature. The Portland crowd, he said, was not as ready to "support" as Burke's "imagination" or Windham's "more sistematical [*sic*] judgment" would indicate.[96] The Portland party was ambivalent about too many matters, and as for the duke, said Lady Malmesbury, he reminded her of the allied general, the Duke of Brunswick; "no party will be led to victory by either."[97]

Of those who participated in these protracted conversations,

---

[94] H.M.C., *Dropmore Papers*, II, 294, 299, Pitt to Grenville, July 27, 1792, Dundas to Grenville, Aug. 9, 1792; Butterfield, *Cambridge Historical Journal*, IX, 314. Portland did not receive the Garter until 1794. Burke worked for Portland's election to the chancellorship. Burke MSS, Sheff., Lord Hawkesbury to Burke, Richard Knight to Burke, Aug. 19, 1792. Portland was elected chancellor on Aug. 27 and was installed on Sept. 27. *Times*, Aug. 28, Sept. 29, 1792. Burke attended the ceremony. Burke MSS, N.R.O., Axiv61a, Burke to Fitzwilliam, Oct. 5, 1792.

[95] Barnes, *George III and Pitt*, 247-52; Butterfield, *Cambridge Historical Journal*, IX, 314-15; Malmesbury, ed., *Diaries*, II, 471.

[96] P.R.O., *Chatham Papers*, 30/8, 103, the King to Pitt, Aug. 20, Nov. 26, 1792.

[97] Burke MSS, N.R.O., Axiv63, Burke to Richard, Jr., Aug. 22, 1792; Burke MSS, Sheff., Richard, Jr., to his parents, Aug., 1792; Minto, *Elliot*, II, 72, Lady Malmesbury to Lady Elliot, n. d., but Oct., 1792.

Burke stood on the loftiest ground, and not entirely because he was the one person who was not seeking office. He alone was exclusively concerned with the principles of coalition, the general conditions that justified it, and the criteria for deciding loyalties. Loughborough also, though influenced by the prospect of office, was able to see that principle was important.[98] Government, he said, ought to be composed of men who loved the constitution. Owing to the French Revolution, the line between parties should henceforth be drawn to separate the assailants from the defenders of the constitution. But the politicians behaved as though they were engaged in typical eighteenth-century ministerial shufflings, with the disposition of offices the only matter of significance.[99] That was why the problem of Fox seemed to them the central issue. Burke vainly advised his friends to agree first on principle and then the problems of Fox and the arrangement of offices would resolve themselves.[100]

Burke's position, rejected by Portland, was logical, consistent, and thorough. By his definition, party consisted of men agreed on principle, and by this definition the Portland Whigs had ceased to be a party. They were a collection of politicians at odds over the great issue of the day, yet trying to ignore their disagreements. Thus, Fitzwilliam accepted appointment as a steward at the dinner celebrating the anniversary of Fox's election for Westminster.[101] Let the issue be made clear, said Burke, let men choose their allegiances accordingly, and if the result was a major political realignment, then so be it. The crisis called for heroic action and justified an "extinction," or at least a "suspension," of former party arrangements. Parties were the practical dispositions of political forces, necessary for the conduct of affairs in a representative legislature, but they should mirror divisions over principle and in that sense be subordinate to general politics. The French Revolution had dislocated former political alignments. New ones must be formed, because "Party ought to be made for

98 Burke MSS, Sheff., Loughborough to Burke, Sept. 15, 1792.

99 Burke MSS, Sheff., Portland to Burke, Sept. 12, 1792, for a criticism of the administration's conduct that revealed the limitation of Portland's understanding.

100 Burke MSS, N.R.O., Aiv34a, Burke to Will Burke, Sept. 3, 1792.

101 *Times*, Oct. 1, 1792. The dinner was held on Oct. 10.

Politics; not Politics for Party Purposes."[102] Burke's rationale of coalition departed far from the political thought and practice of the eighteenth century.

Burke's sense of crisis reflected his reaction to events during the last half of 1792. As early as August 17, referring to the insurrection in Paris, he said that he was as shocked as if he had been surprised.[103] When there followed the suspension of the monarchy, the September massacres, the cannonade at Valmy, which reversed the direction of the war and enabled French armies to take the offensive, the abolition of the monarchy on September 21 and the declaration of the Republic on the next day, the conquest of the Low Countries in November and the issuance of the revolutionary decrees promising French aid to the oppressed peoples of Europe—who, Burke might ask, had correctly judged the character of the Revolution?

It was hard to disentangle the separate strands of events, but there must be no mistaking their meaning. Burke undertook to enlighten ministers. Immediately after the insurrection of August 10, reminding Grenville of the presence of Jacobins in England, Burke advised him against any action that might be interpreted as recognition of the people who possessed power in France.[104] Specifically, he recommended recall of the British ambassador. Grenville's reply was not entirely satisfactory.[105] Though the recall of Lord Gower had already been decided upon when Burke's advice arrived, Grenville was pleased to know that he and Burke agreed upon the need for protecting England from "the contagion" of France. This was not enough for Burke. The "political state of Europe hinges upon" this most important crisis in the history of the world.[106] England must vigorously enter into it and furnish leadership to a disjointed Europe.[107] The only way to check the spread of French ideas was to extinguish them at their source.

The publication in August of a six-penny edition of Part II of

102 Burke MSS, Sheff., Burke to Fitzwilliam, Nov. 29, 1792.
103 Burke MSS, N.R.O., Axiv62b, Burke to Fitzwilliam, Aug. 17, 1792.
104 H.M.C., *Dropmore Papers*, III, 464-66, Aug. 18, 1792.
105 Burke MSS, Sheff., Sept. 6, 1792.
106 H.M.C., *Dropmore Papers*, III, 466-67, Burke to Grenville, Sept. 19, 1792.
107 Burke MSS, Sheff., Burke to Loughborough, Oct. 23, 1792.

the *Rights of Man* was followed by Paine's incendiary *Letter Addressed to the Addressers,* unwittingly giving point to Burke's warnings. In the *Letter* he sneered at parliamentary reform, "a worn-out hackneyed subject," and called for the election of a national convention to rewrite the British constitution. Grenville spoke of the "increased activity and boldness of our Republicans," perhaps prodded by his brother's complaints of governmental laxity toward those who spread "libellous publications"; Dundas reported to Pitt an alarming situation in Scotland, "very bad," which promised to get worse if the "spirit of liberty and equality" continued to spread.[108] Though Burke had company in worrying about the domestic peace of England, only Windham and Loughborough were with him in desiring English intervention on the continent.[109]

While sojourning at Bath, Burke brought together all of his thoughts about domestic and foreign affairs, and in a paper dated November 5 he submitted them to ministers.[110] His argument was restrained and carefully organized, with the conclusions and recommendations following from the premises. Among these were some of Burke's long-held beliefs about the fundamentals of British foreign policy and relations with France. The growth and success of French military and naval power struck at England's traditional national interests, the continental balance of power, the Low Countries, the Mediterranean and Italy, and the Empire. Under any system of government, France was England's natural rival, and under a revolutionary government she was more dangerous than ever before. Urged by the necessity of the times, and justified by European tradition and public law, England should join in a continental alliance, not for the purpose of

108 H.M.C., *Dropmore Papers,* II, 327, 333-34, Buckingham to Grenville, Nov. 8, 15, 1792, Grenville to Auckland, Nov. 13, 1792; P.R.O., *Chatham Papers,* 30/8, 157, Dundas to Pitt, Nov. 22, 1792. For other expressions of alarm see Br. Mus., Add. MSS 37,873, fols. 171-72, 181-82, 183-84, 185-86, Windham to John Gurney, March 20, 1792, J. Anstruther to Windham, Nov. 30, 1792, Lord Mulgrave to Windham, Dec. 1, 1792, Loughborough to Windham, Dec. 1, 1792; Malmesbury, ed., *Diaries,* II, 473-74.

109 Burke MSS, Sheff., Burke to Fitzwilliam, Nov. 29, 1792; Butterfield, *Cambridge Historical Journal,* IX, 317-21.

110 "Heads for Consideration on the Present State of Affairs," *Works,* IV, 381-402; Burke MSS, Sheff., Burke to Fitzwilliam, Nov. 29, 1792. Also a draft in Fitzwilliam MSS, Sheff., F30i.

negotiating with the revolutionary government, but in order to destroy it and to restore the royal system in its entirety, at the same time making certain that her own maritime, commercial, and imperial interests were secured.

Without flatly rejecting Burke's advice, Pitt and Grenville raised qualifications that steered the discussion away from the vital issue of neutrality.[111] They wanted to know whether they could count on the support of the Portland Whigs. Burke could not offer guarantees. He could only say that he believed they would support the government in return for fair treatment and full communication. After talking with Portland, Burke thought he had fairly represented the duke's opinions. Then, at dinner at Loughborough's, with Portland, Windham, Stormont, Carlisle, Malmesbury, Porchester, and John Anstruther, Burke was disappointed. After some pleasant conversation, the company refused to take up the subject of foreign affairs and told Burke and Windham to cease confidential communication with ministers. Undoubtedly, Fox's known disapproval was the source of the reprimand.[112] Fox was also trying to persuade the changeable Portland that there was no international crisis. England should recognize the French republic, tell the French to make the Netherlands independent, and grant civil rights to Dissenters and Catholics, and the Whigs should steadfastly oppose the administration. At least Burke so understood Fox's position.[113] When Burke called Portland "a very wretched man," he echoed Malmesbury, who found the duke *"benumbed* and *paralyzed,"* a man "in a trance."[114]

So far, everything Burke desired had failed—coalition, British entry into the war, and the repudiation of the Gallican wing of the Portland Whigs. In the eyes of Pitt and Grenville he must appear a dupe. He had irritated Fitzwilliam and Portland. Burke wondered how they could be satisfied. They feared breaking with Fox and, of course, did not want the responsibility of destroying

111 Burke MSS, Sheff., Burke to Fitzwilliam, Nov. 29, 1792.
112 Aspinall, ed., *Later Corr. of Geo. III,* I, 630, n. 1, for a statement by Fox of his displeasure.
113 Burke MSS, Sheff., Burke to Fitzwilliam, Nov. 29, 1792; *Times,* Nov. 27, 1792; Malmesbury, ed., *Diaries,* II, 473-76.
114 Minto, *Elliot,* II, 76, Lady Malmesbury to Lady Elliot, Dec. 19, 1792; Malmesbury, ed., *Diaries,* II, 477-78.

the party. Burke did not understand how they could fail to see that it was already destroyed.

The nation seemed in a perilous state when parliament opened on December 13. During November delegates from various English reform societies presented congratulatory messages to the National Convention in Paris. This body was trying to decide the fate of Louis XVI and finally brought him to trial as an enemy of the state. Simultaneously, French armies were continuing their victorious course, buoyed by the decrees of November 16 and 19, which unilaterally repudiated the public law of Europe by declaring the Scheldt River open to navigation and promised French assistance to all people desirous of "recovering" their liberty. Pitt and Grenville were stiffening in their determination to resist continued French aggressions and to honor Britain's treaty obligations toward Holland, though they continued to hope that agreement with France might be reached.[115] Meanwhile, precautions were taken for maintaining domestic peace. On December 7 some of the county militias were embodied. Private citizens were already organizing themselves for the defense of the constitution. On November 20 an "Association for Preserving Liberty and Property" was formed at the Crown and Anchor tavern. The idea spread, and soon other patriotic societies sprang up to preserve the established church as well as government by king, Lords, and Commons.

Against this nervous background occurred the agitated opening sessions of parliament. The King's Speech noticed recent internal disorders and threats to the constitution, confessed "uneasiness" over events abroad, and promised to try to preserve the peace while upholding the honor and national interests of England.[116] The spirit of neutrality was weakening.

In the tempers of the moment, the speech was provocative, and the debate on the address to the king exposed bitter differences. Two questions were paramount—was domestic tranquility threatened, and were England's national interests in jeopardy? The debate in the Commons, December 13-14, was almost entirely within the Whig party. Pitt was not yet reelected after accepting

---

115 Ward and Gooch, eds., *Cambridge Hist. British Foreign Policy*, I, 225-29.
116 *Parl. Hist.*, XXIX, 1556-57.

the wardenship of the Cinque Ports, and Dundas discreetly stayed in the background. As he had promised, Fox came to the House well prepared; his speech opposing the address was circulating as a pamphlet before the echo of his voice died.[117] Burke insisted, as he had been doing since 1790, upon the connection between internal and external affairs.[118] "The French had declared war against all kings," and so the question was "not whether we should carry an address to the throne, but whether we should have a throne at all." He scorned Fox's proposal to negotiate with a regicide republic (the trial of Louis XVI had just begun). On December 15 Fox presented his suggestion as a motion, and for the third day in succession the Commons, mainly the Whigs, debated the French Revolution. Burke summarized his position: there was no way of avoiding war; "I say we are now engaged in actual war" for "the security of England, the interests of Europe, and the happiness of mankind."

In effect, Burke and Windham had delivered themselves over to the government, as Fitzwilliam irritably put it. Yet the earl was so distressed by Fox's performance that, with several others in the party, he left London to escape embarrassment.[119] When Burke and Windham ostentatiously sat on the Treasury Bench, they severed the last formal connection with Fox. Though they did not think of themselves as deserters of Portland, their act embarrassed him. He was willing to make public his dissent from Fox's position, but he told the Lords that in supporting the policy of the government he was not in coalition with it.[120]

Desertions to Pitt took place in spite of Portland's disapproval and Fox's sentimental pleas for party unity in remembrance of the good old days when the group had fought extensions of the prerogative. Before the end of the first week of the session Elliot estimated that about seventy "have already gone over," many of them country gentlemen who, though not party men in the sense of Burke, had formerly supported the Portland connection but

117 Burke MSS, Sheff., Edmond Malone to Burke, Dec. 16, 1792, French Laurence to Burke, Dec. 8 [18], 1792; Malmesbury, ed., *Diaries*, II, 475.

118 *Parl. Hist.*, XXX, 55, 115.

119 Malmesbury, ed., *Diaries*, II, 476, 479.

120 Burke MSS, Sheff., French Laurence to Burke, Dec. 8 [18], 1792; *Parl. Hist.*, XXX, 158-59.

now found their interest better represented by the government.[121] On December 13, for example, Lord Feilding decided to "rally round the throne" even if he had to abandon former political associates.[122] Windham announced his readiness to act from a sense of duty, regardless of the opinions of old political friends. On December 28, during the debate on a bill to regulate the immigration and residency of aliens, Elliot declared his intention to support the government.[123] He doubted whether ever again he could act in concurrence with the associates of Fox. But that did not mean he was joining Pitt. The Old Whigs who had separated from Fox still considered themselves unconnected with the ministry and, as a body, acting under their "ancient chief," Portland.

Burke felt as Elliot did, though he did not like to discuss party affairs in public because in them private friendships were involved.[124] He thought it useful to admit, however, that his breach with Fox had not "impaired," though it had "not improved," his own friendship with Portland. Without abandoning his old jealousy of the prerogative, he desired strong government—a ministry enjoying the king's confidence and the firm support of parliament. If that meant forsaking some of his old friends, he was prepared to do so, and if other political rearrangements were necessary, he was ready to work for them, as his conduct during the past year had demonstrated.

This debate of December 28 was also the occasion of Burke's notorious dagger scene.[125] In the midst of a diatribe against the revolutionaries, who might be expected to "take apprentices to the trade of blood," he drew a dagger from his clothing and melodramatically threw it onto the floor of the House. It was a warning against the murderers of France and their English disciples who had ordered three thousand such daggers in Birmingham. This bit of histrionics, awkwardly performed, made no impression upon the House, but gave the newspapers and car-

---

121 Minto, *Elliot*, II, 85, 87, Elliot to Lady Elliot, Dec. 18, 20, 1792.
122 *Parl. Hist.*, XXX, 9-10.
123 *Parl. Hist.*, XXX, 176-77; Minto, *Elliot*, II, 87-88, 96-98, Elliot to Lady Elliot, Dec. 22, 29, 1792.
124 *Parl. Hist.*, XXX, 181; *Times*, Dec. 29, 1792.
125 *Parl. Hist.*, XXX, 189.

toonists material for satire.[126] Indeed, to some of his opponents
it suggested a precarious state of Burke's mind, although Burke
had more than once indulged in eighteenth-century demonstra-
tive oratory.

These discussions about the state of the nation, against the
background of French military success on the continent and
radical excesses in Paris, where the trial of the king was proceeding, indicated the nervousness and uncertainty prevailing in England by the end of 1792. Men on both sides in the debate on the
alien bill, including Burke, admitted that of the some eight
thousand émigrés in England, less than two dozen were suspicious
or dangerous characters, but the bill's supporters considered even
that small number a threat when the times were so troubled.
The bill itself was more shocking to the eighteenth- than to the
twentieth-century mind; its provisions were less restrictive than
those imposed by all modern governments upon aliens. It contained no suggestion that England would close the doors to
refugees from the continent. Had it, Burke could not have
supported it. His humanitarian sentiments generally, and his
especial sympathy for the victims of the French Revolution, had
already made him active in the organized efforts to provide relief
for them.

Since the first wave of émigrés had come to England in the late
summer and early fall of 1789, Burke had been their friend. To
give one example, Jacques de Cazalès, a royalist leader of the

126 Letters in the Burke MSS, Sheff., amplify Burke's assertion that an order for
daggers had been placed with a Birmingham firm. One, unsigned, of Dec. 29, 1792,
said that 3,000 daggers had been made for Dr. William Maxwell and were shipped
to Calais. J. Overton on Dec. 31, prompted by a newspaper account, wrote of an
order for 10,000 daggers; 4,000 were made and stamped with the words "Rights of
Man," and then the swordmaker, Mr. Thomas Gill, made no more. James Woolley,
a Birmingham swordmaker, gave the fullest account, Jan. 16, 1793. A letter to
Overton from Burke, seeking information about the daggers, was brought to
Woolley, who endeavored to tell Burke the full story. On Sept. 10, 1792, Captain
William Blair introduced Dr. Maxwell, who desired 20,000 daggers. Woolley
informed two other firms, and the three set the same price. But only Gill decided
to take the order, and he worked on it for two months. He completed 3,000, which
were sent to Dover and thence to Calais. On March 6, 1793, Burke read Woolley's
letter to the House of Commons in order to correct a statement of Dec. 28. Dr.
Maxwell protested to Burke, March 6, 1793, asking to see the letter so that he
could defend himself against Woolley's slanders. Burke wrote on March 9 to
Woolley, who referred to this letter and Burke's advice in a reply of March 12.
Woolley said that he could back up his statements.

National Assembly, who came to England with Richard, Jr., when he returned from Coblentz, virtually lived at Gregories for the next few years.[127] Following upon the events of August–September, 1792, the émigrés came in greater numbers and often in desperate need, many having left France with little more than their lives and the clothing they wore. Though their numbers and needs were exaggerated, their hardships evoked widespread sympathy and stimulated organized efforts to provide relief.[128] Among several private committees that opened public subscriptions, the one initiated by John Wilmot, which met at the Freemason's Tavern, was the most ambitious. Burke wrote the "Case of the Suffering Clergy of France," which introduced its appeal for funds.[129] It was both a factual and an emotional account of the terrors in France from which the refugees had fled. It was informed by Burke's characteristic passion and by the tales the refugees had told him. One of the most exciting escapes was that of Jean-François de la Marche, the Bishop of St. Pol. It is not difficult to imagine him recounting his experiences when he visited Gregories early in September nor surprising that he collected at once £20 from Burke and nearly £200 from the neighborhood.[130] Though Burke desired some permanent arrangement for the refugees, such as subsidized settlement in Canada or assisted emigration to Maryland, some temporary measures were immediately necessary.[131] Burke gave generously of his time to the Freemason's Tavern group, and with Fitzwilliam, Walker King, and Dr. Brocklesby, among others, served on its committee. By the end of October the committee had collected nearly £14,000 and was already furnishing quarters, food, and clothing to the refugees. Burke differed with some of his friends on the committee, objecting to publication of information about subscriptions. He feared that even some slight irregularity of émigré

127 Smith, "Burke's Crusade," 215-16, n. 4.

128 On Sept. 17, 1792, the *Times* said the names of 10,000 refugee clergy were on the registry books of the Bishop of St. Pol. But at its meeting on Sept. 20 the Relief Committee at the Freemason's Tavern reported the presence of 1,500 French clergy in England and 1,000 in Jersey, of whom about one-third needed relief. *Times*, Sept. 22, 1792.

129 *Times*, Sept. 17, 18, 1792. Printed in Prior, *Burke* (3d ed.), 393-95.

130 *Corr.*, IV, 4-5, Burke to Richard, Jr., Sept. 9, 1792.

131 *Corr.*, IV, 4-5, Burke to Richard, Jr., Sept. 9, 1792; Burke MSS, Sheff., Burke to Fitzwilliam, Nov. 29, 1792.

conduct might stimulate unfavorable reactions among persons
suspicious of an influx of Catholics. Burke also desired government support for projects of aid and, like his committee, was
critical of what he unfairly thought was official dilatoriness in
getting ready a royal property at Winchester as a residence for a
large number of the clergy.[132] Apart from the purely humanitarian
considerations that brought together in this enterprise the chari-
ties of Englishmen of various religious and political preferences,
the influx of refugees deepened England's growing doubts about
the Revolution and furnished evidence to support the diatribes
Burke had been hurling.

This intense hatred and fear of the Revolution informed all of
Burke's views on public policy. A war of extirpation and restoration, with England leading an allied Europe to victory over the
Revolution, was the object of his desires. To that end, unity at
home was necessary, to be achieved by exposure and suppression
of pro-French sympathies and by the cessation of normal political
opposition to the government. Remembrances of past political differences with Pitt were irrelevant. All who opposed the Revolution must join on that principle, even if to do so meant breaking
up the Whig party, abandoning the Foxites, and forming a
coalition with the government.

Among the Portland Whigs who had abandoned Fox and
declared their support of the government, some, like Burke,
Windham, and Elliot, were leading members of the party though
not then recognized as men of ministerial status. In January,
1793, such men began to desert. Malmesbury went over in
mid-January, followed immediately by Loughborough, who to
Burke's pleasure became lord chancellor, as the first part of a
more comprehensive arrangement.[133] Unsuccessful efforts to extract from Portland more than a vague consent to support govern-

---

132 *Times*, Oct. 12, 13, 16, 24, 31, 1792; H.M.C., *Dropmore Papers*, II, 315, 318,
J. B. Burges to Grenville, Sept. 14, 1792, Buckingham to Grenville, Sept. 23, 1792;
Aspinall, ed., *Later Corr. of Geo. III*, I, 616, Dundas to the King, Sept. 22, 1792;
Henry Ellis, *Original Letters Illustrative of English History*, 2d ser. (London, 1827),
IV, 536-39, Burke to Wilmot, Oct. 2, 1792; MS in Huntington Library, MO658,
Burke to [?], Oct. 16, 1792; various letters in Burke MSS, Sheff, and N.R.O. during
the autumn of 1792, esp. Burke MSS, Sheff., Burke to Fitzwilliam, Oct. 20, 1792.

133 Burke MSS, Sheff., Loughborough to Burke, n. d., but during the negotiation
before he took office, Burke to Loughborough, Jan. 27, 1793; Aspinall, ed., *Later
Corr. of Geo. III*, I, 647, n. 1.

ment measures of which he approved forced the conclusion that he was unable to obey his better judgment.[134] In spite of the duke's indecision, Grenville thought he saw the beginning of a general migration, and Pitt tried to encourage it by letting Loughborough know of his willingness to offer places to Malmesbury, Windham, and Elliot. The last two were not yet ready to accept.[135] The Prince of Wales, who in the preceding May had offered his maiden speech in support of the Royal Proclamation, announced to Portland his decision to support the "public good." Portland received it calmly.[136] He could himself support certain measures for the safety of the country, but he could not give "implicit confidence" to the administration. The prince's action did not excite enthusiasm among friends of government. Provided the prince did not become a nuisance, said Buckingham, he might draw with him some of Fox's "mobleaders."[137]

The defections, which did not yet constitute a formal coalition, were seriously affecting the party. On January 20 the Whig Club, or the remnant of it, declared its loyalty to Fox. Burke and others who thought as he did considered this a challenge. In a hurriedly called meeting on February 10, twenty-one persons signed a resolution to oppose French principles and to support the government "in the present difficult crisis of public affairs," while continuing to acknowledge Portland as their leader.[138] The resolution also spoke for two other persons, absentees, who had sent their agreements. All who signed were members of the Commons and among them, besides Burke, were Windham, Elliot, Frederick North, and Anstruther. Then Burke, his son, Windham, and forty-two other members resigned from the Whig Club, blaming Fox for making their action necessary.[139]

It is difficult to describe precisely the state of affairs at this

---

134 Burke MSS, Sheff., Loughborough to Burke, Jan. 12, 19, 1793; Buckingham, *Courts and Cabinets*, II, 236, Grenville to Buckingham, Jan. 19, 1793; Butterfield, *Cambridge Historical Journal*, IX, 329.

135 Minto, *Elliot*, II, 112, Elliot to Lady Elliot, Feb. 5, 1793.

136 Aspinall, ed., *Later Corr. of Geo. III*, I, 649-52, the Prince to Portland, Portland to the Prince, Jan. 21, 1793.

137 H.M.C., *Dropmore Papers*, II, 369-70, Buckingham to Grenville, Jan. 20, 1793.

138 Br. Mus., Add. MSS 37,873, fol. 201, paper containing resolutions and signatures; Minto, *Elliot*, II, 113-14, Elliot to Lady Elliot, Feb. 12, 1793.

139 Burke MSS, Sheff., Burke to Whig Club, Feb., 1793; George, *Catalogue of Satires*, VII, 20.

time. Windham's attempt must have puzzled his correspondent in Italy, John Coxe Hippisley.[140] The most unambiguous fact was the fundamental difference with Fox, a "difference of feeling that pervaded all our sentiments on the present state of the world." Whether there were two wings of the Whig party in disagreement over principles and the question of supporting the government yet acknowledging Portland as head of the party, or two opposition parties, Portland's and Fox's, or a proadministration faction that considered Portland their leader but temporarily looked to Windham for guidance, or whether the Whigs were drifting while Portland prayed that the disagreement with Fox would somehow go away—the answer at the moment was not clear.

But by this time there was another factor in the situation. On February 1, 1793, France declared war on England. Perhaps the years of indecision had ended.

140 Br. Mus., Add. MSS 37,848, fols. 59-64, March 28, 1793.

CHAPTER XVII

The Anti-Jacobin Crusade

ENGLAND'S INVOLVEMENT in the war, in spite of the ministry's desire to remain neutral, vindicated Burke's preaching. In the House of Commons on February 12, 1793, Pitt's long review of the events leading up to the French declaration proved, said Burke, that ministers had not "precipitated the nation into a war."[1] France had formed a "regular, methodized system for the destruction of the antient order of things throughout Europe" and England at last and inevitably, as a member of the European "commonwealth" had become drawn into the struggle.[2]

The manner of England's involvement and the alleged reasons displeased Burke. He would have preferred that she declare war, even though the French aggression bore out his arguments. He emphasized ideological differences where Pitt ignored them. Burke derided the contention that England went to war over the opening of the Scheldt River, a "chamber pot." For nearly four years his "utmost exertions" had not aroused either the government or the public to the dangers they faced. Fortunately, when the war came, it was not too late for England to defend herself. As a prudent politician, Burke admitted that if England had declared war at an earlier time, the government would not have received at home the support she now would enjoy. His own desire for war had not previously expressed "the feelings of the nation." To hold Burke responsible for creating a warlike temper in

England is to exaggerate his influence and to defy the record of events.[3]

Disagreement about war aims also disturbed Burke. His were clear and simply stated—to extirpate the Revolution and restore a reformed monarchical system to France. Ministers, concerned only about the protection of England's vital interests on the continent and in the Empire, were willing to ignore the internal politics of France. If a short war checked French aggressions and persuaded the French republicans that peace was their interest, if then the French republic promised to be pacific, ministers, seeing no question of England's survival in it, would enter into a treaty with France.[4] Burke would have to differ with ministers not only about the conduct but about the policy and the meaning of the war.

These differences, which were apparent to any who compared Burke's writings with the diplomatic correspondence laid before the Commons by Dundas on January 28, were further exposed during several debates in the weeks following the declaration of war. Burke spoke vigorously on the government side against the antiwar arguments of Fox and his supporters. He admitted that he went beyond Pitt by adding to France's external aggressions her "internal policy . . . as a ground for war."[5] England would be forced eventually "to interfere in the internal government of France" as the only means of obtaining peace. In addition to supporting the government, Burke thought it his duty to convert ministers to his views. This he tried to do, for example, on March 6 in a long conversation with Pitt and Dundas. Pitt listened "patiently and cordially."[6]

Burke opposed the attempt of Fox to divert attention to Poland in order to expose contradictions in government policy. Having

1 *Parl. Hist.*, XXX, 383.

2 Burke MSS, Sheff., undated fragments, B-10, B-10h.

3 For examples of such exaggerated assertions, see Harold J. Laski, *Political Thought in England from Locke to Bentham* (New York, 1920), 256; John Bowring, ed., *Bentham's Works* (Edinburgh, 1843), II, 463; *The Political Writings of Joel Barlow* (New York, 1796), 253.

4 Ward and Gooch, eds., *Cambridge Hist. British Foreign Policy*, I, 230, 235; Watson, *George III*, 363.

5 *Parl. Hist.*, XXX, 435, Feb. 18, 1793.

6 Minto, *Elliot*, II, 121-22, Elliot to Lady Elliot, March 7, 1793.

acquiesced in "the open contempt of the law of nations" shown by Russia and Prussia in the recent second partition of Poland, said Fox, ministers were trying to justify war against France without exhausting the possibilities of negotiation.[7] Burke, whose opposition to France was based on principle, was bound to be embarrassed when he used a circumstantial argument in trying to explain away England's Polish policy. His dilemma was that of the statesman who takes a strong stand for the right and then has to accommodate such a commitment to the facts of practical politics, in this instance, of geography. He had lamented the fate of Poland at the first partition treaty years before, just as he deplored the threats that appeared in 1792.[8] In contrast with the French Revolution, the movement in Poland that produced the constitution of 1791 appeared to him as a great conservative achievement.[9] It would provide the basis for further improvements by giving to the Polish aristocracy the opportunity to be a true nobility rather than enjoy "a sort of wild liberty among slaves." Not even Burke could agree with Russia that the Polish Revolution was an eastern European expression of French Jacobinism.[10] He found a different rationalization. The demands for English intervention against Russia endeavored "by the back door" to draw England into concert with France.[11] More to the point, though a departure from all principle except practicality, was his admission that there was little England could do to aid the Poles. Burke could only "hope for better things" in the East and urge England to concentrate upon "the infinitely more dangerous" tyranny "at our very door."

This view, expressed in the summer of 1792, remained his opinion when Fox raised the question on February 18, 1793. As an abstract question of morality, the partition of Poland was an international wrong against a Christian people. But nations have

7 *Parl. Hist.*, XXX, 431-32.

8 *Corr.*, III, 474, Burke to Richard, Jr., July 29, 1792.

9 *Corr.*, III, 446-51, 472, Burke to Stanislaus II, March 20, 1792, Burke to Richard, Jr., July 29, 1792; R. R. Palmer, *The Age of Democratic Revolution* (Princeton, N.J., 1959), 431-32. Burke's letter to Stanislaus was in acknowledgment of a medal the king had sent to him.

10 Palmer, *Age of Revolution*, 434.

11 *Corr.*, III, 473-74, Burke to Richard, Jr., July 29, 1792.

to "have a predilection for their own safety."[12] Unless the "injury" done to Poland affected Britain's vital interests, she should attend to the threat of revolution and the maintenance of "the balance of power at and near home." This prudential position was theoretically inconsistent with Burke's conception of the unity of the Christian commonwealth of Europe, and he frankly admitted it. Nations, however, unlike judges, could not "act with perfect impartiality, to the exclusion of all ideas of self." They had to perform their duties in order of importance, and the first business for England was the war with France.

That also meant attending to the threats to England's domestic peace. Like the majority of the Commons, Burke rejected Sheridan's challenge to inquire into the seditious practices referred to in the King's Speech. They were self-evident, but lest there be any doubt, Burke cited some instances to prove the existence of an incendiary faction propagating French principles. Fox disputed the accuracy of his remarks. The question of the danger to the British constitution was not settled then, though historians generally have thought the parliamentary reformers were, at worst, merely overenthusiastic and indiscreet. If Burke and Windham, ministers, the people who joined the loyal associations, and probably the majority of Englishmen who concerned themselves with the problem misjudged the reform societies, it is not necessary to believe that these judgments were insincere.

The Traitorous Correspondence Act was one of the early security measures. With Elliot, Burke was consulted privately about the bill. It forbade such commerce and intercourse with the enemy as fell within the statutory definitions of treason. Though it was not as stern as he desired, Burke supported it vigorously. The bill, justified by the emergency and supported by precedents, was not an infringement of constitutional liberties, though like every law it limited natural liberty to some extent. Burke's position was legally and constitutionally sound. The more

12 *Parl. Hist.*, XXX, 433, Feb. 18, 1793. On Jan. 31, 1794, Grey teased Burke over the Polish question. In one of his off-color figures of speech, Burke compared himself and England with an impotent lover whose only strength was desire. Where, he asked, would England find the fleet and the army of 200,000 men necessary to give effective aid to Poland? *Times*, Feb. 1, 1794.

questionable argument concerned the nature of the emergency. The majority of parliament, including Portland in the Lords, concurred in the wisdom and prudence of ministers.

The session saw many such debates. A stubborn minority, led by Fox and Sheridan and Grey and seldom numbering more than fifty, repeatedly questioned the justice and policy of the war and the measures for prosecuting it. The premises of the debates were always the same, whatever the subject, and their contents were therefore often repeated. Two of the most notable were occasioned by Grey's motion of May 6 for parliamentary reform and Fox's of June 17 for reestablishment of peace with France.

Grey's motion, which had been preceded by the presentation of petitions for reform from twenty-two places in England and Scotland, asked for the consideration by a committee of the petition from the Friends of the People.[13] This petition, often cited by later reformers and historians, illustrated the discrepancies and absurdities in the distribution of parliamentary representation. Grey's speech argued for reform on the basis of expediency rather than of right. It was, therefore, almost a rehearsal of the successful arguments of 1830-1832, but the outcome was different, for the times were against the reformers. Grey's motion was beaten 282-41. Though he was present, Burke did not speak against it. We can only guess at the reason.

The opponents of Fox's motion, which was beaten 187-47, were not quite in complete agreement, and the motion was designed to exploit the differences among them. With a view to dissociating England from her allies, Fox desired a pledge against interference with the internal government of France. Pitt carefully avoided it, circumscribing his explanation with various conditions and qualifications. Burke and Windham, however, challenged Fox.[14] Windham considered it one of the objects of the war to establish in France a government with which England could confidently treat. Burke refused to be as credulous as Fox in thinking that England could negotiate with the sans-culottes, or trust them to honor engagements even if a treaty were signed. Burke conceded the difficulties of forcing a particular form of government upon a

13 Printed in *Parl. Hist.*, XXX, 788-99.
14 *Parl. Hist.*, XXX, 1006-13.

country, but in the interest of common safety, citing Vattel, he upheld the right of the allies to attempt it, by war if necessary, when the government of a nation deliberately set out to foster anarchy by subverting the law and religion of other countries. In this speech, Burke established the tone and announced the theme of all of his later writings upon the war and the revolution and marked out the lines of future disagreements with the government he had chosen to support.

Just as in 1790, so in the summer of 1793, few people in England subscribed fully to Burke's views. His earlier assessment of the character of the Revolution and the tendencies of reform in England had now become widely accepted, and at last England was engaged in the war he had long desired, but he was almost alone in advocating a policy of "thorough" conduct of the war. Possibly Englishmen would learn to accept it as they had come to his other judgments. In the meantime he had two functions to perform, one to express his views on the war, and the other to give his support to the government and win friends for it. Events favored his efforts. By the end of the session on June 21 Pitt's parliamentary strength was overwhelming. When the subject was the war or related matters, the opposition was a pitifully small, if valiant, group. Those who had abandoned Fox had in effect coalesced with Pitt for parliamentary purposes, although there had been no announced secession by the heads of the Portland wing. Fitzwilliam and the Duke were still tied with Fox.

Throughout the session Burke and Windham, with other secessionists from the Whig Club, endured from former friends accusations of apostasy and hypocrisy for supporting a minister that they had attacked since 1783. Burke undertook to set men straight about the history of the Portland Whigs. He had parted company with such as Fox and Sheridan, but they were latecomers "who had incidentally joined that party by the way," and they "had no claim upon him."[15] The original members of the old Rockingham connection agreed with him about the war even though some were reluctant to break with Fox. In that sense, Burke insisted, he had not deserted the party. Admitting Fox's

---

15 *Parl. Hist.*, XXX, 555, Feb. 28, 1793.

influence, still Fox had no right to consider a party as "made only for him." If he adopted a line of conduct without consulting the other members, "it might then be supposed that the party was at liberty to leave him." Indeed, many of the party had done so. The Old Whigs who were supporting Pitt in the Commons outnumbered those who stood by Fox, though their position was ambiguous because Portland continued to think of himself as joined with Fox in an opposition party.

The ambivalence of their position was reflected in their private conduct. Their relations with ministers were growing more intimate and confidential. They consulted privately with Pitt on matters of public concern. Elliot, Windham, and Lord Spencer, after refusing offers from Pitt and Dundas, gave the impression that at the proper time they would accept places.[16] Burke, Elliot, Windham, Malmesbury, Lord Beauchamp, and Porchester, with others who opposed Fox, formed a political dining club.[17] At the same time, Burke and his son, his brother and Will Burke (just back from India), French Laurence, Spencer and the Duke of Devonshire, and Frederick Montagu dined with Fitzwilliam and agreed to dine with Portland soon after.[18]

During the summer politics abated. Burke was at Gregories, attending to his farming. He kept up his correspondences, however, and occasionally entertained guests and talked politics, with Grenville at dinner and with Lord Hawkesbury, who spent a night. On September 18 he went to town and attended a royal levee; two weeks later he dined at Wimbledon with Dundas, Pitt, and Sir Gilbert Elliot, who had come from Scotland to accept a mission for the government.[19] Burke seemed to enjoy his new associations; at Wimbledon he was in high humor. "Everyone," said the *Times,* "knows his happy talent at description, and few men are so richly endowed with that fund of humor and genius, which are the charms of society." Elliot, having lost patience with Portland, had decided at last to join Pitt. In September he undertook a mission to Toulon. Burke heartily approved of

16 Minto, *Elliot,* II, 150-51, Elliot to Lady Elliot, June 25, 1793.
17 Minto, *Elliot,* II, 139, Elliot to Lady Elliot, May 3, 1793.
18 Minto, *Elliot,* II, 136, Elliot to Lady Elliot, May 2, 1793.
19 *Times,* Aug. 1, Sept. 19, 20, Oct. 7, 1793.

his acceptance, thinking wrongly that through Elliot he could impress a royalist policy upon Pitt.[20] From this time until his death in 1814 Elliot held one or another foreign and imperial office and died the Earl of Minto.

As for the year past, Burke maintained a self-conscious friendship with Portland while arguing, with Windham's help, the need for united support of a war against Jacobinism.[21] Deluded persons who opposed such a war were likely to become "the instrument" of revolutionary designs. Those who opposed Fox could not be effective by remaining a third party. They might have to join the administration, and their leader might have to accept places, as Loughborough, Elliot, and Malmesbury had done. Portland agreed on the necessity of supporting the war effort but thought he could best do his duty by remaining independent both of the administration and of the Friends of the People.[22]

Burke, in his instruction about the meaning of party, had failed to make one point clear. He had always insisted upon the importance of principle in giving purpose and direction to party efforts. The words "Whig" and "Tory" referred to principle, and as long as the issues had been domestic, the distinction had had meaning. The Whig, loyal to the Revolution Settlement, accepted the constitution embodied in king, Lords, and Commons and "on any public misunderstanding" preferred "the aristocracy and democracy" of the country to the monarch. The Tory at

[20] Minto, *Elliot*, II, 165-75, Burke to Elliot, Sept., Sept. 22, 1793, Windham to Elliot, Sept. 19, 1793. Burke wanted Elliot to place De Cazalès in a position of authority in Toulon. Elliot refused. He did try to do another thing Burke desired, that is, bring the Comte de Provence and his brother to Toulon and give them positions of leadership. Ministers rejected this plan. Burke misunderstood Elliot's position and resolved never to write to him again. But this was because he mistakenly thought that Elliot did not want him to. *Corr.*, IV, 178, Burke to Windham, Oct., 1793. No real breach between them occurred. Burke came to believe that Elliot should resign rather than follow orders conflicting with his own views. Minto, *Elliot*, II, 176-78, Burke to Sylvester Douglas, Nov. 14, 1793. In this instance, Burke misunderstood Elliot's views. Soon after his return to England Elliot visited Gregories, somewhat apprehensive about his reception, but he found "the kindest and most affectionate welcome it is possible to imagine." Minto, *Elliot*, II, 403-405, Elliot to Lady Elliot, June 1, 3, 1797.

[21] Portland MSS, Burke to Portland, Aug. 1, Sept. 29, 1793. The last letter is the one that accompanied Burke's "Observations on the Conduct of the Minority," to be discussed later.

[22] Br. Mus., Add. MSS 37,845, fols. 11, 13-14, Portland to Mrs. Crewe, Aug. 26, 1793, Windham to Portland, Sept. 3, 1793.

such times favored "the prerogative of the crown."[23] By this definition, Burke had been a Whig from the beginning of his parliamentary career and remained one, for he had not changed his views about these domestic constitutional questions, and he never considered it unwhiggish to support the cause of social order.

By 1793 the New Whigs were confusing the old distinctions. As Burke had told Fitzwilliam, if Fox claimed to be a Whig and if "Tory" described a man who desired to preserve social order and the ancient constitution against the French principles which the New Whigs proclaimed, then he himself had no objection to being called a Tory. Indeed, Portland and Fitzwilliam had not abandoned traditional Whiggism any more than had Burke. But in subordinating it to personal friendships or memories of old political antagonisms—that is, in clinging to Fox—they gave a false appearance.

The strained relationship between Burke and Fitzwilliam was complicated by a family matter.[24] Richard, Jr., asked (or demanded) the seat vacated by the death of John Lee, who sat for Fitzwilliam's borough Higham Ferrers. He thought he understood from a conversation held a year earlier that Fitzwilliam had promised it to him. Fitzwilliam did not see how he could have made such a promise when even then he and the Burkes had disagreed about politics. Richard's arrogant announcement that in sitting for Fitzwilliam's borough, he would maintain his independence determined Fitzwilliam. "I cannot bring myself to offer a seat to a young man on those terms on which alone you have declared your intention to receive it." Richard's defense of himself, and particularly of his father, irritated Fitzwilliam further and drove him to an assertion that he probably regretted. Burke had delivered himself to Pitt while Portland and Fitzwilliam were in opposition. That was tantamount to desertion. To give Higham Ferrers to Richard would be another blow at Portland. Fitzwilliam wanted to hear no more of the matter. If,

23 *Parl. Hist.*, XXX, 612, March 22, 1793.
24 Burke MSS, Sheff., Fitzwilliam to Richard, Jr., Aug. 8, 27, 1793; Burke MSS, N.R.O., Aiv16a, Richard, Jr., to Fitzwilliam, Aug. 31, 1793; Fitzwilliam MSS, Sheff., F31a, Portland to Fitzwilliam, Sept. 22, 1793; Minto, *Elliot*, II, 8n., William Elliot to Elliot, n. d.

as alleged, Burke intruded with a sharp letter that drove Fitzwilliam to his bed for several days, the evidence is not in the
papers of either man. Richard, however, offered a dignified, able
defense of his father that, in fact, revealed a good deal less
self-delusion about the state of politics than Portland and Fitzwilliam displayed. In this last word between them on Higham
Ferrers, Richard rightly attributed the political confusion to the
ambiguous conduct of Fitzwilliam and Portland. All the noble
lords could do was reassure one another and admit that neither
really liked Burke's son. Portland said that as far as a seat in
parliament was concerned, he had always thought Richard "labored under a disqualification" for which there was no cure.

By autumn, 1793, the ambiguities seemed to be dissolving. The
Whig aristocrats were withdrawing subsidies to certain newspapers, "winding up the finances of the party," conceding the
likelihood of its dissolution, and admitting the impossibility of
reconciling their political views with those of Fox.[25] In an effort
to clear the air Burke sent Portland a long explanation and
apologia, with a covering letter dated September 29.[26] He had
composed the paper during the last parliamentary session and
now, after reading it over, decided that it accurately expressed his

[25] Butterfield in *Cambridge Historical Journal*, IX, 330; *Times*, Nov. 23, 1793.

[26] "Observations on the Conduct of the Minority, particularly in the last session
of Parliament. Addressed to the Duke of Portland and Lord Fitzwilliam," *Works*,
V, 3-63. The accompanying letter is in Burke MSS., N.R.O., Aivl2, and in the
Portland MSS; a copy of the "Observations" is in the Portland MSS. Portland
acknowledged receipt of it on Oct. 10, 1793. *Corr.*, IV, 161-66. Intended only for
the addressees, the original draft was retained by Burke's secretary, William Thomas
Swift, who, upon surrendering it early in 1796 to French Laurence, assured him
that no copy had been made. *Epistolary Correspondence of . . . Burke and Dr.
French Laurence* (London, 1822), 122-23, Laurence to Burke, Feb. 14, 1797. Yet in
Feb., 1797, it was published under the title "Fifty-Four Articles of Impeachment
against Charles James Fox." For a few days the news of publication was withheld
from Burke, who was then ill, but Laurence finally told him about it and of his
and Walker King's successful application for an injunction to stop publication.
About 3,000 copies had been sold. Burke concluded that Swift must have made a
copy. Burke MSS, Sheff., Burke to Laurence, Feb. 15, 1797. The case against Swift
is not proved by direct evidence. It does not seem likely that if he was the culprit,
he would have supplied a "garbled version" of it, but someone else, whether the
publisher or not, might have "garbled" it and supplied the new title. After
Burke's death, a genuine version was published, Oct., 1797, and sold about 5,000
copies. John Nichols, *Literary Anecdotes of the Eighteenth Century . . .* , VII, 6-7,
George Steevens to Bishop Percy, Oct. 24, 1796 [1797]; *Burke-Laurence Corr.*, 293-94,
Laurence to Loughborough, Sept. 27, 1797.

sentiments. Burke asked only for an acknowledgment of its receipt; he even urged Portland not to read it until he had time for "reflection." If by that time Burke was dead, Portland would be able to know that he had had a "true friend," who opposed "the modern system of morality and policy." It was during this last session, said Burke, that he had finally abandoned all hope of a reconciliation with Fox and a reparation of the breach in the party.

The "Observations" was a long, superficially calm review of the reasons for this conclusion. But under the placid surface Burke's deepest passions ran. There could be no doubt of his remorse over the breach with Fox, the horror that Fox's parliamentary conduct inspired in him, or the genuine sense of moral duty that had urged him to oppose Fox and repudiate his doctrines. Burke no longer could give him the benefit of doubt. If Fox did not speak quite as indiscreetly as his followers, or was content to "make his invectives" and leave it to others "to draw the conclusion," it was because he had "reasons for management and caution" that they did not share. There could be no mistaking his purposes and desires, which, if achieved, would bring ruin upon England and Europe. Nor, on the personal level, could there be any doubt of Fox's complete repudiation of Portland's position on the justice and necessity of the war, or of his political conduct. Stooping low, Burke reminded Fitzwilliam that the Friends of the People had named his borough of Malton as an instance of corrupt political practice. Parliamentary reform was a frontal attack upon the "operation of property in elections," and the reformers would not respect the political leadership of men who opposed reform. The conduct of Fox and his followers in the last session had demonstrated clearly the loss of Portland's and Fitzwilliam's influence in the party that they thought they led. If, by some miracle, the party came into office, not they, but Fox and Sheridan, would enjoy the substance of power.

It would be best, Burke continued, to forget the past and all the reasons that justified opposition to Pitt in 1784. The fact in 1793 was that either Pitt or Fox must be minister, and Pitt enjoyed the plenitude of confidence, of the king, the Lords, and the Commons, and of the public. More than that, in 1793 Pitt was right in his views on public policy. In the interest of the country, Portland and Fitzwilliam belonged with him, not with Fox, Sheridan, Lansdowne, Grey, and Lauderdale.

After reading the "Observations," as well as the accompanying letter, Portland wrote to Burke.[27] The letter must have disappointed its recipient, for, it seemed, the message of the "Observations" had made no impression. Portland admitted the need for extirpating Jacobinism and acting "with any man, at any time, in the cause of good order and of civil society." But he blamed Pitt, at least in part, for bringing on the crisis. He suspected that Pitt retained his old reforming principles and was not ready to repent his past. The war apart, there were too many differences between Portland and the minister to justify "a title for confidence." Portland thought the negotiation of 1792 had shown a "want of good faith"; it was still wanting. Despite differences, mutual confidence remained between Portland and Fox. And so things stood in October, 1793. Portland was not ready, as Burke was, to subordinate everything—friendship and years of political comradeship—to the great issue of 1793.

Unhappily, even ministers seemed as myopic as Portland in failing to see in Jacobinism the overriding issue. In Burke's view, the war and allied victory could bring a lasting settlement to Europe only if the proper war aims were relentlessly pursued.[28] To accomplish them, the allies must forbear territorial indemnities, must support the émigré nobility and keep the principle of monarchy alive by recognizing the Comte de Provence as regent, and must be ready to aid internal opposition to the French Republic. It was foolish to peck away at the fortresses of Flanders when by aiding the revolt in the West the allies could gain in effect 40,000 men.[29] The capture of Toulon was doubly important, because it placed England on the royalist side. Burke

---

[27] *Corr.*, IV, 161-66, Oct. 10, 1793.

[28] *Corr.*, IV, 132-34, 134-36, 136-50, 150-57, 159-60, Burke to Windham, Aug. 18, 23, 1793, Burke to the Comte de Mercy, Aug., 1793, Burke to Sir Gilbert Elliot, Sept. 22, 1793, Burke to Dundas, Oct. 7, 1793; Burke MSS, N.R.O., Aiv22, Aiv7, Burke to General Count Edward Dalton, Aug. 6, 1793, Burke to Col. John St. Leger, Oct. 23, 1793.

[29] Osborn Coll., Box 74, #2, Burke to Dundas, Oct. 8, 1793. When Dundas, in a reply to Burke, acknowledged the importance of the revolt in La Vendée, he confessed that England could give little help except to send supplies. Burke MSS, N.R.O., Aiv10 (6), Oct. 13, 1793.

hoped the Toulon venture would encourage an alliance with the royalists in La Vendée. Perhaps it would bring the recovery of purpose that had been lost when Austria became more interested in territorial gains than in a royalist restoration, when Pitt neglected the émigrés or the Comte de Provence, and when Grenville desired only "some legitimate and stable government."[30]

Against Burke's arguments it has been urged that an attempt to restore the monarchy would have "condemned" the cause in the eyes of Frenchmen, whereas the Toulon venture "bound France to the regicide cause."[31] This judgment is made with the knowledge of the allied failures in 1793. If England and the allies had pushed vigorously the kinds of efforts Burke demanded, the outcome might have been different, because in 1793 it was still early enough to make the royalist cause appear to be the winning cause. Allied blunders gave France time to organize a national defense and so to perpetuate the war for a generation. In the end the war was won only when allied armies penetrated France. Burke, better than the traditionalists who directed allied efforts, saw not only the nature of the Revolution but also the nature of the war that would be necessary to defeat it.

Their failure to see what he understood accounts for the differences between their views and his on strategy and tactics. He asked for greater devotion to an ideal than the allied leaders were capable of. He recommended an ultimate remedy for Europe's troubles to people whose imaginations, feelings, judgments, and conclusions could not "keep pace" with his.[32] Burke complained about this. England was not engaged in the traditional kind of war. In the cause of humanity, Europe was fighting a principle, Jacobinism, and a spirit, Jacobinism. The sources had to be destroyed; as long as Jacobinism subsisted, France would be "a perpetual fund of revolution."[33]

Burke was right in many of his judgments. He perceived the dynamic quality of the Jacobin spirit and the necessity for fighting an ideological war. He understood the uncompromising, aggres-

30 Ward and Gooch, eds., *Cambridge Hist. British Foreign Policy*, I, 242-43.

31 J. Holland Rose, *William Pitt and the Great War* (London, 1911), 119-20, 162-63; Ward and Gooch, eds., *Cambridge Hist. British Foreign Policy*, I, 242-43.

32 Adapting a phrase from Portland's confession. *Corr.,* IV, 162, Portland to Burke, Oct. 10, 1793.

33 *Corr.,* IV, 139, Burke to Comte de Mercy, Aug., 1793.

sive character of the revolutionary government in France and the impossibility of negotiating with it a peace of compromise. He anticipated a long war that would not end until the revolutionary government was overthrown and the Bourbons restored. The history of the next twenty-five years vindicated him. But he made one serious miscalculation, when he thought it possible by military victory to extirpate the spirit of revolution. In the world after 1789, or after 1815, or after Marxism, impulses released by the French Revolution continued to operate powerfully. That is why Burke's philosophy of counterrevolution remained viable; those who embraced it found it relevant in the continuing conflict with the secular, democratic, equalitarian, positivistic liberalism of the nineteenth and twentieth centuries.

Doggedly, Burke continued to press his ideas upon England. When he learned that a declaration of British policy was being prepared, he began another paper, hoping to submit it to ministers in time to influence them, and meanwhile asking Dundas for an opportunity to comment on the declaration before its publication.[34] Dundas was sorry; it was too late. The declaration had already been circulated to foreign governments.[35] Grenville sent a copy of the declaration to Burke, trusting that he would approve of it, and Pitt gave him a private hearing.[36] Oblivious or disdainful of their impatience with him, Burke continued with his own proposals about allied policy.[37] Nations are judged by their deeds as well as their words, and Burke wanted to impress upon ministers his judgment about the proper conduct for England. He repeated that the best way of achieving victory was to support the émigrés and the insurgent royalists of La Vendée. He argued once more for the reestablishment of the old order—monarchy, property, nobility, and church—because in them were the "corporate people" of France, those known to public law. Having

34 H.M.C., *Dropmore Papers*, II, 450-51, Oct. 27, 1793. Burke's paper was his "Remarks on the Policy of the Allies with Respect to France," *Works*, IV, 405-82.

35 Burke MSS, N.R.O., Aiv6, Dundas to Burke, Oct. 29, 1793.

36 Burke MSS, N.R.O., Aiv8, Grenville to Burke, Oct. [28], 1793. Burke had no serious objection to the language of the Declaration, but questioned the timing. The *Times*, Nov. 18, 1793, reported a "very long" conversation between Burke and Pitt on a Sunday morning.

37 "Remarks," *Works*, IV, 407. The first pages were written before the Declaration of Oct. 29 was published, but the paper was not completed until Jan., 1794. P.R.O., Chatham Papers, 30/8, 118, Burke to Loughborough, Jan. 12, 1794.

restored a reformed monarchy, he would leave France a great power. To weaken her internally and externally would invite disorder in Europe for a century, as France would be unable to preserve domestic peace, incapable of playing her part in the European balance, and a prey to ambitious neighbors. This was the wisest part of Burke's counsel, and it anticipated decisions made in 1814-1815. His expectations about the terms of a restoration in France were much less perspicuous. His entrancement with the royalists concealed from him their narrowness, their misunderstanding of the tempers of Frenchmen, and their lack of charity and political wisdom and prevented him from seeing that the restoration of a reformed monarchy, unless accompanied by a reformation of the royalists, would not bring peace within France.

Burke's understanding of the nature of the European state system and of France's pivotal position within it was profound. It was shaped by his study of history and his belief that religion was an essential part of the social structure of a nation or a civilization. Until the French Revolution, Burke's political experiences had concerned national rivalries within the larger system of Europe, but he had always taken for granted a European order whose members had many things in common. More than most of his contemporaries he appreciated the Middle Ages, and his knowledge of that period deepened his understanding of the community of Europe. The French Revolution was a challenge to the unity of Europe, a threat to the principles and the institutions that gave order to the system, and so the war against Jacobinism was a crusade against infidels who would destroy the foundations of Europe, subvert its public law, and, if successful, create a new Europe based upon principles antipathetic to the old. For Jacobinism was to Burke the wrong kind of international influence; it was a propagandizing, atheistic, republican assault against the traditional religious, monarchical, and propertied community of Europe. Burke was correct in thinking the French Revolution a challenge to the eighteenth-century order. The challenge was in part bourgeois—the rising commercial and industrial interests against landed, aristocratic, and royalist domination. In France it took a political form, and because of the nature of the old regime, a violent one as well.

Burke understood the political revolution better than the one that underlay it. The parliamentary reform movement of the 1780's and 1790's was the beginning of a challenge that would not be victorious until 1832. Thus, to put down the enemy in France would not be the salvation of the eighteenth-century order. It was threatened by rising industrialism, and to this threat Burke seemed oblivious. While peaceful, it would nevertheless be effective. The old order would remain in jeopardy even if the allied armies should suppress the French Revolution.

In his "Remarks on the Policy of the Allies," Burke stressed the unity of Europe. He spoke of its public law, and he called Europe a "federative society," a "diplomatic republic." His conception was legalistic and political. Though it was not Vattel who taught him to understand the unity of Europe, Burke quoted extracts from the *Law of Nations* in an appendix. In the "Remarks" he paraphrased Vattel, but in so doing he again simply demonstrated the community between his and the views of a recognized authority in international law.

Religion and property were twin pillars of the European order. In the great crusade against Jacobinism, Burke asked that denominational differences be ignored. The war against France was indeed a religious war, the Jacobins "against all sects and all religions." To stress differences among denominations "in the present state of the world, is too contemptible." "It is for the Christian statesmen, . . . to secure their common basis, and not to risk the subversion of the whole fabric by pursuing these distinctions with an ill-timed zeal." In the "grand alliance" of Europe were different "modes of government," as of religion. But there was agreement in fundamentals, and they must be preserved by a community having as its object the destruction of the common enemy, Jacobinism.

Against this background, Burke's engagement in a delicate diplomatic venture becomes plausible and consistent, though his part in it is easily exaggerated. Unlike his son's mission in Coblentz, this one involved a recognized political entity, not an aggregation of private persons. Burke stated his apparent desire in a single sentence of a letter to John Coxe Hippisley. "I confess, I would, if the matter rested with me, enter into much more distinct and avowed political connections with the Court of Rome than hitherto we have held."[38] Taken out of context, this sentence seemed to measure the depth of Burke's feelings about the French Revolution.[39] If carried into effect, it would return England to a political, though not a religious, communion from which she had been separated since the reign of Elizabeth and would modify the state system Europe had known since the Peace of Westphalia in 1648.

In the summer of 1793 when the question of relations with the papacy was discussed, the British government by its actions had already acknowledged their common interests. George III and his ministers were grateful for the papal admonition urging Irish Catholics to keep the peace, for the papal permission for the British fleet to take on supplies in the papal states, and for intimations that fruitful commercial relationships might be developed with the papal territories, whereas the papacy appreciated England's naval commitments in the Mediterranean and recent concessions to the Irish Catholics.

In Rome, soliciting good will, was a man of business who would be willing to accept the ministry there if one should be established.[40] This was John Coxe Hippisley, who busied himself inside the periphery of diplomacy without unduly offending the men responsible for its conduct. A barrister and doctor of civil law, well known in Italy and Madras, Hippisley was a friend of Windham and of Burke. Elected to parliament in 1790, he supported the Portland party. Late in November, 1792, he went to Italy, ostensibly to spend the winter for his health. Besides his own friends there, he had contacts through his sister, who was married to a Roman nobleman.[41] His status, at least at the beginning of his sojourn, was quite unofficial; as late as August

---

38 Burke MSS, Sheff. and Br. Mus., Add. MSS 37,848, fols. 297-301, Oct. 3, 1793.

39 In his *Monastic Life in the Middle Ages* (London, 1922), 276, Cardinal Gasquet quoted only this sentence and thus created a false impression of Burke's view about relations with Rome. See below, n. 49.

40 H. V. F. Somerset, *Dublin Review*, CCII, 138-48, esp. 144-45; Br. Mus., Add. MSS 37,848, fols. 63, 65, 69-71, 71-75, 113, 114, Windham to Hippisley, March 28, July 31, 1793, Hippisley to Windham, Aug. 24, 1793, Lord Hood to Hippisley, Aug. 5, 1793, Sir William Hamilton to Hippisley, July 13, 1793; Burke MSS, N.R.O., Aiv17, Hippisley to Grenville, Sept., 1793.

41 Br. Mus., Add. MSS 37,844, fol. 11, Windham to Pitt, Oct. 11, 1793; *Times*, Nov. 21, 1792.

24, 1793, the only persons at home who knew his role were Windham, Loughborough, and Andrew Stuart.[42]

Hippisley was arranging for Monsignor Charles Erskine to visit England. This visit would be the fruition of a scheme that the zealous Hippisley had been developing since the spring of 1793. He described it in long, verbose letters from which Windham was to glean information for Pitt and Grenville. In Rome, Hippisley kept in touch with ecclesiastical authorities, including even the pope, and cultivated Prince Augustus Frederick, the sixth son of George III, who, himself desirous of closer relations between England and Rome, encouraged Hippisley's plans for a commercial treaty and advised him to enlist Monsignor Erskine in his campaign.[43] These and other enterprises Hippisley undertook on his own initiative, trusting to Windham and Loughborough to gain the approval of understanding ministers.[44] It was Hippisley who informed the pope of Burke's solicitude for

[42] Br. Mus., Add. MSS 37,848, fol. 103, Hippisley to Windham, Aug. 24, 1793. Somerset, in the *Dublin Review*, CCII, 144, suggests that Hippisley might have enjoyed some kind of official status. This was not so. The fullest account of the ensuing episode, based upon papers in the Vatican Archives, is an appendix to Cardinal Gasquet's *Monastic Life*, 269-330. Gasquet, 271, says the British government chose Hippisley to open communications with the papacy, but a letter of Hippisley's, Dec., 1793, in Gasquet, 281, makes clear that he took the initiative in the "opening up of political communications" with the papacy and received ministerial approval afterward. Sir William Hamilton congratulated Hippisley: it was wise "when you took upon yourself to open a correspondence with His Holiness," 281. The correspondence from the Windham papers cited in the following account reveals Hippisley as a self-appointed diplomat. This is corroborated by a letter from Sir Gilbert Elliot to Portland after the Duke had taken office. Minto, *Elliot*, II, 419-24, Sept. 24, 1794. Elliot, who disapproved of an "avowed communication" between Rome and London, and of Erskine's mission, ascribed the initiative to Rome, where Hippisley, with "the most sincere zeal for the public service and the purest intentions" was cooperating with papal desires. Elliot seemed to locate the responsibility in the Papal Court itself, with Hippisley a very cooperative "English traveller" who, "*de facto*," was "performing all the functions of British Envoy" pending establishment of a mission "*de jure*." Although Elliot's statement raises questions about the origin of the communication, it makes clear that Hippisley did not go to Rome under orders or instructions from his government.

[43] Br. Mus., Add. MSS 37,848, fols. 107-108, Augustus Frederick to Hippisley, June 17, 1793.

[44] Br. Mus., Add. MSS, 37,848, fols. 69-70, 113-14, 155-58, Hippisley to Windham, Aug. 24, 1793, Hood to Hippisley, Aug. 5, 1793, Hamilton to Hippisley, July 13, 1793, Hippisley to Prince of Wales, Sept. 7, 1793; Burke MSS, Sheff., Hippisley to Grenville, Sept. 1, 1793; Burke MSS, N.R.O., Aiv15a, copy of Hippisley to the Prince of Wales, Sept. 7, 1793.

the émigré clergy; Burke learned of this from the pope himself. In a letter of September 7, 1793, Pius VI thanked him for his efforts in behalf of the cause of religion, of the Irish Catholics, and of the Catholic émigrés in England.[45]

Up to this time Burke had not been involved in Hippisley's transactions, but now he was brought into them as plans for the Erskine visit matured.[46] Ostensibly it would be a visit to his family by a Mr. Erskine, in lay garb, who would live like a gentleman at papal expense. Actually, he was to make contacts with leading persons in and out of government, to impress upon Catholic leaders the need for civil obedience, to convey papal gratitude to England, to seek further relaxation of the penal laws, and ultimately to work for closer communication with England, perhaps even for formal diplomatic relations. Burke was one of the persons Monsignor Erskine planned to visit.

Probably to Hippisley's surprise, Burke was less enthusiastic than his friendships towards Catholics, the émigrés, and the cause of religion would lead one to expect.[47] If Hippisley had known of Burke's letter of December 14, 1791, to the Archbishop of Nisibi, he would have been even more shocked at the appearance of retreat from the ideas Burke had then expressed.[48] In that letter Burke had spoken of Europe's community of interest in opposing the spread of the Revolution. The pope, "a Prince of great rank," was a leader in the "Empire of opinion." Mutual understanding among those who loved order was necessary if the "common enemy" was to be checked. When Burke held these opinions and scorned the "beaten routine of old systems," he might be expected to welcome new diplomatic enterprises in this great crisis. But Burke had also warned against entering upon "untrodden paths of policy"; the proposed mission of Erskine in 1793 might be one of them. Burke would have preferred that Erskine wait for an invitation from the British govern-

---

45 Burke MSS, Sheff., and N.R.O.

46 Burke MSS, Sheff., Hippisley to Burke, Sept. 7, 1793; Burke MSS, N.R.O., Aivl4a, Hippisley to Burke, Sept. 18, 1793; Br. Mus., Add. MSS 37,848, fols. 84-106, 139, Hippisley to Windham, Aug. 24, Sept. 4, 1793.

47 Burke MSS, Sheff., and copy in Br. Mus., Add. MSS 37,848, fols. 297-301, Burke to Hippisley, Oct. 3, 1793.

48 Printed by Somerset in *Dublin Review*, CCII, 139-41.

ment.[49] He thought the papal command to Irish Catholics unfair
to them and provocative to the intolerant. In Rome people
mistakenly confused participation in civil disturbances by some
Catholics with disloyalty to the king. Burke asked Hippisley to
correct these impressions. Lest his Roman friends think Burke's
an official opinion, Hippisley was to inform them that under
the British constitution, members of parliament were only private
persons. This remark was aimed at John Coxe Hippisley, M.P.
To the general idea of closer relations between England and the
papacy, that is, to a community of sentiment, Burke gave cordial
support. "Avowed political connections" with the Vatican might
be desirable when other circumstances were favorable, but Burke
did not think the times or opinion were ready for them.

Hippisley felt this blunt rebuff. He offered a vindication of his
conduct, sending copies of his letter to Windham and to Grenville
in the event that others misunderstood his position.[50] To Windham he was indignant and alarmed; Burke, he said, has "mist
before his eyes."[51] Hippisley also began to worry about the
opinions of other people. He feared that Dundas' antagonism,
dating back to his Indian days, might be revived; he disliked the
silence of Loughborough and Sir Gilbert Elliot, whom he thought
Burke may have influenced against him; Grenville's restraint
discouraged him; and he feared that Augustus Frederick and the
Prince of Wales had lost interest.[52] Hippisley's intuitions came
near the mark.[53]

[49] Cardinal Gasquet quotes from the letter of Oct. 3, 1793, only the extract that
speaks generally of Burke's desire for closer relations with the papacy, p. 276, and
gives the impression that Burke enthusiastically endorsed Erskine's mission. The
deceiver was Hippisley. In a letter to the Cardinal Secretary of State, Hippisley
quoted only that much of Burke's letter, and that was all Gasquet saw in the
Vatican Archives. If, as Gasquet says, p. 278, Burke was "quite explicit as to his
view" of the mission, it was rather to oppose than to favor it, as the remainder
of the Oct. 3 letter makes clear. When Somerset, p. 143, overlooked some of
Burke's qualifications, he strengthened the false impression that had originated
as described.

[50] Br. Mus., Add. MSS 37,848, fols. 303-10, and Burke MSS, N.R.O., Nov. 20, 1793.

[51] Br. Mus., Add. MSS 37,848, fols. 311-12, Nov. 27, 1793.

[52] Br. Mus., Add. MSS 37,848, fols. 311-12, 325-27, 333-34, Hippisley to Windham,
Nov. 27, 1793, Hippisley to Burke, Nov. 27, 1793, a Mrs. Lubbock to Windham,
Dec. 28, 1793.

[53] Br. Mus., Add. MSS 37,844, fols. 11, 13-14, Windham to Pitt, Oct. 11, 1793,
Pitt to Windham, Oct. 13, 1793; Add. MSS 37,846, fol. 1, Windham to Grenville,
Oct. 21, 1793.

All of this was after the event. With an appearance of haste, Erskine had left Rome on October 4. Obviously, Burke had nothing to do with the decision to send him to England. Unpersuaded by Windham's attempt to justify the mission, Burke feared that precipitancy and failure to observe proprieties might delay the establishment of open and official correspondence between Rome and England.[54] If the public got hold of the news, anti-Catholic feelings might be aroused and legalistic objections raised. Actually, Erskine's arrival was not secret, and his mission was widely known as one inspired by the pope.[55] Burke at first was displeased with Erskine's conduct. He was too promiscuous, consorting with Catholics, democrats, the Cisalpine Club, and the Friends of the People. Possibly because Erskine was discerning enough to ask his advice, Burke later recanted and told Hippisley he was pleased with the visitor.[56] George III received Erskine and, like Grenville and Pitt, was favorably impressed.[57]

The mission did no harm and accomplished a little good.[58] Erskine stayed in England until 1801, with increased powers as envoy extraordinary. Hippisley was created baronet in 1796 for miscellaneous services, including the negotiation of a marriage in the royal family and his earlier work in connection with the provisioning of the Mediterranean fleet and the landings of British forces in papal territory.

The Erskine episode places Burke's relations with the papacy in proper perspective. His sympathies for Catholics, in the British Isles and in France, were genuine. His solicitude for the émigrés grew out of humanitarian and religious sentiments, though not out of any denominational partisanship. His desire for friendly, and eventually formal, relationships with the papacy, was a part

54 *Burke-Windham Corr.*, 79-82, Burke to Windham. This letter is dated Nov. 8 in Thomas W. Copeland's *Checklist*. But in it Burke spoke of Erskine's deportment, and Erskine only reached England on Nov. 13. Sir Stephen Gaselee, "British Diplomatic Relations with the Holy See," *Dublin Review*, CCIV (Jan., 1939), 4.

55 Gasquet, *Monastic Life*, 283.

56 Burke MSS, N.R.O., Aiv20, Erskine to Burke, Nov. 11, 1794; Br. Mus., Add. MSS 37,849, fol. 17, Hippisley to Windham, Feb. 8, 1794; Gasquet, *Monastic Life*, 287.

57 Burke MSS, N.R.O., Avii6a, Pius VI to Greenville, Nov. 10, 1793; Br. Mus., Add. MSS 37,846, fol. 2, Grenville to Windham, Dec. 31, 1793; Gasquet, *Monastic Life*, 287-88.

58 Gasquet, *Monastic Life*, 288-321; Br. Mus., Add. MSS 37,875, fols. 56-57, Erskine to Windham, May 23, 1795; Add. MSS 37,846, fol. 6, Hippisley to Grenville, March 12, 1794.

of his larger reaction against the French Revolution and his concern for the unity and security of Christian Europe. But apart from expressing himself in general terms, anything he had to do with any aspect of relations with the papacy was fortuitous. His writings, as Hippisley liked to emphasize, were admired in Rome and were cited on one occasion in support of the Holy See's efforts to settle an ecclesiastical question in Corsica.[59] Beyond this, there is little to say. The correspondence of 1793-1794 reduces almost to insignificance Burke's part in the story of relationships with the papacy. As late as November 25, 1796, although deploring the antagonism between Protestants and the papacy, he spoke only generally about ways to mitigate it.[60]

Indeed, it seemed that in the autumn of 1793 Burke's political influence had been reduced almost to insignificance. Virtually a pariah in the estimation of one group in the House of Commons, not a member of Pitt's party though giving it his support, he, the apologist for party in the House of Commons, was a politician without a party. Tolerated by ministers who told him that they appreciated his advice and then pitied him behind his back, he knew he was not in their confidence. He and Sir Gilbert Elliot spent a day in October talking with ministers about the affairs of Europe, and though Burke already knew of Elliot's appointment to a mission to Toulon, the two did not mention it.[61] Nevertheless, Elliot considered Burke "a sort of *power*" in Europe as well as England, a man to whom attention was paid, though his advice was never fully accepted.[62] Perhaps Burke underestimated himself, failing to see, as Elliot saw, that when his advice did not make an immediate impression, *"some part"* of it stuck, perhaps to be of later effect. A few young men devotedly surrounded him— Windham, Walker King, French Laurence. But, as he had told Shackleton's daughter a year before, when he consoled her after her father's death, at his time of life it was not possible to repair the loss of old friends.[63]

One was back, however. William Burke had returned from

---

59 Gasquet, *Monastic Life*, 305-306.
60 *Burke-Laurence Corr.*, 82-83.
61 *Corr.*, IV, 178, Burke to Windham, Oct., 1793.
62 Minto, *Elliot*, II, 122, 136-37, Elliot to Lady Elliot, March 7, May 2, 1793.
63 Osborn Coll., Box 39, #15, B/53, Burke to Mrs. Leadbeater, Sept. 8, 1792.

India during the year, leaving behind some confused accounts but meeting others in England, where the late Lord Verney's niece was in wait for him. In poor health, he stayed out of the way, at Beaconsfield or on the Isle of Wight, as convenience or exigencies might be served. Richard, Sr., was also ailing, nursed in his illnesses by Jane Burke and, when he could, carrying on his legal business with chambers at Lincoln's Inn and performing his duties as Recorder of Bristol.

It was easy for Burke to feel "resentment and indignation" over the discouragements he encountered. He had revealed this at Oxford early in July.[64] He was still irritated by the university's refusal to grant him a degree by diploma after the publication of the *Reflections,* and when Portland, the chancellor, proposed to offer his name for an honorary doctor's degree, Burke refused the honor, suggesting that it be given to his son. Portland was angry but agreed, but the incident "made a great rout." Burke justified his displays of feeling as responses to the "demands of duty" that helped him to avoid "sinking into a state of despondency."[65] Keeping busy in response to these demands also helped, and so did a bit of simple philosophy. Now events "are bad;—now good;—up and down, and with them our poor hearts up and down also. . . . But so it is; and we go on in a perpetual state of fluctuation; following, indeed, our nature, but following not the strongest, but the weakest part of it."[66]

The news from Europe made the autumn of 1793 one of those periods when Burke's heart went "down." The triumph of the Jacobins, the dominance of the Committee of Public Safety under Robespierre, the beginning of the career of the Revolutionary Tribunal, in October the execution of Marie Antoinette, which Burke called a "murder" of "savage and unrelenting cruelty," the hunting down and extermination of the Girondins—that is, the establishment of the Reign of Terror (called by Robespierre the "mainspring of popular government" and by Saint-Just the "complete destruction" of everything opposed to the Revolution) —all of these composed one part of the revolting and melancholy

64 Minto, *Elliot,* II, 153-54, Elliot to Lady Elliot, July 3, 1793; *Times,* July 2, 4, 5, 6, 8, 1793.
65 *Corr.,* IV, 177-78, Burke to Windham, Oct., 1793.
66 *Corr.,* IV, 157-58, Burke to William Burke, [Sept. 15], 1793.

record. The other was the mounting success of the French armies. During the autumn they passed to the offensive, pushing the allies back to the northern and eastern frontier. The suppression of the royalist revolt in La Vendée and, at the end of the year, the recapture of Toulon virtually extinguished royalist hopes for a long time to come.

In Burke's judgment, these "calamitous" events were "disgraceful."[67] England and her allies almost deserved their defeats; their leaders seemed "not equal to the demand" of the times. The allied defeats were political as well as military reverses, the results of refusal to keep steadily in view the true objective of a war unlike "any that has ever existed in the world."

Burke saw only two alternatives—to destroy Jacobinism and to permit "the present order of things" to be destroyed. He rejected any sort of arrangement with a French administration that, even if stable, was formed on "Jacobin principles." He could not agree with Pitt, who was ready to treat with a French republican government if one should be firmly established.[68] Pitt's alignment with the royalist cause by the end of 1793 was, for Burke, too equivocal to guarantee that he would not desert it should expediency and false hopes of peace tempt the allies into treating with the Jacobins.

Burke's position at this time was awkward and embarrassing. A constant object of solicitation by émigrés in London and abroad, and much influenced by their thoughts when ordering his own thoughts upon the war and the revolution, he could not disabuse their exaggerated notions of his influence with ministers.[69] He was not in an official position, his rank as a privy councilor meant nothing, and his membership in the House of Commons little more. Perhaps by his writings he had made his name known to the public, but people at a distance should realize that "a man's importance" was not measured by "the noise he happens to make." A humble clerk in an obscure office might have "fifty times" more influence upon events than Burke.

---

[67] *Corr.*, IV, 205, 212, 218-20, Burke to Windham, Jan. 8, 1794, Burke to Richard, Jr., Jan. 10, 1794, Burke to Woodford, Jan. 13, 1794.

[68] Rose, *Pitt and the Great War*, 162-63.

[69] *Corr.*, IV, 166-69, 187-88, the Comte d'Artois to Burke, Oct. 23, 1793, Burke to the Comte d'Artois, Nov. 6, 1793.

At home the government was commendably stern. Burke approved its policy of suppressing reform activity in the country, transporting for sedition certain Scottish reformers in the summer of 1793 and again in the following January. The great need, as his correspondence proclaimed it, was for a more vigorous conduct of the war. To achieve this, ministers must be strengthened, not merely by verbal support in parliament but by political union carried to the logical conclusion, the sharing of office. During the autumn of 1793 and the early part of 1794 prospects for coalition began to improve, promoted by the discouragements of the war. The negotiations were coy and hesitant, the old uncertainties kept raising themselves, and the approaches resembled the advances and retreats of the dancers in a gavotte.

Burke pursued coalition relentlessly, joined in the effort by the increasing influence of Windham. His rise pleased Burke. Their views about the war were identical, and Windham, in the government, would produce an effect that Burke, in a private station, could not achieve. An office for Windham was part of his idea of coalition. Windham was moving toward this conclusion, disliking as the alternative to coalition the nebulousness of remaining in a third party, even though supporting the war.[70] By November, 1793, Lord Spencer was talking with Pitt about coalition and an office, but the discussion was inconclusive.[71] Portland was still trying to reconcile his sense of duty and his realization of the necessity for vigorous prosecution of the war with his belief in the country's need for a true Whig party.[72] Meanwhile, the Whig Club had dwindled to a rump of its former self.[73]

Portland's efforts to take a position were laborious and painful. For thirty years he had listened to Burke, and when now he described the party, he repeated Burke verbatim.[74] The Whig party, he told Windham, was composed of "persons of independent

---

[70] *Burke-Windham Corr.*, 53-54, Windham to Portland, Sept. 3, 1793.

[71] Br. Mus., Add. MSS 37,845, fols. 122, 124-25, Spencer to Windham, Nov. 11, Dec. 8, 1793.

[72] Br. Mus., Add. MSS 37,845, fols. 15-33, Portland to Windham, Oct. 17, 1793, Jan. 11, 1794.

[73] *Times*, Dec. 13, 1793.

[74] Br. Mus., Add. MSS 37,845, fol. 18, Jan. 11, 1794. Also *Corr.*, III, 384-90, Burke to William Weddell, Jan. 31, 1792, for Burke's description.

minds & fortunes formed [illegible] together by their beliefs in the principles upon which the Revolution of 1688 was founded & perfected, & by their attachment to the present form of our government, to all its establishments & orders, religious & Civil." The Whig found his purpose in the preservation of religion, law, and the social order, his duty in the acceptance of office when the good of his country demanded it, and his interest in the preservation of an independent Whig party capable of serving the public. The questions were now clear. Could the Old Whigs serve best by remaining in opposition or by joining Pitt and abandoning their traditional role? Was Pitt sincere, or was he trying to divide the Whigs in order to achieve his own political purposes? Could the Whigs support the war and other desirable measures from their positions of independence? Was the cost of coalition—the destruction of the Old Whig party—too great?

As for two years past, Fox remained the pivotal person. When Portland wondered hopefully whether the Whig split was only temporary, he had in mind eventual reconciliation with Fox. To Burke, this hope was a delusion.[75] Fox would not part with Sheridan; Sheridan might indeed be sick of his flirtations with revolutionaries; he and Fox might "piece up their own broken connexions in England," but such a patchwork could not include Burke or Windham or Spencer, Elliot or Malmesbury, or the country gentlemen who were already in Pitt's fold.

Amid these confusions, Burke did not attempt to hide his dissatisfaction with the prevailing hesitancy.[76] He was furious with Windham and Spencer, berating them for refusing to take office, and disgusted with Portland and Fitzwilliam.

The coalition seemed no closer when parliament met on January 21 than when it had ended its session six months before. Five days earlier, Pitt showed Windham a draft of the king's speech.[77] Though it misrepresented the trend of the war, the speech pledged England to continue fighting until the peace and safety of Europe had been secured, and implied that the destruc-

75 *Corr.*, IV, 213-14, Burke to Richard, Jr., Jan. 10, 1794.

76 Fitzwilliam MSS, Sheff., F31a, Portland to Fitzwilliam, Dec. 25, 31, 1793.

77 J. H. Rose, "Burke, Windham, and Pitt," *English Historical Review*, XXVII (1912), 711.

tion of the Jacobin system was essential to that end.[78] On January 20 some thirty members of the Portland party met at Burlington House to consider the speech and their line of conduct in the coming session. Burke, dubious about the sincerity of Portland's invitation and fearful that his presence might exacerbate existing differences in the party, attended the meeting only because Pitt urged him to go.[79] There was no occasion for disputes. Instead of Fox, who previously had presided over these presessional meetings, Portland took charge.[80] Burke had the satisfaction of hearing the duke call the war the leading public issue and, with only Robert Adair opposing, pledge himself and his friends to support energetic prosecution of it.

The opening debates were revealing. In the Lords, Portland and Spencer supported the address to the king. In the Commons, Fox moved an amendment recommending peace with France, and Pitt avowed that there could be no peace with the present rulers of France. He did not, however, pledge himself to the restoration of monarchy in that country. If Burke was disappointed in this, at least he could be certain that the disagreements between the Foxites and the Old Whigs were beyond reconciliation. This was reaffirmed by Fitzwilliam on February 17 when he opposed, in Burkean sentiments, Lansdowne's motion for an address asking for peace negotiations with France. Like Pitt, Fitzwilliam did not ask for the restoration of monarchy, but he declared peace impossible until in France there was established "a regular form of government . . . upon which some reliance might be placed."[81] In these debates the government and their parliamentary allies had pronounced their hostility to Jacobinism, to what Fitzwilliam called "French principles and the new-fangled doctrine of the Rights of Man."

[78] *Parl. Hist.*, XXX, 1045-47.

[79] Rose, *English Historical Review*, XXVII, 711; Osborn Coll., Box 74, #25, Pitt to Burke, Jan. 20, 1794; Burke MSS, Sheff., Portland to Burke, Jan. 19, 1794; *Corr.*, IV, 221-22, Burke to Portland, Jan. 20, 1794. This version of the letter is the softer of two drafts in the Burke MSS, Sheff. In the printed version, Burke said his presence might excite "discussion." In the MS version, the word is "disputes." The *Times*, Jan. 21, 1794, reported Burke's presence at a "grand dinner" given by Pitt on Jan. 20.

[80] Greig, ed., *The Farington Diary*, I, 37.

[81] *Parl. Hist.*, XXX, 1408; *Times*, Feb. 18, 1794.

During the first month of the session Burke took no part in the debates. His letter of January 20 to Portland suggests that a sense of futility may have been one reason. Another was the death of his brother during the night of February 4. Although Richard had been in declining health, his death came unexpectedly. He had spent the evening in Duke Street with the Burke family and then returned to his chambers at Lincoln's Inn. A "fit of coughing" seized him and he died suddenly.[82] He was buried in Saint Mary and All Saints Church in Beaconsfield; the plaque on the south wall says of him only that he was "Barrister at law and Recorder of the City of Bristol."

Burke's grief was deep and lasting. He had always felt a sense of responsibility toward Richard; he had shared in his tribulations, taken excessive pride in his accomplishments, and greatly overestimated his talents. In a paper written after Richard's death, Burke eulogized him with characteristic exaggeration.[83] If the death of the brother that he loved and admired left him severely depressed in spirit, it was not only because of the personal loss but because it was in his own family that Burke found the most complete agreement with his views on the troubled times. Shortly before his death Richard had published his translation of a pamphlet on the French Revolution by Mallet du Pan, and a few months earlier his charge to the grand jury in Bristol, attacking the English sympathizers of the French Revolution.[84] Early in 1794, William Burke translated Brissot's address to his constituents, for which Edmund wrote a preface. His own analysis of the nature of Jacobinism was corroborated by one of the leading victims of Jacobin fury, the Girondin Brissot de Warville. No one could doubt Brissot's enmity to royalism and the Christian religion, and his address therefore vindicated Burke and all in England who, in sounding the alarm, had done it for the security of England.[85] For her the chief lesson of Brissot's address was briefly stated: "In a cause like this, and in a time like the present,

---

[82] H.M.C., *Charlemont*, 230, Feb. 20, 1794.

[83] Wecter printed extracts in *Kinsmen*, 71-73.

[84] Wecter, *Kinsmen*, 75, n. 86; *Monthly Review*, n.s., XII, 106, XIII, 93-95.

[85] Wecter, *Kinsmen*, 75, n. 87; *Works*, V, 67-92, esp. 87, 90; *Monthly Review*, n.s., XIII, 227-30.

there is no neutrality. Those who are not actively, and with decision and energy, against Jacobinism, are its partisans."

This statement accurately represents the attitude government was adopting toward the parliamentary reformers. To advocate reform was a seditious practice; to organize in order to promote it was a treasonable conspiracy. And it was the duty of government to suppress such activities. On May 12 a dozen leaders of reform societies were seized and committed for trial. A royal message informed parliament of the order to seize the records of the Corresponding and Constitutional societies. On May 13 Pitt proposed a committee of secrecy to study these records. He and Dundas, Burke and Windham, and seventeen others formed the committee. After a speedy examination of the confiscated papers the committee reported on May 16: "From these [the proceedings of the London Corresponding Society] it appears, that during almost the whole of that period [January, 1792–May, 1794] and with hardly any considerable interval, except during part of the summer in 1792 and 1793, this society has, by a series of resolutions, publications, and correspondence, been uniformly and systematically pursuing a settled design, which appears to your committee to tend to the subversion of the established constitution, and which has of late been more openly avowed, and attempted to be carried into full execution."[86]

This report furnished the evidence to justify a bill suspending habeas corpus until the following February. Pitt said the bill was necessary to hold back the "enormous torrent of insurrection," and Windham thought it would prevent "total annihilation of all property, constitution, and religion."[87] Burke approved of withholding the liberty of the country for a short time in order to preserve it forever. Whatever the protests of the minority, the bill seemed to harmonize with prevailing opinions. By divisions of 201 to 39, 201 to 32, 197 to 33, 132 to 16, and 151 to 37, and finally, on the third reading in the Commons on May 18, by 146 to 28, the suspension of habeas corpus passed. In the House of Lords, where Portland and Carlisle were members of another

---

[86] *Parl. Hist.*, XXXI, 475-76.
[87] Rose, *Pitt and the Great War*, 191; *Parl. Hist.*, XXXI, 546.

secret committee on the reform societies, the bill also carried by overwhelming majorities. The division on the third reading was 92 to 7.

Parliament continued its attacks on the reformers. On June 6 the Commons' secret committee brought in a second report: "The result [of further examination of the seized papers] appears to your committee strongly to confirm all the propositions which they found it their duty, on the outset of their inquiry, to submit to the House, and to leave no doubt of the nature, extent, and malignity of the extravagant designs which have been formed, of the regularity and system with which those designs have been pursued, or of the rapid progress of the measures which have been taken in order to attempt to carry them into execution."[88] Exactly a week later, both houses passed an address demanding the trial of the twelve reformers. The session ended on July 11 with a speech from the throne expressing gratification to parliament for its support of the efforts to achieve victory in the war and to preserve order at home.

During the session, as the debates on these questions widened the cleavage between the Portland and Fox parties, the relations between the Portland party and ministers grew closer. Burke's long efforts to create a community of sentiment were considerably aided by the reverses in the war and by the increasing panic at home. Pitt and Dundas took advantage of every opportunity provided by the growing alarm. Dundas inquired indirectly whether Portland would be interested in the lord lieutenancy of Middlesex.[89] Prior to bringing the Prussian subsidy into the House, Pitt asked Loughborough to learn Portland's opinions of it.[90] After consulting Burke, Fitzwilliam, Windham, Mansfield, and others, Portland promised to support it, even though Loughborough had been forbidden to disclose the details. Pitt occasionally consulted Burke. On April 11 he thought Burke might like to inform his friends of Sheridan's intentions to oppose the bill enabling the king to organize an émigré corps.[91] During this

88 *Parl. Hist.,* XXXI, 688.
89 Br. Mus., Add. MSS 37,874, fol. 10, Evan Nepean to Windham, Feb. or March, 1794. Portland later became Lord Lieutenant of Nottinghamshire.
90 Minto, *Elliot,* II, 383-84n., William Elliot to Sir Gilbert Elliot, March 15, 1794.
91 Burke MSS, Sheff.

time Burke met every Thursday at Burlington House with Windham, Spencer, and other leading Old Whigs.[92]

In May Portland succumbed, with the suddenness one might expect of a man who had lived in indecision for over two years. The panic that produced the suspension of habeas corpus gave the last fateful push. When he told Pitt he was ready to talk about coalition, the ministers were receptive.[93] Portland at once asked Fitzwilliam to come to London to advise on the problem of distributing offices.[94] The earl did not come, using as an excuse for his aloofness his lack of detailed knowledge.[95] His ignorance was of his own choosing, and suggests not only reluctance to enter into a coalition because of distrust of Pitt, but an indecisiveness even greater than Portland's. Yet, after urging Portland to consult Devonshire and Mansfield, he said he was willing to go along if Portland was in earnest. The responsibility in that case would be the duke's. But Portland threw the ball back. When he met with Pitt on June 13, they were unable to conclude anything because the duke did not know Fitzwilliam's opinions.[96] About all that a meeting among Portland, Windham, Spencer, Mansfield, and Grenville amounted to was agreement that there was no insuperable barrier to coalition. Windham insisted upon the presence of Fitzwilliam. Paradoxically, Portland, having at last abandoned Fox and become convinced of Pitt's sincerity, was the most impatient of all to conclude the business. It was, he told Fitzwilliam, the last chance to preserve the constitution, aristocracy, and Whiggism. This was essentially what Burke had been saying all along. The conversion of Portland to this belief was the work of Burke, abetted by events.

Though in frequent association with both Pitt and Portland, Burke had little to do with the conduct of the negotiations. He was not, of course, considered for an office. Instead he was marked for a reward for having helped to create the state of mind that made coalition possible. Pitt was ready to recommend a peerage

92 *Burke-Windham Corr.*, 106.
93 Portland MSS, Pitt to Portland, May 23, 1794.
94 Fitzwilliam MSS, Sheff., F31b, Portland to Fitzwilliam, May 25, 1794.
95 Fitzwilliam MSS, Sheff., F31b, Fitzwilliam to Portland, June 12, 1794.
96 Fitzwilliam MSS, Sheff., Portland to Fitzwilliam, June 14, 1794. The death of the Duchess of Portland on June 3 also delayed negotiations. *Times*, June 5, July 3, 1794.

and a handsome pension that would relieve him of financial
worries.[97] Portland took this as further proof of Pitt's sincerity,
for the rewards to Burke would antagonize the East Indian
interests in these declining days of the Hastings impeachment
and would, while pleasing Burke's aristocratic friends, offend some
of Pitt's own colleagues. Yet there is a qualification that suggests
that Pitt's motives were not purely altruistic. It was not until the
terms of the coalition were settled that Pitt informed Portland
of his inability to persuade the king to grant the peerage unless
the cabinet consented. And Pitt was not prepared to make a
cabinet issue of it.[98]

The details of Burke's reward were deferred while the negotiations for the coalition continued. They involved the usual
leisurely haggling. Fitzwilliam was willing to leave them to
Portland, asking only for clear understanding of the primacy of
foreign affairs.[99] Pitt gave assurance on this point, even to agreeing that the object of the war should be the restoration of the
monarchy.[100] With this, and with Devonshire's acquiescence,
Fitzwilliam at last gave positive consent, and even showed a bit
of enthusiasm for a decision that he was now willing to admit
would preserve the "Old Whigs" and the aristocracy.[101]

But cabinet dispositions were always important. The most
difficult one involved the administration of the war effort. Proper
management of it required more concentrated attention than the
busy Dundas had been able to give to it. At the same time, Pitt
would not give over the management of it to Portland and told
him so frankly.[102] For a moment it seemed that the coalition
would fail. Pitt was in a dilemma.[103] He had to keep the coalition
safe without surrendering the war department to Portland.
Though he trusted the duke, he could not give to him the
confidence he had in Dundas. Grenville was ready to give up the

97 Fitzwilliam MSS, Sheff., F31b, Portland to Fitzwilliam, June 14, 1794.
98 Fitzwilliam MSS, Sheff., F31b, Portland to Fitzwilliam, July 26, 1794; *Windham Papers*, I, 214, Richard, Jr., to Windham, June 19, 1794.
99 Fitzwilliam MSS, Sheff., F31b, Fitzwilliam to Portland, June 15, 1794.
100 Fitzwilliam MSS, Sheff., F31b, Portland to Fitzwilliam, June 19, 1794.
101 Fitzwilliam MSS, Sheff., F31b, Fitzwilliam to Portland, June 23, 1794.
102 Portland MSS, Pitt to Portland, July 5, 1794.
103 H.M.C., *Dropmore Papers*, II, 595-96, Pitt to Grenville, July 5, 1794; Portland MSS, Pitt to Portland, July 5, 1794.

foreign office and take instead the reduced Home Office, but Portland demurred because he wanted Ireland in his purview. After two anxious days agreement was reached, as a result of the king's intervention. Dundas became Secretary of War and Colonies; Portland, as Home Secretary, would manage Irish affairs.[104] Meanwhile the problem of arranging for Windham arose. He began to wonder whether the offer of the Secretaryship at War, formerly merely a ministerial post, indicated a mysterious desire to keep him out of the cabinet. Portland also worried about this, fearing that rumors about disagreement might circulate.[105] The problem was settled by raising the secretaryship to cabinet rank. The other arrangements were simpler, eased by the king's steady cooperation.[106] Fitzwilliam agreed to take the lord presidency, with the understanding that the lord lieutenancy of Ireland could be opened up for him whenever he wanted it.[107] Spencer became Lord Privy Seal, and Mansfield received a cabinet post without portfolio. On July 16 Portland was chosen Knight of the Garter.[108]

These arrangements displeased some persons.[109] Apart from personal factors, it seemed that the Portland crowd had done too well. If it was only a jest to say that Pitt might be outvoted in his own cabinet, it remained true that counting Loughborough, there were six Portland men in a cabinet of thirteen. But Pitt was still prime minister, he possessed the confidence of the king, and more fully than anyone knew at the time, he could count on the loyalty of Portland. The duke was never a threat to Pitt. His accession achieved the purpose Pitt intended, to strengthen the government internally, in its relation with parliament, and in the estimation of the nation.

The coalition of 1794 was the end of an old and the beginning

---

104 Furber, *Dundas,* 103; Philip H. Stanhope, *Life of The Right Honourable William Pitt* (London, 1861-1862), II, 254-55. At first, Portland thought of the lord lieutenancy for himself. *Windham Papers,* I, 259, Mansfield to Windham, Oct. 12, 1794.

105 Br. Mus., Add. MSS 37,845, fol. 41, Portland to Windham, July 3, 1794.

106 Portland MSS, Pitt to Portland, July 3, 1794.

107 Portland MSS, Pitt to Portland, July 2, 1794.

108 *Times,* July 17, 1794.

109 *Times,* July, 1794, *passim* and esp. July 17; *St. James's Chronicle,* July 10-12, 1794; Stanhope, *Pitt,* II, 255; H.M.C., *Dropmore Papers,* II, 597-98, Buckingham to Grenville, July 8, 1794.

of a new era in English party history. Burke recognized this and approved, because he believed that the new arrangements fairly represented the divisions in parliamentary and public thought. They realigned political interests in accordance with changed circumstances, but they recognized significant old principles. The Portland Whigs, giving precedence to the issue of first importance, had joined with Pitt to preserve social order, and in that respect remained true to traditional Whiggism. Other tenets of Whiggism, particularly those of constitutional significance, were for the moment of secondary importance. Why worry about internal constitutional relationships when the constitution itself, and the established social order were in danger?

If Burke was nostalgic to see the passing of the Portland Whigs through the portals of Pitt's Toryism, he did not show it. He had already explained the reasons why he felt the necessity for ending the identity of the old Rockingham-Portland "connexion" even if it meant the end of a political era. In any case, there was a certain appropriateness in the situation. Burke's parliamentary career almost exactly spanned the history of his party. As they had begun together, so they ended together. For during the time when the negotiations for coalition were being consummated, Burke applied for the Chiltern Hundreds, that is, went through the formal procedure for resigning from the House of Commons.

For several years he had contemplated resignation. Now, the Hastings trial in Westminster Hall was ended, and the coalition for which he had helped create "the disposition" was completed, or nearly so.[110] There was nothing more for him to do in the House of Commons. It remained for the House of Lords to render its verdict on Hastings; it remained for his friends in office and in parliament to conduct the war to what at last, it seemed, he had persuaded them and Pitt was its proper object. He had spent nearly fifteen years of prodigious labor in the one enterprise and four years of anguished effort in the other. Whatever the decision of the Lords, Burke had done his duty to humanity and to himself in prosecuting Hastings. Whatever the outcome of the war, England was fighting for the right cause.

110 Grattan, *Memoirs*, IV, 203, Burke to Grattan, March 5, 1795.

Burke's parliamentary work was ended, and the future was in other hands.

On June 25 Pitt wrote him a gracious letter.[111] He regretted Burke's decision to leave the House of Commons, but he wished to comply with his desires and so had given the order appointing him to the Chiltern Hundreds. Lord Fitzwilliam was equally gracious.[112] For the honor Burke had done to Malton by representing it in the Commons, Fitzwilliam was appreciative. The loss was not only Malton's. The House of Commons would miss its brightest ornament and the source of its greatest wisdom.

Fitzwilliam hardly exaggerated. For nearly thirty years Burke had been a member of the House, and almost from the moment he took his seat, an outstanding one. Energetic, eloquent, passionate, sometimes indiscreet, sometimes wise, always jealous of the independence of parliament, he had been a good House of Commons man. Nearly always out of power, he had suffered through the frustrations of futile opposition, always confident that opposition to the government was beneficial to the public interest, though it might harm personal ambitions. Members respected his parliamentary abilities; his opponents had not been able to treat him with indifference; he had to be heard. In an age accustomed to parliamentary brilliance, his was outstanding.

There was still another triumph in store for Burke, the achievement of his fondest desire. Fitzwilliam gave Malton to Richard, Jr. This was the greatest boon one could confer upon Burke.[113] In July, after attending the council when the new ministers formally entered office, Burke and his son journeyed to Yorkshire for the election at Malton and a visit to Wentworth. There can be little doubt that this was one of the happiest and proudest moments of Burke's life.

But it was a very brief moment. Richard, energetic in a feverish way, had always been a fragile person. When he became ill on this trip, he gave way rapidly. His vision blurred by proximity, Burke had no idea of the seriousness of Richard's condition until their return to London. Dr. Brocklesby took charge

111 Burke MSS, N.R.O., Avil0.
112 Burke MSS, Sheff., Fitzwilliam to Burke, June 26, 1794.
113 Burke MSS, Sheff., Burke to Fitzwilliam, June 28, 1794.

of the case. It was unmistakably pulmonary tuberculosis. The Burkes took country lodgings at Cromwell House a little beyond Brompton, and there awaited God's will. As late as August 1 Dr. Brocklesby thought there was no immediate likelihood of death, but this comforting judgment did not strengthen the "feeble & faint" hope of Richard's parents. Burke sought tranquillity in prayer and sustenance in the tactful encouragement of his wife.[114]

The end came pathetically on the morning of August 2. Quoting *Paradise Lost* and trying to assuage his parents' grief, Richard died in his father's arms.[115] He was buried in the church at Beaconsfield. The plaque records only the date of his death, his age, and the fact that he was "Representative in Parliament for the borough of Malton." To Burke, a seat in the House of Commons of the imperial parliament was the highest honor a man could possess.

His son's death was the severest blow Burke ever suffered; he never recovered from it. The memory of his son haunted him, and occasionally he gave way to paroxysms and wept "like a child."[116] He is said never again to have entered the church at Beaconsfield, and even to have avoided the sight of it.[117] As Fitzwilliam told Portland, "nothing will ever administer comfort to his mind, that has not relation to his son."[118] Burke's friends had tolerantly acquiesced in his exalted notions of his son; among themselves they did not speak well of Richard. At this time, however, they were able to offer condolences. Fitzwilliam, by stressing Richard's sense of honor and affection for his family, could be honest.[119] In his grief, Burke was able to think even the

114 MS in Yale Library, Dr. French Laurence to Mrs. William Haviland, Aug. 1, 1794. A Beaconsfield neighbor, Mrs. Haviland was the mother-in-law of Burke's niece, Mary French Haviland. Also *Burke-Laurence Corr.*, 30-31, Burke to Laurence, [July 31], 1794.

115 MS in Yale Library, Laurence to Mrs. Haviland, Aug. 4, 1794; Greig, ed., *The Farington Diary*, I, 66, 67. Walker King wrote the obituary published in the newspapers.

116 MS in Yale Library, Laurence to Mrs. Haviland, Aug. 7, 1794.

117 Peter Burke, *Life of Burke*, 285-86, citing John Heneage Jesse, who heard the story in Beaconsfield.

118 Portland MSS, Aug. 10, 1794.

119 *Corr.*, IV, 224-27, Fitzwilliam to Burke, Aug. 4, 1794. Fitzwilliam sent the letter to Walker King, leaving it to him to decide whether or when to give it to Burke. Osborn Coll., Box 88, #40, Fitzwilliam to King, n. d., but about Aug. 4, 1794.

mildest praise a panegyric. He thanked Grattan for speaking of Richard "as he deserves"; to Fitzwilliam he expressed remorse at having been a burden upon a "Son that never had an equal."[120] And now, when Richard was "upon the threshold of public life," ready to enter upon the career for which his education, his legal practice, his diplomatic ventures, his father's tutelage, and his frank advances to the administration were preparations, and when Burke could enjoy honor, not for his own accomplishments, but as the father of such a son, all was ended.[121] Henceforth, Burke thought of his duty as living for Mrs. Burke who deserved so much as a wife and as the mother of that son. But he kept alive his grief, cherishing it also "as a duty." Charlemont spoke for all the friends—"Poor Burke!"[122]

The pity for him was the greater because in addition to other burdens, his financial circumstances were, if possible, worse than ever. In fact, less than a week after Richard's death, Fitzwilliam sent a draft for Burke, payable to Walker King, because he knew of his acute financial distress.[123] Richard, Jr., had pooled his income with the family's in the common purse. He had also tried, without much success, to straighten out his father's tangled finances. The task was not easy, for Burke's obligations were pressing, the income slender, and the disposition to economize totally lacking. As Richard had told Windham in June when Pitt talked of a pension, "in the abstract" it would be best if his father sold Gregories and "cut himself down to the measure of his means" rather than accept a niggardly reward from the government.[124] But his father had no choice; he would have "to submit," sacrifice "dignity" to "ease," and be thankful for even a small favor. None of this had been settled by the time Richard died. The old worries were passed on to new financial advisers, Walker King and French Laurence, to assuage if they could.

120 Grattan, *Memoirs,* IV, 153, Burke to Grattan, Sept. 3, 1794; Burke MSS, Sheff., after Aug. 4, 1794.

121 Grattan, *Memoirs,* IV, 153, Burke to Grattan, Sept. 3, 1794. For the advances to administration, Burke MSS, Sheff., Richard, Jr., to John King, [Aug.], 1793.

122 Burke MSS, Sheff., Burke to Fitzwilliam, after Aug. 4, 1794; Greig, ed., *The Farington Diary,* I, 187, Jan. 22, 1797; H.M.C., *Charlemont,* 277, Charlemont to Malone, Aug. 7, 1794.

123 Osborn Coll., Box 88, #40, Fitzwilliam to King, Aug. 7, 1794.

124 *Windham Papers,* I, 215, June 19, 1794.

There was nothing to be gained from family resources. Both Richards had died intestate and poor. Will Burke was a financial burden and a legal liability, living under the threat of imprisonment for debt. His will, written at Beaconsfield before he departed for the Isle of Man where he died in 1798 (Somerset House, Walpole 527), confessed his failures, expressed remorse over his inability to help the family, intimated that at last Edmund was impatient with him, and hoped that Edmund would accept his watch. When in response to a plea from the Abbé de la Bintinnaye, Burke said he had not "a single guinea," he was telling the literal truth, though it was not quite the fact that he was unable to borrow money.[125] He had no regular income except £500 a year from his land; his debts amounted to twenty-five or thirty thousand pounds.[126]

In these circumstances, the grant of a pension to aid "this distressed man," as the king called him, was not only an act of generosity but an act of charity. Despite some sneers to the contrary, there was nothing inconsistent in Burke's acceptance of it. Four years after the passage of his civil list act, which regulated the manner of granting pensions, Burke had justified them as a means of enabling the crown to reward public services. Pensions were a "fundamental part of the constitution."[127] When his own pension was being discussed in the summer of 1794, Burke submitted to Pitt a document setting forth his claims.[128] In 1782, in the interest of forming an administration, he had

125 Burke MSS, N.R.O., Avi23, Dec. 20, 1794.

126 P.R.O., Chatham Papers, 30/8, 190, Windham to Pitt, Aug. 13, 1794. The larger figure was Walker King's calculation, a year later. Fitzwilliam MSS, Sheff., F30i, King to Fitzwilliam, Aug. 3, 1795. Before the pension was settled in 1795, King revealed other details of Burke's financial condition. MSS in Yale Library, Burke to King, June 30, 1795, King to Pitt[?], July 2, 1795. Besides tradesmen's debts of about £1,000, Burke faced the demands of other creditors. Among them was the estate of James Ridge, to which Burke, though himself an executor, owed about £1,000. This debt was incurred before Ridge's death in 1784. Burke MSS, Sheff., Burke to [?], Jan. 5, 1796. Besides owing a year's interest on the Gregories mortgages, Burke owed, including arrears of interest, nearly £6,000 to the executors of Garrick's estate. MS in Yale Library, King to Pitt[?], July 2, 1795. Burke had borrowed a good deal more than the £1,000 he had requested of Garrick in 1769.

127 *Daily Universal Register,* April 6, 1786.

128 P.R.O., Chatham Papers, 30/8, 118, dated only 1794 but doubtless during the summer. This document was cited by H. V. Somerset, "Some Papers of Edmund Burke on His Pension," *English Historical Review,* XLV (1930), 110-14.

deferred his own claims and supported instead pensions for Barré and Dunning. Yet he had "in any three months" worked more for the public service than either of them during their entire lives. Somewhat unfairly, Burke pointed to William Eden as another who received rewards for services less notable than his. In any case, a pension for Burke would be no more unpopular than those had been, and was eminently more deserved than the first two. Burke had devoted his life to the public service, and though he admitted he had only done his duty, he had done it at great personal sacrifice. "A total neglect of a man's private affairs is likewise the inevitable consequence of occupations that engross the whole man." This self-evaluation was accurate, even though subjective.

Pitt deserves credit for refusing to take offense from this somewhat peevish paper. He went ahead with the pension, the project of a peerage having been dropped even before Richard's death.[129] Windham, with Walker King, pushed Burke's claim energetically, as Richard had done earlier, asking both for speedy action and generosity. There followed some sticky negotiations about details, but by August 30 Pitt was able to inform Burke of an immediate grant of £1,200 per year on the civil list, the statutory maximum.[130] This was to be assigned according to Burke's wishes, and in the next session of parliament, application would be made for an additional grant "more proportioned to his Majesty's sense of your public merit." According to Burke's desires, this pension was made out for his life and Mrs. Burke's, retroactive to January 5, 1793.[131] On September 20 the king returned to Pitt the signed warrants, happy to help someone who,

[129] The chronology of the documents makes this clear. Fitzwilliam MSS, Sheff., F31b, Portland to Fitzwilliam, July 26, 1794; Portland MSS, Fitzwilliam to Portland, July 26, 1794. Thus, a week before Richard's death, Fitzwilliam said he did not think Burke cared much about the peerage. Rose also pointed out, in *English Historical Review*, XXVII, 714, that the peerage was given up before Richard's death. Yet the notion has persisted that the death of his son caused Burke to lose interest in the peerage, e. g., Bertram Newman, *Burke*, 302, Magnus, *Burke*, 261, and Stanhope, *Pitt*, II, 244. Stanhope, of course, wrote before Rose. Windham continued to hope for the peerage. P.R.O., Chatham Papers, 30/8, 190, Windham to Pitt, Aug. 13, 1794.

[130] *Corr.*, IV, 231. Also P.R.O., Chatham Papers, 30/8, 102.

[131] *Corr.*, IV, 239-40, Pitt to Burke, Sept. 18, 1794. Also P.R.O., Chatham Papers, 30/8, 102.

by his quality of gratitude, compensated for his errors and failings.[132]

Burke's enemies decried the pension publicly and to Burke himself. An unknown correspondent, for example, wrote abusively, denouncing Burke's title to a reward for public service. "Thirty years Service! Gracious Heaven can you be serious in advancing such a claim?"[133] Pitt decided against provoking more opposition, and instead of applying to parliament he arranged for two other annuities from the crown on the West Indian 4½ per cent fund, urged to speedy action by King and William Elliot, who revealed to him Burke's desperate financial condition.[134] One annuity was for £1,350 and the other £1,150, both for three lives and one of them vendible.[135] Though he would have preferred a parliamentary grant, Burke appreciated Pitt's problem. At any rate, he could now face his creditors unafraid and could abandon the dreary recourses he had thought of not long ago, selling off Gregories, paying his creditors a portion of the debts, and seeking asylum in Portugal or America or in a debtors' prison.[136] As he told Pitt, "with the anticipation proposed, and the distribution of the Lives, and the immunity from charges," he could be comfortable and enjoy ease of mind for the rest of his life.[137]

A slight delay in issuance of the royal warrants caused some worried moments while Burke and King were trying to arrange for the management of his debts.[138] King estimated that Burke would be able to raise about £17,000 immediately by assigning the vendible annuity, which would enable him to satisfy his most clamant creditors, and would have £2,500 a year for the rest of his life.[139] By October 28, 1795, all of this was settled, and on

132 P.R.O., Chatham Papers, 30/8, 103, the King to Pitt, Sept. 4, 20, 1794. A copy of the letter of Sept. 4 is in the Yale Library.

133 Br. Mus., Add. MSS 27,916, fol. 68, n. d., but late 1794 or early 1795.

134 MS in Yale Library, King to Pitt, July 2, 1795, enclosing Burke's pathetic letter of June 30, mentioned in the next sentences.

135 Fitzwilliam MSS, Sheff., F30i, Burke to Fitzwilliam, Aug. 8, 1795. An undated letter in the Morgan Library, [?] to Mr. Beauchamp, Gazeteer, lists the three pensions as totaling £3,700.

136 MS in Yale Library, Burke to Walker King, June 30, 1795.

137 P.R.O., Chatham Papers, 30/8, 118, Burke to Pitt, Aug. 2, 1795.

138 MS letter, Burke to Dundas, Aug. 30, 1795, in possession of Mr. L. H. Marshall of Columbus, Ohio, who kindly supplied me with a copy of it.

139 Fitzwilliam MSS, Sheff., F30i, King to Fitzwilliam, Aug. 3, 1795.

that date Burke was able to send his thanks to Pitt and to the king, along with his prayers for a long and victorious reign of his "Royal Benefactor."[140]

In an age when the payment of pensions out of public funds was an established part of the political and social order and indubitably approved by canons of public morality, the justice and propriety of the grants to Burke could earn the disapproval only of those who had a personal or partisan animus against him. Few men of that period had devoted themselves so arduously and unremuneratively to the public service as had Burke. Few politicians were so indifferent to royal or official opinion as Burke. His support of the institution of monarchy during the French Revolution, which naturally the king appreciated, did not mean the abandonment of his earlier position relative to the prerogative and the independence of the House of Commons, and could not fairly be interpreted as a self-seeking endeavor to court the royal favor. Burke was not that kind of person. If royal approval blessed his anti-Jacobin campaign, Burke was pleased, but the approval was simply an added gratification, not the object of his efforts. If the king was pleased to reward him, that too was a gratuitous, if earned, consequence. And if the recipient was poverty-stricken, then the pension was given to a man who not only deserved it but badly needed it.

There is no evidence to suggest implied conditions. There could be no doubt that Burke would continue to support the war and oppose the parliamentary reform movement, or that he would uphold the political coalition. No one intimated that he must therefore approve all of the government's measures. The differences between him and Pitt on the conduct of the war and its purposes were well known. Even before the award of the last two pensions Burke had disagreed sharply with the handling of Irish affairs during the winter of 1794-1795.

His representation as a Judas Iscariot or a sycophant was therefore cruel and maddening as well as untrue. The distortion

---

140 P.R.O., Chatham Papers, 30/8, 118, Burke to Pitt, Oct. 28, 1795, two letters and an enclosure for the King. The mortgages on Gregories continued to trouble Mrs. Burke until shortly before her death in 1812, when she sold the estate to James Du Pre for £38,500. Burke MSS, N.R.O., Avi54, a Mr. Garrison to Mrs. Burke, April 9, 1798, and Magnus, *Burke*, 298.

might have been expected of the caricaturists and the partisan press, but hardly of responsible members of parliament. The pettiness of the Duke of Bedford and the Earl of Lauderdale when they did this in the House of Lords on November 13, 1795, or when Lauderdale asked for a statement of all grants and pensions to Burke cannot be excused on any count. They deserved Burke's masterful reply.

The slanders were uttered during a debate on the third reading of the Treasonable Practices Bill. As Foxites, Bedford and Lauderdale opposed the bill as a threat to constitutional liberties and at the same time defended the French Revolution. Then they dragged Burke's name into the discussion, referring to his pension as an instance of governmental profligacy that, as practiced in France, had helped to bring the downfall of the old regime.[141] They pointed to Burke's apparent inconsistency. A former advocate of economy, he accepted a pension and "in an eminent degree" contributed to bringing on the costly war against France. Of the two, Lauderdale used the harsher language, calling Burke an "apostate" and a "court dependent." Grenville replied at once, acknowledging his part and his pride in helping arrange for the pension. "Never" was "a public reward . . . more merited for the most eminent services."[142] In the House of Commons, the argument continued. After Erskine and Fox complimented Burke obliquely, Windham defended him and the pension, thinking it only demeaned Burke's detractors to talk as they had.[143] Sheridan admitted that if anyone deserved a pension, it was Burke, but he thought it disgraceful for ministers to evade Burke's civil list bill of 1782 by avoiding parliamentary reference of the pension.

Burke decided against discreet and dignified silence. Three months later his reply was published in the form of a letter to Lord Grenville.[144] At first, one might think he had made a mistake to plunge into a new controversy, but upon reading the pamphlet, one must agree that Burke was right. In so far as the

141 *Parl. Hist.*, XXXII, 260-61, 263-64.
142 *Parl. Hist.*, XXXII, 265.
143 *Parl. Hist.*, XXXII, 390, Nov. 16, 1795.
144 "A letter to a Noble Lord on the attacks made upon Mr. Burke and his pension, in the House of Lords, by the Duke of Bedford and the Earl of Lauderdale," *Works*, V, 173-229.

"Letter" referred to the horrors of the Revolution that had inspired his conduct since 1790, it added nothing. But as an apologia, a defense of his political career, and a justification of the self-made man against the snobbery of pseudo-aristocratic privilege, it was a noble effort. Burke wrote in lofty anger one of his best known passages.

I was not, like his Grace of Bedford, swaddled and rocked and dandled into a legislator: *"Nitor in adversum"* is the motto for a man like me. I possessed not one of the qualities nor cultivated one of the arts that recommend men to the favor and protection of the great. I was not made for a minion or a tool. As little did I follow the trade of winning the hearts by imposing on the understandings of the people. At every step of my progress in life, (for in every step was I traversed and opposed,) and at every turnpike I met, I was obliged to show my passport, and again and again to prove my sole title to the honor of being useful to my country, by a proof that I was not wholly unacquainted with its laws and the whole system of its interests both abroad and at home. Otherwise, no rank, not toleration even, for me. I had no arts but manly arts. On them I have stood, and, please God, in spite of the Duke of Bedford and the Earl of Lauderdale, to the last gasp will I stand.

He denied that he had entered into a bargain when he accepted the pension he had not solicited. That much of the noble lords' insinuations was easily disposed of. The main question was the justice of the pension. If Burke did not deserve it, then the Duke of Bedford's censures of him and ministers were proper. But Burke thought he was worthy of the reward, though the services he had rendered to the public were "incommensurable" and had not been undertaken with a view to a pension. In any case, the Duke of Bedford, born the year of Burke's election to parliament, was hardly the person to judge of this. His accusations revealed his lack of understanding of the nature of the crisis of 1780-1782 and the efforts of the Rockingham ministry, of which Burke's reforms were a part, to heal the public "distemper." The duke also had revealed his ignorance of Burke's earlier career and his lack of appreciation for what was Burke's greatest service to England, his labors in the affairs of India.

Who was the Duke of Bedford to be so superior? Burke's

answer to his own question refutes charges that he was a sycophant who regarded all titles of nobility with awe, whether their possessors were true aristocrats or not. Burke's scorn was magnificent. The duke was of the family that rose from modest circumstances to riches as recipients of confiscated lands granted by the crown in the sixteenth century.

These grants to the House of Russell were so enormous as not only to outrage economy, but even to stagger credibility. The Duke of Bedford is the leviathan among all the creatures of the crown. He tumbles about his unwieldy bulk, he plays and frolics in the ocean of the royal bounty. Huge as he is, and whilst "he lies floating many a rood," he is still a creature. His ribs, his fins, his whalebone, his blubber, the very spiracles through which he spouts a torrent of brine against his origin, and covers me all over with the spray, everything of him and about him is from the throne. It is for him to question the dispensation of the royal favor?

This was undoubtedly one of Burke's most effective images, admitting the certain crudity that often intruded into his expression. It was doubly effective for those who knew Francis, fifth Duke of Bedford, as an immensely wealthy man though a frugal playboy. For persons unacquainted with genealogy, Burke supplied a history of the rise of the Russell family, beginning with "a Mr. Russell, a person of an ancient gentleman's family, raised by being a minion of Henry the Eighth." That king, "The lion, having sucked the blood of his prey [the monasteries], threw the offal carcass to the jackal in waiting." Burke used more of such vigorous language to contrast the nature of his own services, his rewards, and the "mild and benevolent sovereign" who granted them, with the services of the original Russell and the nature of the favors he had received from the king whom Burke, thinking adjectives superfluous, merely called "Henry the Eighth." Passing then to the present, Burke admonished the duke to be watchful of his interests. Immensely wealthy in lands and buildings, the duke's properties would be an immediate object of confiscation should England fall. "They are the Duke of Bedford's natural hunters; and he is their natural game." Indeed, the duke should be grateful to Burke. The war he had urged, but of which he certainly could not be considered the author, was a war to preserve a constitutional and social order which could ensure to the duke the rank and riches he had inherited. But if Burke had little to do with bringing on that war, he would support it to the end, and he would never countenance a peace with the regicides. Burke preferred to leave a discussion of that for another occasion, for it was "high matter, and ought not to be mixed with anything of so little moment as what may belong to me, or even to the Duke of Bedford."

Of "little moment" in the historical scale of things, this incident was of the sort that caricaturists and pamphleteers thrived upon. For the former, Burke's "Letter" was "a sensation"; prints castigating both him and Bedford appeared at once in the shops.[145] At least two pamphlet replies were issued, interesting less for their quality than for their sordidness; the epigram they provoked indicated that the public, after the initial excitement, was willing to drop the affair.

> Each Flow'r in Burke's gay Rhetoric smiles
> What in his Answerers do we meet?
> Dragg'd thro' a Length of tedious *Miles*
> We finish with a dirty *Street*.[146]

For, as Burke had said in concluding his "Letter," there were higher matters at issue. If he was no longer a public man, his views interested the public, and from his retirement at Beaconsfield he had much to say about the revived problem of Ireland and the all-embracing question of war and peace with regicide France.

[145] George, *English Political Caricature*, II, 25.
[146] Balderston, ed., *Thraliana*, II, 955 and n. 4. The pamphlets were by William Augustus Miles and Thomas George Street.

CHAPTER XVIII

The Tragedy of Ireland

THE PORTLAND WHIGS did not enter Pitt's government as meek suppliants. In a general way they intended to strengthen it in its prosecution of the war and in the maintenance of order at home, but they also made a bargain that the disposition of offices reflected. Although Burke had nothing to do with cabinet arrangements, he approved of them. Windham, as unenthusiastic as Burke for the Netherlands and West Indian campaigns, began at once to urge upon Pitt the importance of the royalist uprisings in La Vendée. In effect "the minister for co-operation with the *émigrés*," he succeeded in persuading Pitt to give more generous aid to the royalists, though for various reasons a campaign in the West was delayed until 1795.[1] The other ambition of Pitt's new colleagues was to take charge of Irish affairs. With Portland as Home Secretary, and with Fitzwilliam free to decide when he wished to assume the lord lieutenancy, the direct authority over Irish affairs would belong to persons who, Burke thought, could bring peace with justice to Ireland.

Always a delicate problem, Ireland was in deep trouble. The promise of the 1780's had not been fulfilled. If legislative independence had freed the Irish parliament from certain statutory restraints, it had not thereby become a legislature representative of the interests of the Irish people. The Junto or the Protestant Ascendancy ruled it in conjunction with the British administration. At the time the French Revolution began, the Junto had recovered from its temporary reversal during the Regency crisis. Under the Marquis of Buckingham and beginning in 1790 under the young Earl of Westmorland, the Irish administration used its authority to resist the demands of Irish Catholics for a constitutional voice in public affairs. To Catholic discontent were added the grievances of the Protestant Dissenters, who were especially influential in Northern Ireland. After 1789 the French Revolution inflamed this discontent. The Irish problem of the 1790's was no longer isolated from the world outside. In Dublin or in Belfast or in the country, social and political aspirations were manifested in an atmosphere of revolution, and later of war. If the demands were for the kinds of reforms sought in the 1780's, they had a reference and a significance that made the decade of the 1790's different from any that Ireland had previously known. The difference in the temper of the times became more clearly discernible as each year passed, as tension increased amid a developing sense of crisis.[2]

At first the opposition to the Irish government continued to be led by the parliamentary corps headed by Grattan, Charlemont, and George Ponsonby. They formed the Whig Club, which, Burke advised, at a time when "party is absolutely necessary" might prevent the evaporation of the principles of 1688.[3] But to perfect Irish legislative independence by abolishing corrupt practices without reforming parliament or enfranchising Catholics was too mild a program to satisfy persons such as Lawrence Parsons, the young Wolfe Tone, and the notorious Napper Tandy. It was in Belfast, where enthusiasm for the Revolution was warmest, that in 1791 the Society of United Irishmen was founded. Inspired by Tone's pamphlet, it advocated an alliance of Catholics and Dissenters to achieve parliamentary and suffrage reforms and to

1 Watson, *George III*, 368, for the quotation. Also Rose, *Pitt and the Great War*, 259-60; Rose, *English Historical Review*, XXVIII, 87-103; *Windham Papers*, I, 221, 223-27, 231, Spencer to Windham, Aug. 12, 1794, Capt. Sir W. Sidney Smith to Windham, Aug. 13, 1794, Pitt to Windham, Sept. 10, 1794.

2 For the history of the next period see generally Lecky, *History of Ireland*, III, chaps. VI and VII; McDowell, *Irish Public Opinion 1750-1800*, 136-92; Harlow, *The Second British Empire*, I, 627-46; Buckingham, *Courts and Cabinets*, II, *passim;* H.M.C., *Dropmore Papers*, II, *passim;* Mahoney, *Burke and Ireland*, chaps. VI and VII; William T. W. Tone, ed., *Life of Theobald Wolfe Tone* (Washington, 1826).

3 Grattan, *Memoirs*, III, 430, Burke to Charlemont, March 29, 1789.

abolish the system under which England governed Ireland by means of a bought administration and an unrepresentative parliament.

The differences between the Whig Club and the United Irishmen were both greater and smaller than might at first appear. Some of the Whigs, like Grattan, could accept both Catholic emancipation and a mild parliamentary reform, provided they did not dislodge the power of property or disturb the imperial connection. Tone and Tandy sought an independent and republican Ireland. In a word, though both groups were antiadministration, the Whig Club was in the spirit of Burke, the United Irishmen in the spirit of Paine.[4]

The Catholic community was not united. Lethargic since 1783 under the leadership of Lord Kenmare and some of the old aristocracy, the Catholic Committee (a new name for the old Association) did not adequately represent the aggressive, rising Catholic commercial interest. They expected nothing from prayerful appeals to Westmorland's government. The militants quarreled with Kenmare and, headed by the wealthy merchant John Keogh, assumed control of the committee. Keogh and his friends were not radicals. They sought the removal of disabilities so that the propertied Catholics could participate in public life and strengthen the defense against friends of the French Revolution. The Protestant Ascendancy, the pillar of Westmorland's system, saw even this much relaxation as a threat to their control of the Irish political system.

The committee turned to Burke for advice and assistance. In August, 1790, mainly because of his father's reputation, they retained Richard, Jr., as a kind of London agent who could give legal advice and improved literary form to their statements. A Catholic priest, Dr. Thomas Hussey, served as go-between.[5] The immediate object was the preparation of a Catholic petition to the Irish parliament. Richard wrote it.[6] Richard also went to

---

4 Lecky, *History of Ireland*, III, 20.

5 *Corr.*, III, 150-55, the Rev. Dr. Thomas Hussey to Burke, Aug. 13, 1790, John Hussey to Thomas Hussey, Aug. 6, 1790. The initial payment to Richard was 50 guineas. Also Burke MSS, Sheff., Dr. Hussey to Richard, Jr., Aug. 28, 1790. Dr. Hussey had been in London for many years, but these are the first letters to pass between him and the Burkes.

6 Burke MSS, Sheff., B8d, Hussey to Burke, Oct. 3, 1790.

Ireland in the fall of 1790 to spy out the land and make a report to the Catholics.[7] This was the kind of employment that Richard liked and thought he had a talent for; it was also a step forward in a career that he and his father hoped would lead him into the House of Commons—and who could know what, beyond.

The original Irish commission achieved nothing, but Richard made a favorable impression upon the Catholic Committee. In the autumn of 1791 he resumed his employment for them, according to an agreement made before he went to Coblentz.[8] The first objects were in England, to discuss with ministers the affairs of the Irish Catholics and to assist in preparing a petition to the king. Besides repeal of the legal prohibitions that forbade Catholics to practice law or to serve as magistrates and jurymen, the committee desired votes for qualified Catholics in county elections. The appointment of Richard was a tribute to his father, even more obviously than a year before, and a continuation of the effort to involve him deeply in the committee's work.

Along with John Keogh, Richard spent the last three months of 1791 in conversations with Dundas, Grenville, and Pitt. By his own estimate, Richard achieved great success in stating the Catholic cause, even to Robert Hobart, the Chief Secretary to Westmorland, who was in London to "counteract" him. Later, in telling Westmorland that the grant of a limited franchise to Catholics would be the safest course, Dundas used arguments similar to the ones Richard had presented.[9] They stressed the necessity for enlisting substantial Catholics in the cause of constitutional government. Richard seems to have made some impression on Grenville in urging concessions to the Catholics as a means of heading off union between them and the Dissenters.[10] He

7 Burke MSS, Sheff., B8d, Hussey to Burke, Oct. 3, 1790; D. A. Chart, ed., *The Drennan Letters* (Belfast, 1931), 52-53, Dr. William Drennan to Samuel McTier, Jan. 4, 1791.

8 Burke MSS, Sheff., Edward Byrne to Richard, Jr., Sept. 15, 1791. This letter was written before Richard's return from Coblentz; it refers to prior correspondence, which is missing, but see a letter in Burke MSS, Sheff., Richard Burke, Jr., to Dundas, July 23, 1791, in which he speaks of resuming his agency for the committee.

9 Mahoney, *Burke and Ireland*, 167; *Corr.*, III, 490-91, Richard, Jr., to Will Burke, Aug. 17, 1792; Lecky, *History of Ireland*, III, 38-41. But Lecky, III, 36, says that ministers would abandon the franchise for fear of antagonizing the Ascendancy.

10 H.M.C., *Dropmore Papers*, II, 221-22, Grenville to Dundas, Oct. 29, 1791.

had help from an unexpected source. The Marquis of Bucking-ham warned Grenville against the delaying tactics of Hobart and the lord lieutenant and urged concessions to Catholics, even a limited franchise, as a matter both of justice and expediency.[11] However, Buckingham doubted whether the franchise would pass the Irish parliament. On the whole, the impression is clear that Pitt, Grenville, and Dundas, who approved the Catholic Relief Act in England in 1791, were predisposed in favor of the program Richard discussed with them. In a larger sense the approach to a solution of an important part of the Irish problem was being made when Richard set off for Ireland at the end of the year. He carried assurance that Westmorland would be fully informed of Dundas' views, along with an admonition to proceed through the proper channels—that is, through the government of Ireland.[12] If ministerial duplicity is disallowed, then ministerial under-estimation of the Protestant Ascendancy must be admitted.

As the Catholic Committee had expected, Burke offered advice freely, and even beyond their expectations. To Richard he assigned an impossible task, instructing him on the one hand to avoid a breach between the Catholics and the Dissenters and on the other to urge Catholics to accept a franchise with qualifications even higher than the existing ones, rather than support the Dissenters' desire for parliamentary reform.[13] Yet he was ready to admit Catholics to the franchise in corporate towns, which was more than his son or Pitt or Dundas would do.

Burke also presented his views to the public. If his letter to Lord Kenmare, written ten years earlier, was published at this time in Dublin without his consent or disapproval, his long reply of January 3, 1792, to a letter from Sir Hercules Langrishe was published in London and in Dublin early in March.[14] An inde-pendent, though generally a supporter of the government, Lan-grishe was also a known friend of the Catholics and a long-time friend of Burke. The publication of Burke's letter was too late

11 H.M.C., *Dropmore Papers*, II, 237-38, 248, Buckingham to Grenville, Dec. 11, 1791, Jan. 4, 1792.

12 *Corr.*, III, 365-66, Dundas to Richard, Jr., Dec. 25, 1791.

13 *Corr.*, III, 360-64, Burke to Richard, Jr., Dec. 15, 16, 1791.

14 "A Letter to Sir Hercules Langrishe, Bart., M. P., on the Subject of the Roman Catholics of Ireland," *Works*, IV, 243-306. A second edition also appeared in London in March.

to influence opinion in Ireland before parliament took up the Catholic question. Since it represents Burke's views at the time of its composition, it is proper to notice the letter now, rather than in connection with events at the time of its publication.

The "Letter to Langrishe" was intended for a large audience, though it retained a natural, personal tone. It refuted Langrishe's points of difference with Burke on the question of the franchise and on the position of the Ascendancy on Catholic relief. It was closely reasoned, exact in its definitions, careful in its analyses, deeply felt, toward the end warm in its emotions, and firm in denouncing the proscription of whole classes of men. It was mellower, perhaps, than anything Burke ever wrote, a perfect example of political charity, of humanity, of the old sentiment that magnanimity is the truest wisdom in the conduct of social relationships.

The letter almost crossed over the line into inconsistency when arguing for the Catholic franchise. It was saved from that by remaining on the safe ground of property as the qualification for the franchise and for participation in political affairs. Catholics should not possess the franchise by virtue of religion but only as they met the property qualifications and, if they did, should not be excluded from the franchise because they were Catholics. In conceding this point, government would be obeying "the great law of change" and, by anticipating the conditions under which it operated, be able to control it and achieve gradual reform.

Justice and humanity, expediency and circumstances, all agreed that the time for lifting restrictions upon Catholics had arrived. Nothing in the constitution or the coronation oath need bar relief. The Catholics should be a part of the state; to exclude them was to divide it into two bodies and thus to invite perpetual conflict. To restore civil rights to Catholics in Ireland would not be an invitation to papal control any more than it had been in Canada. This restoration would fulfill the promise of the Irish Revolution of 1782, bring stability to Ireland in Church and State, and unite its people in a common interest. Like most of Burke's other writings, the "Letter" had little influence upon events but gained its significance in retrospect as a commentary upon the events.

Burke's letters to his son complement the "Letter to Langrishe" because while it argued the case, they in large part discussed tactics.[15] He advised Richard to be patient, and if things did not go well, to depart with dignity and wait for better times. Perhaps it was moral courage, but it was also Richard's exaggerated self-esteem that made him crash recklessly onward, exacerbating differences among the Catholics. Self-deluded, he thought of himself, "under the name of agent to the Catholics, in effect at the head of a great party."[16] The committee objected to his presumptuousness and dictatorial manner.[17]

Though he advised patience to his son, Burke wanted the committee to be "importunate." The Catholic gentlemen and clergy, servile out of habit and often lacking in intelligence and education, faced formidable adversaries. The Irish administration, which Burke detested, was making an impression on Pitt and Dundas. If Catholic Relief could not be gained quietly, Burke feared that they would give it up and "remain in quiet." This was not a completely fair judgment, but it contained enough truth to justify Burke's advice to go forward with a petition to the king. The committee should not modify its claims, even to the franchise, lest like Kenmare and his friends, they appear interested in the "accommodation of a few gentlemen" and indifferent to the Catholic common people. The well-being of three million Catholics was worth more to Burke even than the maintenance of the established church in Ireland, though he did not think the choice would have to be made. In any case, a Catholic Ireland would remain a Christian Ireland, and that was more important than anything in the Thirty-Nine Articles. If the Catholic Committee remained persistent and united, "reason and justice will prevail."[18]

It hardly seemed so. During January and February, 1792, the Irish Ascendancy won Pitt's and Dundas' approval for concessions much more limited than earlier they had contemplated. Richard lobbied tactlessly, if earnestly, for the committee's program, on one occasion exposing himself to the threat of arrest by the

[15] Burke sent a stream of letters during Jan., Feb., and March, 1792. *Corr.*, III, 367-455, and Burke MSS, Sheff., about Jan. 8, Jan. 12, and Feb. 19, 1792.
[16] *Corr.*, III, 492, Richard, Jr., to Will Burke, Aug. 17, 1792.
[17] Tone, ed., *Life of Tone,* I, 63.
[18] *Corr.*, III, 452-53, Burke to Richard, Jr., March 23, 1792.

sergeant at arms of the Irish Commons.[19] The relief bill that the Irish parliament accepted was not officially the government's, though it represented their views and Hobart seconded it. Introduced by Langrishe, it offered some concessions that were individually of merit but that embodied in a bill seemed almost insulting. Burke said it afforded "no relief." It was "mischievous and insolent" and ought to be rejected.[20] Richard considered it illiberal and vicious, a sop to the Kenmare party, a rebuff to the Catholic Committee, and a proof of the extent to which Langrishe was deceived.[21] The act opened the legal profession to Catholics, legalized mixed marriages, and removed restrictions on Catholic schools and apprenticeships. It was silent about jury service, magistracies, the right to bear arms, and the franchise. Thus, it embodied only the concessions that Westmorland and his Privy Council had agreed to accept from the outset.

The Catholic Committee were displeased and decided to restate their desires. Their petition, from the composition of which Richard was excluded, was rejected on February 20.[22] The vote, 208–23, reveals the strength of the Irish government and the unwillingness of Burke's Irish Whig friends to take up the cause of the Catholic franchise, whereas the manner in which the petition was drawn up showed the committee's lack of confidence in Richard.

This Irish mission was not the personal diplomatic triumph Richard had hoped to achieve. Had he departed in January, as his father had suggested, because the committee's program was doomed to rejection, he might have avoided some of the recriminations he drew upon himself. Richard did not seem to sense the humiliation of being paid two thousand guineas and then being requested to handle committee business only in London. His subsequent actions indicate failure to recognize that the com-

19 To his father, Richard denied being upon the floor of the House; to O'Beirne he admitted trespass; to Will Burke he said he had gone a "few inches" onto the floor. Burke MSS, Sheff., Jan., 1792, late Feb., 1792; *Corr.*, III, 496, Aug. 17, 1792. His father told him to stay away from the Commons. Burke MSS, Sheff., Feb. 19, 1792.

20 *Corr.*, III, 418-19, Burke to Richard, Jr., Feb. 19, 1792.

21 Burke MSS, Sheff., Richard, Jr., to O'Beirne, late Feb., 1792.

22 Mahoney, *Burke and Ireland*, 184; Burke MSS, Sheff., Richard, Jr., to Burke, late Feb., 1792. The petition is printed, *Corr.*, III, 427-28.

mittee wanted no more of him in Ireland, where Wolfe Tone would continue the work he had tried to do.

Yet the events of the following year vindicated Richard's judgment. In insisting upon the full program of the committee, in keeping it alive as the committee's goal, and by condemning the Act of 1792 he helped to stimulate discontent with it. Timid acquiescence, like that of Lord Kenmare, would have encouraged the Irish government to think that further concessions to Catholics could be indefinitely postponed.

When Richard returned to England, he found ministers unreceptive. When Dundas greeted him warmly at a levee, he exhausted the proof of good will he had promised to demonstrate.[23] Afterwards he was unavailable. The Catholic Committee was indignant. Dundas and Pitt had time to consider the plight of African slaves but none for that of the Irish Catholics, complained Keogh, and they were perfectly willing to use Edmund Burke to protect the constitution against radicalism.[24] Rebuffed by Dundas, Richard turned to Grenville.[25] The Catholics, having had enough of the Irish government, were going to petition the king, hoping thereby to present their true situation and hoping also to encourage the English government to assert its authority. These representations did not stir Grenville, and Richard had to report to the committee that England would not intervene. As Burke said, the English government did not desire to keep Ireland suppressed, but the Irish government did, and its will prevailed—or rather the "junto of robbers" who governed Ireland for the lord lieutenant.[26]

In September Richard went to Ireland. His motive was clear enough to Tone—he desired "another 2,000 guineas," or he wanted to increase his nuisance value with the English ministry.[27] He was treated suspiciously. Tone said Keogh thought him an agent of Dundas; William Drennan considered him a pro-Catholic spy sent by Pitt to seek information about the Dis-

23 Burke MSS, Sheff., John King to Richard, Jr., March 3, 1792, Walker King to Richard, Jr., March 20, 1792, Dundas to Richard, Jr., March 21, 1792.
24 Burke MSS, Sheff., Keogh to Richard, Jr., May 17, 1792.
25 *Corr.*, III, 455-62, June 2, 1792; Tone, ed., *Life of Tone*, I, 209-10, Richard, Jr., to the Catholic Committee, June 17, 1792.
26 *Corr.*, III, 524, Burke to Richard, Jr., Sept., 1792.
27 Tone, ed., *Life of Tone*, I, 165-66.

senters.[28] Whatever his capacity or authority, Richard acted with complete freedom, traveling around the country and, he thought, winning support for the Catholic cause.[29]

As he had before, Burke sent advice to his son.[30] He wanted the Catholics to be persistent, even obnoxious, but to avoid force or flirtations with France. Richard should be discreet in talking with the Ascendancy but frank with the committee. He could serve the cause best by encouraging the Catholics to persevere. Their first step should be a petition to the king; there was no point in an application to the Irish parliament until both governments and the public were better disposed toward the Catholic cause. In the meantime the Catholics could strengthen their position by maintaining unity and achieving a reconciliation with the elements among the Irish Protestants who were not infected with French principles. From their actions he knew that the Ascendancy was growing alarmed; if the English government could reverse the traditional order and, for once, force the Ascendancy to yield, the Catholic cause would succeed. Burke seemed not to be aware that both Pitt and Grenville were beginning to think that the concession of the franchise was the only way of pacifying Ireland at a time when England badly needed peace at home in order to protect herself better against growing dangers from abroad.[31]

If upon his return from Ireland in December, Richard was unable to talk with Dundas or to lay a Catholic representation before the king, he and his father found other ways of pressing the Catholic case upon ministers. Burke's effort was a long discourse, historical, didactic, and hortatory.[32] The restoration of the franchise to the Catholics would be an act of elemental justice, attended with beneficent social, economic, and political results. The best security for the peace of Ireland was a Catholic stake in the country. Burke was not ready to promise that having won the franchise, the Catholics would be forever content. "Un-

[28] Tone, ed., *Life of Tone*, I, 180; Chart, *Drennan Letters*, 96, 98, Drennan to Martha McTier, Nov. 20, 25, 1792.

[29] Burke MSS, Sheff., Richard, Jr., to Burke, Sept. 9, Oct. 10, 1792.

[30] *Corr.*, III, 525, IV, 2-3, 10, Burke to Richard, Jr., Sept., Sept. 9, 29, 1792.

[31] Buckingham, *Courts and Cabinets*, II, 220, Grenville to Buckingham, Oct. 11, 1792; Harlow, *The Second British Empire*, I, 638.

[32] *Corr.*, IV, 65-96.

doubtedly" they would eventually ask for more, but until then, prudence dictated this concession. By accommodating themselves to the Catholic franchise, Ireland and England would prepare the way for later enlargements of Catholic liberties. The Catholics would earn them by demonstrating their capacity to use the franchise wisely. Here again Burke was the advocate of gradual change. He denied that each concession to the Catholics would take Ireland one step further toward a popish state. It was better to remove an immediate and known danger than to worry about one "contingent and remote." "By practising the prudence of to-day, we shall be more likely to practise that of to-morrow." The whole point of Burke's argument was a denial of the identity between prudence and inaction, and in making it, he referred only once to the French Revolution as a reason for concessions to the Irish Catholics. The grant of the franchise would be right in itself.

Recognition of rightness did not win the victory for the Catholics. If it was right in 1792-1793 to grant the franchise, it had been right to do so earlier. Circumstances had changed, and these persuaded the English government to force the Ascendancy to yield. The great, overriding circumstance was the French Revolution, and in the winter of 1792-1793 the worsening of relations between England and France. Peace in Ireland was imperative in the presence of dangers from abroad and from pro-French sympathizers among some at home. The assemblage of the Catholic Convention in Dublin early in December was a well-behaved one but nevertheless a demonstration of strength that impressed the governments of Ireland and England. When the delegates of the convention arrived in London bearing the petition to the king, they found their way easier because the Burkes had prepared it for them. The delegates were courteously received because the English government during the two preceding months had made up its mind to grant the Catholics' prayer.[33] On December 17 Dundas announced to Westmorland that the enfranchisement of Catholics was in the interest not only of Irish Protestants but of the Empire as a whole. Whether the Burkes'

[33] Harlow, *The Second British Empire*, I, 638-39; Lecky, *History of Ireland*, III, 126-28, 131.

arguments had converted Dundas, he had adopted their language, and the bill that was passed by the Irish parliament in the spring of 1793 corresponded to their desires. It granted the franchise and eligibility for membership on grand juries, for magistracies, for military and naval commissions, for all but a few civil offices, and for university degrees. The one great gift still withheld was seats in parliament. If only it had been granted, the history of Ireland would have been much different.

Burke was pleased with the Relief Act of 1793, though he did not consider it the complete settlement of the Irish question.[34] Its real importance was that it was a major step toward political equality. Reforms, he said, go in progression, each making the next one easier to achieve, and in the end the Catholics would have to be admitted to parliament. For himself, Burke took no credit for the Relief Act. He thought his son had helped obtain it, particularly as a *"dunn"* with English ministers.

It is difficult to say whether with the Relief Act of 1793 Burke considered that his own concern with Ireland had ended. He hoped for an interval of peace during which the Irish problem in its larger complexity might be put in the way toward ameliora-tion.[35] The qualified Catholics could exercise the franchise and prepare themselves for eventual admission to parliament. He might not live to see it, but he knew it would come and he was ready to support it if an occasion arose. Emancipation was no panacea. It might remove a stigma and so be morally desirable. But under the electoral system, not more than three Catholics could be elected to the Commons even if the legal barrier were removed. Perhaps Burke underestimated the importance of the principle involved; emancipation remained a leading issue until it was achieved in 1829. If emancipation was only a step toward solution of the problem, union between Ireland and England was a "Bold, experimental remedy" that, under the circumstances he knew, Burke considered quite impracticable.

There remained, in the area of politics, one essential reform that was practicable, even if difficult. This was a change in the

---

34 Grattan, *Memoirs,* IV, 113-14, Burke to Grattan, March 8, 1793.
35 Burke MSS, Sheff., Burke to Fitzwilliam, marked "received" Sept. 26, 1794, for this paragraph.

system of governing Ireland. Whether one called that system a "Junto," a "Click," or the "Protestant Ascendancy," one meant a nefarious, corrupt, politically immoral arrangement whereby *"mastership"* over the Irish people was exercised by a small, self-seeking group.[36] This system Burke described as "neither more nor less than the resolution of one set of people in Ireland to consider themselves as the sole citizens in the commonwealth, and to keep a dominion over the rest by reducing them to absolute slavery under a military power, and, thus fortified in their power, to divide the public estate, which is the result of general contribution, as a military booty, solely among themselves."[37] The recent measures of Catholic relief may have removed some burdens from the Catholics, but they remained subject to the Junto. Legislative independence was limited in its effectiveness by the operation of this system, which, in a broader sense, included the king and the administration in England. As the support of the Irish politicians was needed to govern Ireland, they in turn needed support from England to resist the opposition in Ireland. Until this system was destroyed, that country would not be free. As long as the Ascendancy ruled Ireland, only reforms that did not endanger its control would be permitted, and the solution of the basic problems that were social and economic even more than religious would never be attained. "Alas! it is not about popes, but about potatoes, that the minds of this unhappy people are agitated. It is not from the spirit of zeal, but the spirit of whiskey, that these wretches act."[38] Cannot some "poor clown" be "unwilling, after paying three pounds rent to a gentleman in a brown coat, to pay fourteen shillings to one in a black coat, for his acre of potatoes, and tumultously to desire some modification of the charge" and still not be ready for papal control or be an enemy to the king and the British constitution, Burke asked indignantly?

The problem of Ireland was land—oppressive tithes and ruinous rents—and the Irish people deserved relief. But political changes

---

[36] Burke MSS, Sheff., Burke to Sylvester Douglas, after Dec. 31, 1793, for the word "Click"; Burke MSS, Sheff., Burke to Windham, Oct. 16, 1794, for the word "Junto"; "A Letter to Richard Burke, Esq., on the Protestant Ascendancy in Ireland," *Works,* VI, 387-412, written in 1793.

[37] "Letter to Richard Burke," *Works,* VI, 392.

[38] "Letter to Richard Burke," *Works,* VI, 399.

had to come first. Within the framework of an established church and the British constitution, even a Protestant parliament could be a "patriot Parliament," moved by "common reason and common honesty" to frame laws "to suit the people and the circumstances of the country," while preserving an "orderly civil society" under a constitution "favorable at once to authority and to freedom."[39] The Junto must be destroyed; "pluck Ireland out of the unwise and corrupt hands that are destroying us!"[40]

It was to this task that Burke hoped the Whig members of Pitt's government, especially Portland and Fitzwilliam, would dedicate themselves. As lord lieutenant, Fitzwilliam would, Burke thought, be in a position to smash the Junto and prepare the way for the settlement of Ireland's troubles. Indeed, only Fitzwilliam could do it.[41] But before Fitzwilliam became lord lieutenant, there was a desperate period of political negotiations during which the coalition almost came to an early end.[42] The terms of the coalition clearly provided that Fitzwilliam would become lord lieutenant after a brief term as lord president. Though the change would displace Westmorland, Pitt assured Portland that there would be no difficulty, and the lord lieutenancy would be opened "whenever it is agreeable to Lord Fitzwilliam to accept it."[43] If recent history meant anything, the change of men would indubitably mean a change of measures—otherwise the coalition negotiations were "unintelligible."[44]

Fitzwilliam almost at once was ready to go to Ireland. On August 10 he informed Portland of his decision; by August 15 he was wondering whether Pitt had acknowledged his acceptance; on September 4 the *Times* announced that the appointment was settled; and by September 8 Fitzwilliam was asking whether the

[39] "Letter to Richard Burke," *Works*, VI, 402-403.
[40] Burke MSS, Sheff., Burke to Windham, Oct. 16, 1794.
[41] Burke MSS, Sheff., Burke to [?], June 6, 1794.
[42] There is much source material concerning this affair. The Burke, Fitzwilliam, Portland, and Pitt MSS contain many letters, and these, with other correspondence, make the episode one of the most completely documented of any in which Burke was involved. Yet, as will be seen, some essential information is missing.
[43] P.R.O., Chatham Papers, 30/8, 102, July 2, 1794.
[44] Lecky, *History of Ireland*, III, 241-43. Grattan made the same point in the Irish Commons on April 21, 1795, saying he had Portland's word for it. *Times*, April 28, 1795.

king had been informed.[45] Taking Pitt's and the king's approval for granted, he began auxiliary arrangements. At one time it was thought the chief secretaryship would be given to Richard Burke, Jr., but his death removed that possibility. Fitzwilliam offered it to Grenville's brother Thomas, who was then in Vienna, and he accepted.[46] Soon Fitzwilliam was enlisting support for his new measures from George Ponsonby, who was in London, and from Grattan, who quickly came.[47]

But delays intruded, creating first embarrassments and then friction. For no apparent reason, Portland postponed informing Pitt officially of Fitzwilliam's acceptance.[48] Pitt, who doubtless knew of it, was having second thoughts. To change the system in Ireland would mean replacing the Junto, his friends, with the friends of Fitzwilliam.[49] To Burke, of course, this was the crux of the matter.[50] By October he had become so depressed by the delays, uncertainties, and increasing asperities, that he was ready to believe Fitzwilliam would never go to Ireland. In that event the coalition, never solid, would become shakier; if it collapsed, and internal unity with it, Ireland would remain troubled, and England would be unable to play her part as the savior of Europe. These calamities would have a single cause —jobbery in Dublin.

The maneuvers relating to the settlement of Fitzwilliam's appointment produced one of the strangest political performances of the times. Pitt complained because reports of Fitzwilliam's appointment preceded steps toward "creating a Vacancy" for him there.[51] Westmorland was still unprovided for when Portland, early in October, informed Pitt of Fitzwilliam's readiness to go to

45 Portland MSS, Fitzwilliam to Portland, Aug. 10, 15, Sept. 8, 1794.

46 Buckingham, *Courts and Cabinets*, II, 281-83, T. Grenville to Fitzwilliam, Sept. 14, 1794.

47 Portland MSS, Fitzwilliam to Portland, Aug. 15, 1794; Grattan, *Memoirs*, IV, 173-74, Fitzwilliam to Grattan, Aug. 23, 1794.

48 Fitzwilliam MSS, Sheff., F31d, Portland to Fitzwilliam, Aug. 16, Sept. 11, 1794.

49 Fitzwilliam MSS, Sheff., F31d, Portland to Fitzwilliam, Oct. 14, 1794; Grattan, *Memoirs*, IV, 174-78; Buckingham, *Courts and Cabinets*, II, 302, 304-307, Grenville to T. Grenville, Sept. 15, 1794, Grenville to Buckingham, Sept. 27, 1794; H.M.C., *Dropmore Papers*, II, 634, Buckingham to Grenville, Sept. 20, 1794.

50 Burke MSS, Sheff., Burke to Fitzwilliam, Aug. 31, Sept. 9, 1794, Burke to Loughborough, after Oct. 3, 1794.

51 P.R.O., Chatham Papers, 30/8, 101, Pitt to Lord Chatham, Sept. 24, 1794.

Ireland.[52] Fitzwilliam talked with the Ponsonbys and Grattan as though his depature for Dublin was imminent, and they were also meeting with Pitt, in private and at Portland's home. Obviously, Pitt was dragging his feet, trying, under the influence of Dundas, Grenville, and Buckingham, to save the Junto. In all of this he was repudiating original understandings about the terms of the coalition.

The unavoidable consequence was confusion and anger.[53] Fitzwilliam talked ominously about a stain upon his honor. Pitt's performance violated both the letter and the spirit of the coalition. If in talking with Irish opposition leaders, Fitzwilliam had misled them into thinking he would have a free hand as lord lieutenant, that was because he had been misled by Pitt. Portland, impatient with Pitt, wondered why he had accepted office and thought of resignation as the only dignified solution of his predicament. Windham, deploring what he called misunderstanding, tried to mediate. His attempt to present Pitt's case was very weak. When he asked whether it was fair to expect Pitt to accept the proscription of his friends in Ireland, even for the sake of preserving the coalition, Windham was preferring jobbery to the good of Ireland and preferring Pitt to Portland. He urged continued conversations, hoping that somehow Fitzwilliam might sufficiently reduce his demands for changes so that Pitt could accept them without letting down his Irish supporters. Lord Mansfield saw no possibility of such a compromise unless Portland and Fitzwilliam abandoned the original terms of the coalition.[54] He was confident that he could prove in a court of justice that Portland and Fitzwilliam had been assured of the "entire management" of appointments in Ireland.

On October 14 Fitzwilliam issued an ultimatum.[55] He demanded an immediate decision—"am I in the month of October to be appointed to that situation, which in the month of July it was propos'd to me to fill, & the decision whether I should or

---

52 Portland MSS, Fitzwilliam to Portland, Oct. 8, 1794.

53 Br. Mus., Add. MSS 37,845, fols. 45, 47, Portland to Windham, Oct. 8, 1794, Portland to Windham, Oct. 11, 1794; Fitzwilliam MSS, Sheff., F31i, Fitzwilliam to Windham, Oct. 11, 1794, Windham to Fitzwilliam, Oct. 12, 1794.

54 Br. Mus., Add. MSS 37,874, fols. 88-89, Mansfield to Windham, Oct. 12, 1794.

55 Portland MSS, Fitzwilliam to Portland.

should not, left absolutely to my election." There was no doubt about his conception of the terms of the coalition. There was no misunderstanding, only a repudiation of them by Pitt.[56]

On the other side, Pitt was firm.[57] To Dundas and to Windham he insisted that he would not give up the Irish chancellor, Fitzgibbon—that is, he would not smash the Junto. He drew up a memorandum for himself in which he listed points he would not surrender: there would be no new system, either of men or measures or principles, and the lord lieutenancy would not change hands until Westmorland and his Chief Secretary were provided for. Such adamancy may have truly reflected Pitt's mind in mid-October, but Fitzwilliam's contention, that Pitt had indeed repudiated the understandings made three months earlier, was not answered.

By this time the coalition's collapse seemed imminent. The cabinet members worked desperately to save it. Loughborough felt that the continuance of full and frank discussions was the only way to reach understanding.[58] Grenville, who thought Fitzwilliam was wrong about the terms of the coalition, said that if the quandary was the result of "precipitation and indiscretion" rather than design, sincere discussion might find a way out.[59] He offered himself as a sacrifice, but Pitt would not permit him to surrender his post in order to create a vacancy for Westmorland.[60] Pitt seemed to intimate that he would give up some of the Junto if Fitzgibbon were spared.

During this time Burke lived in horror.[61] A ministerial crisis would "complete our ruin." More than anyone, he held the preservation of the coalition essential to successful prosecution of the war against France. For the moment, that was more important than the destruction of the Junto. He hated to think that the quarrel was between Fitzwilliam, "the man in the world I am most obliged to," and Pitt, to whom he owed "strong and

56 Burke MSS, Sheff., Fitzwilliam to Burke, Oct. 21, 1794.

57 Stanhope, *Pitt*, II, 283, 289, 291.

58 Br. Mus., Add. MSS 37,874, fol. 94, Loughborough to Windham, Oct. 16, 1794.

59 Buckingham, *Courts and Cabinets*, II, 312-16, Grenville to T. Grenville, Oct. 15, 1794.

60 P.R.O., Chatham Papers, 30/8, 140, Grenville to Pitt, Oct. 13, 1794.

61 Burke MSS, Sheff., Burke to Windham, Oct. 16, 1794; Br. Mus., Add. MSS 37,845, fol. 59, Portland to Windham, Oct. 18, 1794.

recent obligations." Although the earl had not lately been a model of discretion, his interpretation of the terms of the coalition was correct, and Pitt was mainly to blame for the situation that had arisen. The threat of disaster hovered over all. Burke therefore advised Fitzwilliam to unbend a little, at least to continue conversations. If Pitt would be magnanimous and forgive the precipitancy of Fitzwilliam and his Irish friends, if all concerned would seek clear understanding and, avoiding recriminations, put the national interest ahead of pride, then maybe "God in His goodness" might direct them to a solution. This was the letter of a deeply troubled man. An inner contradiction, admitting justification for Fitzwilliam's resignation, revealed hopelessness, despair, but also a faith in Divine Providence. Two days later Windham reported some improvement in tempers; Portland and Fitzwilliam seemed more acquiescent than formerly.[62] Burke too had changed. Whereas on October 16 he had talked of conversations and of resignations, on October 20 he wanted Portland and Fitzwilliam to stand firmly upon their former demands while thinking of what was best for Ireland.[63]

If Burke's advice would be difficult to follow, his last admonition at least corresponded with his earlier desire for continued discussion. There could be none if Fitzwilliam gave up office. As long as he and the duke were in the ministry the conversations would have to go on. And when, after a talk between Pitt and Portland, it was decided to await the return from Vienna of Spencer and Thomas Grenville, a moment of respite occurred.[64] Meanwhile, appeals to reason were being made. Burke wrote a careful letter, an essay on patriotism, to Loughborough, in whose conciliatory abilities he had great confidence, and Loughborough sent it on to Pitt.[65] If all persons gave their confidence to Loughborough, something might be worked out. Grenville was considering various possibilities, including the retention of Fitz-

[62] Burke MSS, Sheff., Windham to Burke, Oct. 18, 1794.
[63] Burke MSS, Sheff., Burke to Windham, Oct. 20, 1794, Burke to Fitzwilliam, Oct. 21, 1794.
[64] Burke MSS, Sheff., Windham to Burke, Oct. 21, 1794; Buckingham, *Courts and Cabinets*, II, 317-18, Grenville to T. Grenville, Oct. 24, 1794.
[65] Burke MSS, Sheff., Loughborough to Burke, Oct. 23, 1794, Burke to Windham, Oct. 28, 1794, Loughborough to Burke, Oct. 30, 1794.

gibbon, or even of Fitzwilliam's staying on as lord president in
the interest of the common cause.

During this lull, Burke came to town and made his greatest
contribution to a settlement. He and Grattan talked with Fitzgibbon, who had come over from Ireland, and virtually committed
Fitzwilliam to a conciliatory position.[66] The earl was determined
to reform Ireland, they said, though not to the extent of introducing "new Systems," and he would do it in concert with Pitt
who should support his efforts. Ministers should agree to think
only of the future, and if they did, there was nothing to prevent
candid conferences. From this moment steady progress was made
toward agreement. That shrewd politician George III untied,
rather than cut, a Gordian knot. He suggested the rearrangement
of offices to take care of Westmorland.[67] At the same time, George
spoke appreciatively of Fitzgibbon, and because Grattan and the
Ponsonbys had consented to it, Pitt could be assured that they
would raise no controversy about Fitzgibbon in Ireland.[68] When
at the Lord Mayor's banquet a few days earlier Pitt had proposed
a toast to Burke, he seemed to be suggesting that the breach was
healing.[69]

The only absolutely clear term of the compromise that enabled
Fitzwilliam to be sworn in as lord lieutenant on December 10
seems to be the one concerning Fitzgibbon. So far as we know
there was no written agreement or minutes to which the historian
can resort.[70] The sources are not official documents or precise
and written engagements, but private correspondence, which
records the memories and interpretations of the participants, with
their biases forcefully stated. And all of these were made some
time after the event, rather than immediately—that is, after
misunderstandings produced tragedy and men tried to recall what
had actually taken place. There were discussions, and presumably
some understandings were reached in them, if understandings is

[66] Burke MSS, N.R.O., Avi19, Burke to Fitzwilliam, Nov. 7, 1794.
[67] P.R.O., Chatham Papers, 30/8, 103, the King to Pitt, Nov. 13, 20, 1794; 30/8, 102, Pitt to the Duke of Montrose, Nov. 21, 1794.
[68] Burke MSS, Sheff., Fitzwilliam to Burke, Nov. 18, 1794.
[69] *Times*, Nov. 12, 1794.
[70] Grattan thought it ludicrous to expect men of honor to have to talk with a notary public present. The *Times*, April 28, 1795, reporting Grattan's speech of April 21 in the Irish Commons.

the proper word. On December 3 Grattan and several Irish gentlemen dined with Pitt; on December 9 Pitt, Dundas, Loughborough, Spencer, Grenville, Ponsonby, and Grattan dined at Portland's house; and on December 10, following the levee and the Council at St. James's, the cabinet dined at Fitzwilliam's in Grosvenor Square.[71] The curious silence about all except Fitzgibbon, along with the recall to favor of the Ponsonbys and Grattan, seemed to suggest that the Junto's days were numbered. The discussions, before Fitzwilliam left for Ireland, of Irish peerages and pensions as part of the bargain involving Fitzgibbon strengthens this suspicion.[72] At the same time, Fitzwilliam's disapproval of rewards he would not personally approve of hinted at potential misunderstandings. Thomas Grenville's second thoughts about the chief secretaryship also suggested uneasiness, and Buckingham's open disapproval of favors for his old opponents, the Ponsonbys, anticipated the reactions of others.[73]

The understandings or misunderstandings about measures will probably never be cleared up. The truth of Fitzwilliam's and Grattan's later statements on Catholic Emancipation was never denied.[74] The negotiators accepted the desirability of emancipation in the abstract, one part of the cabinet cordially and the other without objecting, according to Grattan.[75] As to tactics, Fitzwilliam agreed not only not to initiate emancipation but to try to prevent others from doing so. If, despite his efforts, the Catholics were determined to "bring it before Parliament, I was to give it a handsome support on the part of Government."[76] Before the earl left England, a foreboding event occurred in Dublin.[77] On Decem-

---

[71] *Times*, Dec. 3, 9, 10, 11, 1794.

[72] Portland MSS, Fitzwilliam to Portland, Dec. 7, 1794; J. H. Rose, *Pitt and Napoleon* (London, 1912), 28-29.

[73] H.M.C., *Dropmore Papers*, II, 653-55, Pitt to Buckingham, Dec. 20-25, 1794, Buckingham to T. Grenville, Dec. 30, 1794; P.R.O., Chatham Papers, 30/8, 117, Buckingham to Pitt, Dec. 29, 1794.

[74] Lecky, *History of Ireland*, III, 262-63.

[75] The *Times*, April 28, 1795, reporting Grattan's speech of April 21.

[76] Quoted in Lecky, *History of Ireland*, III, 262. In a footnote, Lecky quotes a statement made in parliament in 1799 to the same effect, except that instead of saying the support of "Government," Fitzwilliam said "my full support." This was essentially Grattan's version. Grattan, *Memoirs*, IV, 177. Stanhope, *Pitt*, II, 302, says that Fitzwilliam was to refer the question of emancipation to England if the Irish brought it forward. But Stanhope gives no source.

[77] *Times*, Jan. 7, 1795.

ber 24 a meeting of Roman Catholics prepared a petition for complete Catholic relief and resolved to ask Grattan to introduce it into parliament. Fitzwilliam and his princely retinue left Holyhead on January 3, sailing into stormy weather.

Of Burke's relief when the appointment of Fitzwilliam was official there can be no doubt. He was optimistic for Ireland, thinking the Catholic question as good as settled.[78] And a political rupture had been avoided. During the height of the quarrel, he had told Windham that if only a break could be avoided, if only the coalition could endure amicably for another six months, it would become an organic union.[79] That such a union meant the disappearance of the Portland party and therefore the end of the old Rockingham connection, with Pitt established as leader of the new Tory party, Burke was ready to admit. He had no regrets about this, and he hoped for a better future because of it. On December 30, Burke wrote to Windham.[80] He did not mention Ireland, perhaps because he thought its affairs were in good hands. But he had it in mind, as well as the war, when he closed with a wish for "A better year—may we have it."

For nearly a month Burke was silent about Ireland, but some exciting things were happening there.[81] Fitzwilliam arrived on January 4, went through the ceremonies of the reception and Westmorland's departure, and then, already clear about his intentions, proceeded to fulfill them. His actions, said the *Times,* belied assertions that he had accepted office without the power to surround himself with his friends. He had brought over Lord Milton (George Damer) as Chief Secretary, and appointed Burke's friend, O'Beirne, as his private secretary. Among others, he dismissed the attorney general, Arthur Wolfe, the secretary at war, Edward Cooke, and John Beresford, first commissioner of revenue and the second most important member of the Junto. These dismissals made offices available for his friends, especially the Ponsonbys, and Grattan assumed a dominating role in the

---

78 Grattan, *Memoirs,* IV, 181.
79 Burke MSS, Sheff., Oct. 16, 1794.
80 *Corr.,* IV, 251-55.
81 *St. James's Chronicle,* Jan. 8-10, 10-13, 1795; Fitzwilliam MSS, Sheff., F5, fols. 2-4, 5-7, 12-16, Jan. 6, 8, 10, 1795; Buckingham, *Courts and Cabinets,* II, 329; *Times,* Jan. 28, 1795.

House of Commons. On January 22 he moved the address in response to the Speech from the Throne and saw it carried 150 to 2. The Junto was sulking. In the meantime Fitzwilliam tried to keep back the demands for Catholic Emancipation, and with the aid of Lord Shannon he thought at first he might succeed. But as early as January 10 he began to doubt his ability to repress them, and on January 23 he had to inform Portland that the alternative to granting the Catholic demands was trouble.[82] Considering the situation on the continent and the danger of French invasion, Catholic Emancipation was preferable to tumult in Ireland, if one wished to put the matter on grounds of expediency. On January 24 Grattan presented to the Commons the first of a series of Catholic petitions praying for emancipation.[83]

Fitzwilliam's actions and, as it appeared in London, his surrender on the Catholic question, created consternation. The furor over Beresford illustrates the misunderstandings about the terms of the agreement made in London before Fitzwilliam's departure. The earl said he had "distinctly told" Pitt that Beresford must go, and Pitt had not objected.[84] Fitzwilliam reminded Portland that he had remarked to him upon Pitt's apparent acquiescence. Pitt flatly contradicted Fitzwilliam.[85] The dismissal of Beresford violated their understanding. Windham remembered that Fitzwilliam was to take no action on men and measures without first consulting Pitt.[86] Grattan and the two Ponsonbys—but no cabinet members—corroborated Fitzwilliam's view; Windham does not confirm Pitt's; and indeed, Windham's version is not credible, for Fitzwilliam would not have gone to Ireland under such a restriction.[87]

If the facts are in doubt, the consequence was clear enough. In letters of February 14 to both Portland and Pitt, Fitzwilliam demanded support from London, specifically challenging Pitt to

82 Fitzwilliam MSS, Sheff., F5, fols. 23-27, 30-33, Fitzwilliam to Portland, Jan. 23, 29, 1795.

83 *Times*, Feb. 3, 1795.

84 Fitzwilliam MSS, Sheff., F5, fols. 39-40, 58-64, Fitzwilliam to Portland, Feb. 3, 1795, Fitzwilliam to Pitt, Feb. 14, 1795; Lecky, *History of Ireland*, III, 274-75.

85 Fitzwilliam MSS, Sheff., F31e, Pitt to Fitzwilliam, Feb. 9, 1795.

86 Fitzwilliam MSS, Sheff., F31i, Windham to Fitzwilliam, March 5, 1795.

87 See the comment in the *Times*, Jan. 28, 1795, to this effect, and the *Times* of April 28 for Grattan's and Ponsonby's comments.

choose between him and Beresford.[88] By this time Pitt was in the process of choosing, if he had not already made his choice, but other things had happened to influence it.

Fortunately, the appointment to the provostship of Trinity College, vacant since the death of John Hely Hutchinson in the preceding September, was not one of them. Burke, with many others, had been worrying about jobbery in the University since the post had become vacant. He had protested Hutchinson's inappropriate appointment in 1774 because it was a political deal; like the Fellows of Trinity he feared a political appointment that would be an insult to the scholarship and integrity of Trinity College.[89] If Burke had been younger, he might himself have been appointed; even so, there were rumors that he would be.[90] But that was out of the question, and when Dr. Richard Murray was named, there was relief that a scholar instead of a politician or a clergyman received the post. The students rioted joyfully to express their approval.[91] Burke was also pleased by the elevation of O'Beirne to the bishopric of Ossory.

If only offices of state or other public matters could have been disposed of so agreeably—for example, the question of Catholic Emancipation. Fitzwilliam had not mentioned it in the Speech from the Throne, but it was already in the air when Grattan brought before the Commons the first Catholic petition. To the king, who was becoming alert to it, this was the most important of all Irish questions.[92] In the conduct of Fitzwilliam he discerned either a desire to humiliate the old friends of the government or obedience to the "heated imagination" of Burke. The connection between England and Ireland, the king said, would be less disturbed by the dismissal of Fitzwilliam than by Catholic Emancipation. And so George III suggested the ultimate resolution of the problem facing Pitt.

When the king spoke of Burke's influence, he was only talking generally, for Burke had said little about emancipation and

88 Fitzwilliam MSS, Sheff., F5, fols. 58-64, 64-65.
89 Burke MSS, N.R.O., Avi8a, Burke to Loughborough, after Oct. 3, 1794; Burke MSS, Sheff., Burke to Fitzwilliam, Oct. 21, 1794.
90 *Times*, Aug. 15, Sept. 26, 1794.
91 *St. James's Chronicle*, Feb. 5-7, 1795.
92 P.R.O., Chatham Papers, 30/8, 103, the King to Pitt, Feb. 6, 1795.

hardly anything recently. His latest opinion, given in a solicited letter to William Smith, who had circulated it in Ireland, could hardly have been known to the king when he made the statement about Burke.[93] The letter opened with an explanation. Burke's retirement from public life and his consequent ignorance, even of Fitzwilliam's plans, really disqualified him from speaking about particular measures. But he could speak more largely and could reaffirm his support of a religious establishment while denying any danger from popery. The great issue of the times, and Burke's "whole politics," was the struggle against Jacobinism, which was "at inexpiable war" with all religions. Consequently, in addition to the other things they held in common, Anglicans, Protestants, and Catholics were joined in the great cause. Under this circumstance, rather than from any principle of toleration, the Catholic in Ireland deserved to stand on an equal footing with his allies in respect to "the privileges which the fundamental laws of this country give him as a subject." And when the Catholics numbered four-fifths of the population of Ireland, the need for a political equality that could deter them from going over to Jacobinism became all the more urgent. The specific issue of eligibility for seats in parliament was by itself quite trivial, if one thought only of practical, political influence, and for that reason, the folly of opposing such a reform was even more absurd. Continued exclusion would create "jealousy and suspicion" without providing security for established Protestant institutions. The "grand controversy" no longer was between Protestants and Catholics, but between Jacobins and Christians. So, Burke favored emancipation. It is interesting to notice in this letter the absence once again of any discussion of the principle of toleration. As the storm broke around Fitzwilliam, Burke despaired, because he felt that the refusal to grant emancipation would, by dividing Ireland, encourage the growth of Jacobinism. The question of emancipation, like earlier concessions to Catholics, was entirely one of political prudence and expediency, not one of abstract rights.

The persons directly concerned with the problem considered

93 Smith's letter is in *Corr.,* IV, 260-66; Burke's reply, dated Jan. 29, 1795, is in *Works,* VI, 363-73. For the bibliographical details about it, Mahoney, *Burke and Ireland,* 393, n. 13.

it in different lights. The king opposed emancipation out of prejudice; Pitt subordinated it and the question of offices to the needs of politics; Portland, fearful of the future of the coalition, was adopting Pitt's views; and Fitzwilliam considered emancipation a means of preserving order in Ireland and the breakup of the Junto as a point of personal honor and administrative necessity. The support given him by the Ponsonbys and Grattan was already moving parliament to grant government's requests for money and expansion of the armed forces. With their support and the confidence of the English cabinet, he would be able to give Ireland a firm and popular administration even against the opposition of Beresford and "his gang." If emancipation were not granted, Fitzwilliam would be destroyed and so would the peace of Ireland and the security of the British Isles.[94]

His destruction was decided by the British cabinet even while Grattan's bill for emancipation was in their hands and Hussey was imploring Burke to urge their acceptance of it.[95] To Portland, who so handsomely had stood by Pitt, fell the unpleasant duty of announcing Fitzwilliam's recall. On February 21, the same day that Pitt was telling Fitzwilliam that the government could not give up its friends in Ireland, Portland was telling the earl that government had given up on him.[96] The severity of these blows was not mitigated by other letters that Fitzwilliam received.[97] Portland privately expressed his grief, Grenville urged him to remain in the cabinet, Spencer asked him to continue to support the government, and Carlisle, in a provoking manner, beseeched Fitzwilliam to be moderate. Fitzwilliam was the stoic. He asked for early replacement.[98]

Burke knew nothing of these cabinet details. Generally, he was aware of the dangers to Fitzwilliam and to Ireland, he feared

94 Burke MSS, Sheff., Grattan to Burke, Feb. 19, 1795. The quotation two sentences earlier is from Grattan's letter.

95 *Corr.*, IV, 277-81, Hussey to Burke, Feb. 19, 1795.

96 Fitzwilliam MSS, Sheff., F31e, Pitt to Fitzwilliam, Portland to Fitzwilliam. In this letter, Portland asked Fitzwilliam to resign, but two days later Portland wrote a letter of dismissal.

97 Fitzwilliam MSS, Sheff., F31e, Portland to Fitzwilliam, Feb. 23, 1795, a private letter; F31i, Grenville to Fitzwilliam, Feb. 23, 1795, Spencer to Fitzwilliam, Feb. 23, 1795, Carlisle to Fitzwilliam, Feb. 24, 1795.

98 Fitzwilliam MSS, Sheff., F5, fols. 80-86, 86-88, 89-91, Fitzwilliam to Portland, Feb. 25, 26, 28, 1795.

ruin from the efforts in behalf of "Jobbers," and he had some feeling of an approaching climax.[99] But he learned of the recall not sooner than six days after it had been issued. Both Hussey and Grattan wrote the news to him on February 26; on the next day, before he could have received these letters, Burke wrote to Hussey about other matters and did not mention the recall.[100] With the exception of one letter, Burke was not in correspondence with Fitzwilliam up to March 2. The only influence he had upon Fitzwilliam's administration was that stemming from associations with the earl before he left for Ireland, for between his known opinions and Fitzwilliam's preferences there is a close agreement.

When he learned of the recall, Burke wrote at once, advising Fitzwilliam to stay in Ireland as long as he was "permitted" to do so.[101] To give up on the issue of a "Jobb," even for Beresford, might be too hasty an action. And he added, "My heart is almost broken." Fitzwilliam was willing to be patient, but not blind.[102] More than "the support of such an old rotten stinking jobber as Beresford" was involved, however important were he and his family connections. Fitzwilliam could not remain in Ireland to be there when Beresford returned triumphantly from London to prove that Fitzwilliam's government had no authority. And Beresford's rejuvenated presence would ensure the defeat of Catholic Emancipation, which would have carried easily had Pitt supported it. Worse, Ireland was on the verge of revolution. If disappointment over dashed hopes is a cause of upheaval, then Fitzwilliam was correct, for not since 1782 had so clear a "national will"—not merely a Catholic ambition—existed in Ireland.[103] Hussey, remarking to Burke on the "awful gloom" hanging over Ireland, was "terrified" by the prospect of "civil war."[104] People with differing opinions about emancipation agreed upon the dangers to civil order.[105]

Strife might be prevented if the English government could be

99 Burke MSS, Sheff., Burke to Sir Gilbert Elliot, Feb. 24, 1795.
100 Burke MSS, Sheff., Grattan to Burke, Feb. 26, 1795; *Corr.*, IV, 282-83, Hussey to Burke, Feb. 26, 1795, Burke to Hussey, Feb. 27, 1795.
101 Burke MSS, Sheff., Burke to Fitzwilliam, March 2, 1795.
102 Burke MSS, Sheff., Fitzwilliam to Burke, March 4, 1795.
103 Lecky, *History of Ireland*, III, 285, 298-99.
104 *Corr.*, IV, 282-83, Feb. 26, 1795.
105 Lecky, *History of Ireland*, III, 312-14.

persuaded to accede to popular wishes in Ireland. From all sides came expressions of confidence in Fitzwilliam; the Catholics in Dublin drew up a loyal address and sent it to the king by a delegation of three men.[106] They were received graciously by Portland, who presented them to the king. All this was unavailing. The king would only communicate through the lord lieutenant, and ministers would not be persuaded that the Junto's emissaries were misinforming them about conditions in Ireland.

Burke did not at once surrender hope, partly because he was not fully informed. He went to London and sought out ministers, even giving a "great Breakfast" at Nerot's Hotel for certain members of administration.[107] The *Times* wished success to Burke's efforts at reconciliation.[108] Only after "a great deal of useless discourse" did he realize that prospects for emancipation were ended, as was Fitzwilliam's administration.[109] "I can do no more," he told Hussey. If Windham was one of the ministers with whom he talked, the futility of Burke's efforts becomes clear. Windham charged that Fitzwilliam's actions in removing Beresford, promoting the Ponsonbys, and acquiescing in emancipation without permission from London were "in direct opposition to, what I had understood to have been agreed upon, either directly or by implication, in the conversation . . . in Downing Street" just before Fitzwilliam's departure for Ireland.[110] Thus, the differences about the terms under which Fitzwilliam went to Ireland continued to exacerbate the relations among the parties to the agreement. Grattan virtually accused Portland of treachery for abandoning Fitzwilliam after having promised, with Pitt's knowledge, to secure Beresford's dismissal.[111]

These were in the nature of postmortems, for on March 9 Fitzwilliam received his mandate to return to England.[112] Ironically, it arrived on the packet that returned the triumphant Beresford from his successful mission to London. Beresford quickly demonstrated his return to power. He moved into a

106 *Times*, March 5, 1795; also March 7, 10, 11, 12, April 12, 1795.
107 *St. James's Chronicle*, March 3-5, 1795.
108 March 5, 1795.
109 *Corr.*, IV, 289-91, Burke to Hussey, March 5, 1795.
110 Br. Mus., Add. MSS 37,875, fol. 5, Windham to Fitzwilliam, March 5, 1795.
111 Burke MSS, Sheff., Grattan to Burke, March 11, 1795.
112 Burke MSS, Sheff., Fitzwilliam to Burke, March 9, 1795.

renovated suite in the New Customhouse even before Fitzwilliam left Ireland, and one of his sons appeared as a contractor for an Irish loan. Burke, having recovered from the initial shock and despair, was ready to offer his judgment upon the event.[113] He sympathized with Portland's agony, but he blamed him nevertheless for failing to consult his friends, including Burke, and for surrendering so completely to Pitt. For the future, he hoped Fitzwilliam's friends would support him. "How," he asked Devonshire, "can you aristocrats exist if you are not true to one another?" Burke really begged his own question when he admitted that the alternatives were condemnation of Fitzwilliam or abandonment of Portland.

In fact, Fitzwilliam was forcing the choice upon his friends. Irritated by their mild admonitions, especially Carlisle's, whose version of the London conference differed from his own memory of it, and angered by what he considered calumnious and misinformed talk, he decided to present his side of the story. Before he left Ireland, he wrote two letters to Lord Carlisle, who wrote one in reply, and all somehow soon got into print.[114] Though Burke doubted the propriety of the letters, he admired them. They add nothing to the information derived from the private correspondence, but to contemporaries, who of course had not read the correspondence, they were most interesting. Fitzwilliam made two major points. The Catholic question was not the cause of his recall, and this contention he based upon the chronology of the official correspondence. For three weeks after he had informed the British cabinet that emancipation could not be deferred, he heard nothing from them, and took silence to mean consent. Portland referred to the subject first in a letter of February 8. Before Fitzwilliam could have received Portland's letter of February 18, asking for more information on the subject,

113 Burke MSS, Sheff., Burke to Devonshire, March 11, 1795, Burke to Fitzwilliam, March 14, 1795, Burke to Grattan, March 20, 1795.

114 *A Letter from Earl Fitzwilliam . . . to the Earl of Carlisle* (2d ed., London, 1795); *A Letter from a Venerated Nobleman . . . to the Earl of Carlisle* (London, 1795); *A Letter from the Earl of Carlisle to Earl Fitzwilliam . . .* (London, 1795). Fitzwilliam's letters were published first in Dublin. The *Times* of April 2 mentioned Fitzwilliam's distribution of copies among his friends in Dublin and expected their early printing. Also the *Times*, April 6, 7, 11, 21, May 1, for other notices and extracts.

the cabinet had decided to recall him.[115] The dismissal of Beresford was the "grand question," but it was only an excuse.[116] The truth was that Pitt had been insincere in forming the coalition. Fitzwilliam was more blunt on this point in a letter to Burke written while he was preparing his second letter to Carlisle.[117] Pitt, he said, had no intention of keeping faith with the Portland ministers. He had not desired to see Fitzwilliam replace Westmorland but later decided to get rid of Fitzwilliam by sending him to Ireland as a preliminary to dispensing with him altogether. Secondly, Fitzwilliam reaffirmed that his conduct in Ireland was "in perfect conformity" with the agreement made in London before his departure.

If there is no way of determining who was correct about that, Fitzwilliam's assertions about Beresford, the other dismissals, and the Catholic question are persuasive, though in neglecting the king's influence they omit the strongest reason for stressing the question of emancipation. Carlisle's reply was weak, except for his contradictory version of the London conversation. To say that because members of the Junto had not offended against him, Fitzwilliam had no reason for dismissing them, was not only politically foolish but a vacuous idealization of the situation in Ireland. To say that Fitzwilliam violated confidences when he referred to private correspondence was to deny him the means of self-defense. The conflicting judgments about Pitt's insincerity in forming the coalition cannot be proved either way, though Fitzwilliam's opinion is difficult to accept unless one is ready to make a devil of Pitt. Certainly Pitt was neglectful, as was Fitzwilliam, in not clarifying the London agreement by casting it in writing, however unbecoming this might have seemed for gentlemen. In consequence, confusion was unavoidable and so was the necessity of a choice between Beresford and Fitzwilliam. Pitt made his choice, and in the light of later events, it can only be said that it was a bad one.

[115] For a detailed analysis of the chronology, justifying Fitzwilliam, see Mahoney, *Burke and Ireland*, 396-97, n. 78. Mahoney supports Lecky, *History of Ireland*, III, 287-89, 298-300, and refutes Rose, *Pitt and Napoleon*, 31.

[116] When George Ponsonby said that emancipation was only an excuse for recalling Fitzwilliam, he corroborated the first part of this statement. *Times*, April 28, 1795.

[117] Burke MSS, Sheff., Fitzwilliam to Burke, March 21, 1795.

In all of this Burke was on Fitzwilliam's side. He was ready to charge Pitt with desiring to get Fitzwilliam out of the administration in order to remove an opponent of the projected peace negotiations with France.[118] But the act had been performed, and for the future there was the question of Fitzwilliam's conduct to consider. By the end of March, when he left a Dublin draped in mourning, he and Burke had agreed on strategy. The earl would present to the king a short statement that, in making the injury appear as a wrong to the public, would prepare the way for a detailed memorial justifying his conduct in Ireland.[119] While Fitzwilliam delayed his arrival in London on account of his son's illness, Burke was busy with the memorial.[120] By mid-April he had prepared a draft for Fitzwilliam's scrutiny. He was not answering a charge but was making one, which would place Fitzwilliam's enemies on the defensive.

The politicians and the press were still discussing his affairs when the earl arrived in London. In the House of Commons on March 24, Fox, in a debate on the state of the nation, had championed Fitzwilliam, and Pitt, vaguely defending himself, showed embarrassment and reluctance to talk. Six days later in the Lords, Grenville advised against exacerbating Ireland further by discussing the Fitzwilliam episode. The minority did not intend to permit ministers to avoid the subject. Nor did Fitzwilliam or Burke intend to remain silent. The earl's presence in London encouraged ministerial opponents to renew their attacks. On April 15 Fitzwilliam met the king, was received graciously, told his story, and left a paper for George to peruse.[121] It did not impress him.[122] Of his old friends, only Windham seemed to know Fitzwilliam; Portland, when they met, bowed coldly.[123] After Fitzwilliam took his seat in the Lords, wrangles occurred as ministers tried unsuccessfully to prevent discussion.[124] Portland was so wrought up that he became ill; the debate that ministers

118 Burke MSS, Sheff., Burke to Fitzwilliam, received March 22, 1795.

119 Burke MSS, Sheff., Burke to Fitzwilliam, received March 22, 1795; Fitzwilliam MSS, Sheff., F31f, Fitzwilliam to Burke, March 20, 1795, Burke to Fitzwilliam, April 11, 1795.

120 Burke MSS, Sheff., Fitzwilliam to Burke, April 3, 1795.

121 Fitzwilliam MSS, Sheff., F5, fols. 122-32, Fitzwilliam to Grattan, April 25, 1795.

122 Mahoney, *Burke and Ireland*, 265.

123 Fitzwilliam MSS, Sheff., F5, fols. 122-32, Fitzwilliam to Grattan, April 25, 1795.

124 *St. James's Chronicle*, April 23-25, 28-30, April 30—May 2, 1795.

could not prevent was postponed until he could be present.[125] In the Commons, where Joseph Jekyll had threatened a motion for May 1, strangers were excluded from the gallery on that day. In the Irish House of Commons, where Grattan and the Ponsonbys had been trying to bring the subject forward, the new administration of Lord Camden kept control, defeating 155-48 Grattan's demand for an inquiry.[126]

The full-dress debate in the Lords came on May 8, when, with Portland at last present, the Duke of Norfolk moved an address to the king asking for the correspondence on the Fitzwilliam mission. Though Norfolk's speech was an attack upon the administration, his account of the background of the Irish mission censured Burke. Burke's *Reflections* and Paine's reply to it had done "infinite mischief" in creating the panic that led to the coalition of 1794. Of those who formed it, the Portland party had acted from pure but "mistaken principles," whereas Pitt had been guided by cynical motives. The known opinions of the Portland ministers made it unlikely that they would enter a coalition unless changes were contemplated for Ireland. Therefore, it was impossible to believe that Fitzwilliam had contravened an agreement about Ireland, and it was necessary to hold Pitt responsible for the misunderstandings and calamities that ensued. In order to learn the facts, Norfolk moved for the papers. To the assertion that these papers would reveal cabinet secrets, Fitzwilliam replied. The facts involved were already known. What was needed was knowledge of the motives that had produced his recall and challenged his honor. Those who defended Pitt based their case on the prerogative. The recall had been an exercise of prerogative power and ought not be inquired into, especially as no charges had been levied against Fitzwilliam. The issue then became the prerogative versus justice to a man who said he had been injured, or constitutional propriety against equity. The ministerial side was on secure but hypocritical ground, and it also had the votes to defeat the motion 100-25. The best Fitzwilliam could do was enter a protest on the Journals.[127]

125 *Times*, April 30, 1795. This discussion occurred on April 24, the day on which the Lords gave their verdict on the Hastings impeachment.
126 *St. James's Chronicle*, April 25-28, May 9-12, 1795; *Times*, April 28, 1795.
127 *Parl. Hist.*, XXXI, 1521-1530.

The House of Commons on May 19 entertained a similar motion. Lord Milton categorically asserted that Fitzwilliam had followed procedures agreed upon by the British cabinet before he left England, and reminded members once again of the cabinet's long silence on the Catholic question. No one refuted him, but the motion was defeated by a four to one majority. A fortnight earlier the Irish Commons had rejected Grattan's emancipation bill after an eighteen-hour debate. The Junto was in control again.

These debates ended the episode, though it was mentioned in parliament subsequently and though in June Fitzwilliam and Beresford met on the dueling grounds. Stopped by a peace officer before they could fire their pistols, they accepted one another's explanations of the point at issue and shook hands.[128]

Burke was satisfied with Fitzwilliam's conduct and with the parliamentary efforts of his supporters. Of course, in his view, they had the best of the argument. He had long been familiar with the kind of parliamentary situation in which the numerical majority had the weaker case, morally. This was small compensation for the tragedy in Ireland. "My sanguine hopes are blasted," Burke told Sir Hercules Langrishe.[129] He had learned to endure defeats in the "other great, just, and honorable causes" in which he had labored (for example, the recent acquittal of Hastings), but in Ireland the margin had been so close, the times and circumstances had been so propitious for the settlement of the political and the Catholic questions, the benefits that settlement promised were so great, and now the evils that would follow upon the failure so obvious and so imminent that patience in this disappointment would be difficult to achieve. The thing to be feared was the encouragement that Jacobinism would derive from the "ill-humours" in Ireland. For men must not forget that Jacobinism, as it affected Europe and the "state of human society itself," was still the "greatest evil."

[128] Burke MSS, N.R.O., Avi26, Portland to Burke, June 28, 1795.
[129] "Second Letter to Sir Hercules Langrishe on the Catholic Question," *Works*, VI, 377-84, May 26, 1795.

CHAPTER XIX

The World from Beaconsfield

THE LAST TWO YEARS of Burke's life lacked the rhythm of the annual sessions of parliament, which from autumn to early summer since 1765 had given purpose to the other months of each year and regulated even his nonpolitical activities. Free from the domination of the parliamentary calendar and the demands of party, he was not free from the burden that public affairs imposed upon his mind and heart. When, no longer a member of parliament, he retired to his home near the village of Beaconsfield in the summer of 1794, he may have withdrawn from formal participation in public affairs, but he did not fall into oblivion. He remained a prominent person, though a private one. His opinions were sometimes solicited, at other times provoked, as by the Duke of Bedford, and always he felt an obligation to express himself, especially upon the problems of Ireland and the war. The rural quietude of Beaconsfield was not isolation. Burke felt the oppression of events as much as if he had been in Westminster—perhaps more, because he had leisure to ruminate upon them. His letters and formal publications, the expressions of an ill and despairing man, were listened to. After thirty years, the public was too much in the habit of attending to Burke's reflections on the state of the nation; it could not suddenly cease.

In lesser matters too, the public continued to think of him as a man of influence. In retirement his reputation for charity remained undimmed. Kinsmen, friends, and strangers sought his assistance. He willingly gave it when he could, often successfully applying to friends in office for favors and appointments to his suppliants and at other times acting himself, when it was in his power to do so.[1] His readiness and his success in fact multiplied his problems. He complained that he sank "under the weight" of the numerous applications for help.[2] But he did not try to evade them. His generosity added to his burdens. At Gregories, where he had always kept a kind of open house, providing during the French Revolution for numerous émigrés, he now had a crowd of dependents, a train, Gilbert Elliot once said, that would sink anybody else.[3] In the fall of 1795, Burke's home was a veritable "hospital."[4] "Patients" in residence were his niece, Mary French Haviland, who had resided there for three years and had just become a mother and a widow, his brother-in-law's wife, Mrs. Jack Nugent, who was ill, Will Burke, who was also ill, and a Mrs. Burke, the wife of a kinsman.

On this count alone, Burke demeaned himself when "in the silent gloom" of his "forlorn situation," he spoke of dragging on his "degraded & apparently useless existence."[5] It was in fact a very useful existence, not only to his personal dependents but to the public. The idea might be a fitting theme for the last chapter of Burke's life—how, as a private man, he continued to try to serve the public good and to enlarge justice.

Dr. Thomas Hussey attributed to Burke the inspiration for the founding in the preceding year of the College of St. Patrick, the seminary at Maynooth for the education of Irish Catholics for the priesthood.[6] This remark was probably more accurate than Hussey's additional comment that in working with Portland and Lord Camden for its establishment, he was only acting under Burke's

---

1 Examples may be found in the following: Burke MSS, Sheff., Burke to Fitzwilliam, Feb. 11, 1795, Patrick Kennedy to Burke, March 11, 1797; Br. Mus., Add. MSS 12,099, fols. 13-14, Burke to Portland, Nov. 25, 1794; *Burke-Windham Corr.*, 120, 144, 166-67, Sept. 28, Dec. 22, 1794, Sept. 4, 1795; Portland MSS, Burke to Portland, July 1, 1795; P.R.O., Chatham Papers, 30/8, 364, Second Earl of Chatham to Burke, Dec. 21, 1794; Osborn Coll., Box 96, #77, Lord Chatham to Burke, Dec. 20, 1794; Burke MSS, N.R.O., Avi30, Burke to Dr. Brocklesby, Aug. 3, 1795.

2 For the quotation, Burke MSS, Sheff., Burke to [?], dated 1796.

3 Minto, *Elliot*, II, 136-37, May 2, 1793.

4 Burke MSS, N.R.O., Avi34, Burke to the Abbé de la Bintinnaye, Sept. 3, 1795.

5 Burke MSS, Sheff., Burke to Fitzwilliam, Feb. 10, 1795.

6 Burke MSS, Sheff., Hussey to Burke, July 14, 1796.

direction. In 1782 Burke had written Lord Kenmare urging the need for, and the justice of providing, clerical education in an exclusively Catholic institution.[7] The letter, when published in Dublin in 1791, revived the idea, and it was still being discussed in Ireland when Burke urged it upon Grattan in the fall of 1794.[8] A new reason justified it now. The Revolution had driven Irish seminarians from France. The education of priests in Ireland was imperative for the needs of religion and for the struggle against Jacobinism. Grattan agreed with Burke, happier for finding him retaining "the power of being eminently useful."[9] Fitzwilliam sanctioned the idea, if not a specific project, in his Speech from the Throne, and Dr. Hussey assembled Catholic bishops in Dublin to promote it. Upon Fitzwilliam's recall, Burke feared for the project. He had advised Hussey to return to England, but Portland requested Hussey to continue his work for the institution.[10] He therefore stayed on. In April the Irish parliament passed the law authorizing the seminary and appropriated £8,000 to begin it. If Burke's promotion of the institution was helpful, his advice on details was neither entirely practicable nor wise. For example, it was necessary to accept three judges and the lord chancellor as members of the Board of Trustees, though Burke opposed such an intrusion by the Protestant Ascendancy. His strongly expressed opinions, which became known to the Irish government, proved to Edward Cooke that Burke, "the chief, if not sole, mover of all the measures with respect to the Irish Catholics," secretly desired to establish a popish influence in Ireland.[11]

Despite his reservations, Burke had to wish the college well, and he sent a gift of books in the name of his son, Hussey's "late dear friend."[12] Occasionally thereafter, Hussey consulted him

[7] "A Letter to a Peer of Ireland on the Penal Laws against Irish Catholics," *Works,* IV, 219-39.

[8] Grattan, *Memoirs,* IV, 155.

[9] *Corr.,* IV, 244-46, Oct. 1, 1794.

[10] *Corr.,* IV, 292, 296-98, Hussey to Burke, March 10, 1795, Burke to Hussey, March 17, 1795.

[11] *Corr.,* IV, 295-306, Burke to Hussey, March 17, 1795; Lecky, *History of Ireland,* III, 366-67, including the quotation from a letter of Burke.

[12] Br. Mus., Add. MSS 33,101, fol. 191, Burke to Hussey, June 9, 1795; Burke MSS, Sheff., John Thomas Troy (Archbishop of Dublin) to Burke, July 13, 1795, expressing the thanks of the trustees.

about the affairs of the college, and Burke offered advice.[13] He wanted to be sure that money was spent for the proper things, food, clothing, and above all, good instruction. But he took a narrow view that was, as Lecky says, sacerdotal. His preference for an exclusively Catholic institution, like that of the statute establishing Maynooth, by its protectiveness may have helped to diminish the confidence between denominations that had grown so much in the preceding decade.[14]

The middle 1790's were years of stress for Burke and strain for England in many ways, and even when hardships did not personally affect him, Burke was concerned about them. One that disturbed England in 1795 was called "scarcity" by contemporaries —a compound of bad harvests, wartime exigencies, rising prices, declining real wages, and acute physical distress among certain groups and in various areas of the country. In an uncertain way, men saw a relationship between economic adversities and political discontents; the stoning of the king's carriage to and from the opening of parliament on October 29 was accompanied by cries of "Bread," "Peace," "No Famine," and "No War." Although the government responded to disorders by passing the severely restrictive Seditious Meetings and Treasonable Practices acts, it also took account of the bad economic conditions that in part stimulated the disturbances these acts were aimed against. The King's Speech noticed the scarcity; on November 3 the House of Commons named a select committee to inquire into the high prices of corn. Later, Samuel Whitbread offered a bill to empower justices of the peace to fix minimum wages for agricultural laborers. Generally, the Commons admitted that it was undesirable for government to interfere with "the unassisted operation of principles," as Pitt expressed it; even those who favored the bill did so as a concession to urgency rather than as a matter of policy.[15]

When Burke entered the discussion by addressing to Pitt a paper on the subject, he took a position not much at variance with the consensus of the House.[16] Though Pitt acknowledged in-

---

[13] *Corr.,* IV, 328, Burke to Hussey, Nov. 28, 1795; Burke MSS, Sheff., Hussey to Burke, Jan. 21, 1796.

[14] Lecky, *History of Ireland,* III, 361-65.

[15] *Parl. Hist.,* XXXII, 700-715, Dec. 9, 1795, Feb. 12, 1796.

[16] "Thoughts and Details on Scarcity," *Works,* V, 133-69, Nov., 1795.

debtedness to his readings on economic matters, Burke's paper doubtless among them, it would be impossible to attribute to his influence any noticeable impact upon Pitt's thought. Burke's views were neither unusual nor deserving of special attention as a contribution to economic thought. Fox, for example, told the House of Commons that wages ought to be determined by the humanity of employers rather than by compulsory measures. Concerning the foreign trade and international relations of normal times, Burke adhered to the traditional protectionist and balance of power policies. Concerning the domestic economy, he opposed governmental interference with the "operation of principle"; that is, he upheld supply and demand as the law governing the sale of commodities and labor. When the laborer was incapable of offering his services in the market, Burke recommended private charity. If his views embodied a mixture of mercantilism, *laissez faire,* and rural paternalism, then so far was Burke from nineteenth-century Cobdenism, and so much was he in agreement with the settled views of his own age.

Attempts to connect Burke with the teachings of Adam Smith are quite unnecessary, and in fact obscure the social emphasis of Burke's thought. When in 1772 Burke had himself moved the repeal of statutes against forestalling and regrating, and in 1787 had opposed an unsuccessful effort to revive an old act against forestalling, and in 1795 when he began his "Thoughts" by saying, "Of all things, an indiscreet tampering with the trade of provisions is the most dangerous," he expressed views that were in harmony with the spirit of the age, as the actions of the House of Commons demonstrated. His views were coincidentally and superficially in agreement with Smith's because his also were "thoroughly in sympathy with the humors of his time."[17] If self-interest harmonized with the public interest in economic matters, then the *Daily Universal Register* was merely malicious when it

17 Betham-Edwards, ed., *Autobiography of Young,* 302-13, Burke to Young, May 23, 1797; *Daily Universal Register,* May 17, 25, 1787; *Works,* V, 133; *Parl. Hist.,* XXVI, 1769, May 16, 1787. The last quotation concerning Smith is taken from A. W. Coats, "Adam Smith: The Modern Reappraisal," *Renaissance and Modern Studies,* VI (1962), 28, quoting Joseph Schumpeter, *History of Economic Analysis.* Coats goes on to say, 29, that Smith "synthesized the ideas of his predecessors and his contemporaries,"

asked whether Burke opposed restrictions upon forestalling for fear that "the lean produce of his own farm should be forced into Smithfield." Burke's statement of the doctrine of natural identity of interests reads like Smith's, but has different implications. Where Smith spoke of the influence of the "invisible hand," Burke described the identification as a divinely ordered obligation upon men, "in pursuing their own selfish interests, to connect the general good with their own individual success."[18] Burke's concept of the general good contains a conscious social purpose which is central rather than coincidental. Burke made the achievement of identity between private and public interests a social responsibility, whereas Smith, as an individualist, thought of identity as something that would occur in an impersonal, automatic fashion. For both men, however, private judgments would be more efficacious than governmental fiat.

Burke's "Thoughts" was a social commentary concerned with domestic problems rather than an economic tract. He ignored the plight of the increasingly numerous manufacturing laborers.[19] His concern, natural for a landed gentleman, was exclusively with the problems of the farmer and the agricultural laborer. Their economic relationships and obligations, as employer and worker or superior and inferior, were part of the providential order, to be governed by natural laws rather than artificial interferences. Supply and demand and the operation of the market place regulated wages and prices; "an overdoing of any sort of administration" was "meddling with the subsistence of the people." The laboring people would always be poor "because they are numerous." Burke did not mean that the condition of "the animal man" could not improve. It had in England in his time, and it could continue to improve. But how and when was not for government to determine. Though he did not entertain an idea of an iron law of wages, Burke's economic doctrine approached fatalism. He did not think of himself as professing a dismal science. He merely accepted what he considered to be the natural order of things.

18 *Works*, V, 141.
19 In this respect, too, Burke was like Smith, who, says Coats in *Renaissance and Modern Studies*, VI, 37, "was unaware of the incipient industrial revolution" and, 39, was "essentially a pre-industrial economist."

He escaped materialistic determinism by returning to his doctrine of providence and by insisting that freedom of choice, when made in a moral context, ought to have in view the general good.

Intended only for Pitt, the "Thoughts" somehow became known to other persons. Sir John Sinclair, President of the Board of Agriculture, encouraged Burke to publish it and sent Burke some of the board's publications with Arthur Young, who visited Burke in May, 1796.[20] Burke had no intention of publishing it. In his conversations with Young, he repeated his dislike of government regulation of wages and prices and spoke of the "mischief of our Poor-Laws," which the justices of neighboring Berkshire had recently converted into a system of indirect wage support. Burke seems this early to have understood the effect of a change that, by 1833, became generally a system of supplementing wages out of the rates. Had he lived in the age when Benthamite doctrines were at their highest influence, Burke undoubtedly would have supported the Poor Law Amendment of 1834, unless, that is, his humanitarian feelings had overridden his economic views.

For, despite the apparent harshness of his "Thoughts," there was in his social philosophy a large place reserved for the virtue of charity. Because Burke placed strict limitations upon the responsibilities of the state, he left the more room for private relief of the poor and the distressed.

Distress often arose from poverty, but poverty might result from various causes. Thus, the French Revolution brought distress to many people, and Burke did his best to relieve it. One such effort was a project for educating the children of émigré nobles. It originated in protest against a government plan for moving some of the French clergy from Winchester, where they were comfortably situated, to the former Haviland residence at Penn.[21] This house, only three miles from Beaconsfield, was in the custody of the Barracks Office. Burke thought it unfit for the assigned purpose. Out of his concern in the winter of 1795-1796 grew an idea for a different use of the house. He discussed it with Mrs.

[20] Burke MSS, Sheff., Sinclair to Burke, April 25, 1796; Betham-Edwards, ed., *Autobiography of Young*, 256-58.
[21] Prior, *Burke* (3d ed.), 499; Buckingham, *Courts and Cabinets*, II, 341; Portland MSS, Burke to Portland, Sept. 15, 1795; P.R.O., Chatham Papers, 30/8, 118, Burke to John King, Sept. 17, 1795; *Burke-Windham Corr.*, 167-68, 170, Burke to Windham, Sept. 15, 1795, Burke to Portland, Oct. 3, 1795.

Crewe, who was at Gregories for an early spring visit.[22] She gained the willing support of the Marquis of Buckingham and delivered to him the plan of the project that he sent on to Pitt.[23]

Burke summarized it as "the attempt of a private person, more full of zeal, than of means, to serve the meritorious French."[24] He envisaged a school in the Haviland house to accommodate sixty boys and their tutors. A board of trustees would govern it, the Committee of French Emigrants would pay over out of allowances the guinea a month that each emigrant child received, an émigré committee would select the boys and decide upon the curriculum, and "a gentleman in the neighborhood," namely Burke, would be not only a trustee but the "agent and steward" of the trustees and the émigré committee. The government would pay £50 per month for its upkeep and £1,000 for furnishing the house. In return, Burke engaged "that these boys shall be well fed, lodged, clothed and instructed" in military science as well as in civilian subjects, so that if restored to their country, they would be ready to take places of leadership. At the very least, the boys would be saved from growing up in "bad society" or being "trained to Botany Bay or the gallows."

The project sounded simple enough, but petty difficulties arose. Burke found that "with all these dukes, marquises, cabinet-ministers, secretaries of state, and secretaries at war, cast-off lord lieutenants of Ireland and their secretaries . . . with the aid, too, of all the lady-marchionesses and lady-knights of the shire" such trifles as the fifty pounds a month seemed insurmountable obstacles.[25] Before he could decide about "Burke's school," Pitt had to consult with Grenville and Portland; after two weeks he was able to tell Buckingham that the payments of money could be arranged for.[26] Buckingham prodded Pitt, urging the school as a humanitarian act for Burke's own benefit and, facetiously, as a means of keeping his mind occupied before he published his

22 *Corr.*, IV, 331-36, Burke to Mrs. Crewe, Feb. 26, March 3, 1796.

23 *Corr.*, IV, 337-41, Buckingham to Pitt, March 10, 1796, and enclosure of Burke's plan. This letter in MS, P.R.O., Chatham Papers, 30/8, 117, is dated March 11, 1796.

24 Burke MSS, Sheff., B10d, a MS describing the project. Also Osborn Coll., Box 74, #8, Burke to Lady Buckingham, Nov. 23, 1796.

25 *Corr.*, IV, 334, Burke to Mrs. Crewe, March 3, 1796; Osborn Coll., Box 88, #40, Burke to [Mrs. Crewe], March 18, 1796.

26 Burke MSS, Sheff., Pitt to Buckingham, March 11, 24, 1796.

intended attack upon the government's efforts to make peace with France.[27] If too slowly to satisfy Burke, the wheels of government turned. By the end of March the house at Penn was available, and Burke was buying supplies for the school.[28]

Other difficulties appeared. It was not always possible to honor requests for admission—for example, when the boy was a Protestant, or even when he was sponsored by people as important as Lady Jane Douglas.[29] Indeed, Burke found to his embarrassment that the admissions were decided in a manner quite unlike his original plans.[30] He complained when selections were made without his knowledge. "The poorest country school-master would have been favoured with some better account of his pupils." It turned out that Buckingham was making selections. The marquis was conciliatory and assured Burke that the final voice was his. This was important because Burke felt that the Bishop de St. Pol had been interfering with selections to serve his own purposes, honorable though they might be. Burke found it necessary to impose some of his ideas about curriculum upon the recalcitrant priest in charge of instruction, the Abbé Jean-Marin Maraine.[31] The abbé favored a purely French education under his full control; Burke, as a kind of "guardian" of the boys' interests, insisted upon some admixture of English and of English methods of instruction. He would not permit the school to be run like a seminary of monks, as the bishop desired, nor would he let the boys be foreigners in England.[32] He and the bishop disputed about tutors. Two sent by the bishop were incompetent, and when Burke proposed another, the bishop objected. He meant well, but he was not easy to get along with; Burke regretted having permitted him a voice in choosing masters.

[27] P.R.O., Chatham Papers, 30/8, 117, March 22, 1796. Buckingham referred to Burke's letters on the regicide peace, the first of which was published during the autumn.

[28] Burke MSS, N.R.O., Aviil3, order from the Barracks Office, March 29, 1796, and Aix19, inventory of goods.

[29] *Corr.*, IV, 354, Burke to Mrs. Crewe, Nov. 8, 1796; Osborn Coll., Box 88, #40, Burke to Walker King, Jan. 25, May 16, 1797.

[30] Buckingham, *Courts and Cabinets*, II, 345, Burke to Buckingham, May 24, 1796; Burke MSS, N.R.O., Avi43a, May 26 and 29, 1796; Burke MSS, Sheff., Buckingham to Burke, June 12, 1796.

[31] Burke MSS, N.R.O., Avi42a, Burke to Maraine, May 2, 1796.

[32] Burke MSS, Sheff., Burke to Hussey, May 25, 1796; Osborn Coll., Box 74, #35, Burke to Laurence, [summer], 1796.

Buckingham upheld Burke, informing him and the bishop that Burke had final authority, with the French committee only an advisory group.[33] Even Mrs. Crewe became a nuisance.[34] "Too fond of business," she was trying to take over the school, said Burke. He would have preferred that she withhold financial support if she did not approve of his plans. He assumed the unpleasant task of writing frankly to her. Apparently his letter had more effect than he expected, for there is no evidence of further trouble between them. The Treasury added to Burke's troubles by its delays in repaying monies he had advanced.[35]

Despite these difficulties, Burke was pleased with the school. The twenty-five boys and three tutors who took up residence in May, 1796, found decent accommodations and wholesome food. The boys were dressed neatly in blue uniforms with white cockades inscribed "Vive le Roi." Burke saw them nearly every day; he felt sure "that if they are left to me for six months, a set of finer lads, for their age and standing, will not be seen in Europe."[36]

The school remained a monument to Burke's vision and charity. As a trustee for the government, he continued to supervise it as long as he lived, or rather, as long as his health permitted. In his will he commended the school and the boys who attended it to the care of the surviving trustees.[37] Supported out of the British Treasury until the restoration of the monarchy in France, and afterward by the French government, the school functioned until August 1, 1820.

Hovering over all of these events was the shadow of a war that had become for Britain a succession of defeats and for Burke

33 Osborn Coll., Box 88, #40, Burke to Walker King, [summer], 1796; Burke MSS, N.R.O., Avi43a, Buckingham to Burke, May 26 and 29, 1796.

34 Osborn Coll., Box 88, #40, Burke to Walker King, [early summer], 1796.

35 Burke MSS, N.R.O., Avi50, Charles Long to Burke, July 8, 1796, Avi45, Burke to Walker King, July 26, 1796; Osborn Coll., Box 88, #40, Burke to King [?], June 4, 1796.

36 Buckingham, *Courts and Cabinets*, II, 343, Burke to Buckingham, May 24, 1796.

37 MS copy of will in Morgan Library, codicil, Jan. 30, 1797. The codicil of the copy in Somerset House (Exeter 477) is dated Jan. 29, 1797. The codicil is in fact a new will rephrasing in legal language the literary document Burke had composed as his will in 1794. Though one folio page thus replaced three, the codicil contains not only the new clause concerning Penn School but also a clause making clear that Richard, Jr.'s, property, of which Burke had become possessed, was to go to Mrs. Burke along with all of her husband's.

a continuous disillusionment. The downfall of Robespierre and the end of the Terror in the summer of 1794 did not, as Mallet du Pan said, inaugurate the counterrevolution that Burke and the émigrés desired.[38] There would be no restoration of monarchy, and the war would continue as the French armies pressed their attacks along the frontiers. Besides losses in the Low Countries, Britain suffered other blows—peace between France and three of Britain's former allies, Prussia, Holland, and Spain, reverses in the West Indian campaign, and in the summer of 1795 a miserable failure in an invasion of La Vendée by British and émigré forces.[39] Yet Britain had protected and advanced her commercial and colonial interests. In the autumn of 1795 the King's Speech announced that she was prepared to balance off accounts and to negotiate with France "for a general peace on just and equitable terms." About this there were differences within the cabinet. Portland and Windham were not congenial to the idea of giving up the cause of the monarchy, nor was George III. When Grenville went along with Pitt in thinking that recent changes within France gave hope of successful negotiations, the king acquiesced reluctantly. There followed three unsuccessful efforts during the last eighteen months of Burke's life, one in the spring of 1796 conducted by William Wickham at Berne, another in Paris by Malmesbury late in the year, and the third in the summer of 1797 at Lille, where Malmesbury was when Burke died.

Burke was unhappy and displeased with the conduct of the war and infuriated at the idea of peace with regicide France. He expressed his views bitterly in a series of "Letters to a Member of Parliament on the Proposals for Peace with the Regicide Directory of France."[40] Of the letters, the "Fourth" was not

[38] H.M.C., *Dropmore Papers*, II, 616, Mallet du Pan to the Earl of Elgin, Aug. 3, 1794.

[39] Burke hoped for much from this expedition. If it failed, prospects would be black indeed. Burke seemed to anticipate failure; at least, he had little faith in the leadership of Count Joseph de Puisaye, and said that to Windham. Osborn Coll., Box 2, #1, Burke to William Elliot, June 21, 1795.

[40] *Works*, V, 233-508, for the letters numbered "First," "Second," and "Third," and VI, 9-112, for the so-called "Fourth," which is the only one to name Earl Fitzwilliam as the member of parliament to whom they were addressed. See also *Works*, VI, 3-7, and *Journal and Correspondence of Lord Auckland*, III, 317-19, 320, for letters between Burke and Auckland, and P.R.O., Chatham Papers, 30/8, 118, Burke to Pitt, Oct. 28, 1795.

published until 1812, though it was the first to be written. In October, 1795, in a pamphlet, Lord Auckland suggested peace with France. Burke reacted with a letter of December-January, 1795-1796 to Fitzwilliam. The formality of its style corroborates other evidence that Burke wrote it with publication in mind, though he also desired privately to encourage Fitzwilliam in the House of Lords to oppose the peace negotiations. By mid-January, 1796, Burke was far advanced with this letter and was planning another, telling Fitzwilliam that the first would not be sufficient for his purposes.[41] What he was working on in March seems to have been still this letter.[42] The reason for cessation of the printing, which had begun, and of the writing is not revealed in Burke's correspondence. Possibly the march of events and the beginnings of negotiations in Switzerland dated it, and so, despite the desire of friends to see it published, and Stockdale's offer of £1,000 for it, he discarded it and began another, the one that became the "First" letter, discussing the actual negotiations. After this he wrote a "Second" letter, and both appeared in October, 1796. A "Third" was published posthumously in November, 1797.[43]

The so-called "Fourth" letter is a proper introduction to the three that were published first, because it combatted the idea of negotiation. Regicide France was no longer a member "of the commonwealth of Christian Europe" and was no more a proper object of diplomatic approaches than were "the ruffians, thieves, assassins, and regicides" who governed there, now wearing court dress instead of sans-culottes. Enmity to all "civilized nations" was their creed; between the regicides and "our humanity, our manners, our morals, our religion" there was a fundamental antagonism. Their atheism made them dangerous by definition. The Christian religion and the Established Church were the foundations of English laws and institutions; if the foundations

---

41 Burke MSS, Sheff., Burke to Fitzwilliam, Jan. 16, 1796.

42 *Burke-Laurence Corr.*, 48, 51-52, Laurence to Burke, March 15, 26, 1796. In the belief that Burke had not arranged for publication, John Stockdale asked to publish the letter, sight unseen. Osborn Coll., Box 88, #40, Stockdale to Dr. Brocklesby, April 8, 1796.

43 On Jan. 9, 1797, he was working on it. *Corr.*, IV, 423, Burke to Windham. The editors of the *Corr.* refer this remark to the "fourth" letter, meaning the fourth to be written and the "third" in order of publication.

were destroyed, the constitution was gone. The security of the moral and social order of England, and of Europe, required the destruction of the regicide regime. During the late spring and summer, having laid the first letter aside, Burke worked on two new letters on the regicide peace. By the end of July he had finished them and departed for Bath, leaving to French Laurence the duty of seeing them through the press.[44] He gave to them the timeliness that his earlier letter to Fitzwilliam would have lacked had it been published, but he continued the discussion of principles that lifted the letters above the level of topical pamphlets.

The argument, the sentiments, the tone, even much of the language of the "First" and "Second" "Letters on the Regicide Peace" had appeared in one or another of Burke's earlier writings on the Revolution. In the "First," the philosophical premises about the natural order of the universe with its "laws universal and invariable," the "occasional interposition and irresistible hand of the Great Disposer," the essentially moral nature of politics, and the obscurity of the "internal causes" that affect the fortunes of states and societies inform Burke's views about the "awful drama of Providence now acting on the moral theatre of the world." Because he was "at the end" of his career, Burke could play no part in "the unravelling of the intricate plot." But at least he could offer his judgments to younger men such as Fitzwilliam. His advice was to avoid the "fundamental error" of thinking that it was "in our power to make peace" with France, "this monster of a state," or with the *"armed doctrine"* that England was at war against. The failure of Wickham's negotiations proved Burke's contention. The British government properly terminated the episode when it found no alternative but "to prosecute a war that is just and necessary." Unfortunately, the government continued to grasp at straws, defying the sounder instincts of the majority of the 400,000 people who constituted the "natural representatives" of the nation. These people naturally desired peace, though they would reject it if they fully understood that peace with regicide France was a threat to all

[44] *Burke-Laurence Corr.*, 57, 67, 69-71, Burke to Laurence, Aug. 26, Sept., 1796, Laurence to Burke, Oct. 13, 14, 1796.

that was "dear to them." That was why Burke thought it necessary to teach them that their true interests could not lie in making peace with regicides, Jacobins, and atheists.

The "Second" letter developed this theme. From his analysis of the character of the Revolution, Burke deduced its unsettling effect upon the Christian community of Europe. This letter was a kind of postscript to the *Reflections,* added six years later to show that his opinions of the nature of the Revolution had not changed. Events since 1790 gave substance to his original judgment that the Revolution and the Christian order could not exist together on the same continent. Burke concluded with the promise of another letter that he had already begun, upon the dangerous "internal state" of the European nations. His project had grown upon him during the year since Auckland's pamphlet. He seems to have desired to end his life, which he now felt was nearly finished, with a last great charge to the moral consciousness of Europe.

The problem Burke described for the public in these letters was a dilemma.[45] He had not resolved it, but at least he had made its content clear. There could be no peace with honor with regicide France, but there was no likelihood of an early destruction of the republican regime. Unpleasant as was the prospect of a long war, people seemed to appreciate Burke's defiant and frank acknowledgment of it. They read his pamphlets eagerly and approvingly; thirteen editions were issued.[46] It was a matter of indifference that an old antagonist ridiculed his letters.[47] Simpkin, who had defended Hastings, thought it unfortunate that the impeachment was ended. Were it still going on, Burke might be too busy getting "rid of his bile" against Hastings to fulminate about matters of state in his efforts to prove

> . . . that a government recently made,
> Is always a nuisance, that never can plead

---

[45] Burke MSS, Sheff., Burke to [?], Oct. 26, 1796.

[46] Burke MSS, Sheff., Burke to Fitzwilliam, Oct. 30, 1796, Thomas Townshend to Burke, Nov. 6, 1796, Fitzwilliam to Burke, Nov. 10, 1796; Br. Mus., Add. MSS 37,876, fols. 251-54, William Elliot to Windham, Nov. 22, 1796; William B. Todd, "The Todd Collection of Edmund Burke," *The Burke Newsletter*, III, 101.

[47] *Letters from Simpkin to his Brother Simon,* 27.

>   Prescription, in favour of plunder and trade:
>   And he says, 'tis a maxim in politics true,
>   Old robbers ought never to tolerate new.

Pitt seemed to be in closer agreement with Simpkin than with Burke. The antithesis between their conceptions of the war, with Burke pleading for a royalist crusade, made agreement impossible either about the conduct of the war or the time for terminating it. In the fall of 1796 Pitt thought there was an opportunity to end it, and even before Burke's pamphlets appeared, Malmesbury was on his way to Paris with terms for negotiation. Burke was incensed. Malmesbury had taken a long time to get there, said Burke, because "he travelled all the way on his knees."[48] Of course, Burke expected the negotiations to fail, and he was not shocked when on December 19 the Directory ordered Malmesbury to leave Paris within forty-eight hours. He was "kicked out of Paris," said Burke, simply because the Directory, true to their nature, desired to continue the war and sought any excuse to justify their continued belligerency. Burke thought his government accepted too calmly, in fact meanly, this treatment of its agent and therefore of itself. He intended to say something about this to the public; he was already at work upon another letter, and Rivington was setting it in type as Burke wrote.[49]

The "Third Letter," as Burke had told King, fulfilled the promise of the first two by showing that England did indeed have the resources for continuing the long war in which she was engaged. This letter was more than a political tract; it was an economic analysis of the condition of England and the British Empire. No "absolute necessity," growing out of economic conditions, justified a "mendicant diplomacy." England was rich. Her people had demonstrated their readiness to pledge their money and resources to the support of the war. England's increasing

---

48 Bickley, ed., *Diary of Sylvester Douglas*, I, 92, Oct. 28, 1796.

49 Burke MSS, Sheff., Burke to Fitzwilliam, Dec. 28, 1796; Osborn Coll., Box 88, #40, Burke to Walker King, Dec. 30, 1796. The opening pages of Burke's "third" letter are a scornful analysis of the government's communications to parliament respecting the rupture of negotiations and Pitt's speech on the subject. *Works*, V, 384-427; *Parl. Hist.*, XXXII, 1406-64. This letter was not published, however, until Nov., 1797.

population, her fruitful agriculture, her growing capital and manufactures supported her ability to continue the war. Indeed, the nation had thus far exerted only a small part of her strength. In earlier wars she had made greater proportionate efforts and now, considering her increased resources, was capable of larger efforts than ever she had made before. The navy was Britain's "right arm," but land forces in Europe, to which England had hardly contributed, would have to strike the blow that would "reach the heart of the hostile mischief." The 280,000 men kept in the British Isles for "an inert and passive defence" should be thrown into an offensive war. Burke may have misjudged the potentialities of a royalist effort in a war for the restoration of monarchy, but he was certainly correct in insisting on mobilization of all of the nation's economic resources behind a mighty offensive directed at France herself. Again, he may have been optimistic in his expectations of Allied unity, but he was correct in thinking that such unity, inspired by aggressive British leadership, was the way to bring the war to a successful conclusion. Not only had Burke early appreciated the character and strength of the Revolution, but he also, better than most of his contemporaries, understood what was needed to win the war against it. His despair in 1797 grew out of his disillusionment with the quality and the purpose of the war effort, not out of a hopeless belief that England had not the national capacity to win the war. It was the duty of Britain's constitutional rulers, their responsibility "to conscience and to glory," to the "existing world" and to posterity, to a tribunal to which "kings and parliaments . . . [and] nations themselves, must one day answer" to wage mighty and victorious war against the enemy of the Christian order of Europe.

This discouragement over the conduct of the war was of a kind with that over the affairs of Ireland, of which he wrote and thought much during his last months.[50] The last of his pieces to

---

[50] It would be tedious and repetitious to follow Burke's gloomy correspondence on the subject. There was much of it, especially with Lord Fitzwilliam, and though concerned with current events, it reflected Burke's long-held views about the nature of and remedy for the problems of Ireland. Yet six weeks before he died, he told Fitzwilliam that he had no recommendations for Ireland. Osborn Coll., Box 88, #40, May 16, 1797.

be published in his lifetime was a "Letter on the Affairs of Ireland," written in May, 1797.[51] In it he repeated his basic beliefs. The root of Ireland's troubles was the Protestant Ascendancy. The cure was the destruction of the Junto. This, he said, was what he had told ministers the last time he had discussed the problem of Ireland with them. It was the Junto who perpetuated the opinion that the safety of Ireland demanded the exclusion "of the mass of their countrymen" from government and insisted that the connection with England could endure only so long as a "very small number of gentlemen" remained "in possession of a monopoly of that kingdom." Emancipation of Catholics, a thing necessary in itself, though perhaps not immediately, was separable from parliamentary reform in Ireland. Burke desired above all to perpetuate the connection between Ireland and England, and he would domicile the superior power in *"imperial* politics" in England. Ireland, "locally, civilly, and commercially independent," could then look to England "in matters of peace or of war" and, joined with her, could be safe, prosperous, and contented. Magnanimity in politics, Burke had said over twenty years before, was not seldom the truest wisdom, and the thought applied as well to Ireland as to America. That lesson, learned too late for settlement of the American problem, was not applied to the Irish problem in Burke's lifetime. Fortunately, perhaps, he died before the climax of the troubles he deplored.

Though the dominant mood of these last months was discouragement, or even gloom, expressed often with anguish, it was not pessimism. Burke abandoned neither his faith in Divine Providence nor his confidence in England's strength. He did not foresee an early end to troubles, but he described the means and policies within England's capacity and choice by which justice and order could be attained. If Burke had been a pessimist, he could not have believed that it was within England's power to triumph over the troubles she was enduring.

The anguish of Burke's last months was intensified because his health was rapidly declining. His poor physical condition exaggerated adversities and, by contributing to despondency, discouraged him from essential precautions, such as maintaining nourish-

[51] *Works,* VI, 415-29.

ment, which would keep up his physical strength. He felt keenly the death of Lord John Cavendish, who, by helping bring him to Rockingham's attention over thirty years before, justified Burke's remark that his entry into political life was under Lord John's "auspices."[52] His death seemed to emphasize the unhappy fate of the Portland party, the old Rockingham connection, after the coalition with Pitt. Burke had worked for the coalition, hoping that the Portland ministers would be able to influence Pitt's policies on the war and on Ireland. They had not, though on the first Windham had tried. The recent breach between Fitzwilliam and Portland and the increasing friendliness between Fitzwilliam and Fox were tragedies to Burke.[53] Against them, the entry of French Laurence into the House of Commons was only a personal gratification. It seemed to Burke that the integrity of politics had weakened. He had always been able to believe that the Rockingham-Portland party stood for principles. He had expected Pitt to perpetuate the tradition by committing the new Tory party to an antirevolutionary creed. Instead, Pitt had betrayed the purpose of the coalition, in part because of Portland's mismanagement of affairs.[54]

And so in Burke's letters occur expressions of bitterness and avowals of readiness to die. The grant of an East India Company pension to Hastings stirred him deeply. How, he asked, could he earnestly defend the present order of things when rewards were dispensed to murderers and peculators?[55] "I am sick of many griefs—it is time I should go to my long repose." He stayed close to Beaconsfield, seeking what pleasure he could find in his farming, almost his only consolation. He could not stand to go to London with "its Indian corruptions and its Jacobin peace."[56]

It is not easy to determine how hard he fought for life. Perhaps a resolute will would have made no significant difference. His inactive tuberculosis, arrested during his boyhood country life,

52 Burke MSS, Sheff., Burke to Dudley North, Dec., 1796. Cavendish left a bequest to Burke and remitted some bonds. Osborn Coll., Box 88, #40, Burke to Walker King, March 27, [1797].

53 Burke MSS, Sheff., Fitzwilliam to Burke, Aug. 30, 1796; Burke MSS, N.R.O., Avi52, Burke to Laurence, May 12, 1797.

54 Burke MSS, Sheff., Burke to Fitzwilliam, Sept. 2, 1796, Burke to Laurence, Dec. 23, 1796.

55 Burke MSS, Sheff., Burke to Walker King, March 11, 1796.

56 *The R. B. Adam Library*, I, 22, Burke to John Coxe Hippisley, Jan. 22, 1796.

flared again. Though only a "shadow" of himself existed, he went to Bath in the summer of 1796, on Fitzwilliam's and Windham's insistence, and found some relief from the gnawing pains in his stomach.[57] Windham thought he was yielding to discouragement and could get well if he set his mind to it. Burke respected his friends' desires, but he really did not care if he lived.[58] He had become so weak that he spent most of his days on a couch and dictated his letters. "I am not long for this world," and he did not regret to leave it, he told Dr. Hussey.[59]

Though he retained interest in affairs and in his old friends, he had no desire for new acquaintances. At the end of 1796 he made an exception, to meet James Mackintosh—a meeting that resulted in an important description of Burke near the end of his life.[60] Trained at Edinburgh as a physician, at twenty-three Mackintosh moved to London, where he became associated with the radical interest in the metropolis. His *Vindiciae Gallicae* was, from an intellectual and analytical viewpoint, the ablest of the replies to Burke's *Reflections,* the only one, said Samuel Parr, that made much impression on the "better educated classes." Mackintosh served briefly as secretary to the Friends of the People. A trip to France in 1792 seems to have begun his conversion from a sympathizer to an opponent of the Revolution.

It was Mackintosh's favorable reviews of his "Letter to a Noble Lord" and the first two "Letters on a Regicide Peace" that renewed Burke's interest in him. Through the good offices of Laurence, and after an exchange of letters, Burke invited him to Gregories, though he was somewhat suspicious of his former opponent.[61]

I forgot to speak to you about Mackintosh's supposed conversion. I suspect by his letter, that it does not extend beyond the interior

---

[57] Burke MSS, Sheff., Burke to Fitzwilliam, April 26, July 11, Aug. 27, 1796, Windham to Burke, July 17, 1796; *The R. B. Adam Library,* I, 23, Burke to Dr. Caleb Parry, Jan. 29, 1797.

[58] *Corr.,* IV, 360, Burke to Mrs. Crewe, Nov. 23, 1796.

[59] *Corr.,* IV, 379, Dec., 1796.

[60] The following account is based on Robert James Mackintosh, ed., *Memoirs of . . . Sir James Mackintosh* (London, 1836), I, 45-92, and Sir James Mackintosh, "A Discourse on the Law of Nature and Nations," *Miscellaneous Works* (London, 1854), I, 345-92.

[61] *Burke-Laurence Corr.,* 106-107, Burke to Laurence, Dec. 25, 1796.

politicks of this island, but that, with regard to France and many other countries, he remains as frank a Jacobin as ever. This conversion is none at all; but we must nurse up these nothings, and think these negative advantages as we can have them. Such as he is, I shall not be displeased if you bring him down; bad as he may be, he has not yet declared war along with his poor friend *Wild* [John Wilde] against the Pope.

Burke saw in Mackintosh a promising recruit in the war against Jacobinism and was ready to make an effort to complete the conversion.

From his account, Mackintosh enjoyed his holiday visit with Burke. He found the sick man in good spirits, full of wise and eloquent talk, and exceedingly well informed about public affairs. What he learned during this visit, combined with his careful reading of Burke's writings, enabled Mackintosh to form some judgments about the nature and content of Burke's thought.[62] Burke was not an acute or precise thinker. He had a "discursive understanding" and took a "comprehensive" rather than a minute view of problems. His mind operated in the middle region between the "details of business, and the generalities of speculation"; he climbed high enough in political discussion to gain a commanding view but never so high as to get lost in the clouds. His was a "comprehensive understanding [which] discovers the identity of facts which seem dissimilar, and binds together into a system the most apparently unconnected and unlike results of experience." Burke never departed far from circumstance or experience; his principles and his theory "lay in the immediate neighbourhood of practice"; his object was not truth but utility. Burke was one of the great teachers of "civil prudence." This mode of thought operated from a set of premises of natural law, "as fixed and inevitable as the order of nature," which made justice the end of civil society.[63]

62 Mackintosh, ed., *Memoirs of Mackintosh*, I, 69-76, 92.
63 Mackintosh, *Misc. Works*, I, 350, 392. In his "Discourse," Mackintosh cites Burke and clearly places him in the natural-law tradition, with Cicero. Mackintosh' analysis, undated but probably about 1799, is in essential agreement with one of the latest studies of Burke's thought, Canavan's *Political Reason of Edmund Burke.* Except for the word "utility," all of these phrases from Mackintosh are used in one variation or another by Canavan.

As to practical, political questions, Mackintosh thought there was close agreement between Burke's views and the ones he himself expressed later in his "Discourse." Perhaps Burke would be more reluctant to try to define liberty, as it was a practical matter related to circumstances. But they shared suspicion of democracy because no power outside the sovereign people could check their will. It was more prudent to place "efficient sovereignty" in the control of a natural aristocracy, to be exercised through a parliament adequately representing the important "interests" of the nation, with the people serving as a check upon its abuse. Mackintosh summarized concisely the essential qualities of Burke's thought.

Shortly after Mackintosh's visit, Burke's health and spirits declined another stage. On January 9, 1797, he told Windham that he was merely waiting for the will of God.[64] But at the urging of friends he went again to Bath. There Dr. Caleb Parry and Brocklesby diagnosed his "disease" as "a want of proper motion in the alimentary canal" and, returning to the ancient doctrine of the humors, as a "redundancy of *atra* Bilis."[65] In fact, Burke suffered from tuberculous enteritis.

Though he was so weak that he could hardly walk, his mind was lucid and active. He wrote or, rather, dictated many letters, about the war, Ireland, and politics, to Fitzwilliam, Windham, Hussey, and Laurence, and he worked on his "Third" letter on the regicide peace. By the end of March and from then until the middle of May, he seemed to improve. Then began a rapid decline, and he left Bath before the end of the month to return to Beaconsfield and await death.[66] Sir Gilbert Elliot visited him early in June and found him emaciated, taking hardly any nourishment, yet talkative and interested in the affairs of the world.[67] Steadily he grew weaker. On July 6, he talked with Windham about Hastings and Sir Elijah Impey. He read and admired William Wilberforce's *Practical View of Christianity*. On

64 *Corr.*, IV, 421, Jan. 9, 1797.

65 Br. Mus., Add. MSS 37,843, fols. 137-38, 141-42, Parry to Windham, Feb. 17, 1797, Edward Nagle to Windham, Feb. 22, 1797.

66 *Corr.*, IV, 436, 448, Burke to Windham, March 30, 1797, Burke to Mrs. Crewe, May 21, 1797; MS in Harvard Library, Jane Burke to [?], May 8, 1797.

67 Minto, *Elliot*, II, 404-405, Elliot to Lady Elliot, June 3, 1795.

one occasion he alarmed his attendants. He told Edward Nagle that he wanted to be buried "unknown, the spot unmarked & separate from his son, wife and Brother on *account of the French Revolutionists*."[68] This was no indication of a wandering mind. To the last Burke retained his hatred of Jacobinism and his distrust of its works.

Late at night on July 8 he conversed with friends and read from Addison, seeming in good spirits. Toward midnight he was being assisted to bed when he collapsed, struggled briefly, and soon expired. A pulmonary embolus, brought on by his prolonged immobilization, was probably the final cause of his death.[69]

He was buried on July 15. According to the directions in his will, the funeral was a simple, private one in the church at Beaconsfield. About thirty friends attended, along with some sixty members of the neighborhood friendly society that Burke had sponsored and belonged to.[70] His pallbearers were Portland, Devonshire, Fitzwilliam, his neighbor Lord Inchiquin, Sir Gilbert Elliot, Loughborough, and Henry Addington, the Speaker of the House. Among other old friends who attended were Dr. Burney, Frederick North, Walker King, Laurence, Dudley North, and Philip Francis. On the second day after the funeral, some of them who had been staying at Bulstrode with Portland visited Penn School "in honor of Mr. Burke."[71]

On the south wall toward the west end of Saint Mary and All Saints Church in Beaconsfield is a tablet. It reads: "Near this place lies interred all that was mortal of the R't Honourable EDMUND BURKE Who died on the 9th of July, 1797 aged 68 years . . . And of his widow Jane Mary Burke who died on the 2d of

68 Br. Mus., Add. MSS 37,843, fols. 195-96, Capt. Woodford to Windham, July 6, 1797.

69 I am indebted to my friend Irving F. Kanner, M.D., for the diagnosis, based upon epistolary descriptions, of Burke's illness and the cause of his death. A diagnosis at such a distance of time must be tentative, but that which is given here seems the likeliest.

70 Osborn Coll., Box 74, #24B, account by Laurence. A "friendly society" was a private, voluntary benefit society to which members paid weekly contributions for sickness and burial benefits. Ironically, Dr. Richard Price had done much to work out the mathematical tables that provided reasonably sound actuarial bases for friendly societies.

71 Percy A. Scholes, *The Great Dr. Burney* (London, 1948), II, 160.

April 1812 Aged 78." Below is a profile of Burke and the words: "Edmund Burke, patriot, orator, statesman, lived at Butler's Court, formerly Gregories, in this parish from 1769 to 1797. This memorial, placed here by public subscription, records the undying honour in which his name is held. July 9, 1898."

Burke's bones do not lie immediately below the slab.[72] After the funeral the body was transferred to another coffin and buried elsewhere in the church. The grim command to Edward Nagle had been obeyed.

In his will Burke asked forgiveness of all whom politics had estranged from him. This would include Fox, with whom he refused formal reconciliation shortly before his death. To his political friends, Burke wished success. He left Gregories to his wife, and she lived there until her death. Shortly before, she sold it, and at last Burke's debts were extinguished.[73]

---

[72] Copeland, *Our Eminent Friend Edmund Burke*, 90-91; Bertram D. Sarason, "Edmund Burke's Burial Place," *Notes and Queries*, n. s., II (Feb., 1955), 69-70.

[73] In her will, drawn in June, 1811 (Somerset House, Oxford 209), a year before her death, Mrs. Burke directed her executors to sell Gregories and all of the personal property which she did not specifically bequeath, and from the proceeds to pay off the mortgages on Gregories, to pay off her husband's and her son's debts, to pay £500 on the debts of Richard, Sr., to pay her monetary bequests of £34,000, and to provide two life annuities of £100 each and one of £20. I do not know whether Mrs. Burke was overly optimistic.

CHAPTER XX

Afterword

DURING THE PAST two decades there has been a remarkable quickening of interest in Edmund Burke, reflected by an extraordinary number of publications about him. Not that he had ever been dropped from the active file of historical personages. To every generation since his death he has had something to say, and in all of them there have been persons who thought him worthy of attention. But for the unusually keen current interest in Burke there are some reasons that ought to be noticed.

Some of the young men who knew and admired Burke in his later years lived on into the second quarter of the nineteenth century. From their memories they transmitted their personal knowledge of Burke to the generation of De Tocqueville, of Disraeli and Gladstone, even of Lord Acton. Considering that Gladstone did not die until 1898, it may be said that an oral tradition one generation removed from immediate recollection of Burke lasted almost until the twentieth century. This tradition was overlapped by the generation of John Morley. The last perhaps of the Gladstonian Liberals and an interpretative biographer of Burke, Morley lived until 1923.

In the nineteenth century, Burke's collected writings, available in numerous editions, were much read and widely admired. A succession of critics praised his literary style. Mackintosh, William Hazlitt, and Coleridge could remember him, whereas Matthew Arnold, Leslie Stephen, and Morley read Burke in longer perspective. On the continent Burke inspired the counterrevolutionaries such as Joseph de Maistre or Gentz; in England in an age when the Benthamite influence was at its height, positivists such as Thomas Buckle and Liberals such as Morley gave to Burke's thought the prevailing utilitarian construction. The Victorians, proud of England's accomplishments in the art of governing and boastful of her parliamentary system, thought Burke's writings a storehouse of practical, prudential political wisdom and his active career in the House of Commons, especially before 1785, an example of commendable opposition to illiberal government.

Such a view of Burke reflected the experience and the preferences of a utilitarian, Whiggish England. When nineteenth-century interpreters recalled that during the French Revolution Burke was in conflict with Enlightenment doctrines of natural rights and progress, and in certain respects seemed no longer the Burke of the 1770's and 1780's, they worked out explanations. Morley, for example, said simply that Burke's judgment of the French Revolution was wrong because he was inadequately informed about his subject. Buckle went to the extreme of saying that the Burke of the 1790's was a different man, possibly deranged. The inadequacy of these apologies and the failure to provide a substantial foundation for Burke's so-called "conservatism" (a word avoided in the present study), meant that inevitably he fell under the suspicion of the aggressive political forces, "liberalism" and "progressivism," of the late nineteenth and early twentieth centuries. Best remembered for his *Reflections on the Revolution in France,* to some persons Burke was merely an opponent of change and therefore not a useful guide in an age when reform was in the air, unless one chose to emphasize his pre-Revolutionary career.

These difficulties arose because Burke had been placed in a false position by his utilitarian interpreters. They did not see that he possessed ethical norms based upon the tradition of natural law, and in consequence they did not fully appreciate why his position on the French Revolution was philosophically identical with his positions on the other leading public issues of his period. Steadily he had represented not the incompatibility between natural rights and utilitarianism but the hostility of the natural-law tradition to the scientific materialism and the legal positivism of the Enlightenment. The recent identification of Burke with the natural-law doctrine places him centrally in the great, continuing engagement between two philosophies of man and society and has contributed to the contemporary revival of interest in Burke.

But there are other important reasons for the Burke revival. They are quite separate from interpretations of his political philosophy and important enough by themselves to have brought about a renewed interest in him. The deposit at the Sheffield Central Library and in the Northamptonshire Record Office of the great Fitzwilliam manuscript collections alone would have stimulated scholarly Burke studies. The many publications during the past dozen years based in small or large part upon these collections attest to their richness and to the number of scholars who have journeyed to use them. Then, these manuscripts became accessible at a time when a strong interest was developing in eighteenth-century English political studies. Sir Lewis Namier's two epoch-making books on politics at the beginning of the reign of George III were published in 1929 and 1930, but they did not have their full effect until after World War II. A new generation of scholars, brought up on Namier's teachings and able after the war to carry out historical research and writing, found a great store of unexploited manuscript materials relating to their rapidly growing field of eighteenth-century political history. Obviously, a politician as active and outstanding as Burke had been deserved a place of prominence in the new studies. Some who were interested in Burke's role in eighteenth-century politics were almost hostile to a philosophical approach.

Coinciding with or closely following these events came the fruitful work of Hoffman, Leo Strauss, and Stanlis. Among others, they elaborated the interpretation that identifies Burke with the natural-law tradition. Another group, called the Neo-Conservatives, quickly appropriated these teachings and joyfully adopted Burke as their intellectual forebear who connected them with the medieval and classical traditions of natural law. Modern conservatism, whether moderate or extreme, finds in Burke's thought powerful opposition to the positivism, nominalism, and materialism of modern liberal thought.

Only a large book could tell all of this in full detail. This one has not gone beyond the time of Burke's death except in this brief afterword, to indicate the reasons why Burke has continued to interest people. Upon scholars of various disciplines, including English literature, political philosophy, politics, and public address, among others, his spell is stronger, perhaps, than ever before. To the person interested in the philosophical issues underlying the public problems of the twentieth century, Burke remains important. But the attention directed to Burke's philosophical genealogy should not obscure another important matter. Burke belongs to the history of politics as well as to the history of political philosophy. The two interests join in him. For as Burke the philosophical politician said, the art of government, concerned with the eternal problems of civil and moral order, with in a word justice, exercises "all the great qualities of the human mind."

CARL B. CONE, the author of this book, is professor of history at the University of Kentucky. A native of Iowa, he received his undergraduate and Ph.D. degrees at the State University of Iowa; he has also undertaken postdoctoral study at Yale University. Mr. Cone is the author of *Torchbearer of Freedom: The Influence of Richard Price on Eighteenth Century Thought,* published in 1952 by the University of Kentucky Press. The first volume of *Burke and the Nature of Politics,* subtitled *The Age of the American Revolution,* appeared in 1957.

BURKE AND THE NATURE OF POLITICS was composed and printed in the Division of Printing of the University of Kentucky. It is set in Linotype Baskerville, with headings in ATF Bulmer. The book is printed on Warren Olde Style antique wove paper and bound in Holliston Roxite cloth by the Grand Rapids Book Manufacturers, Inc.